COINS

AN ILLUSTRATED SURVEY
650 BC TO THE PRESENT DAY

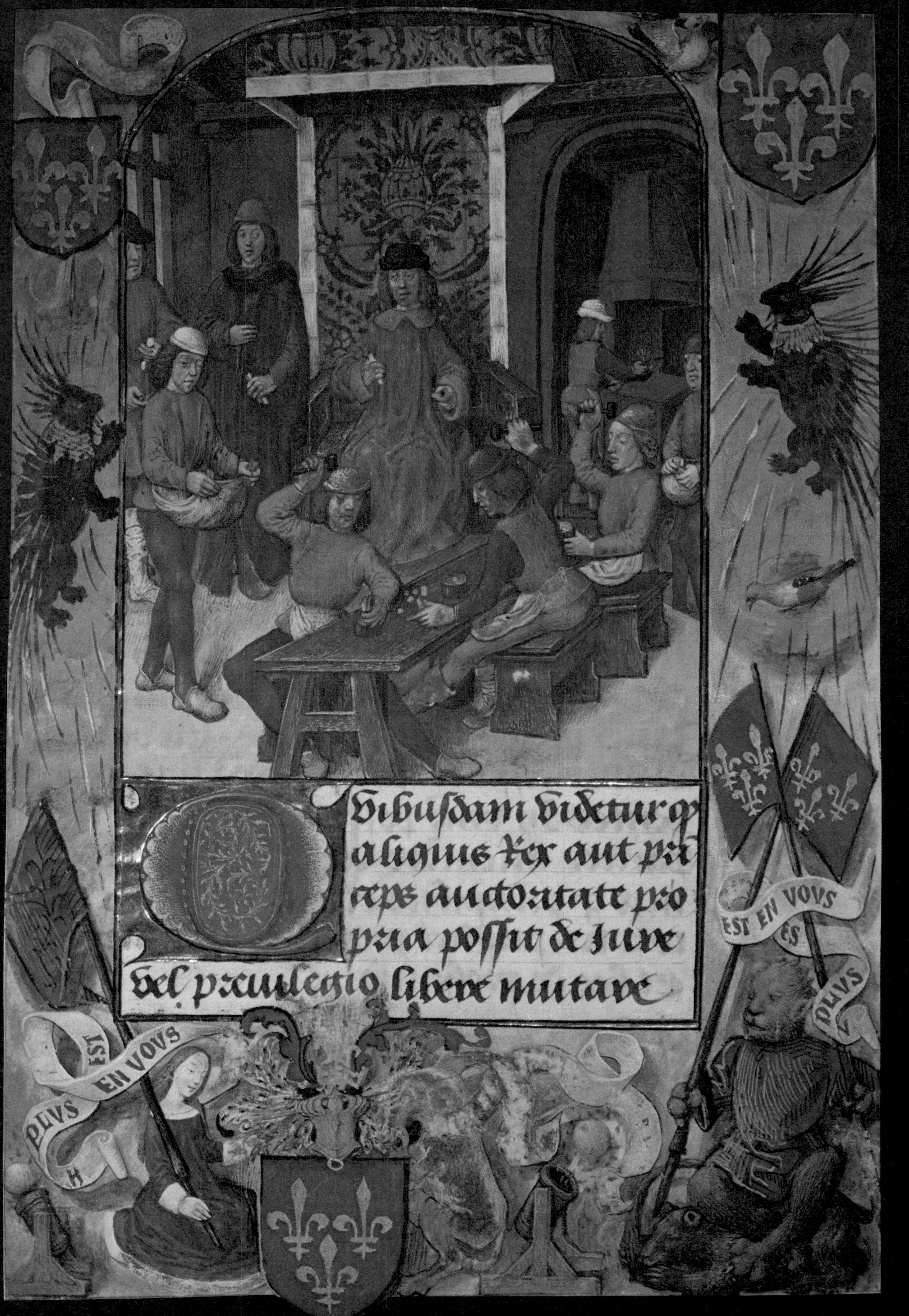
uibusdam videtur q
aliquis Rex aut pri
ceps auctoritate pro
pria possit de iure
vel privilegio libere mutare
EST EN VOUS
PLVS
PLVS EST EN VOUS

PUBLISHED IN ASSOCIATION WITH
BRITISH MUSEUM PUBLICATIONS LIMITED

COINS

AN ILLUSTRATED SURVEY
650 BC TO THE PRESENT DAY

General Editor: Martin Jessop Price

Methuen

New York · London · Toronto · Sydney

Coins.
Includes index
1. Coins—History. I. Price, Martin, 1939-
CJ59.C64 737.4'09 80-13028
ISBN 0-416-00691-4

First American edition
Published in the United States of America by
Methuen Inc.
733 Third Avenue
New York, N.Y. 10017

Phototypeset by Tradespools Limited, Frome, England
Printed in Hong Kong

House Editor: Glyn Thomas
Designer: Karel Feuerstein

Half-title page:
An 'owl' minted at Athens (**116**)
Frontispiece:
The royal mint, depicted in Nicolas Oresme's
de Moneta, about 1490.
Title page:
Pavilion d'or of Edward the Black Prince, struck
at Poitiers in the fourteenth century (**798A**).
Following page:
Gold 10 ounce coin, minted in Japan
in 1860 (**1469**).

CONTENTS

FOREWORD

For over 2500 years coins have provided a standard medium through which services and labour may be rewarded and commercial exchanges may be transacted. Today we are accustomed to using coins only of relatively low value; but just as gold sovereigns and Krugerrands are well recognized as a means of storing wealth and of protecting it against inflation, so in the past coins of gold and silver, often with enormous purchasing power, acted mainly as a means through which wealth might be stored or transferred. The payment of armies, the collection of taxes, the distribution of gifts: these are all aspects of daily life for which coins are ideally suited, and the important role of coins in the day-to-day transactions of the economy is reflected in the care and attention paid to their production.

All coins are the product of three separate decisions. It is the economist or state treasurer who normally decides an issue of coinage is required; it is the politician or ruler who decides what designs are placed on the coins; and it is an artist who carries out those designs. Each of these stages involves the discussion of quite different problems, and the resolution of each is bound closely to the time and place of the issue. Coins are thus inseparable from the history of the state that issued them, and at the same time they provide a sequence of miniature pictures that trace the history of art from the seventh century BC to the present day.

No single book can adequately cover the whole history of coinage; but this volume sets out to illustrate through more than 2000 photographs the main trends of coinage in its many different facets; and the accompanying essays show how the coins relate to their cultural and historical background. This arrangement gives a more comprehensive view of coinage and is more easily assimilated than any previously published. By way of introduction John Porteous has provided a general account of the development of coinage throughout the world, and some of the coins there illustrated will be found again in later sections, where they occur in the full cultural context of their issue. Miriam Balmuth has added an account of the development of the concept of money to the point at which coinage evolved, setting the scene for the historical and geographical sequence of the following essays.

In order to facilitate the reproduction of the details of the coins, and to increase an appreciation of their role in the history of art, many of the coins are shown enlarged. On the black-and-white photographs indication of the actual size is given by the amount of the enlargment (× 2 and × 3 for double or three times actual size respectively); where no such indication is given, the coin has been reproduced actual size. Certain coins have been shown at both their actual size and enlarged; these have been indicated by '× 1, × 2' or '× 1, × 3'. In certain illustrations, such as of notes, the dimensions in millimetres have been appended instead. In addition there is a list at the back of the book giving the details of the illustrations including for each coin its maximum size in millimetres and its weight in grammes. This allows immediate comparison of the size and weight of different coins at different periods. The colour photographs heighten the artistic effect, and although they have not been shown at their actual sizes, their dimensions can be found in the list of illustrations, and the section frontispieces usually select a detail from a coin to emphasize its sculptural quality. Most coins, of course, have a design on both sides, but in an attempt to give as wide a coverage as possible often only one side of the coin is shown. Where both are illustrated, the letters A (indicating the obverse of a coin) and B (indicating the reverse of a coin) have been used to link the photographs to the single caption, and in certain cases, related coins have also been treated in this manner. The combination of a rich photographic record and concise explanatory essays enables a subject that is often reserved for the specialist attentions of the scholar to be presented in a manner that is both informative and exciting.

Martin Price

I

THE NATURE OF COINAGE

John Porteous

In 1971 the Government of the Seychelles required a new coin of the value of five rupees. It was specified that the reverse design should incorporate all the elements of the badge of the Sey-
1 chelles, namely an island, a palm-tree, a sailing-boat and a tortoise. Norman Sillman, the designer called upon by the Royal Mint in London to execute this commission, may well have been dismayed at being asked to cram all these objects, together with a mark of value, on to the reverse of a medium-sized coin; but no doubt the Government of the Seychelles believed that it had commissioned a truly original piece. Actually, it had done no
2 such thing. As long ago as 1676 a silver gulden of Duke Johann Friedrich of Brunswick-Lüneburg, an uncle of King George I of Great Britain and so an ancestor of the sovereign in whose name the new five-rupees was issued, contained all the same elements except the tortoise; and on coins of another ancestor, Mary
3 Queen of Scots, a tortoise figured with a palm-tree.

One might conclude that it is now impossible to invent an entirely original coin-type. Yet though the three coins of Scotland, Hanover and the Seychelles have so much in common, still each is typical of its own age and society. This is most obvious in the metals, the sizes and the techniques of manufacture. But consider also that on the Scottish coin the tortoise is actually climbing the palm-tree, a feat which does not occur in nature! In the sixteenth century men were fascinated by allegory and magical emblems, while they knew next to nothing of natural science. In our own contrasting age any mint in the world would reject out of hand a design which showed a tortoise climbing a tree.

On another occasion in recent years an authority which had a fine romanesque crucifix somewhere in its small territory, proposed that this should be used as the reverse design for a new coin. It so happens that, while the cross was a standard type for
5 the whole coinage of medieval Latin Christendom, the crucifixion is rather rare; but the decision not to accept the proposal was made not because of that but because it was thought embarrassing to put Jesus on a coin at all since some might be offended by this association of God with commerce. So far had feeling changed since, in a more devout age, the most commercial people in Europe, namely the Venetians, placed a Christ in glory on every piece that left their mint.

It is part of the interest of coins that they reflect so much of the age and civilization which made them. This is true in some degree of any artefact, but the reflection which we get from coinage is especially vivid. This is because it is, so to speak, stereoscopic. Coinage has a dual nature. Functionally it is the instrument of daily exchange, the common drudge between man and man. Symbolically it is an expression of sovereignty, and one of the very few such which is visible and permanent. An issue of coin is one of the most indestructible of man's works. There are rulers known to history only by their surviving coins. It is not for nothing that coins are almost always among the objects ritually laid under the foundations of buildings.

Naturally governments attach great importance to the appearance of their coinage and to the image of themselves which they project thereby. Yet they still have to make their coins fit for their economic function. Every minting authority therefore is constrained by the suitability of metal, size and shape, and even by the range of intelligible or (as we have seen) permissible symbolism. Above all, there is the constraint of continuity: it is almost a condition of a coin's acceptability that it does not differ overmuch from what has gone before.

For this reason, although coins exist in so many various forms, they can all be shown to have developed, one from the other, by the slow processes of evolution and cross-fertilization. Every issue has more in common than it has points of difference with
the coins already in circulation. A basic conservatism has 6
marked the minting policy of even the most revolutionary 7
governments.

There are three main roots from which coinage has grown. Three civilizations, the Greek, the Indian and the Chinese, have independently concluded at a certain stage of their development that stamped metal is the most convenient form that can be given to money (see the table on page 11).

Of the three, the Chinese was the most unchanging and the most impervious to outside influences. Indian coinage, by contrast, has been so susceptible to Greek, Roman and Islamic influences that some have questioned whether there is an indigenous Indian coinage tradition at all.

Greek coinage has had the most various progeny. It is the direct ancestor, through Rome, of all western coinage; and through the Seleucids, the Parthians and the Sassanians, of all Islamic coinage. Eventually, by its association in the last four centuries with the expanding economy of western Europe and America, this coinage tradition has shouldered out all the others. All modern coinages are now derived from the western stock, and only vestiges of the others remain. Even so, while this western or Greek-derived tradition has expanded geographically, the actual role of coinage, both economically and sociologically as a source of pride or shame to governments and peoples, has greatly diminished. In no country is coinage now the

Gold sovereign of Henry VIII of England, 1543.

1 Seychelles, Elizabeth II, 5-rupees, 1971.

2 Johann Friedrich, Duke of Brunswick-Lüneburg, gulden, 1676.

3 Mary Queen of Scots, ryal (30 shillings), 1566.

4 Venice, Doge Pietro Gradenigo, gold ducat, 1289.

5 Mantua, Duke Frederick Gonzaga, silver scudo, 1536–40.

6 Russia, Tsar Nicholas II, 3-kopeks, 1915.

7 Russia, communist Republic, 3-kopeks, 1924.

8 China, Han dynasty, 5-grains, 118 BC.

9 China, Qing dynasty, standard coin 1889.

10 India, stamped silver ingot, fourth century BC.

11 India, 5-pice, 1959.

12 India, gold dinar of Kanishka, second century AD.

13 Silver didrachm struck by Themistocles as dynast of Magnesia, about 460 BC.

14 Electrum stater stamped with the seal of Phanes, 600-580 BC.

13A×3

13B×3

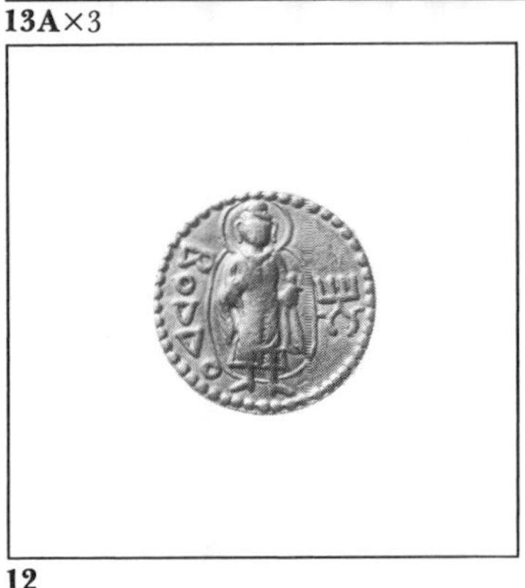

12

14

essential embodiment of money, as it was in the sixteenth or even the nineteenth century.

The coinage of China received no influences from outside until
it was effectively superseded by a western type of coinage in the
late nineteenth century. It was derived from utensil currencies of
1417-1421 knives and hoes, and the earliest Chinese coins are knife-shaped
and hoe-shaped objects in cast bronze. The classic Chinese coins
8 are made of cast bronze, are round, and have a raised rim with a
square hole in the middle. The hole, which incidentally was
present in the handle of the knife-money, had two functions. In
minting it served for the insertion of an iron bar or axle, on which
many coins at a time could be rotated while the rough edge left
by the casting was filed away. In circulation the hole served to
string coins together in lots (typically of about 1000). Chinese *cash*
p.294c normally circulated in this multiple form. The broad rim
protected the face of the coins as they hung together on their
string, so wear was minimal. In the nineteenth century, coins of
the Tang and Song periods were to be found, rim to rim on these
9 strings, with cash just minted by the Manchu emperors of the
Qing dynasty. Through all this time the coins were scarcely
changed in appearance. There was no type but only the
inscription to change, arranged round the square hole.

It must be admitted that Chinese coins reflect little of Chinese

Trends in coinage

A simplified diagram showing the parallel chronology and the main streams of coinage

BC 650
Lydia
Greeks
Persia
Rome
India
China
Alexander the Great 336-23
Celts
Hellenistic kingdoms
Parthia
Roman republic
Han dynasty 206 BC-AD 220
Augustus 27 BC-AD 14
Roman empire
Kushan dynasty
Sassanian empire
Tang dynasty 618-907
Foundation of Constantinople 330
Western Europe
Byzantine empire
Gupta dynasty
Islamic dynasties
Delhi sultanate
Song dynasty 960-1272
Seljuks
Mongols
Ottomans
Mongols 1271-1368
Fall of Constantinople 1453
Mogul empire
Ming dynasty 1368-1644
Americas
'Milled' coinage
European traders
Qing dynasty 1644-1911
17th century
Influx of Western silver
British empire
1980 AD

15 Thurii, Italy, distater, about 375 BC.

16 Antimachus, King of Bactria, tetradrachm, about 190-80 BC.

17 Silver didrachm of Rome, about 300 BC.

18 Denarius of Rome, 54 BC.

19 Denarius struck for the Roman emperor Augustus, about 20-15 BC.

20 Sestertius of Caligula, Rome, AD 37-41.

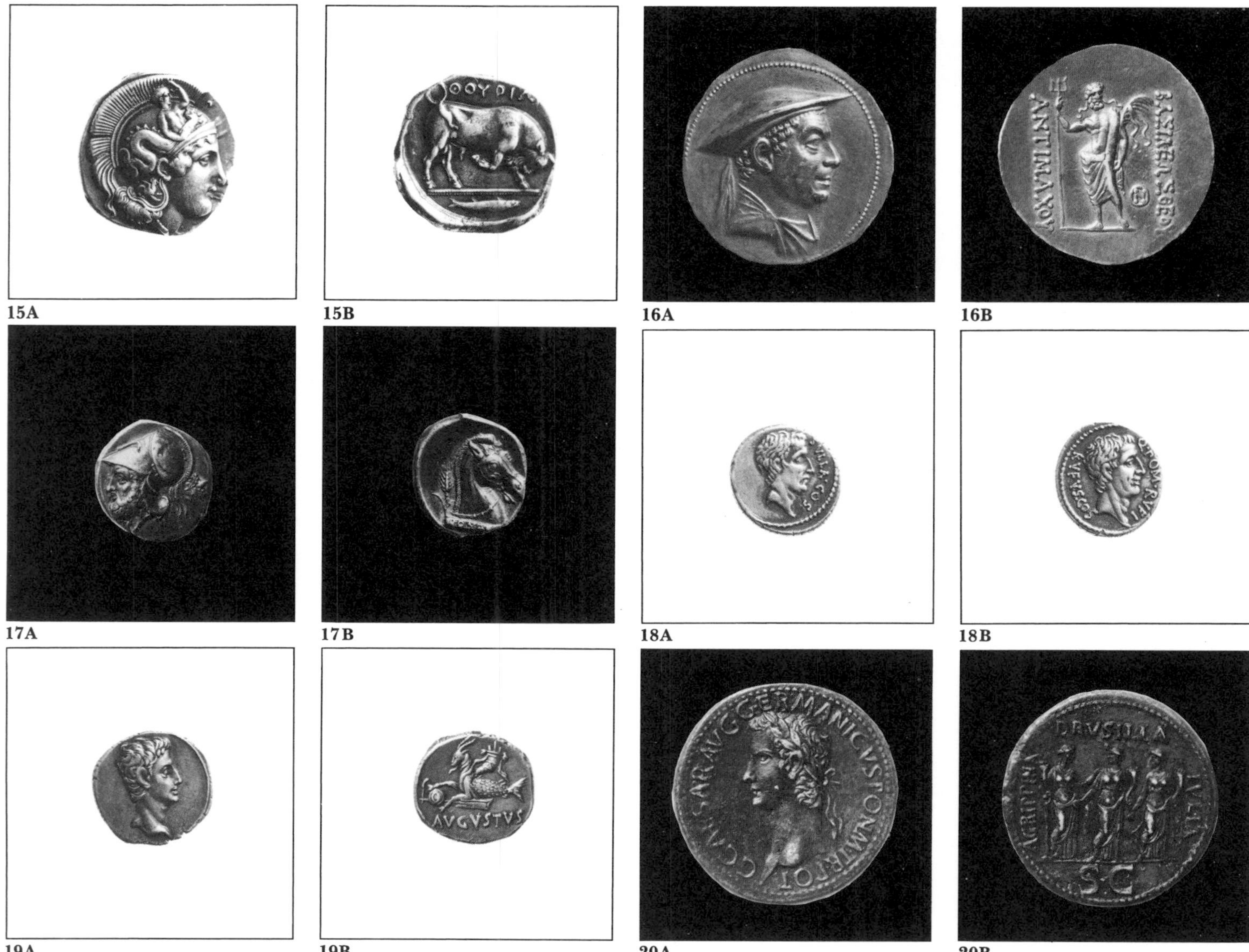

15A **15B** **16A** **16B** **17A** **17B** **18A** **18B** **19A** **19B** **20A** **20B**

civilization except its conservatism and its bureaucratic
efficiency and continuity. The interest of such humble coins
circulating in an immense and wealthy society centres on their
economic function. It seems that in China, as in our present
world, coins were only the small change of economic life, and
1439 that the people who invented the concept of paper money some
500 years before any others always thought of coined money as
representing only a tiny part of their community's liquid wealth.
So we have the curious paradox that while the physical form
taken by coinage today is everywhere western, stemming from
the Greek, the actual use we make of it is more akin to that of the
ancient Chinese.

The earliest Indian coins are roughly cut rectangular pieces of
10 silver, stamped on both sides with a number of separate punches.
Their dating is difficult: it is probable that the earliest at least
pre-date Alexander's invasion of India in 327 BC, and the
minting of Greek-type coins by Indian rulers which followed.

After that invasion, it is difficult to distinguish the native element from the foreign in Indian coinage. Three characteristics have persisted, namely a predilection for square coins, a somewhat dumpy fabric, and the practice of producing coins with multiple stamps. The first and last of these stem directly from the primitive coinage. Square coins were minted by the
Indo-Greeks, by the Moghuls, by the British, and are even now **11**
struck by the Indian Government. Coins struck with several
punches were made as late as the eleventh century by Hindu
dynasties in the Deccan. The heavy, dumpy fabric, which is
perhaps the most striking characteristic of Indian coinage from
the time of the Guptas until the nineteenth century, may
however be an inheritance from the Greeks. It is this above all
which distinguishes Islamic Indian coinage from that of the rest **1414**
of the Islamic world, and the colonial coinages of Bombay and
Goa from the British and Portuguese coinage at home.

The types which appear on Indian coins are derived from the
alien tradition of the west. The portrait of the ruler, the figure of **12**
a deity with his divine attributes, the circular inscription, or, on
the coins of Islamic rulers, the inscription filling the whole field **1403**
on both sides, come entirely from Greek coinage and its
successors. The divinity may be Vishnu on his serpent or **1387**
Lakshmi on her lotus; the ruler may be wearing the high boots of
a Kushan warrior; the inscription may be in the exquisite
calligraphy perfected at the courts of Jahangir and Shah Jehan. **1397**
The treatment and the subject matter may be Indian, but the
idea that a coin should carry subject matter of this kind and
arranged in this way was not originally Indian at all.

The earliest Greek coins, or coin-like objects, are cast blobs of **61**

21 Cologne, billon antoninianus struck by the Gallic usurper Tetricus I, about AD 272.

22 Constantius I, mint of Siscia, billon follis AD 293-305.

23 Constantine I, mint of Siscia, gold medallion struck AD 306-07.

24 Mithradates I of Parthia, silver tetradrachm, about 140 BC.

25 Shapur I of Persia, drachma, AD 241-72.

26 Umayyad imitation of a Sassanian drachma, Merv, AD 651-52.

27 Arab imitation of a Byzantine gold solidus, Carthage, AD 704.

28 Umayyad Caliphate, silver dirham struck at Wasit, AD 726-27.

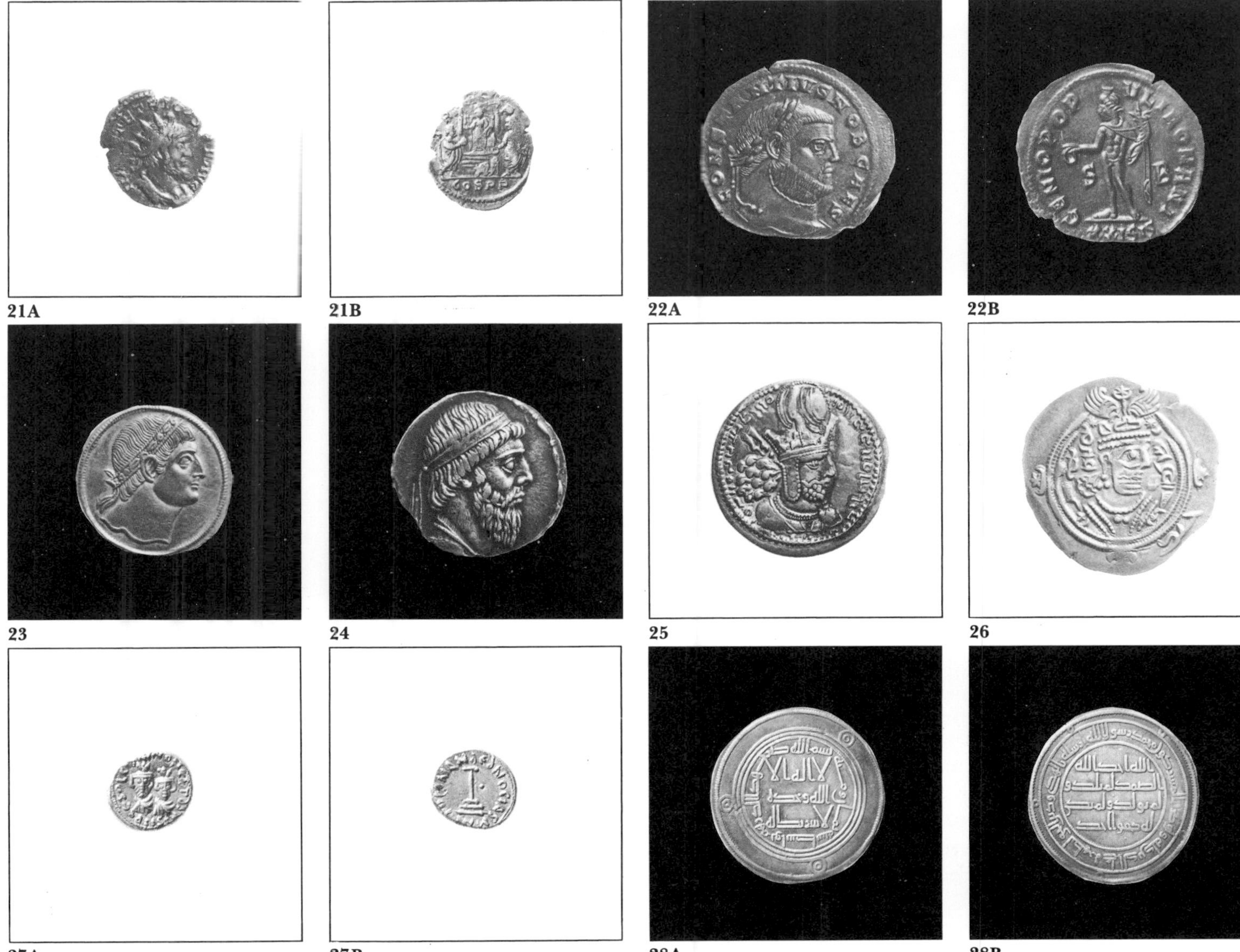

21A **21B** **22A** **22B** **23** **24** **25** **26** **27A** **27B** **28A** **28B**

metal struck on the reverse with a small square punch. They are as primitive in their way as the first Indian coins, but they did not stay like that for long. First, the Greeks engraved in intaglio
13 the surface on which the metal was placed to be struck. This was the origin of the obverse die. Then they began to elaborate, and finally to engrave in detail, the punch with which they struck the coin; which became in due course the fully-developed reverse die.

Both in technique and in intention the engraving of the dies for the earliest Greek coins bore many similarities to the older one of seal-making. A primitive Greek coin was metal sealed to serve as
14 money. One of the earliest bears the seal-like inscription: 'I am the badge of Phanes'. Phanes on this evidence is the first of a long but intermittent list of named moneyers and coiners.

The extraordinary characteristic of Greek coinage is the speed with which it developed from the primitive level as sealed lumps of metal, to become a perfect, if minor, art-form. By 550 BC the techniques were still primitive, the style stiff and archaic though full of promise. The fifth century saw the minting of the most beautiful coins ever made.

The earliest Greek coins have a simple design, usually a single natural object, animal or vegetable, on the obverse and just the punch-mark on the reverse. The object was usually a badge symbolising the state which issued the coin, chosen either because that state was noted for a particular animal or crop, or because the design was associated with a deity to whom the state paid special devotion. In practice the association was often dual: the immediate motive was pious, but a city's choice of one deity rather than another was conditioned by its natural resources and physical situation.

From such beginnings it was natural to introduce into the
reverse punch a small engraving showing the head of the divinity 124
whose badge appeared on the other side. Nor was it long before this head, as it became larger and more ambitious in its treatment, was transferred to the obverse, which was the die that took less wear. The badge was moved to the reverse. Thus the
classic Greek coin was evolved with a head on the obverse and a 15
badge (initially set into the square frame of the reverse punch) on the reverse. Only Islam, among the nations which have followed the western tradition, has broken free from this pattern.

The exceptional beauty of classical Greek coinage is due to a number of factors, technical, economic and aesthetic. Technically the important point is that Greek coins, struck on cast blobs of metal, are very thick but not very broad. It was thus possible to get great depth of relief into the die without too much danger of its breaking up in the striking. Economically, perhaps the

29 Ilkhanid dirham of Abu Sa'id, dated 732 of the Hijra era (= AD 1331-32).

30 Hussayn of Isfahan, 4-shahi silver piece, 1703-04.

31 Constantinople, Justinian I, bronze follis, AD 538-39.

32 Gold histamenon of Basil II and Constantine VIII, Constantinople, 976-1025.

29 **30A** **31A** **31B**

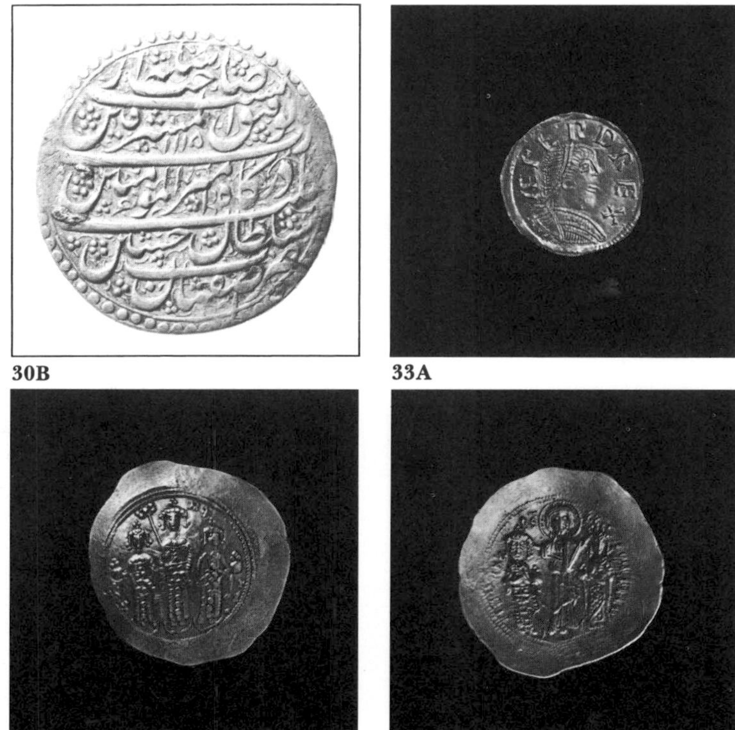

30B **33A** **32A** **32B**

most important point is that most Greek coins are struck in silver, which is the perfect coinage metal, less dazzling than gold, but rich and soft enough to take a sharp impression. Also few of the Greek city-states were large or wealthy. Their coinages therefore were quite small; small enough for a very few exquisitely cut dies to suffice for a whole issue. Aesthetically, the special quality of Greek coins lies in a clearly perceived vision of the ideal. The figures on them, whether a god's head, a dancing
87 nymph or a racing chariot are seen in depth and isolation as the essence of divinity, of the dance or of the race. Nothing else distracts the attention, no pictorial effect, no narrative, no personal or princely display. Even the inscription is played down, often faintly engraved where the main figure is bold.

The first personal note to creep in is the artist's signature on a
95 few coins of the late fifth and early fourth centuries. The coins of
99 Euainetos and Kimon at Syracuse and those of Theodotos at Clazomenae are among the greatest treasures of Greek numis-
139 matics not because of the signature, since nothing is known of these artists except that they signed these coins, but simply because they are among the most beautiful ever made.

There were two principal heirs of Greek classical coinage tradition: Rome and the Hellenistic kingdoms of the eastern Mediterranean. The innovations of this period were portraiture, personality and political content. With these, coins become less beautiful but more interesting.

The best Hellenistic portraits, those for example of the early Bactrian kings (which promoted the Greek influence in Indian coinage), or of the first Seleucids, are very fine. But the faces of
16 those wary middle-aged princes are miles away in spirit from the ideal heads of Dionysus on coins of Naxos or of Apollo on coins of Clazomenae.

Rome originally had its own Italian pecuniary tradition, lumps of cast bronze representing cattle-money, which are
220 hardly true coins. The earliest true Roman coins are also of cast bronze, but otherwise they are Greek in form, round and having a god's head (Janus) on one side and a symbol (a prow) on the other. Under Campanian influence Rome turned to a struck coinage in silver. But specifically Roman features remained for a 17
time, including a system of marks of value which reflects the exactness of Roman administration.

Roman coinage was in the hands of junior magistrates drawn from the leading families of the republic. These families were patriarchal, their most profound feelings centred upon ancestor-worship and their household gods. In the last century of the republic, the personal influence of the moneyers made its mark on the coinage, giving a stronger character to what was originally a rather uninteresting Greek sub-species. Many Roman coins of this epoch show portraits of ancestors which draw directly upon the sternly realistic and unidealized death- 18
mask traditions of the Roman *familia*. The reverses are vignettes of scenes in the life of famous ancestors. 246

In a sense the first imperial coinage was an extension of this. The imperial *imago*, distributed to the cities of the empire as the model for imperial statues and coin-portraits, was a kind of super 19
household god for a whole people. One consequence was an extraordinary realism in this imperial portraiture. The profiles of 20
the emperors from Augustus to Marcus Aurelius are among the best known features in the world, instantly and individually recognizable not only to their contemporaries but also to almost anyone educated in the Renaissance tradition from the fifteenth century to the early twentieth. These emperors have been strikingly characterized by Tacitus, Suetonius and Gibbon. But the reason why they have become as visually familiar to many people as television personalities is that their powerful unflattering portraits were reproduced in their millions and have survived in their thousands on the gold, the silver, and the bronze of the Roman mints.

No special claim can be made for the aesthetic merits of the reverses of Roman imperial coinage. They provide a fascinating record of official policy, for which they are the principal

33 Penny of King Alfred, 871-99.

34 King John, penny struck at London 1216.

35 Edward I, penny struck at Bristol, 1279.

36 Silver bracteate pfennig struck by Siegfried, abbot of Hersfeld, 1180-1200.

37 Philip VI of France, écu à la chaise, 1337.

33B **34A** **34B** **35A**

36 **37A** **37B** **35B**

historical source; but the engraving is feeble, the figure-drawing
467 poor and the disposition of the figures pedestrian.

We know little of the men who made these coins. Work in the public mint, like nearly all manual labour in Rome, was done by slaves. It was usually worse to be a public slave than a private one, and mint work, hot, noisy and hard, was reckoned to be among the worst forms of servitude. The higher class of work, such as engraving, was performed, we may guess, by freedmen of the class which dominated the fields of skilled labour and the arts.

The work of the mint-slaves must have been especially hard in
the years of the great Roman inflation, when they struck the
debased antoniniani in their thousands of millions. The sheer
21 quantity of this coinage is enough to explain the deterioration
which took place in its appearance. Indeed it is surprising that
the successive monetary reforms led to any improvement. Yet,
for the coins of Diocletian and again for those of Constantine the
mints developed a style and technique with lower relief and
thinner coins, which coped with the immense volume in a
tolerably handsome way. Nevertheless the output of this era is
22 grim and uniform. The tetrarchs all look much alike with their
square skulls, their bristly scalps and their staring eyes, though
23 the actual coins are well-made. By contrast the Constantinian
emperors look more refined and remote. The reverse types are
less interesting and varied than those of the earlier empire.
Christian motifs are slow to appear after Constantine's conversion. The well-ordered system of mint and *officina* marks is
characteristic of a strictly ordered and bureaucratized society.

Three later coinage groups are directly derived from classical coinage, that of the Parthians and the Sassanians in the east, Byzantine coinage, and that of the barbarian invaders of western Europe.

The coins of the Arsacid rulers of Parthia are essentially
24 Hellenistic coins of an oriental cast. Those of the Sassanians who
superseded them are more rootedly oriental. Those of the earliest
Sassanian kings, hieratic bearded figures in profile whose 25
elaborate crowns are their most individual feature, are the finest
produced anywhere in the third and fourth centuries, far
superior to coins of Rome in quality or design. With the earliest
of them a new feature is evident: Sassanian drachmae are flatter,
thinner and broader than contemporary Roman coins or those
of their Arsacid predecessors. Those of the last Sassanians, less 1218
distinguished in engraving and design than the earlier pieces, are
very broad and thin and are evidently struck on blanks which
have been cut from hammered sheets of metal.

The change in Persia had important consequences. Sassanian
coinage was the pattern for the first Arabic silver coinage in the
seventh century, and with the spread of Islam this fabric became 26
normal for the whole of the Mediterranean world. It was
adopted also by the Carolingians and in medieval Latin 637
Christendom the practice of cutting coin blanks from thin sheets
of metal was universal until the introduction of machinery and
the rolling mill in the sixteenth century.

The origins of Islamic coinage are to be seen in the very
earliest imitative pieces: the gold are copies of Byzantine solidi, 27
the silver copies of Sassanian drachmae. Soon the Koranic
prohibition of the making of images led to a major change. In a
reform in 696 the caliph 'Abd al Malik introduced purely
epigraphic types for both silver and gold.

Islamic calligraphy has lent surprising variety to Islamic
coinage in its fourteen centuries of almost completely image-free 28
existence. The arrangement of the inscriptions, in lines, in
concentric circles, framed in a square or a hexagram, or free-
standing, and the different scripts, the rugged Kufic, the 29
versatile and flowing Nashki, the architectural Thuluth and the
graceful Nastaliq, have allowed an infinite number of combina- 30
tions. The aesthetic range is almost as wide as that of figurative
coinage, and with its low relief requirement the Islamic style has
been less badly affected by modern mass-productive minting 48
techniques than the coinage of other cultures.

38 Silver testone of Galeazzo Maria Sforza, Duke of Milan, 1468-76.

39 Testone of Milan, Charles V, Holy Roman Emperor, 1536-56.

40 Florence, Alessandro de Medici, testone, 1532-36.

41 Henri II of France, teston au moulin, 1553.

42 Louis XIII, écu blanc, 1643.

38A **38B** **40A** **40B** **42A** **42B**

39A **39B** **41A** **41B**

Byzantine coinage is originally late Roman, and late Roman too is the high degree of mint organization illustrated by the reverses of the copper coins of the first monetary reforms. These
31 are given over entirely to conveying practical information: value, date, mint and workshop number. They are arguably the most utilitarian coin types ever, making even the stark reverses of the Benthamite era in mid-nineteenth century Europe seem frivolous by comparison.

Such a utilitarian concept of coin design left little room for the introduction of Christian motifs, but this changed. The cross was introduced as the principal reverse type on the solidi of Tiberius
558 Constantine. A hundred years later Justinian II introduced the bust of Christ as the principal obverse type, relegating his own portrait to the reverse. During the iconoclastic period, this bust was removed again, but the triumph of the iconodules was signalled by the return not only of Christ but subsequently of the
32 Virgin Mary and of lesser saints. The Byzantine coinage became virtually a treasury of little icons. For a time even the emperor's name disappeared from the copper coinage. The folles of the tenth and eleventh centuries are a strange contrast to those of Anastasius and Justinian I. They contain no useful information whatever, no value, no date, no mint; just the bust of the Saviour
602 on one side and on the other the title, Jesus Christ the King of kings. They might serve as the coinage of the Kingdom of Heaven, and were indeed conceived as the coinage of the one Christian commonwealth.

Two other aspects of Byzantine coinage may be noticed. The appearance of so-called scyphate, that is to say saucer-shaped, coins which appeared about the year 1000. It began with the gold, and under the Comnenian emperors extended to all metals, but it was never used for all coins. It was nevertheless a normal feature of Byzantine and related coinage until the thirteenth century. It must have been extremely impractical. Scyphate coins cannot be stacked, and their obverse (convex) side tends to take a wobbly impression and wears badly.

The other late Byzantine phenomenon is overstriking. This is the process of placing old coins in the die rather than melting them down and recoining with fresh blanks. It always results in ugly coins, since the old impression is never completely effaced by the new.

It is curious that the Byzantines, whose coinage was in so many respects consistent, handsome and well-ordered, should have produced these two aberrations, the most impractical and the most unsightly coins in the history of minting.

Like that of Byzantium, the coinage of the barbarian invaders of western Europe was late Roman in origin. Its charm, if it can be called that, consists in the fresh but naive attempts to imitate classical models, in which it compares in style and feeling with the coinage of the Celts, who had similarly tried to copy Greek models some 600 years earlier.

Ninth-century European coinage took on that flat fabric we have already noticed in the coinage of Islam. Some of this coinage is still classical in aspiration but most of it is less
ambitious and largely epigraphic. 33

The coinage of the next four centuries is characterized by its simplicity. It is simple in its uniform denomination, the silver denier or penny; in its manufacture, struck by dies made with simple, not to say crude punches; and in its design, which consist

43 Silver crown of the English Commonwealth, 1652.

44 Danzig, Sigismund III of Poland, ort, 1621.

45 George III of Great Britain, pattern penny from the Soho mint, 1797.

46 Gold sovereign of George III, 1817.

47 Elizabeth II, sovereign, 1979.

43A **43B** **45A** **45B**

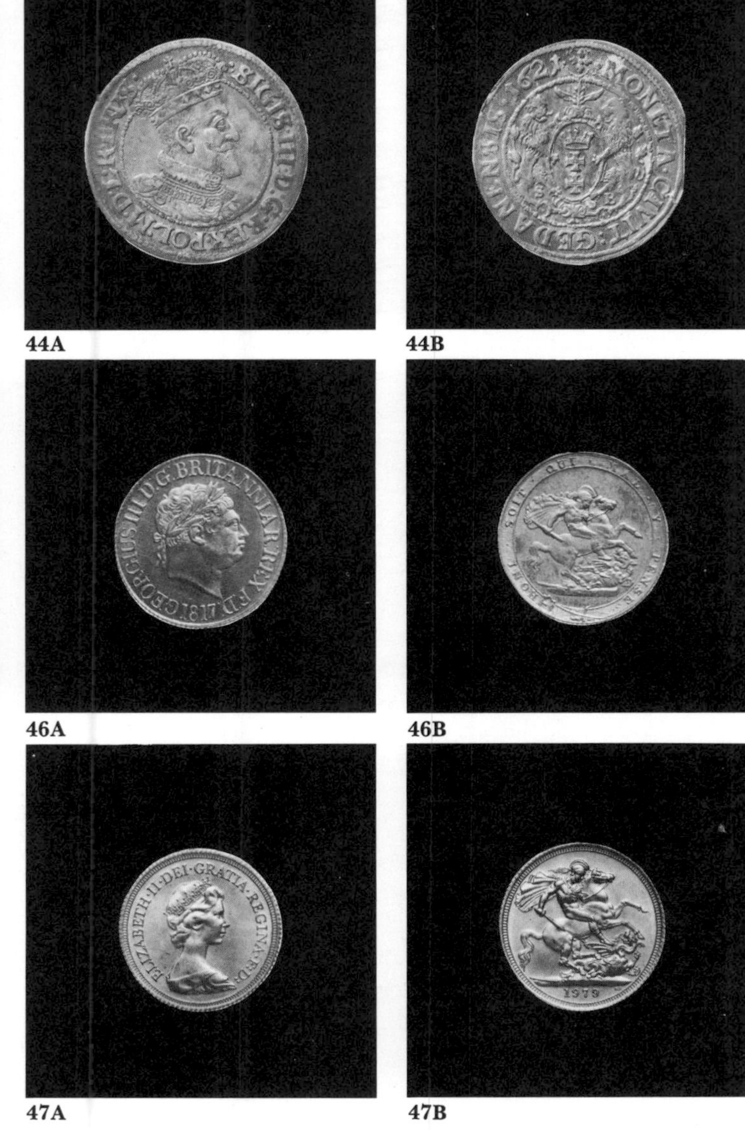

44A **44B** **46A** **46B** **47A** **47B**

of monograms, letters, symbols (the cross especially) or, at its
34 most ambitious, schematic heads or buildings. A common phenomenon is the immobilization of types, the establishment of
35 a certain design and inscription to keep them unchanged for centuries. This is a phenomenon not unknown in our own day, the Maria Theresia thaler and the reverse of the British gold
47 sovereign being examples. It is due more to the economic conservatism of the users than to poverty of invention on the part of the issuers.

Poverty of invention is nevertheless a characteristic of early medieval western coinage. Only in one part of Europe did the mints rise above it to produce coins worthy to set beside their romanesque abbeys, their illuminated manuscripts and their enamels. This was in Germany east of the Elbe, where there was developed an extraordinary technique of coinage, wafer thin but
36 very broad. These coins, today called bracteates, were struck with only an obverse die, the upper 'die' being lined with some soft but resistant material such as leather. The metal was so thin that the impression was clearly visible on both sides, coming through in intaglio on the reverse. The existence of some bracteates less sharply struck up than others from the same die suggests that a number were struck at one stroke; thus only the one nearest the die would receive a sharp impression.

The broad flan of the bracteates gave the die-engravers more scope than the conventional twelfth century penny for imaginative design, and the sharpness of impression taken by the thin metal (on the bottom coin at least) allowed for delicacy of detail.
733 By no means all bracteates are of fine quality, but the best are as satisfying in their way as a romanesque capital carved in miniature.

Bracteates are naturally very fragile. Their life expectancy in circulation can have been no more than that of a modern banknote.

If coinage be taken to reflect the civilization from which it comes, the early middle ages come across as poor economically, poor in technique, and poor in invention. A change comes towards the twelfth century with the commercial revolution and the minting of gold and larger silver coins. Although made by the same techniques as earlier, the dies for these later pieces, especially those for the gold, are of more elaborate and careful workmanship.

Since the new coins were bigger, their thin broad flans gave scope for inventive design. The coins of the great Italian 785
commercial republics were comparatively plain, but the kings of France and England and the princes of north-western Europe indulged in a bold display of heraldic exuberance. The first gold coins of these rulers were struck just as gothic art was beginning its last and most ornamental flowering. They share the delicacy 37
of contemporary illuminated manuscripts, compensating for their absence of colour by the extreme richness of the pure beaten gold. As the fifteenth century drew on, some of these coins also displayed a touch of contemporary religious sentiment, as in 805
the Annunciation on the French *salut* or the shield-bearing angels on the coins of Hainaut and Burgundy.

What the magnificent late gothic coinage lacks is sculptural relief. This was to be developed in the coinage of Italy, which never fully took to the elaborate gothic style. From the thirteenth century it was more influenced by classical, or in the case of

4 Venice, Byzantine models. In the time of the emperor Frederick
783 II serious attempts were made to emulate the coinage of imperial
Rome. Even in the fourteenth century a new interest in the
human form and a much more careful treatment of relief is
shown occasionally.

Pisanello's first portrait medals were cast in 1438. Before 1464,
Francesco Sforza ordered a realistic portrait for his coinage at
38 Milan. The courts of Mantua and Ferrara, closely related to
Milan by political and matrimonial ties, were quick to follow.
811 The first portrait coin appeared at Venice in 1472, and at papal
815 Rome in the papacy of Sixtus IV. A similar spirit infused the
reverse types as the stiff and formal figures of the saints, Saint
John at Florence and Saints Peter and Paul at Rome, took up a
more relaxed and natural stance.

For the first time since the days of ancient Greece, named die-engravers were employed at the Italian mints. None at first were sculptors of the foremost rank and the precise association of particular artists with particular coins is a dubious area of numismatic scholarship. But that certain artists worked at certain mints, Cristoforo Foppa known as Caradosso at Milan, Gianfrancesco da Parma known as l'Enzola at Ferrara, Bartolomeo Melioli at Mantua, and Emiliano Orfini of Foligno at
Rome, is known beyond doubt. A generation later, artists of
higher reputation, though not necessarily greater achievement,
39 were employed. Benvenuto Cellini engraved dies for Popes
40 Clement VII and Julius III and for Duke Alessandro de' Medici
at Florence; his rival Leone Leoni worked at Milan for the rival
court of Charles V. Both produced coins of the highest quality. 'Your Holiness may boast a coinage superior to any of the ancients' said Benvenuto to Clement VII. He was probably unfamiliar with ancient Greek coins. His and Leone's coins were at least as good as the best Roman pieces, with portraits as powerful yet more subtle than the best Roman work. Their real superiority lay in their handling of the reverses. Leone's rather imitate the Romans in subject matter, but are better handled. Benvenuto's are both more imaginatively conceived and better engraved.

Benvenuto is the most distinguished artist in modern times to have devoted any of his talent to die-engraving, and he has left a full account of it in his autobiography. He did not find it easy. He reports the frequent breaking of dies and we can see ourselves, in the die-flaw behind the duke's nose on all extant specimens of the *testone* which he made for Alessandro de' Medici, that he was not always successful in overcoming these difficulties.

The experiments of Benvenuto and Leone in engraving dies of sculptural quality were not the only new developments in minting practice in the early sixteenth century. The afflux of precious metals, first from central Europe and later from America, led to the minting of broader and heavier coins and in greater numbers than before. First there was the testone
weighing about 10 grammes and 30 mm in diameter, and later
826 the thaler weighing about 30 grammes and up to 45 mm in
diameter. Cutting circular blanks for such large coins and striking them in quantity was a laborious process, and inventive minds, including Leonardo da Vinci's, turned to devising ways of doing it by machine.

Various machines were invented. Leonardo's was for cutting blanks. The problem lay in bringing together and improving the half-developed techniques for rolling out metal to the required thickness, for cutting out blanks and for striking them. The whole process was finally perfected in Germany, but first put into practice in France. Under the chief direction of Aubin Olivier as chief engineer, a mill was established in 1551 at the point of the Ile de la Cité with all the accompanying machinery, including a screw-press for striking.

As is often the case with new inventions, the very first work
produced by the Moulin des Étuves, as this establishment was 41
called, was some of the best ever done. This was in spite of, or perhaps because of, the difficulties which had to be overcome. These included trouble over rolling metal to the right thickness, and a tendency for the dies to break under too heavy pressure from the screw-press. The moneyers who practised the old methods were not above adding to these problems by Luddite obstructionism.

The next 100 years saw the establishment of similar mints elsewhere, often in the face of similar difficulties. Nowhere did the change-over proceed altogether smoothly: in general the pattern was for there to be a retreat from the new method after a tentative start and then a resumption of the experiment a generation or more later. So in France the Moulin des Étuves fell into desuetude in the 1560s and milled coinage was only re-
established by Jean Varin in 1641. In England milled coinage 42
was only established for good in 1662. However in the interven-
ing years the best contemporary engravers and engineers were 911
always associated with experiments with the new method:
Nicolas Briot, who moved from Paris to London to work as
medallist for Charles I, Thomas Simon, who was chief engraver 43
in England under the Commonwealth and conducted numerous
experiments with the engineer Peter Blondeau, and Samuel 44
Ammon in Danzig, distinguished as the first engraver since
Theodotos and Pythodoros to sign his coins.

The mill and screw-press were not the only new mechanical methods. In Germany a technique of engraving the dies on rollers was developed. A strip of metal was run through them and then the finished coins were cut out of the strip. This technique was adopted in 1566 at Hall, a silver mining centre in Tirol, and subsequently by other Habsburg mints. Many thalers and lesser coins from central Europe have the slightly cambered
and elongated form which this method produces. 867

The high point in the achievement of the western European mints was reached during the period 1470-1670. These were centuries of rising confidence in the arts and technology. The first hundred years were also a time of immense economic expansion, financed by an increasing money supply which largely took the form of coins. It was impossible to conduct a siege or a war, to found a new colony or a new religion, without leaving a mark on the coinage which was needed to finance these activities. It is no coincidence that in the next phase of economic growth, which was financed more by paper money and credit, there was a marked decline in the interest and beauty of contemporary coins as they played an increasingly subsidiary role.

Eighteenth century coinage was still mostly handsome enough, but the allegory and fantasy were gone, and with them the profusion of religious and philosophical inscriptions which had characterised the coins of the Reformation and Counter-
Reformation eras. On the obverse of the typical eighteenth 914
century coin there was generally a bust, well-proportioned to the size of the coin. On any given set of coins the same bust would be

48 Saudi Arabia, 4-gurush, 1956-57.

49 France, silver 2-francs, 1902.

50 France, cupro-nickel franc, 1960

48A

48B

49

50

subtly reshaped for every denomination to suit the scale of each piece, even the smallest. The legend was generally a recital of increasingly elaborate titles, and the reverse design a heraldic or
915 other conventional device. All was well-ordered, sedate and uniform.

The industrial revolution brought with it new minting techniques and the French revolution new ideas in coin design and symbolism.

45 The new techniques, first developed by the English engineer, Matthew Boulton, centred upon the replacement of the hand-driven screw-press by a press which was powered by steam. This and the development of new and stronger alloys for die-manufacture, meant that more coins could be minted, faster and more accurately.

Once again a new technical development stimulated an artistic revival. The change occurred in the heyday of neo-classicism, a style to which the clean-cut appearance of the coins made by the new industrial process was especially suited. The ponderous busts of the post-baroque gave way to neat profile
1035 heads, truncated at the neck. At the same time, in response to the surge of nationalism, heraldry on many coins gave way to more popular national symbols. On Matthew Boulton's British copper coinage Britannia took on her classic form with her Union Jack shield, her trident and her men o' war. Liberty made her first appearance on the coins of the United States, and Marianne on
46 those of the French republic. In 1817 Benedetto Pistrucci produced his George and Dragon, a paradigm of neo-classical design and the last coin-type to establish itself, by its association with a coin of first rate commercial importance, as an immobilized type.

The sovereign of 1817 was the coin with which the gold standard made its debut on the monetary scene. One aspect of the gold standard is that coins of all other metals take their value not from their intrinsic worth but by fiat of the issuing government. Their value cannot therefore be assessed by recourse to the scales but must be marked on each coin. Nineteenth century coinage is distinguished by the prominence given to the mark of value, a characteristic which has continued into the twentieth. Indeed it is now all the more necessary, since most coins have no intrinsic value whatever. Significantly only
47 coins minted for the international bullion market are free from this utilitarian requirement, which proves so inhibiting in coin design by its creation of severe limitations.

The advances in minting technology since 1800 have almost all led to a deterioration in the aesthetic quality of coins. Minting has always been a mass-productive process, but the volume has had to be increased enormously and quantity is bad for quality. Nowadays the artist who designs a coin is separated physically by at least six processes from the coin which leaves the mint. He makes a plaster model, maybe a hundred times larger than the coin which is planned. This is reproduced by electrotype in a synthetic material, which is placed in a reducing machine, which engraves a punch, which makes a matrix, which is touched up by engravers at the mint and then used to make punches to make the dies which strike the coins. This is a long way from Benvenuto's hand-engraving of his own dies. The most sensitive of original designs is coarsened by this succession of industrial processes.

Another adverse factor since the 1914-18 war has been the cheapening of coinage. Many fine coins have been struck in bronze, but the best have been struck in gold and silver, which are precious metals not just because they are rare but because they are pleasing to the eye. Nearly all coins today are struck in base metal, and a high proportion of those in nickel or more of cupro-nickel. Nickel is exceedingly hard, it will not take a detailed impression or subtle relief, and it reflects light in a capricious and disagreeable manner.

An interesting example of the degeneration of modern coinage is to be seen in the current French franc. In 1897 a new design was commissioned for the franc and the prize was awarded to Oscar Roty for the Semeuse, a figure of Marianne which broke
away from the tired neo-classicism of the 1850s which had **49**
sufficed for the Third Republic until then. She symbolized the life-giving force of France as experienced in the great national recovery after the debacle of 1870. In the inflationary period after 1918, the Semeuse disappeared from circulation; but she was still remembered as a symbol of resurgent France and sound money. When therefore Charles de Gaulle wished to strike this
note at the time of the monetary reform of 1960, he ordered that **50**
Roty's design should be used again. Alas, on the later coins the delicate art nouveau draperies have lost their flowing line and the faint rays of Roty's rising sun have almost disappeared in the glare of the cupro-nickel reflection. Yet the very fact that a great statesman found it worthwhile to revive the coin at all, shows that even in the age of the slot-machine, coins have still kept some of their age-old prestige.

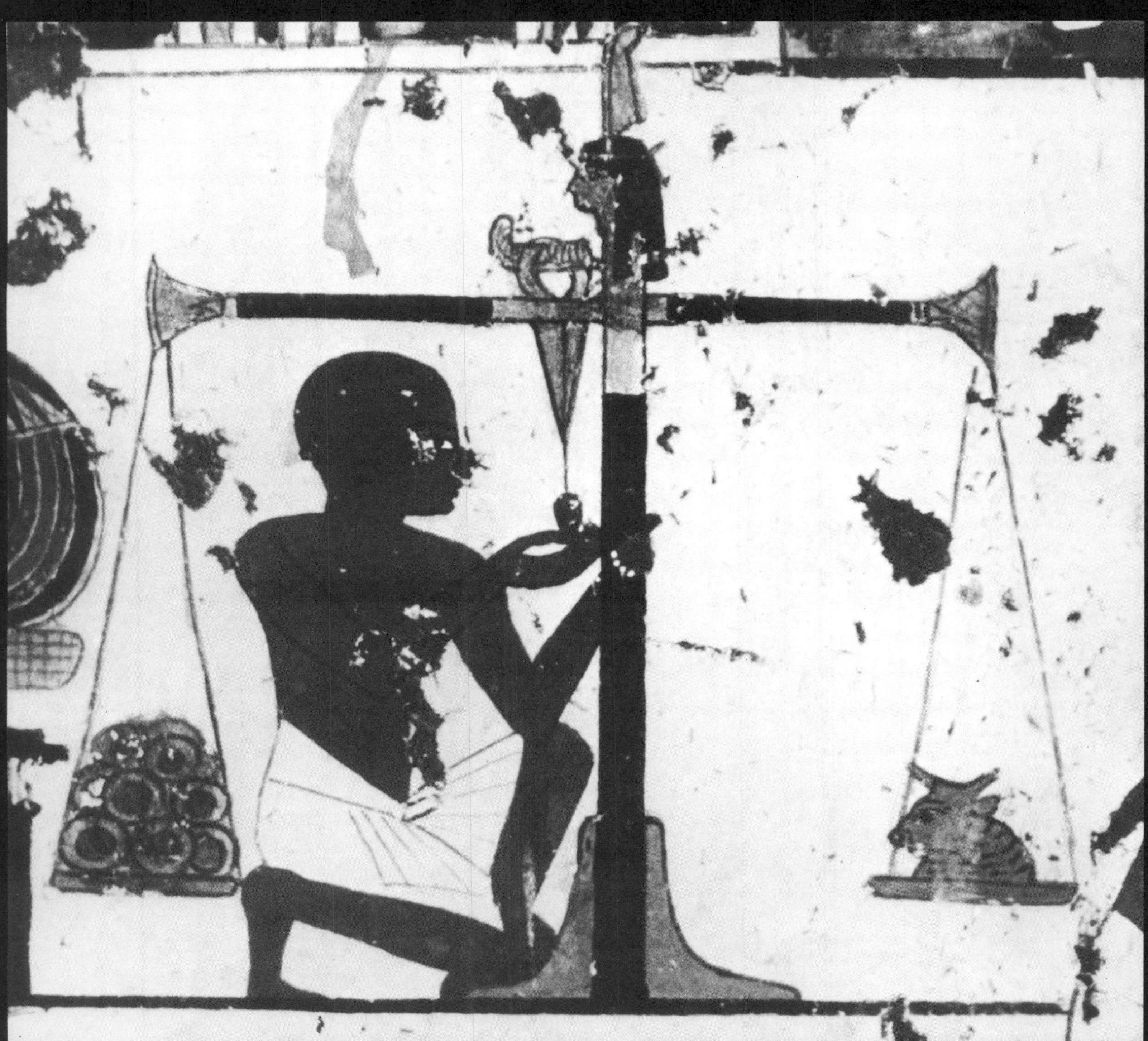

II
MONEY BEFORE COINAGE

Miriam Balmuth

From time immemorial, people have been giving and receiving in exchange goods, services, animals and even other people. Trade is considered by anthropologists to be a fundamental and universal aspect of human behaviour and one that has characterized society from the earliest times. An appropriate question for a volume on coinage is: 'How did people trade before the earliest coins were produced?' The answer is complex and varied, but ultimately traces the evolution of trade from barter to coinage.

The Greek philosopher Aristotle asked the same question in the fourth century BC, at a time when coinage had already been in continuous use for over 300 years. He describes barter, the system in which one commodity is traded for another without restriction, as the earliest kind of trade and a function of nature. In time, he goes on to explain, the growth and expansion of trade and the importation and exportation of goods required some kind of mutually acceptable, useful and portable commodity as a medium of exchange. He suggests that metal was used as that commodity, at first having its value determined by size and weight, but then, after a time, being stamped with an indication or assurance of its value, in order that it not be necessary to make a separate measurement of size or weight for each transaction. This man-made law or social institution illustrated to Aristotle a development from nature to culture and the dichotomy between the two, a subject of endless fascination to him. It also accounts for the Greek word for coin, 'nomisma', derived from the word for law or custom, 'nomos'.

This answer was one worked out by theoretical deduction, and it is possible today to give some substance to these theories. Information and insight gained through archaeological and anthropological studies have enabled us to reconstruct the path of development in trade and exchange. Barter persists as an effective and universal practice even today. The mutually acceptable commodity used as a medium of exchange, however, has had a vast range, extending from natural to manufactured items, and from the utilitarian to the luxurious: crops from the earth, cattle, wine, butter, cloth, shells or slaves are just a few of the kinds of goods that have acted as payments, some very recently. During the Second World War, cigarettes were accepted in Sicily in preference to Italian lire, and in agricultural communities, produce and certain tools are always acceptable as currency.

A form of exchange that lies outside Aristotle's experience and theorizing is the gift which is given in the expectation of some kind of return. This has been part of a social ritual in some tribal societies up until the first generation of this century. The potlatch of the North American Kwakiutl Indians was a ceremonial festival based on the lavish gifts of the host and the assumed return exceeding his presentation. Because of excessive borrowing to make the presentations, the potlatch began to contribute to so much impoverishment that it was outlawed by the Canadian government. The mutually accepted commodity used as a medium of exchange at the time was the blanket, which also acted as the standard of value. This means that everything was either paid for in blankets or in other objects whose value was measured in blankets. Before the institution of blankets as the medium of exchange, the function had been served by wampum in the form of strings of shell beads or by furs.

Since coins first appeared around the Mediterranean, it is appropriate to consider the development here of the concept of metal both as the medium of exchange and the standard value. Archaeological finds of inscriptions specifying payments have made it possible to reconstruct in part the nature of exchange in the Near East from as early as the late third millennium BC since they furnish information on administrative procedures, legal penalties, wages, loans and interest as well as other economic activities of the urban centres of the earliest civilizations. The successive political states in Mesopotamia have been an especially rich source of this kind of textual information and have also provided the material which may actually have been used for the payments.

Hoards of small pieces of silver or broken or cut-up silver jewellery have been found in the Sumerian and Akkadian levels of the Mesopotamian plain, dating them to the middle of the third millennium BC or just after. They serve as vivid illustrations for the earliest texts which refer to payments in silver **51,52**
fragments or broken or cut silver, such as the one pictured in which is recorded the transfer of 'Silver broken, the property of Urdulkugga.' Other cuneiform tablets from the same city, Nippur, which thrived in the century before 2000 BC during the third dynasty of Ur, give accounts for loans and payments in terms of grain or cattle, but for the most part the references are to silver shekels. Like the weighed silver, the grain or cattle acted either as the actual payment or as the standard according to which equivalents were expressed. In time, however, silver became the almost universal standard. It could be stored, reused and divided, and its value was not as dependent on seasonal variations as that of crops or cattle. Its use by weight is a practice confirmed by the word 'shekel'. The meaning of the verbal root 'šql' is 'to weigh' in all Semitic languages, hence the original

Weighing gold rings at Thebes, Egypt, fourteenth century BC.

51 The most widespread expression of exchange in the Mediterranean area from the third millennium BC onwards was silver by weight. From a recent excavation at Tell Taya in Mesopotamia comes one of the earliest known hoards of silver, cut-up and broken, in a form that lends itself to a transaction requiring weighing. From literature contemporary with the hoards, we read of the money carried in jars or bags.

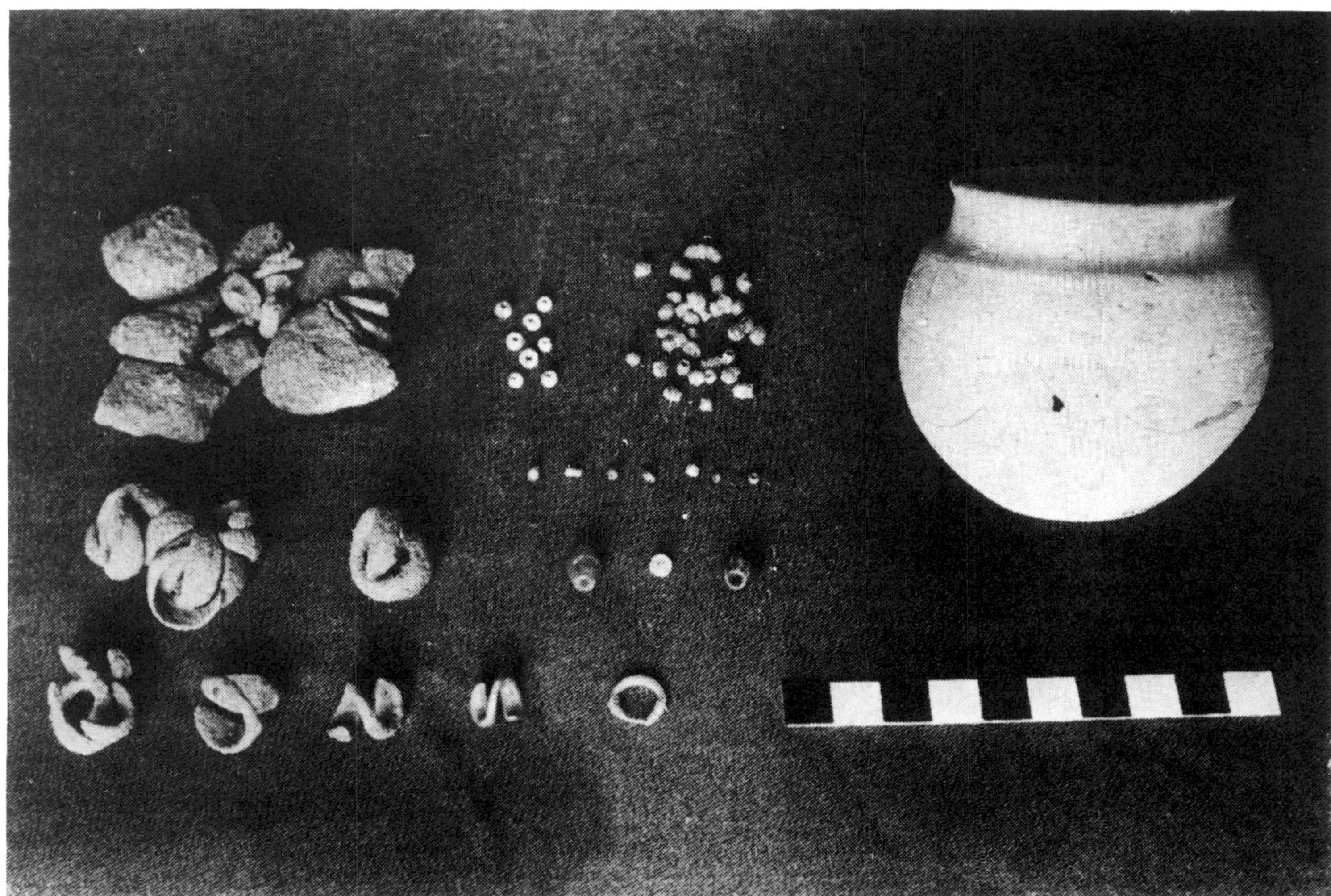

51

meaning of unit of weight which later came to mean denomination. This is equally true of the Greek 'talent' and is most visible in the English 'pound'. Likewise, the Semitic word for silver, 'ksp', came to mean money, just as in the French 'argent'.

The shekel was the smallest whole standard unit of weight in a sexagesimal system in Mesopotamia; there were 60 shekels in a mina and 60 minas in a talent, the largest denomination. In other areas of the Near East, the relationship varied according to tradition or ease of foreign trade. Further variations existed within one system when shekels appeared simultaneously with shekels of the sanctuary or shekels current with the merchant, both known from Old Testament sources. In addition, royal shekels or heavy shekels are known and silver and good silver seem to be used as variants. The earliest reference to a payment in the Old Testament is the 400 shekels of silver, current with the merchant, which were weighed out for Abraham's purchase for land in which to bury Sarah (*Genesis* 23:15-16).

The archaeological evidence which supports these texts and interpretations of exchange before coinage is the discovery of scale pans and scale weights and the hoards of precious metal not only from Mesopotamia, but from other Bronze and Early Iron Age civilizations in the Near East: Egypt, Syria and Palestine as well as peripheral areas. These hoards, made up of variously sized and shaped ingots and often including pieces of jewellery, appear to have been used for exchange by weight. This use is not only known from as early as the third millennium BC but extended to long after coins had become common in Greece, in areas which did not mint their own coins. From the sixth century BC on, some of the Near Eastern hoards of silver used in exchange actually contained minted silver coins from Greek cities, used as bullion.

For more specific illustrations, it is instructive to survey the textual and material remains of one ancient site. The important Late Bronze Age city of Ugarit on the coast of northern Syria, was known only from references in ancient inscriptions until 1928, when its remains were stumbled upon in the village of Ras Shamra. For over 50 years now, French archaeologists have been excavating the city and its adjoining port, uncovering a thriving cosmopolis of the fourteenth century BC. Clay tablets with cuneiform writing have been found in great number in the royal palace, some still in the oven describing emergency conditions when the city was finally destroyed at the end of the thirteenth or beginning of the twelfth century BC. The tablets are a rewarding source of information not only about trade and exchange, but of the structure of the palace economy and its relation to the population. Tribute and taxes are paid in wine or in silver shekels; there are inventories with prices attached; wills, fines and rations; and guild quotas and guild allotments. Most of the prices are expressed in silver shekels or heavy silver shekels. One illuminating text, treating the distribution of purple wool in specific amounts, reveals a talent of 3000 shekels, unlike the more symmetrical Mesopotamian talent of 3600 shekels. The 4:1 relationship of gold to silver can also be extrapolated from an administrative text. Literary and poetic texts are equally informative. In two different epics, the heroes weep: what they weep is compared to fractional shekels, ¼ or ⅕, which course down their cheeks to the ground. In a poem describing the preparations of the wedding of two deities, the full use of a scale is recounted, revealing the thorough familiarity with weighing that allows its functions to be transferred to poetry, as each member of the bride's family attends to a different aspect of balancing the scale-weights against a treasure.

52 From the Sumerian city of Nippur have come a large quantity of cuneiform tablets with information on the financial activities of the community. This tablet specifies a payment in broken silver made before five witnesses. Dating from the third dynasty of Ur, around the twenty-first century BC, this inscription is one of a group which constitutes the earliest known reference to exchange by weighed silver.

53 Pieces of silver were found adhering to the scale pans shown, perhaps from a hoard being weighed out as a payment. The hoard shown was considered part of a jeweller's stock by the excavator, but it is ideally suited for exchange as well. Ugaritic tablets document just such exchanges in the administrative texts, poems and epics found in the royal palace from the fourteenth century BC.

54 The use of scales, balances, and weights must have been a daily activity among Egyptian merchants. The ring-shaped objects to be weighed out may actually be a kind of negotiable currency. An Egyptian wall painting from Beni-Hasan.

52

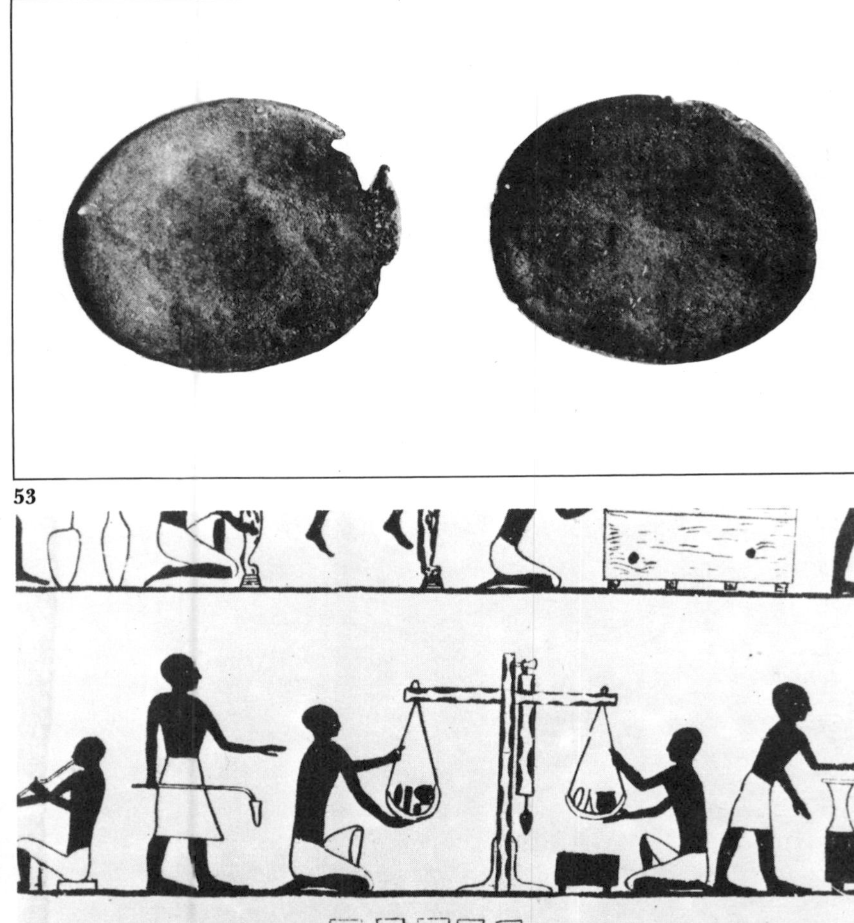

53

54

The archaeological evidence supporting the text is particularly
53 strong in Ugarit. Scale trays made of bronze have been found in identical pairs. Scale weights of a wide variety have also appeared as geometrical stone shapes, a large inscribed bronze bull and a bronze representation of a human head. Certain of the weights have been used to calculate that 50 shekels equalled the intermediary weight known as a mina, and that there must have been 60 minas in a talent, since the written accounts have already confirmed a 3000-shekel talent. In one instance, a complete set of weights lay beside two bronze scale trays as they were excavated, together with tiny grains of silver. Silver again is the material of a hoard containing jewellery such as earrings and finger rings, miniature animals, and cut-up and folded pieces of metal. The composition of the hoard is similar to the others known from this period after the middle of the second millennium BC from other East Mediterranean sites. A later hoard from this same site belongs to the realm of coinage proper since it contains not only silver ingots but also Archaic Greek coins from cities of northern Greece and Cyprus. The later hoard is one of many known from the sixth century BC until the institution of coinage by Alexander the Great in the Near East in the fourth century BC and is an eloquent illustration of the continuation of the monetary practice of weighing the silver in this area even though coins were acceptable payments on presentation in Greece. Even the Greek coins in the hoard were exchangeable by weight only, their stamp of guarantee notwithstanding. In Southern Italy, a mixed hoard of this kind is known from
60 Taranto, where it was buried around 500 BC.

From Egypt comes evidence for the storage and transportation of the material used for payments. An eleventh century BC tale, written on papyrus and now in Leningrad, is of the journey of Wen-Amon who travelled by sea to Lebanon to buy timber for a ceremonial barge for his god. An early anti-hero, Wen-Amon, had more adventures than success. He carried jars and sacks filled with gold and silver for the payments he would make if he were ever to reach his goal. These were counted in *deben*, an
Egyptian unit of weight. Even earlier than Wen-Amon, Egyptian 54
tomb paintings showed scenes of weighing metal for exchange, with both metal rings and scale weights visible in the painting. An actual 'crock of gold' in the excavator's words, was found at Tell el-Amarna filled with ingots of gold and silver and rings of silver. The site is precisely datable to a 17-year period in the first
half of the fourteenth century BC and the find illustrates the 55
continuity of storage of precious material suitable for exchange in pottery vessels.

This kind of storage is known as well from several hoards from Palestine between the fourteenth and eleventh centuries BC, such as one from Beth Shan discovered with the pot in which it was found and one from Megiddo with traces of bronze mesh bags around it. Even later hoards, including those of ingots mixed with Greek coins are often found in ceramic containers. On the island of Bahrein in the Persian Gulf, the ancient Dilmun known from early inscriptions has been found. At a level of later occupation, about the beginning of the sixth century BC a pot was found containing silver ingots, pieces of cut jewellery, some whole rings and earrings and remains of woven cloth. The fifth-century BC Greek historian Herodotus wrote of a quaint custom among the Persians illustrated by Darius' tribute from Europe in gold, which he had melted down and poured into pots. When the pots were filled, the king would break them and then cut off pieces of gold when he needed money.

Five undecorated clay pots were the storage containers for

55 Like other hoards found in a pot, the gold and silver from the fourteenth century BC capital of Pharoah Akenaton at Tell el-Amarna may have been stored for future exchange to be transacted by weight with the help of a scale.

56 A significant inscription from eighth century BC North Syria within the Assyrian power sphere; the name of King Barrekub of Zinjirli marks a round silver ingot, one of three such found. Unmarked ingots of the same size and shape as well as smaller pieces of silver were part of the large hoard found in the royal palace. Since the inscribed ingots conform to an official weight standard, they can technically be considered coins.

57 The stock-in-trade of a jeweller or silversmith made ideal currency for exchange in the Mediterranean world where silver by weight is the most widely documented form of trade. The material found in five jars in biblical Eshtemoa consist of earrings, finger rings and nose rings in addition to amorphous broken pieces. The bezels, or seal parts, of the finger rings have an especially coin-like appearance.

57

56

58

59

over 25 kilogrammes of silver found at the biblical site of
Eshtemoa. Partly pieces of jewellery and partly amorphous
57 ingots, the silver seems ideally suited to exchange by weight. Of
special interest is the shape of the bezel or seal part of the finger
rings. These are so similar to coins in size and shape that they
may possibly be thought of as one source of inspiration for the
final appearance of coins. The inhabitants of Eshtemoa were
among those given gifts by King David from the spoils of the
Amalekites (I *Samuel* 30) and while it is tempting to think of the
silver as part of the spoils, the hoard may date from the eighth
century BC, too late to correspond to the biblical reference.

From as far east as Persia, a hoard has been found of silver both in bar-shaped ingots and in smaller pieces that seem to have been cut off from them. These were found along with rings in a large bronze bowl at the site of Nush-i Jan and have been interpreted as currency to be negotiable by weight in the same manner as the other hoards here discussed. The find is dated to the seventh century BC, the century in which coins first began to appear in the Greek world.

An eighth century hoard from North Syrian Zinjirli, a city that
was actually ruled by Assyria, has elements reminiscent of past
hoards as well as some which seem to anticipate aspects of Greek
coinage. From the palace of King Barrekub in the last decades of
the century was found a large amount of silver in cut pieces,
56 thicker folded pieces and several discs. Three of the discs were
inscribed with the name of the king, who was a vassal of the
Assyrians. Their weight corresponds roughly to that of the

55

58 Silver bars, buns and cut-pieces were found together in a bronze bowl at Nush-i-Jan in Persia, where they were put together for exchange in the seventh century BC, the time when coins first began to be struck in the Greek world. The different shapes may mean that they were intended for separate markets.

59 In a literate society, the mark of identification on a seal is name, sometimes position and sometimes descent, with or without a device or emblem. This eighth century jasper seal found in Megiddo shows a lion striding left with the inscription above and below the animal: 'Of Shema, servant of Jereboam'. The type, inscription and arrangement of elements are all forerunners of Greek coins.

60 The earliest hoards of coins usually contain also the ingots and fragments of silver that were hoarded in the centuries before coinage. This clearly indicates the similarity of function between coined and uncoined silver. Objects from a hoard found at Taranto, Italy in June 1911, originally deposited about 500 BC.

60

Assyrian system, and it is still unclear whether they were intended for circulation or were just part of the palace treasure. The seal of the king was also found in the palace, complete with the royal insignia. Another eighth century seal was found at Megiddo and in its subject matter, composition and inscription is another clear anticipation of the type yet to come on early
59 Greek coins. A lion striding across a ground line with letters above and below is strikingly similar to the early electrum stater
62 from Ephesus struck about a century and a half later.

Since controlled weight is one of the characteristics of early Greek coinage and its successors, emphasis has been placed on metal exchanged by weight. Another kind of payment existed at the same time, however, as the hoards which had to be weighed for each transaction: exchange by unit or what is known as 'utensil money'. The value of the cauldron or axehead in such negotiations would not be dependent on weight, but on the unit itself which already possesses the value of use and recognition. Some early Near Eastern inscriptions confirm such items as copper utensils given as payments in which weighing plays no part, but more evidence comes from Archaic Greece, where as late as the sixth century BC some fines were still being reckoned in cauldrons and tripods. The use of the word 'obol' for a small coin denomination is another demonstration of exhange by unit since in its original form, it means a spit or pointed instrument and retains that meaning in literature until the fifth century BC, implying that spits had the exchange value that was eventually transferred to the small coin.

Not surprisingly, cattle also served both as medium of exchange and standard of value in weight-free transactions. In the Iliad of Homer, first written down in the eighth century BC, prizes were offered for the games described in the twenty-third book. Among them are cauldrons, tripods, horses and mules and oxen, women, and even a piece of iron. The awards listed for a wrestling match were a tripod worth 12 oxen for the winner and a woman talented at handcrafts worth four oxen for the loser. In the sixth book of the Iliad, the hazard of uneven exchange is pointed out in the account of two warriors from opposing sides, Diomedes and Glaucus, who make a sentimental exchange of armour: a gold suit worth 100 bulls for a bronze one worth nine!

The analysis of ancient texts and materials has made it possible not only to trace an evolution from barter to the use of coins, but also to see the contributions to the final product made by the processes introduced in the Near East. The first is the 60
institution of a standard measure of value, whether by unit, measurement or weight. Another is the establishment of a precious metal (silver) as that standard, in a manner that allowed complete flexibility and reusability, controlled by weight and continuing in use even after the appearance of the earliest coins. The type and inscriptions of the earliest coins have been discovered on the earlier seals of identification, and their composition, shape and size come as no surprise after viewing many Bronze Age hoards. It was, indeed, inevitable that these characteristics would be combined to produce the world's first coins . . . but that is the starting-point of the next chapter.

III

THE FIRST THREE CENTURIES OF COINAGE

Martin Price

In the foundations of the temple of Artemis at Ephesus the excavators discovered a rich deposit of votive offerings enclosed within the earliest structure on the site. Amongst the statuettes and jewellery were 87 coins, all of electrum, an alloy of silver and gold which is found in a natural state in the valley of the Pactolus river in western Asia Minor. Most of the coins bore a design on one side only, and all were recognized to be from amongst the earliest coins ever made. The find appears to substantiate the statement of the fifth century BC Greek historian Herodotus that 'the Lydians were the first people we know to have struck and used coinage of silver and gold.' King Croesus of Lydia (561-46 BC) gave generously towards the construction costs of the temple of Artemis, and this allows us to date with certainty before 550 BC all the objects found in the substructures. From the available evidence the first coins may be dated to the late seventh century BC, certainly no earlier than 650 BC. The first reference to coinage in literature is a donation of 2000 staters for military expenses made to the poet-statesman Alcaeus by the Lydians in the early years of the sixth century BC.

61 It is the punch struck into the ready-weighed lump of precious metal that differentiates a coin from a rough nugget of bullion; and the pattern or design engraved on the punch, or in the anvil onto which the coin is struck, identifies the issuing authority. In this way the design that appears on the coin has its origin in the
59,62 personal seal. A great variety of types and denominations exists amongst the earliest electrum coins; but most of the issues must have been very small. The coins were all of electrum, although silver and gold objects were found beside them in the deposits of the temple of Artemis. It may be assumed that electrum was preferred for coinage; and the fact that the amount of gold in the alloy was sometimes reduced to as little as 30%, without perhaps affecting the value at which the coin circulated, implies that profiteering was one reason for striking coinage. The practice of countermarking (stamping an already existing coin with a small
120 device, personal or official) began with the earliest Lydian electrum, and is a sign that some further guarantee was required before a coin would be readily accepted in transactions.

The middle of the sixth century BC saw a revolution in
68 coinage. In Lydia Croesus substituted pure silver and gold coins for the earlier electrum; and at about the same time the cities of
69,70-72 Athens, Aegina, and Corinth in mainland Greece, and Sybaris and Metapontum in Italy, began for the first time to strike coinage, all using silver as the coinage medium. The different techniques used for these early coinages show that the process of minting evolved independently in different geographical areas; but the idea of coinage, with the implications that the same weight of metal could be worth more as a coin than as a nugget, must have been known to any who had travelled to western Asia Minor in the 50 or more years before the time of Croesus.

Silver had long been recognized to be a valuable metal, convenient as a medium for commercial transactions; but judging from existing objects and hoards, it does not appear to have been available in large quantities before the mid-sixth century BC. Silver in its natural state could only be mined in Spain (Tartessus) or central Europe; and it is silver extracted from lead ores by a process of cupellation that provided the metal for ancient coinage. It is very probable that technological improvements in extracting silver resulted in the increased exploitation of silver-bearing lead ores in mining areas such as Laurion near Athens and in Macedonia and the Greek Islands; and this new availability of silver led to the striking of coinage throughout Greek lands.

Hoards of coins found in Palestine and Egypt in the late sixth century and early fifth century BC show that Greek coinage travelled extensively to the eastern Mediterranean, where clearly the silver was more valuable than in the Aegean basin, even after any overvaluation imposed by the minting authorities. In the
East the carefully worked coins were treated as bullion metal, 113
roughly chopped to test their purity or cut into fragments whenever a transaction so required. The carefully weighed monetary units were disregarded, and the same hoards contained rough nuggets of silver side by side with the coins. In Italy and Sicily silver was also imported from the Aegean; but the need for the city states to retain control over the imported silver led to their striking their own coinage, often overstriking coins of other cities with new types. In South Italy, Crete, and other areas where silver was difficult to obtain, the coins remained in the area where they were minted, and did not circulate in the same way as the coins of states which had easy access to silver. This in turn indicates an even greater amount of overvaluation of the coin against the current value of bullion silver.

Weight was always a major consideration with coins of precious metals, and the intricate variety of weights of early Greek coins reflects the many traditions that existed in a world broken into small city-states. Each coin was carefully weighed according to the weight system that each city had adopted; but in the Greek world as a whole there was a multitude of different systems. The basic unit of weight in the Aegean area, however,
long before the first coins were minted, was the *drachma* 74
('handful'), and the different weights accorded to the drachma –

The nymph Arethusa engraved by Kimon, Syracuse, about 410 BC (**95**).

79 Six unciae (hemilitron), one of the earliest bronze coins struck in Sicily, normally attributed to the city of Himera, about 430 BC.

80 Bronze hemilitron of Acragas, about 420 BC. The crab and shell symbols emphasize the maritime position of the city.

81 Syracuse, Sicily was one of the first cities to adopt small, light coins of bronze, but on this series there is no mark of value. Possibly a hemilitron, about 410 BC.

82 Ear of barley on a bronze obol of Metapontum, Italy, about 360 BC. The inclusion of the name of the denomination leaves no doubt as to the value at which the coin circulated.

83 The fish-tailed monster Scylla, who delighted in the destruction of ships, and the mussel shell, indicate the importance of the sea in the life of the city. Cumae, Italy, stater about 450 BC.

84 Thurii was a pan-hellenic colony founded on the site of Sybaris in 443 BC. The head of Athena marks the part played by Athens in the foundation, and the bull recalls the coinage of Sybaris (**69**). A figure of the Scylla decorates Athena's helmet. Distater, about 375 BC.

85 Heracles, the legendary founder of Croton, is named *oikistes* (founder) on this stater about 420 BC.

86 Victory seated on a stone base, holding a bird. Terina, stater about 400 BC.

87 The lively cutting of this decadrachm of Acragas is a masterpiece of late fifth century BC workmanship. It was probably struck to commemorate the victory of Exainetos in the Olympic games of 412 BC. The racing quadriga is adapted from contemporary Syracusan coins, popular throughout Sicily. The eagles clutching their prey is a common motif on the coins of Acragas of all metals.

80

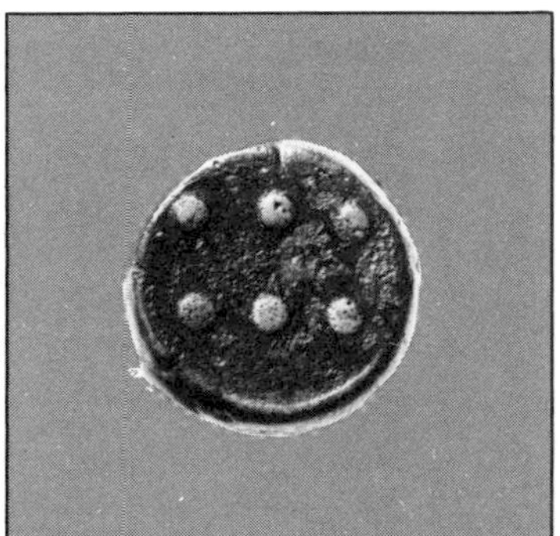

79

82×2

83×2

84A

84B

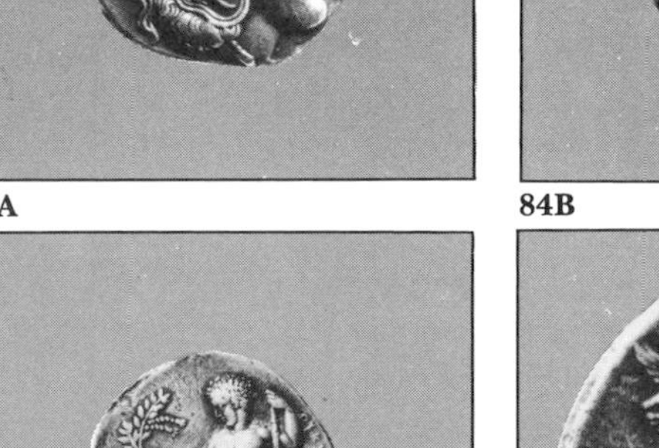

85

86×2

87A×2

88 At Catana, north of Syracuse, the engraver Heracleidas signed this magnificent adaptation of Kimon's facing head (**95**) for a head of Apollo with laurel wreath. Tetradrachm, about 405 BC.

89 The man-headed bull, the personification of the rushing waters of the river Gelas, is used as the badge of Gela throughout the fifth century BC. Tetradrachm, about 475 BC.

90 The racing chariot first adopted at Syracuse was borrowed by many Sicilian states. On this tetradrachm of Himera the name of Pelops, founder of the Olympic games, and the palm of victory, link the issue with the victory of Ergoteles of Himera at Olympia in 464 BC.

91 The personification of the city of Himera offers sacrifice in her sanctuary, while the satyr, the devotee of Dionysus, wades knee-deep in the basin of a fountain. A charming tetradrachm, about 415 BC.

92 The mule chariot celebrates the victory of Anaxilas of Messana at Olympia, and the hare and head of Pan recall the connections of the city with Messene in the Peloponnese. The types instituted by the tyrant Anaxilas were retained throughout the fifth century BC even after his expulsion in 461 BC. Messana, Sicily, tetradrachm, about 430 BC.

93 Magnificent early classical engraving, celebrating the rich vineyards of the area, with the head of the god Dionysus linked with the horse-tailed Silenus, squatting to drink the fruit of the vine. Naxos, Sicily, tetradrachm, about 460 BC.

88

89

81

90

87B×2

92A

91

92B

93

107 At Abdera, Thrace, the badge of the city was the griffin, and about 375 BC the staters inscribed 'in the period of office of Polykrates' depicted the fine cult image of Artemis the Huntress, from the goddess's temple in the city.

108 Amphipolis was founded in 436 BC to defend Athens' interests in Macedonia; but it soon became a seat of hostility to her. The facing head of Apollo on a tetradrachm of about 360 BC has all the soft charm of mid-fourth century work, and was struck a little before the destruction of the city in 357 BC.

109 The coinage of Mende continued throughout the fifth century BC until a decree from Athens insisted that all members of the Delian confederacy should adopt Athenian coinage, about 425 BC. This tetradrachm of about 430 BC shows Dionysus with his drinking cup, reclining on an ass; and, on the reverse, the vines for which Mende was famous.

110 The Chalcidian League, centred on Olynthus, dominated the politics of Macedonia until its dissolution in 348 BC by Philip II. Gold stater of the League, about 350 BC, depicting Apollo and his lyre, and dated 'in the period of office of Eudoridas'.

111 The small island of Peparethus in the north-west Aegean produced few tetradrachms; but this exquisite personification of Boreas, the north wind which to this day brings the grapes to ripeness, was used about 490 BC to symbolize the importance of viticulture in the island's economy.

112 Larissa in Thessaly issued a large number of drachmae in the late fifth and fourth centuries BC for local circulation. The facing head of the personification of the city was adopted in the mid-fourth century BC.

113 Delphi was not a major mint, but all the examples of this issue of tridrachms of about 480 BC depicting ram-head drinking cups and dolphins, were found in Egypt. Once the coins had left Greek lands, they were used only as nuggets of silver, often, as in this case, chopped to test the purity of the metal.

107A 107B 108 109A

109B 110A×2 110B×2 111

112×2 113

115A×2 115B×2 114×3

116 117×2 118 119×2

114 An inscription at Delphi records full details of the coin issue of 336 BC to which this didrachm in the name of the Amphictionic Council belongs. Apollo is shown seated on the sacred stone, the omphalos, with his lyre and tripod.

115 The Boeotian cities of central Greece used their distinctive shield as a badge for the staters of all cities. In the mid-fourth century BC Thebes adopted a fine amphora as reverse type, and the names of officials responsible for the issues are given a prominent place. On this example EPAMI is probably the great Theban general Epaminondas, who led the Thebans to supremacy in Greece from 371 BC until his death in 362 BC.

116-119 The enormous issues of 'owls' of Athens (**116**) struck from silver mined at Laurion, spread throughout the Mediterranean in the fifth and fourth centuries BC. The coins were so commonly used that local issues were often struck either copying directly the coins of Athens or adapting the types for local requirements. **117** Stater in the name of the dynast Täthiväibi, Lycia (Lycian script), about 425 BC; **118** Tetradrachm in the name of the satrap Mazaces, Babylonia (Aramaic script), about 330 BC; **119** Tetradrachm in the name of King Artaxerxes III of Persia, struck in Egypt (Demotic script), about 340 BC.

120 This fine portrait of a Persian *satrap* (governor) is presumed to be that of Tissaphernes, minted on the occasion of his payment to the Spartan fleet at Miletus in 411 BC. The reverse directly copies that of an Athenian tetradrachm, but consciously replaces the name of Athens with the letters BAS (*Basileos*, the Great King of Persia). Like many of the coins of Athens with which it was found in Cilicia, it was countermarked during circulation with the Aramaic letter *heth*, probably a banker's mark, a practice of giving a personal guarantee to a coin, adopted from before the time of Croesus.

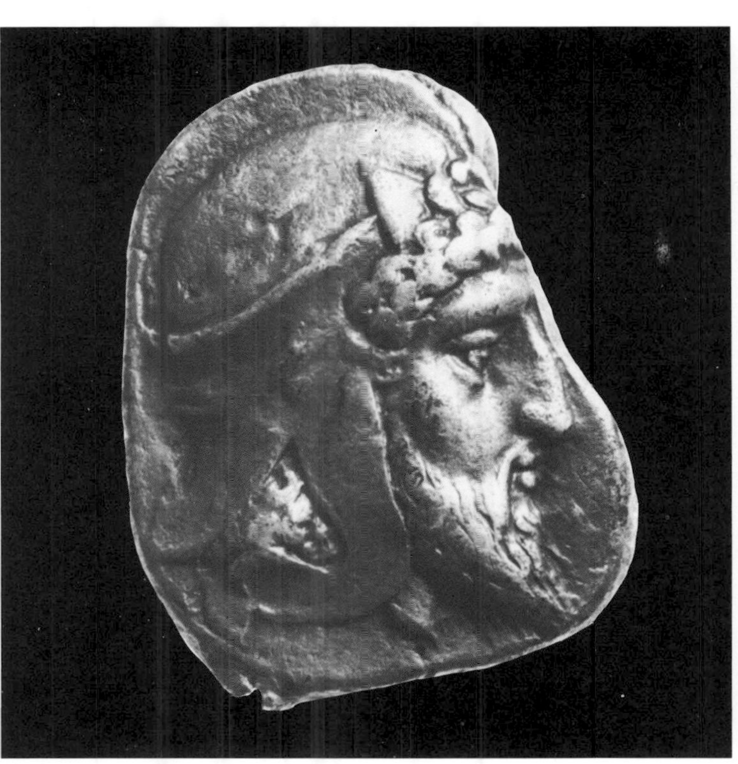

120A×3

120B×3

Hoards represent deposits buried in ancient times, which for one
60 reason or another were never recovered until turned up by
chance in modern times. When a mixture of coinages which had
134 circulated together were buried in this way, the study of one
hoard can throw light on the history of many different coinages.

There are some coinages, such as that of Athens, which because of the lack of variety in the designs can only be dated somewhat vaguely; and there are some coins that cannot at present even be attributed to a mint city. Normally however an inscription in the design allows an accurate identification of a coin's origin. The design was itself an official emblem, consciously chosen at a particular time to be placed on the coinage; and this, linked with the fact that the date of a coin can usually be accurately established, makes coinage a fascinating contemporary commentary on the history of the city. At the same time many of the cities that struck coins were by no means in the forefront of the history that has been transmitted to us by the
Greek historians; and coins are therefore a primary historical 109
source for this period, reflecting through their types and weights both the religious beliefs of the citizens, and also the political affiliations of cities of which even the sites may now be uncertain.

Coins were struck when needed and when metal was avail-

121 Fourteen talents (84,000 drachmae) of gold from statues of Victory on the Acropolis were melted with several talents of gold bullion to provide an emergency coinage at Athens 407-406 BC, when the Spartans had cut off supplies of silver from the mines at Laurion. This gold half-drachma (= six silver drachmae) belongs to that issue.

122-123 The economic crisis at the end of the Palopennesian War forced Athens to adopt base-metal coinage. The silver plated coins were issued officially. The small bronze pieces which are found with a large variety of types, have every appearance of being privately issued tokens. The emergency coinage was demonetized about 393 BC. **122** Silver plated drachma of Athens with bronze core, 406-405 BC; **123** A knuckle bone design on a bronze 'kollybos', late fifth-century BC.

124 This silver stater about 500 BC was one of the first on which Corinth introduced the head of Athena as a reverse type. Thereafter the combination of Pegasus and head of Athena remained constant, illustrating the changing styles of art of the fifth and fourth centuries BC.

125 Many colonies of Corinth in north-west Greece and other cities in Magna Graecia adopted the stater of Corinthian types, with subsidiary symbols and letters indicating the mint of origin. Staters of Ambracia, mid-fourth century BC.

126 The monster chimaera, 'body of a lion, tail of a snake, and she-goat in the middle,' (Homer, Iliad VI. 181), was regularly used on the silver coinage of Sicyon in the Peloponnese. Stater, about 380 BC.

127 The important coinage of Elis reflects that city's role as president of the Olympic games. The eagle tearing at the throat of a lamb has been placed as the device of a shield, suited exactly to the round flan of the coin. Stater, about 380 BC.

128 In 365 BC the Arcadians seized the sanctuary of Zeus at Olympia in order to wrench from the people of Elis the presidency over the Olympic games. During the games of 364 BC the Eleans invaded the sanctuary unsuccessfully; but the Arcadians began to

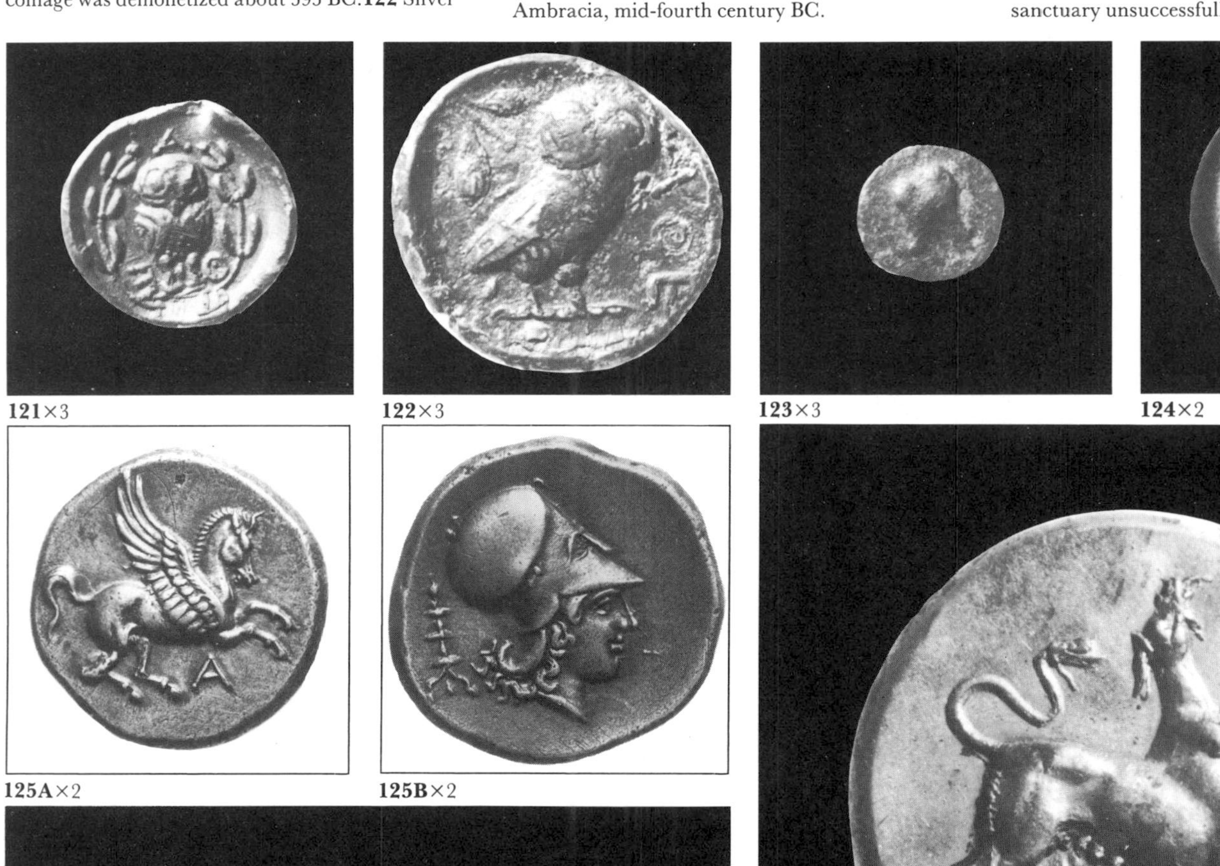

121×3 122×3 123×3 124×2

125A×2 125B×2

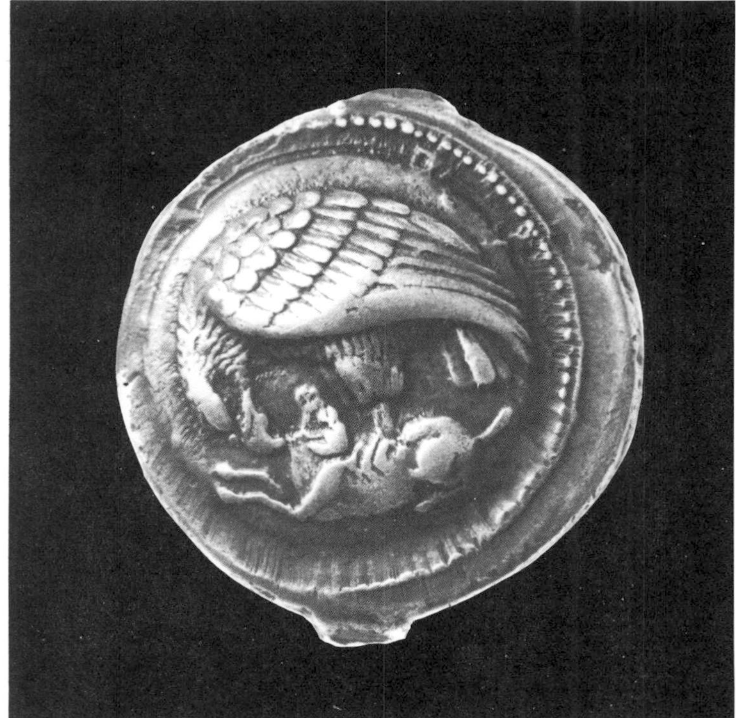

127×3

128×3 129×2

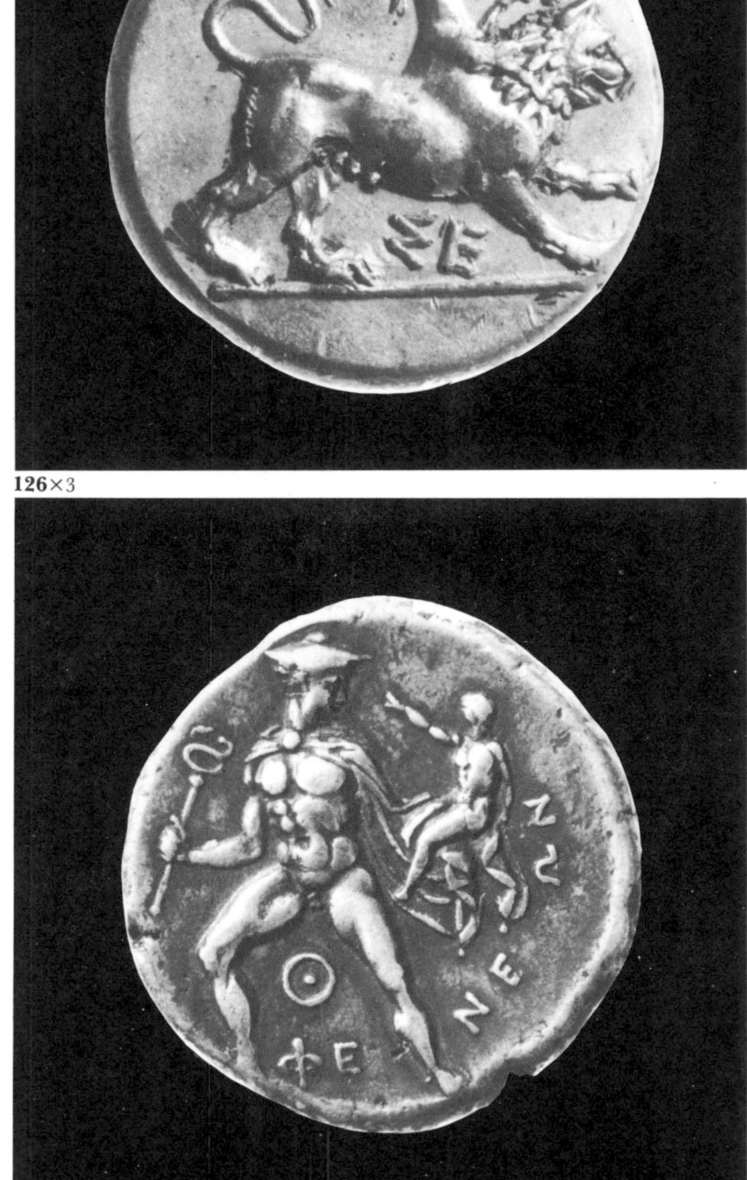

126×3

130×3

use the sacred treasures to pay their troops, and Elis soon regained control. This gold coin of 'Pisa' (= one silver stater), depicting the head of Olympian Zeus, belongs to this short period of Arcadian 'protection'.

129 The Arcadian League of cities produced only one issue of staters, depicting the figure of the god Pan seated on a rock inscribed OLY(mpia). This is of the mid-fourth century BC, and must also belong to the time of the Arcadians' capture of Olympia 365-64 BC.

130 Pheneus in Arcadia, though a city of little importance in Greek history, employed a major artist to engrave this figure of Hermes with the child Dionysus for an issue of staters about 360 BC.

131-133 Cretan coinage circulated only within the island, but some 30 cities struck their own coins. The silver coinage of the late fifth and fourth centuries BC are remarkable for their choice of designs:
131 The Minotaur, Cnossus, stater, about 425 BC; **132** Heracles fighting the Hydra, Phaestus, stater, about 325 BC; **133** Aeneas, founder of Aptera as well as of Rome, Aptera, stater, about 350 BC, signed on the obverse by the engraver Pythodoros.

134 In 416 BC the Athenians captured the island of Melos and killed or sold into slavery all the inhabitants. An important hoard of silver staters, from which this example of about 420 BC comes, was hidden in that year and never recovered.

135 The city of Panticapaeum in the Crimea was gateway to the gold and grain of South Russia. The head of the satyr symbolizes the rich fertility of the area, and the griffin, the legendary guardian of the gold, stands on the ear of barley. Stater, about 350 BC.

136 Electrum stater of Cyzicus depicting the omphalos of Delphi (**114**), the centre of the Greek world, about 450 BC. The tunny, the badge of the city, is always present on constantly changing designs.

131×3

132×3

133×3

134×2

135A×2

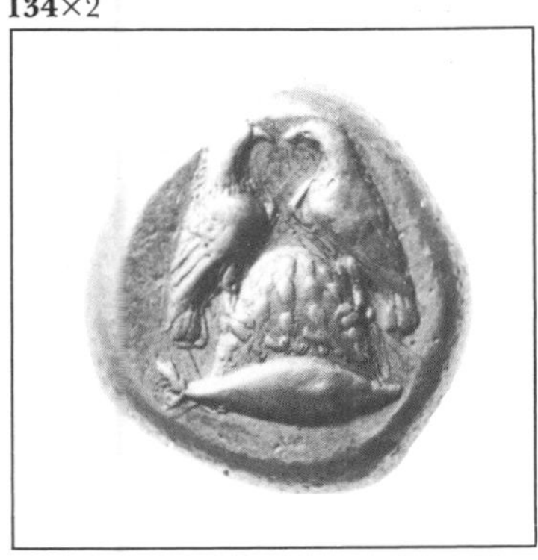

136×2

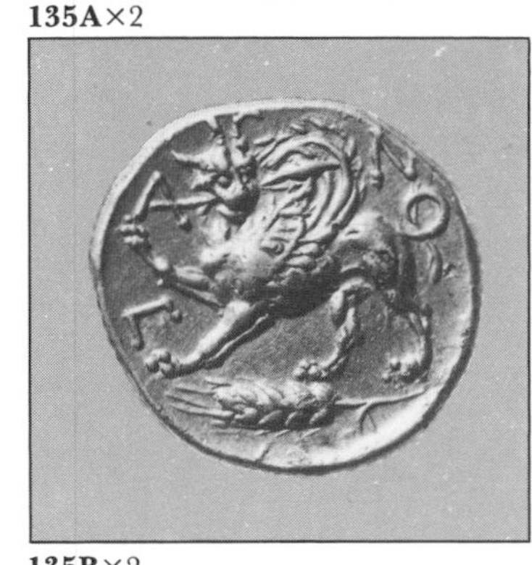

135B×2

able; but some states, notably Sparta, consciously rejected the idea of coinage. Others clearly relied on the circulation of foreign coins, and an agreement between Phocaea and Mytilene, preserved in an inscription of about 400 BC, shows that the cities shared the striking of an electrum coinage, each undertaking it for a year in turn. Coinage patterns changed: the intense mining activity that provided silver for the Macedonians in the early fifth century—Alexander I enjoyed an income of 6000 drachmae a day from one mine alone about 480 BC—appears to have exhausted the available ores, and from 460 BC only the cities of Acanthus, Mende and Abdera produced more or less continuous coinage in Macedonia. In the Peloponnesian War, supplies of silver to Corinth were cut about 430 BC resulting in a break in her otherwise copious coinage; and the allies of Athens appear to have struck no coinage in the decade 425-15 BC as the result of a decree imposing the general use of Athenian weights, measures and coinage throughout the confederacy.

In Sicily and Italy, after slow beginnings, the idea of coinage **83-99**
gained momentum from 480 BC and the care and attention lavished on the medium has left a magnificent series of miniature sculptures from a wide range of cities. The invasion of Sicily by Carthage (410-400 BC) brought a sudden end to minting at most

137 The named portrait of the Persian Pharnabazus was struck at the Greek city of Cyzicus, as the tunny below the prow indicates. Tetradrachm probably struck 396-95 BC.

138 Lampsacus issued an important sequence of gold 'Darics' with changing designs of great beauty. Here Victory erects a trophy of war, about 350 BC.

139 This magnificent tetradrachm of Clazomenae is signed by the engraver Theodotos on the obverse, echoing Sicilian precedents. About 380 BC.

140 Themistocles is best known for his part in building up the Athenian navy, which resulted in the defeat of the Persian Armada at Salamis in 480 BC. He was however expelled about 471 BC, and the Persian king made him tyrant of Magnesia, Ionia. This stater of Magnesia of about 460 BC bears his name around a figure of Apollo.

141 In the fourth century the tetradrachms of Rhodes formed a major currency in south-west Asia Minor, using the *rhodos* (rose) as play on the name of the island. The gold issue here illustrated belongs to the time of Alexander the Great, about 330 BC.

142 Maussollus, tyrant of Caria 376-53 BC is famous for his tomb at Halicarnassus, constructed by Greek artists. His coinage also shows his Greek inclinations, although the figure of Zeus Labraundeus with his double axe is a local god, whose cult was centred on Mylasa. Stater about 360 BC.

143 The gold 'Daric' introduced by Darius I of Persia to replace the posthumous coinage of Croesus at Sardes, Lydia, became an international currency. The stylized figure of Darius himself firing a bow marks this as one of the first issues, about 500 BC.

139A

137A

137B

139B

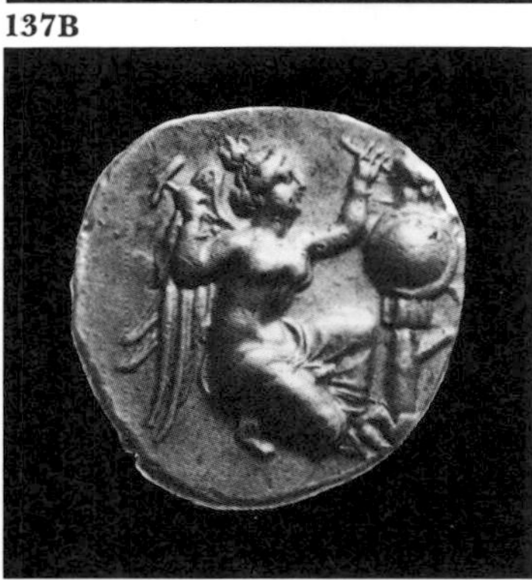

138×2

141A×2

141B×2

144 There is no Achaemenid coinage from Persepolis, Babylon, or Susa; but in the western empire the siglos (shekel) struck with the Darics at Sardes, provided an official Persian coinage. The type depicting the king with bow and sceptre began under King Xerxes, and continued unchanged for over a hundred years. This is from about 460 BC.

145 The Persians permitted the dynasts of Lycia to strike important coinages in silver. This stater of Khäräi, probably minted about 420 BC, is one of the first coins to adopt a regal portrait.

146 The early portraits of Lycian rulers are spectacular. Perikles (380-60 BC) adapted the Syracusan model of Arethusa (**95**) to provide a dramatic representation of his own features. Stater, about 370 BC.

147 The figure of Apollo sacrificing at an altar is clearly Greek in origin; but the inscription is in a local script not yet deciphered. Side, Pamphylia, stater mid-fourth century BC.

148 Aphrodisias in Cilicia produced only one issue of staters, about 350 BC. It depicts the patron goddess of the city, Aphrodite, holding a flower and enthroned between two sphinxes.

149 The Aramaic inscription proclaims this to be an issue of Pharnabazus as satrap of Cilicia; and the helmeted head reflects the nature of the coinage, minted at Tarsus in preparations for the re-conquest of Egypt 397-94 BC.

150 Tarsus was an important military centre for the Persians. The name of Datames in Aramaic identifies the seated satrap inspecting an arrow, with the winged sun-disc of Ahuramazda emphasizing his Persian origins. On the obverse the great sky god of Tarsus, Baal, holds emblems of fertility, the whole surrounded by a wreath of stylized lotus flowers. This stater, like **149**, was probably issued during operations against Egypt, 378-72 BC.

140×2

143×3

144×3

142×3

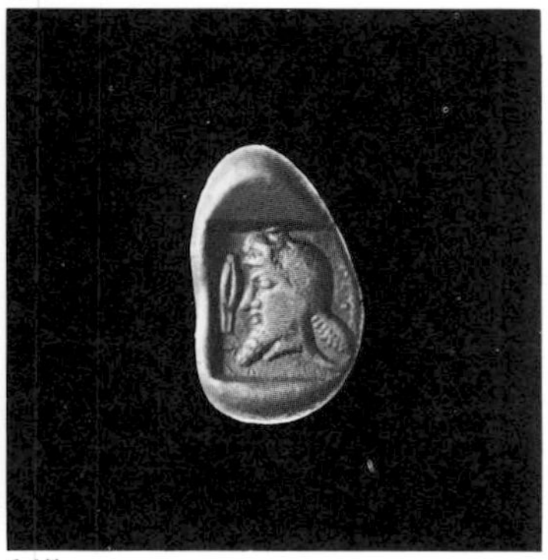

145

147

148

146×3

150A

150B

149×3

151 The power of the Persians is the theme of this stater struck at Tarsus for Mazaeus, 351-34 BC, and names him as 'satrap of the territory beyond the Euphrates,' in the Aramaic inscription.

152 The mint of this tetradrachm depicting a satrap in combat has not yet been discovered. It appears to have been made in Phoenicia in the mid-fourth century BC, perhaps at the time of the revolt of the cities of that area against Persia.

153 Europa is shown clutching the bull that brought her from Sidon in Phoenicia to Crete. The inscription giving the name and title of the king is in Cypriote characters. Stater of Timochares, King of Marium, Cyprus, early fourth century BC.

154 The Great King of Persia is driven in a chariot of oriental form, and a figure in Egyptian dress walks behind holding a sceptre. Double shekel of Ba'lshallim II, King of Sidon, Phoenicia, 385-72 BC.

155 This shekel of Tyre about 400 BC underlines the oriental nature of some 'Greek' coins. Melqart, the great god of Tyre equated by the Greeks with Heracles, rides over the sea on a hippocamp; and on the reverse the owl, familiar from the coinage of Athens, is given the Egyptian symbols of royal power, the crook and flail.

156 Judaea made rare issues of small silver coins both before and after the conquest of Alexander. This 'drachma' may be identified by its Aramaic inscription naming Judaea, and it depicts a deity on a winged wheel, similar to that seen by the prophet Ezekiel, which thus illustrates Jewish traditions.

157 There was little coinage in Egypt under Persian rule apart from direct imitations of Athenian tetradrachms; but under king Nectanebo II (359-43 BC) gold 'Darics' were issued with the hieroglyphic signs heart and windipe (*nefer*), collar with beads (*nub*) = fine gold.

158 The facing head so popular in the fourth century was used at Cyrene, Africa, for the features of the local god Zeus Ammon on a stater about 360 BC. The silphium, a medicinal plant, was used as the badge of the city.

151 152×2 153 155A 154×3 156×2 155B 157×2 159A×2 158A×3 158B×3

159 Philip II of Macedonia adopted the head of Apollo from the coinage of the Chalcidian League (**110**) for his gold staters, and the racing chariot recalls his victory in the Olympic games of 356 BC. It was not until late in his reign, about 340 BC, that he began to issue gold coinage, and most examples are posthumous. Stater, about 340 BC

160-161 The silver staters of Philip II were to have a dramatic influence on the Celtic coinages of Europe. His first coins were struck soon after his accession in 359 BC with head of Olympian Zeus and king on horseback, or, as on this example, a victorious jockey. A large coinage was issued during his lifetime (**160**, about 345 BC), but the coinage was continued after his death for a few years (**161**, 336-35 BC) and was resumed by Philip III (323-17 BC) and successors.

162 Alexander the Great (336-23 BC) adopted the Attic standard as being more international, with his 'ancestor' Heracles and the seated figure of Zeus as his chosen devices. This tetradrachm was struck with the same symbol prow and at the same time as **161**.

163 Alexander's gold coinage looks forward to victory. The helmeted head of Athena is on the obverse, and the figure of Victory holding a mast from the great battle of Salamis reminds the Greeks of that victory. Stater, about 330 BC.

164 As the Macedonian forces marched eastwards defeating the armies of the Persians, new mints were set up to produce coinage for Alexander. This stater is marked as being from the Phoenician town of Sidon, about 323-22 BC.

165 A decadrachm struck probably at Babylon about 330 BC celebrates Alexander's victories over the Persian East. On the obverse Alexander on his horse Bucephalus drives back the oriental war elephant; and on the reverse, Alexander with the thunderbolt of divine power is crowned by Victory.

166 New varieties of coins are continually being discovered. This tetradrachm issued with the decadrachm (**165**) about 330 BC was unknown until 1973. It depicts a figure adapted from Persian sigloi, holding a long bow quite unlike any Greek weapon.

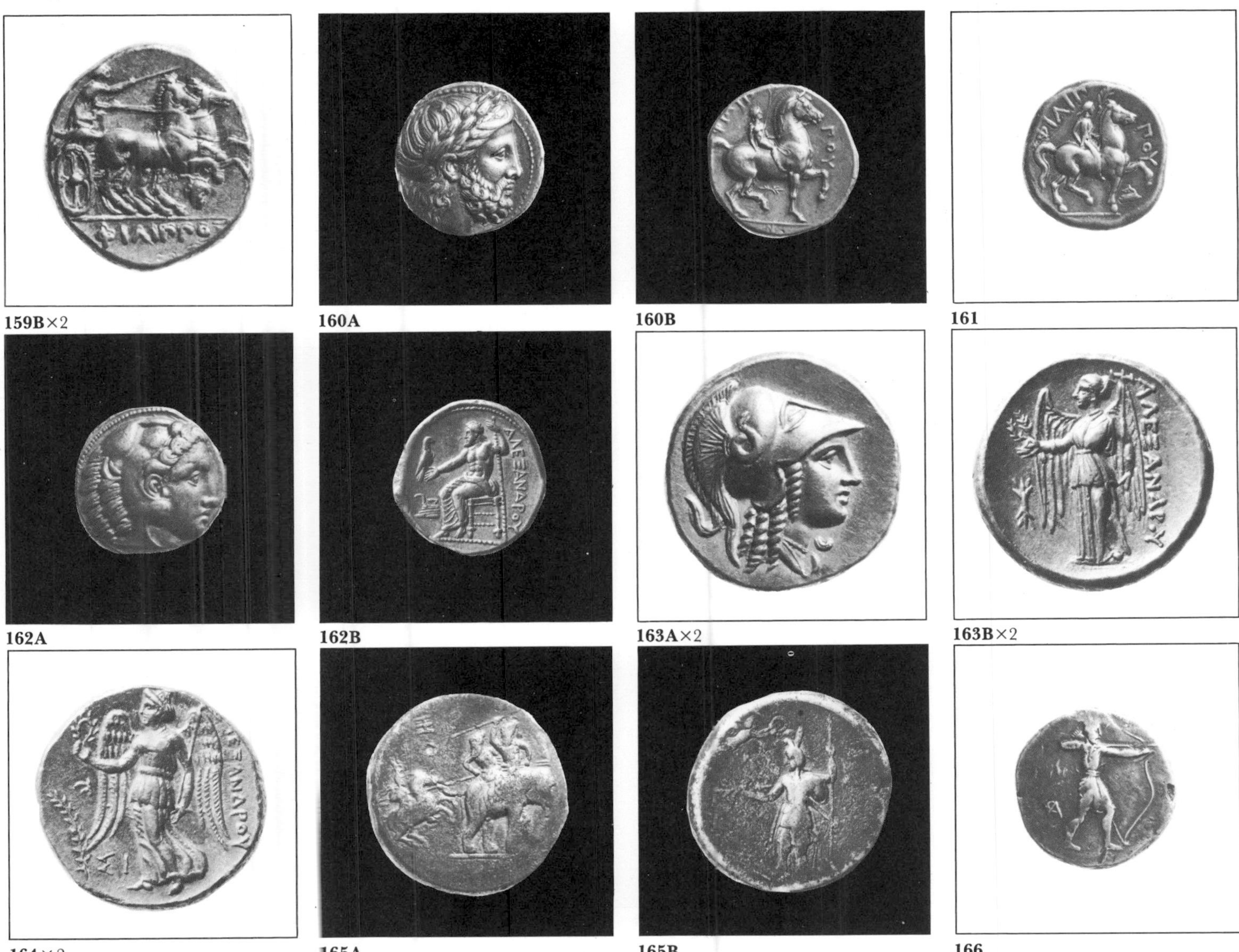

159B×2 **160A** **160B** **161**
162A **162B** **163A**×2 **163B**×2
164×2 **165A** **165B** **166**

101,102 cities, and only Syracuse with a series of silver decadrachms and
gold 100 litrae retained a precious metal coinage into the fourth
century. This too came to an end about 375 BC, and until the
liberation of Sicily by Timoleon in 344 BC bronze issues alone
were struck. Carthage, through her bases in Western Sicily,
provided the silver tetradrachms for the Greeks.

The fourth century BC saw coinages blossom in Greece and
the eastern Mediterranean. It is impossible to generalize concerning the particular reasons for cities adopting the practice,
but many coinages can be seen to be military in nature. In 356
BC, following a precedent set by the Arcadians at Olympia in
128,129 365-64 BC, the people of Phocis seized the treasury of Apollo's
sanctuary at Delphi and produced a series of coins for the
payment of their mercenary troops. The large coinage struck by
159,160 Philip II of Macedonia (359-36 BC) reflects the great military
activity of his reign. By conquering the neighbouring cities of the
Chalcidian League, and by exploiting anew the mining areas of
Mount Pangaeum, he was able to exert an influence over the
whole of Greek affairs. By the end of his reign he had established
a new regular coinage in gold, which his successor Alexander the
Great (336-23 BC) was to increase. Enormous coinages of silver
and gold accompanied Alexander's conquest of the East, and as
the riches of Persia were seized, mints were established to enable
Alexander to keep his army in the field. The wide circulation 163-166
that the 'owls' of Athens had achieved through trade was gained
for the coinage of Alexander by force of arms. Like his Persian
predecessors, he sought to foster local coinages for local use; but
for reasons that were both political and economic, he extended to
the whole empire the use of his royal coinage.

The description 'Greek' coinage embraces the coins of the many cities and cultures with which the Greeks were in contact. The drachma-sized sigloi (shekels) of the Achaemenid kings of Persia, and coins inscribed in the local scripts and tongues of the eastern Mediterranean, circulated alongside coins struck at Greek cities with designs derived from Greek mythology. Coinage thus reflects, perhaps better than any other medium, the many artistic and cultural traditions to be found in the 'Greek' lands surrounding the Mediterranean.

IV

THE HELLENISTIC KINGDOMS AND COINAGES 323-170 BC

Ian Carradice

The empire of Alexander the Great did not survive intact for long after his death in 323 BC. The most powerful and ambitious provincial governors fought for control of parts or the whole of it, and after some 40 years of wars there emerged a new Greek world in which the territories formerly united by Alexander were now divided into separate kingdoms interspersed with semi-independent and independent city-states. The 'Hellenistic Age' is the label traditionally given to the period during which these kingdoms were formed, flourished, and then declined until absorbed by the new empire of Rome in the first century BC.

The most important of the Successors were all former generals and companions-in-arms of Alexander. Cassander held Macedonia, Antigonus and his son Demetrius Poliorcetes ('The Besieger of Cities') fought for Greece and Asia Minor, Lysimachus formed an empire based in Thrace, Ptolemy held Egypt, and Seleucus controlled vast areas in the East. Respect for their former leader and for the popular acceptability of his coinage, as well as political expediency (because they all depended upon a connection with Alexander for the legitimacy of their rule) prompted the Successors to continue producing coins of the types and in the name of Alexander the Great. But these men all shared essentially the same ambition, to establish kingdoms and found dynasties. Each adopted the title of *Basileus* (King), and although some continued to exhibit conservative tendencies, others, in particular Ptolemy and Demetrius, soon began to employ more personal or dynastic types on their coins. This development culminated in the widespread adoption of regal portraiture.

Portraits on earlier coins had largely been confined to Asia
145,146 Minor, where they had appeared occasionally on issues of
120 Lycian dynasts and Persian satraps. However, Alexander's
creation of an empire involving, as it did, the absorption of eastern ideology, followed by its disintegration into separate kingdoms, provided both the conceptual and political ingredients for a full development of the art of portraiture in the Greek world. The portrait became the dominant type on the coins of the Hellenistic kings because coinage was the principal vehicle available to the ancient State for projecting the image of its sovereignty; and this was now embodied in the King's person.

The model for the Hellenistic portrait on coins was the head of
162 Heracles on the ubiquitous 'Alexander' tetradrachms. This
image must have become so closely assimilated with the memory of Alexander, now deified, that it was probably widely regarded as a representation of him. When the first true portraits of the posthumous Alexander then appeared on the coins of the Successors, he was adorned with, and indeed sometimes almost concealed by, attributes of divinity. Similarly, the first of the
Successors' own portraits are characterised by a profusion of 168,169,172
symbols which identify the ruler with one god or another. The Hellenistic portrait, which was the model for the Roman and the ancestor of the modern portrait on coins, thus began essentially as a representation of divinity, but of a divinity that in the new political climate of the period could now be manifested in the identifiable features of a man. Alexander's coin types also strongly influenced the reverse designs on Hellenistic coinage.
Very common are profile views of various seated deities, which 174
were based ultimately on the Zeus reverse of Alexander's tetradrachms

By 275 BC the main political divisions of the Hellenistic East were established. The coinage of the ensuing period reflects the new political organization and provides evidence for economic conditions in the Hellenistic world.

The three major dynasties were the Antigonids in Macedonia, the Seleucids centred in Syria and the Ptolemies in Egypt. The Antigonids and Seleucids retained Alexander's Attic standard for their coinage, with the tetradrachm being the principal denomination. So also did the lesser kingdoms of Asia Minor and the eastern kingdoms of Parthia and Bactria which seceded from the Seleucid Empire in the mid-third century. Meanwhile, the many autonomous cities and leagues of cities in Asia Minor and
Greece continued to strike 'Alexander' gold and silver coins, and 204
their northern neighbours produced similar pieces copying the
types of Lysimachus. The lasting popularity of these coins, 205
particularly the 'Alexander' tetradrachms, can be compared with that of the Athenian 'owls' in the days before Alexander. Coin hoards of the period indicate that they circulated throughout the territories from mainland Greece to Bactria, alongside the somewhat more regionalized contemporary regal coinages.

Egypt, however, was outside the main Hellenistic coinage zone. Ptolemy I had begun to develop a policy of economic isolation for his country which included, before 300 BC, a reduction in the weight standard of the tetradrachm. Ptolemy's successors continued this policy and henceforth the Ptolemaic
coinage usually circulated alone within Ptolemaic territories. It 183,184
is also distinguished from neighbouring Hellenistic coinages by other special features including an extensive production of large
denominations in gold and of very large bronze pieces. 189

Outside Egypt the Attic tetradrachms and, in much lesser numbers, gold staters, enjoyed universal circulation; but they were accompanied, especially in Greece and the Aegean, by local

Portrait of Alexander the Great, Pergamum, about 280 BC (**173**).

167 This 'Alexander' tetradrachm was struck in Babylon, 323-17 BC, in the name of Philip III (Arrhidaeus), Alexander the Great's retarded half-brother. Until his death in 317 BC, Philip was supported by the army as joint ruler of the Empire with Alexander's posthumously-born son, Alexander IV.

168 A portrait of Alexander with the ram's horn of Ammon which is visible under the elephant headdress on this tetradrachm of Ptolemy I. In his lifetime, Alexander had claimed that Zeus Ammon (the Hellenized Egyptian ram-god) was his spiritual father. Alexandria, about 300 BC.

169 The aegis of Zeus lends divinity to the subject, but this portrait of Ptolemy has been cut with brutal realism. The reverse type of eagle on thunderbolt further emphasizes Ptolemy's desire to be associated with Zeus. Alexandria, after 305 BC.

170 Cassander (319-297 BC) used familiar Macedonian types on his coins. This horseman reverse had been introduced by Philip II (**160**). Macedonia, after 305 BC.

171 On this tetradrachm of Demetrius Poliorcetes the obverse type celebrates the destruction of Ptolemy's fleet in 306 BC; Victory blows a trumpet over the broken beak of the enemy's ship. Poseidon, depicted in aggressive pose on the reverse, was, not inappropriately, Demetrius' patron deity. Struck at Salamis.

172 The bull's horn of Poseidon decorates the portrait of Demetrius, the first ruler in Europe to place his own image on coins. The diadem was reputedly an invention of the god Dionysus; it was used by the Hellenistic kings to denote royal power. Thebes, 289-87 BC.

167A×3

167B×3

169A×3

169B×3

or regional coinages whose smaller denominations in silver adhered to various different weight standards. Thus, for instance, in mainland Greece and the Peloponnese in the late third century BC Attic 'Alexander' and regal Macedonian tetradrachms circulated alongside local 'Corcyrean' drachmae and reduced 'Aeginetic' triobols. Meanwhile, drachmae and didrachms of a 'Rhodo-Phoenician' standard shared the currency market with Attic tetradrachms in the Aegean Islands. Rhodes itself produced at the same time Rhodian silver coins and Attic 'Alexanders'. The picture is less confused further east and in the north where the Attic standards established by Alexander almost exclusively dominated the currency of the region.

The most noticeable physical characteristic of coins in this period is that they gradually become thinner and broader. This is particularly evident on the tetradrachms whose larger surface area now provides the die-engravers with greater scope for their designs and more room for detailed inscriptions, dates and
symbols. The systems of dating involve the use of a sequence of **265**
letters used as numerals, with eras based either on the year of the
beginning of a dynasty or of the freedom of a city, or on the year **211**
of accession of a king. The portrait is the standard type on the coins of the monarchies, apart from Macedonia which for a time

173 Lysimachus had access to large resources of wealth and his coins were issued in very large numbers. The head of Alexander as Zeus Ammon is thought to be a copy of a famous portrait by the sculptor Lysippus.

174 The Athena type on the reverse of Lysimachus' coins has been much imitated on coinage, mainly via Roman intermediaries, ever since. Compare Britannia (**422, 936**). Pergamum, 297-81 BC

175 The anchor in the field identifies the issuer of this 'Alexander' tetradrachm as Seleucus. He had an anchor-shaped birth mark on his thigh, and this symbol became the official badge of the Seleucid dynasty. Aradus, Phoenicia, about 310 BC.

176 The elephant represents one of the great strengths of Seleucus' battle line – the war elephants. The horse's head may depict Alexander's famous steed Bucephalus ('Ox-head'), or it may simply be a reference to cavalry. Apamea in Syria, where this bronze piece was minted in about 300 BC, was the main Seleucid arsenal.

177 This helmeted head carries attributes of Poseidon (the bull's horn and ear) and Dionysus (the panther skin). It has been identified as a portrait of either Seleucus, who minted the coin, or Alexander. Susa, about 300 BC.

178 While he was establishing an independent kingdom at Pergamum the enterprising Philetaerus issued coins with a portrait of Seleucus, whose overlordship he recognized. Struck after 281 BC.

179 This gold stater was struck in Athens by the tyrant Lachares when he was defending the city against Demetrius Poliorcetes in 297-95 BC.

168×3 **170**×2 **171A** **172** **171B** **174**×3 **173** **175** **176A**×2 **176B**×2 **177** **178** **179A**×2 **179B**×2

180 The head of Apollo on the obverse, and on the reverse the letters PO, together with the rose which provides a pun on the name of the issuing city, identifies the mint of Rhodes. This didrachm was minted by the magistrate Aristonomos about 300 BC.

181 The cities of Crete continued to strike extensive issues of coinage in the Hellenistic period. The labyrinth, relating to the legend of the Minotaur, on the reverse of this stater identifies the mint of Cnossus. About 300 BC.

182 Ptolemy III 'the Benefactor' in this remarkable portrait is adorned with attributes of Helios (crown of rays), Poseidon (trident) and Zeus (aegis). The Ptolemaic gold coinage includes a varied and attractive series of portraits, whereas the obverses of the silver tetradrachms are virtually confined to representations of Ptolemy I.

180A×2

180B×2

181A×2

181B×2

182

183 The importance of dynastic continuity to the Ptolemies is well expressed on this gold octadrachm of Ptolemy III (246-21 BC). On the obverse are portraits of Ptolemy II and his sister-wife Arsinoe, together referred to as 'divine brother and sister'; the reverse has their parents Ptolemy I and Berenice, who are 'gods'.

184 The extensive regal bronze coinage issued by the Seleucid kings was supplemented by sporadic local production. Alexandria Troas, later third century BC. Compare **186**.

185 Head of Berenice II, wife of Ptolemy III, wearing veil and diadem. A bee on the reverse of this piece indicates that it was struck at Ephesus, which at this time was part of the Ptolemaic domain.

186 This seated Apollo type, introduced by Antiochus I (280-61 BC), became the standard reverse design on Seleucid tetradrachms. The grazing horse in the exergue identifies the mint of Alexandria Troas where this piece was struck under Antiochus Hierax (246-27 BC).

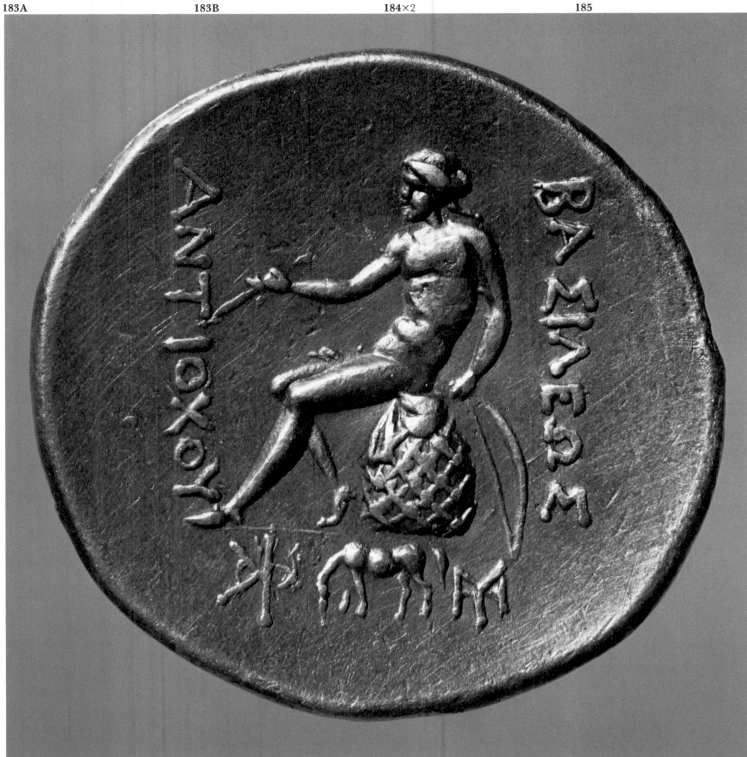

183A

183B

184×2

185

186

THE HELLENISTIC KINGDOMS AND COINAGES 323-170 BC

198 The silver drachmae or 'victoriates' of Dyrrhachium in Illyria have types derived from the coins of Corcyra. Two magistrates are named: Ariston on the obverse; and on the reverse Damen, to whom the symbols on the obverse also relate. 229-100 BC.

199 The first coins ever to be struck in Sparta were modelled on those of the major Hellenistic monarchies. This tetradrachm portrays King Nabis (207-192 BC). The deity with whom he associated himself is Heracles, whose seated figure, presumably copying a celebrated statue, also appears in identical pose on Seleucid and Bactrian coins.

200 Philip V (220-179 BC) revived the use of portraiture on coins of the Macedonian kingdom. This tetradrachm employs a representation of an archaic statue of Athena Alkidemos, the city goddess of Pella, for the reverse type.

201 The famous Roman general T. Quinctius Flamininus defeated Philip V at the battle of Cynoscephalae in 197 BC. Afterwards he issued a rare series of gold staters commemorating his victory, which is alluded to on the reverse. The head of Flamininus is the first portrait of a living Roman to appear on coins.

198A×2

198B×2

201A×2

201B×2

199A×3

199B×3

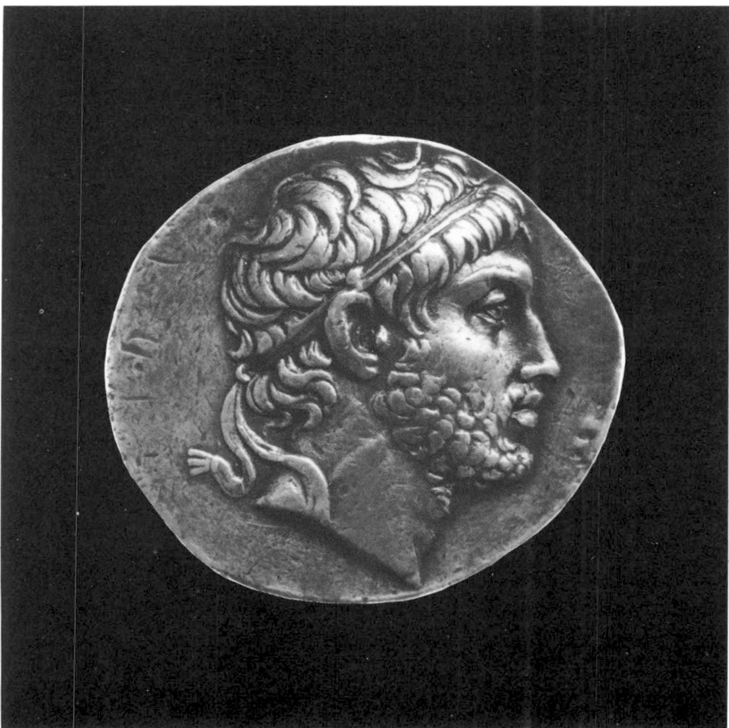

200A×2

200B×2

202 Antiochus III 'the Great' regained for a time the eastern territories of the Seleucid Empire lost by his predecessors, but after his defeat by the Romans at Magnesia in 190 BC he lost most of Asia Minor to the Pergamene kingdom. This tetradrachm was struck at Ecbatana, about 200 BC.

203 The mass-produced tetrobols of Histiaea are often carelessly struck. A maenad, a devotee of the god Dionysus, with pine-cones in her hair provides the obverse type; the reverse has the nymph Histiaea seated on the stern of a ship.

204 This 'Alexander' tetradrachm was struck at Smyrna, Ionia, in the early second century BC.

205 The letters BY inscribed on the throne on the reverse identify Byzantium, the most active mint striking 'Lysimachi'. Mid-second century gold stater.

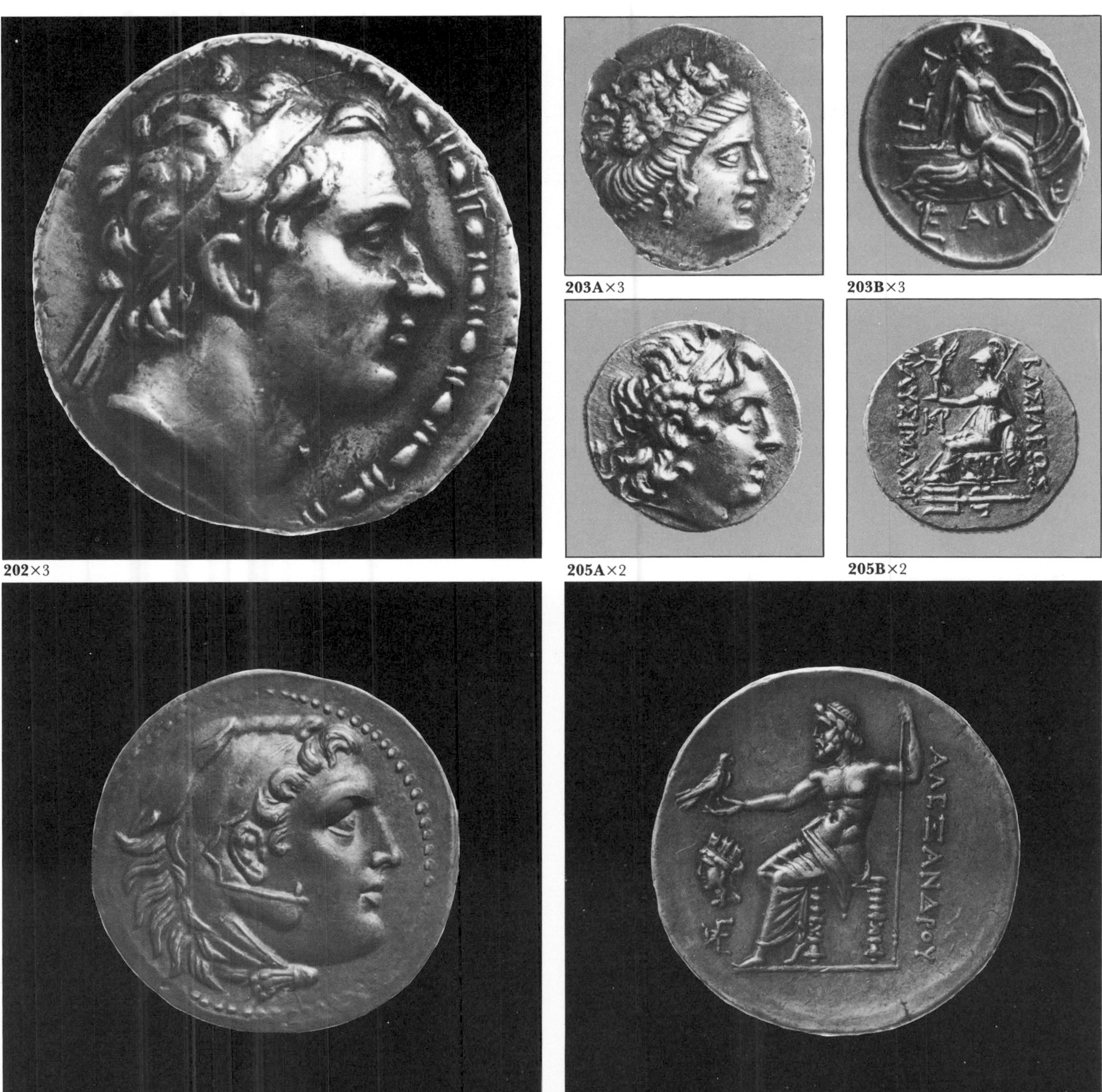

202×3

203A×3

203B×3

205A×2

205B×2

204A×2

204B×2

abandoned its use. On the other hand, the autonomous cities and leagues naturally did not employ portraits. On high value currency the 'Alexanders' or 'Lysimachi' were the usual types; but the more powerful Leagues and city-states, such as Rhodes, also produced local types. Otherwise, local or regional types are
203 mainly in evidence on the smaller silver coins of the cities and
260 leagues of mainland Greece and the Aegean area, and on the bronze pieces produced for local circulation. Many cities which
185 were under the control of the monarchies, were allowed to strike in bronze.

Early in the second century the stability of the Hellenistic East was shattered by the arrival of Roman armies. In 197 BC Philip V of Macedon and in 190 BC Antiochus III of Syria suffered crushing defeats. Many cities in Greece and Asia Minor were formally given their freedom by the Romans who then returned home. The physical appearance of the coinage of these regions was not greatly affected by these events. The major changes in types (in particular the appearance of the 'wreath' coins, which 259
were once thought to have started soon after 190 BC) seem now 261
not to have taken place until after 168 BC. But the changed circumstances did lead to important shifts in coinage production. In mainland Greece, for instance, huge numbers of Histiaean

206 A fine portrait of Perseus (179-68 BC), the last Macedonian king.

207 The Seleucid King Antiochus IV (175-64 BC) called himself 'god incarnate' and provoked great hostility in Judaea by rededicating the Temple at Jerusalem to Zeus. On this coin Antiochus is portrayed as Helios. The mark of value, a very rare feature on Hellenistic coinage, is a monogram composed of Δ (= four) and X (= chalkoi). Struck at Nisibis, Mesopatamia.

208 The legendary warrior and philosopher-king Menander (about 160-40 BC), portrayed here on an exceedingly rare tetradrachm, was the only Bactrian king whose name survives in native Indian literature.

209 The drachma was by far the most popular denomination used by the kings of Cappadocia. This particular issue is extremely numerous: it has been attributed to Ariarathes V (163-30 BC).

210 This newly discovered gold octadrachm portrays Ptolemy VI and his mother Cleopatra I, who acted as regent during her son's minority. Alexandria, about 180 BC.

206×2

207×3

208×3

210A×3

209A×2

209B×2

211 A typical late-Ptolemaic tetradrachm struck in debased silver by Ptolemy XII (80-51 BC). The obverse bears an idealized portrait of Ptolemy I. The letters L (Egyptian symbol for year) and KZ (= 27) in the reverse left field, date the coin to 55-54 BC; on the right are the letters ΠΑ, the mint signature of Alexandria.

212 The later Seleucid portraits on coins become formalized and characterless, but the personalities they portray are not without interest. This unusual obverse depicts Antiochus XI and his brother Philip. For just a few weeks in 93 BC they held Antioch, but they were defeated by a cousin, Antiochus X, and in attempting to make his escape after the battle Antiochus XI is said to have drowned in the River Orontes.

211A×3

211B×3

210B×3

212×3

203 tetrobols suddenly appear, possibly because they were used by the Roman armies in the area. Also, there was a great increase in the production of 'Alexanders' and 'Lysimachi'. In the later
204 third century the leagues of cities in Greece and the Aegean area
205 revived their usage; and when the newly freed cities of Asia Minor regained the right to strike their own coins, they also adopted these well-established types, suggesting that conservatism and economic realism for the time being overcame any urges they might have had to proclaim their newly won autonomy with the traditional profusion of local coin types.

The Roman victory over Perseus, King of Macedon, at Pydna in 168 BC brought to an end the Macedonian monarchy and heralded a new era in Greek coinage. However, the Seleucid and Ptolemaic monarchies survived, although their later history is one of gradual but continuous decline and disintegration. However, the proud portraits of their kings and queens continue to adorn their coins as do the heads of rulers on the corresponding coins of other eastern monarchies.

V

ROME AND THE HELLENISTIC WORLD

Andrew Burnett

In the Hellenistic world, coins were made of gold, silver and
bronze, and of these metals silver was by far the most important.
It was minted to meet a variety of public expenses, of which the
213,214 most significant was military pay, whether of a regular army or
of mercenaries. Public works, such as roads, buildings and
aqueducts, had also to be paid for with cash, and other items
242 such as purchases of corn might arise from time to time.
Consequently, it was only the more important states and towns
which issued silver regularly and on a large scale, while smaller
or dependent towns tended to mint sporadically and on a small
scale. Some towns were even too small to have their own mint
and would get larger towns to mint silver or bronze on their
behalf.

Sometimes a state or ruler ran out of money and was forced to
make too many coins out of too little silver, and so had to alloy
261,273 copper or some other base metal with the silver. The cistophori,
for example, were made of almost pure silver in the second
century, but by about 70 BC they were only 80% fine. Such
292 debasements might well be short-lived if they occurred in
wartime (both the Romans and Carthaginians resorted to
debasement in the Hannibalic War 218-02 BC) but sometimes
coinages never recovered. For example, Ptolemy XII was
forced to debase his silver coinage in 53 BC to meet the cost of
the massive bribes he had paid to have himself restored to the
Egyptian throne, and the Egyptian coinage never regained its
purity, even under the Roman empire. A curious consequence of
such debasements was that occasionally the currency of one
area, such as Syria in the late first century, could consist of coins
266,276 of different fineness. This foreshadows the coinage of the Roman
empire, the fineness of which varied widely from province to
province; and of course the debasements of the Hellenistic world
were to provide a ready precedent for the Roman emperors when
they were later faced by equally pressing financial problems.

A shortage of cash could also be met by the issue of gold coins.
163,164 Gold staters had been minted in large numbers by Alexander the
Great, but after his death their issue was less regular and was
reduced in scale. Some of the kingdoms of his successors, such as
Syria, minted gold fairly often, but only Ptolemaic Egypt and
Carthage had a plentiful gold coinage. Otherwise it was minted
only rarely and usually in emergencies: the Romans had to use it
269 in the war with Hannibal, and other examples are Mithradates
VI, or the Syrian Alexander Zabinas (129-23 BC) who coined
gold obtained from melting down the statue of Victory from the
treasury of Zeus at Antioch. Similarly, the vast expenditure of
the civil wars of the late Republic caused the different factions to
mint gold throughout the Mediterranean, and this widespread
use of gold led to its establishment as one of the staple metals of
the Roman empire.

The final legacy of the Hellenistic world to the Roman empire
was an extensive bronze coinage. Bronze was adopted in Greece
and Asia Minor by the first half of the fourth century and in
Syria and Egypt slightly later. In Africa, at Carthage, it began in
about 300 BC, and in Spain about a hundred years later. From
the third century there was an enormous increase in the scale of
its production, and some governments such as Rome and the
Syrian kings issued huge quantities. Sometimes, as with silver, it
was minted to meet public expenditure – the Roman army was
paid in bronze until the middle of the second century – but a
number of small issues seem to have been privately inspired. A
good case can be found in the coinage of Paestum, where some 230
coins portray a lady known from inscriptions to have been a
benefactress of the town: presumably she paid for the coins to be
made as gifts to the people of Paestum.

There were a number of different systems of denominations for
these coins. In the West the Romans adopted the South Italian
system of bronze obols (the sixth of a drachma), but at the same 82
time they used their own system of the *as* and its subdivisions.
After 225 BC the latter system prevailed, and it quickly spread
throughout Italy and to Spain. In Sicily it co-existed with the
Sicilian system whereby one talent of three denarii equalled 120
litrae; presumably therefore the as, which circulated extensively
in Sicily, was worth 2½ litrae. Further east the picture is more
complex, although the obol was fairly universal. It was, however,
subdivided in different ways, e.g. into four tetartemoria at
Athens or into eight chalkoi in Syria. Significantly, Roman 207
denominations (the denarius and the as) seem to have played no
part in Greece or further east until the Roman empire, and even
then they co-existed and were integrated with the Greek systems
of silver and bronze values.

'Bronze' is a word loosely used to denote any copper-based
metal, and it is more correct to distinguish between pure copper;
bronze, which was composed mainly of 70% copper, but with
the addition of significant quantities of tin and lead; and brass,
which was called orichalcum in the ancient world and which
usually contained 75% copper and 25% zinc. As bronze was the
commonest base metal at the time (it was used, for instance, for
statues and other metalwork), it was a natural metal to use for
most of the earliest 'bronze' coins. But shortly after 100 BC the
application of the cementation process enabled metalworkers to
produce brass by adding zinc to copper, and from this date the

Zeus wearing a wreath of laurel, Samos, about 170 BC (**255**).

213 Timoleon's expedition in 344 BC was paid for with coins of Corinth and her colonies. Timoleon minted similar coins, but with the legend 'of Syracuse', at Syracuse after his capture of the city.

214 During the first Punic War (264-41 BC) the Carthaginians minted large silver five-shekel coins with the head of Tanit (the supreme goddess of Carthage) and a flying horse derived from Corinthian coins (**213**).

215 The portrait of Hiero II, king of Syracuse (275-15 BC) and great ally of Rome, is based upon contemporary coins of the Hellenistic east (**172**).

216 Towards the end of the fourth century Metapontum in south Italy adapted the head of Athena on Corinthian coins (**213**) to represent the legendary founder of the city, Leucippus.

217 Locri in Italy minted coins in 286-82 BC, which have the earliest representation of the goddess Roma, who is shown seated, crowned by *Pistis* (Good Faith).

218 The first Roman silver coins (about 300 BC) have Mars and his sacred animal, the horse. The obverse is inspired by Corinthian coins (**213, 216**).

219 A Roman currency bar (about 275 BC) with an elephant and a pig (not shown). They refer to the war with king Pyrrhus (281-72 BC), who was the first to use war elephants in Italy.

213A×2 **213B**×2 **214A** **214B**

215×2 **216**×2 **217**×2 **218A**×2 **218B**×2

219

220 In about 225 BC the heavy cast bronze coins of Rome adopt the types of Janus and a prow. These remained the standard designs for over a century.

221 Roughly cast bronze coins (*aes grave*) were made by towns in central Italy: Todi, for instance, produced some with a frog seen from above. Mid-third century BC.

222 The Carthaginians minted coins in Spain in the late third century. This head has been identified as Hannibal, but it is probably the Punic god Melqart.

223 Capua struck rare silver coins with Zeus and his sacred bird, the eagle, in her revolt from Rome (216-11 BC). The Oscan inscription reads *Capw*.

220A

220B

221

222

223A×2

223B×2

earliest brass coins so far identified appear in northern Asia Minor. Brass with its attractive yellow-gold colour spread
274 quickly through Asia: Phrygia had a bimetallic system of brass and bronze by the middle of the century, and these metals were later used by the emperor Augustus for his Asian coinage. During his reign brass was also adopted at the mint of Rome, and later it spread further west to Spain, although it never replaced bronze there.

Such was the general nature of Hellenistic coinage. In the east it was dominated by the Hellenistic kings, as has already been described. In the west it at first reflected the history of the wars between Carthage and, at first, Syracuse and, later, Rome. These wars flared up in the later fourth century BC when Timoleon, with the support of Corinth, set out to revive the fortunes of the Greek cities of Sicily. As a result there was a great burst of minting activity just after 350 BC: Carthage opened two
101 new mints for tetradrachms in Sicily, and supplemented their products with gold minted in Carthage itself. Timoleon brought large numbers of Corinthian coins, which for the next 40 years
213 made up more than three-quarters of the silver currency of Sicily. Some two decades of peace ensued until Timoleon's role as champion of the Greeks was taken up by Agathocles of Syracuse (317-289 BC), and in his wars against Carthage he made the first Syracusan tetradrachms for almost a hundred years. He also minted electrum (debased gold), matching the similar coins of Carthage, and from his reign Syracusan coinage came to dominate the currency of Sicily. In this period too Syracuse changed the weight system of her large denomination silver coinage and introduced a system based on the litra, later adopted by the Romans as their unit, the *scruple*.

Despite the fact that the First Punic War (264-41 BC), during which Rome replaced Syracuse as the main adversary of Carthage, was a war about Sicily, Roman coinage did not reach the island for another generation, but instead was confined to the Italian peninsula where it had begun some 40 years before. Until the end of the fourth century the Romans had used bronze by weight as a measure of value (and perhaps as a means of payment) and had even occasionally used the coins of other states. But in about 300 BC they made their first coins, silver coins whose execution differs only in the legend ROMANO from
the contemporary Greek coins of South Italy. This adoption of **216,218**
the Greek practice of coining is probably a reflection of the growing and self-conscious Hellenisation of Rome at the time.

At first Roman coinage consisted of four elements: struck silver and bronze coins of the Greek type (didrachms and obols),
large cast bronze bricks (so-called 'aes signatum') and large **219**

224 Just before 300 BC Taranto in south Italy made some beautiful gold staters depicting the goddess Hera. The reverse represents the Dioscouri, the patron deities of Sparta, and refers to the help given by Cleonymus of Sparta to the Tarentines in their war against the neighbouring Lucanians.

225 A Carthaginian half shekel has the head of Tanit and a horse. It was minted in south Italy, probably at Locri, during the Punic occupation.

226 One of the earliest Roman denarii. It was made in Sicily (Agrigento?) and signed by the magistrate C Al. in about 210 BC. The head is of the goddess Roma, and the reverse shows the Dioscouri, who according to legend had helped Rome in an earlier hour of need (the battle of Lake Regillus in 496 BC).

227 Roman 'victoriates' have the head of Jupiter and a figure of Victory (hence 'victoriate') crowning a trophy. They were made extensively in the Hannibalic War and until about 170 BC. The significance of the monogram on this piece of about 210 BC is not clear.

228 Some of Rome's allies contributed coins to her war effort. Teate in south Italy puts Athena and her owl on some of her coins.

224A

225A×3

225B×3

224B

226A×3

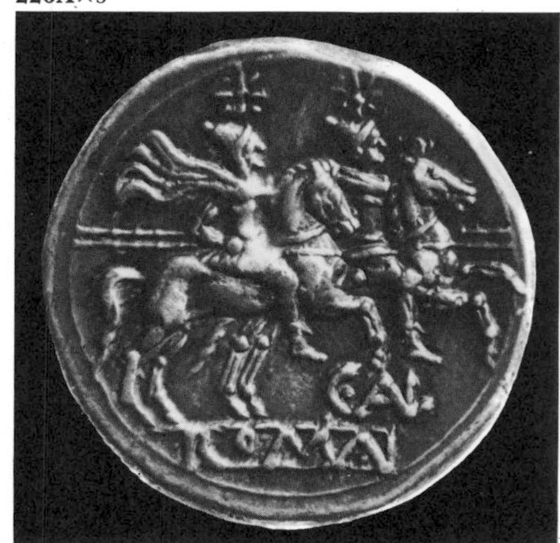
226B×3

229 A struck bronze as, with the traditional types (**220**), is of a particular series distinguished by the wreath symbol above the prow. Uncertain mint, about 205 BC.

230 The only non-imperial lady to appear on 'Roman' coins, Mineia, is depicted on a semis of Paestum near Naples, in the late first century BC.

231 Catana, in Sicily, minted many bronze coins during the Roman Republic, including some with a crude head of Jupiter Ammon.

232 Lepcis Magna in north Africa made coins which refer to the town's patron deities, Heracles and Dionysus. The obverse has the head of Dionysus and the reverse the club of Heracles. The neo-Punic legend refers to the town. First century BC.

233 A denarius minted at Osca (modern Huesca) in Spain, in the early second century BC, with the name of the town in Iberian script. This was the most prolific Spanish mint, and it has been thought that it gave rise to the Roman phrase 'Oscan silver' to denote Spanish denarii, but the phrase may mean only 'coin with funny writing' (**223, 249**).

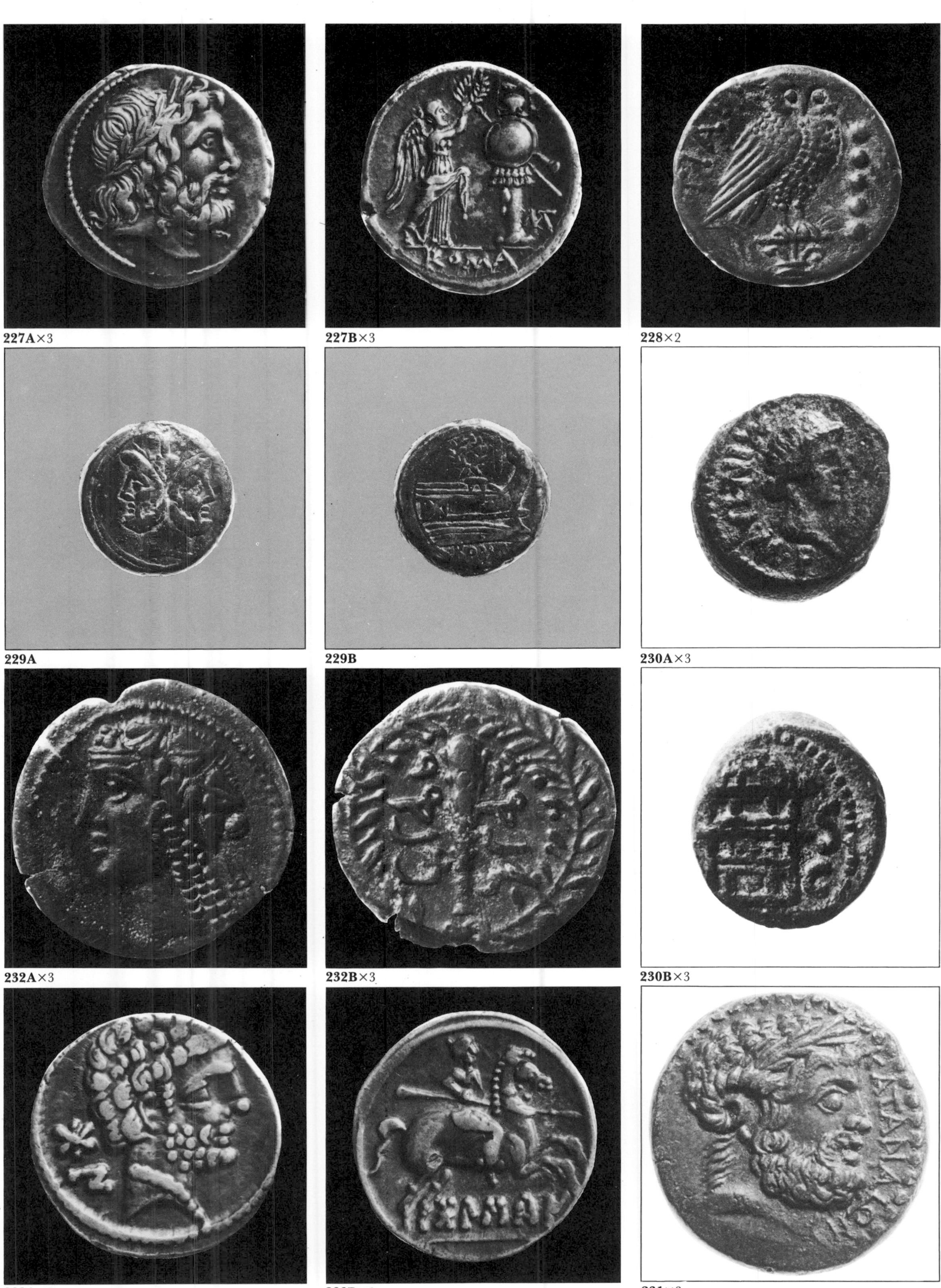

227A×3 **227B**×3 **228**×2

229A **229B** **230A**×3

232A×3 **232B**×3 **230B**×3

233A×3 **233B**×3 **231**×3

234 A bronze coin of Obulco (modern Porcuna, near Corduba) has the head of Apollo and a plough and corn ear. The Latin inscription on the obverse names the town, while on the reverse are the names Situbolai and Urkail in Iberian script. Second century BC.

235 The island of Ibiza produced many bronze coins with a figure of the god Bes, since the island's name probably means 'Island of Bes' in Punic.

236 The Roman moneyer C. Val(erius) Flac(cus) marked his coins with the number XVI (= 16) after the revaluation of the denarius. The reverse has one of the standard types of the second century, Victory in a chariot, perhaps referring to the Roman conquest of Macedon in 168 BC. Minted about 140 BC.

237 The half as or semis (hence the value mark *S*) always had the head of Saturn, while the reverse had the usual prow. Issued by the moneyer T. Quinctius in about 130 BC.

238 The denarius issued by P. Nerva in about 112 BC shows a Roman voting scene. One voter receives a ballot from an official, while another places his in the ballot box.

239 P. Nerva also issued this quadrans (3/12 of the as, hence the three pellets) with the normal types: a head of Hercules and the prow.

240 A moneyer called Philippus (about 113 BC) makes a punning allusion to his name by using the head of King Philip of Macedonia. The 'portrait' is entirely imaginary.

241 The quaestor (Q) Fundanius minted quinarii in 101 BC. This denomination was now called the victoriate and took its types from the earlier coins of that name (**227**). To the traditional type he added a Gallic trumpet to the trophy, referring to Marius' recent victories over the Cimbri and Teutones.

234A×2 **234B**×2

235×2 **236A**×2 **236B**×2 **237A**×2

238×2 **239A**×2 **239B**×2 **237B**×2

240×2 **241A**×3 **241B**×3 **242**×2

242 Denarii were specially struck in 101-100 BC to allow the quaestors Piso and Caepio to purchase corn (AD FRV EMV). They are shown seated on their thrones, and the ear of corn refers to their task.

243 Sulla issued some aurei, and in 80 BC one variety showed his equestrian statue. The head of Roma may imply that he intended to restore the Republic rather than retain power for himself.

244 L. Roscius Fabatus (64 BC) made coins with serrate edges, a fashion which was quite common at the time and which was probably intended to allay public suspicions of forgery: it implies that the coin is good silver throughout. Each pair of his obverse and reverse dies were always related (here both refer to Isis; her headdress and her rattle). When one die broke the other must have been thrown away or reengraved. The types refer to Fabatus' home town, Lanuvium.

245 When he was aedile in 58 BC and made coins, M. Scaurus recorded how four years before Aretas III, king of Arabia (here symbolised by the camel), had submitted to him. In fact Aretas bought off Scaurus with a huge bribe.

246 A denarius issued by Sulla's son Faustus in 56 BC shows the surrender of the Numidian king Jugurtha to his father. It is likely that the coin type has been copied from Sulla's signet ring.

247 Faustus was also one of Pompey's legates, and some of his coins show three wreaths, symbolizing Pompey's triumphs for his African, Spanish, and eastern victories; above is the golden crown he was voted in 63 BC. The globe represents the world.

248 In the mid-first century moneyers sometimes used portraits of earlier members of their families. Pompeius Rufus in 54 BC has the head of Sulla.

243A×2

243B×2

244A×2

244B×2

245×2

246×2

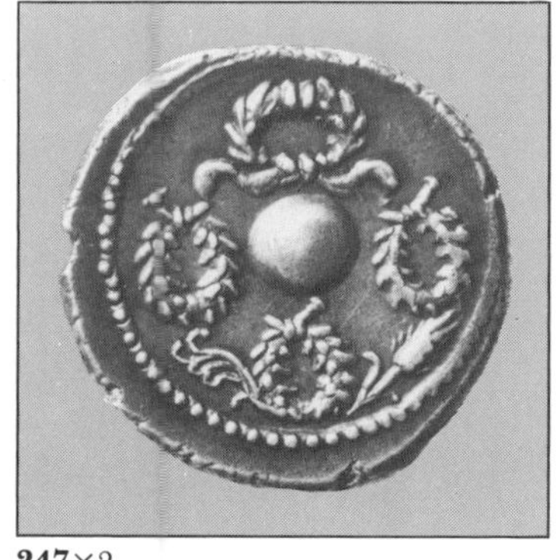
247×2

248×2

220 round cast coins ('aes grave'). For several decades these coins were made only sporadically. There was little or no denominational relationship between the different elements, and the metals had different functions: silver was for South Italy and bronze for central Italy. But from about the middle of the century the coinage became more unified and by the 230s BC all the elements could have the same issue mark, e.g. a club, showing that they were produced as a single series. Just before the war with Hannibal (218-02 BC) this unity was emphasized when cast and struck pieces were made with a similar janiform
220 head on the obverse; and but for the financial catastrophe of the war this pattern and structure might well have remained for the later Roman coinage.

Despite their loss of Sicily in the First Punic War and other subsequent setbacks, the Carthaginians pursued a vigorous policy of expansion, acquiring large financial and military resources in Spain. War broke out when Hannibal set out from Spain to cross the Alps and invade Italy, and after he had won a
223 series of brilliant victories, some Italian cities such as Capua and Syracuse went over to him and made coins to help him. Most of Italy, however, remained loyal and, although he scored some more notable successes, Hannibal was shut up in the toe of Italy. It was only a matter of time until he had to cross to Africa, where he was finally defeated at the battle of Zama (202 BC) by Scipio. His campaigns were financed partly by coins minted by allies like Capua and partly by Punic coins; some of these were minted
225 in Italy and Sicily, but others were transported from Carthage. The Romans had entered the war with silver and bronze coins linked by their common use of the janiform head, and the vast expense incurred by Rome is reflected in the huge increase in the minting of silver, the production of an emergency gold coinage, and then the rapid reduction in the weight and purity of the silver. The weight standard of the bronze collapsed as well. This catastrophic effect is not really so surprising, as Rome was fighting in Italy, Sicily, Sardinia and Spain and had to mount an expedition against Macedonia. For a time Rome may have even run out of money and lived on credit, but from about 212 BC she
was again able to issue silver. The new coins: the denarii, **227**
victoriati, quinarii and sestertii, together with accompanying bronze and occasional gold pieces; were made at many mints.
Apart from Rome, there were two mints in Sicily, one in **226**
Sardinia, one in south-east Italy and probably others which have
not yet been identified. In addition some of Rome's allies issued **228**
coins to help.

After the successful outcome of the Hannibalic war the production of Roman coins was centralized at Rome, and the overwhelming majority of coins used in Italy were produced
there, although a few places like Velia or Paestum made small **230**
issues of bronze until the age of the early empire. In Sicily too a
number of cities like Syracuse made intermittent issues of bronze **231**
in the second and first centuries BC, and even until the reign of Tiberius (AD 14-37). The part of Africa (Tunisia) which was incorporated into the Roman world after the destruction of Carthage in 146 BC followed a similar pattern. Silver was
provided mainly by Rome, while some cities made fairly small **232**
bronze coinages. Spain, which had been acquired by Rome in the Hannibalic war, had a native coinage of much greater importance. Only here in the West was there a systematic silver
coinage, the Iberian denarii, which were minted for about a **233**
hundred years from the early second century. They were made at a number of centres, mainly in the Ebro valley or in the south, all with similar types. The analogy of the cistophori suggests that they were minted to meet the expenditure of the Roman state rather than that of local communities, although it is not clear why they should have been made only in certain areas. The
Spanish cities also issued large quantities of bronze with types **234,235**
that are occasionally inspired by Roman coins but usually indigenous, and these can acount for 50% or more of the bronze circulating in Republican Spain. From the reign of Augustus the number of towns minting declined, and Spanish coinage came to

249 Rome's Italian allies rebelled in 91-87 BC. Their coins copied the physical fabric and often the types of Roman coins, but here the design is original: the bull of Italy tramples the wolf of Rome underfoot. The legend means 'Italy' in Oscan script.

250 L. Plautius Plancus puts Victory leading a chariot on his coins, copying a famous painting by Nicomachus, which his family owned at the time. Minted in 57 BC.

251 In 46 BC T. Carisius portrayed the patron goddess of the mint, Juno Moneta. On the reverse are coining tools: a die above an anvil, tongs for handling blanks and a hammer for striking.

252 Although quinarii were occasionally minted (**241**), silver sestertii (quarter denarii) were made only in 210 BC and 90 BC until they were revived by Caesar. The types used by Palikanus in 45 BC probably represent a money pot and one of the *tesserae* which bankers like his father used to certify the good quality of coins they had examined.

253 In 90 BC L. Piso made asses by feeding a strip of connected blanks between the dies to stimulate a fast rate of production.

254 In the early second century the Thessalian league minted drachmae with the head of Zeus and the figure of Athena Itonia. The league was established in 196 BC when Rome freed Thessaly from Macedonia, and the Nicocrates named on the obverse may have been the league's commander in 182 BC.

255-256 A recently discovered tetradrachm from Samos (about 170 BC) has a head of Zeus and his wife Hera. A comparison of contemporary Zeus heads (**254, 257, 258**) shows the variety of different styles and engraving abilities to be found in different parts of the Greek world at the same time.

250×2

251A×2

251B×2

252A×3

252B×3

249

253

254A

254B

255

256

257 When Macedonia was defeated in 168 BC it was divided into four regions. The silver mines were in the first region which minted these very rare tetradrachms before the Roman senate closed the mines. They have the head of Zeus and Artemis on a bull (she was a principal deity of Amphipolis where this coin was minted).

258 The Achaean league of cities in Greece made a federal coinage in the second century. The head of Zeus is common to all cities, but each had their own reverse. Here we have Pegasus for Corinth, soon to be razed by the Romans when the league rebelled in 146 BC.

259 In the early 160s BC Athens inaugurated a new style of coinage, although employing her traditional types (**73, 116**). Inscriptions call them coins 'of wreath-bearing attic silver'.

260 Some 20 other communities also made 'wreath coins'. Tenedos, an island off the Turkish coast, uses a striking conjoined male and female head, while the double axe within the wreath is the traditional badge of the island.

257A×3

257B×3

258A×2

258B×2

260A

260B

259A×2

259B×2

261 In about 175 BC the kings of Pergamum replaced their coins with 'cistophori' from several royal mints. The name means 'box-bearing', referring to the Dionysiac chest from which a snake slithers. The bow-case entwined with snakes alludes to Heracles. The Pergamene dynasty claimed descent from Dionysus and Heracles. Pergamum mint, about 165 BC.

262 At about the same time, Rhodes introduced a new style of coin, on the same new weight standard. The new coins were called *plinthophoroi* (brick-bearing), from the incuse square on the reverse. They were made until the first century BC: this one dates to the late second century BC.

263 The child king of Syria, Antiochus VI (145-42 BC) is shown wearing the radiate crown of the sun-god. Tetradrachm minted at Antioch, 144 BC.

264 Tryphon (142-39 BC) murdered Antiochus VI and usurped the Syrian throne. The reverse of this coin has a helmet with an ibex-horn.

265 In 141 BC the Syrian king Antiochus VII gave the Jews the right to strike coins. The first ones were made 10 years later at Jerusalem, and they have the anchor for Syria, and the lily for Judaea. The Greek number ΑΠΡ (181) means the 181st year from the beginning of the era of the Syrian kings (312 BC).

266 The city of Tyre in Phoenica was freed from Syrian domination in 126 BC, and began to mint a lengthy series of shekels of pure silver with the head of Melqart and an eagle. Jews used them to pay their temple tax, since Jewish law forbade the representation of humans, and this prohibition ruled out the other coins of the area. The number ΔΚ (24) means the 24th year from the freedom of the city (= 102 BC).

261A×3

261B×3

262A×2

262B×2

266A

266B

263×2

264×3

267 Along the Black Sea coast many cities made bronze coins with the same types for Mithradates. Several proclaim his alleged descent from the hero Perseus: here the hero holds the head of the gorgon Medusa, while her decapitated body lies behind Amisus, about 90-85 BC.

268 Mithradates VI. At the beginning of his empire-building in 89 BC he adopted a portrait with wild flowing hair. This departure from normal Hellenistic practice was a deliberate attempt to make him look like Alexander or Dionysus, another conqueror from the east. Minted in 75 BC.

269 Athens was captured by Mithradates and in 88-86 BC made silver and even gold (as here) coins for him. They have the usual type compare (**259**), but have his name 'King Mithradates' on the reverse.

270 Mithradates' son-in-law Tigranes, king of Armenia, took the opportunity to help Mithradates and to enlarge his own realm by overrunning large areas of Roman territory, including Syria. At Antioch he made tetradrachms which portrayed him wearing an Armenian tiara.

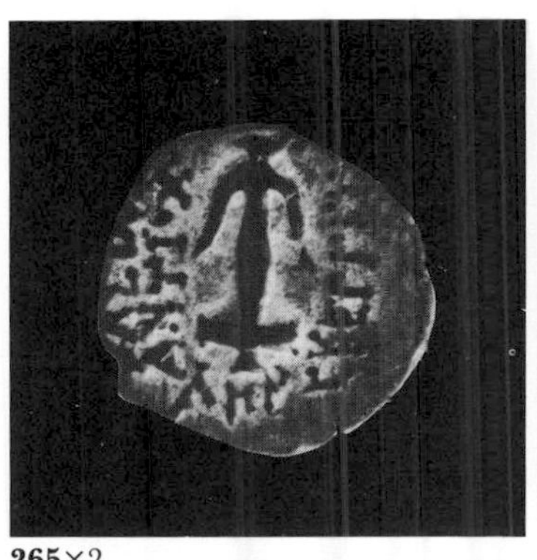

265×2

267

269A×2

269B×2

268×2

270×3

an end early in the reign of Claudius (AD 41-54). The currency
of the peninsula was then provided by locally made imitations of
Claudius' metropolitan coins, and this change probably reflects
a deliberate decision to bring the local coinages to an end and
replace them with imperial issues.

With the exception of Spain, all these local coinages were
restricted in scale, and the great bulk of the currency of the West
consisted of coins from the mint of Rome. For the last two
hundred years before the empire, Rome made large issues of
227 silver; at first the victoriate predominated, but from the middle
of the second century its place was taken by the denarius. The
regular minting of the denarius seems to coincide with the
decision to pay the army in silver rather than bronze, and from
this time the number of denarii minted may well correspond with
the numbers of soldiers under arms (a Roman legion cost 1.5
million denarii a year). Silver was of course also used to pay for
242 public works and for the distribution of subsidized and free corn
to the population of the capital.

In the third century BC the Roman coinage was probably
controlled by the censors (the magistrates responsible for letting
public contracts), but–perhaps in the Hannibalic War–control
passed to the senate with the senior financial magistrate (the
quaestor) and the junior magistrates (the *tresviri monetales*), the
moneyers who were actually in charge of the working of the mint.
These moneyers often added to the coin type a reference to
themselves. At first this might take the form of a punning symbol 229
or a monogram, but later fuller forms of their names appeared. 236
Towards the end of the second century the freedom of the
moneyer to add to the type took a dramatic step forward when
the traditional types were replaced by individual types which
often had political relevance. Coin types might then comment on
contemporary events, or they might advertise the origins and
family history of the moneyer himself (e.g. the successes,
achievements and even, later, portraits of ancestors or parents).
This variety of types began as a result of a law in 139 which
enforced secret ballotting at Roman elections. The moneyership 238
suddenly became more popular among the Roman nobles, since
coins provided an opportunity for the self-advertisement which
now became necessary to launch a successful political career.
From the time of Marius moneyers began to refer also to the
achievements of famous men who were not related to them. The 241
major figures of the late Republic, such as Pompey or Caesar, 247
later dominated the coinage, and the propaganda function of
coins reached a peak in the civil wars of the late Republic and in
the reign of Augustus.

Despite the huge variety of types which resulted from each of

271 Many tetradrachms were minted in Macedonia by the Roman quaestor (Q) Aesillas, perhaps to pay expenses incurred to meet the threat of Mithradates VI. The obverse has the head of Alexander the Great; on the reverse the club is the symbol of Heracles, and is accompanied by a money chest and the quaestor's chair of office. Early first century BC.

272 The campaigns of Mithradates and Tigranes were eventually ended by the Roman general Pompey. He refounded the city of Soli (opposite Cyprus on the Turkish coast), and was commemorated on coins of the city.

273 In 58-48 BC cistophori were made with names of the Roman governors (including even Cicero!). Lentulus Spinther, the proconsul of Cilicia in 56-53 minted this one at Apamea.

271A×3

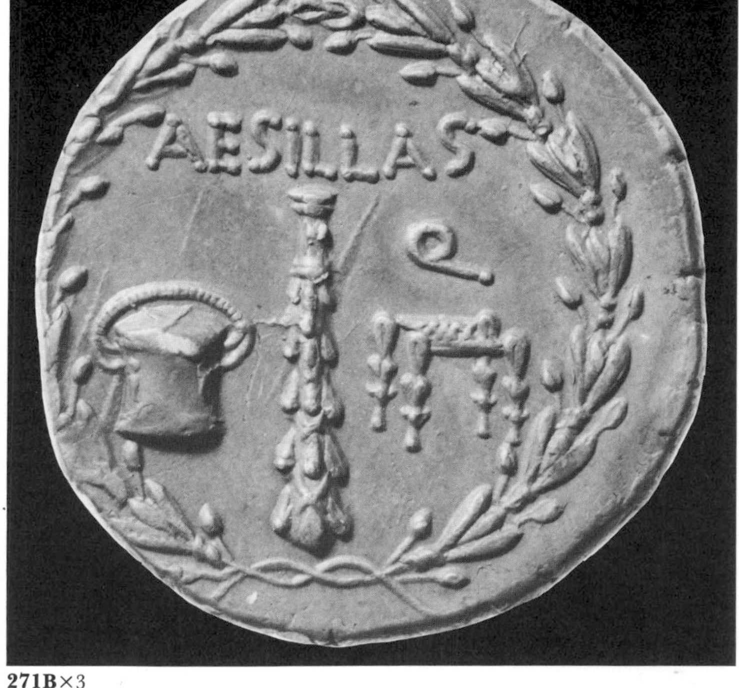

271B×3

272×3

273×3

three annual moneyers using at least one separate design, the denarius was a very stable coinage: its weight and (with a solitary exception) its fineness remained constant throughout the period. The only important change was monetary: at its inception it was worth 10 asses, but in about 140 BC it was revalued at 16, a change which probably gave official recognition to the fact that the market price of a denarius in terms of asses had risen substantially in the period since 212 BC.

Unlike the silver, Roman bronzes nearly always had standard types, the head of a god and the prow of a ship (Roman
237,239 schoolboys would shout 'heads or prows' when tossing coins). It was issued in six main denominations:

1 as = 2 semisses = 3 trientes = 4 quadrantes = 6 sextantes = 12 unciae.

Bronze was issued in large quantities in the second century, but
after 100 BC its production almost ceased. There was an issue at **253**
a reduced weight in the 80s, but afterwards, with the possible
exception of coins of Octavian in 38 BC, none was made at Rome **296**
until the reign of Augustus. The bronze currency of the period consequently consisted of old coins, many of which were extremely worn.

The standard designs allowed the engraving of their dies to

274 As well as silver cistophori, Asian cities minted large numbers of bronze coins, although these have only the names of the city magistrates. Apamea produced a series of brass coins with Athena and an eagle. Minted in 56 BC.

275 The Roman conquest of Crete by Metellus (69-63 BC) was one of the rare occasions where an eastern conquest was marked by a special and 'Roman' coin type. At Gortyn tetradrachms were minted with a head identified by the inscription as 'Roma'. The elephant's head on her helmet is the badge of the Metelli.

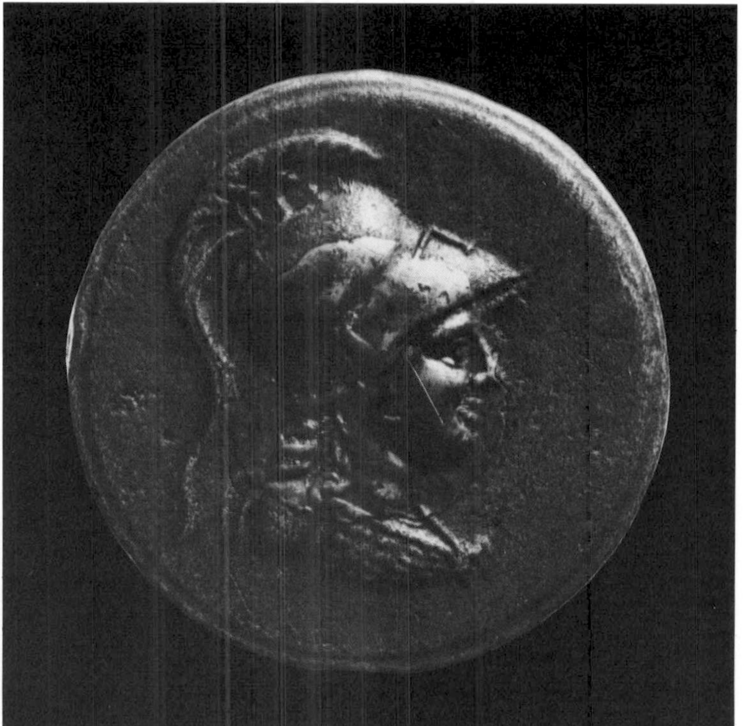

274A×3

274B×3

275×3

become rather stereotyped, and the difficulty of striking such large pieces (at first more than 50 grammes in weight) contributed to their rather rough appearance. In addition, the blanks were prepared by casting metal into two moulds, and since these moulds were often not properly aligned the coins tended to have an odd lopsided appearance. The physical appearance of silver was much better, and it remained fairly constant, although there
244 were one or two short-lived variations. Technically the quality of die engraving fell, largely as a result of mass production of coinage from about 200 BC: the engraving is often crude compared with Hellenistic work, and the introduction of many varied and often complicated types accentuated the decline. The heavy-handed use of the drill, for instance, resulted in a blobby effect on the coins. Only in the first century did the influence of Hellenistic art begin to be felt as a result of the eastern commercial contacts and interests of some moneyers, and with the reign of Augustus Rome produced a fine Hellenistic coinage for the first time. In general, Augustus reserved to himself the right to issue coins in precious metals, but allowed the senate the right to issue token coins in brass and in copper. Most of the large value coins of Augustus were struck at a single mint in
Lyons, France. **297**

The coinage used and produced in the eastern Mediterranean provides a strong contrast with that of the West. Roman involvement in the east had begun at the end of the third century in Illyria, and Roman armies quickly became involved in Macedonia, Greece and Asia Minor. Roman policy was, however, generally passive, responding only to the need to balance the power blocks of the east rather than following a deliberate programme of expansion. Intervention was usually followed by a new arrangement of the existing territories of leagues or kingdoms rather than by direct annexation. In the same way the pre-existing coinages continued and the Romans did not introduce their own. Indeed their presence at first had no effect at all on the coinages of the East, except that the ones they may have used to pay their own expenses were greatly increased in number.

In the period of the Third Macedonian War (171-68 BC), however, a profound change occurred in the coinage of Greece and Anatolia. In the first place all earlier coinages disappeared—not only the regal coinages of Macedonia or Pergamum, but also the huge number of posthumous coins of Alexander the Great and of Lysimachus with Alexander's portrait. Secondly, new coinages replaced the old. A group of these, issued by some 20 cities, all have the same basic pattern. The obverses have the
head of a deity and the reverses a design surrounded by a **259,260**
wreath. These new coins clearly are a recoinage of the silver

287-288 Pompey's son Sextus used Sicily as his base against Octavian. In 43-40 BC he struck superb aurei there with his portrait. The reverse has the facing heads of his father and brother.

289 The 'fleet' bronzes of Antony, struck in Greece by his lieutenants in the mid 30s BC, included the first bronze sestertii, or four as, coins. They are distinguished by the four hippocamps, the Greek numeral 4 (Δ) and the symbol IIS (= 2½ the original quarter of a denarius) for sestertius, linked by a line.

290 Antony and Cleopatra appear on shekels minted in about 34 BC somewhere in Phoenicia. The coin commemorates the open liaison between them, after he had rejected Octavia.

287

288×2

289

290A

290B

291 Cleopatra was more attractive when younger: a coin minted at Ascalon in 49 BC shows here aged 20.

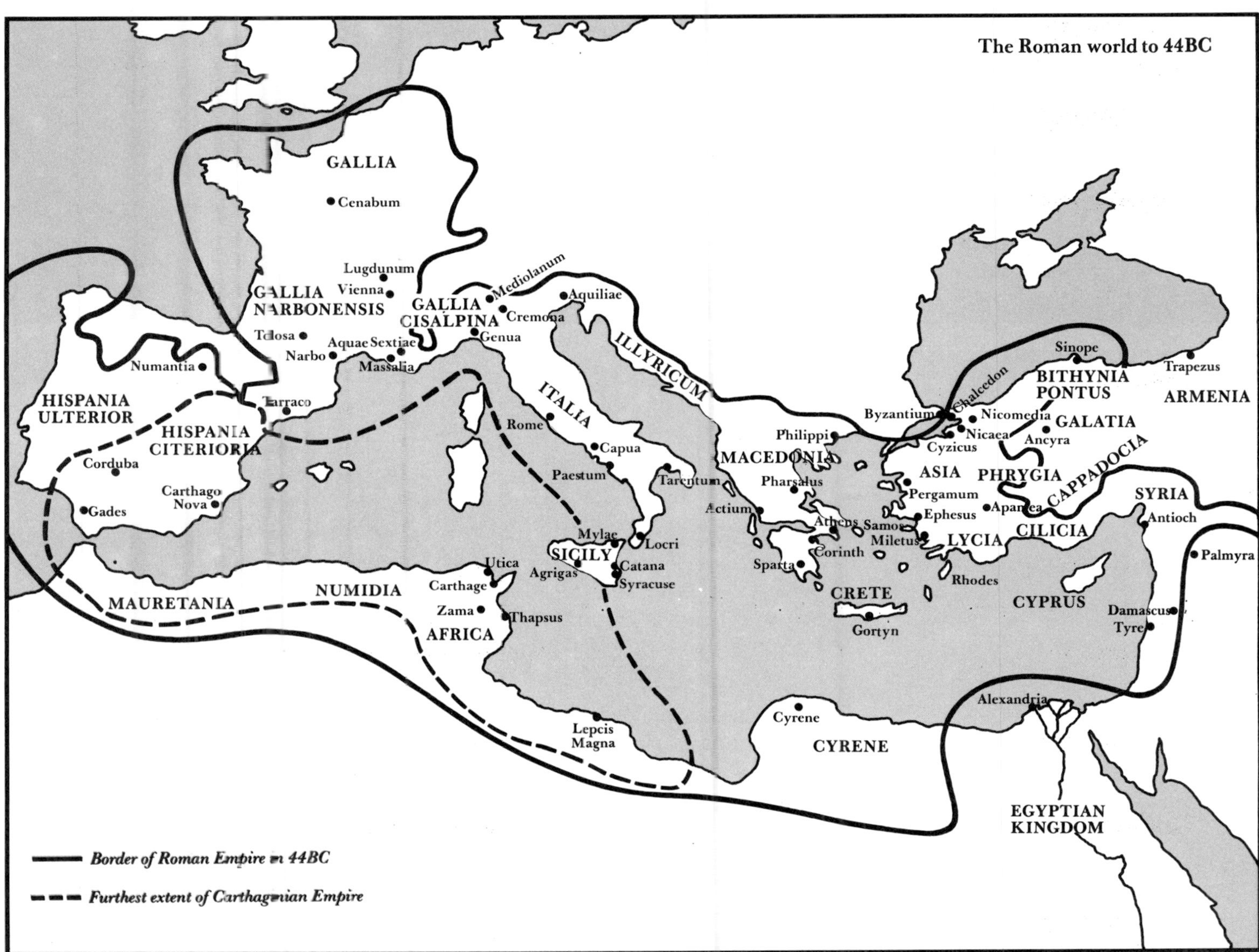

291×3

local coinages of these areas, many of which (including those of Athens and Asia) stop at about this date, and one later finds a similar preference for denarii rather than local denominations during the Severan civil wars. This preference enabled the leaders of the different factions to advertise their claims since denarii had a long tradition of varying types, while the essence of **286**
local coinages was the standardization of their types. One of the most dramatic consequences of this intoduction of Roman coins was the widespread use of Roman portraits on coins. Caesar had decided to put his head on coins in 44 BC as if he were a Hellenistic king, and his precedent was quickly copied by his **284**
successors. The leaders of the different parties in the civil wars regularly placed their portraits (however unflattering) on coins just like any Hellenistic usurper; and after Actium, of course, the use of the portrait became a standard feature of the Roman imperial coinage.

This proliferation of precious metal coinages was supplemented by a vast increase in the quantity of bronze coin, since bronze too was used to meet the expenses of warfare, including military pay. Occasionally it was minted in the name of the different leaders, but usually it consisted of the normal issues of **289,296**
cities, magnified in number. In one small area of Spain no less than 60 cities may have produced coins, and as far as can be seen

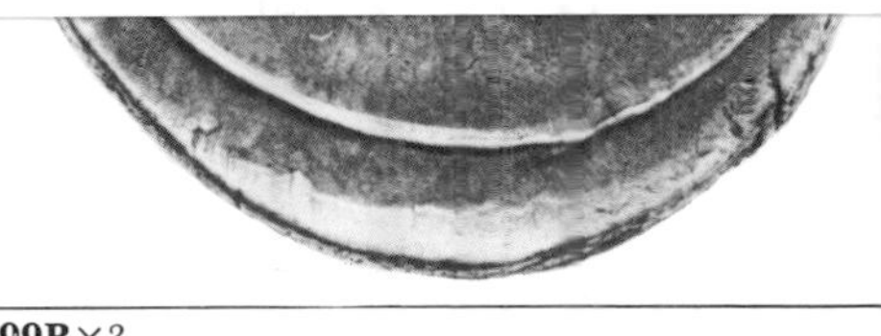
299B×3

300A×2

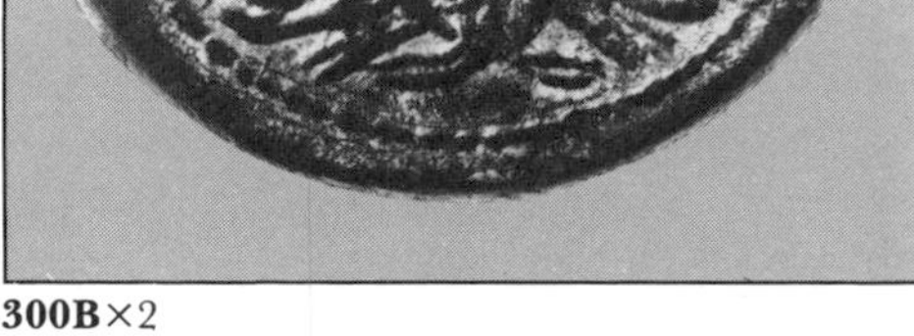
300B×2

from the pattern of the few datable bronze coinages of the east, much the same is true there. Sometimes these civic coins would
293,298 replace their normal types with references to the warring dynasts or their commanders, and sometimes even have their portraits.

After the battle of Actium, Octavian, later called Augustus, emerged as the sole ruler of the Roman world. The ending of the civil wars in itself naturally brought a reduction in the widespread production of coinage, and it seems that Octavian himself also made a deliberate attempt to reduce this chaos of coinage. This is implied by a conversation supposed to have taken place between him and Maecenas when they considered the possibility of stopping cities from using their own coins and making them use imperial ones. An attempt to do just this was made in the early 20s BC with Augustus' CA coinage, which was **300**
centrally minted to a standard design and which circulated throughout Asia and Syria. The attempt was not, however, successful, and the pattern of coinage resumed its former nature; but now nearly every coin had the head of the emperor Augustus, and this profound change marks the beginning of the coinage of the Roman empire.

292 The famous legionary denarii of Mark Antony, struck to pay his troops on the eve of the battle of Actium (31 BC). Antony was running out of money and had to debase these coins to only 85% fine.

293 The legates of the principal contenders also struck coins in many places: Atratinus minted coins at Sparta (as here), fleet bronzes (**289**), bronzes somewhere in north Greece, and bronzes at Enna and Lilybaeum in Sicily. The use of the portrait follows from its use by the major leaders.

294 In Cyrenaica the governor Lollius minted coins (perhaps during the civil wars) with the head of Zeus Ammon, the principal deity of Cyrenaica, and the official chair of a Roman magistrate.

295 After Augustus' victory the portraits of legates (**273**) continued to appear on coins for some time. Here we have Cicero's son at Magnesia in Asia, perhaps in the 20s.

VI

THE CELTS

Daphne Nash

By the end of the third century BC the Celts were established in northern Europe from Britain to the Black Sea and from southern Germany to the Pyrenees. They were the first to strike coinages in barbarian Europe, even in areas such as the north Balkans where they were an ethnic minority. The earliest Celtic coinages were struck between 250 and 190 BC; issues of this period are found in the Danube basin, northern Italy, the
304 Rhineland and several areas of Gaul, and they were of gold and silver of high purity and heavy weight. Their types reflected their authors' familiarity with contemporary Greek and Macedonian coinages, and their chosen models were at first copied very closely.

By far the most widely used prototypes were coins of Philip II of Macedon (359-36 BC). His silver tetradrachms were preferred by the eastern Celts, and his gold staters by the Gauls of the Rhineland and France. Familiarity with these and other Mediterranean prototypes is most likely to have resulted from the widespread use of the Celts as mercenaries by Philip and his successors and by Greek cities, from the fourth to the second centuries BC. Although coins of Philip II and Alexander III (336-23 BC) were the most frequently used models for Celtic coins, the coinages of other cities and kings were also used,
302 notably Thessalian Larissa and kings Lysimachus of Thrace, Patraos and Audoleon of Paeonia in the east, Massilia in northern Italy, Emporiae and Rhode in southern Gaul, and Tarentum in the Somme area of northern France.

The date of the early Celtic issues in the Danube area is known from hoards which also contain well-dated Greek and Macedonian coins; in Gaul in the absence of such hoards, chronology depends heavily on typological arguments.

After an initial period of close imitation, a large number of distinctive issues of gold and silver were struck during the second century BC in many Celtic areas. In most cases they can be divided into clearly differentiated series with pronounced local or regional distributions which reflect their use by specific Celtic communities. Six main regional divisions of Celtic coinage can be recognized: the eastern (Danubian) region from the Black Sea to the Alps where the silver tetradrachm was the basic unit; the
305 Po Valley with drachmae based on the coinage of Massilia; Bohemia with gold staters derived from coins of Alexander III
309 and Philip V of Macedon; the Rhineland and central Gaul with gold staters based on those of Philip II; north-western France
318 with half-staters derived from the coinage of Tarentum; and south-western and southern Gaul with silver coins based on
315 drachmae of Emporiae and Rhode in Spain. The choice of particular prototypes must partly have been governed by the content of the types; the eastern Celts and the Gauls chose types with horses, whether ridden, driven, free-standing or winged, which probably reflects the interests of the Celtic aristocracy, who were fine horsemen. (Notable exceptions to this rule of preference were the Cisalpine Celts and the peoples of Bohemia and southern Germany.) The dominant coinage metal was partly determined by preexisting conventions in the composition of wealth in each region, and partly by the local availability of precious metal ores.

The types used in all areas were still therefore related to Mediterranean prototypes, but in an increasing number of cases the connection was indirect and traditional. The majority of new issues now took their inspiration from other Celtic coins, and there is no reason to suspect that their authors were familiar with the Mediterranean coinages which supplied the original models.

The fineness and weight of precious metal coins in all areas declined in successive stages during the second century as the volume of coins which were struck increased. Some of the finest products of Celtic die-engravers' art belong to this period, and a few rare examples of literacy occur, as on an Illyrian tetradrachm inscribed SASTHIENI in a local script, or a Gaulish gold stater inscribed EIQITIVICO in imperfect Roman characters. Normally, however, the letters which appear on coins have no phonetic value, and were either purely ornamental or were included as traditional features of coin design.

Non-Celtic communities in close contact with the Celts began to strike coinages barely distinguishable from those of their neighbours. Most important among these were the silver drachmae of the Veneti in the north-east of Italy and the coins of some Alpine populations, which shared the type and weight standards of the Cisalpine Celts, and in the east the coinages of the Geto-Dacians in the Danube basin, and the tetradrachms from the Black Sea coast imitating coins of Thasos.

Developing contacts with the Roman Republic are reflected in the choice for the first time during the later second century of some Roman prototypes: tetradrachms of Macedonia Prima in the Balkans, and Republican denarii in the Rhone Valley and parts of southern France.

The widest geographical extension of Celtic coinage occurred during the first century BC. In most areas important changes in the coinage took place, related to contemporary social and political developments. In general there were fewer issuing authorities than before, but most of them struck unprecedentedly large coinages. Gold coins became increasingly debased every-

Celtic design derived from a Greek chariot (**159**) on a stater from the Moselle valley about 100 BC (**323**).

301 With types derived from tetradrachms of Philip II of Macedon (**160-61**), this tetradrachm from southern Transylvania, struck about 200 BC, has preserved the basic Macedonian types without the inscription, and a severed human head has been substituted for the original mint-mark.

302 Fourth century silver coins of Larissa (**112**) presented the facing head of a nymph on the obverse and a horse on the reverse. Celtic tetradrachms which adapted these types were struck in south-western Romania in the years around 200 BC. This is the only extensive Celtic series to display a facing head.

303 Large issues of debased silver coinage were struck in the Danube basin from 125 BC until the mid-first century. This type, from south-eastern Romania, illustrates the very perfunctory execution of coin dies typical of this late phase. The head of Zeus has been reduced to a few suggestive dots and lines, as has the horse on the reverse.

304 Tetradrachms of Alexander III (**162**) and Philip III (**167**) showed a head of the young Heracles in a lion-skin headdress, and on the reverse a figure of Zeus, with sceptre and eagle, seated on a throne. A long series of tetradrachms and drachmae modelled on the coins of Alexander the Great and Philip III was struck in south-eastern Romania and northern Bulgaria from 225-180 BC. Reverse dies are numerous, but few obverse dies were used. As they cracked and were worn by the strikings, they were repeatedly re-engraved or gouged out until they became an almost formless cup. This coin shows an early stage in the process of disintegration.

305 Drachmae of Massilia with a head of a nymph and a standing lion were chosen as model for the native silver coinage of Cisalpine Gaul. The Insubres around Milan struck one of the earliest of these in the late third century BC. The reverse (shown here) retains meaningless elements of the Greek legend ΜΑΣΣΑ.

301A

301B

302

303

304A×3

304B×3

305×2

306×2

306 Imitations of Roman Republican denarii became common in Pannonia and the Danube basin in the mid and late first century BC. In Pannonia the Eravisci struck a series in the later first century which are inscribed with a version of their tribal name; the types are adapted from first century Roman denarii.

307 The Boii in southern Slovakia began to strike a silver coinage on the eastern tetradrachm standard around 60 BC, with coins inscribed BIATEC. BVSV came later in the first century BC. Roman influence on die design is very marked; on two occasions denarii were followed closely as models, but the winged female centaur is Celtic in inspiration.

308 Heavy silver coins with legends in the Roman alphabet were struck in Noricum (Austria) during the first century BC. The charging horseman is found on denarii of the Roman Republic, but Celtic taste is exhibited in the elaborate crest on his helmet and on the obverse, which shows a horse with a tree-like structure behind it, ultimately derived from the head of Zeus on Danubian tetradrachms.

309 Gold staters of Alexander III with helmeted head of Athena and standing victory (**163**), and tetradrachms of Philip V (**200**) with a figure of Athena, provided models for the gold coinage of Bohemia and Moravia in the second century BC. In this area the stater was divided not into quarters but into thirds, sixths, ninths, and twenty-sevenths. Here Athena has been reinterpreted as a male warrior, and the vestiges of the Greek legend have lost all meaning.

310 The last descendants of the Athena Alkis tradition were first century BC gold coins of the Boii known as Mussel staters because of their shell-like appearance. About 60 BC the last dies of the series were inscribed with the name of the same Biatec who inaugurated the inscribed silver tetradrachms of the Boii in Slovakia.

307A×3

307B×3

308

309A×3

309B×3

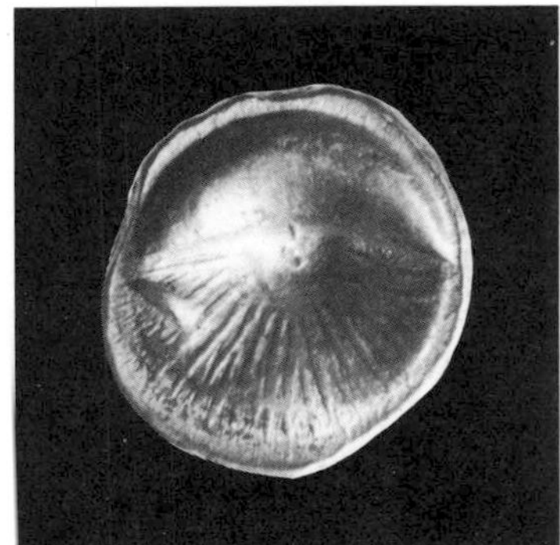

310×2

where, as did silver in the Danube region. New types were widely adopted, in many cases unrelated to traditional models, although still in most areas preserving the head and horse formula. Geographical distributions of coins are usually well defined, and may often be related to the known or supposed extent of territories of peoples with increasingly centralized political structures. For the first time Celtic coins are commonly found in settlements, and in some hillforts evidence has been found for coin manufacture, undoubtedly under the supervision of the rulers of the community.

During the first century BC small silver fractional coins and bronze token currency began to be issued in western and central
332 Celtic areas, a development which is connected with the emergence of town life and increasingly complex administration in this period. By the mid-first century bronze coinages were abundant in Gaul and were probably issued for local use at most settlements of substantial size.

The influence of Rome was widely felt in the first century BC.
307 The first silver coinages of the Boii and the kingdom of Noricum to the north and east of the Alps were struck on the eastern Celtic
308 tetradrachm standard, but used Roman Republican denarii as models for their types. Denarius imitations of lighter weight became common in the eastern region later in the first century, ultimately superseding the debased tetradrachm coinage. In Gaul and southern Germany local silver weight standards gave way in many areas to coinages on a standard weight of just under
two grammes (roughly equivalent to the Roman quinarius), and 330
Roman Republican coin types were commonly used as inspira- 331
tion for coinage types in all metals. There is widespread evidence for literacy among die engravers during the first century. Various alphabets were used – Italic scripts in Cisalpine Gaul, the Alps and Rhone Valley, Greek in parts of Gaul, and above all Roman in Bohemia, Noricum, the Danube region, Gaul and Britain.

In every area, wars with Rome provoked unusually high levels of coin production to pay for armies and associated expenses. In Gaul, the Belgic tribes struck large gold stater coinages on a common weight standard and with interrelated types for the duration of the war with Caesar (58-50 BC), and the Armoricans
in western Gaul struck enormous issues of base gold and silver 336
billon staters on a similar basis. Elsewhere in Gaul the war elicited large gold and silver coinages from the major states of central and eastern areas, for the payment both of auxiliary contingents in Caesar's army and for Gaulish armies to resist him.

The Roman conquest of the Celtic provinces put an end to the

311 In southern Germany in the first half of the first century BC gold staters were struck by the Vindelici and their neighbours on a Gallic weight standard but with types related to the northern Mussel stater tradition. The triquetra may be seen as three revolving birds' heads sharing a central eye. Later specimens are of silver billon and finally bronze.

312 The Germani on the right bank of the Rhine struck a number of important silver coinages in the first century BC on or below the Romano-Celtic 'quinarius' standard, and with types which are partly Roman and partly Celtic in inspiration. This type has Roman origins, but the soldier on the denarius has become a bird-man carrying a Celtic torque. The chevron border recalls that of contemporary gold staters of the same region (**311**).

313 Silver tetradrachm coinage was struck by the Celts in Hungary (Pannonia) during the second century BC, based on the types of Philip II. The standard of design and engraving was high; but the diecutters were illiterate and the Greek letters used can have had no phonetic value. The triskeles was a common element of design on Celtic coins of all areas.

313

311×2

312A×3

312B×3

314 In the southern Alps around Genoa in the first century BC, small silver coins were struck with types ultimately derived from the Cisalpine drachma. They may have been issued by a Ligurian rather than a Celtic authority.

315 Drachmae of the Greek colony of Rhode on the Catalan coast of Spain furnished the prototype for the earliest Celtic silver coinages of south-western Gaul around 200 BC. The Greek coins showed a head of a nymph and on the reverse a rose seen from below. In the Celtic series the rose gradually became a wheel or a simple cross with decoration in the quarters.

316 Silver cross coinages were the principal currency of the Garonne basin and south-western Gaul in the second and first centuries BC. There are several distinct series: that of the Volcae Tectosages showed an axe in the lower left-hand quadrant. The obverse shows a Celtic interpretation of the dolphins in front of 'Arethusa's' face on coins of Emporiae ultimately derived from Syracuse (**98, 99**).

314

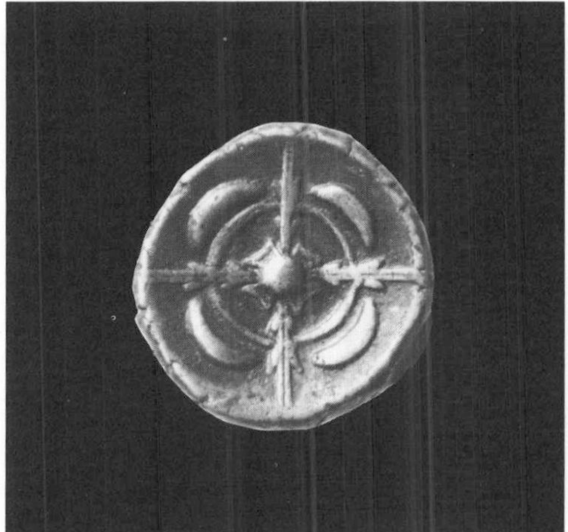

315×2

316A×2

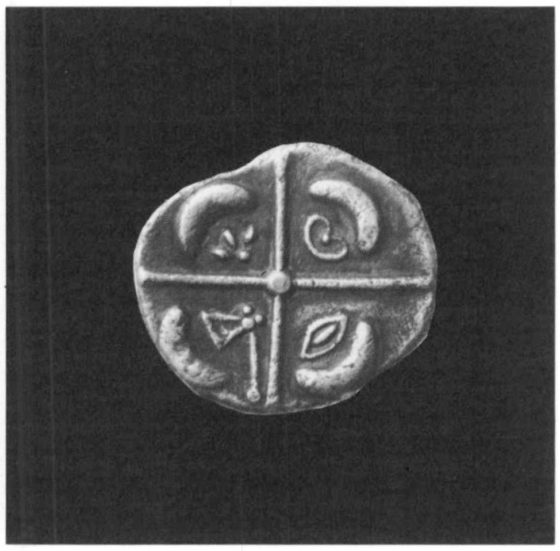

316B×2

317 During the first century BC a number of silver coinages related in weight, type and method of manufacture to the cross coinages were struck in areas further inland. The Ruteni of Rouergue substituted a Celtic boar for the cross, but the flan was prepared, like many cross coinages, by chopping strips or sheets of silver into roughly rectangular pieces of the right weight.

318 Massilia's colony Emporiae in Spain furnished models for silver coins in southern central Gaul, inland from the area of circulation of the cross coinages. The earliest imitations of Emporitan drachmae with standing horse and flying victory were struck around 200 BC in Spain and southern Gaul. The Gaulish series reduced the victory to a figure of eight and showed the horse prancing.

319 Late third century drachmae of Emporiae replaced the earlier standing horse and victory with a Pegasus. The first century silver coinage of the Elusates of south-western Gaul shows a very stylized version of Pegasus in which the wing is reduced to a linear pattern. The obverse type has lost almost all resemblance to the head of Ceres on early Gaulish silver coins of Emporitan type from which it is derived.

317×3 **318**×3 **319**×3

320×3 **321A**×3 **321B**×3

322×3 **323**×2 **324**×2

325×2 **326A**×3 **326B**×3

320 Iberian denarii struck inland from Emporiae were the ultimate model (**233**) for a large series of silver coins with horseman reverse struck in Central Gaul in the later second century BC, and closely related to Gallic drachmae of Emporiae type.

321 The dominant model for Gaulish gold coinage was the stater of Philip II which showed a head of Apollo wearing a laurel wreath, and a galloping biga with charioteer (**159**). Some of the earliest Celtic versions were struck in the Rhineland, Switzerland, and Burgundy before 200 BC, and faithfully reproduced their models in every detail.

322 The earliest gold coinage near Bordeaux was struck around 200 BC. The Celtic engravers have reproduced the heavy features of Apollo and linear style of the reverse characteristic of the products of the Macedonian mint signed with trident symbol (**159**), but the result is unmistakeably Celtic. The trident symbol continued to be used on second century gold staters of western Gaul.

323 By the late second century BC links with Macedonian coinage had become very distant in Gaul. In the Moselle valley a gold coinage was struck with a wreathed head in the Apollo tradition; but on the reverse the chariot was replaced by a human-headed horse and floating driver.

324 The earliest gold coinages of the Somme valley were third century half and quarter staters modelled on coins of Tarentum. In the mid-second century a new gold stater coinage was struck on wide flans. It retains elements of the Tarentine series, such as the treatment of the hair of Apollo, but also borrows from the Philip tradition, especially on the reverse which shows a horse with winged victory and the vestiges of a chariot.

325 Later second century BC coins of central Gaul show only distant echoes of the Philip tradition. This series from Touraine or Berry retains the charioteer and a token wheel from the original chariot, and the thunderbolt which was among the mint marks copied onto the earliest Celtic gold coins.

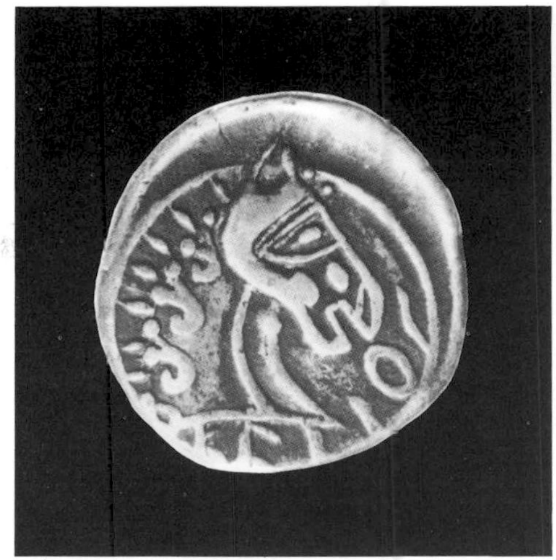

327×3

326 Armorican gold coinages display some of the finest products of pre-Roman Celtic art. The Veneti used the early coinage of the Moselle valley (**323**) as the model for the reverse of their late second century coinage. The head of Apollo has been interpreted as a severed head placed on a support visible under the neck truncation; the four small heads on cords probably have mythological significance.

327 Celtic silver coins were not struck in the Rhone valley until the second century BC. The earliest issues show the head of a horse on the reverse, probably copied from late third century Punic coinages. Names of rulers or magistrates such as KASIOS are inscribed in a north Italian script.

328 In the first century BC the Allobroges struck a silver coinage with a mountain goat reverse.

329 Rome made treaties with some of the Celts in the upper Rhone valley and eastern Gaul in the 120s BC. Soon afterwards some of them abandoned their debased gold coinages and began to strike silver coins on a weight standard close to the Roman quinarius. Either the Aedui or the Lingones struck a large and enduring coinage with a helmeted head derived from Roman denarii (**236**). Greek script was used for the name ΚΑΛΕΤΕΔΟΥ, which was progressively abbreviated until it disappeared altogether.

328×3

329A×3

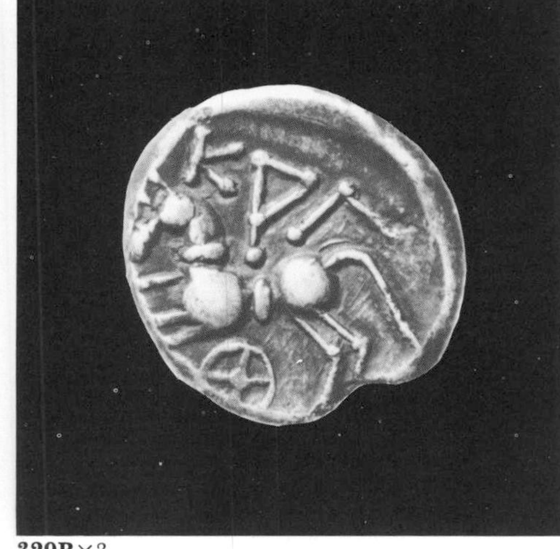

329B×3

issue of most precious metal coinages. Gaul was taken by Caesar by 50 BC, and after that date no gold coinage was struck and little silver. Danubian coinages also came to an end in the mid-first century, probably in this case as a result of the conquests of the Dacian king Burebista. Gold and silver coinages north of the Rhine in Germany continued to be issued until the later first century BC, while Bohemian and Norican isues were struck until the Roman conquest of Pannonia and Noricum in the last decade of the century.

After the Roman conquest precious metal coinage was no longer struck in Gaul except by a few Belgic and central Gaulish authorities who issued silver coins of 'quinarius' weight during the 40s and perhaps early 30s BC. Their authors were sometimes
341 Roman citizens and it is likely that the coinages were destined to be used as pay for the expenses of the new provincial administration, and especially the Celtic contingents in the Roman armies whose task of subduing northern and western Gaul continued long after Caesar's departure. In contrast, bronze coinage flourished after the conquest and was issued in unprecedented quantites not only in central Gaul where it it had long been in use, but in Belgic Gaul where it was a recent development. Celtic bronze coinage came to an end in the last decade BC with bronzes of GERMANVS INDVTILLI L and some uninscribed issues found on northern settlements and in Roman legionary camps on the Rhine.

Britain was the last major Celtic area to adopt coinage and the last to cease striking it. Gold coins from Belgic Gaul were transported to southern Britain in significant quantities during the first century BC, partly no doubt as an aspect of the historically documented spread of Belgic authority in the area, but also as payments for British services to the Belgae including military help. Coins of the Somme region, which in the mid-first
century was under the authority of the Ambiani, were the most 338
numerous imports, and a stater type of c. 75-60 BC provided the model for the earliest gold and silver coinages in southern
Britain. These earliest British coinages probably belong to the 343
decades immediately before Caesar's conquest of Gaul. From about 40 BC, and for just over a century, the rulers of southern Britain produced abundant coinages in gold, silver and bronze; many that were issued were inscribed with their names and mints, thus enabling a rudimentary history of the period to be reconstructed.

South of the Thames a strong dynasty was founded by Commius soon after Caesar's conquest of Gaul and his departure from the sphere of Roman authority. His gold coinage was modelled on staters of the Belgic Suessiones struck during Caesar's war. Commius' sons Tincommius (20 BC-AD 5),
Eppillus (AD 5-10) and Verica (AD 10-40) ruled the Atrebates 345
and Regni in southern Britain from centres at Chichester and Silchester, and struck large and varied gold and silver coinages which are strongly Romanized in type and bear fully literate Latin inscriptions. Their small change was in silver.

North of the Thames an uninscribed gold coinage of Celtic
design contemporary with that of Commius was succeeded by 346
coins of Tasciovanus (20 BC-AD 10) which were influenced by 347
Roman types. Tasciovanus' sons Cunobeline (AD 10-40), Epat- 348
ticus (AD 25-35) and Caratacus (AD 25-30) also struck large Romanized coinages from centres at St. Albans, Colchester and, in the case of Epatticus, somewhere south of the Thames. Coinages of this dynasty north of the Thames and those of the contemporary rulers of Kent had bronze coins as their lowest denominations.

330 One of the largest 'quinarius' issues of eastern Gaul in the first century BC was struck in the name of SOLIMA. The legend appears both in Greek and Roman alphabets, reflecting its authors' familiarity with Greeks through Massilia and with the Romans.

331 A prominent Sequanian noble, Togirix, struck a very large silver 'quinarius' coinage which circulated widely at the time of the Caesarian war, accompanied by cast bronze (potin) fractions. His career as a supporter of the Romans is illustrated by his coinage. His silver coins are Celtic in type although with a literate Latin legend; his bronze coins show a head wearing the helmet of a Roman auxiliary cavalry officer, and finally silver coins struck after the conquest name him as Julius Togirix, indicating that he had by then received Roman citizenship.

332 In eastern and central Gaul token coinage was commonly manufactured by casting strips of coins in clay moulds more or less crudely impressed with the types. The coins had a high tin content and were cut apart when removed from the mould. One of the earliest such potin coinages was that of the Aedui, first issued early in the first century BC. The types were derived from struck bronze coins of Massilia showing a head of Apollo and a butting bull, which was reinterpreted as a horned quadruped of indeterminate type.

330A×3 **330B**×3 **331**×3

332A×3 **332B**×3 **333A**×3

333B×3 **334**×3 **335**×3

336A×3 **336B**×3 **339**×2

333 Many first century gold coinages in Gaul depart widely from the earlier Philip tradition. The Arverni first struck a gold coinage in the first century BC, and it was issued in great quantities during Caesar's war. Many dies show familiarity with Roman techniques and the Latin alphabet. The prancing horse is found with a wide variety of subsidiary symbols.

334 In the first century BC the Bituriges Cubi of central Gaul struck gold inscribed staters and a parallel bronze coinage. Their silver coinage, struck at a separate mint, is largely uninscribed, but the latest issue–which may belong to the early 40s BC–is inscribed CAMBOTRE and shows a very Romanized version of their traditional silver reverse type.

335 The Carnutes struck an unusually prolific and varied bronze coinage during the middle and late first century BC. Many types are modelled on Roman Republican denarii, and the names of several rulers or magistrates appear including the pro-Roman Tasgetios, mentioned by Caesar. His name has been spelled with the cursive form II for E, a common occurrence on northern Gaulish coins.

336 During the Caesarian war many Armorican peoples issued increasingly debased gold or silver billon coins on a common weight standard. The boar and the human-headed horse are among the motifs most frequently used by this highly distinctive school of engraving.

337 The Parisii of Paris struck a substantial gold coinage in the earlier first century BC. The design owes something both to Armorican art and to the wide flan staters of the Ambiani (**324**).

338 The Ambiani appear to have been the wealthiest of the Belgae and struck three successive gold coinages between the mid-second century and Caesar's war. The second, shown here, began as a greatly simplified version of the wide flan staters (**324**), and was struck in the first half of the first century BC; it was replaced by a new uniface series during the Caesarian war.

339 The Belgae north of the Seine joined forces to resist Caesar's campaigns from 58-50 BC, and struck gold coinages on a common weight standard to meet the expenses of the war. One of the most important from the Treveri, shows a large eye.

337A×2

337B×2

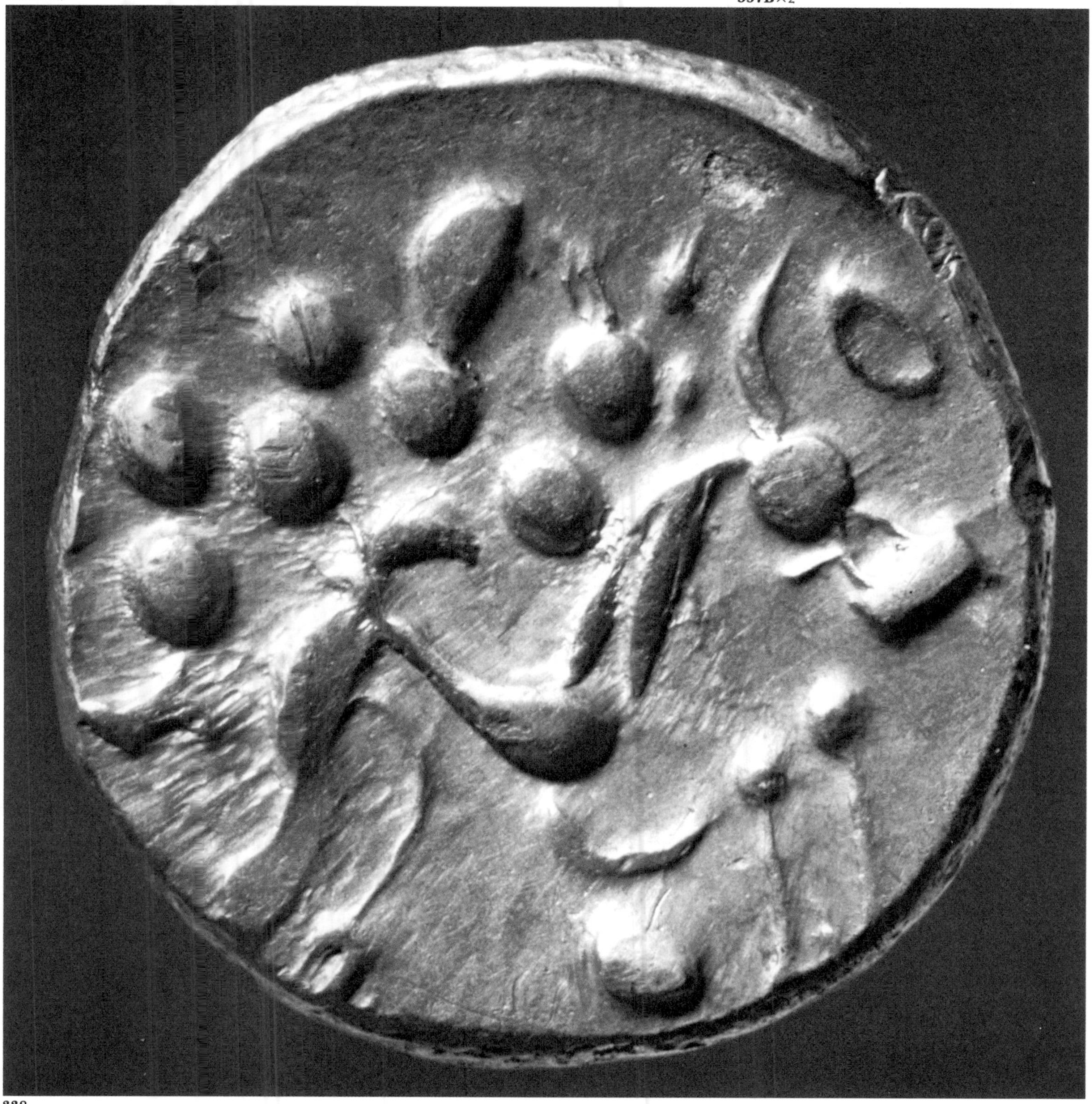

338

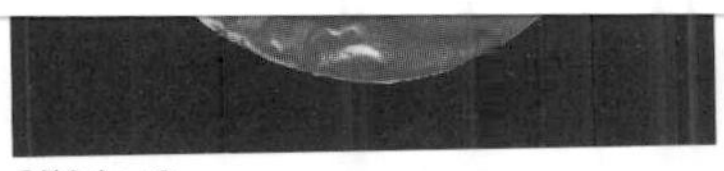

350A×2

350B×2

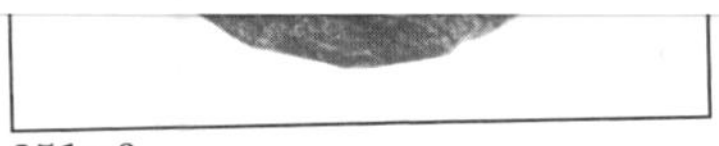

351×3

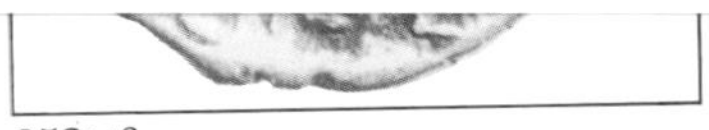

352×3

There were substantial coinages in other areas of Britain, none of which show very significant Roman influence in their choice of types or execution, except in the use of Roman letters for inscriptions during the first century AD. The most important of
350-353 these coinages were struck by the Durotriges, Dobunni, Iceni and Coritani. All were in existence by 40 BC and were issued until the mid-first century AD when Celtic coinage finally came to an end.

353A×2

353B×2

340 The Remi were a weak state until Caesar raised them to the heights of political prestige in return for their cooperation. They had not the resources to strike a precious metal coinage of any importance, but issued very large quantities of well-designed potin coins. A small figure bears a spear and torque; the reverse shows a bear-like animal and a brooch.

341 Until the Roman conquest the Pictones of western Gaul struck a base silver coinage of Celtic type in the Emporitan tradition. Duratius, a Pictonian noble, helped Caesar and after the war appears to have received Roman citizenship. Under his new name Julius Duratius he struck one of the postconquest 'quinarius' coinages. A tristyle temple of rather Classical appearance is shown in silhouette above the horse.

342 An Arvernian noble, Epasnactus, also collaborated with Caesar. His postconquest silver coinage displays his Roman tastes: the obverse is copied from Republican denarii, and the reverse portrays an elaborately equipped auxiliary soldier.

343 The earliest British gold coins were struck in the first half of the first century BC, and took their types from staters of the Belgic Ambiani (**338**).

344 In Britain, potin coins were confined to the lower Thames valley and north Kent. They were modelled on first century BC potins of the Senones in Gaul, but their thin flat fabric was unknown on the continent.

345 Verica is named in Latin as son of Commius on this gold stater. Some of his dies may have been engraved by a Roman diecutter. The vine leaf corresponds with the corn ear on contemporary gold staters of Cunobeline on the other side of the Thames.

346 Tasciovanus' principal mint was at Verulamium (Saint Albans). The types of this silver coin are derived from a denarius of Augustus struck at Lugdunum in Gaul, about 16 BC.

VII

THE ROMAN EMPIRE AND PROVINCES

Ian Carradice

In the first two centuries AD the Romans governed one of the largest empires known to history. The Roman Imperial coinage circulated in one form or another throughout, and indeed far beyond, the vast territories bounded by this empire. In the fifteenth century surviving examples from the Imperial coinage issues produced by the principal mints of the Caesars were the first ancient coins to capture the imagination of the Renaissance humanists. These coins have retained their popularity with scholars and collectors ever since; but more recently it has been recognized that a full appreciation of the Roman coinage of the Imperial period demands a consideration of all the issues produced under various authorities in the many mints located throughout the empire.

The coinage of this period has traditionally been classified under two convenient, but artificial, labels. 'Roman Imperial' coins were produced in the principal mint (usually Rome itself) or mints of the empire. They are always inscribed with Latin legends and they circulated extensively, in some cases throughout the empire. 'Greek Imperial' coins were struck in innumerable mints mainly in the eastern half of the empire. They usually have Greek legends and, in comparison with the 'Roman Imperials', their circulation was much more restricted. In these two coinages, in their interrelationships and in their similarities and differences, lies the story of money in the Roman Empire.

Augustus (27 BC-AD 14) was responsible for establishing the
354-359 essential coinage system of the empire. At first he struck coins at
a number of centres, but later, although he permitted local coinages of varying importance to continue, he concentrated production of large value currency in a single mint in the West. This mint, which was at Lyons in France probably until the reign of Nero (AD 54-68), when its responsibility for precious metal coinage was moved to Rome, produced gold coins for the whole empire. It also produced the bulk of the silver coinage, although in the East certain long-established mints continued to issue silver Greek coins under the emperor's authority. In AD 68-69 army revolts and resulting civil wars caused an outbreak of
384-388 regional gold and silver issues struck by rival factions, but the
eventual victor, Vespasian (AD 69-79), then centralized production again at Rome. Here it remained until the death of Commodus in 193 led to another series of civil wars and a further outbreak of provincial coinage issues in precious metals.

In the West the striking of bronze coinage in small provincial mints was gradually curtailed after Augustus and it ceased completely in the reign of Claudius when the last remaining mint, Ibiza, was closed. The Roman bronze coinage was then issued from the main mints at Rome and, from the reign of Nero, also at Lyons until, apparently under Vespasian, the Lyons mint was also closed. These Roman bronze coins sometimes travelled as far as the eastern parts of the empire, but there they were far outnumbered by the locally struck bronze coinage, production of which continued until the late third century.

The authority by which the Roman Imperial coinage of the West was struck has long been a question for discussion. The emperor's direct control over gold and silver issues has never been doubted; but it has often been thought that the Senate retained at least some measure of control over the bronze coinage
in the early Imperial period. The letters SC for *Senatus consulto* **355**
('by decree of the Senate') would seem to imply that this was indeed the case, but it is unlikely that this authority was anything more than a formal administrative concession. The designs on Roman Imperial bronze coins almost invariably
relate to the emperor and there can be little doubt that he held **358**
ultimate authority over coinage policy.

The government official who had overall responsibility for Imperial coinage was the emperor's financial secretary (*a rationibus*). There were also various officials in charge of the working of the mints and the striking of coins. The mints were divided into separate workshops (*officinae*). The coins produced by each *officina* were distinguished in the early empire probably by their use of different reverse types. This facilitated the checking processes that were necessary to ensure the maintenance of standards and to prevent fraud within the mint. The commonness of forgeries of denarii, silver-plated on a copper core, indicates that the ancient production of false Roman Imperial coins was a flourishing business.

In the East the question of authority for coinage production is more complicated than in the West because of the profusion of local and regional issues. The emperor undoubtedly had the final say in coinage policy, but many different categories of coins were produced, authorised by various bodies. Most important were the silver issues. The provinces of Egypt, Syria, and Asia produced tetradrachms on a regular basis, and city mints, notably Caesarea in Cappadocia, also frequently issued silver coins struck to Greek standards. All these coins, together with the major bronze issues from the same mints such as the
Alexandrian bronzes, the CA coins of Augustus, and the SC **300**
coins of Syria, have a definite 'official' character. They should be **363**
regarded as 'Imperial', though in most cases, especially the Egyptian issues from Alexandria, their circulation was restricted to the area of origin.

The harbour at Ostia on a sestertius of Nero AD 64-66 (**378**).

THE ROMAN EMPIRE AND PROVINCES

424 This bronze from Alexandria has a fine late portrait of Hadrian. The engaging reverse type depicts the Alexandrian triad of deities above an eagle. Sarapis and Isis face each other with their son Harpocrates (Horus the infant), personification of the ideal child, between them. Dated AD 134-35.

425 Portrait of Faustina I, wife of Antoninus Pius, with her hair braided and arranged elaborately around her head.

426 The reverse of this sestertius records the successful conclusion in AD 164 of Lucius Verus' Armenian campaign. Verus, flanked by soldiers, crowns Rome's protegé, Sohaemus.

427 Marcus Aurelius and his wife Faustina II were blessed with many children. On this sestertius the empress is clearly assimilated with Felicitas. AD 161(?).

424A

424B

426×2

427A

427B

428A×3

428 Marcus Aurelius broke with recent tradition by nominating as successor his own son, Commodus, instead of adopting a worthy candidate from outside his immediate family. On the reverse of this aureus of AD 175 Commodus Caesar is depicted distributing largesse. This popular act is frequently represented on the Imperial coinage.

429 The commonest reverse type on the important coinage of Caesarea in Cappadocia depicts the holy Mount Argaeus, the volcanic peak 13,000 feet high overlooking the city. Didrachm, Marcus Aurelius.

430 This large bronze piece celebrates the 'alliance' between the cities of Laodicea and Pergamum, represented symbolically by their patron deities Zeus of Laodicea and Asclepius. The exergue legend proclaims 'concord'. Marcus Aurelius.

428B×3

429A×3

425

429B×3

430A

430B

Moreover, it should be noted that many of the deities and personifications on the coinage owe their presence to a connection with the emperor. There is also an abundance of direct references to contemporary events provided by the coins. Imperial accessions are recorded, including those of short-lived usurpers; wars are fought; victories are proclaimed (but not defeats); triumphs are commemorated; new buildings are dedicated; and popular legislation is announced.

The types on the coins of the eastern provinces are no less interesting. Indeed, so mixed was the coinage issued in the East, and so diverse were the traditions of the people, that the range of types is even more extensive than in the West. The types vary according to the authority behind the coinage, and the purpose for which it was produced. The major 'Imperial' issues are dominated by the emperors. These coins were, on a smaller scale, the counterpart in the East of the great Imperial issues of the mint of Rome; they therefore had the same propagandist functions. The portrait of the emperor is ever-present on the obverses, but reverse types vary greatly. Thus, for example, Syrian issues are characterized by a relentless repetition of the
same simple reverse types, whereas Alexandria utilizes a vast 424
range of reverses, both local and Roman (or 'International'). The 'Imperial', 'Provincial', and 'civic' (but not the 'autonomous') coinages all tend to show a great interest in the Imperial family whose portrayal by them provided a means of proclaiming local devotion and loyalty to the emperor. It is not certain how knowledge of Imperial portraits circulated; but a comparison of coins from different areas suggests that various models were being used. The coins themselves provided portraits from which others might be copied, and in general the importance of

VIII

ROME: SEVERUS TO DIOCLETIAN

Andrew Burnett

Commodus was murdered on New Year's Eve 192, and after the brief reign of his successor Pertinax, civil war broke out between Septimius Severus in Pannonia, Albinus in Britain, Julianus in Rome, and Niger in Syria. After a few years Severus emerged as victor, and founded a dynasty for which he claimed descent from the Antonines and which lasted until 235. Thereafter there was a quick succession of military emperors, and the great difficulty of meeting the threats to the empire from the barbarians in Europe and the Persians in the East led to the fragmentation of the Roman world. The West was held by a series of Gallic usurpers from 260 to 274, and much of the East was in the power of the kingdom of Palmyra. Unity was restored by the emperor Aurelian (270-75) and despite revolts such as that of Carausius (286-93) in Britain it was preserved until the reorganization of the empire under Diocletian.

This history is reflected in the coinage which during the third century makes the transition from the stable but varied currency system of the early empire to the uniform coinage of the late empire inaugurated by Diocletian. This transition was made as the result of two parallel tendencies–the cessation of all bronze coinage (and therefore also of most of the eastern civic issues) and the gradual replacement of the various silver denominations of the East with a single one (the denarius and later the antoninianus) minted at several mints throughout the empire. Gold too was minted at these new mints, ending the former monopoly of Rome.

The civil wars after 192 caused an extensive production of denarii and aurei from a number of mints in Syria and the East. The Persian wars, on the other hand, seem at first to have been financed mainly by local silver denominations: Gordian's wars
453 saw the final issue of drachmae and didrachms from Caesarea, and earlier the campaigns of Caracalla brought a huge increase in the number of Syrian tetradrachms and the mints which
448 produced them. Soon after this the eastern silver production returned to the sole mint at Antioch, but from the middle of the third century Latin antoniniani, a purely Roman coinage, were minted there, as well as Greek tetradrachms. The minting of tetradrachms ended a few years later, and Antioch then became an important mint for the production of antoniniani. There had been an earlier tendency for denarii to be minted more regularly in the East, but these mints were fairly short-lived: a mint for denarii and aurei was established in 218 by Elagabalus, perhaps at Nicomedia, and lasted for some five years, while there may also have been an eastern mint during the reigns of Gordian III and his successor Philip. But the first permanent mint for antoniniani in the East was Antioch, whose importance was second only to Rome. Another regular eastern mint, probably at Cyzicus, started work later in the 250s, and there was also a brief issue from Tripolis later in the century.

The need to have supplies of cash at hand to pay large concentrations of troops also accounts for the opening of mints in another area, the Balkans. Here the threat came from over the Danube, from the Goths, and this danger is reflected in the appearance of city defences on the coinage of Balkan cities. A mint at Siscia began under Gallienus (253-68) and Aurelian established two more–a short-lived one, of which the location is unsure, and one at Serdica which remained active into the fourth century. Viminacium may also have been a mint, but the coins attributed to it from 253 may have been made elsewhere,
perhaps in Milan. Milan does at any rate become an important 463
mint in the reign of Gallienus. His campaigns in Gaul against the Germans brought a new mint into existence there (probably at Trier), and it was taken over during the revolt that brought to power the Gallic usurpers, who added a second mint. After his reunification of the empire, however, Aurelian relied on a single Gallic mint at Lyons and this mint soon became extremely productive. Finally Aurelian opened another mint in Italy, at Ticinum (Pavia).

The opening of all these new mints reflected the difficulty of controlling the empire and its gold and silver coinage from a single central point, and it led to a great increase in the quantity of silver coins in circulation. At the same time the productivity of the old mint at Rome was stepped up by increasing its six *officinae*
(workshops) to 12. The reason for this increase in production 461
was the continuous debasement of the silver, since as its value fell it had to be made in greater quantities (a grim parallel to the currency of today). Despite the occasional but hopeless attempt to reverse the process, debasement progressed rapidly from the reign of Severus until it reached its nadir in about 270. As the purity and weight of the silver decreased, so the weight of the gold coin fell, no doubt to preserve the relationship of one aureus to 25 denarii. Claudius II (268-70), however, took over from the usurper Postumus the idea of stabilizing the weight of the aureus and abandoning the fixed relationship between gold and silver, and the stability and independence of gold remained a feature of Roman coinage. The bronze too was debased: the weight of sestertii fell and their more valuable constituents (zinc and tin) were replaced by cheap lead. Thus bronze coins came to be composed once more of the leaded bronze which had been the normal coin metal before the introduction of brass coins some

The Roman Emperor Probus, AD 276-82 (**475**).

446 In 204 Septimius Severus minted an aureus showing Hercules and Dionysus, the *di patrii* (patron deities) of his African birthplace, Lepcis Magna.

447 The first antoninianus, so-called after Caracalla who was named Antoninus by his father Severus as part of their claim to be descended from the Antonine dynasty. Minted in 215.

448 A silver tetradrachm of Caracalla minted at Loadicea (Syria) in about 210. Many similar coins were minted at several Syrian mints to pay the expenses of the Persian wars.

449 Coins of Tarsus in Cilicia commemorate the shipment of corn (*seitos*) to the city, perhaps from Egypt. Minted about 215.

450 Augusta Traiana in Thrace has a fine representation of its gateway. Minted for Caracalla, about 200.

451 A denarius of Elagabalus minted in 218-19 in the East, at Antioch or Nicomedia. The reverse shows a triumphal car carrying the sacred stone of Emisa shaded by four umbrellas with the legend 'to the divine sun god Elagabal'. It demonstrates Elagabalus' attachment to the cult of the god Elagabal, whose chief priest he was and from whom his name is taken. Similar types do not, however, appear at Rome until late in his reign.

452 A sestertius of Gordian II, emperor for only three weeks in 238.

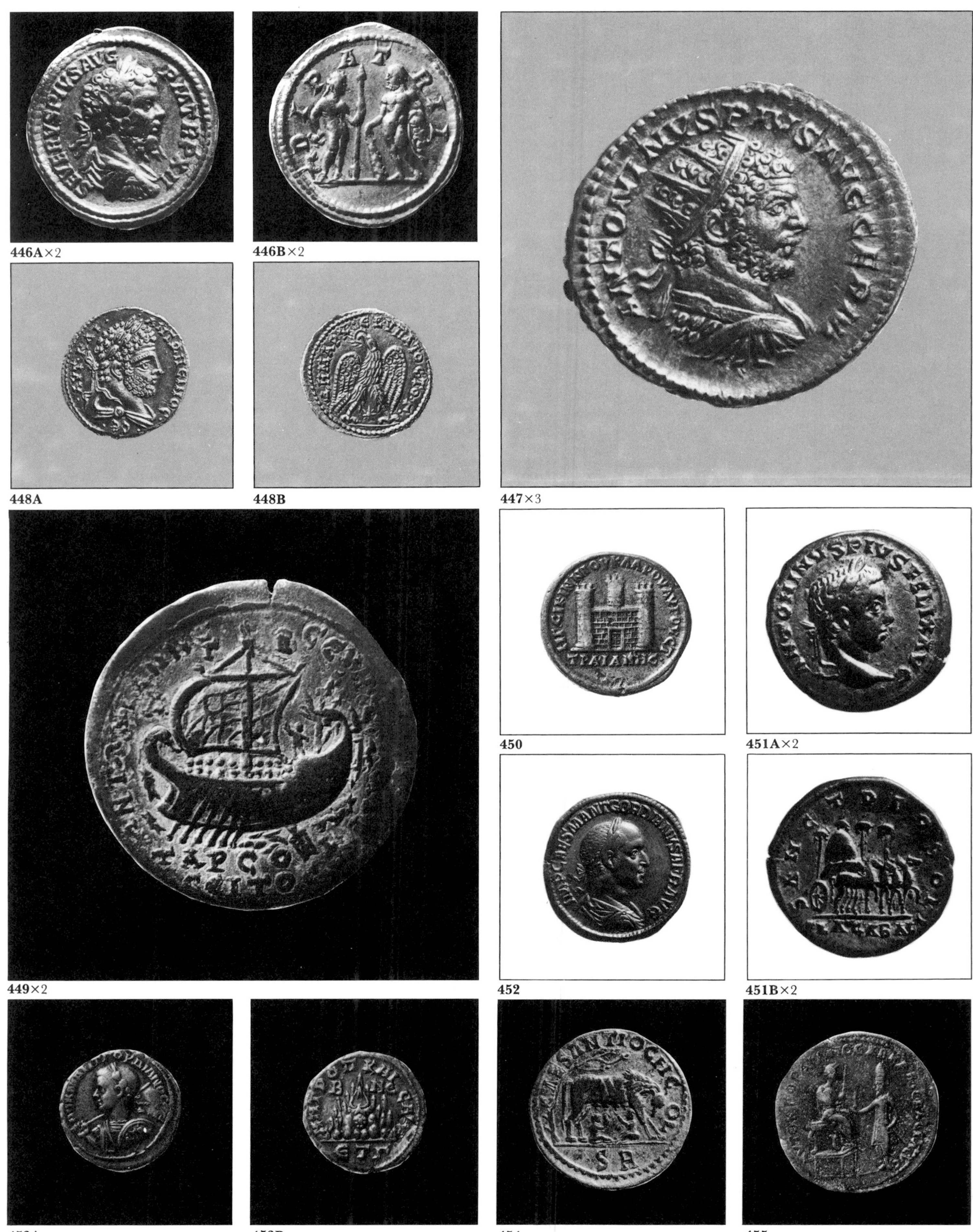

446A×2 **446B**×2 **448A** **448B** **447**×3

449×2 **450** **451A**×2 **452** **451B**×2

453A **453B** **454** **455**

453 To pay for his war against the Persians Gordian III minted silver at Caesarea in Cappadocia. The reverse shows Mount Argaeus, the sacred mountain (**429**). Didrachm, minted in 240.

454 At Antioch in Pisidia a large bronze coinage was produced during Gordian's campaigns. This coin portrays the foundation legend of Rome (the wolf suckling Romulus and Remus) and its choice reflects the town's pride in its status as a Roman colony.

455 During his campaigns Gordian III restored Abgar X as king of Edessa in Mesopotamia. The dependent status of the king is clear: Gordian is seated, while Abgar stands before him.

456 Some Syrian silver tetradrachms of Philip (244-49) have the usual types and legends (compare **448**), but an unusual style which is like that of the mint of Rome. Moreover the words MON(ETA) URB(IS) below the eagle imply that the coins were made at the 'mint of Rome' and were then shipped out to Syria to be put into circulation there.

456A×3

456B×3

350 years before. The fall in standards at Rome was mirrored in the provincial coinage: mints such as Caesarea produced brass coinage with a decreasing percentage of zinc, and at the same time the weights of the coins fell. At Sparta, for instance, a 4-as coin of Commodus weighed about 10 grammes, whereas one of
465 Gallienus weighed only about 5. An essentially similar process took place in Asia Minor where coins were countermarked with numerals to give them new higher values.

The fall in the value of bronze led, as in the case of silver, to an increase in production. The Rome mint made large numbers of sestertii in the early third century and similar coins were also made in the Balkans, at Viminacium for instance. The period also saw the most abundant production of civic bronzes in the East: approximately 50 towns had coined for Claudius (AD 41-54), but for Caracalla (198-217) the number was well over 200, and moreover, the level of output for each city was greatly raised. This increase, however, preceded and was linked with the end of bronze coinage in the empire, either because the purchasing power of bronzes became negligible with their low denominations, or because the intrinsic value of the silver coin fell below the intrinsic value of the bronzes which were supposed to be of lower value. At Rome bronze ceased in about 260, and in Gaul the usurper Postumus made no sestertii after about 262. At Alexandria the last bronzes were struck in Gallienus' twelfth year (264), while in Greece and the near east the number of cities which had coins made fell dramatically at about the same time. During the reign of Gallienus there were over 100 mints, but for his successor Claudius II (268-70) and for Aurelian (270-75) there were only five. The city of Perga in Asia struck the last civic coins under the emperor Tacitus (275-76). Thereafter the only current coins of the empire were the gold and silver issues from the imperial mints, and the billon tetradrachms of Alexandria in
482 Egypt.

Another consequence of the debasement of the coinage was the introduction of larger denominations. In 215 Caracalla had made heavier gold and silver coins characterized by the radiate crown (of the sun) worn on the portrait. Imperial ladies would have a corresponding crescent (of the moon) under the portrait. The new silver coins, today called *antoniniani* or radiates, were at first made for only a few years, but from 238 their production was resumed and they replaced the denarius as the staple silver coin. Denarii continued to circulate for a little over 10 years, but during the reign of Trajan Decius (249-51) they were withdrawn from circulation and many were used as 'blanks' for restriking
with new types as radiates. At the same time Decius introduced a 467
larger bronze coin, marked like the silver with a radiate crown, but these double-sestertii were not again made (except by Postumus). As well as these larger silver and bronze coins, multiple aurei were also minted, some of which were very large
and were mainly used as presents from the emperor. 464

By the reign of Aurelian (270-75) the coinage of the empire consisted mainly of gold and debased silver coins, which were produced at a number of mints and which circulated throughout the empire, although Egypt retained its separate currency. In early 274 Aurelian made a general reform of the coinage,
although the details of this reform are obscure. The reform was 472
at least partly technical, as the flans of the coins became broader, flatter, and more circular. The style of engraving also changed. The abysmal efforts of recent years were replaced by a much neater execution, for instance of letter forms (compare **461** with **472**). The engravers themselves were also changed, perhaps as a result of the revolt of the moneyers which is said to have taken place at this time, and in the West they were replaced by a new school at Rome, Milan and Siscia. From this time too begins the
activity of a remarkable engraver at Serdica. 479

The most problematic feature of Aurelian's reform is the addition of the numbers XXI to his coins. A very large number of theories have been advanced to explain them and most scholars (but by no means all) can only agree that they are value marks of some sort. What sort? Were the coins now valued

457 Trajan Decius (249-51) introduced the double sestertius; but this new denomination was not a success and was only used otherwise by Postumus in Gaul some 10 years later.

458 Decius minted consecration coins celebrating former emperors such as Antoninus Pius, to replace the images of them which were lost from circulation when he withdrew the denarii.

457

458A×2

458B×2

The Later Roman Empire

Eboracum
BRITANNIA
Londinium
ATLANTIC OCEAN
Cologne
Parisii
Treveri
Argentorate
GALLIA
Lugdunum
Milan
Emona
Siscia
PANNONIA
Aquincum
Singidunum
Pavia
Massalia
Ravenna
Caesaraugusta
Tarraco
HISPANIA
Cordova
Carthago Nova
Rome
Neapolis
Tingis
Caesarea
Hippo Regius
Carthage
AFRICA
Theveste
Hadrumetum
Lepcis Magna
Sabrata
Division of Empire in AD 395
Border of Roman Empire
DACIA
THRACIA
BLACK SEA
Constantinople
Dyrrachium
Hadrianopolis
MACEDONIA
Larissa
Corinth
Athens
Cyzicus
Sardis
Nicaea
Ancyra
PHRYGIA
Laodicea
PISIDIA
COMMAGENE
Caesarea
Samosata
Nisibis
Tarsus
Edessa
CILICIA
Antioch
Palmyra
Ctesiphon
Byblos
Damascus
Tyre
Jerusalem
MEDITERRANEAN SEA
Alexandria
Petra
AEGYPTUS

459 Valerian became emperor in 253 and soon appointed his son Gallienus to rule with him. Both emperors are portrayed together on coins of Anazarbus in Cilicia in 254. The obverse has a portrait of Valerian in good style.

460 By way of contrast the portraits of Gallienus, his wife Salonina and his son Valerian II are here so crude that they are unrecognizable. Panemoteichos, Pisidia, about 256.

461 Towards the end of Gallienus' reign the Rome mint made a series of coins commemorating various gods as protectors of the emperor: for instance Diana with her sacred animal, the deer. XI on the reverse refers to the eleventh workshop of the mint. Note the poorly formed letters: the Ns are only three vertical lines, while the As look like Hs. About 266.

462 The finest Roman coin portrait: the Gallic usurper Postumus (260-69).

459A×2

459B×2

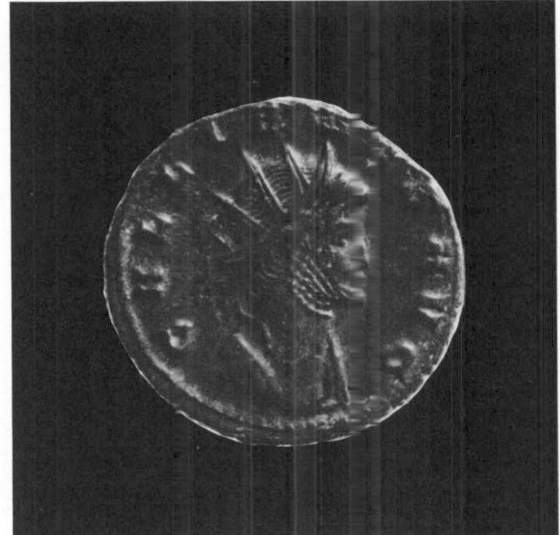

461A×2

461B×2

460

462

463 An antoninianus of Gallienus from the Milan mint is one of the first to identify its mint: M on the reverse for Mediolanum (Milan), and T for *Tertia Officina* – the third workshop. The reverse is typical of the banal types of the third century, a seated figure of Concord. Minted about 265.

464 Later in the third century the minting of large gold coins became more common. As an accession gift in 268 Claudius II made this fine eight-aureus.

465 An eight-as coin of Gallienus from Sparta. The value is inscribed on the reverse (AC H), which has a bronze statue of Athena.

466 Uranius Antoninus, a Syrian usurper in about 253 purified the silver coinage of Syria which was previously very debased. This piece has the bust of the sun god Elagabal on the reverse (compare **451**), perhaps implying that Uranius was in fact the priest of Elagabal, Sampsigeramus.

467 Some of the most repellent of all Roman coins were minted by Regalian, a usurper who struck coins, using earlier denarii as blanks, at his headquarters in Carnuntum, Austria. Minted about 261.

468 Postumus' coins show that he was devoted to Hercules. In about 267 his devotion became identification and he is shown, as Commodus had been before him, as Hercules. Like the hero he is naked and carries the club and lion skin. The reverse

463A×2

463B×2

464

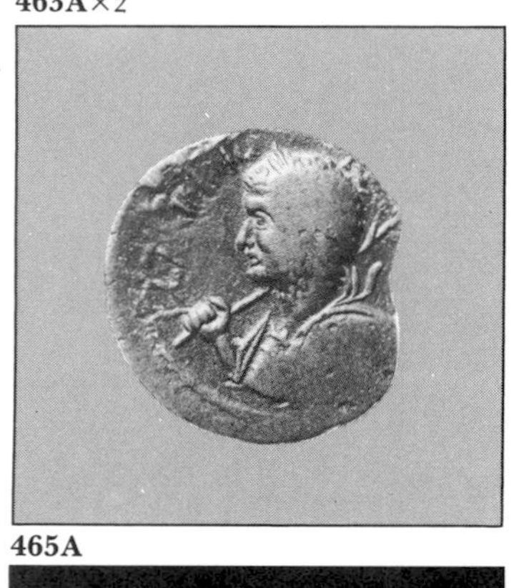
465A

465B

466A

466B

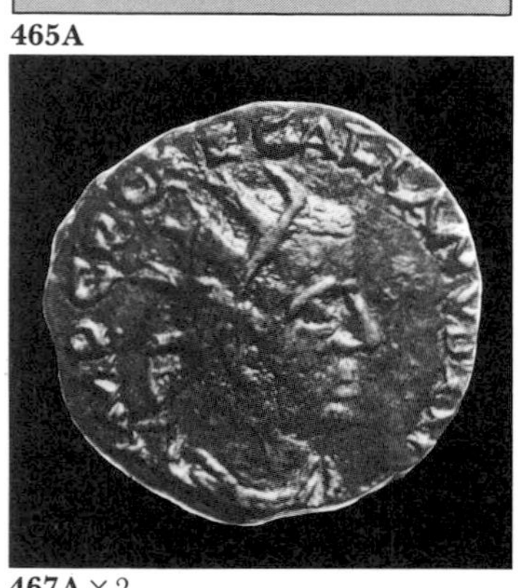
467A×2

467B×2

468A×2

468B×2

469A×2

469B×2

470A×2

470B×2

471A×3

471B×3

472A×2

472B×2

shows Hercules' weapons (bow, club and quiver), and is copied from a coin of Commodus.

469 The Gallic usurper Victorinus (269-71) has a distinctive nose. His most common reverse type is Peace; the V to her left stands for his name.

470 The accession of Tetricus II as ruler of Gaul is perhaps commemorated on extremely rare coins of his father from the Cologne mint. Father and son are shown taking their imperial vows in front of a temple of Rome. Tetricus I, about 272.

471 In 270-85 huge numbers of more or less barbarous imitations of coins were produced in western Europe. This one crudely copies coins of Tetricus; the reverse legend Pax is misspelled PX.

472 A reformed coin of Aurelian from the Rome mint, with the value mark XXI and R as the mint signature. The reverse type attests Aurelian's devotion to the sun god. The Persian and Gallic captives refer to the reduction of the Palmyrene occupation of the East and of the Gallic usurpers of the West.

473-474 Vabalathus, king of Palmyra, ruled Syria and the mint of Antioch. He issued coins with himself and the emperor Aurelian. Minted about 271.

475-479 In the late third century the obverse bust became more varied on coins. As well as the usual right-facing portrait, the emperor could be shown as consul facing left (**475**), in heroic fashion, seen from the rear, naked and with spear and shield (**477**) or facing left with spear and inscribed shield (**478**). A remarkable engraver at the mint of Serdica described emperors with extraordinarily flattering legends such as 'To Probus, the emperor for ever' (**479**) or, earlier, 'To our god and lord the emperor Aurelian'. All these are coins of Probus (276-82) from the mints of Siscia (**475**), Ticinum (**477-478**), and Serdica (**479**).

476 Probus portrays 'Siscia faithful to Probus the emperor' seated between two river gods (the Savus and the Colopis), as this mint town was situated at the junction of two rivers. Reverse of **475**.

480 Carausius, the usurper in Gaul and Britain (286-93), had an ugly appearance. This coin, minted at London, has the type 'Peace of the Emperor', which dominates his coinage and is one of the particularly unsubtle pieces of propaganda typical of the third century and its usurpers (compare **469**).

481 Carausius hoped to be declared co-emperor with the legitimate emperors Diocletian and Maximian, and this unfulfilled hope found expression at Carausius' second British mint (Colchester?) with the rare coins which show all three together. The legend is 'Carausius and his brothers'.

482 In the last 20 years before Diocletian's coinage reform the only non-standard coinage in the empire was the base silver tetradrachms of Egypt. Those of Diocletian are particularly abundant, and this one has the personification of the mint city, Alexandria.

473×3

474×2

475

477

476×3

478

479×2

480A

480B

481×2

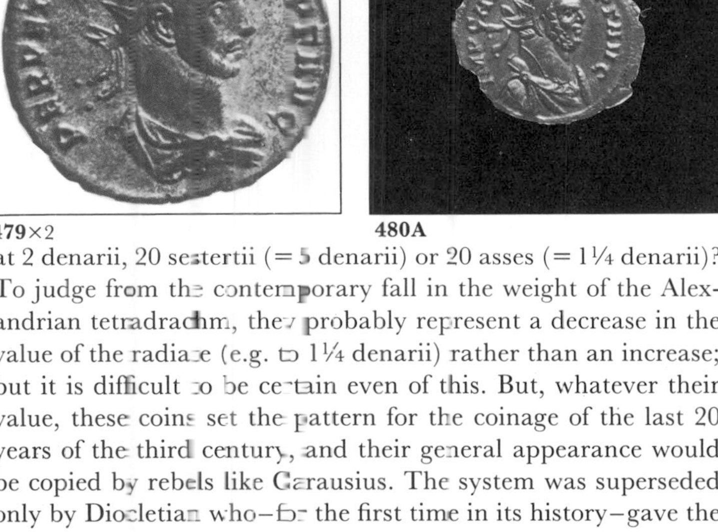

at 2 denarii, 20 sestertii (= 5 denarii) or 20 asses (= 1¼ denarii)?
To judge from the contemporary fall in the weight of the Alexandrian tetradrachm, they probably represent a decrease in the
value of the radiate (e.g. to 1¼ denarii) rather than an increase;
but it is difficult to be certain even of this. But, whatever their
value, these coins set the pattern for the coinage of the last 20
years of the third century, and their general appearance would
480 be copied by rebels like Carausius. The system was superseded
only by Diocletian who–for the first time in its history–gave the
whole Roman empire one unified currency.

482A×2

482B×2

IX

FROM THE CLASSICAL TO THE MEDIEVAL WORLD 300-700

John Kent

The late empire saw the last trappings of republican form stripped from the Roman monarchy. But the elaborate ritual which now separated the emperor from his subjects came in the end to have a paralytic effect on government. A strong and active ruler found that he was no longer fully informed, while a weak one became the puppet of court juntas. At best, late Roman government tended to be headed by a committee of top men whose immense influence, variously exerted, produced vacillating and on the whole ineffectual policies. The harsh economic fact that a declining population must in an unchanging system produce a declining revenue was never accepted, and coercion was the order of the day. Despite a genuine intention to rule in the public interest, an all-pervading corruption and inefficiency ensured that government was feared and disliked, and as successive areas fell under non-Roman rule, there is little evidence that the masses regretted the change. The concept of a Roman Empire, however, long outlived its reality in the minds of educated men, especially the Christian clergy, and still vestigially survives in the Roman Catholic Church.

Coinage faithfully reflects the new concept of the emperor. The feature of early Imperial portraiture had been its individuality; in principle, each ruler was recognizable by portrait alone. In the early years of the new system, effigies of brutal insensitivity warned subjects of the eastern emperors of the dangers of
483,484 disobedience; but after 325 a bland, impassive face implied the 'permanence' of an emperor raised above mere human affairs and faithfully reflected his isolation from reality. During the fourth century effigies were still crudely characterized as 'young',
485-487 'old', 'stout', 'slight', 'bearded'; but after the usurpation of Magnentius (350-53) the truly individualized portrait disappeared for two and a half centuries. The traditional representation of the emperor in armour and military cloak remained normal, though his depiction in the robes of a consul sometimes
488 marked the years when he assumed that distinguished office. The spectacular games and distributions of money on these and other occasions of public rejoicing were an important aspect of the fragile public relations between emperor and people.

The late Roman monetary system was based on the rocketing inflation of the denarius, its unit of account. Attempts to maintain a constant relationship between the gold aureus and its base silver sub-multiple had ceased in the reign of Gallienus (260-68); thereafter the gold coin remained a more or less stable commodity, while lower denominations fluctuated in size and weight according to theories and requirements which cannot now be known. The stability of the gold coinage was often emphasized in the early fourth century by including in the 489-491
legend a statement of weight. After 366, greater concern was felt for the fineness. Silver coinage, which had lapsed into a base billon between 250 and 270, never really re-established itself as a 492
vital part of the currency. Its heyday came between about 348 and 400, but there was probably a constant difficulty in establishing a satisfactory relationship with both gold and base billon.

The very base silver coinage of the first two decades of the fourth century was the lineal descendant of the silver of the early empire; that of the following three decades, of Diocletian's own short-lived fine silver issues. When the base silver coins were struck in more than one denomination, it was usual for the larger pieces to contain higher percentages of silver–up to 3%. This seemingly small addition should not be underestimated; the market ratio of silver to bronze was 100:1, and the addition of 3% silver to copper quadrupled the value. A law of 349 shows that it was worth people's while to melt down such imperial coin and extract the silver. After 364 it seems that base silver coinage was discontinued and that all low-value coins were made in bronze alone. The base silver coins were treated before issue to give them a superficial silvery apperance. This rarely survives on casual finds, but is more frequently seen on pieces from large hoards or from the dry soil of Egypt.

During the first two centuries of the empire it was often the practice of the mint to celebrate the emperor's achievements and aspirations by appropriately designed reverse types. By the third century it is unusual for reverses to display more than a banal selection of gods and personified virtues. The few literary references to Roman coin-types suggest however that the public readily misunderstood even obvious allusions; and since a basic technique of propaganda is the endless repetition of a very small number of simple themes, it is not surprising that the late imperial coins drastically restricted the range of types and legends. How and to what extent new coin-types and inscriptions were disseminated and explained to the public is not known; but the process may be related to the inscribed tableaux depicting 'The Valour of the Emperor' and the like, which the Prefect of the City of Rome exhibited in the Circus. Most early imperial reverse legends are simply descriptive of the type. More characteristic of the late empire are legends which complement the 493
main type. Many inscriptions are drawn from the language of acclamation–'Glory', 'Hope', 'Salvation of the Romans', 'Hurrah for the wedding' and so on. A favourite theme is that of 494,522
the imperial vota, sometimes as part of a larger type, sometimes

Portrait of the Ostrogothic king Theodohad 534-36 (**540**).

483 Licinius I (308-24). Gold aureus, Nicomedia mint.

484 Contrast the intense, worldly features of Licinius with the serene, heaven-seeking portrait of his conqueror. Constantine I (306-37). Gold medallion, Siscia mint.

485 Note the small head of the boy-emperor, and the typical western empire reverse. Valentinian II (375-92). Gold solidus, Trier mint.

486-487 Two usurpers publicize their unfamiliar features, and emphasize their Christianity:
486 Magnentius (350-53). Bronze 'maiorina', Amiens mint; **487** Vetranio (350). Billon 'maiorina', Siscia mint.

488 The imperial visit to Rome in 357 celebrated at one time Constantius' 35th anniversary and his ninth consulship; it was perhaps the greatest pageant of the late empire. Constantius II (337-61). Gold solidus, Rome mint.

489 Galerius (Caesar 293-305). Gold aureus, Antioch mint.

490-491 Preoccupation with weight. Ξ and LXXII denote respectively pieces weighing 1/60 and 1/72 pound. Constans (Caesar 333-37). Gold solidus, Antioch mint.
491 Gratian (367-83). Gold solidus, Constantinople mint.

492 The preoccupation with fineness: OB–*obryziacus* (made of fine gold); PS–*pusulatum* (refined silver). Valens (364–78). Silver 'siliqua', Trier mint.

483×2 **484** **485A**×2 **485B**×2

486A×3 **486B**×3

487A×2 **487B**×2 **488**×2 **489**×2

490×2 **491**×2 **492A**×2 **492B**×2

493 The personification of Victory defined as 'the security of the State'. Valens (364-78). Bronze coin, Arles mint.

494 The young emperor is acclaimed: 'Our Lord... Emperor of Emperors'. Gratian (367-83). Gold solidus, Arles mint.

495 In the late empire, celebrations of *vota* were occasions of extra 'voluntary' taxation to be spent on bonuses to the army. Although regular in principle, their dates were often manipulated for political reasons. Constantius II (337-61). Silver 'siliqua', Arles mint.

496 In 354, an ill-expressed law had the effect, perhaps unintentional, of demonetizing all existing small change in Gaul and Britain; public reaction was to overstrike large numbers of the old authentic coins with home-made dies of the new type. False *Fel. Temp. Reparatio* type (**508**) overstruck on genuine *Urbs Roma* (**506**) c. 355.

497 Julian the Apostate (361-63) ordered that each city should have its official weigher; from his reign down to the early fifth century runs the series of bronze weights for gold coin bearing the imperial portrait. Bronze solidus weight, reign of Honorius, 395-423.

498 After direct Roman rule ended in 410, Roman coins ceased to come to Britain. Perhaps clipping helped to eke out surviving silver. Clipped silver 'siliqua' of Valens (**492**).

493×2 **495**×2 **496A**×2 **494**×3 **496B**×2 **497A**×2 **497B**×2 **498A**×3 **498B**×3

495 on their own. Vota were the public prayers offered every five years (more or less) for the continuance of the emperor's reign. They originated in the reign of Augustus himself, and figured intermittently on the coinage from the mid-second century onwards.

We are so used to the idea of coinage as a public utility that it requires an effort to appreciate that Roman coinage was created solely for the benefit of the government, and served commerce only incidentally. Its function was to pay state functionaries, especially the soldiers, and acquire goods and services for the government beyond what could be obtained by mere requisition. In the late empire it was the practice to pay out in gold, and gold coin is therefore more abundant than in earlier times. It was the government's desire to recover this gold coin as quickly as possible, and to this end money-changers were supplied with small change in order to 'cash' the very high value gold coinage. These were then returned to the treasury, and more change supplied. Under Valentinian III (425-55), the money-changers were required to buy gold solidi from the public at not less than 7000 nummi apiece, and to sell them to the treasury for 7200 nummi. There were many irrational aspects to the public acceptance of coin. It had to be enacted by law, for example, that all genuine gold coins had to be taken at the same value, regardless of date or diameter! The discounting of metallically equal coins by date was practised in India as late as the eighteenth century.

Forgery and other malpractices were rife in late Roman times. It was believed that the moneyers themselves produced false coin. This would presumably be distinguishable only by weight and alloy; but there are also a great many forgeries whose bad style betrays the amateur hand. The forgery of gold coin was a constant problem. The great waves of imitations which sometimes swamped the base metal and even the silver coinage, seem
however to have been evoked by abrupt changes of monetary 496
policy and arbitrary recoinages. Clipping was scarcely a prob- 497
lem, when the gold coin was accepted by weight as much as by tale, though local conditions in early fifth-century Britain led to
the general clipping of the numerous silver coins in circulation. 498
This should be distinguished from the random cutting-up of surviving fourth-century bronze coins in order to accommodate them to the size of their tiny successors from the fifth century.

The late Roman coinage was to a great extent the outcome of a series of expedients, few of which proved durable. For the first 10 years of his reign Diocletian (284-305) maintained with but little change the system inherited from his predecessors. Gold coins (aurei) were struck at two standards, 1/50 pound (rarely) and

499-500 Diocletian asserts the patronage of victorious Jupiter, Maximian wears the lion-skin head-dress of Hercules: **499** Diocletian (284-305). Gold medallion, Nicomedia mint; **500** Maximian (286-305). Billon medallion, Rome mint.

501 The numeral XCVI denotes a weight standard of 1/96 pound but surviving coins fall far below this and do not even achieve the average weights of Nero's denarii. Maximian (286-305). Silver 'siliqua', Pavia mint.

502 The 'follis' sometimes bears the 'mark of value' XXI, suggesting an identity of denomination with Aurelian's radiate; if this was an attempt at deflation, it soon failed. Constantius I (Caesar 293-305). Billon 'follis', Siscia mint.

503 'As long as our emperors flourish, Carthage is happy'; a nice combination of provincialism and patriotism. Galerius (Caesar 293-305). Billon 'follis', Carthage mint.

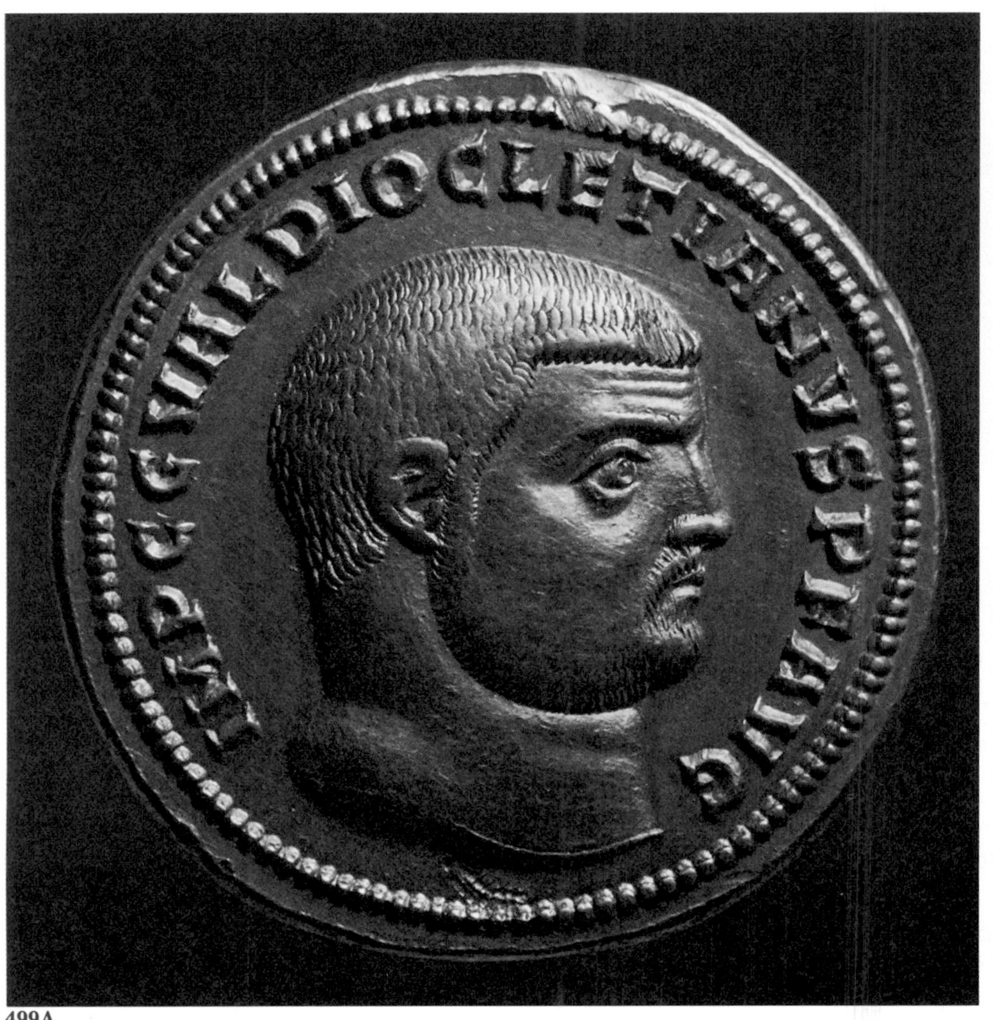

499A

501×3

502A×2

502B×2

499B

503×2

504 In 318 the 'follis' coinage was replaced by descendants of Diocletian's 'siliqua' (**501**), so base as to suggest an annual inflation rate in excess of 15%. Constantine I (306-37). Billon 'centenionalis', London mint.

505 *Urbs Roma*. Billon 'centenionalis', Lyons mint 330-35 (see **507**).

504A×3

500A

504B×3

505A×3

500B

505B×3

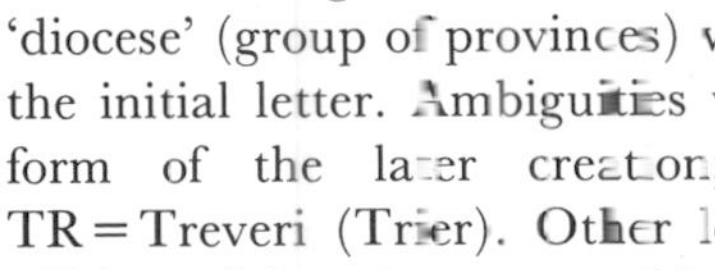

521A×2

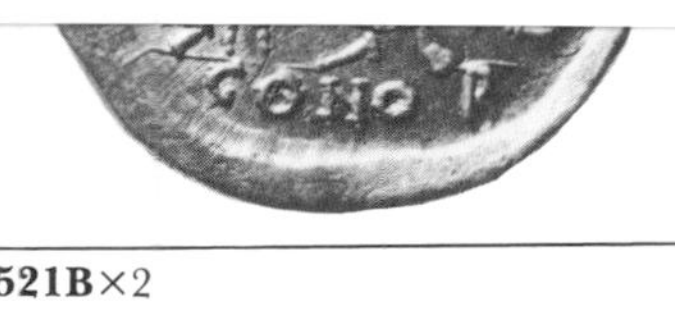

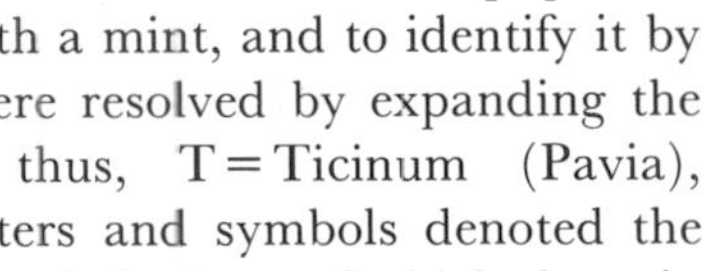

521B×2

The use of an identical type from one end of the empire to the other no doubt made necessary the specific identification of each mint. The original scheme seems to have been to equip each 'diocese' (group of provinces) with a mint, and to identify it by the initial letter. Ambiguities were resolved by expanding the form of the later creation; thus, T=Ticinum (Pavia), TR=Treveri (Trier). Other letters and symbols denoted the officina of the mint responsible, and the issue of which the coin was a part. The whole establishment was sometimes defined as *Sacra Moneta*, The Sacred (i.e. Imperial) Mint.

Inflation, however, remained rampant. It was tackled some-

name. All appear on the coins along with his wife and mother. Constantine accepted Christianity at the time of his seizure of Rome in 312; but the pagan gods, especially Mars and the Sun God, do not disappear from the coinage for a further five years, and few overtly Christian symbols or types are found.

Constantine could not halt inflation, but he did stabilize the gold and silver coinage. The gold *solidus* of 1/72 pound which he established about 308 lasted without significant change into the eleventh century, and his silver coinage arrangements of 325 did not finally disappear for almost 300 years.

Constantine's family ruled until 363. There were several substantial changes in the billon coinage. The most ambitious was the three-denomination scheme of 348, in which each coin
differed not only in weight but also in fineness. The whole issue 508
was linked by the legend FEL TEMP REPARATIO ('The
Golden Age Restored') and the theme of the self-renewing 509

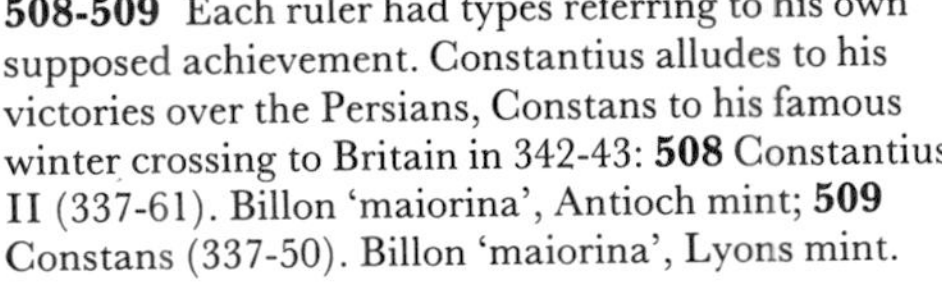

506 The last empress to have a characterized coin-portrait. Fausta, wife of Constantine I (307-25). Gold double-solidus, Trier mint.

507 The dedication of Constantinople (Byzantium, Istanbul) in 330 was commemorated by a very large issue of coins without imperial portrait, but naming the two capitals. The reverses refer to the cities' origins: Romulus and Remus (**505**), and the naval victory of Byzantium in 324.

508-509 Each ruler had types referring to his own supposed achievement. Constantius alludes to his victories over the Persians, Constans to his famous winter crossing to Britain in 342-43: **508** Constantius II (337-61). Billon 'maiorina', Antioch mint; **509** Constans (337-50). Billon 'maiorina', Lyons mint.

510 His subjects found Julian slightly comic, unlike his dignified predecessor Constantius II; this coin-type, too, was mocked, but we do not know exactly what idea the Bull, 'Security of the State', was intended to convey. Julian the Apostate (361-63). Billon coin, Constantinople mint.

511 On eastern solidi 'Imperial unanimity' was oddly personified by the city of Constantinople; it was used for almost half a century with little change. Theodosius I (379-95). Gold solidus, Constantinople mint.

523 After 435, the *vota* for Theodosius III's thirty-fifth anniversary became immobilized and were meaninglessly copied well into the sixth century. Leo I (457-74). Gold semissis, Constantinople mint.

524 The imperial monogram is often the only way of identifying these little coins. Marcian (450-57). Bronze coin, Constantinople mint.

525 Anastasius (491-518). Bronze follis, Constantinople mint.

526 Anastasius' reform was modified by Justinian in 538. He increased the weight of the 40-nummi piece from about 17 to 23 grammes and caused the year of the emperor's reign to be inscribed, at least on the larger denominations. Justinian I (527-65). Bronze follis of 538-39, Constantinople mint.

527 Constans, hard pressed by the Arabs, promises recovery and a complete Christian victory. Constans II (641-68). Bronze follis of 641-42, Constantinople mint.

528 An eastern nobleman introduces the eastern facing bust to the western coinage. Anthemius (467-72). Gold solidus, Rome mint.

529 The last western emperor struck solidi of purely eastern type; in his last years the style was abominable. Julius Nepos (474-80). Gold solidus, Milan mint.

530 Together with similar bronze coins, this is among the earliest issues to name a barbarian king and omit the imperial authority. It comes from the end of Odovacar's reign, when he had irretrievably quarrelled with the emperor. Odovacar (476-93). Silver 'half-siliqua', Ravenna mint.

531 This coinage has reminiscences of first, second and fourth century prototypes, and is a remarkable example of antiquarianism. Zeno (474-91). Bronze follis, Rome mint.

523×2

524×3

526A

526B

525A×2

525B×2

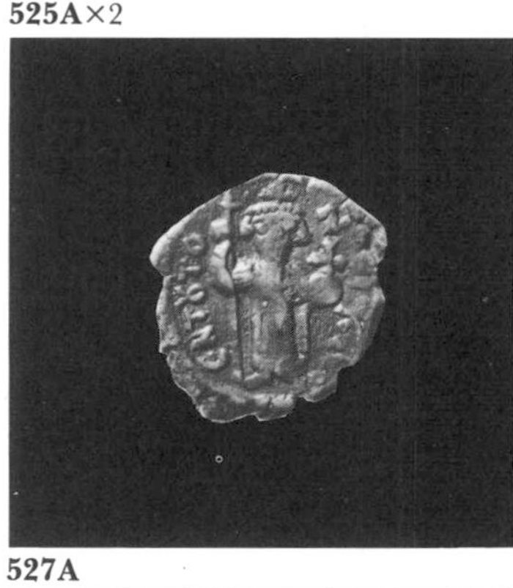

527A

527B

529A×2

529B×2

528×2

530A×3

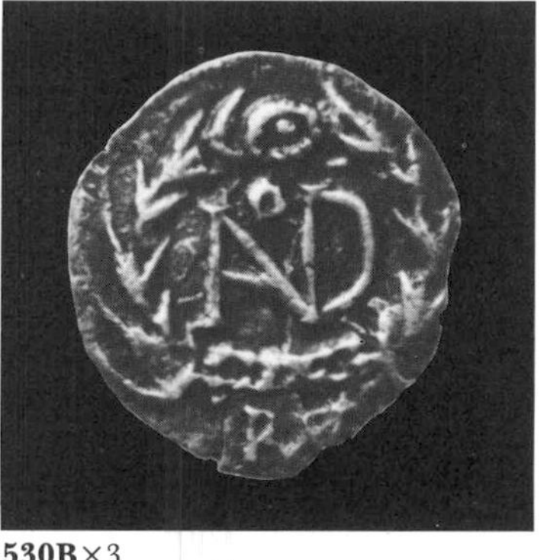

530B×3

531

532 Theodoric (489-526). Gold triple-solidus, Rome Mint.

533 Note the monograms denoting mint and royal name. Theodoric. Gold solidus in the name of Anastasius (491-518), Rome mint.

534 Ostrogothic gold solidus in the name of Justinian I (527-65). Struck 527-35, Rome mint.

533A

532

533B×2

534A×2

534B×2

535 Justinian I (527-65). Gold solidus, struck 535-46, Rome mint.

536 Athalaric (526-35). Silver coin, Rome mint.

537 Titulature, and the design of both sides of Italian solidi were updated when Rome was regained by the emperor. The obverses of the silver coins remained unchanged, but the name of the Ostrogothic king was replaced by a mark of value. Justinian I (527-65), silver coin of 120 nummi, struck 535-46, Rome mint.

538 Note the imperial-style bust, and the acclamation 'May you flourish forever!' Totila (541-52). Bronze coin of 10 nummi, Rome mint.

535A×2 **535B**×2

536A×3 **536B**×3

537A×3

537B×3

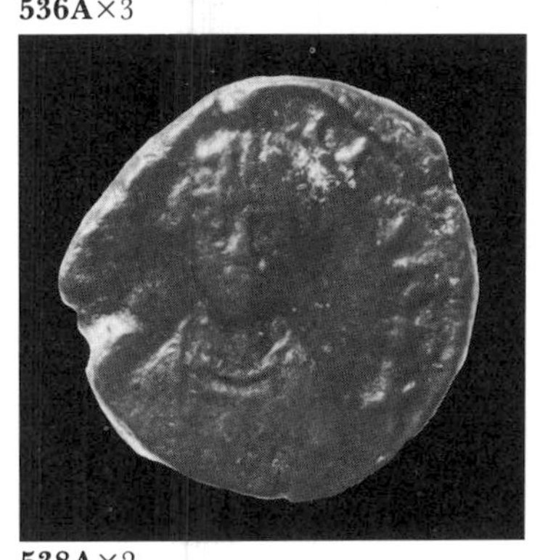

538A×2

538B×2

phoenix. Rebel emperors in the 350s provide the first overtly Christian types and inscriptions but it was the last emperor of
510 the line, the pagan Julian (361-63), who produced the most enigmatic type, a fine bull.

The last part of the fourth century shows an increasing division between the eastern and western parts of the empire. Coinage types are now usually distinct, and the bronze issues often quite unrelated in weight. The last important change carried out in concert by the two emperors was in 365, when, as a consequence of reforms in Treasury procedure, the letters OB began to appear on almost all gold coin and the mintage of gold was largely restricted to a special Treasury mint.

The immobilization of inscriptions and types became more apparent. After 365 there were few western solidi without the type of 'Emperor(s) and Victory' and the legend VICTORIA
485 AVGG(G) and few silver 'siliquae' without the personified city
511,541 of Rome. Almost all Eastern 'siliquae' bore vota inscriptions.

The reign in the western empire of Honorius (395-423) was both symptomatic and critical. The long survival of the feeble-minded emperor, puppet of successive juntas, ensured that even his most active successors could never again truly take charge of the empire's affairs. The break-up of the empire now began. Usurpers were supported now by the remains of the once-mighty provincial armies, now by groups of invading barbarians.
512,513 Imitative coinage begun at this time was the forerunner of a long series in the names of late emperors whose titular supremacy the Visigoths and other peoples acknowledged.

Economic and political collapse now went hand in hand. The copious issues of silver and bronze were reduced to a mere trickle, and the volume of gold coinage declined as the empire's area and resources contracted. Characteristic of the fifth century is the greatly increased coinage of *tremisses*, thirds of the gold solidus; this small but highly valued coin was to be the principal denomination of the barbarian kingdoms of the sixth and seventh centuries.

During the long and disastrous reign of Valentinian III (425-55) the uniform appearance of the gold coinage assured by the reforms of 365 disappeared, to be replaced by distinctive styles,
local to each mint. Though types remain constant, variations in 514-516
legend began to be found, particularly at Milan, which seems to have had a special dependance on the Commander-in-Chief ('Magister Militum', 'Patrician') of the western armies; not surprisingly, it grew steadily in importance as the emperors grew weaker. From the reign of Majorian (457-61), the Commander-
in-Chief in Gaul had a similar, but much smaller mint. In the 517
second half of Valentinian's reign began the principal issue of
Visigothic solidi and tremisses; they soon acquired an evil 518,519
reputation for baseness, and their poor quality was seen as foreshadowing the disastrous defeat of 507, by which the Visigoths lost most of southern Gaul to the Franks.

The less calamitous history of the eastern empire is reflected in its more stable monetary history. The already apparent tendency to immobilize types was accentuated; solidi for instance have
almost invariably the armed facing bust of the emperor, while 520
from the middle of the fifth century there were few that did not
carry the design of 'Victory and cross'. Even types for special 521
occasions, such as imperial weddings, were stereotyped from 522,523
reign to reign. The bronze coinage of these years consisted
almost entirely of very large numbers of tiny pieces. 524

In 498 Anastasius (491-518) carried out an important reform of the bronze coinage. As finally achieved, it involved the creation of four higher denominations above the tiny nummus. The 40, 20, 10 and 5-nummus pieces were respectively given the Greek marks of value M, K, I and E, and this system lasted well
into the eighth century. From the time of Justinian, the weight of 525-527
the 'follis' declined until after 660, whereafter it became very erratic.

The imminent fall of the western empire became clear to all in the 460s, and there were sometimes long interregna when the government was carried out nominally in the name of the eastern

539 Coins of 'Unconquered Rome' sometimes name the Gothic king on the reverse. Ostrogothic. Anonymous bronze follis, early sixth century, Rome mint.

540 The finest coin-portrait of the sixth century – but of a discreditable and unremarkable ruler. Theodahad (534-36). Bronze follis Rome mint.

541-542 Contemporary copies of Honorius' silver were struck in southern Gaul and Africa. The latter are considerably more common than originals: **541** Honorius (393-423). Silver 'siliqua', Ravenna mint; **542** African imitation of **541**.

543 This series avoids naming a specific ruler, but is not necessarily Vandalic. African. Anonymous bronze coin, first half of fifth century, Carthage mint.

544 Silver coins of the Vandal kings bear marks of value in denarii. Gunthamund (484-96). Silver coin of 100 denarii, Carthage mint.

545 Vandalic. Anonymous bronze coin of 42 nummi, c. 500, Carthage mint.

539A

539B

541×2

542×2

540×3

emperor. After such an occasion, Leo I (457-74) appointed a
distinguished east Roman, Anthemius (467-72) to try and
528 recover the desperate position; eastern support could not,
however, save him for long. A second eastern nominee, Julius
Nepos, became emperor in 474; between 475 and 476 he was in
529 Dalmatia, a refugee from the Army of Italy, but from 476 to 480
he seems to have been recognised again as western emperor.
After his death there were no more emperors in the west.

Odovacar, once Commander-in-Chief of the Army of Italy,
now ruled there as king. At first his gold and silver coins were
struck in the names of Nepos and the eastern emperor Zeno
(474-91). However, in 488 Zeno dispatched Theodoric and his
Ostrogoths and, after bitter fighting, Odovacar was overcome
530 and slain in 493. Italy was thus incorporated into the Ostrogothic
domains under the rule of Theodoric.

531 The Ostrogoths began to coin in the name of Zeno after their
occupation of Rome in 489. The long reign of Theodoric (489-
532 526) spanned those of Anastasius (491-518) and Justin I (518-
527) at Constantinople. Only a unique triple solidus bears the
king's name and effigy; the rest of the gold and silver coinage is
533 purely imperial, bearing at most the royal monogram. Much
early coinage was struck at Milan, but in the later years of his
reign only the Rome mint was used, and it continued in sole use
down to Justinian's invasion of Italy in 535.

An imperial coinage of gold, silver and bronze was struck in
Rome between 535 and 546, slightly but significantly disting-
534-537 uished from similar Ostrogothic issues. Under their vigorous
king, Totila (Baduila, 541-52) the Ostrogoths reoccupied Rome
538 in 548; it is interesting, however, that the royal name was not put
on gold coinage, although the name of their enemy Justinian was
replaced by that of the long-dead Anastasius. During the rule of
539 the Ostrogothic kings in Italy a number of anonymous bronze
coinages were struck with obverses honouring 'Unconquered
Rome' and 'Fortunate Ravenna'.

When the Byzantines lost Rome, the coinage of precious

543A×3

543B×3

544A×2

544B×2

545A

545B

546 The Vandalic bronze coinage was supplemented by old sestertii and asses engraved with the numerals LXXXIII (83) and XLII (42). They are mostly Flavian, and perhaps largely came from a single hoard. Bronze sestertius of Vespasian (69-79), engraved in Africa c. 500 with the numeral LXXXIII (=83 nummi).

547 Carthage modelled its practice on that of Constantinople (**525**); it began to develop unusual features later in the century (**561**), but under Justinian was not very active after the first few years of the reconquest. Justinian I (527-65). Bronze follis, Carthage mint.

548-550 Successive emperors differentiated by effigy and type as well as legend: **548** Justinian I (527-65). Gold solidus, Constantinople mint; **549** Justin II (565-78). Gold solidus, Constantinople mint; **550** Tiberius II (578-82). Gold solidus, Constantinople mint.

546×3

547A×2

547B×2

548A×2

548B×2

549A×3

550A×3

550B×3

549B×3

551 The pressing needs of the war against Persia and later the Arabs, led to the minting of church plate into coins, appropriately inscribed DEVS ADIVTA ROMANIS ('God, help the Romans'). Heraclius (610-41). Silver 'hexagram', Constantinople mint.

552-553 The junior emperor is placed at the left hand of the senior; as Caesar, Valentinian III stands undiademed, as Augustus, he is diademed and enthroned. Theodosius II (402-50). Gold solidi, Constantinople mint.

554 The emperor adopts the role of Christ's viceroy on earth. Justinian II (first reign, 685-95). Gold solidus, Constantinople mint.

551A×2

551B×2

552×2

553×2

554A

554B

555 Leo was senior to his father Zeno. Leo II and Zeno (474). Gold solidus, Constantinople mint.

556 Justin I and Justinian I (527). Gold solidus, Constantinople mint.

557 Sophia was the veritable power behind Justin's throne. Justin II and Sophia (565-78). Bronze follis of 575-76, Cyzicus mint.

558 Constans had three sons, Constantine (IV), Heraclius and Tiberius. Constans II (641-68). Gold solidus, Constantinople mint.

559 Leontius II (695-98). Gold solidus, Syracuse mint.

560 Justinian II (first reign, 685–95). Bronze follis, Syracuse mint.

561 Maurice (582-602). Gold solidus of 586-87, Carthage mint.

562 Gold solidus struck by Heraclius in 608-09 at Carthage, at the start of his revolt against Phocas.

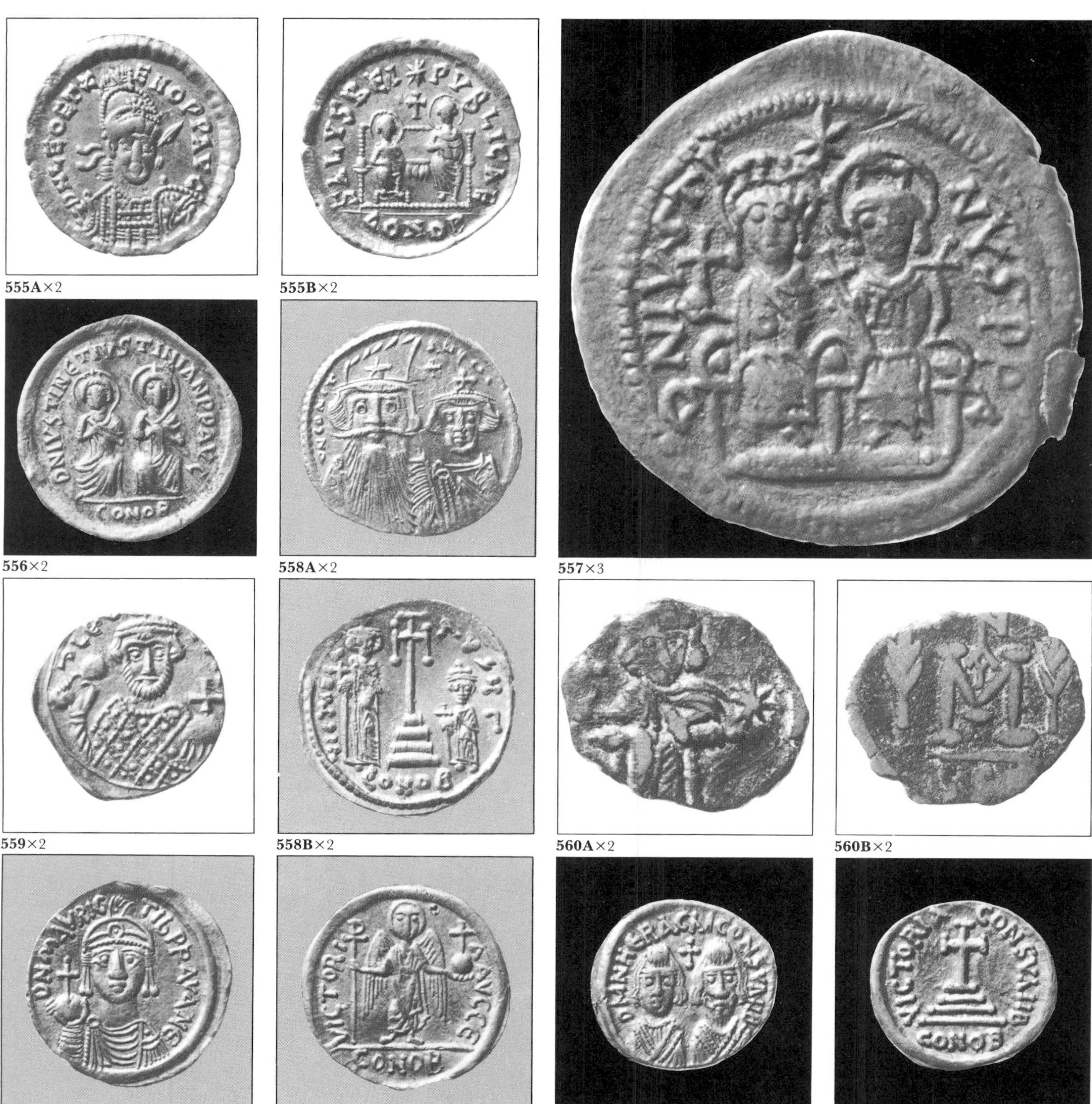

555A×2 555B×2 556×2 558A×2 557×3 559×2 558B×2 560A×2 560B×2 561A×2 561B×2 562A×2 562B×2

metals was transferred to Ravenna, where the mint remained after the fall of the Ostrogothic kingdom. Types did not change, but the new mint had a curious and quite distinct linear style in low relief. Little is known for certain about the bronze of this period, which very rarely bears a mint-mark, but it seems to have emanated from several centres which rarely conformed to a common type or style. Italian bronze under the Ostrogoths and the restored empire frequently bore marks of value expressed in Latin rather than Greek (XL, XX, X and V nummi).

Africa, so important to Rome as a source of corn, was already
541 held only with difficulty in the reign of Honorius (395-423), to
which period belongs an extensive series of rather base silver
copies of his Ravenna 'siliquae'. To this time, or perhaps shortly 542
after, dates a neat series of bronze coins inscribed DOMINO
NOSTRO, DOMINIS NOSTRIS ('To the honour of our Lord, 543
Lords'). They were minted at Carthage, which fell into Vandal
hands in 439. The earliest inscribed coins of the Vandal kings are
small silver and bronze pieces of Gunthamund (484-96). Like the 544
Ostrogoths, the Vandals issued anonymous bronze coins; these
naturally honoured the personification of Carthage, and were
arranged in the unusual set of denominations: 42, 21 and 12
(nummi). There is no indication that the Vandals ever struck 546

563 Constantine IV (668-85) and his brothers Heraclius and Tiberius. Gold solidus of 678-79, Carthage mint.

564 Tiberius III (698-705). Gold solidus, struck in Sardinia.

565 Early Arab coins in Africa were totally given over to drastically abbreviated Latin inscriptions praising God and stating their African origin. Gold solidus struck in 704-05 by the Arab conquerors of Africa. Compare **1235**.

566 Maurice (582-602). Gold tremissis, Ravenna mint. This type was copied by the Lombards (**567**).

563A$\times$3

563B$\times$3

564A$\times$3

564B$\times$3

565A$\times$3

565B$\times$3

566A$\times$2

566B$\times$2

gold coin at any point in their history.
When retaken by Justinian's armies in 533, Carthage was at
547 once re-established as an imperial mint.
Whereas the imperial effigy in the East throughout the fifth
century had been largely stereotyped, each emperor between
Justinian I (527-65) and Leo III (717-41) has a coin-portrait
sharply differentiated by insignia or by features. Typological
development however was slow. On the bronze there was
548 virtually no change. On the gold, the facing Victory of Justinian
was discontinued by his two immediate successors in favour of
549 the personification of Constantinople and the jewelled cross of
550 Calvary respectively. Justinian's type was revived by Maurice
(582-602). and Phocas (602-10), but the cross returned with
Heraclius (610-41) and remained until well into the eighth
century. There was little silver coinage until the time of
551 Heraclius, when the heavy (6.5 grammes) *hexagram* was created.
Hexagrams were rarely struck after about 670, and later pieces
generally very closely resemble contemporary solidi; the denomination was discontinued in about 720.
From the late fourth century onwards it was not unusual for
the eastern empire to be ruled by more than one emperor at a
552,553 time. Such co-emperors were at first represented individually on
obverses, though they might appear together on reverse types. In
555 474 Leo II and Zeno were named together on obverses of the
gold coinage, though there remained only one bust. This
convention lasted down to the joint bronze coinage of Justin I
556 and Justinian in 527; gold coins of this reign introduced the
principle of depicting as well as naming both sovereigns, a
practice that developed in succeeding reigns, sometimes includ-
556 ing the empress. Three, and sometimes four emperors might be
represented (though not all named) on the crowded family coins
557 of Heraclius and his successors (610-85). A deeply significant
and slightly bizarre development came under Justinian II (685-
554 711), last of his dynasty. In 692 he placed on the obverse the bust
of 'Our Lord Jesus Christ, King of Kings', relegating himself as
'Servant of Christ' to the reverse. Although the religious scruples
of Iconoclasm meant that the representation of Christ as the real
ruler of the Byzantine empire did not survive Justinian's death, it
was revived in the ninth century and indeed underwent further
important development.

The Byzantine empire was in theory 'Roman' right down to 1453. The eastern empire had always been largely Greek-speaking, and by the sixth century, even the conservative administration had abandoned much of its Latin. The coinage proved most conservative of all; though its language became for the most part Greek in the course of the eighth century, Roman letters were used to express legends into the eleventh century. The first wholly Greek inscription comes from the reign of Constans II (641-68): EN TOYTO NIKA ('In this (sign) conquer'). This alludes to the 'vision' that turned Constantine the Great to Christianity and seems appropriate to the formidable Constans, who had adopted 'Constantine' as his official name. Individual letters are much influenced by manuscript forms and can be difficult to read, but it is the deplorable style and execution of the sixth and seventh centuries that has until recently discouraged most collectors.

The coinage of Italy and Africa steadily diverged from the
main stream during the seventh century. By its close, Italian
gold was largely struck at Syracuse, and had become both base 559
in alloy and light in weight; corresponding bronzes were totally 560
different from their eastern counterparts and are identified by
the imperial monogram. African solidi began to be dated by the
annual 'indiction' (the imperial financial year) during the last
quarter of the sixth century. At the same time, while retaining a 561
correct weight, they began to be made steadily smaller in
diameter and of much greater thickness. These dumpy coins
continued to be made down to the loss of Carthage to the Arabs
in 698. Even after that, similar pieces were struck in Sardinia, 562,563
while in Africa the Arabs themselves produced for a short while 564
coins of similar fabric, but totally given over to drastically

567 Lombardic copy of a gold tremissis of Maurice (**566**).

568 This is based, in a crudely stylized form, on contemporary Byzantine coins; see, for the bust, **547**. Visigothic gold tremissis in the name of Justinian I (527-65).

569 Several of Liuvigild's coins refer to sucesses in the civil wars of his reign; this evokes his capture, with God's help, of Seville–CVM D(E)O OPTINVIT SPALI. Liuvigild (568-86). Gold tremissis, Seville mint.

570 Wamba (672-80). Gold tremissis, Tarragona mint.

571 Early Arab coins in Spain are based on their African issues (**565**) and not upon Visigothic models. Gold solidus struck in 716-17 by the Arab invaders of Spain.

567A×2

567B×2

568A×2

568B×2

569A×2

569B×2

570A×2

570B×2

565 abbreviated Latin inscriptions praising God and stating their African origin.

The Lombards invaded Italy in 575, and for a century and
566 more relied on imperial Italian coinage for their main needs. Numerous imitations of this coinage in gold and silver are
567 attributed to the Lombards, but inscribed regal and ducal issues are not found until the very end of the seventh century.

A period of rule by an Ostrogothic noble revitalized the Visigothic kingdom after the disaster of 507. Coinage shares in
568 the revival, with fine gold solidi (rare) and numerous tremisses. The outstanding Visigothic king was Liuvigild (568-86), and it was he who established a national coinage with the names of both king and mint. Shortly before the end of his reign, Liuvigild introduced the type with a crude facing bust on both sides and, despite the development of distinct provincial styles, there was a fair degree of uniformity throughout the 79 mints of the kingdom. After the middle of the seventh century the profile bust came back into partial use. The mint-name is usually accompanied by a royal epithet: 'The Pious', 'The Just', 'The
570 Victorious'. From the reign of Wamba (672-80) the king's name is prefixed by the abbreviated formula IN DEI NOMINE ('In God's name'). The Visigothic kingdom was overthrown when Roderic was defeated by the Arabs in 711, but a shadowy king, Achila, reigned for a few years longer in the extreme north-east. As in Africa, the victorious Arabs issued for a short while a gold
571 coinage with Latin legends.

The Burgundians had lived in the Rhone valley as allies of the Romans from the middle of the fifth century, but they cannot be shown to have issued a coinage until well into the reign of Gundobad (473-516), their most famous king. A series of solidi and tremisses in the name of Anastasius (491-518) is shown to belong to his reign by the existence of similar pieces bearing the
572 royal monogram. Tiny silver and bronze coins of this king have
573 been found, the bronze having the mint-mark LD (Lyons). Similar gold coins in the names of Anastasius, Justin I and Justinian are known, with the added monograms of the two following kings, Sigismund (516-24) and Gondemar (524-34); the latter was expelled by the Franks, who thereafter ruled in Burgundy.

The coinage of the Merovingian Franks takes its humble origins from the rare little silver coins attributed to the late fifth-century Roman generals in northern Gaul. Not until the absorption of the Burgundian kingdom in 532 can a Frankish gold coinage be recognized–tremisses of Burgundian style but without royal monograms, bearing the name of the Byzantine emperor Justinian I (527-65). Successful looting coupled with 574
boundless pride and ambition led King Theudebert I (532-48) to coin gold solidi and tremisses resembling those of Justinian, but bearing his own name. Rather base gold coins, mostly tremisses, imitating the imperial coins of Ravenna, fill the third quarter of 575
the sixth century.

Substantial subsidies of Byzantine gold during the last quarter of the sixth century enriched the kings and stimulated coinage, 576,578
especially in Provence. Elsewhere the coinage was frequently illiterate, but when inscriptions can be deciphered, they generally bear the name of a moneyer (*monetarius*) and mint. There 577
were hundreds of such 'mints': cities, royal estates, churches, and even a place describing itself as a wood! Many were ephemeral, others seem to have combined to employ the services of the same die-engraver, and perhaps workshop. 579,580

Royal control must have been minimal, and it is remarkable that standards of weight and fineness achieved the consistency they did. An abrupt reduction in the weight of the tremisses from about 1.4 grammes to 1.25 grammes took place about 575; it is indicated on the coins by the frequent inscriptions VII (XXI on solidi), denoting a coin weighing seven siliquae as opposed to the Imperial standard of eight.

Gold fineness dropped steadily but slowly until after 630, when the cessation of Byzantine subsidies caused it to plummet in a few years from around 70% to a bare 30%

572 Gundobad (473-516). Gold solidus in the name of Anastasius (493-518).

573 Gundobad (473-516). Bronze coin, Lyons mint.

574 The Byzantines were indignant at this breach of the monopoly of the imperial name, and for the next 80 years the names of kings occur only rarely. Theudebert I (532-48). Gold solidus.

571A×3 **571B**×3 **572A**×2 **572B**×2

573A×3 **573B**×3 **574A**×2 **574B**×2

575 Literacy and better gold returned to the Frankish coinage towards the end of the sixth century; this piece has a blundered obverse legend but a literate reverse, naming the mint. Gold tremissis struck at Lausanne c. 580.

576 Gold solidus struck at Marseilles in the name of Maurice (582-602).

577 Gold tremissis struck at Paris. This coin bears the name of the famous moneyer Eligius (Saint Eloi). Clovis II (639-57).

578 After c. 575, numerous solidi and tremisses were struck in Provence. The name of the emperor was retained down to c. 615, when it gave way to that of the Frankish king. Chlothar II (584-629). Gold solidus, Marseilles mint.

575A×3

575B×3

576A×6

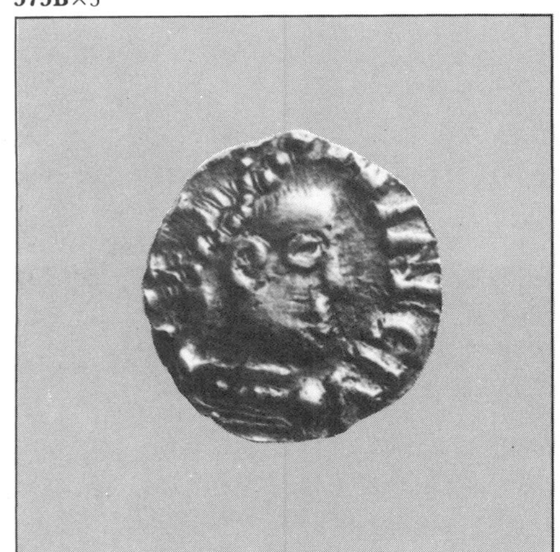

577A×3

577B×3

576B×6

579 This style is very characteristic of the area south and west of Paris; much may be the work of a single craftsman. Gold tremissis struck c. 610 at Orleans by the moneyer Augiulfus.

580 Two 'mints' named on a single coin; rare die-links also suggest that not all coins were struck at the place whose name they bear. Gold tremissis struck c. 600 for the cities of Sion and Susa.

581-582 An Anglo Saxon coin and its Roman model. Pada and his anonymous successors based many of their designs on this one original. The reverse of **485** was also copied. **581** Gold tremissis struck c. 650 by the moneyer Pada. **582** Crispus (317-26). Billon 'centenionalis', London mint.

578×2 **579A**×3 **579B**×3

580A×3 **580B**×3 **581A**×3

581B×3 **582A**×3 **582B**×3

Frankish gold coinage gradually petered out after the middle of the seventh century, and by the end of the century had everywhere been replaced by silver deniers.

Visigothic, and especially Frankish, coins came to England with increasing frequency during the later sixth and early seventh centuries, but there is little sign that they had much monetary function; many have been mounted as jewels. The first English coinage is known almost entirely from the Crondall hoard; it seems to date from the 630s and to be associated with the kingdom of Kent. It followed the Frankish tremisses very closely in gold standard and weight, but based its designs to a considerable extent on Roman coins found by chance; Roman types exercised then and later a fascination for the English coin-die engravers without parallel in other contemporary coinages.

As in France, the gold coinage soon became base and petered
out being replaced by the silver 'pennies' commonly but
erroneously known as 'sceattas'. The transition from gold to
silver is typified by coins bearing the runic legend 'Pada', 581
presumably the name of a moneyer. Pada's coin designs are
based, with infinite skill, variety and imagination, on those of a
base silver 'centenionalis' of Crispus (317-26). His work formed 582
the prototype for many later 'pennies'.

X

BYZANTIUM AND THE CHRISTIAN LEVANT 717-1453

Philip Grierson

The coinage of the Byzantine Empire, from the accession of Leo
the Isaurian in 717 to the fall of Constantinople in 1453, falls into
three periods, the second and third much briefer than the first.

The three and a half centuries from 717 to 1092 form a
recognizable unit during most of which only a single denomination was being struck in each of the three traditional metals,
gold, silver and copper. There was a transitional phase in the
eighth century during which this simplification of the monetary
system was being accomplished and another, in the eleventh
century, during which it was in process of disintegration.

The second period, which began with monetary reforms
carried out by the Emperor Alexius I Comnenus in 1092, is
characterized by a new pattern of denominations, mainly distinguished from each other by differences in alloy instead of in
weight. In its main lines it continued down to the mid-fourteenth
century, when the gold *hyperpyron* was replaced by a heavy
denomination of silver, though it had been somewhat modified
earlier in the century by the introduction of lighter silver
denominations. The third and final period, characterized by an
even more developed silver coinage, continued down to the
capture of Constantinople by the Turks in 1453. If Byzantium's
neighbours be taken into consideration, however, it is more
convenient to make a division between the second and third
periods in the late thirteenth century, at the time of the
reintroduction of silver instead of that of the disappearance of
gold, and this is what will be done here.

The standard Byzantine gold coin since the time of Constantine the Great had been the solidus, or *nomisma* in Greek. Up to
the eighth century it had been supplemented by its half, the
semissis, and its third, the tremissis. Both of these had ceased to
be struck for commercial purposes at Constantinople by the mid-
eighth century, though they were minted for ceremonial distributions down to at least the reign of Leo VI (886-912). They
continued to be struck in the Italian mints of the Empire down to
the times when these were lost, the mainland mints of Ravenna
and Rome in 751 and 781 respectively, the Sicilian mint of
Syracuse in 878.

The solidus was thus left in possession of the field, though as
time passed it changed appreciably in appearance. Under the
Isaurian dynasty (717-97) all vestige of portraiture disappeared
and the imperial effigy, almost invariably a bust, was rendered in
severely linear terms. The cross was replaced as reverse type by
583 another emperor or emperors, first, under Leo III, by his son
Constantine V, subsequently by all early members of the dynasty.
This representation of deceased rulers on the coins was a
novelty, but the reason behind it was family feeling and not any
objection by Leo and his successors to the cross, their iconoclastic prejudices being directed solely against images of Christ and
the saints. Nor did it affect the coinage of the West. 584,585

After the definitive restoration of the cult of images in 843, at
the conclusion of the Iconoclastic Controversy, a bust of Christ 586
took the place of both cross and imperial colleague, and
thereafter the cross never reappeared on Byzantine gold coins.
The normal obverse type for the future was to be a bust or a 587
seated image of Christ, often representing some well-known icon.
Occasionally the image of Christ was replaced by one of the
Virgin, but more often, from the reign of John I onwards, she
was shown accompanying the figure of the emperor on the
reverse. In the tenth century there was an occasional return to 591
characterized portraiture which became normal in the eleventh,
but the low relief of the coins and the fact that the emperor was
invariably shown facing instead of in profile, as on Roman coins,
limited the possibility of individual representation. Throughout
the ninth and tenth centuries the emperor is shown in civil 586-90
costume, wearing either a *chlamys* (cloak) or a *loros* (consular
scarf), but military attire came back into fashion in the eleventh 592
century.

Three major changes came about in the later Macedonian
period. First, under Nicephorus II, a gold coin slightly lighter in
weight than the customary nomisma was introduced, so that
there were henceforward two forms of nomisma, a heavier coin
known as a *histamenon* or *stamenon* and one about 0.25 grammes
lighter known as a *tetarteron*. At first these were of the same size 590
and design, so that it was virtually impossible to distinguish
between them, but in the eleventh century the histamenon was
made larger and thinner and the tetarteron smaller and thicker, 591
so that the difference was made clear to users. The coins also
became more varied in their details. Second, starting in the 593
1030s, the debasement of both forms of the nomisma began. It
was at first quite small, involving a reduction from 24 carats to
about 20 carats in fineness, but it subsequently became much
more pronounced, especially after the great military disaster of
Manzikert in 1071. By 1081, when Alexius I Comnenus came to
the throne, the gold coins were only about eight carats fine, and
by 1092 they had been debased out of existence. Third, ca. 1040,
the histamenon began to be struck slightly concave. Coins of this
type were described by contemporaries as *trachea*, the term
'scyphate' employed by some modern numismatists being a
misnomer. The original purpose of this curious fabric is dis-
puted, but it eventually came to serve for distinguishing base

The Byzantine emperor Alexius I 1081-1118 (**604**).

583 Gold solidus of the Emperor Leo III with his son Constantine V, associated co-emperor in 720. Leo's appearance is shown unchanged on his coins throughout his 24 year reign, but Constantine, who was only two in 720, is first shown as a small child and then progressively older. This coin must date from the late 730s.

584 Base gold solidus of Constantine V and his son Leo IV minted at Rome in the 750s. The reverse type and inscription are still those of the previous century, and the design and execution are much rougher than at Constantinople. The *Manus Dei* blessing the two sovereigns is very unusual at this period.

585 Sicilian gold coins of this period, though of good quality, were struck to a lower weight standard than that of the capital and are of very small module and very thick, perhaps in order to discourage their export from the island. Obverse of a gold semissis of Theophilus struck in Sicily in the 830s.

586 Gold solidus of Michael III, struck after the end of his mother Theodora's regency in 856. The bust of Christ is copied from that of Justinian II's coins (**554**) but the style is notably cruder.

587 This is the first appearance of a seated figure of Christ on the coins, and probably represents the mosaic image which decorated the apse behind the imperial throne in the main reception hall of the Great Palace. Gold solidus of Basil I, the first ruler of the Macedonian dynasty, with his eldest son Constantine, who died before him in 879.

588 The Emperor Alexander in 912 changed the traditional design of the miliaresion by placing a bust of Christ at the intersection of the cross of the reverse type. Later emperors, as Nicephorus II Phocas (963-69) on this coin, replaced this with their own portraits.

583A×3

583B×3

584A×3

584B×3

585×3

586A×3

586B×3

587A×3

coins from ones of pure metal in much the same fashion as some countries in the nineteenth century used a central hole to differentiate coins of nickel from ones of silver.

The silver coin of the middle Byzantine period, known as a *miliaresion*, differed completely from its seventh century predecessor, being based in its fabric on the Muslim dirham and so ultimately on the thin silver coin of Sassanian Persia. It is broad, thin, and like the dirham basically epigraphic in character, with
594,595 the emperor's name and title, inscribed in letters across the field, substituted for his bust or seated figure. It took over from the solidus the traditional cross-on-steps which had been crowded off the gold by the bust of the co-emperor. The miliaresion seems originally to have been intended as a ceremonial coin, for during the first century of its existence it was never struck in the name of a single emperor, and so in each reign cannot have antedated the association of a co-ruler.

Although the weight of the miliaresion was several times modified, its design remained practically unchanged for two centuries. In the tenth century, the emperors began to place their busts either in a medallion on the cross itself or in the field, and the details of the cross were altered and made more elaborate. The earliest miliaresion, that of Leo III and Constantine V, was accompanied by a smaller one-third piece, but fractions were subsequently abandoned and only revived in the eleventh century. The designs of the later issues, more especially those of the fractions, broke away from the austere pattern of the earlier ones, and frequently show busts or standing figures of Christ, the Virgin, or the emperor.

The fate of the copper coinage resembled that of the gold in that it saw the elimination during the eighth century of all

589 The absence of any attempt at portraiture and its use of a virtually linear style were in accordance with the traditions of the mint, and underline the exceptional character of **596**. Reverse of a solidus of Constantine VII struck in association with his son and successor Romanus II between 945 and 959.

590 The flan is already appreciably larger than that of the traditional nomisma, and the crown suspended above Basil's head probably alludes to the opening victories of the campaigns against the Bulgarians that were to earn him the nickname of 'the Bulgar-Slayer'. A histamenon of Basil II and Constantine VIII dating from the first years of the eleventh century.

591 The reverses of an histamenon and a tetarteron of Constantine IX (1042-55), each enlarged three times, show how these two varieties of the nomisma, though differing only slightly in weight, had become distinct from each other in size.

587B×3

588×2

589×3

590A×3

590B×3

591A×3

591B×3

592 The design of this histamenon, showing the emperor Isaac I Comnenus (1057-59) with a drawn sword, was adversely commented on by contemporaries, who held that authority derived from the divine will and thought it unfitting for a general to advertise the true source of his power.

593 The niceties of Byzantine protocol are exhibited in this histamenon, which shows on one face Christ blessing the marriage of Constantine X's widow Eudocia Macrembolitissa to Romanus IV, and on the other the standing figures of Michael VII and his brothers Constantius and Andronicus, her sons by Constantine. It is these who have the place of honour on the convex side of the coin, even though Romanus IV was to be the effective emperor.

594-595 Silver miliaresion of Constantine VI and his mother Irene, and obverse of one of Leo V. The concept of an inscription in several lines replacing a figured type reflects Muslim influence, as does the broad, thin flan of the coin. There is a significant change in the inscriptions, however, for in the last line *basilis* (emperors) has been expanded to *basilis Romaion* (emperors of the Romans). Since Leo's predecessor Michael I had in 812 recognized Charlemagne as Emperor, it was thought desirable to emphasize the full title of the Byzantine emperors on the only type of coin then easily legible.

592

593A×2

593B×2

594A×2

594B×2

595×3

596 A very similar portrait occurs on an ivory at Moscow. The reverse marks the first use on the coinage of the so-called Pantocrator image, showing Christ with his raised right hand in the sling of his cloak and the Gospel Book in his left hand clasped against his body. Gold solidus of Constantine VII struck in 945 as a special issue, when the emperor was briefly sole ruler after the deposition of his colleague Romanus Lecapenus and his sons.

597 By the ninth century most of the traditional symbols on the reverse have become meaningless, for no fraction of the follis was being struck, the Xs no longer represent a date, and since there was only a single officina it was pointless to specify that the coins were struck in the first of these (A). Copper follis of Irene, struck between 797 and 802.

598 The emperor is shown wearing a headdress with a peacock plume known as a *tufa*, which was worn in triumphal processions and in this case commemorates a victory over the Arabs in Asia Minor. The reverse design marks the abandonment of the traditional mark of value in favour of an inscription across the field, as on the silver. Copper follis of Theophilus, of a type inaugurated in the early 830s.

596A

597A×2

597B×2

598A×2

596B

598B×2

599-601 The obverse type of the follis, up to 970, was the facing representation of the emperor, usually a bust but sometimes seated or standing, in company with some or all of his colleagues if he had any. The three coins shown here show Basil I seated, Basil's son Leo VI, and Romanus I, the last of these being intended as a personal likeness.

602 Anonymous follis of the type introduced by John Zimisces in 970 and described by numismatists as Class A, having on the obverse the bust of Christ Pantocrator and on the reverse an inscription meaning 'Jesus Christ, King of Kings.' The varying symbols placed above and below the inscription, and in Christ's nimbus and on the cover of the Gospels, were probably changed on an annual basis and were intended to date the coins.

603 An anonymous follis of Class C showing a standing figure of Christ which can be identified with an icon known as the Antiphonetes especially venerated by the Empress Zoe, which dates the coin to the 1040s. The letters IC XC NIKA ('Jesus Christ, conquer') in the quarters of the jewelled cross on the reverse form an acclamation prominent in the liturgy and sometimes used on coins in the eleventh and twelfth centuries.

599A×2

600×2

601×2

599B×2

602A

602B

fractional denominations, so that only the follis was left. Pentanummia and decanummia were last struck under Constantine V and half-folles under Leo IV, the final issue of the halves dispensing with a specific mark of value (K) and having instead
597 the M of the follis, from which the coin is distinguished by being only half its weight. Follis issues in the eighth century are of very varying weights and were presumably very unstable in value, though how they were reckoned in terms of the *nomisma* we do not know. The use of the M mark of value on the reverse, which had originally indicated a value of 40 nummi, lasted into the ninth century, but with no lower fractional coinage in existence it
598 had by then become completely meaningless, and the Emperor Theophilus in the early 830s abolished it in favour of an inscription in several lines across the field like that already used on the miliaresion. With varying obverse designs, largely
599-601 depending on the number of co-emperors at any given time, this established the pattern of the follis for the next century and a half. Since under Theophilus's father Michael II the follis had been made a substantially larger and heavier coin (eight grammes) than it had been at the beginning of the century, Theophilus apparently thought there might be room for a revived half-follis, but though struck in some quantity in the 830s the denomination was discontinued after his death.

The external appearance of the copper coinage changed suddenly in 970, when John Zimisces, apparently as a gesture of repentance–he had attained power through the favour of the twice-married regent Theophano and the particularly brutal murder of his predecessor Nicephorus Phocas–replaced the
602 imperial bust on the follis by one of Christ and the imperial name and titles by the pious inscription 'Jesus Christ, King of Kings'. These so-called Anonymous folles continued to be struck for just over a century, initially with several changes of weight but none of design, but from the 1040s onwards with a variety of different religious types and inscriptions. Constantine X in the 1060s 603
revived 'imperial' folles, and Anonymous Folles and those bearing the names and representations of successive emperors continued to circulate together for the next half-century. Since the Anonymous coins bear no imperial names they cannot be precisely dated, but the order of issue is known from overstrikes and the later ones can be approximately dated through their overstriking on coins of particular emperors. The coins were reckoned 288 to the nomisma, 12 to the miliaresion, and the later issues are very low in weight, presumably to keep this value steady during the period of debasement of the gold.

A new phase of Byzantine monetary coinage opened in 1092, with a coinage differing completely in appearance from its predecessor. Instead of three clear-cut denominations of gold, silver and copper, it had three of alloyed metal and one, or sometimes two, of copper. The alloyed coins were all concave and theoretically of the same weight, that of the old nomisma histamenon, so that their differentiation in value was effected by their being of different fineness. Only the base gold coins have any claim to beauty: the others are for the most part of poor design and badly struck. The concave fabric in itself made it virtually impossible for complete details of the designs and lettering to be reproduced, since the concavity and convexity of the dies would rarely match each other exactly and blurring through double striking frequently resulted from the repeated blows that were necessary if anything more than the central part of the designs was to register on the flans.

The highest denomination, the equivalent of the old nomisma, was known as a hyperpyron, the name implying that it was of 604,605

604 Reverse of a hyperpyron of the Emperor Alexius I Comnenus, struck after his great monetary reform of 1092. He wears a gorgeously embroidered and jewelled cloak, and a *Manus Dei* emerges from a cloud to touch his crown.

605 Hyperpyron of Manuel I, of the mid-twelfth century. The inscription styles him *despotes* (Emperor), and *Porphyrogenitus* (Born in the Purple), as a sign of his imperial descent.

606 The emperor is shown being crowned by the Archangel Michael instead of by a *Manus Dei*. This denomination is only distinguished from the full hyperpyron by its colour, which is usually dark grey or black owing to the corrosion of the silver in its alloy. Electrum one-third hyperpyron of Isaac II, struck between 1185 and 1195.

607-609 The similarity of fabric between these copper coins and the gold tetartera of the preceding century is very clear (**591**). Copper tetartera of Alexius I and of his son and successor John II.

610 This is markedly different in style from the coins of Constantinople, where most imperial issues were struck. Billon trachy struck in Cyprus by the usurper Isaac Ducas Comnenus in the late 1180s.

603A×2 **603B**×2 **604**×2

605A×2 **605B**×2 **607**×3

606A×2 **606B**×2 **608**×3

609×3 **610A**×2 **610B**×2

611 Hyperpyron of Michael VIII Palaeologus, who recovered Constantinople for the Greeks in 1261, showing him being presented to Christ by Saint Michael. The Virgin was regarded as the patroness of the city, which is why she is here shown surrounded by the city walls and six of its forts.

612 Hyperpyron of John III Vatatzes, emperor of Nicaea, minted at Magnesia in Asia Minor. The types of his gold coins repeat some of those employed a century earlier by John II, but they are markedly cruder in design and they often bear privy marks–in this case, a pellet above Christ's throne–in the field.

613 Long-bearded portrait of Tancred, one of the leaders of the First Crusade, on a follis struck while he was regent of Antioch during the absence of his uncle Bohemund in the West. The coin is overstruck, as are many of the folles of this period, which explains the blurring of the design.

611A

611B

specially pure gold though in fact it was only 20½ carats (854/1000) instead of 24. The third-hyperpyron, basically a
606 revival of the old tremissis, was a coin of the same weight but only 7 carats fine. It was formally known as a 'nomisma trachy asperon', but was more commonly called by some nick-name based on its type. Below it was a coin of base silver (billon) which confusingly bore the same name, but contemporaries called it more briefly a *trachy* or a *stamenon*. It at first contained about 6% silver and 94% copper, and was reckoned 48 to the hyperpyron, but later much further debased and only 120 to the hyperpyron. Finally, at the bottom of the scale, there was a flat
607-609 copper coin, much smaller than the follis of the Macedonian period, which from its resemblance in size and fabric to the gold tetarteron of the eleventh century was called a tetarteron or tarteron despite the difference in metal and in value. A half tetarteron was struck from time to time, usually in copper but briefly under Alexius I in lead.

The coins of the Comnenid and Angelid periods bear no mint-marks and the bulk of them were certainly struck at Constantinople, but the evidence of style and distribution patterns show other mints to have existed from time to time, Thessalonica being the only one that can be identified with reasonable certainty. The coin types are mainly traditional, but new saints, usually of a military character–Saint Michael, Saint George,
605 Saint Theodore, Saint Demetrius–make their appearance, as does a seated Virgin and a bust of the Infant Jesus filling the field. The reverse type frequently shows two figures, but these are no longer the emperor and his expected successor–the only coin showing a co-emperor is a special issue of 1092–but the emperor and some heavenly personage, usually either crowning him or handing him a sword or other piece of insignia.

In the late twelfth century what remained of the Byzantine Empire was beginning to fall apart. Cyprus became independent
610 under a pretender of the Comnenus family; the outlying region of Trebizond, which had enjoyed a certain degree of independence in the time of Alexius I and even minted copper coins on its own, revolted in 1203, the Slavonic kingdoms of Bulgaria and Serbia began to take shape in the northern half of the Balkan peninsula. In 1204 the capital itself was attacked and captured by the soldiers of the Fourth Crusade, who thereupon partitioned between themselves as much of the Empire as they were able. Constantinople became the seat of the so-called Latin Empire. Greece and the islands were divided up between Venice and a number of Frankish and Italian adventurers. But a Greek state survived in Western Asia Minor, its ecclesiastical capital being Nicaea but its power being based on the region round Magnesia much further south, and other Greek states emerged at Epirus and Trebizond. In 1222 Thessalonica was conquered by Theodore Angelus Comnenus Ducas, despot of Epirus; the 'empires' of Nicaea and Thessalonica were united in 1246; and in 1261
Michael VIII Palaeologus, founder of the last Byzantine 611
dynasty, recaptured Constantinople.

The Greek states at first continued the pattern of the Comnenid-Angelid period, but only the Emperors of Nicaea, and
that only from John III (1222-54) onwards, minted hyperpyra. 612
These became in time somewhat baser than their predecessors, and the lower denominations, though they retained the concave fabric and were thus in theory 'full-bodied' coins, were by now of silver and copper instead of electrum and black billon. Only Trebizond in the mid-century diverged from the traditional
pattern, replacing its concave issues by a large and very 622
characteristic coinage of flat silver *aspers*. This brought it into 620
line with the Seljuqs of Rum, who dominated central and 1267-69
southern Asia Minor, and with the kingdom of Little Armenia. The Latin Empire seems to have practically confined itself to concave copper coins, struck not in the names of its own rulers but in those of the various Byzantine emperors of the second half of the twelfth century, so that many can only with difficulty be distinguished from the authentic coins of these rulers and from the earliest coins of the Tsars of Bulgaria, which followed the

614-616 Three of the military or related types found on billon deniers of the Crusaders in Syria and Palestine. The first, a normal castle, is on a coin of John of Ibelin, lord of Beyrout. The helmeted head of a knight wearing chain armour is the normal obverse type of the deniers of Antioch. The third coin shows the Church of the Holy Sepulchre on a denier of Jerusalem.

617 Obverse of a gold bezant struck at Acre in the 1250s, after the pope had forbidden the minting by Christians of imitation Arabic coins referring to Muhammad and employing Muslim religious formulae. The new coins bear on them a cross and an affirmation, in Arabic, of the Christian faith. Compare **1278**.

618 Reverse of a bezant of poor quality gold struck by Hugh II of Cyprus between 1253 and 1267. The king is shown in Byzantine costume, as on coins of Isaac Ducas Comnenus (**610**), but his crown is of western pattern.

619 Soon after 1285 Henry II of Cyprus followed the Western fashion in striking heavy silver gros, known as *besants blancs* (white bezants), with a seated ruler and the Lusignan lion as their types.

620 The kingdom of Little Armenia preceded the Latin states in minting heavy coins of good quality silver. The Armenian inscription on this tram of Leo I, struck in the first years of the thirteenth century, gives his name and that of Sis, the capital of the kingdom, where the coin was minted.

621 Silver dirham of Queen Rusudan of Georgia, struck at Tiflis in 1230. The inscriptions are partly in Georgian and partly in Arabic, the three large letters in the centre being RSN, those of her name.

612A **612B** **615**×2 **616**×2

613×2 **614**×2 **617**×2 **618** **619A** **619B** **620A**×2 **620B**×2 **621A**×2 **621B**×2

same pattern. A few new types appeared, notably a long series involving a winged emperor, and some further saints, notably Saint Tryphon (venerated at Nicaea) and Saint Nicolas. The types of the black billon coins were changed very frequently, in some cases perhaps annually, in contrast to the relative stability of the twelfth century.

If the Latin Empire struck to the Byzantine pattern the same was not the case with the Latin states of Greece proper, where, probably after an initial period of imitations, deniers of the western type began to be minted by the mid-thirteenth century by the Villehardouin in the Morea and by the local Frankish rulers of Athens and Thebes. The dominant model was the
675 French *denier tournois*, with the so-called *châtel tournois* as its
characteristic type. By the end of the century this was almost the only coinage being struck.

In adopting western patterns the Franks in the Aegean area were following the example of their predecessors in the Holy Land, though there had been some initial local variants. The northern states of Antioch and Edessa, which had been in Byzantine hands until quite recently, were provided initially
613 with copper folles, with religious types and inscriptions in Greek,
though with some admixture of military themes essentially western in inspiration. These folles, however, were replaced in the 1130s by billon *deniers* related to those also issued by the kingdom of Jerusalem and the princes of Tripolis, and in both cases they were supplemented by fairly extensive supplies of coin brought with them by the Crusaders from western Europe,
614 mainly from France. The local types are predominantly military:
615 a helmeted head, a castle, an arrow, with the 'castle' in some
616 cases representing a specific building, notably the Church of the
Holy Sepulchre or the so-called Tower of David, i.e. the Dome of the Rock at Jerusalem. Most of the gold that was minted took the form of *besants sarrazinas*, i.e. imitations of Arabic dinars with blundered legends, but in the 1250s these were replaced by coins
617 that were Arabic in script and language but Christian in content.

622 Silver asper of Manuel I of Trebizond (1238-63), with his figure balanced by that of Saint Eugenius, the patron saint of the city, who is shown on virtually all its coins.

623 Hyperpyron showing Christ blessing Andronicus II and his grandson Andronicus III, struck during the 1320s or 1330s. Its crude design and lettering, and the irregularity of its shape, show how little care was taken in striking the now badly debased gold coinage. The obverse design continues that of the hyperpyron of Michael VIII, (**611**) but the number of forts on the wall of Constantinople has been reduced to four.

624 Basilicon showing Andronicus II associated with his son Michael (IX), who predeceased him in 1320. Its resemblance to the silver ducat of Venice, whose weight it reproduces, can be seen by comparing it with **744**.

625 Silver hyperpyron of John V, struck in the third quarter of the 14th century. The idea of a central type surrounded by two circles of inscription was borrowed from western groats, where it formed a common pattern.

626 Half silver hyperpyron of Manuel II, John V's son and successor, very crude in its design and lettering.

622A×3

622B×3

623A

623B

624A×2

624B×2

625A

625B

The kings of Cyprus struck base gold coins of Byzantine pattern, **618**
but by the end of the thirteenth century had replaced these by
large silver coins corresponding to the western *groat*. **619**

In close touch with the Crusader states was the Christian kingdom of Little Armenia, situated in what is now south-eastern Turkey at the head of the gulf of Alexandretta. It issued an abundant coinage of silver trams, together with a little gold
and a fair amount of copper. The Christian kingdom of Georgia **620**
in the Caucasus likewise minted coins of silver and copper, for **621**
the most part Byzantine in inspiration. The rulers of Trebizond managed to remain independent of the restored Empire after 1261, by which date they had already replaced their original
concave coinage of billon or copper with abundant issues of flat **622**
silver aspers that continued down to the fifteenth century and were much imitated by their Georgian neighbours.

The last phase of Byzantine coinage is characterized by a return to silver. Gold hyperpyra continued to be struck down to the middle of the fourteenth century, but the coins were progressively of baser metal. Those of the later years of the reign
of Andronicus II–these were the last to be minted in any **623**
quantity–being only 12 carats fine and often reddish in colour owing to the amount of copper in the alloy. There were also, in the first half of the century, very large issues of concave copper coins, the types being apparently changed annually. They in consequence exhibit great variety of design, but the quality of their striking is so poor that several specimens of any one type are necessary before all the details of its designs can be plausibly reconstructed. Small flat coins of billon or copper supplied the need for small change.

The great innovation of the period was the return to silver. Soon after 1300 the Emperor Andronicus II began the issue of
silver coins known as *basilica*, copied from the silver ducats of **624**
Venice and differing completely in appearance from the concave **744**
coins of the previous century. These continued to be struck in quantity for some fifty years, though with some reduction in

627-628 Two small coins of Mytilene, of uncertain denomination, showing a mingling of western and Byzantine themes. Both have as their reverse type four Bs, the badge of the Palaeologids, but one has on the obverse a double-headed eagle, also a Palaeologid emblem, while the other has an *Agnus Dei*, familiar as a coin type in the West (**792**) but never used at Byzantium. The Gattilusi, who ruled Mytilene, were Genoese in origin, but had received the island by imperial grant in 1355 and intermarried with the imperial family.

629 Gigliato of Rhodes of Pierre de Cornillan, struck in 1354/55, showing the Grand Master, wearing the cowled cloak of his Order, kneeling before the cross on steps that symbolized the hill of Golgotha. The reverse is copied from the gigliato of Naples-Provence but the four lis in the quarters of the cross are omitted and the shield of the Order replaces the lis at the extremities of the cross-arms (**750**)

630 The deniers of Chios had from the first a castle as their type, but in 1413 the city authorities received a grant from the western Emperor Sigismund which entitled them to surmount this by a crowned eagle, as on this gros.

631 Gros of Henry II of Cyprus, of the early fourteenth century, when this type replaced that of the earliest gros (**619**). It continued to be used with few variations–a sword instead of a sceptre, a shield in the field, a different type of throne–down to the end of the Lusignan dynasty.

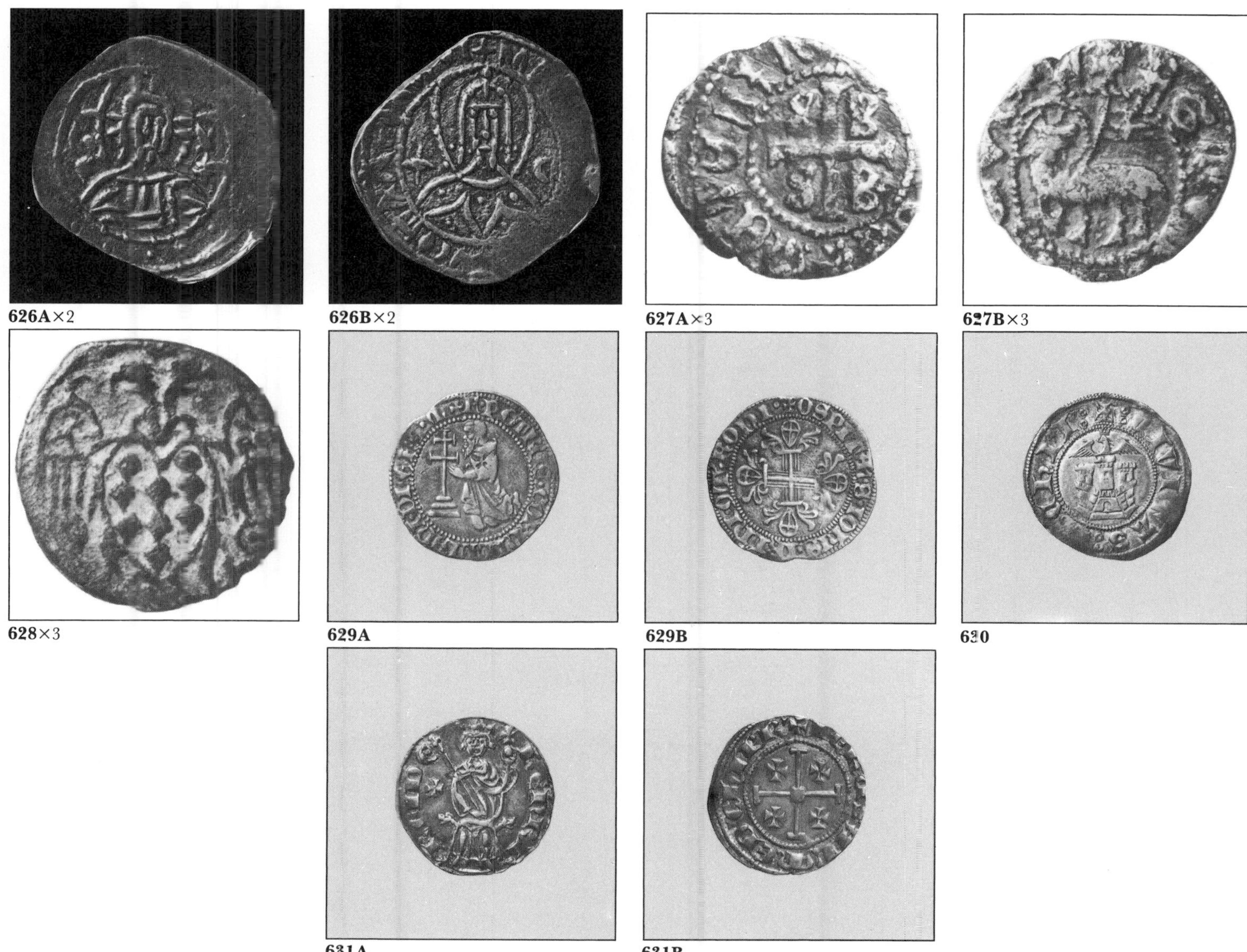

626A×2 **626B**×2 **627A**×3 **627B**×3 **628**×3 **629A** **629B** **630** **631A** **631B**

weight during the period and in any case being only subsidiary
to the gold coinage still in existence. Some time in the third
quarter of the fourteenth century both gold hyperpyra and light
625 silver basilica were replaced by heavy silver hyperpyra which
weighed about nine grammes and so were twice the size of the
largest silver groats being struck in western Europe. These in
626 turn, with appropriate fractions, lasted down to the end of the
Byzantine empire in 1453, though only one of the fractions has so
far been recorded for the last emperor, Constantine XI. This
final coinage of Byzantium forms a strange contrast to that of
Latin Christendom, for at this time the coins of most Western
mints were remarkable for their variety and beauty. The silver
hyperpyra on the other hand bear no more than schematic
representations of the emperor and Christ and their lettering and
standard of striking are extremely crude. Their only merit is that
they were of good quality silver.

Byzantine imperial coinage was anyway, in its last phase, struck on a much smaller scale than that of earlier times, for the Empire by the late fourteenth century was reduced to small areas around Constantinople and Thessalonica and in the southern Morea. Its coinage had therefore to compete with that of the Christian states left behind by the Fourth Crusade. These made
some use of gold, with ducats copied for the most part from those
of Venice and often of inferior quality. Their currency was
mainly one of silver groats below which circulated various
denominations of billon and copper whose relationships are little 627,628
understood and whose very names are sometimes unknown. The
most important coins were those of the Knights of Saint John, 629
who had settled in Rhodes in the first decade of the fourteenth
century, but large *gros* were also struck at Mytilene, on the island
of Lesbos, a fief of the Genoese family of the Gattilusi, and on the
island of Chios, also a Genoese possession. 630

Outside the Aegean area there remained an important Latin
coinage in the island of Cyprus, which enjoyed considerable
prosperity in the last two centuries of the middle ages, partly by
virtue of its own resources in wine and sugar plantations and
partly through its being a convenient stopping place for Italian
merchants trading with Syria and Egypt. The characteristic
types of its gros, which were minted in great abundance, were a 631
seated monarch and the arms of the kingdom of Jerusalem, a
cross potent with four crosslets in the quarters. The coins
continued to be struck down to 1489, when Catherine Cornaro,
widow of the last Lusignan king, sold the island to Venice and an
independent Cypriote coinage came to an end.

XI

WESTERN CHRISTENDOM 700-1450

Philip Grierson

Scholars are accustomed to divide the coinage of the Middle Ages into three periods characterized respectively by the gold tremissis, the silver penny, and the silver groat and gold florin. The first of these periods has been covered in Chapter Nine. The sections that follow will deal with the periods of the penny and the groat and florin, but for convenience that of the penny has been subdivided into three, so as to treat separately the story of its origins and the features of the pennies known as bracteates.

The Origin of the Penny

The characteristic and, for several centuries, virtually the only coin of Latin Christendom in the Middle Ages was the penny, initially a coin of pure silver weighing between one and two grammes and in its most typical form, as established by Charlemagne on the Continent and by Offa in England, some 15/20 mm in diameter, making it the size of the present penny but much thinner. It was called in Latin by the old name of 'denarius', whence French 'denier' (Italian 'denaro', Spanish 'dinero') while in English it was called a penny and in other Germanic languages a *pfennig* or some such word.

The silver denier was introduced in the Frankish kingdom about the middle of the seventh century, providing a currency unit more convenient than the tremisses with which it first circulated concurrently, but which it in due course replaced. The earliest deniers resembled the tremisses in general appearance
632 and like them bore the names of mints and moneyers, but being of inferior value less care was taken over their manufacture so that in due course their types were reduced to crude designs or monograms. Many of them were of the same weight as the tremisses, i.e. 1·3 grammes, the equivalent of 20 barleycorns, but some are lighter, about 1·1 grammes corresponding either to the Roman scruple or to 20 wheatgrains. The earliest English
633 pennies, traditionally called sceattas by British numismatists through a mistaken identification with units mentioned in a few legal texts, do not greatly differ from their Frankish counterparts.

Pepin the Short, the first king of the Carolingian dynasty, abolished the lighter variety of deniers and apparently ordered that the coins in future should bear some reference to his newly
635 acquired sovereignty, but otherwise left their designs to the discretion of the moneyers. His coins are a fraction larger (16 mm) and thinner than the deniers of the late Merovingian. period, probably to accommodate the royal initials more satisfactorily. Charlemagne went a little further than his father in
636 prescribing the precise form which his name on the coins was to take, and later (793-94) undertook a thoroughgoing monetary reform, establishing a heavier 'novus denarius' to be struck to the same design throughout his kingdom and including the name of the place where each coin was struck, but no moneyer's name. Minting was now formally a royal monopoly and great efforts were made to establish the use of coin for all monetary purposes throughout the kingdom, though with little success beyond the Rhine.

At the end of Charlemagne's reign a new type of penny was 638
introduced, with an imperial bust and either some local design and a mint name or a temple facade accompanied by the inscription XPISTIANA RELIGIO. Realistic portraiture, how- 639
ever, was foreign to the aesthetic preconceptions of the time, and Carolingian coin types, apart from the relatively simple temple design which was revived by Louis the Pious and used by many of his successors, tend to be epigraphic in character, with no more than a royal monogram or a mint name in the field. A gold coinage was briefly revived by Louis the Pious, presumably for 640
reasons of prestige.

Although Louis' gold coins enjoyed a local success in Frisia, where they were imitated during several decades, the reforms of Charlemagne can be said to have inaugurated several centuries of silver monometallism—of penny currency, indeed, for halfpennies (known as obols) were struck at only a few mints—in Latin Christendom. No multiples of the penny were struck at all, the 'solidus' (French 'sou', Italian 'soldo') or shilling of 12 pennies and the 'libra' (French 'livre', Italian 'lira') or pound of 20 shillings or 240 pennies being simply monies of account. The traditional relationship between them originated in the eighth century, the ratio of penny to shilling being determined by the commercial ratio of silver to gold—the 'reduced' tremisses of 20 grains was a shilling by Germanic reckoning—and that of penny to pound deriving from the number of pennies struck to a pound weight of silver. The system of reckoning that resulted was used over most of Europe down to the French Revolution, and in Great Britain down to 1970.

Meanwhile a parallel evolution had taken place in England. Offa of Mercia became overlord of Kent in the 770s, and before he died in 796 the transition had been made from pennies 16 mm
in diameter to appreciably larger ones of 19 mm resembling 642
those introduced on the Continent in 793-94. The English coin, however, were lighter, weighing 24 barleycorns or 'Troy' grains (1·4 grammes)instead of 32 wheatgrains (1·7 grammes), and since the great majority were minted at Canterbury it was
thought more useful to mark them with moneyers' names instead 643

Gold noble of Edward III of England, 1327-77 (**800**).

632 Denier of the abbey of St Martin of Tours, of the second half of the seventh century, with the name of the mint (SCI MARTIN) and that of the moneyer Vincter.

633 Anglo-Saxon penny ('sceat') of the late seventh century, handsomely designed but with a meaningless inscription.

634 Another Anglo-Saxon penny of the late seventh or early eighth century. Here not only the inscription but the types, ultimately copied from those of some fourth century Roman coin, are meaningless, being degenerate versions of a profile head and the square head of a standard bearing a *vota* inscription.

635 The earliest coins of the Carolingian dynasty were extremely crude. This penny has no more than the king's name PIPI(nus) and an RP standing for *rex Pipinus*.

636 The obverses of Charlemagne's first type of coinage are the same throughout his kingdom, but the reverses vary greatly and were evidently designed locally. The moneyer responsible for this coin opted for an abbreviation of *rex Francorum*.

637 Charlemagne's reformed coinage of 794 follows a regular pattern for both the obverse and the reverse. The name of the mint–METULLO is Melle, near Poitiers, where there was an important silver mine–surrounds the king's monogram as it appears on royal charters.

638 Charlemagne's last coinage, struck after his imperial title had been recognized by Byzantium (**595**), gives him the title IMP(erator) AVG(ustus) and has a laureate bust copied from a Roman coin. This coin with its type of a ship, was minted at Quentovic, a Channel port that has since silted up.

639 During the 830s, under Charlemagne's son Louis the Pious, a church facade copied from the temple represented on many Roman coins and now surrounded by the inscription XPISTIANA RELIGIO, dominated the coinage and greatly influenced coin designs in the future (**677-678**).

632A × 2 **632B** × 2 **633A** × 2 **633B** × 2

634A × 2 **634B** × 2 **635A**×2 **635B**×2

636A×2 **636B**×2 **637A**×2 **637B**×2

638A×2 **638B**×2

640A × 2 **640B** × 2 **639**×3

640 Louis the Pious' rare gold coins conformed in weight to the Byzantine solidus but had designs suggested by ancient Roman models. They seem to have been used as much as ornaments as currency, which explains the mount that surrounds this specimen.

641 Early portrait penny of Offa of Mercia c. 790 bearing the name of the moneyer Ethelwald.

642 Heavier penny struck at the end of Offa's reign in the king's name – the M above his name stands for *Merciorum*, continuing the *rex* beneath – and Archbishop Aethelheard of Canterbury.

643 Penny of King Burgred of Mercia (852-74) struck at Canterbury, with the name of the moneyer, WULFEARD MONETA(rius) on the reverse. The designs of English coins of the ninth century are much more varied than are those of France.

644 Penny of King Alfred without name of moneyer but bearing the monogram of London (LVNDONIA). There is a great contrast in style between this bust, directly based on some late Roman model, and that of **643.**

641A×2 **641B**×2 **643A**×2 **643B**×2

642A×2

642B×2

644A×2

644B×2

of with place-names as in France. The coinage of the Mercian
644 kings was overtaken in importance by those of Wessex in the course of the ninth century, with substantial Viking coinages in
645 the Danelaw being added at its close.

The remaining major state in Latin Christendom was the kingdom of the Lombards and here Charlemagne's conquest resulted in the establishment of the silver penny as the coinage of north and centre of the peninsula. Lombard coins themselves were virtually all gold tremisses; there was virtually no silver, and the only solidi and folles were a few struck during the Lombard occupation of Ravenna between 751 and 756. Since the Lombards had entered Italy only in 568, pseudo-imperial coins continued to be struck by them to a much later date than was the case in France. Only under Cunincpert were the pseudo-Mauri-
646 cian tremisses of Lombardy replaced by royal coins bearing the
647 king's name, and a little later a municipal coinge, mainly struck at Lucca, replaced the pseudo-imperial coinage of Tuscany, bearing the blundered name of the Emperor Constans II. Only under Aistulf was Tuscan coinage brought under royal control.
648 The coins of the final Lombard period were of seriously debased gold and very light in weight.

This gold coinage was taken over by Charlemagne in 774 and continued in his own name down to 781, when it was formally demonetized and replaced by silver denari on the Frankish pattern. These were continued by Charlemagne's successors for the next century and a half, sometimes with mint-names, usually Milan or Pavia, sometimes without them. There was also at Rome a remarkable papal-imperial coinage. Pope Hadrian I,
649 under whom the papacy became effectively independent of Byzantium, struck coins in his name alone, as did his successor Leo III during the first four years of his pontificate. But the imperial coronation of Charlemagne in 800 gave the Frankish emperors a legal status at Rome, and for the next 170 years, until the coinage came to an end, Roman denarii were struck in the joint names of both pope and emperor save during imperial vacancies, when the popes minted in their names alone.

In southern Italy, divided between Byzantium and the Lombard duchy (later principality) of Benevento, the use of gold lasted longer. The Byzantine provinces naturally continued to use the coinage of the Eastern Empire, though dukes of Naples
sometimes minted copper coins in their own name. The dukes of 652
Benevento had from about the beginning of the eighth century struck pseudo-imperial solidi and tremisses of base gold, at first with their own initials or some other symbol in the field but after the downfall of the Lombard kingdom, when their duke Arichis
assumed the title of prince, with their full names. In the 790s, 653
however, Grimoald III followed the example of the Franks and the papacy in adding silver denari, and after the middle of the ninth century the gold coinage was discontinued and only the silver denari remained.

The Period of the Penny

The period between the tenth and the thirteenth century saw a great expansion of Latin Christendom: into Scandinavia, into central and eastern Europe, into the Iberian peninsula, and into the eastern Mediterranean. Since in the course of the eighth and ninth centuries the silver penny had become the characteristic coin of the West, one aspect of this political expansion was the adoption of the penny in virtually all the lands now acquired for Catholicism.

The evolution of the penny during these centuries followed a number of different paths. In England the tendency was towards unification, till eventually a single royal coinage found itself without rivals. In France there was a breakdown of royal control, so that by the date that the Capetians supplanted the Carolingian dynasty (987) the royal coinage was only one amongst a host of feudal rivals. The same occurred in Germany, though the breakdown there was slower in coming about and more far-reaching when it did so. In other countries royal control was in

645 Most of the pennies struck by the Vikings in the Danelaw have a letter or a cross as their types, but the obverse of this coin of Anlaf Guthfrithsson, struck at York, c. 940, has the raven which figured so often on Viking banners.

646 The 'national' Lombard coinage dates from 690, when Cunincpert's defeat of a rival was ascribed to the intervention of the Archangel Michael, who is here shown on one of the king's tremisses.

647 In the early eighth century a transitional coinage began to be struck at Lucca, with tremisses combining a monogram of the city (LVCA) with a reverse type and meaningless inscription carried over from their pseudo-imperial predecessors.

648 King Aistulf in the 740s generalized Tuscan coin types throughout his kingdom, and struck tremisses with the name of the mint and his own name preceded by DN (for *Dominus noster*, 'Our lord'), a familiar title from Roman imperial coins.

649 Pope Hadrian I (772-95) issued coins with his own facing bust and a cross on steps which followed in general the Byzantine pattern (**584**), but fell into line with the coinage of the Franks in being silver denari.

650 Later papal denari, which were generally struck in association with the reigning emperor, have as their normal type a monogram, as is the case with this coin of John VIII, who was pope 872–82.

651 An exception to the usual design of papal coins was this denaro, of Benedict III in association with the Emperor Louis III (901-03), showing the facing bust of Saint Peter and a rebus incorporating the letters RO and a hand (*manus*), i.e. *Romanus*.

652 A heavy copper follis of Duke Sergius I of Naples (840-61) with a bust of Saint Januarius, the patron saint of Naples, and his own half-figure in Byzantine costume copied from a follis of the Emperor Theophilus (**598**).

645×3

646A×2

646B×2

647A×2

647B×2

648A×2

648B×2

649A×2

649B×2

650×3

651A×2

651B×2

652A

652B

653 Tremissis of Grimoald III of Benevento, of Byzantine pattern, showing how between 787 and 792 the prince was briefly compelled to recognize Charlemagne's suzerainty by placing DOM(inu)S CARL(us) R(e)X on his coins.

654 Penny of Ethelred the Unready struck during the 980s, with a *Manus Dei* between an alpha and an omega protruding downwards in benediction from the clouds. The reverse legend gives the name of the moneyer as Oscytel and the mint as London.

655-656 Pennies of Harold (**655**) and William the Conqueror (**656**) showing how these monarchs were presented to their subjects. Whether either is a likeness is debateable, but William is indeed known to have been beardless and somewhat forbidding in appearance.

657 Penny of Henry I of England. The details of the elaborate reverse types, typical of the coins of this period, were like the obverse designs changed from one issue to the next.

658 'Short Cross' penny struck by a moneyer Ilger at London towards the end of King John's reign (1216). The coin bears the name of John's father, Henry II, but is known to be later.

653A×2 **653A**×2 **654A**×2 **654B**×2

655×3 **657A**×3 **657B**×3

656×3 **658A**×3 **658B**×3

general better maintained, though rarely with the same success as in England.

Debasement, whether by reducing the weight of the coins or by the addition of copper to the silver of which they were made, became general in the eleventh century, though here again there were exceptions. The term 'billon' was applied to such coins once their fineness sank below 50%. Despite common Frankish or English origins there was enormous diversity of type, checked in some mints, especially in those which had come into existence by usurpation, by the practice of immobilization, i.e. the reproduction of coin types and inscriptions unchanged long after they had ceased to be relevant. In others it was enhanced by the practice of what were called *renovationes monetae,* i.e. 'renewals of the coinage' at frequent intervals as a fiscal device. Such renewals involved the withdrawal of the coin type circulating at the time and its replacement by another, which had necessarily to be different from it in appearance.

England was one of the earliest countries in which such
renovationes are heard of, but although they date there from the 654
late tenth century the type changes take place within fairly 656
narrow limits, since it was customary for the obverse type of the 657
penny to be a royal bust, either profile or facing, and for the
reverse to be some kind of cross. Only in the second half of the
twelfth century was the custom of frequent type changes
abandoned, with first the so-called 'Short Cross' penny, then the 658
'Long Cross' penny, and finally the Edwardian penny 659
introduced in 1279. The two first of these were left in circulation
for many decades and the Edwardian type of penny effectively 660
for several centuries. English pennies, from the late eleventh
century onwards, despite the many changes in type of the early

659 'Long Cross' penny of Henry III, struck by the moneyer Robert at Cambridge. This type replaced the 'Short Cross' penny in 1247 and had a cross extending to the edge of the coin so that it would be less likely to become clipped in circulation.

660 Penny of Edward I struck at a temporary mint opened at Bristol to assist in the recoinage of 1279. By this time the bulk of English coins were struck at London and Canterbury.

661 Scottish penny of the late twelfth century struck by the moneyer Ailbodo at Perth for William I. It was the same weight and fineness as the English penny, so that the two could circulate together, but is much inferior in workmanship and general appearance.

662 Berwick penny of Alexander III of Scotland, imitated from the sterling of 1279 but with a profile bust instead of a facing one and mullets (spur rowels) instead of the pellets of its English counterpart.

663 Irish penny of King John struck by the moneyer Robert at Dublin, the triangular settings being intended to differentiate from English coins.

659A×2

659B×2

660A×2

660B×2

661A×3

662A×3

663A×3

661B×3

662B×3

663B×3

issues, were of uniform weight and fineness, which led them to be called *sterlings* (French 'esterlins') from a Middle English word meaning something stable or firm. From the late twelfth century onwards they had a considerable circulation on the continent, since by that time they were one of the few coinages of pure silver remaining in the West and so were readily acceptable beyond the
661-663 frontiers of the state that produced them. The same good reputation was shared by Scottish and Irish pennies.

The predominant coinage of England's closest neighbours in the Low Countries in the late twelfth and the thirteenth centuries
664 were small pennies known as *mailles*, only half the weight of their Carolingian and early feudal predecessors. They were struck
665 partly by such feudal princes as the counts of Flanders and the bishops of Liège, and in the north by the bishops of Utrecht and the counts of Holland, but also by the towns, presumably under
the authority of one or other feudal overlord. English and even 666
Scottish and Irish sterlings circulated as multiples of these small
coins and affected the designs of many of them. 667

The denier coinage of France, on the other hand, derived from that of the Carolingian empire and was little influenced by
English models. The commonest obverse types were ones 668-67
derived from the Carolingian royal monograms or from coins of Louis the Pious with a legend across the field. Profile or facing busts occur in some series, and in a large group of coins from north-western France are wonderfully transformed into designs whose origins and significance one could never guess unless one could trace every step in their evolution. Occasionally there are other types, such as the angel on coins of Valence and the Carolingian temple, transformed into a kind of castle termed by
numismatists the 'châtel tournois', on deniers of the abbey of 675

664-665 Typical small deniers of the kind struck in the southern Netherlands between the middle of the twelfth century and the second half of the thirteenth. These two were minted at Bruges (664) and Ghent (**665**).

666 The northern Netherlands had a more developed minting tradition than that obtaining in the south in the twelfth and thirteenth centuries, as this penny of Bishop Dirk of Utrecht (*Traiectum*) suggests.

667 Dutch pennies of the second half of the thirteenth century were modelled partly on those of Scotland, partly on those of England. Later they were still more definitely Scottish in character.

668-669 Obverses of thirteenth century coins of Champagne and Anjou, showing how types that originally consisted of monograms have been transformed into a comb and a key between two fleurs de lis respectively.

670 A denier parisis of King Louis VII, with the LVDOVICVS REX of the legend continued by FRANCO(rum) in the field. This design is typical of the epigraphic types favoured in the royal mints.

671 The profile head of Saint Maxime is accompanied by an inscription asserting the archbishopric of Vienne to be the greatest see in Gaul (*maxima Galliarum*), a claim going back to a temporary papal grant in the fifth century.

664A×3 **664B**×3 **665**×3 **666A**×3

667A×3 **667B**×3 **668**×2 **666B**×3

669×2 **670**×2 **671A**×2 **671B**×2

Saint Martin of Tours. This design was one that had a great future in French coinage, for the 'denier tournois' was made the basis of the more important of the two monetary systems employed by the Crown and its design was adopted for the 'gros tournois'. Heraldic designs are relatively rare. The normal reverse type was a cross, sometimes with pellets or stars, or an alpha and omega, in its quarters.

The coinage of Germany over the same period is one of much greater complexity. Minting rights were generously conceded by successive emperors to bishoprics and great abbeys in the tenth and eleventh centuries, till eventually, by a mixture of concessions and usurpations, the number of minting authorities
677 became enormous, much larger than in France. There was
678 initially much reliance on the old Carolingian 'Temple' type, which in the end set off a whole series of imaginative representations of churches. Profile busts were comparatively rare save in
679 the eleventh century, but facing ones were common, and there
680 was great use of the seated figures of churchmen or laymen, the
684 former usually holding a sword and a banner or sceptre, the
685 latter a crozier and book. The sterling, even in its Irish variety,
686,687 was widely imitated in the Lower Rhineland and Westphalia. Further south there was extensive coinage of *Handheller*. In regions where frequent 'renovationes' were practised there was

widespread use of animals, whether real or fabulous. The 688
standard of the striking often fell below that of the quality of the 689
designs, which was in general much superior to that of France: 690
parts of the legends and types are off flan or have failed to register, and in many places flans were used that were much too thin. This led, in many parts of the country, to the abandonment of any attempt to provide a design on both sides, resulting in the 691
bracteates which are described in the next section.

It was in the late tenth and early eleventh century that the minting of pennies spread to Scandinavia. The main initial 692,693
influence was Anglo-Saxon, but some Danish coins are Byzan- 694
tine in inspiration. Polish coins mainly derived from those of Germany, and in the twelfth century are characterized by their 695-697
small, neat fabric. The earliest Russian coins are in part 698
Byzantine in inspiration. Bohemian coinage was very important from the tenth century onwards, since there were rich silver 699
mines in the country. After a long phase of mingled Anglo-Saxon and German influence it developed on lines of its own, at first with crude representations of kings or Saint Wenceslas, but 700
subsequently exhibiting an extraordinary variety of complex 701,702
themes, very delicately reproduced and often difficult to interpret. Hungarian coins were initially crude and uninteresting imitations of those of Bavaria, but are later of great variety, 703-707

672-673 Two twelfth century deniers of the mints of Saint-Aignan and Vendome showing the way in whch a profile head could be transformed by repeated copying into a quite meaningless design.

674 This strange-looking angel on a twelfth century coin of Valence in southern France evolved out of the facing Victory on late Roman gold coins.

675 Denier tournois of Saint Louis. This type of coin, with its *châtel tournois*, was taken over by the French crown when Touraine was annexed by Philip Augustus in the early thirteenth century, and was struck at many other mints beside Tours.

676 Denier of Duke Robert of Burgundy struck at Dijon in the late thirteenth century. It was only this century that heraldic types became at all common on French feudal coins.

677-678 Two of the forms assumed by the Carolingian 'temple' in Germany, with the columns replaced by the name of Otto I (ODDO) on a coin of Saxony (**677**) and by that of a moneyer Elin on a Bavarian coin of Regensburg (*Regina civitas*) (**678**).

679-680 Portrait coins of two eleventh century German emperors, one of Regensburg showing Henry II in profile and the other of a Low Country dynast who has taken the facing head of Henry IV.

672×2

673×3

674×3

675A×3

675B×3

676×3

677×2

678×2

679×3

680×3

681A×3

681B×3

681 Penny of Archbishop Anno of Cologne (1056-75) with a stylized representation of the walls of Cologne and its great cathedral within.

682-683 Ecclesiastical and secular rulers as depicted on thirteenth century pennies of Bishop Otto of Würzburg and his neighbour Sophia, regent of Hesse for her son Henry I.

684 Penny of Aachen representing Frederick Barbarossa and the great Palace Chapel, founded by Charlemagne, which was to feature on later coins of the same mint (**766**).

685 Late thirteenth century penny of Gerhard of Osnabrück showing the mitred figure of the bishop seated with a dragon beneath his feet.

686 Penny struck at Dortmund by Rudolf of Habsburg, the first emperor after the end of the Great Interregnum in 1273, and markedly Irish in its design.

687 Copies of the Edwardian sterling usually follow their model very closely, but this Aachen penny of the Emperor Louis IV substitutes an eagle for the initial cross of the legend and another for the three pellets in the second quarter of the cross on the reverse.

682×3

683×3

684A×3

686A×3

685×3

684B×3

686B×3

687A×3

687B×3

maintaining a very high standard of design and execution which
was carried over into the period of the groat and into parts of the
north Balkans subject to the Hungarian Crown.

The penny coinage of north and central Italy in the period of
the penny is of little artistic interest, the types usually involving
708 no more than one or more letters, or sometimes a personal or
mint name, in or across the field, though there were a few
exceptions. Much more interesting was the coinage of the south
and of Sicily, where first a group of states, and eventually a
united kingdom, were created by the Normans. The area was
outside that of the penny and virtually remained so throughout
the Norman period apart from the import of coins from outside.
The domestic coinage was a mixture of Latin, Byzantine and
Muslim elements. The gold coinage was essentially Arabic,
whether minted on the mainland or in Sicily, but in due course
the 'Arabic' was reduced to a meaningless sequence of strokes,
dots and circles, and eventually Latin legends were introduced.
The coins were known as *taris*, from an Arabic word meaning **711**
'fresh', i.e. of good quality, and after the mid-twelfth century **712**
they ceased to conform to any regular weight standard, their **713**
types guaranteeing the quality of their gold (16⅓ carats in Sicily)
and not making them a specific denomination. One of the few **715**
silver coins, the *ducalis* of Roger II, was purely Greek in aspect, **716**
while its fractions were partly Latin, partly Arabic. The copper **717**
coinage was initially Byzantine in inspiration, based on the follis.
The last Lombard duke of Salerno was already striking *follari* on
a substantial scale. His example was followed by his Norman
successors, with a great variety of designs, some original, some **718**
borrowed from antiquity, and in Sicily making much use of
Arabic inscriptions. It was only after the Norman dynasty was

688 A type of penny known as a 'heller,' with an open hand on one side and a cross on the other, was first minted at Hall (Swabia) in the thirteenth century, and rapidly became one of the most popular coins of south-western Germany. The D on this specimen shows it to have been minted at Dillingen by the bishops of Augsburg.

689-690 Fantastic animals are common on south German coins of the thirteenth and fourteenth centuries, as on these Bavarian and Carinthian pennies.

691 Penny of an unidentified south German bishopric, possibly Passau, showing how on very thin coins struck at some mints it was possible for the obverse and reverse types to partially obliterate each other.

692 Imitation of an English penny of Ethelred II struck at Sigtuna by Olaf Tryggvason, the effective founder of the kingdom of Sweden.

688×3

689×3

690×3

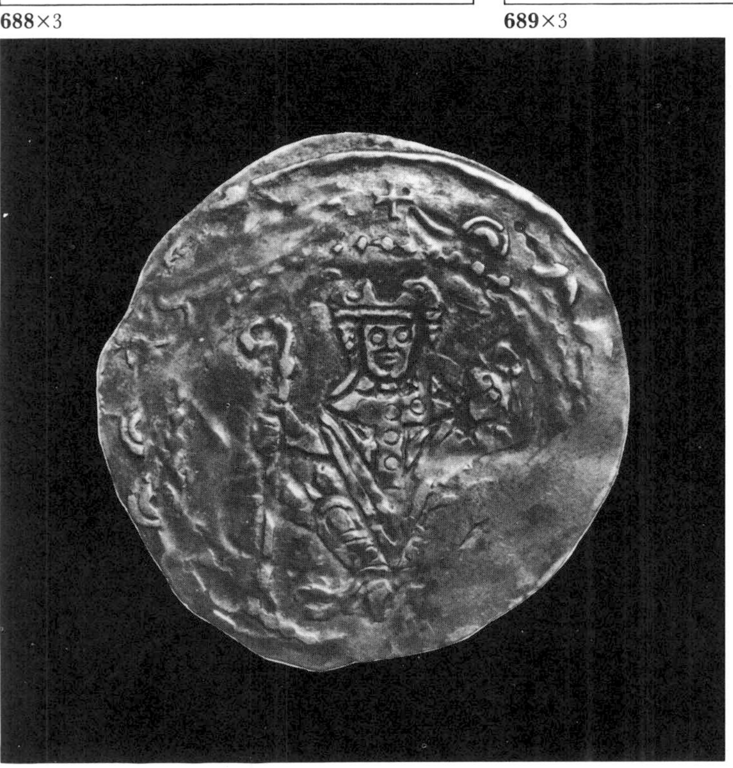

691A×3

691B×3

692A×3

692B×3

693 Danish penny of Harthacnut, struck at Lund in the late 1030s and looking back to an Anglo-Saxon model, and ultimately in part to a Roman one.

694 Danish penny struck in the late 1040s with purely Byzantine types, the reverse being copied from an extremely rare gold coin showing the Emperor Michael IV receiving a standard from St Michael.

695 One of the earliest Polish coins a penny of Boleslas Chrobry of the early eleventh century. The 'church' on the reverse is directly copied from a common north German coin type of the late tenth century.

696-697 The types of the small Polish pennies of the twelfth century show a diversity of secular and ecclesiastical figures, often linked with animal designs such as this bird of prey carrying off a hare.

693A×3 **693B**×3 **694A**×3

695A×3 **695B**×3 **694B**×3

696A×3 **696B**×3 **697**×3

replaced by that of the Hohenstaufen in the 1190s that billon denari corresponding to those in use elsewhere began to be minted.

Spain and the Crusader lands in the eastern Mediterranean also represent acquisitions of Latin Christendom at the expense
721 of the Muslims. Crusader coinage has been dealt with in the
722 previous chapter. The basic coinage of the Spanish states was one of billon denar related to those of France, usually with a
1305 profile bust as obverse type, but gold coins imitated from those of the Muslim dinar or double dinar were struck in Barcelona in the early eleventh century and in Castile in the late twelfth. León and Portugal both introduced gold coinages of the Muslim
723 standard but with figured types. There was no copper coinage, however, since the Byzantine connexion which explains the existence of that of the kingdom of Sicily was absent in Spain.

Bracteates

One of the most unusual types of penny was the *bracteate*. The word bracteate, from a Latin word meaning a leaf, was invented in the 17th century to describe the one-sided paper-thin silver coins which were minted in parts of Germany and some 724
neighbouring countries in the later Middle Ages. The coins were in fact pennies, valued and counted in exactly the same way as ordinary two-sided coins.

Bracteates were struck with a single engraved die against a backing of leather or some soft metal like lead, and some were thin enough for several blanks to be placed on top of each other and struck simultaneously. Their ultimate explanation, as noted already, was the decline of the penny, for as the flans became thinner the impressions of each die affected both sides of the coin

698 Srebrennik ('silver coin') of Prince Vladimir of Kiev dating from about the year 1000. It is of the same dimensions as the Arab dirhams and Byzantine miliaresia that were familiar in south Russia, and the crude bust of Christ is a tribute to the recent conversion of the country, but the trident-like design of the reverse has not been satisfactorily explained.

699 The earliest Bohemian pennies were generally based on Bavarian or Anglo-Saxon models, but occasionally, as with this penny of Duke Boleslav II of the late tenth century, developed types of their own.

700 The imitative phase was followed in Bohemia by coins involving the busts or standing figures of the duke or St Wenceslas, the patron of the country. This penny of Duke Bratislav I was struck in the 1040s.

701 Later in Bratislav's reign the module of the pennies was reduced, as can be seen from this specimen, and the designs were regularized, though with no change in weight.

702 A further development occurred in the twelfth century when, as a result of frequent 'renovationes', the coins become very varied. This coin, of the last decade, shows on one side a half figure in an arch, on the other Saint Michael slaying the dragon.

698A×2 **698B**×2 **699**×2 **700A**×3 **700B**×3 **701A**×3 **702A**×3 **702B**×3 **701B**×3

so that they spoiled each other. On many half-bracteates, indeed, the impression of the lower die is often reduced to a few traces of design and lettering and that left by the upper one is the only one to be clear. These half-bracteates, as they are termed, remained the standard type of penny in some parts of Germany, notably in the south, but in other places it was found simpler to abandon any attempt to produce a lower impression at all. The two main bracteate areas included most of north-eastern and south-western Germany, the northern area (Lower Saxony, Brandenburg, Meissen) extending northwards into Scandinavia and eastwards into Silesia and Bohemia, the southern (Swabia) including most of what is now German-speaking Switzerland.

The bracteates which resulted are most characteristic of the century c. 1150-c. 1250, though a few good ones were still being struck in the second half of the thirteenth century and the fabric was carried on in some places, for very small pennies or *heller*, till the end of the middle ages and even beyond. Bracteates vary in size from about 15 mm to about 45 mm, but the very large ones, which were struck during only a few decades and are limited to a small region of Thuringia, were too fragile to be economically viable. Those of more moderate dimensions (c. 25 mm) are less fragile than one would expect, especially when struck in very high relief, and the small *Hohlpfennige* ('hollow pennies') of parts **743**
of northern Germany and Scandinavia in the fourteenth and fifteenth centuries were quite resistant to wear and handling. The same is true of the small uniface heller widely used in the **830**
Rhineland in the fifteenth and sixteenth centuries.

Bracteates are extraordinarily varied in design, in part because the larger flans of the main series offered great opportunities to artists, in part because many come from areas

703-704 The obverse of Hungarian coins of the mid-eleventh and mid-twelfth century respectively show how the designs were progressively simplified, and the way in which they could be constructed with the aid of very few punches.

705 By the second half of the thirteenth century a marked change in Hungarian coin types had come about, largely as a result of increasingly close relations with Italy. The eagle on this penny of Bela IV is copied from that of the augustale (**783**)

706 Penny of Louis the Great, son of Charles Robert (**774**), with the standing figure of St Ladislas, a notable warrior king of Hungary of the late eleventh century, and the shield of Hungary-Anjou.

707 Denier of Ladislas IV of Hungary (1272-90) struck for the banat of Slavonia, having as types the marten which was the symbol of this province.

708 Italian denari commonly has as their types letters or legends in the field, but Frederick Barbarossa's reformed *imperialis* of Milan (**709**) (MED/IOLA/NVM), created in the 1150s, is a great improvement on the *papiensis* of Pavia of a century earlier (**708**).

703×3

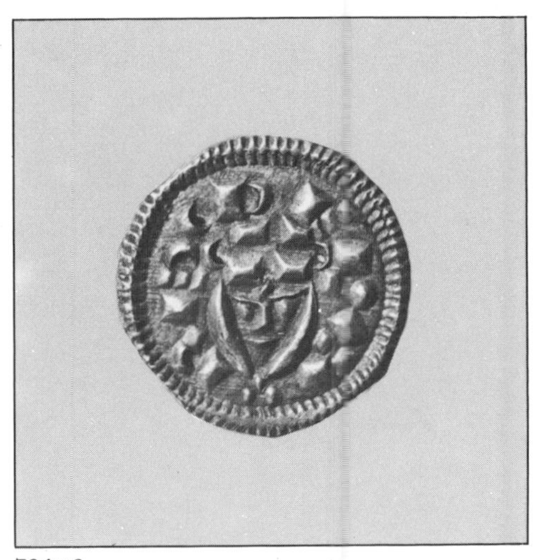

704×3

705A×3

706A×3

706B×3

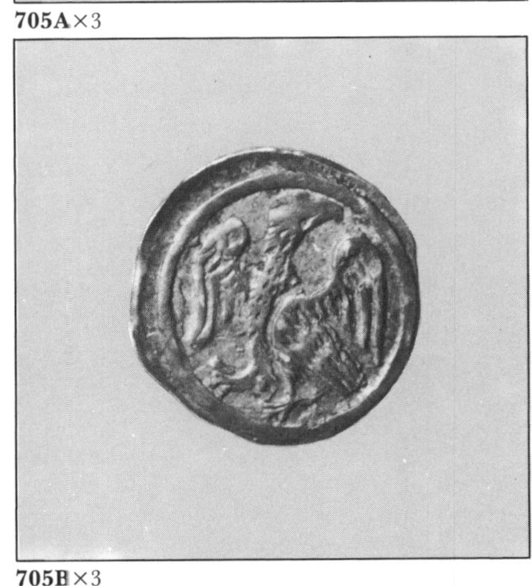

705B×3

707A×3

707B×3

708×3

where renovationes were frequent. Archbishop Wichmann of Magdeburg is reported as having carried out his recoinages at intervals as short as six months. Many bracteates are veritable masterpieces of Romanesque art. Sovereigns are usually shown crowned and other secular rulers wearing helmet and mail,
727 armed with sword and shield or holding the banner by which titles to fiefs were normally conferred. Often there are two
729 figures, sometimes for good reasons–a ruler and his consort, an abbot and the layman who exercised secular functions on his behalf–sometimes for none. The bracteates of ecclesiastical princes usually show the bishop, or the abbot or abbess, or the
733 patron saint of the see–Saint Maurice at Magdeburg, Saint
734 Laurence at Merseburg, Saint Stephen at Halberstadt–or sometimes both. Many types are a play upon the name of the
736 place where they were minted–an eagle at Arnstein, a falcon at
Falkenstein, a linden branch at Lindau–whether the object 737
depicted was a part of the local heraldry or not. What started as a personal badge may become the mark of a particular mint, as
was the case with the lion on bracteates of Brunswick. Quite 738
apart from the individual types the bracteates of certain regions can exhibit features of their own–heavily cusped borders in eastern and sharp, pointed edges in western Swabia, annular borders surrounded by a circle of pellets or squares and crosses further south–which although not universal enable the regions from which they originated to be easily recognized.

Most bracteates are anonymous or bear no more than a
meaningless jumble of letters which were the best that an 725
illiterate die-sinker could produce. But in many series there are one or two types that are signed, usually with the ruler's name only, but sometimes with that of a mint as well, and these

709 An imperialis of Frederick Barbarossa, which is a great improvement on **708**.

710 The ecclesiastical mints of Aquileia and Trieste, produced in the thirteenth century denari of great elegance more German than Italian in their design. This coin of Givard of Trieste breaks up the seated figure of the bishop into a pattern of intersecting or inverted triangles.

711-712 The obverses of two taris of Roger II (1101-54) struck in Sicily (**711**) and at Amalfi (**712**). The Sicilian one, struck while Roger was only count, gives his name and title and the mint and date of the coin, the date by the year of the Hijra; the second, of very base gold, has his initial accompanied by an inscription reading 'Roger the King'.

713 Multiple tari struck by Frederick II as king of Sicily before his imperial coronation in 1220. In contrast to the accurate Arabic inscriptions of Sicilian gold coins of the first half of the twelfth century, the legends have by now degenerated into a meaningless succession of strokes, dots and annulets. The reverse has the victory acclamation IC XC NIKA (**603**).

714 Obverse of a multiple tari struck by Frederick II after his imperial coronation, with the pseudo-Arabic inscription now replaced by F.IMPERATOR.

709A×3

709B×3

710A×3

711×3

712×3

710B×3

713A×3

713B×3

716A×3

715A×2

715B×2

716B×3

715 The ducalis of Roger II of Sicily shows the king standing in company with his son Roger, whom he had created duke of Apulia. The king wears Byzantine imperial costume, including a crown with long pendilia. The letters beside the cross give the date when the coin was introduced as AN(no) R(egni) X, i.e. 1140, the AN being run together.

716 One-third ducalis of Roger II, with a Latin legend giving its value and an Arabic one giving the date as 550 AH (AD 1140-41) and the mint as 'the city of Sicily', i.e. Palermo.

717 Follaro struck at Salerno by Robert Guiscard, the Norman adventurer who had made himself master of south Italy, showing his own bust wearing Byzantine costume and a view of the city with the legend VICTORIA.

718 Follaro struck at Mileto in south Italy by Roger, younger brother of Robert Guiscard, who became count of Sicily and conquered the island in the 1090s. Unlike **717**, it is essentially Western in design, the armour and accoutrements of the count being exactly like those of Norman warriors in the Bayeux Tapestry.

719 Billon denaro of the Emperor Frederick II struck at Brindisi during the 1240s giving him the imperial title on the obverse and that of king of Jerusalem and Sicily on the reverse.

714×3

719A×3

719B×3

717A×3

717B×3

718A×3

718B×3

720 The complex elements that contributed to the culture of Norman Sicily is illustrated by this small copper coin, for it combines a lion's mask copied from a coin of classical Messina of the fifth century B.C. with a reverse (not shown) having an Arabic inscription reading 'King William the Second.'

721 Cornado of John I of Castile, with the castle of Castile and the letter S of the mint of Seville. This coin dates from the late fourteenth century, but the same designs had been used intermittently on Castilian coins from the twelfth century onwards.

722 Gold alfonsino of Alfonso VIII of Castile, with a cross, the letters ALF, and an Arabic inscription setting out the tenets of the Christian faith and giving the king the title 'Emir of the Catholics.' It is dated Year 1227 of an era established under Augustus and widely used in Spain down to the fourteenth century. Year 1227 corresponds to AD 1189.

723 Morabitino of Sancho I of Portugal (1185-1211), with the five shields that became the arms of the country and represented the five Moorish kings killed in the battle of Ourique (1139) which marked the creation of the kingdom of Portugal.

724 Half-bracteate of the bishopric of Worms struck in the third quarter of the twelfth century. A trace of the cross of the reverse type is just visible through the thinness of the flan.

720×3

721A×3

721B×3

723A×3

722×3

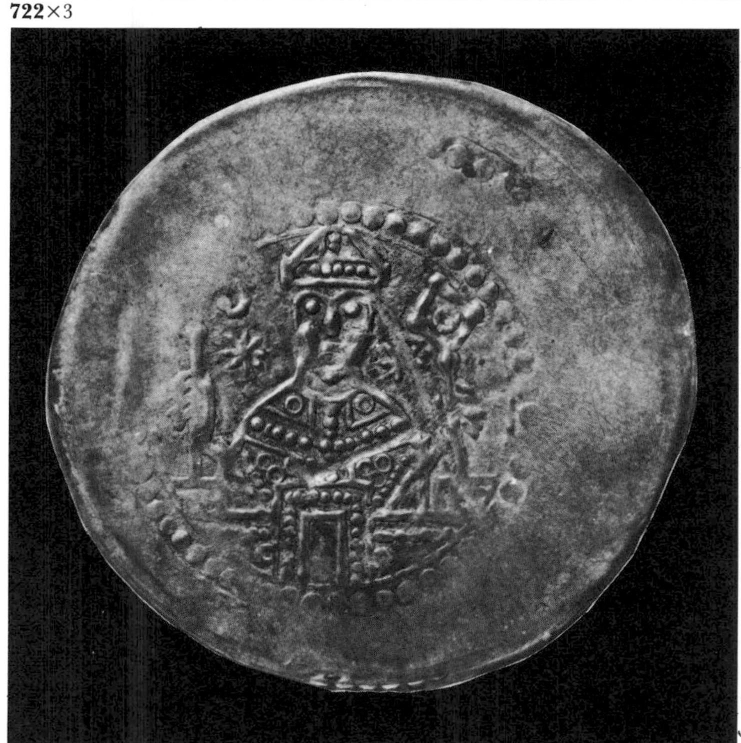
723B×3

724×3

725 Bracteate of Conrad the Great, margrave of Meissen (1127-56), very typical in its depiction of the margrave in military attire, but crude in its design and fabric. On this specimen an illiterate die-sinker has reduced the inscription to a meaningless series of letters.

726 Bracteate of Albert the Bear, margrave of Brandenburg (1134-70), as count of Anhalt, showing his half-figure, with sword and banner, in an architectural setting. It comes from the Freckleben hoard.

727 Bracteate of Albert's son and successor Otto I (1170-84), giving his name and showing him seated with sword and banner.

728 Bracteate of Albert the Rude (1265-1314), landgrave of Thuringia, with the mint name of Gotha (GOTA) in the border. A knight on horseback was a favourite type of the landgraves, but the weight of this coin (0·37 grammes) is only half that of the bracteates at the start of the thirteenth century.

729 Bracteate of the Emperor Frederick I Barbarossa (1152-90), struck at Frankfurt am Main, the nearest point to the Rhine at which bracteates were used. It shows himself and his wife, Beatrix of Franche-Comté.

725×2

726×2

727×2

728×3

729×[illegible]

provide a key to the identification of the others. Later bracteates often have heraldic types, like the uniface heller referred to in the preceding section. Dating depends as a rule on hoard evidence, helped out by considerations of style. Mints would often be unknown without the help of written evidence. Some attributions remain uncertain, especially those of small bracteates with such simple types as a facing head or a standing armed figure, since these could occur independently to die-sinkers in a number of places: one can then only identify the mint of a particular specimen with certainty if its approximate provenance is known. The small uniface bracteates, heller or 'Hohlpfennige' of the end of the Middle Ages usually have heraldic types, but even those do not always provide certainty.

The groat of the later Middle Ages

By the second half of the twelfth century the traditional, silver denier or penny was in many parts of Europe so light and debased that it was no longer useful for large-scale commerce. This situation was at its worst in Italy, despite
709 Frederick Barbarossa's introduction of the improved *imperialis* at Milan in the 1160s. Venice was already one of the most important commercial centres in the West, but its denaro, a tiny concave coin as thin as an eggshell, had sunk to 13 mm in diameter and weighed no more than 0·4 grammes. Since it was only 250/1000 fine, it contained no more than 0·1 grammes pure silver. The Catalan *diner de doblenc* likewise contained only 0·1 grammes silver, and the French denier tournois of Philip Augustus barely 0·3 grammes.

The remedy was not the abolition of the penny, which was long to maintain its usefulness as small change, but the introduction of heavier silver coins and, at a higher level, coins of gold. 'Heavy' is of course a relative term, and the purchasing power of silver in the Middle Ages was so high that even the heaviest of the new denominations, the English groat (4·7 grammes) was still substantially lighter than the modern five-pence piece, though like the penny it was very thin and consequently much larger in area. The new coins were generically known as 'denarii grossi', 'large pennies', or in the vernacular as 'grossi', 'gros', 'groschen', 'groat', etc., though they often had local names based on their designs or on the names or titles of the authorities responsible for their issue. They initially corresponded in value to some commonly used multiple in the system of account, usually 12, 20 or 24 pennies, the choice depending on the degree of debasement of the local penny, though in many places, as further debasement of the penny

730 Another bracteate of Albert the Bear, this time in company with his wife Sophia of Winzenburg. This particular coin evidently meant a great deal to the margrave, for when his tomb was opened in the eighteenth century some specimens were found buried with him.

731 Another bracteate of the Emperor Frederick I, struck at the imperial mint of Nordhausen in north Thuringia. The bracteates of this mint, which are exceedingly large and thin, regularly show the seated figures of Frederick and his wife. This variety is usually dated c. 1225, in the reign of Barbarossa's grandson Frederick II, since it made up the bulk of the Ringleben hoard of about this date, but it is certainly earlier.

732 Bracteate of Siegfried, abbot (SIGERIDVS ABB) of Hersfeld (1180-1200) in eastern Hesse, one of the most important abbeys of western Germany. Its bracteates at this period are of exceptional delicacy and refinement of workmanship.

733 Bracteate of Wichmann of Seeburg, archbishop of Magdeburg (1152-92), showing a half-figure of Saint Maurice, with sword and banner, under an elaborate arch. The inscription describes the saint as DVX, since he was commander of the Theban Legion reputedly massacred by the Emperor Maximian in Gaul for its refusal to sacrifice.

730×2

733×2

734×2

731×2

732×2

735×2

736×3

734 Bracteate of the bishopric of Halberstadt of the third quarter of the twelfth century showing Saint Stephen, the patron saint of the see, seated on a folding stool ornamented with lions' heads and holding a stole in his outstretched arms.

735 The city of Mainz lay outside the bracteate area, but this bracteate of Archbishop Henry I (1142-53) was minted at the important episcopal seat of Erfurt (EPPESFORDI) in Thuringia. It shows the half-figure of the archbishop (HENRC) with his hands raised in supplication to Saint Martin.

736 Bracteate of Walter II, count of Arnstein (1133-66) in the eastern Harz region. Walter's bracteates are of a variety of designs incorporating an eagle (*Aar* in old German) and are for the most part anonymous, but one type gives his name and title.

737 Bracteate of Lindau, on Lake Constance, dating from the 1240s and showing the Emperor Frederick II holding two linden branches, a pun on the mint.

738 One of the many types of lion-bracteates struck by Henry the Lion, duke of Saxony (1142-80) at Brunswick, where he erected the lion monument that still exists. The inscription has many mistakes.

739 Bracteate of the south German bishopric of Augsburg of the last quarter of the twelfth century.

737×3

738×2

739×2

occurred, they quickly became worth more. The earliest grossi were of pure or nearly pure silver, so that in addition to serving local needs they were acceptable in international trade in a fashion that most pennies had ceased to be.

The designs of the new coins were in part traditional, in part new. Some issuing authorities did no more than expand the types of the old pennies to fill the larger flans, or else retained the traditional designs at their old size while supplying them with a decorated outer border or an additional circle of inscription. Others were more adventurous, and since it was in the later medieval centuries that heraldry came into its own, it is not surprising that some coins were furnished with elaborate heraldic devices, either in the form of a shield or of arms occupying the entire field. Elaborate crests or personal devices sometimes replace coats of arms. Direct ruler representations are exceptional, save when they were carried over from preceding penny types, but busts of patron saints, or their standing or seated figures, are shown on coins of many ecclesiastical and some secular mints. Great pains and skill were lavished on designs and lettering, the letters in particular being admirably executed, with a tendency to what British numismatists term 'Lombardic' letters, i.e. rounded As, Es, Ms, and Ns to replace the square ones of earlier times.

The earliest multiple of the denaro, that can be dated with any
744 precision was the Venetian *ducato d'argento*, initially worth 20 or 24 pence and created in 1201 to facilitate the payment of wages to the workmen taken on by the Venetian shipyards for constructing the fleet intended to transport the soldiers of the Fourth Crusade to their destination. It weighed 2·1 grammes, and so was half as heavy again as the English sterling. The Milanese grosso was introduced at about the same time, smaller grossi at Genoa perhaps a little earlier. By the 1230s grossi weighing between 1·5 grammes and 1·7 grammes were being
745 struck at many places in north Italy (Verona, Parma, Bologna,
747 Reggio), and by the end of the 1230s at half a dozen mints in Tuscany, the latter being all of the same weight and fineness so as to be interchangeable with each other.

These coins were all very light, not much heavier than the English sterling. Heavier grossi were introduced at Rome in the
748 mid-thirteenth century, first a twelve-penny coin weighing 3·5
749 grammes and subsequently, under Charles I of Anjou, a 'grosso rinforzato' of 20 pennies (4·2 grammes). Charles was already ruler of south Italy, where he had successively defeated and killed the last Hohenstaufen rulers, Manfred (1266) and Conradin (1268). In 1278 he introduced a silver *saluto* of 3·4 grammes, to which a pendant was added in 1282 in Sicily after the Sicilian Vespers in the form of the *pierreale*, both coins being of the same design as the corresponding issues in gold. Charles II of Anjou
replaced the carlino by the still heavier *gigliato* (3·9 grammes) in 750
1303. In central and northern Italy, however, lighter coins were preferred; the grossi of such cities as Milan and Genoa rarely exceeded 3·5 grammes, and smaller coins, such as the grossi of
Bergamo and Como, the *soldino* (12 pennies) of Venice, and the 751
bolognini struck at many mints in eastern Italy, proved in many 753
places more useful. This is true also of Tuscany, the preference for lighter silver coins being in part explained by the fact that Italian gold coins, modelled on the florin, were also lighter than those north of the Alps.

Silver multiples began to be struck outside Italy quite early in the thirteenth century, the first being a six-penny piece introduced at Marseilles in 1218, but the more important ones all
date from its second half, the French gros tournois from 1266, the 756
petits gros of Flanders, Hainault and perhaps Brabant from 1269, the croat of Barcelona from 1275. The petits gros of the
Low Countries served as a bridge between the sterling and the 757
gros tournois, but as a denomination they did not last very long, being supplanted almost everywhere by heavier coins derived
initially from the gros tournois, which acquired an immense 760
international reputation and in some places continued to be imitated into the second half of the century, long after it had been replaced by other denominations in France. Later groats are more original in their types, whether struck in the Low Countries or in the borderlands of Lorraine and the Three Bishoprics.

The monetary history of Germany in the fourteenth century seems curiously to repeat its history in the Carolingian period. Just as the Carolingian penny failed to secure adoption beyond the Rhine, so in the fourteenth century did the groat. This was
not true of the Rhineland itself, though even here the groat was 765
only introduced in the 1330s or 1340s, much later than in Italy and France. The earliest coins were as heavy as the gros tournois, but the later coin characteristic of western Germany
was the much lighter *albus* or *weissgroschen*, of poorer quality silver 767
but blanched before issue, a circumstance that explains the 'white' of its names. The commercial interests of the Rhineland states led to a long series of monetary conventions, beginning in the 1370s, for the issue of gold and silver coins of the same weight and fineness and almost identical in design which would be acceptable currency the whole length of the *Pfaffenallee* ('Priest's alley'), as the Rhineland was sometimes called because of the dominant role of the ecclesiastical principalities along its banks. Groats of varying designs were widely struck in the whole area between the Netherlands and the lower Rhine.

Beyond the Rhine valley and such adjacent regions as Hesse

740 Bracteate of Bishop Eberhard II of Constance of the mid-thirteenth century. It is copied from an imperial bracteate of Ulm, but has substituted a mitre for the emperor's crown and provided the bishop with a crozier.

741 Bracteate of the Frauenmünster (nunnery) of Zurich of the early fourteenth century, with the facing bust of the abbess and the name of the mint.

742 Bracteate struck at Todtnau in the Black Forest by Albert III of Austria in the late fourteenth century, showing a helmet between the Habsburg shield and the initial of the mint.

743 Saxon Hohlpfennig of the mid-fifteenth century with the Landsberg shield.

744 Silver grosso (*ducato d'argento*) of the Venetian doge Ranieri Zeno (1253-60). The seated Christ and the hieratic pose of the standing figures, which represent the doge receiving a banner from St Mark, are strongly Byzantine in character. The design remained unchanged, save in respect of the doge's name, for over a century and a half.

745 Grosso of Bologna, struck in the thirteenth or early fourteenth century. The inscription ENRICVS refers to the Emperor Henry VI, who granted Bologna the right of minting in 1191, and is

740×2

741×3

742×3

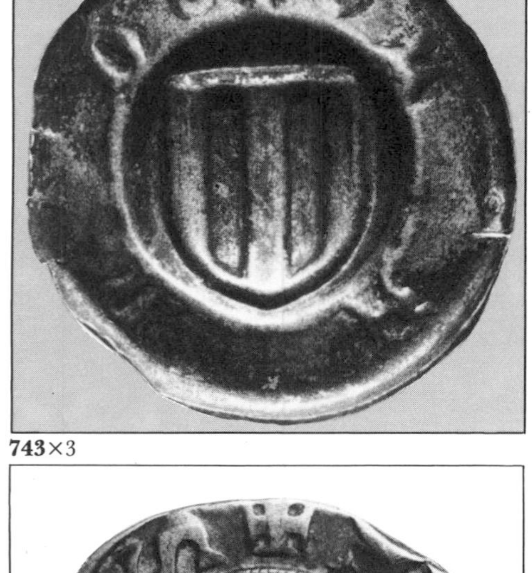

743×3

744A×3

744B×3

745A×3

745B×3

746A×3

747A×3

747B×3

746B×3

continued by the IPRT (for *imperator*) in the field. The large A completes the name of the city in the inscription (BONONI–A).

746 Grosso of Pisa of the mid-thirteenth century, with the initial of Frederick Barbarossa, who granted Pisa the right of minting, and the Virgin.

747 Florentine grosso of the same size and weight as the Pisan coin showing Saint John, the patron saint of the city, and the fleur de lis (*flos*) which was the punning device of Florence.

748 Brancaleone d'Andolò, who came from Bologna to Rome as governor with the title of Senator in 1252, introduced this grosso having as types a seated figure of Roma and a lion, the latter perhaps a reference to his own name. The inscription ROMA CAPUT MUNDI affirms the claim of the city to universal dominion.

749 Reverse of a grosso rinforzato of Charles of Anjou, brother of Saint Louis of France, who became Senator of Rome for the second time in 1270. The design is basically that of the preceding coin, but the pose of the lion has been changed and there is a French fleur de lis above it.

748A×2

748B×2

749×2

the penny continued in general to be the only coin that was struck, and it was only in the mid-fifteenth century that important mints like Münster, Nuremberg, and Würzburg began to strike shillings or other multiples of their own. To this general rule there were two major exceptions, for the new
769 discoveries of rich silver mines in Central Europe made possible
770 the creation of two coinages of major importance, the *Pragergros-*
771 *chen* and the *Meissnergroschen*. The 'groat of Prague' was introduced in 1300, with the help of moneyers from Italy, to exploit the products of the mine of Kutna Hora east of the capital. The Meissnergroschen of the dukes of Saxony, who were margraves of Meissen and could exploit the rich mines of the *Erzgebirge* ('Ore mountains'), followed in 1339. The role they played in German commerce is very apparent from the extent of the countermarking of specimens in the fifteenth century, when the Pragergroschen became very debased, especially in the time of the Hussite wars, and many towns of Westphalia, Franconia, Swabia and Saxony called them in for assaying and stamping as a method of distinguishing those of good quality.

In northern Germany multiples of the penny began to be struck from the 1340s onwards, but the preference there was for
772 smaller coins known as *witten*, i.e. 'white' coins. Just as the coinage of the Rhineland came to be regulated by the monetary conventions promoted by the Rhineland Electors, so the issue of witten by the different cities was regulated by a long series of monetary conventions organized between Lübeck, Bremen, Wismar, Hamburg and neighbouring towns. The witten became the dominant coin in Scandinavia and the east Baltic region, though the Teutonic Knights in East Prussia preferred a *schilling* of 1·7 grammes.

The use of the groat reached south-eastern Europe partly by way of Hungary, partly through Italy. The typical Hungarian coins of the later middle ages were the small pennies, often beautifully designed and struck, alluded to in an earlier section, but heavy grossi were minted by the first two sovereigns of the
775 Angevin dynasty. The first coinages of the kingdoms of Serbia
776 and Bulgaria were, not surprisingly, modelled on those of Byzantium since they were break-away provinces of the Empire, but the early billon or copper trachea were quickly replaced by grossi modelled on those of Venice, with a seated figure of Christ on the obverse and Saint Stephen and the king standing on the other. Later the ruler is shown alone or with a secular colleague,
777 and either seated, standing, or on horseback. The principalities of Wallachia and Moldavia and the coastal cities of the Adriatic had their own coinages either autonomous or under the suzerainty of the larger neighbours, and there is an abundant
778 Bosnian coinage having picturesque armorial types and characterized by its elaborate Gothic lettering. The coinages of Greece, the Aegean area and Cyprus have already been described.

There remain in the West, the British Isles and the Iberian peninsula. After a false start in 1279, a groat and half-groat were 779
successfully introduced in England in 1351, and in Scotland in 780
1357. In Spain, as we have seen, the Catalan groat began in 1275. Alfonso X of Castile had tried in the mid-thirteenth century to supplement the traditional billon coinage with several denominations of silver, but only the smallest unit of 1·4
grammes seems to have enjoyed any success and the Castilian 781
and Portuguese *reales* date from the reigns of Peter the Cruel and 782
Fernando in the second half of the fourteenth century. Both countries had in addition abundant and complicated coinages of billon, in sharp contrast to England, where groats and pennies remained always of good silver. This was not entirely to the advantage of its users, since it meant that the halfpenny and farthing became so small that they were easily lost, besides being so difficult to strike that the moneyers neglected their issue.

Gold Coinage of the later Middle Ages

The groat provided users with currency units more convenient than pennies and corresponding usually to a value of 12 pennies, though varying on either side to as high as 24 pennies or as low as four pennies. Parallel to the revival of silver was that of gold, with coins often corresponding in value to £1.

During the period of the penny there was sporadic use of Muslim and Byzantine gold coins in the West, but the only domestic production of any consequence was limited, as has been seen already, to formerly Muslim lands in the Mediterranean area. It is therefore not surprising that it was the kingdom of Sicily which saw the first gold coin of the later middle ages which was to become widely known north of the Alps. This was
the *augustale* of the Emperor Frederick II, but despite its beauty it 783
was not of pure gold, and the resources of the kingdom were
insufficient to launch either it or its successor, the so-called *reale* 784
d'oro of Charles of Anjou, on the international market.

This destiny was reserved for the Florentine *florin* ('fiorino 785
d'oro'), created in 1252, and its counterpart, the Venetian *ducat* 786
('ducato d'oro'), which followed it in 1284. They were coins of pure gold of identical weight, that of the Florentine prototype having been chosen to give it the value of £1 in Florentine currency of the day and the weight of the Venetian coin to make it equal to the florin, though it corresponded domestically to 60
shillings instead of 20 shillings. A third coin, the *genovino d'oro*, 787
created like the florin in 1252 and of the same weight, was never internationally of the same importance.

750 Gigliato of Robert the Wise, king of Naples. Introduced in 1303 and struck in both Naples and Provence, this coin circulated widely in the Aegean area and imitations of it were struck by various Turkish emirates in Asia Minor.

751 Grosso of Bergamo of the second half of the thirteenth century. The obverse is copied from that of Frederick II's augustale (**783**), while the reverse represents the city perched on its high hilltop overlooking the plain of Lombardy.

752 Obverse of an early grosso of Milan, struck by the commune in the mid-thirteenth century and having as type the seated figure of St Ambrose, bishop of Milan in the late fourth century, who became its patron saint.

753 Soldino of Andrea Dandolo, doge of Venice (1343-54), a coin struck to supply the need for something intermediate between the grosso and the denaro. The letter in the reverse field is the initial of a moneyer.

754-755 Tuscan grossi of the fourteenth century are more elaborate in design than their thirteenth century predecessors. The two obverses shown here are of a grosso guelfo of Florence of a type introduced in 1346 (**754**) and a grosso of Siena of the second half of the fourteenth century (**755**). Each bears a privy mark in the field – it is on the reverse of the Sienese coins – to show exactly when it was struck.

750A×3

750B×3

751A×3

751B×3

The area of influence of the ducat was the eastern Mediterranean, where imitations were struck by several of the Aegean principalities and where it was in due course to provide the
1317 weight standard for the *altun* of the Ottoman Turks and the
ashrafi of the Safavids in Persia. That of the florin was the West, where the activities of Florentine wool merchants and bankers made it for the century after its creation the most widely known gold coin. In the 1320s it began to be imitated – over 150 direct imitations have been recorded – and its reputation eventually suffered, for some of the imitations, notably those of the kings of Aragon, were of inferior gold. Florin and ducat between them are two of the most influential coins ever issued, for at home the florin continued of unchanged weight and fineness until the downfall of the Florentine Republic in 1533 and the ducat of Venice down to the Treaty of Campo Formio that ended Venetian independence in 1797.

Two states beyond the Alps, France and England, tried to follow the example of Florence, but while Henry III's gold 20-pence piece of 1257 was a failure and Louis IX's *écu d'or* of 1266 did not do much better, later French gold coins were successful.
Philip IV issued first a *petit royal assis* and subsequently a masse **788**
d'or whose larger flan makes it the starting point of most of the **789**

756 Gros tournois of St Louis, struck between 1266 and his death in 1270. The coin is the same design as the denier tournois (675), with the addition of a border of 12 fleurs de lis – the coin was worth 12 deniers – and a religious inscription.

757 Petit gros of a type introduced in 1269 by Margaret of Constantinople, countess of Flanders and Hainaut, and struck at Valenciennes. It was equivalent in value to two English sterlings or two-thirds of a gros tournois.

758 The kings of Aragon were also counts of Barcelona, and this croat of Barcelona struck by James II (1291-1307) gives him the royal title. The design is little more than an enlargement of that of a type of penny introduced by his grandfather James I in 1258.

752×3 **753A**×3 **753B**×3 **754** **755** **756A**×3 **756B**×3 **757A**×2 **757B**×2 **758A**×2 **758B**×2

759 Obverse of a petit gros of Brabant, of the same weight and fineness as those of Flanders and Hainaut, struck by Margaret's contemporary John I. The Archangel Michael was the patron saint of Brussels, where the coin was minted.

760 Gros au lion struck at Ghent by Louis I of Flanders (MONETA FLAND) after a monetary agreement between him and John III of Brabent in 1339. Its design was basically that of the French gros, but with the lion of Flanders substituted for the châtel tournois and ivy leaves for the fleurs de lis in the border.

761 One of the many types of gros struck under John the Good, king of France (1350-64) is this gros à la fleur de lis florencée, introduced in 1358 and worth 15 deniers. In the course of the fourteenth century the fleur de lis replaced the châtel tournois as the main element in the types of French royal coins.

762 Groat of a type introduced in 1365 by Louis de Male, count of Flanders, having for type the Flemish lion wearing a helmet, whence its popular name *botdrager* (pot-wearer).

763-764 Obverses of the groats of two neighbouring states in Lorraine showing their respective rulers in clerical and princely attire: Thierry of Boppard, bishop of Metz (1346-84) (**763**) and Charles II, duke of Lorraine (1390-1431) (**764**).

765 Obverse of one of the earliest groschen of Cologne, of a type introduced by Archbishop Walram of Jülich in 1343. As with **760**, the type is basically French in inspiration, but here it is an episcopal bust that replaces the châtel.

759×3

760A **760B**

761A **761B**

762A **762B** **763** **764**

765×3 **766**×3

766 Turnogroschen struck at Aachen in the late fourteenth century, showing the Emperor Charlemagne with a halo–he was canonized in 1165–and the characteristic arched imperial crown supporting the great church whose construction he had begun in the late eighth century.

767 Albus or weisspfennig struck by Werner of Falkenstein, archbishop of Trier, between 1404 and 1407. The arms above the half-figure of St Peter repeated in the shield on the reverse, are those of Trier and Minzenberg, a possession of the Falkenstein family.

768 Obverse of a shilling of Gottfried IV of Limburg, bishop of Würzburg (1443-58). The obverse shows Saint Kilian, the patron of the see, the sword he bears being an allusion to his martyrdom in the late seventh century.

769 Pragergroschen of King Wenceslas II of Bohemia struck between 1300 and the king's death in 1305. The type, with the royal crown and the Bohemian two-tailed lion, continued to be used for the next two centuries, but the later issues are seriously debased.

770 Pragergroschen of Wenceslas IV countermarked in the mid-fifteenth century with the city arms of Ulm.

771 Meissnergroschen of Frederick II of Saxony, which formed a German counterpart to the Pragergroschen., The two are obviously related in design, but the cross fleury in quatrefoil of the Meissnergroschen reverse derives ultimately from that of many French gold coins.

767A×3

767B×3

768

769A

769B

770

771A×3

771B×3

772 Witten of Hamburg of a type introduced in 1387. These coins were of the same value as the English sterling, and formed the chief denomination circulating in the area of the Hanseatic League during the late fourteenth and early fifteenth century.

773 Shilling of Winrich of Kniprode, Grand Master of the Teutonic Order (1351-82) in Prussia, bearing the shields of the Grand Master and of the Order. It was struck with no change of design from its creation under Winrich to well into the sixteenth century, and was one of the most important coinages of north-eastern Europe.

774 Gros of Charles Robert, king of Hungary (1308-42). Its inspiration was the gigliato (**750**), despite its different reverse type. Charles Robert was a grandson of Charles II of Anjou, who had introduced the gigliato at Naples.

775-776 Serbian grosch of Stephen Decanski (1321-31) (**775**), and obverse of one of Stephen Dushan after he had assumed the title of Tsar in 1346 (**776**). The latter shows him being crowned by two angels.

772A×2

772B×2

773A×2

773B×2

774A×3

774B×3

775A×3

775B×3

777 The influence of Western coinage reached as far as the modern Romania, and determined the purely Western types of this silver dinar struck in the late fourteenth century by Vladislav I, prince of Wallachia. Though the inscription is in Latin it gives him the Slav title of voivode (waiwode).

778 Groschen of the last Bosnian ruler Stephen II Tomasevich, who was put to death by the Turks in 1463, showing the standing figure of Saint Gregory Nazianzen and the royal shield with crown and mantling.

779 Groat of Edward III of England, of a type introduced in 1351 which continued unchanged to the end of the Middle Ages. It goes back to the design of the sterling penny (**660**), with borders added, but its details were largely copied from a groat of John III of Brabant, one of Edward's allies in the opening phases of the Hundred Years War. Although much heavier than the continental gros, the high weight and good silver content of the English penny meant that it was worth only four pennies, instead of the 12 pennies or more of its counterparts abroad.

776×3

777A×2

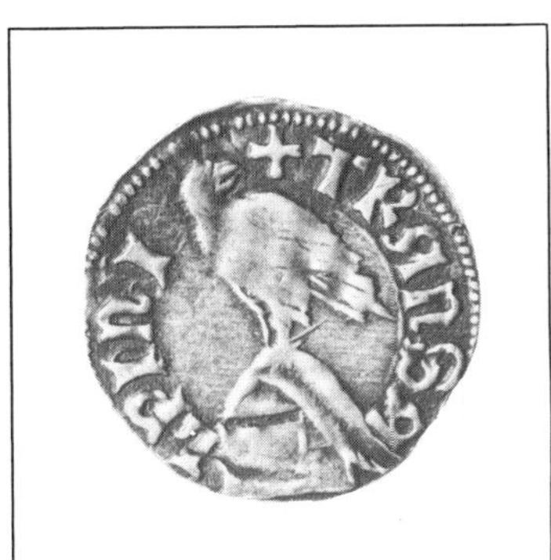

777B×2

778A×2

778B×2

779A×3

779B×3

subsequent gold coinage of western Europe north of the Alps. The French tradition over the next 90 years was to be one of coin
789 usually weighing between about four and five grammes and
790 some 3 cm in diameter, showing the king standing, seated, or on
791,792 horseback, but some coins had such purely religious types as an *Agnus Dei* or a figure of Saint George. Only after 1385 did the
793 type settle down to a simple shield (*écu*), bearing the royal fleurs de lis, which with some exceptions, and small modifications from time to time, dominated French gold coinage down to the end of the Middle Ages.

Fitting counterparts to the French royal coinage were the feudal coinages of the Low Countries and of Guyenne. Flanders was one of the richest states in Latin Christendom, and its gold 795
coinage in the fourteenth and fifteenth centuries was one of great 796
richness and variety, the types being partly imitated from those of France but partly original, making abundant use of heraldic 797
devices, notably of the lion of Flanders. Guyenne for its part was an appanage of the English crown, and in the middle decades of the fourteenth century, under Edward III and the Black Prince, 798
its gold coinage vied in splendour with that of the Low Countries.

The two remaining major states of the Atlantic West were

780 Groat of David II of Scotland, imitated from the English groat but preserving the profile bust of the Scottish penny (**662**). The interior inscription on the reverse gives Edinburgh as the mint.

781 Castilian groats were of French inspiration but often had a crowned royal initial as their main type, as is the case with this Castilian silver real of Peter the Cruel (1350-69). The sea-shell accompanying the arms of Castile-Léon on the reverse shows it to have been minted at the port of Corunna.

780A×2

780B×2

781A×2

783A

782 Real of King Fernando of Portugal (1367-83), with a crowned FR (for *Fernandus rex*) and the mint initial L (for Lisbon) on the obverse and the traditional five shields (**723**) on the reverse.

783 Gold augustale of the Emperor Frederick II, struck at Brindisi and Messina from 1231 onwards. The design, inspired by a classical model, is in much higher relief than was usual in the Middle Ages, but the portrait is idealized and cannot be regarded as a likeness.

781B×2

782A×2

782B×2

783B

784 Gold reale of Charles of Anjou as king of Sicily, struck between 1266 and 1278. It preserves the high relief of its model, the augustale, but the element of portraiture is much stronger. It was succeeded in 1278 by a coin much more medieval in inspiration and type (**805**).

785 Gold florin of Florence struck in 1332-33. The type of the florin remained unchanged, save in small details, from 1252 to 1533, but the symbol above St John the Baptist's hand was changed at six-monthly intervals and identifies the magistrate in charge of the mint during each period.

786 Gold ducat or *zecchino* (sequin) of the Venetian doge Pietro Gradenigo (1289-1311), showing the kneeling doge receiving a banner from Saint Mark.

787 Obverse of a gold genovino of Genoa, struck in the late thirteenth or early fourteenth century. The sea-shell at the end of the inscription is an unknown magistrate's or moneyer's mark.

788 Obverse of the petit royal assis of Philip IV of France, minted in or shortly after 1290. The coin is of the same size and weight as the gold florin, and was intended to circulate on a par with it.

789 Masse d'or of Philip IV, minted in or shortly after 1296. The coin takes its name from the sceptre

784A×3

784B×3

785A×3

787×3

788×3

789A×3

789B×3

(*masse*, 'mace' in English) held by the king. It was twice the weight of the florin but of poorer gold.

790-791 More elaborate representations of the French king appear on the royal d'or of Philip VI (1328), (**790**), with the king wearing royal robes and pointing at his sceptre, and his écu à la chaise (1337) (**791**) showing him seated on a richly decorated Gothic throne wearing armour and holding a sword and shield.

792 Philip IV, near the close of his reign, introduced a small gold coin, 29 mm in diameter, having as its type a representation of the Lamb of God and consequently known as an agnel. When John the Good introduced this larger coin of the same type in 1355, it was somewhat irreverently known as a mouton d'or.

793 This écu d'or of Charles VI, of a type introduced in 1385, is typical of later French royal coinage. The mints are customarily differentiated from each other by a pellet underneath one of the letters of the inscription. One underneath the 26th letter, as on the specimen here, indicates the mint of Villeneuve, outside Avignon.

785B×3

786A×3

786B×3

790×3

791×3

792×3

793×3

794 John the Good struck in 1360 a franc à cheval to pay his ransom after his capture at Poitiers, the name signifying that by it he became *franc* (free). This is the origin of the term franc as a coin-name.

795 The vieil heaume of Louis de Male, count of Flanders, minted in 1367. Its elaborate design, with the ducal helmet surmounted by a coronet and a winged gargoyle, makes it one of the showiest as well as one of the largest of medieval Flemish gold coins.

796 Flandres d'or of the same Louis de Male, minted in or soon after 1369. The type was suggested by the franc à pied introduced by Charles V of France in 1365, but differs in its details.

797 The Low Country taste for highly decorated gold coins lasted into the fifteenth century, contrasting with the plain shield of the contemporary French royal series. This lion d'or of Philip the Good of Burgundy, struck for Brabant at Malines, is of a type introduced in 1354 in his four Low Country principalities.

798 Pavilion d'or of Edward the Black Prince, struck at Poitiers in the 1360s and showing the prince pointing with a significant gesture at his sword in a virtual parody of the way in which the French king

794

795

796×2

797A×2

797B×2

798A

points at his sceptre on some of his coins (**790**). The ostrich feathers which appear in both the obverse and reverse fields still form part of the badge of the Prince of Wales.

799 Dobla de cabeza ('with a head') of Peter the Cruel, king of Castile (1350-69). The S in the reverse field is the mark of the mint of Seville.

800 Obverse of a noble of Edward III of England, giving him the title of king of France and so struck between the introduction of the coin in 1344 and his abandonment of this title under the terms of the Treaty of Bretigny (1360). The type with the king in a ship was basically an allusion to English seapower in the Channel, but may refer specifically to the English victory over the French at Sluys in 1340.

801 Goldgulden of Frederick III of Saarwerden, archbishop of Cologne, minted at Deutz in virtue of a monetary convention concluded in 1385 between the four Rhineland Electors. The shields on the reverse are Cologne-Saarwerden in the centre, Minzenberg (for the archbishop of Trier) and Mainz to the left and right above, and the Palatinate-Bavaria below.

799A×2

799B×2

800×3

798B

801A×2

801B×2

810×2

tradition of minting in gold, however, lapsed in the early fourteenth century, partly because of Florentine competition, and did not revive again till the 1430s. Further north, in Rome, the Senate for over a century minted imitations of the Venetian
806 ducat, but these were succeeded in due course by a papal
807 coinage. Tuscany remained under the domination of the florin, though Siena minted gold on a respectable scale and Lucca and Pisa on relatively small ones. In the north there were important
gold coinages at Milan, especially after the rise of the Visconti, 808
and at Bologna and Genoa. Italian gold coins are almost without 809
exception of good weight and fineness, and so close to each other 810
in weight as to be mutually interchangeable; but, although commercially admirable, they lack the splendour of royal and feudal gold struck beyond the Alps. The great commercial cities were intensely proud of the good quality of their gold coins, but saw no need to use them as vehicles of personal display.

802 Goldgulden struck at Frankfurt am Main by the Emperor Sigismund before he received the imperial title in 1433. The majority of his gold coins have, as here, the imperial orb and cross, commonly called the *Reichsapfel* (Imperial apple), for reverse type. The obverse is copied from that of the preceding coin.

803 Gold florin of John Hunyadi, regent of Hungary between 1446 and 1452. The obverse shows Saint Ladislas, an eleventh century king of Hungary, with his axe, and the reverse the arms of Hungary quartered with that of the Crown and the raven of the Hunyadi family.

804 Gold florin of the Emperor Charles IV as king of Bohemia (1346-78). He wears an 'open' (i.e. non-imperial) crown, and the reverse shows the same Bohemian lion as the Pragergroschen (**769**).

805 Carlino (or saluto) d'oro of Charles of Anjou, with a representation of the Annunciation. We know from a letter that has survived that the king took a personal interest in the design and striking of the coin.

806 Angevin rule in Sicily was ended by the Sicilian Vespers in 1282, and the three-year reign of Peter of Aragon and his wife Constance, granddaughter of Frederick II, saw the issue of handsome pierreali with the shield of Aragon and the Hohenstaufen eagle.

XII
EUROPEAN COINAGE 1450-1797

Edward Besly

From the middle of the fifteenth century, a number of related developments combined to transform the coinages of Europe into what may be described as modern coinage. New discoveries and exploitation of precious metals led to a vast increase in the amount of coin available, ending the European 'bullion famine' of the first half of the century. This increase was largely in the production of silver and the principal feature of the period was the striking of large silver denominations, some equal in value to current gold coins. The introduction of larger coins coincided with the artistic developments of the Renaissance and the types and styles of the coins changed dramatically. The technical problems of producing large numbers of heavy coins accelerated the development of mechanical methods for the production of flans and the striking of coins.

The first major increase in supplies of precious metals came around 1450, when the Portuguese gained access to the gold-bearing regions of West Africa; this gold had hitherto reached Europe overland, so its acquisition by Portugal and the discovery in 1481 of the rich gold-source of Guinea not only boosted the amount of gold available but shifted the economic balance to the west and north of Europe, with the development of Antwerp as an important bullion market. The gold brought back to Europe
859 from Africa was coined by the Portuguese as the *cruzado* and later
as the *Português*, worth 10 cruzados.

At the beginning of the sixteenth century, the African gold was supplemented by gold acquired by the Spanish in the New World. At first the amounts were not great but the conquests of Mexico in 1519-27 and Peru in 1532-41 gave the Spaniards the accumulated gold stocks of the Aztec and Inca civilizations,
864 which were coined first as *doubloons* and subsequently as *escudos*
865 and *pistoles*.

While the major increase in gold supplies came from outside Europe, that of silver came initially as a result of new technology and discoveries within Europe. Around 1450 a new technique for separating silver from argentiferous copper ores and the improvement of drainage techniques allowed many old mines to be reopened, while at Schwaz in the Tirol and in the Erz Gebirge range in Saxony and Bohemia new, productive seams were discovered. The example of Archduke Sigismund of Austria, who
824 in 1486 struck the first silver coin equal in value to the gold
gulden was rapidly followed in Hungary, Switzerland and by several German states; of these, the only sizeable issues were
825 those of the Elector of Saxony. In 1519, the Bohemian counts of
Schlick, whose mine at St. Joachimsthal became the most productive in the area, struck the first St. Joachimsthaler
guldengroschen, an extremely successful coin whose name, 826
abbreviated to -thaler, provided the generic term for the subsequent large silver coins of the Holy Roman Empire. The
Habsburgs, with their control of much of southern Germany, 833
Bohemia, Hungary and Silesia, produced extensive coinages. In
the north, the Saxon duchies and those of Brunswick-Wolfenbüt- 834
tel and Brunswick-Lüneburg-Celle (later the Electors of Hanover) were the principal beneficiaries, though some minor nobility such as the counts of Mansfeld and of Stolberg possessed long-lived mines.

With the growing importance of silver, successive Holy Roman Emperors attempted to exert their authority over the production of silver coinage, as an extension of their existing control over the striking of gold coinage. The disputes thus engendered lasted throughout the sixteenth century, with a succession of Imperial edicts attempting to regulate the standards and values of the silver thalers and their divisions. These edicts ran counter to the interests of the mining states, who generally ignored them. Since 1512, the Empire had been divided into economic circles (Kreise–see map) in an attempt to standardize the monetary systems of different areas; the authorities of each circle met twice yearly to co-ordinate issues and to regulate circulation of foreign coinage. Control of the minor denominations rested with the circles, subject to limits on the quantities which could be struck (see for instance the various
manifestations of the groschen). In the mid-sixteenth century, 829,831,832
the number of circles was reduced by combining the two Saxon circles; Westphalia and the Rhenish circles; and the Austrian, Bavarian, Franconian and Swabian circles. The Burgundian circle, though nominally part of the Empire, pursued its own separate monetary policies. Germany did not achieve full monetary union until the mid-nineteenth century; but the circle system went some way to reducing the chaos of the late middle ages and unifying accounts and coinage on a regional basis.
The striking of coins of the 'odd' denominations, such as ⅔, 846
⅓-Thaler, in Germany during the second half of the seventeenth century had the merit of uniting the various systems of account: at this period ⅔-*taler* equalled 1 *gulden*, 2 *marks* or 32 *schillings*.

German and Austrian silver output continued rising until the 1530s, reaching a peak output of perhaps three million ounces per annum. Thereafter output declined steadily; at the same time imports of New World silver began to rise rapidly, reaching around ten million ounces per annum by the end of the century. In the face of such an abundance of silver, it was not economic to

Heinrich Julius, Duke of Brunswick-Wolfenbüttel, 1609 (**834**).

819 Copper bezant struck by order of M. A. Bragadin, Venetian commander in Famagusta, during a long but unsuccessful defence of the city against the Turks in 1570. After the siege he was flayed alive by his captors. Venice finally surrendered sovereignty of Cyprus in 1573.

820 From the early sixteenth century, the traditional new year's gift of the Doge to his Council consisted of specially-struck coins, oselle, a name derived from *uccelli* (birds), which were formerly given. An osella of Doge Aluise Pisani (1735-41) minted in 1735.

821 Savoy, ducatone of Carlo Emanuele I, 1588. The reverse type, depicting the duke as a centaur, celebrates the capture of the marquisat of Saluzzo.

822 Naples, copper cavallo of Ferdinand I (1458-94). The first successful modern copper coinage of Europe: the obverse type imitates the heavily-debased Roman antoniniani of the late third century (**461**).

819A

819B

822A×2

822B×2

820A×2

820B×2

821A×2

821B×2

823 Swiss coins usually depicted the arms of the issuing authority and the local patron saint, here Saint Nicholas of Myra, better known as Santa Claus. Switzerland, city of Freiburg: silver dicken, end of the fifteenth century.

824 The Austrian Archduke Sigismund (1439-89) started to strike large silver coins (½-guldiner) at Hall in the Tirol in 1484. His guldiner (guldengroschen), illustrated here, was the first silver coin equivalent in value to the gold gulden and forerunner of the German thaler-series. It was also sometimes known as an unzialis, from its weight of one ounce.

823A×3

823B×3

824A×2

824B×2

and as a development from the portrait-medal. The modern portrait-medal originated with the work of Pisanello, whose first example, of the Byzantine Emperor John VIII Palaeologus, was cast in 1439. In the succeeding decades the medal became a popular means of commemorating the individual, being portable, reproducible and durable–advantages not shared by paintings. The first Renaissance portrait-coin was a ducat struck by Francesco Sforza of Milan soon after 1450; this was not a success artistically, since the coin was neither big enough nor thick enough for a successful relief portrait of the type hitherto produced by casting. The introduction of testoni and double
ducats after 1470 provided the ideal opportunity for the success-
ful introduction of portraiture onto the coinage. Both Venice and
Milan depicted their rulers on their first testoni; the latter **38**
proceeded to issue a fine series of depictions of the Sforza family
and, subsequently, of Louis XII of France. Other states early to **812,813**
issue portrait coins included Ferrara, Mantua, Naples, and the
Papacy, the grosso of Sixtus IV being exceptional in this context **815**
in its successful depiction of the Pontiff in shallow relief on a thin
flan. The republics of Venice and Florence avoided portraiture **816**
(as did the republican Swiss) with the exception of the single
issue of Doge Nicolo Tron.

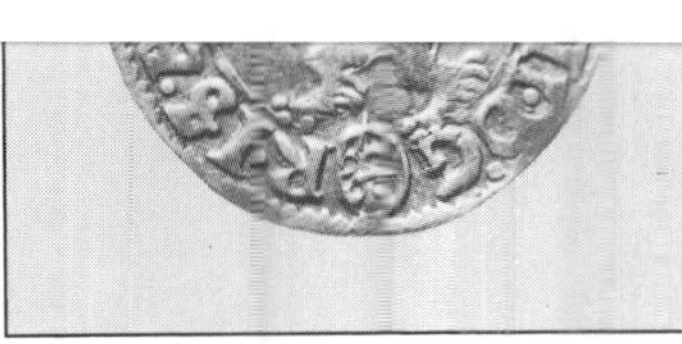

833A×2

833B×2

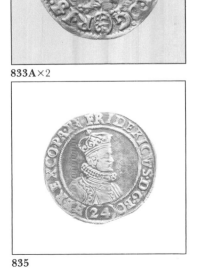

835

836

834

825 Saxony, guldengroschen struck at Annaberg 1500-08 in the names of Friedrich III der Weise (the Elector), his brother Johann and cousin Georg. These coins were later known as klappmützentaler, an allusion to the headgear of the dukes shown on the reverse.

826 In 1519, the counts of Schlick opened a mint at Saint Joachimsthal (Jáchymov) in northern Bohemia, striking Saint Joachimsthaler guldengroschen in the name of King Louis II of Hungary-Bohemia. The Schlicks' benefit from this successful coin was short-lived: in 1528, Ferdinand I 'nationalized' the mint.

827 The Diet of Augsburg in 1551 suppressed the coinage of thalers and substituted a reichsgulden of 72 kreuzers. This example, struck at Augsburg by the counts of Stolberg, follows the specification laid down by the edict and displays its value. The system was modified in 1559 to one based on a reichsguldener of 60 kreuzers.

828 The attempt to suppress the thaler was resisted by the Saxon mining states and in 1568 the striking of thalers was once again authorised. The new reichsthaler of 68 kreuzers supplanted the guldener. Reichsthaler, 1569 of Saxony-Altenburg-Weimar, Duke Johann (1554-73).

829 The standard groschen of the Rhenish circles was known as the albus and valued at 1/28th of the 1551 reichsgulden. Albus of Lothar von Metternich, Archbishop of Trier 1599-1623, struck at Coblenz.

830 By the sixteenth century, the shrunken pfennig was usually struck one-sided, with distinctive regional types. Pfennigs of the Upper Rhine were known as 'schüsselpfennige', from their dished shape. Schüsselpfennig of Pfalz-Zweibrücken, Count Wolfgang (1532-69).

EUROPEAN COINAGE 1450-1797

837 In Saxony and Brandenburg, many unofficial mints were opened, striking low denominations in billon or copper. Tin-coated copper pfennig of Frankfurt-am-Oder, 1622.

838 By 1622, the coinage of Germany was in total chaos, and by common consent a return was made in 1623 to a regular coinage based on a reichsthaler of 90 kreuzers. To reassure its users, this 1623 thaler of Saxony-Weimar bears the message 'of the old weight and fineness.'

839 Despite the conditions of the Thirty Years War, the artistic standards of some coinages remained high, exemplied by this portrait-thaler of Johann Georg II, Bishop of Bamberg 1623-33.

840 The Imperialist general Albrecht von Wallenstein was rewarded for his services with the duchy of Friedland in Bohemia, with minting rights, in 1625. Further successes brought him Sagan and Mecklenburg (1627-28). Thaler 1629, struck at Jičín.

841 After the intervention of Gustav Adolf in 1630-31, Swedish armies marched rapidly through Germany. The Swedes struck gold and silver coinages at several of the towns they captured. Thaler 1632, struck at Augsburg.

842 The length and destructiveness of the Thirty Years War are reflected in the relief with which the Brunswick Duke August greeted the withdrawal of Imperial troops. Bellthaler, Wolfenbüttel 1643.

843 The brilliant mercenary general Bernard von Sachsen-Weimar achieved considerable success fighting with the Swedes and subsequently the French. He died in 1639 at Breisach, but in 1655 his remains were returned to Weimar, an event commemorated by this 1655 quarter-thaler of Weimar.

844 By the mid-seventeenth century, the ducat had replaced the goldgulden as the standard gold coin of the Holy Roman Empire, although the latter continued to be struck by some states for commemorative purposes. Ducat of Christian, Margrave of Brandenburg-Bayreuth, 1642.

837×2

838

839×2

840×2

842

843

841A×2

841B×2

845 The remote principality of Transylvania remained fiercely independent of both Habsburgs and Turks until 1690, striking coinage from its own supplies of gold, as well as thalers. Ducat of Georg Rakoczi, 1646 struck at Alba Iulia.

846 The Saxon mining states, meeting at Zinna in 1667, created a new standard with a debased thaler of 90 kreuzers. This was not struck, the largest silver coin being the ⅔-thaler (or gulden) of 60 kreuzers. Saxony, ⅔-thaler of Elector Johann Georg III, Dresden 1682

847 The Diet of Ratisbon had fixed a new value of 96 kreuzers for the thaler in 1667; the southern states refused to accept the Zinna standard and continued to strike reichsthalers. Thaler of Emperor Leopold I ('the Hogmouth', 1658-1705), Vienna 1671.

848 With two systems in operation, some German states debased their coinage. Count Gustav of Sayn-Wittgenstein went further, issuing base gulden which imitated those of states which coined in fine silver, until his mint was forcibly closed by the Elector of Brandenburg in 1688. Sayn, 16 gute groschen (⅔-thaler) 1676, imitating the coinage of Stolberg.

849 In 1690, a new standard was established at Leipzig based on the speciesthaler of 120 kreuzers (2 gulden). This became the accepted Imperial standard for over half a century. Anhalt-Bernburg, thaler 1746 of Duke Victor Friedrich.

850 The Leipzig standard was accepted by the southern states in 1693. The Franconian circle countermarked overvalued gulden of the Zinna type to circulate at 60 kreuzers (½-thaler under the new system). Countermarked gulden of Montfort, Count Anton II, 1690.

851 Apart from Westphalia, the use of copper coinage did not become widespread in Germany until the eighteenth century. Pfennig scheidemünze of Duke Karl of Brunswick-Wolfenbüttel, 1743.

852 The coinage of Hanover reflects both British and traditional German types. 12-mariengroschen (⅓-thaler) of Georg III, Zellerfeld 1783.

844A

844B

845A

846A

846B

847B

845B

848

849

850

851×2

852A

852B

847A

853 The last major change to the Imperial coinage took place in 1753, when Bavaria and Austria issued a new thaler, the conventionsthaler. Each coin bore a clear indication of its standard, 10 thalers to the Cologne mark of silver. City of Nürnberg, conventionsthaler, 1768.

854 The 'Maria Theresia dollar' became a much sought-after trading coin in East Africa and the Near East. To supply this demand, thalers of this type were struck at many mints (including Brussels, London, and Paris) until as recently as 1961. Maria Theresia, thaler struck at Günzburg in Burgau, 1780.

855 Prussia remained outside the monetary conventions of the Holy Roman Empire, striking a baser thaler (which eventually was to form the basis of nineteenth-century German silver coinage) and her own gold denominations. The Prussian system of mint-letters (A=Berlin, etc.) survives in the present-day coinages of East and West Germany. Prussia, Friedrich II, double Friedrichs d'or, Berlin 1750.

856 Following their success at Mohacs (1526), the Turks occupied most of Hungary. They pushed further westward but were halted by the successful defence of Vienna in 1529. Ducat of Vienna besieged.

857 Taken by the Dutch in 1610, Jülich fell to the Spaniards under Spinola after a siege of five months in 1621. The Dutch governor Pithan struck coins from whatever silver was to hand, in this case a worn-out dicken of the city of Worms. Jülich, coin issued by Dutch defenders, 1621.

858 During the revolt of Franz Rakoczi in Hungary (1704-08), the rebels struck coinage at a number of mints. Copper poltura, Kremnitz 1706.

853×2

855A

855B

856×2

857

854A×2

854B×2

858A

858B

859A×2

859B×2

859 Around 1450, Portugal gained access by sea to the West African gold which had hitherto reached Europe by land. The cruzado, the first modern trading coin, was first struck in 1457 by Alfonso, using the African gold, to finance a crusade against the Turks. Portugal, gold cruzado of Alfonso V (1438-81).

860 Tostão of Manuel I (1495-1521), valued at five vintems or 100 reis; the Portuguese equivalent of the testone, from which it derives its name. The conservative Portuguese coinage retained these types throughout the sixteenth and seventeenth centuries.

861 The discovery of the Minas Gerais goldfields in Brazil in 1693 transformed the economic position of Portugal. Valued in Brazil at 4000 reis, the moeda (known in Europe as the moidore) circulated in Europe at 4800 reis because of the higher European gold:silver ratio. Moeda d'oro, Pedro II, struck at Rio de Janeiro, 1703.

862 Portraiture was not used on the Portuguese coinage until the reign of João V (1706-50). Dobra of four escudos, José I, 1753.

863 The 1497 Pragmatic of Medina del Campo abolished previous Spanish monetary systems and introduced a coinage based on the maravedi. The Pragmatic laid down that every coin should bear the mark of its mint and a symbol denoting the assayer responsible. Spain, Ferdinand (1495-1516) and Isabella (1495-1504), silver real of 34 maravedis struck at Burgos.

864 After the deaths of Ferdinand and Isabella, this type continued to be struck using the Aztec and Inca gold from the New World. The double excelente, exactly equivalent to two Venetian ducats, found wide favour in Europe under the name 'doubloon.' Ferdinand and Isabella, gold double excelente, Toledo mint.

860A

860B

861A

861B

862×3

863A

863B

864A

864B

Many of the earliest large gold and silver coins elsewhere in Europe differed little from their medieval predecessors, retaining their characteristic gothic lettering and heraldic devices but engraved on a larger scale (see for instance, the grote reaal of
872,873,823 Holland, the snaphaan of Guelders and the dicken of Freiburg). Portraiture spread rapidly and was usually accompanied by a transition from gothic to Roman lettering for the legends. In England, however, where realistic portraiture of the Italian type
899 was introduced on Henry VII's testoon, gothic lettering persisted until the reign of Mary (1553-58), for example on the
901 Edward VI crown of 1551. Reverse types became generally less ornate, usually consisting of the coat of arms of the issuer; *anno domini* dating of coins became widespread.

During the first half of the sixteenth century Italy, though no longer an important economic power, nevertheless produced some of the finest coinage. Artists famous in other fields were employed to cut the dies for coins of prestige, which were not designed for heavy circulation. Benvenuto Cellini was employed
817 first by Pope Clement VII and subsequently by the Medici at Florence. Leone Leoni cut the dies for the coinage of the
814 Emperor Charles V as Duke of Milan; both artists also made famous contributions to the development of medallic art. Later in the century the striking of larger coinages as a result of the diversion of Spanish silver bound for the Netherlands through Italy led to a deterioration of artistic quality but the opportunity provided by the larger denominations led to some fine experiments such as the *ducatone* struck by Carlo Emanuele I of Savoy 821
in 1588.

In the German lands a different tradition of portraiture was established during the sixteenth century. Instead of the idealized portraits of the Italian type, there was more emphasis on the rank and authority of the issuer, who was frequently depicted on horseback or half-length in armour, in association with symbols of his power such as a sword and often turning to face the onlooker. Such portraits were not so flattering to the subject but 828
can give one a much better idea of the characters involved than can an idealized profile. Far from both Italian and German influence, countries such as Poland and the principality of Transylvania developed their own distinctive styles of portrai- 845
ture and coinage. Of European monarchies, Spain and Portugal are exceptional: portraiture is virtually absent from the Spanish coinage from Philip II (1556) until 1709, although it was used on 870
the coins of Spanish possessions such as the Netherlands. In 862
Portugal there was no portraiture before João V (1706-50). In the late seventeenth and eighteenth centuries, increasing standardization of production methods and portrait styles through-

865 In 1536, Charles I (the emperor Charles V), concerned about the outflow of bullion from Spain, replaced the excelente with a lighter, 22-carat coin, the escudo, whose double, the pistole became a coin of international importance by the end of the century. Pistole of Philip III (1598-1621), Seville 1611.

866 Machinery was installed at the Segovia mint in 1587 and produced excellent coinage in marked contrast to the ill-struck pieces imported from Mexico and Peru. Silver eight-reals, Segovia mint 1590.

867 The monetary system established in 1497 allowed for indefinite multiples of the real and the escudo. The roller presses at Segovia produced magnificent coins of 50-reals for use as presentation pieces during the reigns of Philip III and Philip IV. Note the use of an altered reverse-die of 1617. 50-reals, Segovia 1618.

868 During the reign of Philip IV (1621-65), the Spanish coinage was virtually reduced to one of copper. Variations in the price of copper led to frequent revaluations of existing coins. This eight-maravedis of 1625 was revalued by countermarking to 12-maravedis in 1641.

865A×3

865B×3

868A

868B

869A

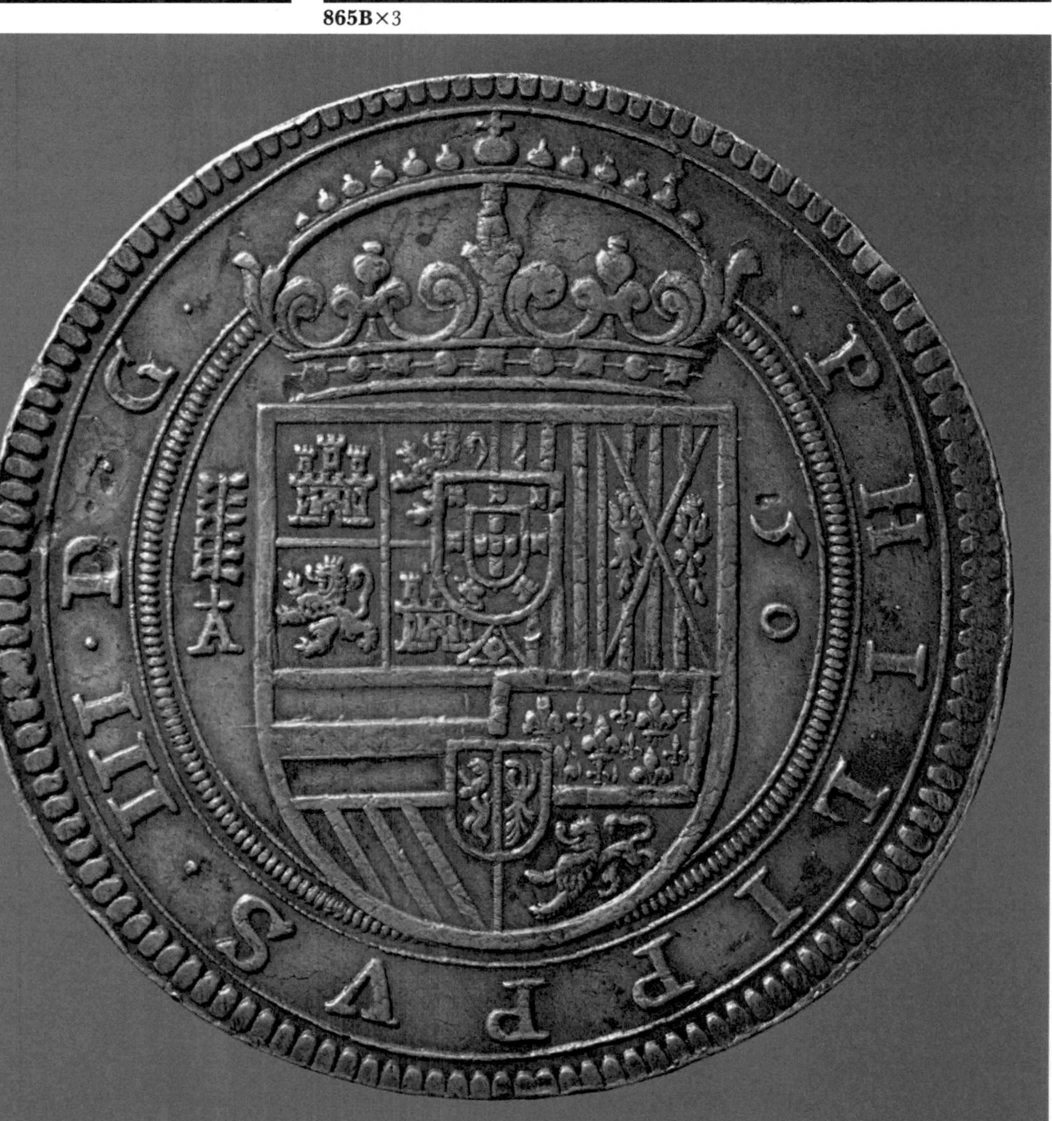

867A

869 During the war of the Spanish succession the Austrian pretender, Archduke Charles, took the name Charles III and issued two-real pieces at Barcelona from 1707 to 1714. Two-reals, Barcelona 1708; the monogram mimics coins of Charles II.

870 Apart from crude portraits of Philip IV, portraiture disappeared as a regular feature of Spanish coinage in the seventeenth century, although Spanish possessions in the Netherlands continued to strike portrait coins. Portraiture reappeared on the Spanish coinage itself with an issue of Philip V in 1709, becoming common on the coins of Charles III (1759-88). Eight-maravedis of Charles III, 1773.

866A×2

866B×2

867B

870A

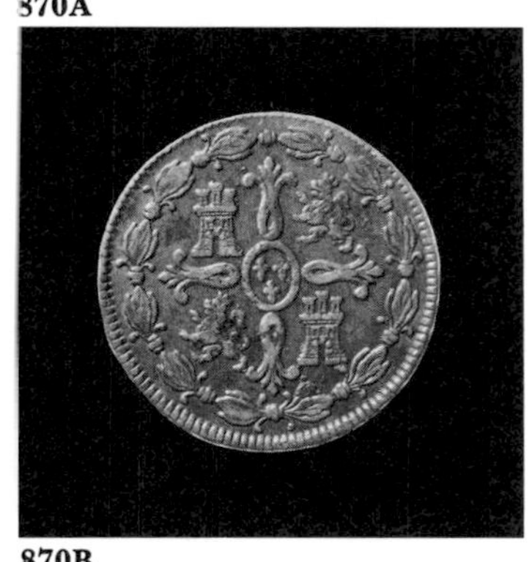

870B

869B

871 The Pragmatic of 1497 was a Castilian ordinance but most provincial issues were struck to the same standards as the Castilian series. Valencia, however, continued to strike its own types and denominations until 1707. Silver croat of Valencia, 1684.

872 Burgundian Netherlands, gold grote reaal 1487, struck at Dordrecht by Maximilian I as regent for his son Philip the Handsome. Although this coin was short-lived, it was imitated by Henry VII of England in his gold sovereign of 1489, a type which survived throughout the sixteenth century.

873 The first large silver coin of the Netherlands, issued in 1509, the snaphaan was equivalent to the Italian testone, but retained the gothic lettering and heraldic designs typical of medieval coinage. Guelders, Duke Karel van Egmond (1509-38), snaphaan.

874 This first Netherlands silver coin equivalent to the gulden was introduced by Charles V in 1540. Flanders, Charles V (1516-56), Karolusgulden minted at Bruges.

871A×2

871B×2

872A×2

872B×2

873A

873B

874A×2

874B×2

875 The first copper coin of northern Europe, the korte bore a remarkable resemblance to its forerunner from Naples. Flanders, copper korte 1549, minted at Bruges.

876 The first major coin of the Dutch Estates, issued from 1575, took its name from the rampant lion of Holland which formed its obverse type. It became a popular trading coin in the Near East. Holland, leeuwendaalder 1504.

877 In the uncertain conditions of the revolt and the subsequent war with Spain, the northern provinces each issued their own coinages, despite attempts to unify the currency by the Earl of Leicester. Foreign coins were frequently imitated: gold rosenobel of Overijssel (Transisulania) c. 1582-86, copying an English ryal.

878 Guelders, 10 stuivers 1606 (equivalent in value to the contemporary English shilling). In 1606 the coinage of the United Netherlands was unified and based on gold ducats and rijders and the silver rijksdaalder, current for 47 stuivers

875×2

876

877A×2

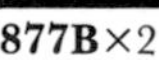

877B×2

878A

878B

out Europe lent a degree of 'sameness' to the major European coins; a profile bust, often ornate, became the universal portrait-type.

The many and diverse authorities striking coins within the Holy Roman Empire produced a correspondingly large variety of reverse types. Of these, the commonest simply bear the (often complex) coat of arms of the issuer or the Imperial eagle; patron
842 saints and views of cities were also common. The striking of multiple-*thalers* as *löser* (or as presentation-pieces) gave the opportunity for elaborate engraving; the series struck by the Brunswick dukes depicts towns, the countryside and the activities of the silver mines as well as bearing some impressive
834 obverse types.

The technical problems of producing heavy coins gave impetus to the development of mechanical methods during the sixteenth century. The first thalers and similar large coins were produced by the traditional method of hammering. Quite apart from difficulties of producing round flans of accurate weight, striking by hand could no longer produce the force necessary for the designs on each die to be properly impressed on the thick silver flans. Many of the early thalers are weakly struck or show signs of double-striking where several blows have been necessary. The sixteenth century developments, initially in South Germany, of machinery for producing improved blanks and more even striking were not everywhere accepted; roller-presses were in use at Hall in the Tyrol by 1566 and were successfully installed at the Spanish mint of Segovia in 1587. In France and 866
England, however, attempts to introduce 'mill money' were defeated by the conservatism of the established moneyers and it was not until the seventeenth century that gold and silver were struck mechanically in these countries. From a stylistic point of view, the advent of machinery forced attention to be paid to all aspects of coin design. This meant that the lettering, hitherto the most neglected part of a design and the principal sufferer from poor striking, was now considered as part of the design as a whole and improved considerably in quality. The use of coinage 866,889
for transactions of all sizes brought its own problems; there existed a demand for small change which the mints often failed to satisfy. Apart from the lack of profits involved, there were technical problems to the production of small coins which were supposed to contain their theoretical value of silver. During the middle ages, mints had at first coped with rising silver prices by reducing the weight of the coins and had subsequently debased the coinage. By the fifteenth century, however, this meant that the smallest coins were almost pure copper, with a silver content that could not easily be verified. It was a simple matter for the

879 The gold rijder, originally current for just over 10 gulden, was equivalent to the recently-introduced English unite of James I, emphasising the important links between the two countries (see **904**). By the mid-eighteenth century its value had risen to 14 gulden. Gold rijder, Utrecht 1760.

880 In 1694, coins of denominations one, two and three gulden were added to the Dutch coinage; the gulden (or florin) remains the Dutch unit of account to the present day. Holland, gulden (20 stuivers) 1748.

881 The smallest Dutch denomination of the eighteenth century (valued at ⅛-stuiver) simply displays the arms and name of the issuing province. Holland, copper duit, 1739.

879A

880A

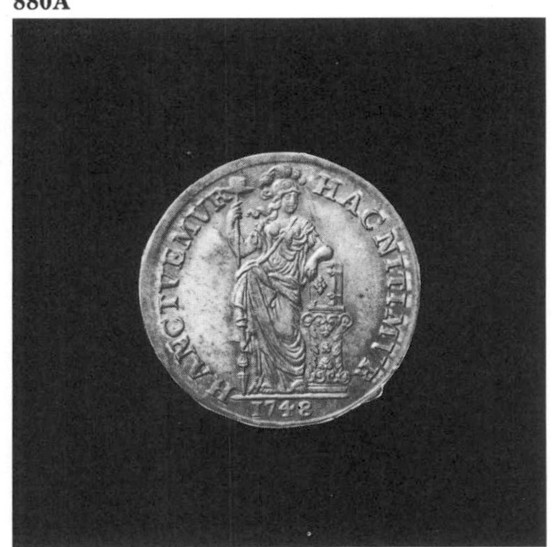

880B

879B

881A×2

881B×2

882 Originally a billon coin, the liard of 12 mites was first struck in copper in 1580. Flanders, copper liard, 1590.

883 The patagon, equivalent to the Dutch rijksdaalder, was introduced in 1612. With its heavier companion the ducaton the patagon circulated widely in both North and South Netherlands. Brabant, patagon 1618 of Albert and Isabella (1598-1621).

884 By the treaty of Utrecht (1713) Belgium passed to Austria, who governed the country until it was occupied by the French in 1794. ½-escalin of Maria Theresia, struck at Antwerp (mintmark, a hand), 1750.

885 Apart from 12 years of truce (1609-21), the United Netherlands were in constant conflict with Spain until 1648. In 1625, as part of the wider war in Europe, the Spanish general Spinola besieged and captured Breda. Breda besieged 1625, silver 60 stuivers

882A×2

882B×2

885

883A×2

883B×2

884A×3

884B×3

886 An improving financial position led Louis to issue France's first large silver coin in 1514. It was derived from Louis' earlier issues as Duke of Milan (**813**) but was of a lower artistic and technical standard. France, teston of Louis XII (1497-1515).

887 The coinages of Brittany and Dauphiné conformed to the French regal system but retained the use of local types. Teston de Dauphiné, François I (1515-47), struck at Romans.

888 An important innovation of François I was the introduction in 1540 of a system of mint-marking by letters. This 'transitional' écu à la croisette was struck at Paris, identified by the letter A, but retains the traditional 'point-secret' (under the 18th letter of the legend).

889 Though technically a success, the introduction of machinery met fierce hostility from the established moneyers and the Monnaie au Moulin was subsequently restricted to the production of medals and jetons. An attempt to set up a mechanized mint in England in 1561 was similarly frustrated. Henri II (1547-59), mill teston 1553, Monnaie au Moulin.

890 Henri III (1574-89), the last Valois king, struck testons initially but by an ordinance of 1575 replaced them with the first French silver francs, of which this example was struck in 1583 at Toulouse.

891 On the death of Henri III, the towns of the Catholic League elected as King Charles, Cardinal de Bourbon, in opposition to Henri de Bourbon. Although Charles X died in 1590, the towns of the League continued to strike in his name until 1597. Charles X, ¼-écu, Dinan 1594.

892 Deniers and double deniers tournois were first struck in copper in 1575; mechanical striking was restricted to copper until the reign of Louis XIII. The Monnaie au Moulin was transferred to the Louvre in 1600. Double tournois of Henri IV (1589-1610), Paris 1603.

886×3

887A×3

888×3

887B×3

889A

889B

890A

890B

893 France finally authorized a thaler-weight silver coin in 1641, valued at 60 sols. The dies for these coins were engraved by Jean Warin. Louis XIII, écu blanc (louis d'argent), Paris 1643.

894 In 1649, a new copper coin, the liard of three deniers, was created by Louis XIV. Unfinished strip of liards (reverse) 1654

895 A product of the Réformations of Louis XIV, this coin still bears traces of its previous type, an écu aux huit LL, struck at Troyes (S). Louis XIV, écu aux palmes, Dijon (P) 1695.

896 The copper coinage of the reigns of Louis XV and XVI consisted of sols, demi-sols and liards (12, six and three deniers respectively), created in 1719. Sol of Louis XV, Strassburg 1773.

897 After the French Revolution (1789), coinage continued to be struck in the name of Louis XVI until his death in 1793. This 'constitutional' coinage was struck from dies by A. Dupré, using a design selected by painter J.-L. David; 15 sols, Paris 1791.

898 Of coinages struck by independent territories in France the douzième d'écu of Anne-Marie-Louise of Dombes (1650-93) became a popular trading coin in the Levant. Several Italian states took advantage of this popularity by issuing base imitations with the legends altered (for instance to PVLCHRA VIRTVTIS IMAGO); but such imitations eventually undermined the type's acceptability. Dombes douzième d'écu 1664.

891×3

892A×2

892B×2

893A

893B

894

895×2

896A

896B

897A

897B

898A×2

898B×2

899 Henry's large silver coin, introduced in 1503-04, was named after its Italian prototypes and was worth 12 pennies, the shilling of the £-s-d accounting system. England, testoon of Henry VII (1485–1509).

900 The last English ecclesiastical coinages were struck during the reign of Henry VIII (1509-47), who closed the episcopal mints at the time of the dissolution of the monasteries. This groat struck at York bears the initials and badge (a cardinal's hat) of Thomas Wolsey, and was technically illegal, since the episcopal mints were not allowed to strike coins greater than half-groats.

901 Following the disastrous debasements of the English coinage by Henry VIII, the first attempts at reform under Edward VI included a silver crown of five shillings, issued in 1551 as a gesture of intent by the administration and the first English silver coin of the same value as a current gold coin.

902 Scotland, portrait-ryal of thirty shillings 1565 of Mary and Henry Lord Darnley, after their marriage.

903 An exceptional example of the intricate low-relief style of engraving on English coinage of this period. Elizabeth I (1558-1603), pound of twenty shillings, initial-mark woolpack (1594-6).

904 The reverse legend, FACIAM EOS IN GENTEM VNAM (I will make them one people), a quotation from Ezekiel xxxvii,22, refers to the Union of England and Scotland on James's accession in 1603. Gold unite of James I (1603-25), second coinage, mintmark lys (1604-05).

905 The first copper coinage in England was produced in 1613 by Lord Harington, who had been granted letters patent by James I. Following Harington's death in 1614, the patent eventually passed to the Duke of Lennox. Farthing tokens continued to be produced until 1644 but were much counterfeited and were unprofitable to their makers.

906 During the seventeenth century, the ratio between English and Scottish coinages was 12:1, so Scottish 12-shilling pieces circulated as English shillings, the mark of value serving both

899

900A

900B

911A

901×2

902

903

904

906

denominations. Charles I (1625-49) Scottish 12-shilling piece.

907 This quasi-medallic coin, never produced for circulation, shows similarities to continental types (**834**), both in the type and in the wealth of detail in the design. Pattern crown by Rawlins, Oxford 1644.

908 Pontefract, under Colonel Morrice, was the last Royalist stronghold in England, and resisted the efforts of Cromwell himself from June 1648 to March 1649. Later coins of the siege, struck after the death of Charles I, bear the legend POST MORTEM PATRIS PRO FILIO. Pontefract besieged, shilling 1648.

909 The 'English Republic' struck a coinage of one type only in all denominations. This plain utilitarian design (nicknamed 'breeches money' from the two shields on the reverse) was revolutionary in its use of the vernacular in the legends. In 1656-58 a trial coinage was designed which bore Cromwell's portrait, but was never produced in circulation quantities. Commonwealth (1648-60), shilling 1652.

910 No official copper coinage was produced in England during the period 1648-72 and the shortage of small change was compensated by the production of local tokens, illegal but tolerated since the Government had no practical alternative. Towcester, Northampton: farthing token of William Bell, dyer.

911 The new gold coin, which finally settled at a value of 21 shillings, remained the standard gold coin of Great Britain until 1816. The elephant symbol, the badge of the African Company, denotes that this specimen was made of gold from Guinea (W. Africa), which gave the coin its name. Charles II (1660-85), Guinea 1663.

912 In 1672, production of regal token coinage was started, first in copper and subsequently in tin, which was more profitable. These coinages were widely counterfeited: the brass plug in the flan was an unsuccessful attempt to deter forgers. The edges were inscribed NVMMORVM FAMVLVS – the servant of the coinage. Charles II, tin farthing 1684.

911B

905A×2

905B×2

907

908A

908B

909A

909B

910A×2

910B×2

912A

912B

913 The English silver coinage was completely recoined in 1696-97. Old, worn and clipped coin was redeemed at face value, the loss incurred being made up by the proceeds of a tax on windows. Five temporary provincial mints assisted with the recoinage. William III (1694-1702), halfcrown, Bristol 1697.

914 Following the Act of Union (1707), the English and Scottish coinages were united, the latter being restruck at Edinburgh using dies and puncheons sent from London. In 1709, the Edinburgh mint was closed and production centralised in London. Anne (1702-14), Edinburgh shilling 1709.

915 The practice of indicating the source of the metal continued on English coinage until the reign of George II. Coins of Anne with VIGO, and of George II with LIMA, were struck from bullion captured from the Spanish at Vigo Bay (1702) and by Anson in South America (1739-43). The silver for this 1723 shilling of George I was supplied by the ill-fated South Sea Company.

916 The shortage and poor quality of official small change led to another period of unofficial coinage in Britain in the eighteenth century (**945**). Such pieces often bore allusions to current political and social affairs. Halfpenny token of W. Gye, Bath, Somerset 1794. The edge inscription reads PAYABLE AT W GYE'S PRINTER BATH.

917 This new design, introduced in 1787, acquired the name 'spade' guinea from the shape of the shield. It was imitated extensively by the makers of brass advertisement and gambling counters. George III, guinea 1794.

918 After his deposition in 1688, James II financed his Irish operations by the issue of fiduciary coinage made from bronze (gun-metal) or copper. Ireland, 'Gun Money' shilling, August 1689.

913×2

914×3

915×3

916A

916B

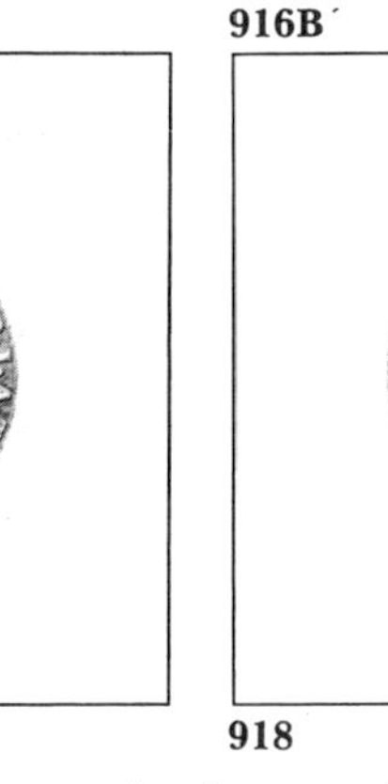

917

918

mint to issue a coin tariffed well in excess of its true value or for a forger to omit silver altogether. In England, which had maintained a currency of fine silver, the problem was different: halfpence and farthings had by 1500 become so small that they were difficult to handle and easily lost.

The solution gradually evolved throughout Europe was to recognize the token nature of small change, which was issued in copper, brass or tin and backed by guarantees of convertibility and limitation of quantity. There was an experiment with copper
822 currency at Venice in 1463, but the copper *cavallo* of Naples,
struck by Ferdinand I (1458-94) is generally regarded as the first modern European copper coin. It was also the Habsburgs who introduced copper coinage to northern Europe when Charles V
struck the *korte* in the Netherlands in 1543. In France, where 875
copper coinage was first produced in 1575, the use of the unfavoured Monnaie au Moulin to produce it resulted in copper coinage of a finer style and execution than much of the
contemporary silver. 892

In England, proposals for coinage in base metal and copper were first made towards the end of the reign of Elizabeth I (1558-1603). The first token currency was made during the reign of James I (1603-25), when letters patent were granted to Lord

Harington in 1613 for the production of copper farthings.
905 Harington and his successors made these tokens throughout the reigns of James I and Charles I. Under the Commonwealth (1649-60) a few silver pennies and halfpennies were struck but there was no authorized copper coinage. Local needs were met by illegal token halfpennies and farthings struck by town
910 councils and traders; a return to regal coinage in copper was
912 made in 1672. A similar shortage of regal small change in the second half of the eighteenth century led to forgery of current coins and to an extensive local coinage of token pennies and
916 halfpence between 1787 and 1797; the shortage was finally remedied by Boulton's copper coinage of 1797. A similar
936 flowering of unofficial tokens occurred in Paris in the years immediately following the Revolution.

A further problem related to a monetarized economy was faced by authorities who ran short of silver, for whatever reason. During the sixteenth and seventeenth centuries, developments in fortifications still matched those in aggressive firepower and the formal siege remained an accepted part of warfare, of which there was plenty, both between and within European states. At a local level, there was often the need to pay troops either on campaign or defending a city or to preserve 'normal' life within a besieged city. Early examples of siege coinage are those of Tournai, besieged by Charles V in 1521, and Vienna, attacked
by the Turks in 1529. These coinages were usually hastily- 856
produced and struck (often one-sided) on crude flans. Some were struck to existing weight-standards but others were more in the nature of 'promissory notes' to be redeemed at the end of the prevailing emergency. Such promises often could not be kept:
their issuers were frequently defeated or even killed. The revolt 819
of the northern Netherlands (1568-1648) and the Thirty Years
War (1618-48) both produced a large number of siege-coinages, 857,885
as did the English civil war of 1642-49. 908

Necessity-coinages include those struck to pay campaigning
troops in Ireland, Poland and by the Hungarian rebels of Franz 918,930,858
Rakoczi. Following the siege of Malta by the Turks in 1565, the Grand Master Jean de Vallette struck a copper coinage to pay
workmen building the fortifications of his new capital of Valetta; 818
the promise NON AES SED FIDES ('Not base but true') borne by these coins was kept when sufficient silver was raised and the redeemed coins were subsequently again used as minor denominations of the Maltese currency.

The Thirty Years War was the most destructive European war before our own century: what started as a German war precipitated by the dispute over the Bohemian succession expanded into a vast conflict involving most major European

919 In Northern Germany, Holstein and Denmark, the unit of account was the mark of 16 shillings; the Danish thaler rose from three to six marks under Christian IV, following successive debasements of the skilling. In 1618 the basis of Danish currency became the krone of eight marks. Denmark, Christian IV, mark 1606.

920 From 1450 until the nineteenth century, Norway was united with Denmark and relegated virtually to the status of a province. Norwegian coinage followed the Danish standards but retained its own distinctive types; daler 1654 of Frederik III.

921 Portraiture in Scandinavian coinages followed the traditions of Germany and Poland, the former exemplified by this half-length portrait of Queen Christina of Sweden on a daler struck at Stockholm in 1641.

922 'Plate money' was issued in Sweden for over a century, from 1644 to 1758. Although the use of a copper 'value-currency' was clumsy as a means of exchange, plåtmynt was a successful way of marketing Sweden's large copper reserves. As the price of copper increased, the weight standard dropped; some examples are countermarked with higher values following a 50% rise in the price of copper in 1718. Sweden, Karl XII, ½-daler plåtmynt 1710.

919A×3

919B×3

920A×2

920B×2

923A

923B

924A×2

924B×2

923 Shortage of silver led Baron Görtz, the finance minister of Karl XII to issue token copper dalers from 1715 to 1719, some of which even bore his own portrait. The majority bore the figures of classical gods, such as this 'Mercury' daler of 1718.

924 In 1528, Sigismund I reformed Poland's much-debased currency and produced a coinage in gold and fine silver. The reform also saw the introduction of naturalistic portraiture to the Polish coinage. Silver 3-grosze struck at Danzig, 1540.

925 Polish thalers appeared in the second half of the sixteenth century. This thaler, struck for Poland under Stefan Bathori, provides a splendid example of the fine, exotic portraiture of the Transylvanian princes. Thaler 1586, struck at Nagybanya.

926 During Sigismund III's reign (1587-1632), successive debasements of the minor coins meant that the thaler rose in price from 36 to 90 grosze. 6-grosze minted at Danzig in 1599.

922

925

926A

926B

921×2

powers in an attempt to forestall Habsburg ambitions of
hegemony in Europe. The German coinage at first went through
a terrible period of debasement and clipping from 1619 to 1622 836,837
before settling down to a remarkable stability for the rest of the
war; the troops of the various armies lived off the land in the
regions in which they operated and there seems to have been
adequate silver available for the coinage which was required, for
instance by Wallenstein who tried to create an organized and 840
properly paid Imperial army. The coinage of the period reflects,
among others, the Spanish operations in the Netherlands; the 857,885
intervention of the Swedes; growing war-weariness; and, after 841
the Peace of Westphalia the posthumous return home of
Bernhard von Sachsen-Weimar. 843

More widely, the seventeenth century saw a dropping-off in fresh silver supplies as the diminishing amounts of New World silver were increasingly diverted to the Americas and the Far East. The Spanish coinage itself was heavily debased and elsewhere in Europe the continuous conflicts of the first half of the century exhausted national treasuries. Minor denominations were often heavily debased, while ducats and thaler-sized coins, which continued to be struck in good alloy, rose to high prices in terms of the smaller coins. In Poland John Casimir (1648-68) tried to improve his finances by the issue of over-valued *tymfs* and

927 John Casimir (1648-68), Torún ducat 1654; valued at 5, later 6½ zloty. The Polish gulden or zloty was the sixteenth century unit of account of 30 grosze, originally equal in value to the ducat.

928 To bolster his treasury, John Casimir issued debased gulden (known as tymf after the mintmaster) of 30 grosze (about three times their intrinsic value) and copper solidi (shillings) at his Crown and Lithuanian mints. Lithuanian solidus, 1661.

929 From 1697 to 1763 Poland was ruled by the Saxon Electors Friedrich August I and II, who reigned as August II and III. Very little coinage was struck in Poland; most of the coinage was supplied by the mints of Dresden and Leipzig, striking Saxon denominations. ⅔-thaler, Dresden 1700.

930 From 1772 to 1795, successive partitions between Austria, Prussia and Russia caused Poland to disappear altogether from the map of Europe. Franz II (1792-1835), copper 3-grossi struck at Vienna for the use of Austrian troops fighting in Poland in 1794.

931 During the sixteenth and seventeenth centuries, the kopek (worth 2 dengi) was the standard Russian coin, the unit of account being the rouble of 100 kopeks. Kopeks were struck on flans prepared from silver wire, whence the curious shape of these coins. Russia, Moscow kopek of Mikhail Feodorovich (1613-45).

932 During the reign of Alexei Mikhailovich (1645-72) an unsuccessful attempt was made, in 1654, to circulate roubles made by overstriking thalers. More successful was the 1655 reform, whereby counterstamped thalers (yefimki) circulated at 64 kopeks, their intrinsic value. Yefimok 1655, made from a 1639 thaler of the city of Rostock.

927A

927B

929A×2

928A×2

928B×2

930A

930B

929B×2

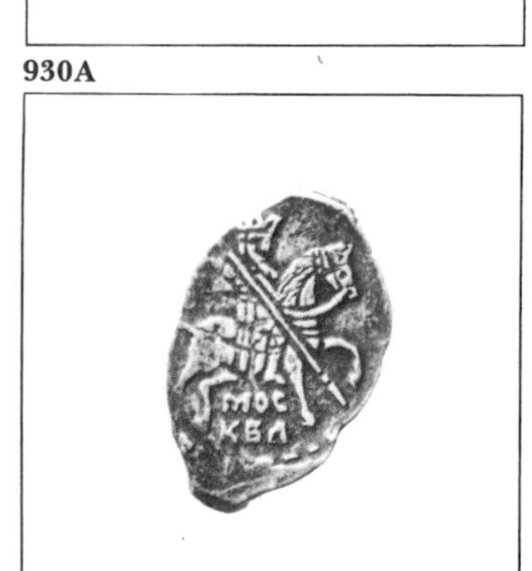
931A×2

931B×2

932

933A

933B

934×2

933 By the end of the seventeenth century, reduction in weight of the kopek made it possible for Peter the Great to issue a new rouble in 1704 equivalent in value to contemporary European thalers, as part of a complete reform of the Russian currency. Peter I (1689-1725) rouble, Moscow 1705.

934 During the seventeenth century, gold coins were only minted in Russia as military presentation-pieces. Following Peter I's reform, gold coins were produced for circulation; first the chervonets (equivalent to a ducat), later the 2-rouble piece, approximately equivalent to a zolotnik ($\frac{1}{96}$th pound). Peter II (1727-30), gold 2-roubles 1727.

935 Plentiful supplies of copper made it an important metal in the coinage of eighteenth century Russia. An issue of plate-money in 1725-26, however, failed to emulate the success of its Swedish prototype. Five kopeks of Catherine II (1762-96), Kolyvan 1784

935A×2

935B×2

928 of solidi (schillings) made from copper rather than the billon previously used. The Russian Tsar Alexei Mikhailovich issued during the period 1655-63 kopeks of copper rather than silver to finance military actions. Both moves were unpopular; both Polish and Russian copper coins were widely counterfeited while in Russia resistance to the copper kopeks culminated in rioting in Moscow which forced a return to coinage in silver. For this, the
932 *yefimki* of 1655 were melted down and restruck as kopeks.

The France of Louis XIV experienced a severe shortage of bullion at the end of the seventeenth century and developed an ingenious system for stretching available supplies. The écu was issued at 66 sols and then successively devalued by edict and called in at 50 sols, to be restruck and reissued bearing a new type and again valued at 66 sols. To save minting expenses, the coins were not melted down; the new types were simply struck onto the existing coins. This practice continued from 1689 until the beginning of the reign of Louis XV (1715); the products of
895 these 'Réformations' often bear clear traces of the types they succeeded.

During the reign of Christina (1632-54), Sweden experienced simultaneously a shortage of silver and a glut of copper, which led to one of the most bizarre necessity-coinages of the period. In 1644 a coinage was issued in copper, which contained its full market-value of the metal: the plåtmynt or plate-money, struck at the mining centre of Avesta. The largest of such pieces, of ten dalers, weighed 19.7 kilogrammes. This impractical-seeming currency was an effective method of marketing the copper and
922 issues of plåtmynt continued until the middle of the eighteenth century. When Russia started to exploit her own reserves of copper, she emulated Sweden by issuing copper roubles and fractions but the issue was short-lived. During the reign of Karl XII (1692-1718), his finance minister Baron Görtz attempted to improve Sweden's finances by the issue of copper token-dalers (mynttecken); the experiment was a disastrous failure, all the 923
more so since plåtmynt (a value-currency) was still being produced. On the death of Karl XII, Görtz fell from power and, held responsible for the failure, was executed.

Another ingenious monetary experiment was carried out in France during the years 1715-26. Following the accession of the young Louis XV a Scotsman, John Law, was made Fermier des Monnaies. Faced with an appalling lack of silver, Law devised a system which attempted to abolish transactions in coin and replace them with paper money. The system failed, because the issues of paper were not backed by any genuine resources; however, the copper sols, demi-sols and liards introduced by 896
Law in 1719 remained a part of the French currency system until after the Revolution of 1789.

It is with the eighteenth century that the heyday of silver coinage in Europe begins to draw to a close. Supplies of silver to Europe continued at a high rate from the Mexican mines, whose lower-grade ore could still be worked profitably using native labour. However, the exploitation of new discoveries of gold in Brazil from 1693 and in the nineteenth century were to lead to a 861
concentration on gold as a standard of value. Already in the 1139
eighteenth century gold became the most important coinage 46
metal in England, thanks to her trade with Portugal and the Far East. At the same time, the development of credit and paper currencies, which started to gain momentum in the late seventeenth century, began to relegate the coinage of everyday transactions to the token status it occupies today. 944

SOHO

XIII
MODERN COINAGE

Anthony Dowle

On 24 August 1793, at a time of increasing political and economic confusion, the National Convention of the French Republic authorized a copper coinage based on the *livre* divided into 10 *decimes* and in turn, the decime divided into 100 *centimes*–in other words a decimal currency. The move followed the example of the young republic across the Atlantic, the United States of America, and was perfectly in keeping with the militant and reforming zeal of revolutionary France. Only one denomination, as it happened, was struck, a 5-decimes and this, somewhat medallic in appearance and generally surviving in good state, was made in such paltry numbers that it has to be considered a symbolic souvenir. Nevertheless it marks a turning point in the monetary history of France and further reforms led to the creation of the *franc*, divided into a 100 centimes, and in 1803 to the adoption of a monetary system not only decimal but also bimetallic, with the ratio of gold to silver clearly fixed by law at 2:31, 3100 francs being struck from a kilogram of standard gold and 200 francs from a kilogram of standard silver. Subsequent to the reform of 1803 a full range of denominations appeared, in the name and with the portrait of Napoleon, First Consul of the Republic since 1799, and they comprised 40-francs and 20-francs
1034 in gold, a large silver 5-francs and a series of smaller divisional
coins. Copper coins had been struck in large numbers a few years earlier, certainly sufficient quantities to meet the needs of the country, and so none were made with the profile of Napoleon.

The monetary system of Napoleon, with some modification, prevailed until the present century and even to this day a link can be seen between the coins currently struck at the Hotel de Monnaie in Paris and a currency created over 170 years ago. Decimalization spread in the nineteenth century, slowly at first but increasingly rapidly as its advantages became more widely recognized and, with its belated adoption by Great Britain in
944 1971, is now universal. The franc is still, of course, the unit of
1052 account in France but has also extended its domain to Belgium,
1046 Switzerland, and, a legacy of empire, to Madagascar and much
of French-Speaking West Africa. Moreover coin design in France, despite occasional concessions to modernity, has remained firmly rooted in tradition: the figure of Hercules, with Equality and Liberty standing at either side, shown on the current 50-francs first appeared on the French coinage in the
49 closing years of the eighteenth century; the francs and ½-francs
1040 now circulating display 'the Sower', that familiar symbol of the
50 Republic dating from the 1890s, and are also of practically
identical size to the coins of these values struck under Napoleon.

However, such similarities as exist between the current coinages of France and elsewhere and those struck before the Great War are superficial; the appearance of continuity, where it occurs, masks the transformation that has taken place. The
Spanish 5-pesetas may show once more the head of a Bourbon 1102
and still be called a *duro* in the streets and cafes of Madrid; but, of small size and made of an alloy of copper and nickel, it is a pale shadow of the large silver 5-pesetas of 80 years ago, let alone the silver coin originally known by this name, the almost universally esteemed and accepted Spanish dollar. The gold sovereign or pound sterling of Great Britain was once legal tender in countries as different as Bulgaria and Canada; it now survives to all intents only as a paper currency diminished by inflation and subject to the fluctuations of exchange rates. While the rouble of the Soviet Union has only its name in common with the silver coin of czarist Russia, certainly not its metallic content or its purchasing power.

Gold still plays its part in the international transactions of central banks, but has not been seen in circulation virtually anywhere since the early days of the First World War. The trauma of the war shattered the gold standard and with it the traditional role of coinage to provide, in the phrase of the economist, 'a store of wealth and a standard of value'. Silver coins have lingered on almost to this day and as late as 1967
Switzerland was producing silver francs and ½-francs as a 1056
general issue; while France, in contradiction to all trends, has recently resumed the striking of large-size silver coins which at least in theory are intended to circulate. On close examination, the more gradual disappearance of silver from the monetary systems of the world is a reflection of reforms in the nineteenth century which reduced the status of silver coins to that of small change, legal tender to a limited amount, and also the low commercial price the metal commanded until recent years. The passing of silver coins marks no more than a sentimental break with the past, and is certainly unnoticed by bankers and those merchants who years earlier would have known the weight and fineness of almost every gold and silver coin in Europe.

Coinage has a function in the modern world: to serve as a means of exchange on a minor scale, and it matters not at all whether struck in cupro-nickel, bronze or aluminium; convenience and public acceptability are the prime considerations and perhaps only the fear of forgery has prevented the appearance of coins made of plastic. It is a function, it should be said, that is not without importance and the traveller to Italy in the last decade can testify to the problems caused by a famine of small change and the various and sometimes curious makeshifts

Britannia on a twopenny piece of George III, 1797 (**936**).

955 Royal portraits have not invariably appeared on European base metal coins, indicating their secondary status. Sweden, Carl XV, copper five-ore, 1861.

956 These large and handsome silver coins ceased to appear after the monetary reform of 1873. Sweden, silver rigsdaler, 1871.

957 Sweden, Gustav V five-kronor, 1935, struck for the 500th Anniversary of the Swedish Parliament, the Rigsdag.

958 Sweden, Charles XIV, silver rigsdaler, 1827.

959 Sweden, Charles XIV, copper two-skilling, 1836.

960 Denmark, Christian VIII, speciedaler, 1840.

961 Denmark, Christian IX, gold 10-kroner, 1873.

962 Finland has produced commemorative coins only since the last war; as might be expected they are distinctly modern in design. Silver 10-markkaa, 1967, commemorating 50 years of independence.

963 Finland, silver 10-markkaa, 1970, for the centennial of the birth of Passikivi.

964 The symbolism seen here needs no explanation, the designs found on later coins of the Soviet Union have been less interesting. Soviet Union, silver rouble, 1924.

955

956A

956B

958

957×2

959×2

960

961×2

962

963

964×2

965 Showing the Imperial family, and commonly called 'the Family Rouble', these pieces were struck in 1835 and 1836 in rather small numbers for presentation purposes. Russia, Nicholas I, 1½-roubles, 1836.

966 Platinum coins, first struck in 1828, were not a success and after 1845 were discontinued. Russia, Nicholas I, 12-roubles, 1843, struck in platinum.

967 Russia, Nicholas II silver rouble, 1907.

968 Large and heavy copper coins were struck in considerable numbers in Russia during the first half of the nineteenth century. Nicholas I, copper 10-kopeks, 1836.

969 For most of the nineteenth century portraits did not appear on Russian coins, except for a few commemorative issues; this is a pattern struck at the Soho mint in Birmingham. The fine bust of Alexander, with an abundance of skilful detail, was the work of Conrad Heinrich Kuchler. Russia, Alexander I, silver rouble, 1804.

970 Russia, Nicholas I, silver 1½-roubles, 1839, commemorating the Battle of Borodino monument completed that year.

971 Russia, Alexander II, gold five-roubles, 1855.

972 In Russia's Polish dominion revolts took place in 1830 and 1863. No coins were issued during the second rebellion, but this five-zloty was struck in 1831 during the first insurrection.

965A×2

965B×2

966

967

968

970A

971×2

970B

969

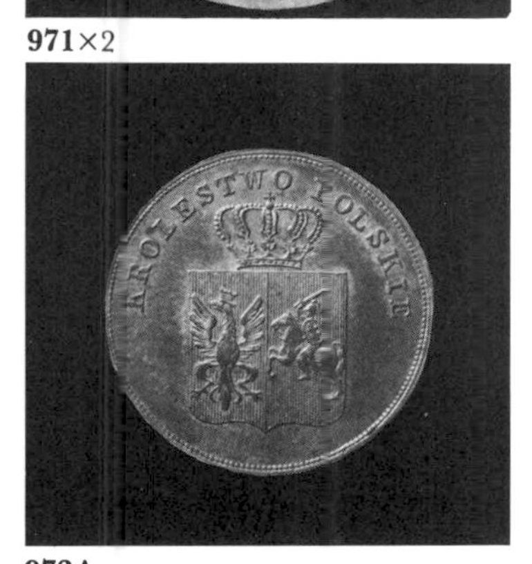

972A

972B

991 This charming study of 'Fame' was designed by the Austrian medallist and sculptor Rudolph Marschall. Austria, Francis Joseph, gold 100-corona, 1908, for the sixtieth anniversary of the reign.

992 Austria, Republic, gold 100-schillings, 1926. 64,000 were struck. Gold coins such as this did not circulate.

993 The modern Republic of Austria has issued a great many commemorative coins in recent years, this two-schillings of 1928, struck on the centenary of the composer Franz Schubert's death, was the first.

994 The temporal authority of Bishoprics such as Gurk, together with their right to strike coins, entirely disappeared in Germany and Austria in the early years of the nineteenth-century. Austria, Bishopric of Gurk, silver thaler, 1801, issued by Count von Salm-Reifferschleid.

995 The Kingdom of Westphalia, comprising much of Hesse-Cassel, Brunswick and eventually a considerable part of Hanover, was created in 1807 and Jerome, Napoleon's youngest brother, was placed on the throne. The monetary system was originally on the French model but opposition forced a reversion to the traditional German systems. Silver 5-franken, 1808.

991

992

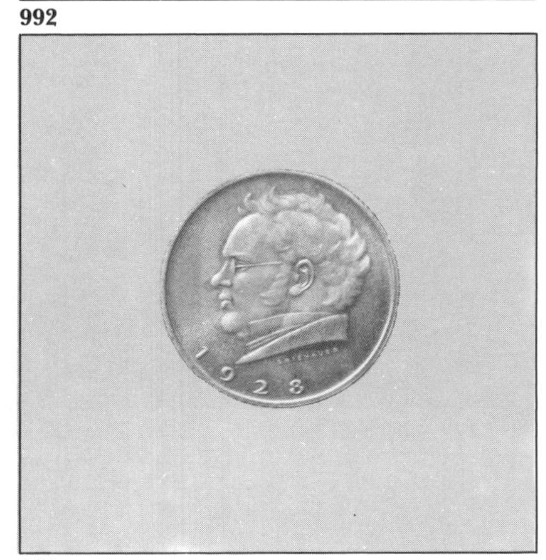

993

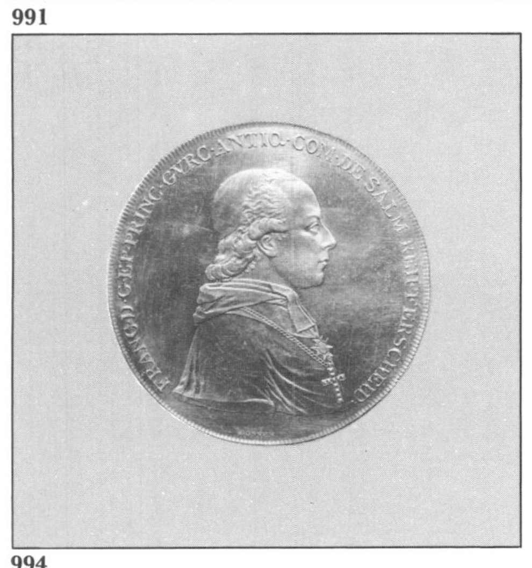
994

995

996

997

998

999

996 Hanover is the modern name for the former electorate of Brunswick-Luneberg. In 1714 the Elector George became King of England and the two states had a common ruler until 1837. This thaler of 1830 was struck with silver from the Clausthal mines.

997 Hanover, William IV of Great Britain, silver ⅔-thaler, 1834.

998 The kronenthaler, based on a standard of 9·08 to the fine mark, originated in the Austrian Netherlands in the eighteenth century and was struck mainly by the states of South Germany. Baden, silver kronenthaler, 1832.

999 Ludwig I of Bavaria struck a considerable number of commemorative thalers and double-thalers based, curiously enough, on the now defunct standard of the conventional thaler of the eighteenth century. This example, issued in 1832, commemorates the choice of Prince Otto of Bavaria as the first King of Greece.

1000 Bavaria, two-thaler, 1839, commemorating the erection of a statue of Maximilian, first Elector of Bavaria.

1001 Frankfurt, one of four Free Cities in Germany, was annexed by Prussia in 1866. Monetary conventions in 1837 and 1838 established the gulden as the unit of account, coined on the basis of 24½ to the fine mark, in many German states. Frankfurt, gulden, 1838.

1002 Frankfurt, silver two-thalers, 1866.

1003 Many German subsidiary coins were struck in base silver. Frankfurt, billon six-kreuzer, 1853.

1004 Until the adoption of the gold standard in 1871 German gold coins were struck for international trade. Hamburg, gold ducat, 1867.

1005 Prussia, silver two-thalers, 1840.

1000

1006 A bewildering variety of states existed in Germany in the nineteenth-century and coins were struck according to several different monetary systems. Conventions in 1838 and 1857 created a degree of unity; this two-thalers of Saxony, dated 1858, was struck on the basis of the system established in 1857.

1007 Saxony, thaler, 1871. Germany has a long tradition of commemorative coins, this piece was struck to celebrate the Prussian victory over France in 1871.

1008 In 1871 the German Empire, comprising 25 states, was created and the gold standard replaced that of silver, with the mark as the unit of account. Gold and large-size silver coins continued to be struck by the states of the Empire, this gold 20-marks was struck by Anhalt, a Duchy in central Germany.

1009 Karl Goetz, one of the most famous of twentieth-century medallists, designed and struck this pattern three-marks for Bavaria.

1010 Prussia, William II, gold 20-marks, 1896.

1001

1002

1003×2

1004×2

1005×2

1006×2

1007

1008×2

1009

1010×2

1030 Belgium, silver medal, 1880, commemorating the 50th anniversary of the Kingdom. This piece is of the same weight as the 5-francs, but it has no mark of value and is usually considered to be a medal. It was also struck in copper and gold.

1031 The Congo was not annexed to Belgium until 1908 but was ruled directly, and with much cruelty, by Leopold II. Congo Free State, silver two-francs, 1887.

1032 During both World Wars the war effort demanded the use of iron and zinc for coinage in Germany-occupied countries such as Belgium. Belgium, 25-centimes, 1918.

1033 Silver 50-francs, 1958, struck for the Brussels Fair. For many years Belgium has struck coins with legends in Flemish as well as French.

1034 France, Napoleon as First Consul of the Republic, silver five-francs, 1803.

1035 France, Napoleon, gold five-francs, 1807; a silver denomination struck in gold almost certainly for presentation purposes.

1036 A rare essay struck at Paris in 1815 and designed by Pierre Joseph Tiolier. Louis XVIII, silver five-francs, 1815.

1030

1031×2

1032×2

1035

1033×2

1034

1037 Struck in 1848, the first year of the Second Republic, the design seen on this French five-francs was first used during the First Republic.

1038 In 1849 France issued coins showing the head of Ceres, Goddess of the Earth and protectress of Agriculture. France, five-francs, 1849; designed by Oudine, the winner of a competition organized the previous year to choose a design for the new national coinage.

1039 France, Napoleon IV, five-francs, dated 1874, a privately issued souvenir, struck at Chaux-de-Fonds in Switzerland.

1040 One of the best known representations of the French Republic, 'la Semeuse' appears on this two-francs of 1902; it was the work of the eminent French medallist Louis Oscar Roty.

1041 France, an officially sanctioned token in aluminium-bronze struck by the chambers of commerce.

1042 Something of the spirit of 'la Belle Epoque' is expressed by this essay struck in 1897 and designed by Louis Eugene Mouchon, a celebrated French medallist.

1043 'Genius writing the Constitution', a design that first appeared on French coins at the end of the eighteenth century, is seen on this gold 20-francs of 1874. The coin had the same weight and fineness as the 20-francs of Napoleon I.

1044 France, cupro-nickel 100-francs, 1954; before the Second World War this denomination had been struck in gold, an example of the ravages of inflation. These coins were replaced in 1960 by the so-called 'heavy' francs.

1045 Algeria, Constantine, aluminium 10-centimes, 1922; one of a large variety of tokens issued after the First World War due to the shortage of legal tender coinage. These pieces appeared both in France and her colonial possessions.

1036

1037

1038

1039

1040

1041

1042

1043×2

1044

1045

Bi-metallism came under pressure in the middle years of the
1098 century. Important discoveries of gold in California in 1848 and Australia in 1851 upset the balance between the two metals; the commercial ratio of their value was transformed, and the bi-metallic states experienced an increasing substitution of gold for silver in their monetary systems. It has been estimated that as many as 500 million silver 5-francs were exported from France between 1848 and 1860; remarkably, they continued to be struck at Paris, and sometimes Strasbourg, but in such small numbers that the impression is given that this was largely a symbolic gesture and it became necessary to strike tiny gold 5-francs. Efforts to stabilize the situation of France, Belgium, Switzerland and Italy, already in de facto currency union, led to the formation in 1865 of the Latin Union. The bi-metallic system was maintained by the contracting states, under pressure from the French. However, only the silver 5-francs remained unlimited legal tender, retaining a fineness of 0·900; the smaller divisional coins came under effective government control – they were reduced to 0·835 fine, legal tender to 50 francs, and the numbers issued strictly proportional to population levels. The free coining of gold and silver continued and each state agreed to receive into their respective treasuries unlimited quantities of gold coins and silver 5-francs struck under the terms of the convention by any of the contracting parties.

The principle of bi-metallism, despite the proven disadvantages, seemed secure. Greece became a member of the Latin Union in 1867. In the following year, although never adhering to
the convention, the Spanish government introduced an identical 1097
monetary system with the peseta, divided into 100 centimos, as
the unit; as did Romania, with the *leu* as the coin of account. 1081
Serbia and Bulgaria followed suit in 1878 and 1880, but by this time the falling commercial price of silver was unbalancing the system as effectively as the previous rise in value. Within a few years of the formation of the Latin Union the contracting states closed the doors to the reception of privately owned silver and suspended the coining of the 5-francs. Spain adopted a similar policy and ceased to accept silver on individual account in 1878, though the 5-pesetas retained its full legal tender status and continued to be struck in large numbers until the turn of the century.

The decline in the importance of silver as a monetary medium was paralleled by the rise of gold; and, as the nineteenth century drew to a close, the latter, stimulated further by the new discoveries of the metal in the Yukon and South Africa, was

1046 French Union, Madagascar, aluminium two-francs, 1948.

1047 Tunisia adopted the monetary system of France in 1891. Gold 20-francs, 1909.

1048 The Comoro Islands, in the Indian Ocean, came under French protection in 1886. A small issue of silver and bronze coins were struck in 1890. The islands were later joined administratively with Madagascar.

1049 The invasion of Switzerland by French armies in 1797 led to the creation of a centralized state with a single monetary system. Helvetian Republic, silver 4-franken, 1799, struck at Bern.

1050 Until the adoption of a new federal constitution in 1848 the Swiss cantons were virtually independent states with the right to strike coins. Appenzell, silver four-franken, 1816.

1051 Geneva, silver five-francs, 1848.

1052 In 1850 Switzerland adopted the monetary system of France. Five-francs, 1850.

1053 Switzerland, gold 20-francs, 1894.

1054 Switzerland, five-francs, 1925; the portrait is of William Tell.

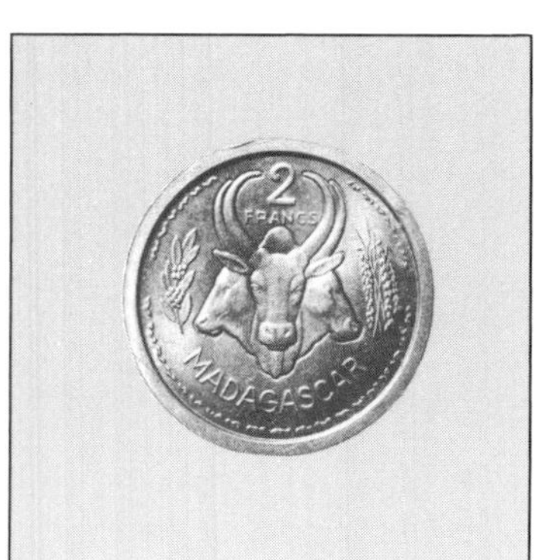

1046

1047×2

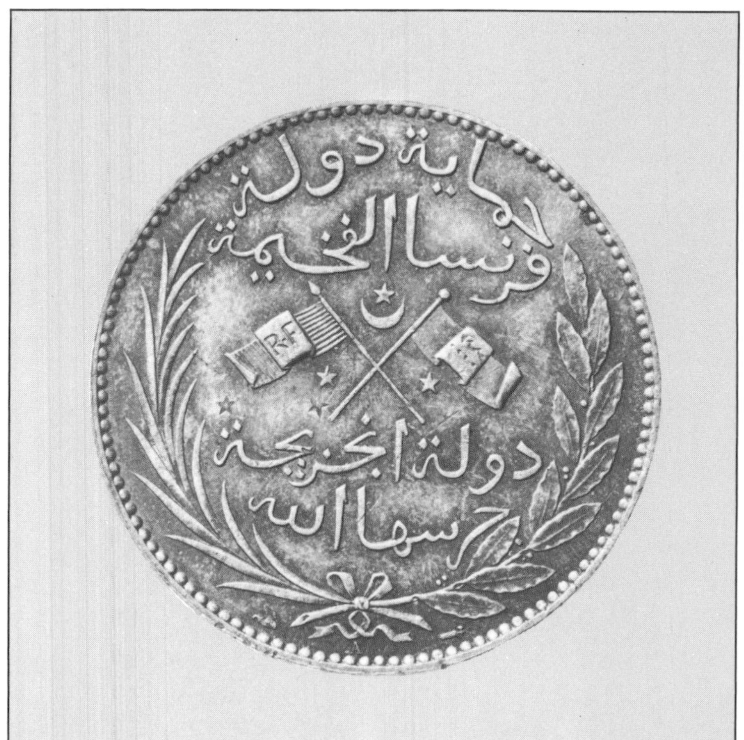
1048×2

1049×2

1050A

1050B

1051

1052

1054×2

1053A×2 1053B×2

1055 The issue of large silver coins to commemorate various Federal Shooting Festivals is a distinctive feature of the modern coinage of Switzerland. Five-francs, 1881, Fribourg Shooting Festival.

1056 Switzerland, silver two-francs, 1959. Switzerland struck silver coins until 1967; this design first appeared in 1874.

1057 The Republic of Italy was created in 1802, with Napoleon as President; in 1805 it was dissolved and became the Kingdom of Italy. The fine head of Napoleon seen here is reminiscent of the portraiture found on some Roman coins; the coin is extremely rare and is probably a pattern. Republic of Italy, gold doppia, year two (1805).

1058 The Cisalpine Republic was founded in 1797 by Napoleon but was dissolved in 1799, after the capture of Milan and Mantua by the Austro-Russian army. Napoleon restored it in 1800. This coin, a silver 30-soldi of the year nine (1801) commemorates the Peace of Luneville and the independence of the Republic.

1059 The Subalpine Republic was formed in 1800 after the Battle of Marengo. This gold 20-francs commemorates the French victory.

1055×2

1056

1057

1058

1059×2

struck in increasing quantities. In 1854 Portugal followed the example of her old ally, England, and adopted the gold standard–even legalizing the circulation of British sovereigns. The newly united German Empire, a rapidly growing military
1008 and industrial power, also adopted gold in 1871 and created a decimal coinage on the basis of the mark; silver was abandoned by Sweden, Norway and Denmark when between 1873 and 1875
954 the Scandinavian Monetary Union was formed to establish a common currency with the *krone* as the unit. Even beyond
1153 Europe gold was gaining ascendance, in North and South America and also in areas where silver alone traditionally held sway, and countries such as Japan and India embraced the gold standard in 1879 and 1899 in imitation of the European nations.

The supremacy of gold coinage was not to last. In reality it had largely been replaced by paper and, inevitably doomed perhaps for economic reasons, was dealt a mortal blow by the First World War. Within weeks of the outbreak of hostilities the convertibility of paper was suspended by the belligerent powers–an example followed, as the war proceeded, by most of the neutral nations–and gold ceased to circulate as currency. A return to the gold standard in the nineteen twenties did not greatly alter the situation. In Great Britain it was possible to convert paper to gold, but not to sovereigns, only bars with a minimum value of about £1700–a figure that few could afford and pointless with its export prohibited. Some states, on the other hand, adopted the gold exchange standard and convertibility of notes was not to coin but the paper currency of some other country maintaining the gold standard.

Gold coins have been struck since 1914–including a number
47 produced during the temporary restoration of the gold standard–and indeed they continue to appear. Many are strictly commemorative or token issues serving no more than a symbolic function; a few are merely medals in disguise, aimed cynically at a collectors' market. Other issues, among them the sovereigns of Elizabeth II and the Austrian restrikes of earlier imperial coins, are simply bullion in a convenient form. There is a sense, it could be argued, in which gold coins such as the sovereign or the Swiss 20-francs have never entirely ceased to be money; but in practice they have ceased to function as coinage in any traditional sense.

Coinage has, without question, a reduced role to play in today's world, its place usurped not only by paper money, but increasingly with the growth of banking, by such mechanisms as
the cheque and the credit card. Nevertheless, the demand for 1182
some means of exchange for minor transactions has not diminished; quite the reverse. In the largely rural and often isolated communities of the pre-industrial age the need for coinage, though existing, was far less than in the rapidly expanding towns and cities of nineteenth century Europe; barter survived in Iceland even as late as 1900. For a variety of reasons shortages of small change have occurred from time to time: in Germany, during and immediately after the First World War, and recently in Spain, following the death of Franco. Situations such as these are exceptional and advances in mint technology since the eighteenth century have provided the means to produce coins of uniform weight and fabric at a speed and on a scale unknown to generations living before the Industrial Revolution. Between 1861 and 1867 Italy produced nearly 1000 million bronze coins, while the annual output of the London Mint stood at 145 millions in 1900 and as high as 652 millions in 1943.

The improvements in minting techniques that made these achievements possible were pioneered in the eighteenth century
by a Birmingham manufacturer, Matthew Boulton, and the 936
Scottish engineer James Watt. Boulton, an entrepreneur of genius with a commendable passion for excellence as well as efficiency, constructed in 1786 at his Soho works a number of coin presses using steam power. Coining machinery powered by steam was exported to Russia in 1799, which became the first state to own such equipment, and subsequently to Denmark and Spain. In 1797 Boulton was given the important contract to strike the British copper coinage, and in 1810 the machinery he

1060 Cisalpine Republic, silver scudo, year eight (1800). The two figures represent France and Italy and the coin celebrates Napoleon's victory at Marengo; it is a good example of the influence of neo-classicism on the coins of the period.

1061 In 1797 Napoleon used the internal struggles of the Republic of Genoa to introduce a provisional government and in 1798 formed the Ligurian Republic. This gold 96-lire of 1805 was the last coin struck before the republic became part of Napoleon's Kingdom of Italy.

1062 Lombardy, Provisional Government, gold 40-lire, struck at Milan in 1848 during the popular uprising of that year against Austrian rule.

1063 Lombardy and Venetia, Ferdinand I of Austria, silver scudo, 1840, struck at Venice.

1064 Lucca, silver lira, 1838.

1060

1061A

1061B

1062×2

1063

1064×2

1065×2

1066

1067

1065 Eliza Bonaparte, eldest sister of Napoleon, and her husband Captain Felix Baciocchi ruled the principality of Lucca and Piombino when this copper five-centesimi of 1806 was struck.

1066 Joachim Murat was made King of Naples by Napoleon, he was the most loved of all the kings that the French Emperor imposed on the European states. Naples and Sicily, silver 12-carlini, 1810.

1067 The monetary system of Sardinia was identical to that of France at this time. Sardinia, silver five-lire, 1820.

1068 The papacy lost its sovereignty in 1870 and, of course, the right to strike coins; this piece is no more than an interesting privately struck memento. Papal States, Leo XIII, silver five-lire, 1878.

1069 This is a large gold coin of the Latin Monetary Union formed with France, Switzerland and Belgium some years earlier. Italy, 100-lire, 1880.

1070 Italy, silver five-lire, 1861, struck in the year that Italy became united.

1071 Italy, silver 20-lire, 1928, to commemorate the tenth anniversary of the end of the First World War.

1072 Eritrea, now a province of Ethiopia, was an Italian colony from 1890 until 1936 when it became part of Italian East Africa. This silver five-lire was struck in 1891.

1073 The small mountain kingdom of Montenegro became part of Yugoslavia after the First World War. Prince Nicholas I, gold 100-perpera, struck in 1910, which was the year Nicholas became king.

1074 Serbia, now an autonomous republic within Yugoslavia, achieved full independence in 1887 after years of Turkish domination. Cupro-nickel 10-para, 1884, struck while the country was still under suzerainty of Turkey.

1068

1075 After the First World War the issue of gold coins was largely a symbolic gesture. Yugoslavia, Alexander I, gold 20-dinara, 1925.

1076 A typical modern coin of Eastern Europe. Socialist Federal Republic of Yugoslavia, aluminium-bronze 10-dinara, 1955.

1077 Albania became a modern nation state in 1912, and many of her coins clearly show the influence of those of Ancient Greece, such as this fine design, by the Italian artist Romagli. Two-franka ari, 1926, struck at Rome.

1078 A large and impressive gold coin, typical of the period. Bulgaria, Ferdinand I as Prince, 100-leva, 1894.

1079 Before the last war fashionable artistic trends rarely influenced coin design. This Bulgarian silver 50-leva of 1934, in the 'Art Deco' manner, is an exception.

1080 This commemorative differs little from countless similar coins issued in the last decade. Bulgaria silver five-leva, 1970, honouring Ivan Vasov.

1069A  **1069B**  **1071A**  **1071B**

1070  **1072A**  **1072B**  **1073**

1074×2  **1075×2**  **1076×2** 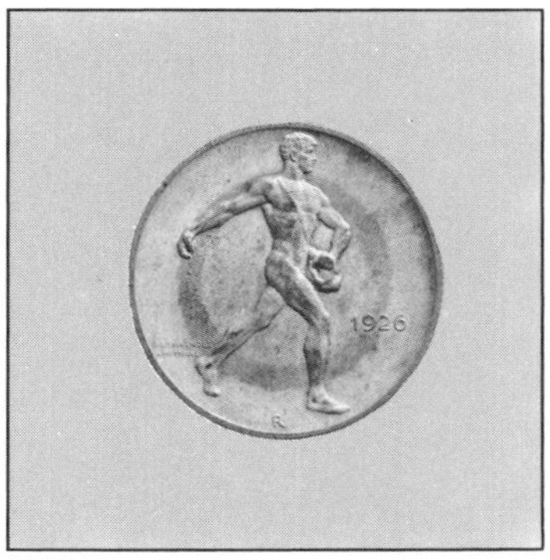 **1077A**

1078  **1079**  **1080**  **1077B**

1081 Romania, the ancient Roman province of Dacia, adopted the monetary system of the Latin Union in the second half of the nineteenth century. This gold 20-lei had the same weight and fineness as similar coins of France, Belgium, Italy and Switzerland; it was struck in 1890.

1082 Although struck in rather shallow relief, this charming study of Queen Marie of Romania in her coronation robes is a good example of better twentieth century coin portraiture. Romania, Ferdinand I, 50-lei, 1922, coronation issue.

1083 Greece, copper 10-lepta, 1828, struck shortly after the achievement of independence.

1084 Greece, Otto, silver five-drachmae, 1833.

1085 Greece, silver 20-drachmae, 1930. An ancient Greek coin served as a model for the designs seen here.

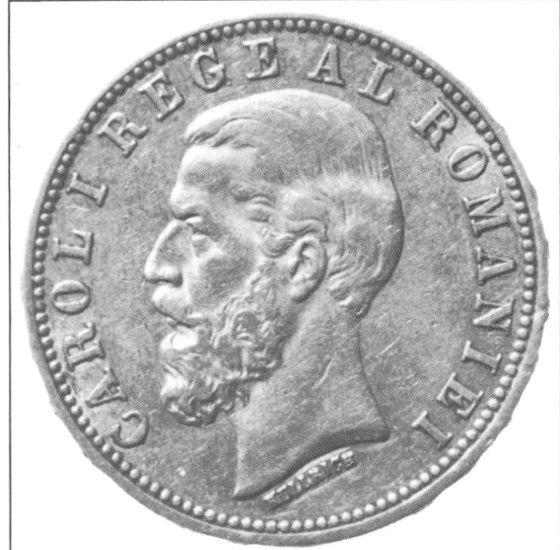

1081×3

1082×3

1083

1084×3

1085A×2

1085B×2

1086 Greece, copper-nickel five-drachmae, 1971.

1087 The Ionian islands were ruled jointly by Russia and Turkey when this copper coin was issued. Ionian Islands, copper one-tazeta, 1801.

1088 Crete, silver five-drachmae, 1901.

1089 Cyprus, Victoria, 18-piastres, 1901.

1090 The resemblance between this portrait and that seen on contemporary French coins is remarkable. Spain, Joseph Napoleon, gold 320-reales, struck at Madrid.

1091 Barcelona, silver five-pesetas, 1813, struck during the French occupation.

1092 Crude coins, simple pieces of stamped silver more or less circular, were issued at Gerona during the War of Independence. Gerona, Ferdinand VII, duro, 1808.

1093 Disorder in Spain following the adoption of a liberal constitution in 1820 led to the intervention of the French in 1825 when this coin was struck; the legend reads 'Valencia besieged by the enemies of Liberty.' Spain, Valencia, four-reales, 1823.

1086A×2

1086B×2

1087×2

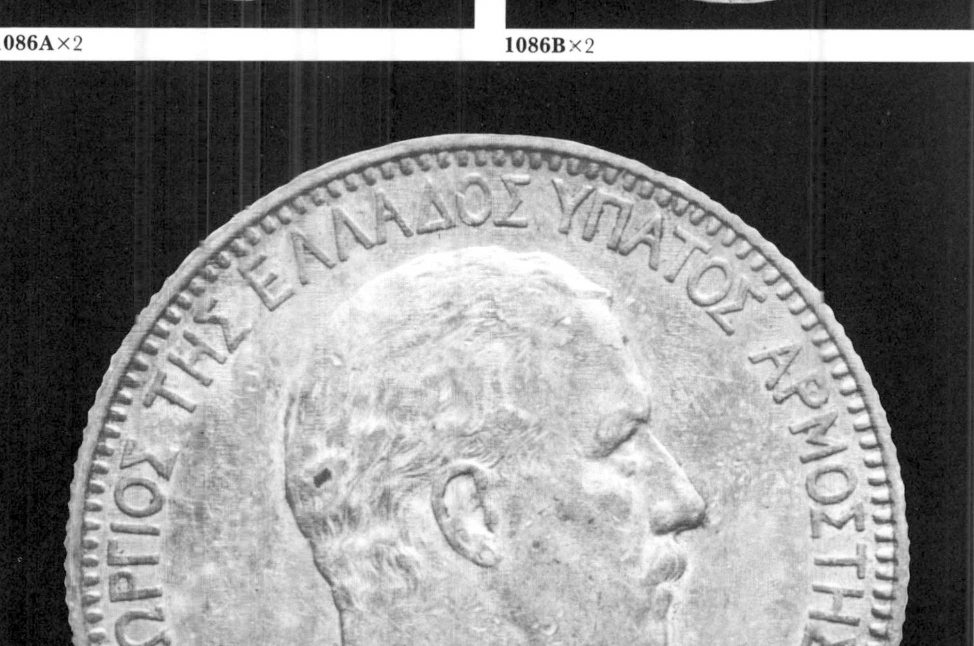

1089×[illegible]

1088×3

1090

1091

1092

1093×[illegible]

1094 Spain, Isabel II, silver 20-reales, 1850, Madrid mint.

1095 Struck during a widespread revolt against central government, this coin, struck during the siege of Cartagena, reminds us of the strength of regionalism in Spain. Spain, Cartagena, five-pesetas, 1873.

1096 This coin, struck in the name of the Carlist claimant to the Spanish throne, was a private and unauthorized issue. Spain, Charles VII, five-pesetas, 1874.

1097 Spain adopted the monetary system of France in 1868, but never formally adhered to the Latin Monetary Union. Alfonso XIII, gold 20-pesetas.

1094×2

1095×2

1096×2

1097×2

perfected was installed at the Royal Mint in London, duplicating almost exactly that existing at the Soho works, Birmingham.

The output of the Soho mint included copper coinages for Bermuda and the Bahamas, a variety of issues struck on behalf of the East India Company, and a beautiful series of denominations for the Sierra Leone Company's colony for freed slaves in West Africa. Boulton's machinery in the Royal Mint was used to strike the entire British regal coinage of the last years of George III. Boulton had the perception to employ two engravers of considerable skill, for a short time a Frenchman, Jean Pierre Droz–who was later to become General Administrator of the Coins and Medals of France and keeper of the Mint Museum in Paris–and later Konrad Heinrich Kuchler, a native of Flanders; and the Royal Mint had the good fortune to have the services of a
masterful artist, Benedetto Pistrucci. The coinages produced 938
with the new presses were not only technically superior to issues prevailing elsewhere, including the contemporary coins of France where innovations in minting had also taken place, but in many cases are of a delicacy of detail and loveliness of design that puts to shame many of the humdrum issues of our century.

Boulton's machinery was in operation at the British Royal Mint until 1882. By this date, however, coin presses developed

1098 Extensive discoveries of gold were made in Australia in the middle of the nineteenth century. The low price the miners obtained for their gold led to the striking of these private gold coins, with an indication of their weight on the reverse; by the time they were struck the banks were offering a fairer price to the miners and only very few were produced. Port Phillip, gold one-ounce, 1853.

1098

earlier in the century by the German engineer Diedrich Ulrich were in more general use. A heavy fly wheel squeezed the upper die down on the blank, instead of a blow with a hammer, and they were considered quieter and less burdensome on the dies than Boulton's models. The new press was first exhibited at the Dusseldorf Diplomatic Congress of 1820, and by 1876 200 had been sold. In 1845 the mint at Paris installed one, with some modifications, and several were later acquired by London.

In countless ways minting processes have progressed since the revolutionary use of steam by Matthew Boulton: automatic machines for weighing and counting coins have been developed; techniques for the testings of alloys have been brought practically to perfection; and the reducing machine–which makes possible the rapid reproduction of dies from an original plaster model of large size–has long been in general use.

Although the last two centuries have witnessed considerable improvement in the manufacture of coins and an almost bewildering variety of issues, this has not been matched, regrettably, by consistent excellence in design, and even innovation has been fitful. The interpretation of Britannia found in the 944
current 50-pence of the United Kingdom differs little from that 936
seen on the copper coins of the early nineteenth century. The

1099 Spain, Isabel II, four-pesetas, 1894; privately struck in London for an English collector Reginald Huth and one of a series of 13 similar pieces.

1100 Spain, peseta, 1933, the only denomination struck in silver by the Second Republic.

1101 Spain, copper-nickel 25-pesetas. Dated 1957, the year the issue was authorized, this coin was struck in 1959; the true date is found on the reverse in a small star.

1102 Spain, Juan Carlos, copper-nickel 5-pesetas, 1975.

1103 John Prince Regent, later to become King John VI of Portugal, struck this gold pesa of 1808 in Rio de Janeiro; these coins circulated in Brazil and Portugal.

1104 Portugal, gold pesa, 1826. The pesa was equivalent to 6400-reis, but Pedro IV revaluated it to 7500-reis when he came to the throne.

1099

1100×2

1101×2

1103×3

1102×2

1105

1104A×2

1104B×2

1106×2

1105 Portugal, Carlos I, silver 1000-reis, struck in 1898 to commemorate the four hundredth anniversary of the discovery of India.

1106 Portugal, silver 10-escudos, 1932.

1107 Terceira is one of the nine isles that form the Azores Archipelago, discovered by the Portuguese navigator Diego de Silves in 1427. Terceira served as base for Dom Pedro of Brazil during his campaign against the tyrant Dom Miguel of Portugal. In 1828 Dom Pedro declined the throne in favour of his daughter Maria. This brass 80-reis was struck in 1829 when she was living in exile in the island. Maria was proclaimed Queen of Portugal in 1834.

1108 The People's Republic of Angola was a Portuguese colony until 1975; discovered in 1482 by Diego Cao, Angola was a major centre of the slave trade. Nickel-brass 50-centavos, 1928.

1109 It was not until 1873 that the first real banking facilities were established in South Africa; in the following year a small issue of gold ponds, made legal tender at the same value as the British sovereign, were coined from gold mined at Lydenfields. However, it was not until some years later that a full range of coins were issued by the South African Republic. South African Republic President Burgers, pond, 1874.

1110 Ethiopia, silver tallero, based on the Austrian thaler of Maria Theresa, the accepted trade coin of the region. The modern coinage of the country, struck at Paris, was first produced in 1894 for the Emperor Menelik II.

1111 Katanga, a province in the mineral-rich south of the Congo, broke away from the rest of the country in 1961 and maintained a precarious independence for two and a half years. This five-francs was struck at the time.

1112 A large number of copper tokens were issued in Australia in the nineteenth century to alleviate the shortage of small change. Penny, Stewart and Hemmant, drapers of Brisbane.

1113 A distinctive national Australian coinage was not produced until 1910. Florin, 1910.

1114 Australia adopted the decimal system in 1966; 50-cents, 1970, commemorating the two hundredth Anniversary of the arrival of Captain Cook.

1107

1108

1109×2

1110A

1110B

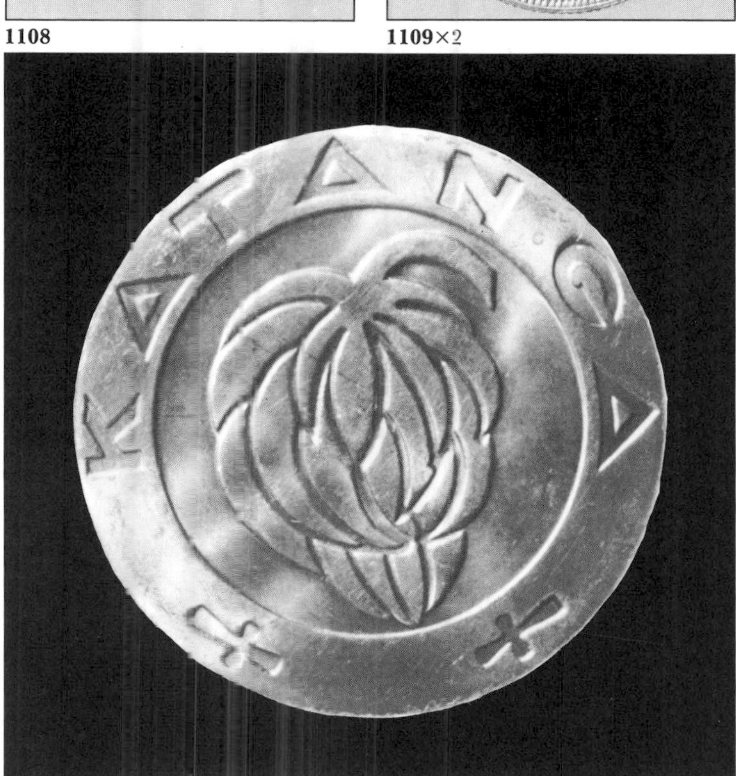

1111×3

1112

1113

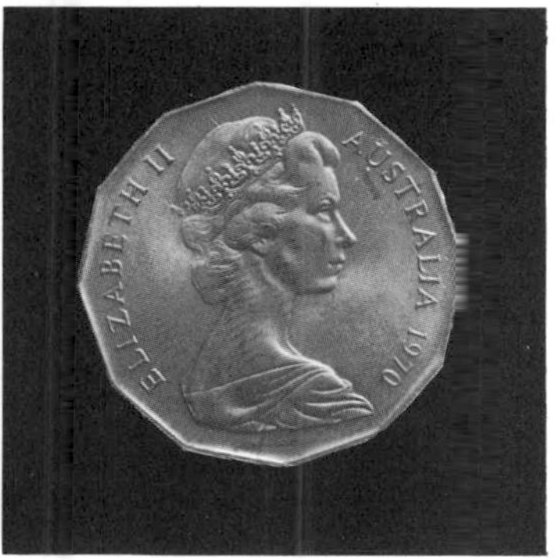

1114A

1114B

German mark of the present day remains the drab coin it was during the German Empire and in France, a country where change and some notice of artistic currents might have been expected, a similar reluctance to break with tradition prevails. Coins are both utilitarian and symbols of authority and there are political as well as practical reasons why changes in their visual appearance should be slow to take place. Where innovation in design has occurred, it has not always been entirely successful, and it could be argued that the clichés of modernism are no more appealing than empty patriotic symbolism. Certainly the mass-produced coinage of our day seems to please no one and has been much criticized, to a great extent justifiably; none the less it should not be forgotten that a coin struck in cupro-nickel, for example, will never possess the same dignity as one struck in silver; nor that a medieval penny has an appeal, enhanced by age, quite unrelated to artistic merit.

The final judgment on the coinage now produced, including the modern commemoratives, is best left to prosterity. However, it can safely be said that the last two centuries have seen a number of issues of considerable charm, and not a few of real distinction, whether inspired by classical prototypes, like many of the coins of Italy and Greece, or in a much more contemporary idiom. 1085

AQUE V
PLUS
1732

XIV

THE WESTERN HEMISPHERE

T. V. Buttrey

None of the peoples of the Western Hemisphere knew the use of coinage before the appearance of the European explorers and colonists. Trade was carried on either by direct barter, or through the medium of natural products or manufactures, such as wampum (threaded beads) in North America, cocoa beans in Mexico, and cloth in South America. The European colonists needed coinage for their own internal trade, and for dealings with the mother country; and, in the event, to control trade with the natives who were compelled to deal in a medium to which they had no easy access. In this the Spanish of Mexico and Peru were especially fortunate, for they settled areas rich in silver and gold, whereas the British and French in North America found no precious metal sources to speak of, and the Portuguese in Brazil were no better off until the very end of the seventeenth century.

The Spanish American colonies produced a variety of coinages of good quality and in large quantity partly for their own use, partly as a convenient form in which to export bullion to Spain in payment of taxes and duties, or to the Far East in exchange for the exotic goods which Mexico transshipped to Europe. So plentiful and convenient were these coinages that they became current even in the non-Spanish parts of the two continents of the New World, and formed the historical foundations of most of the coinages still in use there today.

The Spanish American coinage, first struck at Mexico City in 1535, was based on the silver *real*, struck ultimately in denomina-
1115 tions of eight reales – the dollar size 'Piece of Eight' – 4, 2, 1, ½, and ¼. Its fineness was expressed in a pre-decimal system in which pure silver was of 12 dineros, each divided into 24 granos. Until 1772 the colonial real was 11 dineros fine, or 916·6 thousands; after that date, 10 dineros 20 granos or 902·7 thousands fine.

The gold *escudo* was, after the early eighteenth century, struck to the same weights as the silver and the same system of multiples, but from an alloy of 21 carats, equivalent to 875 thousands fine. Since one escudo was worth 16 reales, the coinage was bimetallic and the ratio between gold and silver defined theoretically as 16·5:1.

To maintain the quality of the coinage, its definition was fixed for all the colonial mints alike by Spanish law, and the types tended to conservative repetition from mint to mint and over the years. It is rather in fabric that the series of colonial coinages are distinguished. The earliest silver was struck on thin round flans, without a collar, so that it still has a faintly medieval aspect. After the middle of the sixteenth century larger denominations were more frequently struck, on thicker flans. But these *macu-*
1116 *quinas* or 'cobs' were simply cut from cast sheets or cylinders, so that they were highly irregular in shape, their outlines did not correspond to the dies, and the uneven thickness of the planchet often made full striking impossible. These singularly ill-made and unattractive pieces were for almost 200 years the monetary expression of the gold and silver riches of the Indies. It was only in 1732 that a new and impressive type, that of the pillar dollar, 1117
neatly struck on a round and regular flan, provided a handsome silver coinage which issued from several mints for 40 years and circulated around the world. These, and the bust type eight reales which followed until 1825, were struck in enormous 1118
quantities. They were to be the model not only for the pesos of the Spanish American republics, but for the U.S. silver dollar.

The end of Spanish domination in Mexico, Central America and South America had no immediate effect on the single monetary system which had operated throughout this enormous 1122
area. On the contrary, the major mints continued to strike for the various independent nations within which they were now located. The Spanish types, however, had to be changed or modified to accord with the new political realities, so that republican types were imposed on what had recently been an 1128
imperial coinage. In some cases a new coat of arms replaced the portrait of the Spanish king; in others the Liberator, or the 1133
President of the republic (the invariable title, although their powers ranged from the benignly constitutional to the dictatorial). The republican mints also began by maintaining the Spanish monetary system based on the real and escudo. Theoretically, therefore, the coinages of the new nations could have been interchanged freely from the Rio Grande in the north to the tip of South America, and to a limited extent were. But this happy state of affairs could not last. Political fragmentation led to economic and monetary individualism, so that even where such movements of coin were not officially discouraged, the national coinages soon differed so greatly one from another as to make easy interchange impossible. Thus by the end of the nineteenth century Mexico still maintained the Spanish weights, fineness and to an extent denominations, and thus guaranteed the acceptability of its eight reales in the Far East. But the silver coinage of Chile had been debased from the Spanish 902·7 thousands fine to 500 thousands; that of Venezuela had been converted to the standard of the Latin Monetary Union; while ultimately several nations of Central America and the Caribbean accommodated their coins to the system of the U.S., whose coins 1132
circulated commonly in those areas. The coinages of several nations without mints were usually small, and the bulk of their circulation was provided by the coins of colonial and republican

The Pillars of Hercules on a Spanish 'dollar' from Mexico, 1732 (**1117**).

export for use elsewhere. Dozens of varieties of the cut and counterstamped coinages are known. Although the major source was the Spanish American eight reales or fractions of pillar or bust type, examples are also known made from French écus, Brazilian gold, and U.S. silver and bronze of all denominations. By the end of the nineteenth century most of these had passed from circulation, and the colonies severally used coinages largely based on the European with a strong admixture of Mexican and U.S., although the U.S. possessions in the West Indies (Puerto Rico, Virgin Islands) have never had their own coinages under that administration. Since the Second World War the newly independent nations which were formerly British or Dutch

tokens. After the colonies gained their independence in 1783 the half-pennies were taken as the model for coinages in copper struck in the names of several of the new states. There was no national mint, nor any facility for coining in silver or gold. But 1147
after the acceptance of the Constitution of the United States in 1787, in which coinage was reserved to the new federal government, a mint was established in Philadelphia, then the 1148
capital city of the nation. From 1793 onwards a fairly regular coinage appeared in the name of the United States.

Three characteristics of the earlier U.S. coinage are to be noted. First, the size of issues was often small and never

1115 One of the earliest coins of the Americas, struck at Mexico City in the name of (but slightly later than) the Spanish monarchs Charles and Johanna (1516-55). The obverse type is the royal arms with figures of lion and castle (León and Castille), appropriate specifically to Spain, but the reverse type of the Pillars of Hercules and the legend PLVS VLTR(A), 'More beyond', indicates the extension of Spanish sovereignty to the New World.

1116 The misshapen macuquina or 'cob' coinage was presumably produced because the Spanish colonial mints were unable to cope with the quantities of gold and silver extracted from the mines of Mexico and South America. Gold eight-escudos, Lima, Peru, 1713.

1117 Although the type of the Pillars of Hercules had been in use almost 200 years before its appearance here, the well-struck eight reales with the two hemispheres of the Old and New Worlds have come particularly to be called pillar dollars. Identical types were used for the smaller denominations of four, two, one and half reales. Mexico City, 1732.

THE WESTERN HEMISPHERE

1119 Although the silver coins of the Spanish American mints were struck in large quantities and used literally throughout the world (**1448**), the gold coinage was not insignificant. The portrait of the Spanish king first appeared on the gold coinage, and was often more finely engraved than ever it was on the silver.

1120 The Spanish colonial mints, like those of Spain itself, also struck proclamation medals, celebratory pieces produced in small quantities on memorable occasions such as the accession of a new king. Although not regular coin issues, many were struck on coin flans and even provided with marks of value. Their frequently worn condition shows that they did circulate as money. Minted in Mexico, 1789.

1121 During the several wars of independence, which often made transportation and communication very hazardous, the Spanish authorities were forced to open branch mints whose products were occasionally rather crude. The revolutionaries struck their own coins or countermarked those of the official regime.

1119

adequate to provide for public need. As a consequence foreign coin continued to circulate widely until 1857. Second, while in intrinsic value the new coinage was deliberately based on the Spanish American coinage rather than the British, in denomination it was decimal, the first fully decimal coinage ever struck, with denominations ranging from the copper ½ and 1 cent, through silver of 5 cents to the dollar of 100 cents, and gold from
1153 1 dollar (ultimately) to 20 dollars. Still, the reality was that the Spanish American coin continued to form the bulk of the silver circulation, a fact which is reflected in the regular appearance of prices of 3 cents and 6 or 6½ cents, the decimal equivalents of the ½ real and 1 real. Third, the typology of the U.S. coinage was extremely limited: until the middle of the nineteenth century all coins of whatever metal and denomination bore two of only three authorized types, namely Liberty (bust or figure), eagle, value in wreath; and even thereafter change was very slow to come. As an extreme example, the reverse type of the quarter dollar was the figure of an eagle from the first issue in 1796 until a new type appeared in 1976 to celebrate the Bicentennial of Independence.

In all these respects, however, the coinage of the U.S. is now much changed. After the Civil War there was an enormous expansion of the coinage, caused by the economic growth of the nation, the opening of the west, and the discovery of quantities of gold and silver in the west. New mints were opened to handle the enlarged coinage, which has served internal circulation almost entirely. While some U.S. coins have regularly circulated in the border areas of Mexico and Canada, and in the West Indies, the coinage has never been intended for export (as for example that of Mexico was over several centuries). The monetary system remains unaltered from that which developed in the nineteenth

1122 In Mexico as elsewhere a republican type was introduced in 1823, the eagle holding a snake and perched on a nopal cactus, a type which, with great conservatism, was used on all denominations in all metals and which has endured to our own day with various changes of style. Ultimately 14 different Mexican mints struck these issues, all maintaining identical types, but indicating the specific authority by including the mintmarks and assayer's initials.

1123 The French intervention of 1861 brought the Austrian Archduke Maximilian to an artificial throne as the Emperor of Mexico (1864-67). His coins were ostentatiously European in manner: struck not to the real but to the decimal system of 1 peso = 100 centavos; with reeded edge where the Mexican republican coins had a dotted semicircle pattern; and with portrait and arms types in imitation of the coins of Napoleon III, who had supported Maximilian.

1124 Mexico experimented with another reeded edge peso after Maximilian's fall, the 'Balanza' type, so-called from the scales of justice on the reverse. Although exactly equivalent in silver content to the traditional eight reales, its differing type and slightly smaller diameter caused it to be rejected in the Far East, whither so many millions of eight reales had made their way in trade. For commercial reasons, therefore, it lasted only from 1869-73.

1120

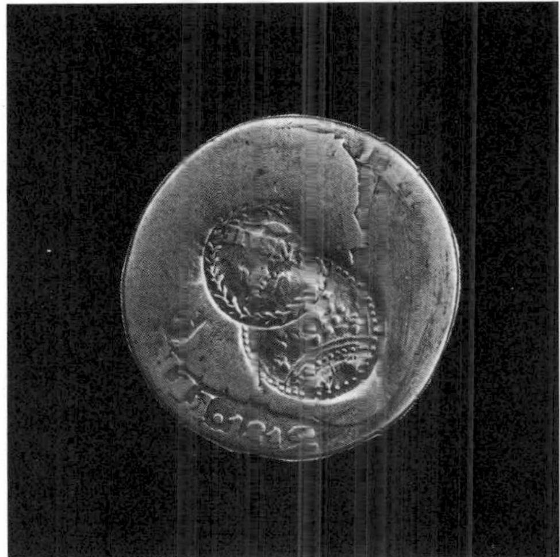
1121

1122

1124

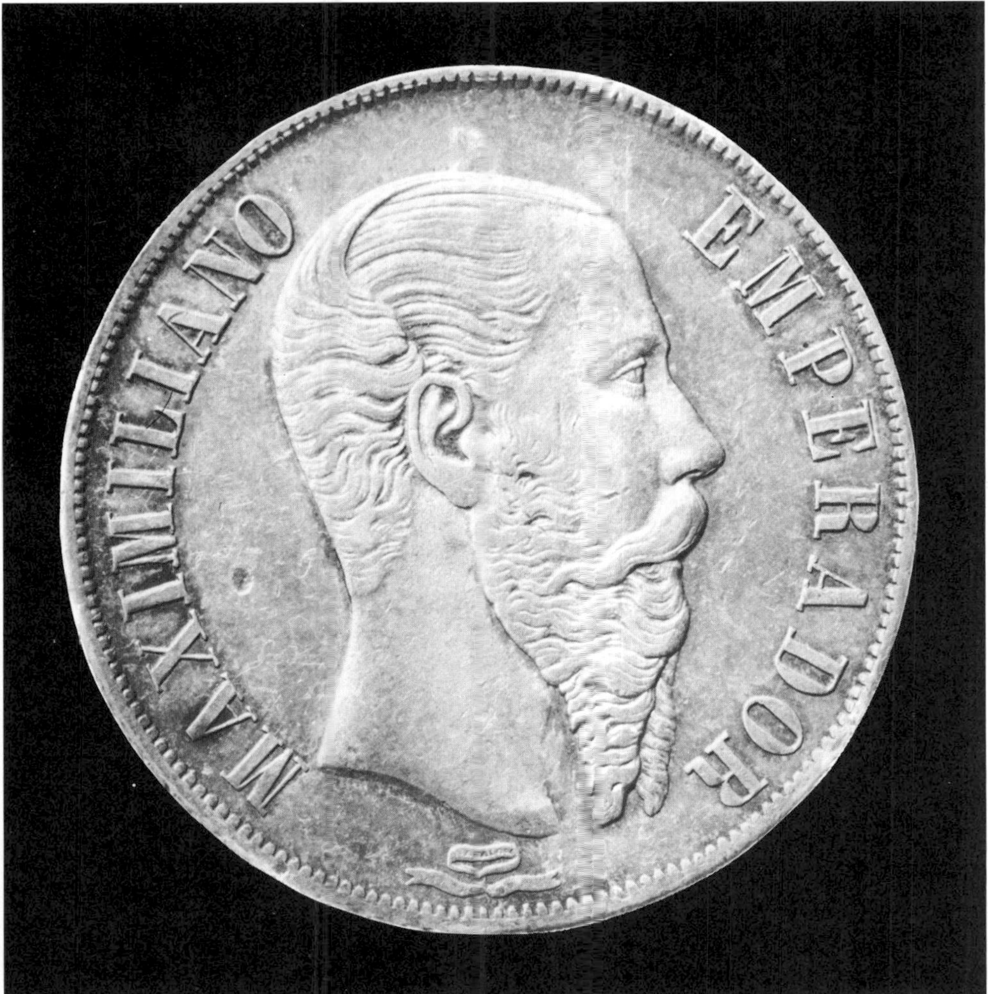

1123A×3

1123B×3

1125 In spite of a large coinage of gold and silver at the various mints, the Mexican small change was often in disarray, and had to be eked out with state or local bronzes, or even private issues. This is one of countless so-called 'Hacienda tokens' issued to facilitate trade on the lowest level of the circulation.

1126 The revolutionary period of 1914-18 again saw the production of coins locally by the various forces, although most of their money was now issued as boundless quantities of paper. The most notorious of the revolutionary coins was the silver peso struck in Durango by the Constitutionalist army opposed to the central government of General Huerta. The coin bears the encouraging legend, 'Muera Huerta' (Death to Huerta).

1127 The continuing depreciation of the peso, and the rising price of silver, has compelled Mexico to strike coins of ever less precious metal content and greater face value. The most highly valued silver coin ever struck in Mexico is the most recent, the 100 peso piece.

1128 The new type of the Central American Republic was imposed on coins of Spanish denomination struck at Guatemala, Tegucigalpa and San José in Costa Rica. On the obverse the national legend and date fall where the regal legend and date had been, and on the reverse are the customary

1126×3

1125×2

1128

1127×3

1129

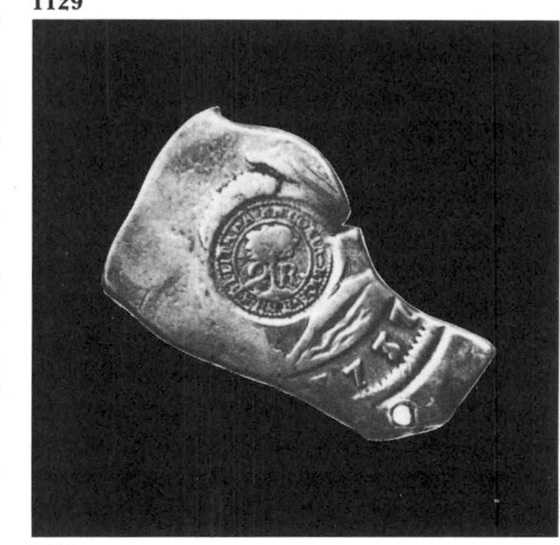
1130

mintmark, denomination and assayer's initials, with the addition of the guarantee of fineness which had not been openly stated on the colonial coin, '10 dineros 20 granos'.

1129 The strains imposed on the coinage after the dissolution of the Central American Republic are illustrated by this piece struck at Tegucigalpa in what became the Republic of Honduras. The coinage continued to bear the types of the Central American Republic, but the indication of fineness is missing, for the metal became debased silver and even copper.

1130 A great many Spanish colonial coins continued to circulate in the nineteenth century, often quite worn and of doubtful value. In 1846 those circulating in Costa Rica were restruck with local dies reading 'Habilitada en Costa Rica' (Validated in Costa Rica) to permit their continued use.

1131 The tradition of an intrinsically valuable coinage is nowhere better illustrated than in the coinage of Panama which began as late as 1904. All denominations were struck in silver 900 thousands fine, down to the 2½ centésimos with a diameter of only 10mm, the smallest precious metal coin to have been struck in the Western Hemisphere.

1132 The influence of U.S. coinage can be seen in the debased provisional 5-peso of Guatemala struck in 1923, whose types are clearly an imitation of the U.S. Lincoln cent then current (**1154**).

1133 Continuity between the colonial and the independent coinages is well illustrated by this early eight soles of the Republic of Bolivia. The reverse type substitutes a local emblem (including the llama) for the Spanish royal arms, but the obverse portrays the liberator Bolívar in lieu of the Spanish king, a usage suggestive of the reestablishment of monarchy in a local line (which actually happened briefly in Mexico in 1822).

1134 In spite of their many mints, some of the republican coinages were designed and struck at traditional mints in Europe. The earliest bronze coinage of Venezuela was designed by William Wyon and struck at London and Birmingham.

1135 The tradition of presidential portraiture was continued in this modern silver coin of Paraguay, struck in 1968 to celebrate the new presidential term of President Stroessner.

1131×1,×3

1132×3

1133×3

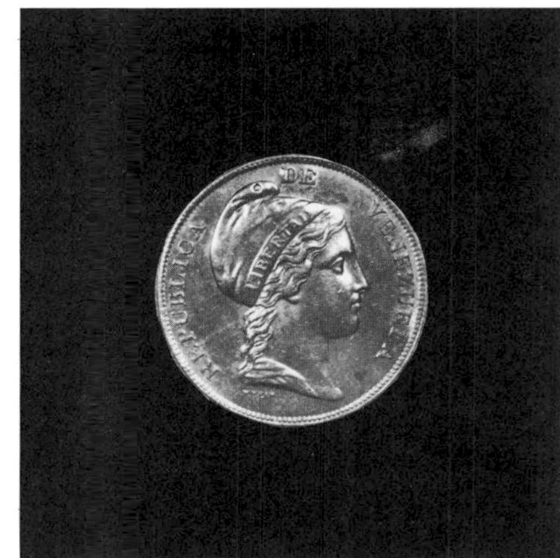

1134

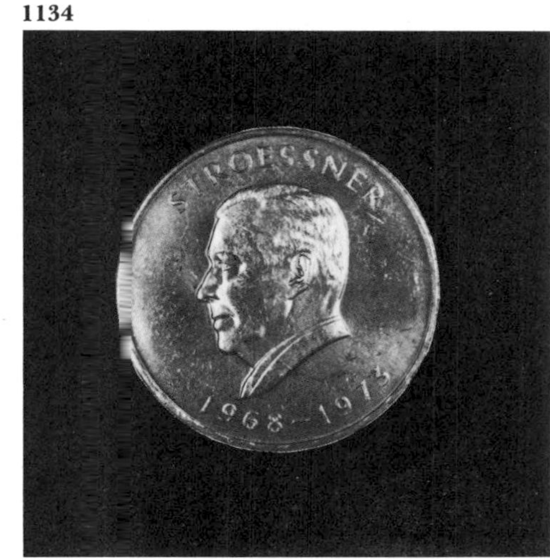

1135

1136 The coinages of South America have tended to the conservative in both type and style, and include relatively few commemorative or celebratory issues. This silver 1000 pesos of Uruguay, struck in 1969 in honour of the F.A.O., is particularly unusual, bearing a highly stylized version of the traditional sun-burst obverse, and a reverse with incuse legends and agricultural symbols as type.

1137 This Chilean 100 escudos of 1974, struck in nickel-brass and of no intrinsic value, is evidence of the collapse of the Spanish colonial coinage system in that country under the pressures of nineteenth and twentieth century inflation. Its theoretical value, reached after several drastic revisions of the Chilean monetary system, is equivalent to 100,000 nineteenth century silver pesos.

1138 The acceptability of the colonial cobs is demonstrated by their wear in circulation or, as here, by their having been countermarked with Portuguese denominations for use in Brazil.

1139 Although the Brazilian gold coinage was late to appear, the high alloy of 22 carats made it acceptable in the West Indies and North America in competition with the Spanish. The dobra of 12,800 réis, equivalent to the eight escudos, was popularly known as the 'Joe' from its royal legend, IOHANNES D.D. Dobra, João V, 1732.

1136A

1136B

1137×2

1138×2

1139×2

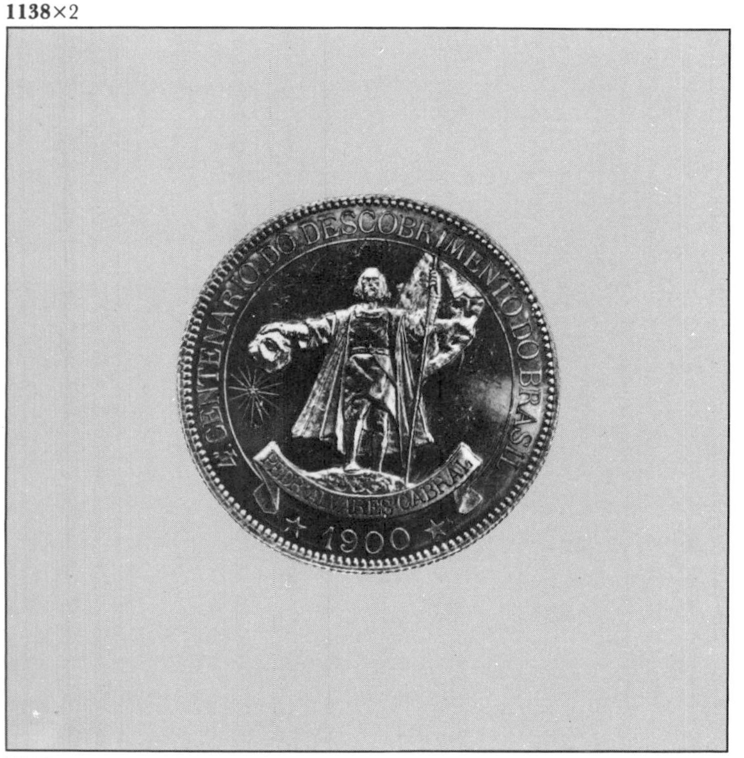

1140

1141×3

1140 In 1900 Brazil celebrated the four hundredth anniversary of its discovery by the Portuguese admiral Pedro Álvares Cabral, with a series of commemorative coins, the chief, of 4000 réis, being the largest struck in the Americas up to that time.

1141 The earliest coins struck specifically for the British West Indies were produced privately in London c. 1616 for the Bermudas. Although resembling contemporary English coins, their metal is base and their type appropriate to the islands – the hog which was found running wild in numbers after having been abandoned there by a Spanish ship in the sixteenth century.

1142 The cut and counterstamped pieces typically bore no date, which must therefore be derived from independent documentation, and often no denomination or even mark of issuing authority. This Spanish colonial eight reales piece, however, was counterstamped for the island of Grenada early in the nineteenth century, and given a local value of four 'bitts' for each cut third.

1143 The earliest copper coinage of Haiti reflects the French tradition from which it derives, even years after the expulsion of the French, in the legend 'Liberté Égalité', the type of the fasces, and particularly the use of the local revolutionary era as the date, a specific imitation of French usage (**1034**).

1144 Some of the modern states of the Caribbean have been provided with coinages whose types and styles mark a distinct break with tradition. Those of the British Virgin Islands illustrate indigenous birds.

1145 The earliest coins struck in North America with full types were the shillings of the Massachusetts Bay Colony. Their crude style is owing to the dies having been cut locally. These shillings are dated 1652, but were struck later.

1146 The first attempt at a coinage for the colonies as a whole was the dollar intended by the Continental Congress in 1776. The original 13 colonies which were to become the United States are represented as the links of an unbroken chain, with the legend 'We Are One'. On the reverse is the admonitory emblem of the sundial and the legend 'Fugio' (I Flee) a device said to have been designed by Benjamin Franklin. The coin was never officially issued because of a lack of silver bullion.

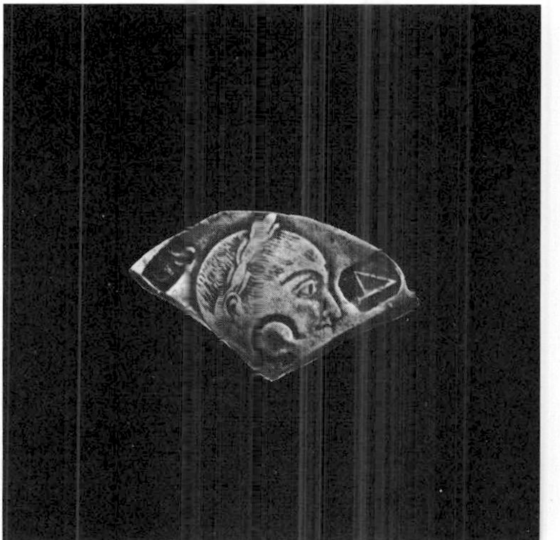

1142

1143×2

1144×2

1146×2

1145A×3

1145B×3

1147 This copper of the state of Vermont, 1788, was conveniently struck from dies prepared from punches originally intended for the counterfeiting of British halfpennies. The obverse portrait of George III now represents Vermont, and the reverse type of Britannia seated is taken as Liberty.

1148 The earliest issue of the national mint at Philadelphia intended for general circulation were the cents of 1793, coppers based on the British half pennies. The obverse figuration of Liberty for this and most succeeding U.S. coins was a deliberate decision of the Congress, in order to avoid the implications of monarchy which the portrait of the President might suggest.

1149 Because a limited number of types were fixed by law, the U.S. coinages of the nineteenth and much of the twentieth centuries have been conventional in the extreme. These half dollars of 1861 and 1863 are representative of a great deal of U.S. coinage.

1150 The early U.S. mints were small and incapable of coping with new discoveries of gold and silver, from which they were quite distant in any case. Many private nineteenth century gold coinages are known, particularly from Colorado and California prior to the establishment of the mints of Denver and San Francisco. This piece was struck by Mormon settlers in Utah, where there never was an official mint.

1151 The Civil War saw the disappearance of gold and silver from circulation and the circulation of masses of paper money of which that of the Confederate States ultimately became worthless. A brief attempt at a distinctive Confederate coinage is represented by this half dollar struck at the New Orleans mint in 1861 after the secession of Louisiana. Only four examples are known the obverse hardly distinguishable from the Federal coinage.

1152 Perhaps the most impressive of American coins was the silver dollar, of which the type struck by the millions from 1878 to 1921 provided the standard coin of the American West.

1147 **1149A** **1150** **1148**×3 **1149B** **1151** **1152** **1153A** **1153B**

century as far as regards danominations and modules (save for
the new small flan dollar), but as everywhere gold is no longer
struck and silver has been replaced by copper-clad and then by
cupro-nickel.

As to types, two innovations in this century have added a
certain variety, namely the introduction of portraits of historical
1154 figures, and the free invention of celebratory types for the
commemorative half dollars. The Lincoln cent was the first U.S.
coin intended for general circulation to bear the head of an
historical person. It was introduced in 1909 on the centenary of
Lincoln's birth, and has continued to be struck with the obverse
type unchanged to this day. Such a stereotyped issue has long
since become conventional and uninteresting but at the time its
introduction was controversial. The portrayal of an identifiable
individual was a numismatic innovation of great seriousness,
and Lincoln in particular offended the Southern survivors of the
Civil War; the style was antitraditional in being derived from Art
Nouveau; and the designer, Victor D. Brenner, initialed his
work, contrary to U.S. coinage usage. But the move to obverse
portraits was renewed with the Washington quarter dollar
1156 introduced in 1932 on the bicentenary of his birth, and today all
1157 current coins bear the head of some historical figure. Additionally typological variety obtained in the commemorative half
dollars, first struck in 1892 to celebrate the Columbian Exposi-
tion. Intended largely for collectors rather than for general
circulation, they have commemorated the anniversary of colonial
settlements, state and local constitutions, events of war and 1155
peace etc.

Colonial Canada was briefly provided with coin by the French
in the late seventeenth century, but in general her story was that 1158
of the rest of North America: the gold and silver circulation was
composed of European and (later) U.S. coins, and even by
Spanish American, while copper was a random assortment. The
population was small, and Canada itself not a political unity
until 1867, so that even after a regular coinage was introduced by 1159
the British in 1858 it was struck for five different provinces:
Canada, New Brunswick, Newfoundland, Nova Scotia and
Prince Edward Island. And it was struck in England, for not
until this century did Canada have its own national mint. After
confederation the coins of the Dominion were a regular series of
drab types, the head of the sovereign and the value in a wreath.
Only with the introduction of the silver dollar in 1935 did
imaginative new types begin to appear on the coins of Canada,
largely for provincial or civic centennials. A complicated series of
non-circulating 5 and 10 dollar silver coins has been struck to
finance and commemorate the Montreal Olympics. 1162

1153 In an attempt to enliven the standard types of American coinage President Theodore Roosevelt induced the sculptor Augustus Saint-Gaudens to design a new 20 dollar gold piece. His earliest efforts (1907) at a facing figure of Liberty were in such high relief that the coin was unsuitable for circulation, but even in lower relief the types were a striking and encouraging variation on the traditional.

1154 In style the Lincoln cent was a notable departure from the academic traditions of U.S. coinage. Most of the legends run vigorously across the flan, rather than following its curve, the letter forms (note especially E and M) are idiosyncratically stylized in the manner of Art Nouveau, and the traditional reverse wreath has been reduced to two schematic ears of wheat.

1155 This commemorative half dollar is a typical example from among some 50 different types and issues. Struck in 1920, it celebrates the three hundredth anniversary of the landing of the Pilgrims in Massachusetts in 1620.

1156 Today all U.S. denominations bear the heads of historical figures. The best known is perhaps that of the Kennedy half dollar, which has been collected about the world in memory of the President.

1157 The most recent innovation in the U.S. coinage is the dollar first issued to circulation in 1979. It departs radically from all earlier dollar coins in its small module and polygonal shape, and is the first regularly circulating piece to bear the head of a woman, Susan B. Anthony, the nineteenth century reformer and campaigner for women's rights.

1155×2

1158 The earliest coins to be struck for use specifically in Canada were French 5 and 15 sols in silver, minted at Paris in 1670. The French and British never established a mint in Canada, so that all coin had to be imported until the twentieth century.

1159 In the earlier nineteenth century private tokens were widely used in Canada to supplement the official circulation. Some were struck in England, others such as this sou token (of which there are many varieties) were produced locally.

1160 The first coins of the Dominion of Canada to be struck at the official Canadian mint at Ottawa were the issues of 1908. Although all the coinage of the Dominion had hitherto been designed and struck in Britain, the modules and denominations of the coins were similar to those of the U.S., whose coins circulated widely in Canada.

1161 During the Second World War a shortage of nickel forced the substitution of other metals in the base coinage. This 1943 five-cent piece was struck in a brass alloy called tombac.

1162 In celebration of the Montreal Olympics of 1976 the Ottawa mint has produced a number of silver coins for sale to collectors.

1154A×3

1154B×3

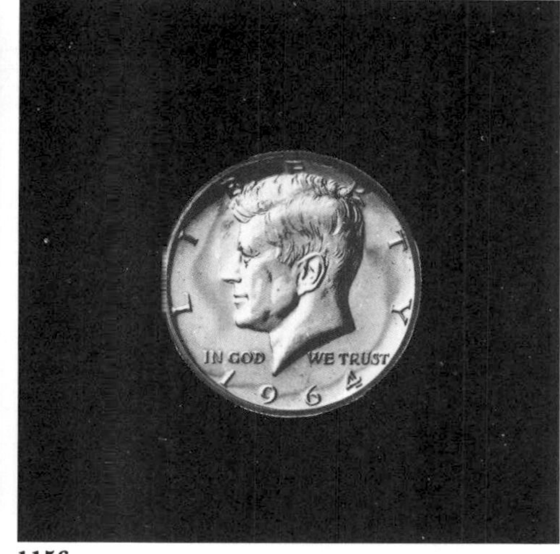

1156

1157×2

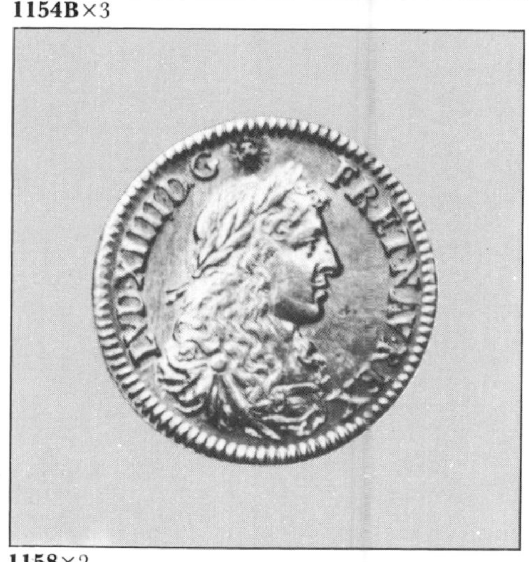
1158×2

1159×2

1160×2

1161×2

1162

SIX POUNDS
THIS BILL of Six
is emitted by a LAW of
passed in the Fourteenth
King GEORGE the Third. Datec
HONI·SOIT·QUI·MAL·Y·PENSE
DIEU ET MON DROIT
SIX £
SIX POUNDS
NEW-Jersey.

XV

PAPER MONEY

Virginia Anderson

Paper money is today widely regarded as a major determinant of economic trends; it evolved, however, more as a symptom than a cause. Arising from the need to create credit for economic and political purposes, paper currency emerged in haphazard fashion with little geographical or chronological sequence: for instance, notes circulated in China as early as the twelfth century, but were not adopted in Europe till the seventeenth and eighteenth centuries. Nevertheless, a broad pattern may be discerned. Almost invariably paper money was issued to promote trade or wage war when specie was scarce; early experiments were therefore tentative, temporary, and of limited application. Enthusiasm for the convenience of notes often outweighed prudence in their management, and bankruptcy was a dismal commonplace of nineteenth century commercial activity. Paradoxically this resulted not in a retreat from paper money, but in a more positive and rational attempt to make it work. Thus from the late nineteenth and early twentieth centuries note issue has been increasingly subject to government control and made the privilege of central financial institutions.

It is a common misconception that paper currency is a relatively modern development. Credit transfer notes were issued in China in the eighth century, and by the end of the
1439 twelfth century notes were circulating as a substitute for copper.
The practice spread to other eastern countries in the middle ages as the Mongols carried notes to Iran, Korea and Vietnam. However, China was an innovator in the use of paper money; elsewhere widely circulating notes did not appear until the seventeenth century. Again, the East led the way. Traders in the Osaka province of Japan facilitated business by issuing notes which by 1630 were circulating in other provinces. In Europe, too, a merchant was responsible for the first paper money. Johann Palmstruch, a Livonian trader, founded the Stockholm's Banco in Sweden in 1656, and in 1661 the first notes were issued. They were called credit notes, but were in fact banknotes much as we know them today—non-interest-bearing, freely transferable, and payable on demand. The enterprise put into practice a contemporary theory succinctly expressed by the English economist William Petty in a dialogue written in 1682:

Question 26 What Remedy is there if we have too little money? Answer: We must erect a Bank.

Too little money: it was a recurring problem, obstructing the course not only of trade, but also of war. In Petty's own country, the Bank of England was founded in 1694 as a vehicle for raising and administering a loan to the King to finance war with France. Depositors could if they wished accept repayment in the Bank's own notes, payable to bearer. At about this time, military aggression prompted the earliest American notes. Strictly speaking, these issues were neither American nor English, but colonial; specie earned in trade was appropriated by the mother
country, and from 1690 onwards the colonies financed military 1163
expeditions with local bills of credit. Somewhat ironically, the first national American paper currency was authorized in 1775 by the Continental Congress to conduct the Revolutionary War against Britain.

In many countries, the first note issues were launched with more imagination than sense; all too frequently, depreciation and bankruptcy were the rewards of over-issue and inadequate provision for redemption. The pioneering Stockholm's Banco, for example, had to cease note issue in 1668, and the value of the American Continental Currency was scornfully recorded in the phrase 'not worth a Continental'. The first French experiences of paper money were similarly disastrous. Early in the eighteenth century, an ingenious Scot by the name of John Law issued assignats backed by land and attempted to convert the national debt by the sale of shares. Initially, public confidence brought buoyancy to the scheme, but by October 1720 stock was flooding on to the market and Law's financial empire crashed. A second
issue of assignats was undertaken in 1789, this time backed by 1166
sales of church lands. It was equally abortive; note issue soon soared ahead of property sales, further emissions were prohibited, and the printing presses smashed in February 1796.

Despite these growing pains, paper money was more widely adopted in the later eighteenth and the nineteenth centuries.
More European countries began issuing notes, and in Britain 1167
and America private banks flourished. In the absence of legal restrictions on the extent of issue, many overreached their credit, but new banks constantly sprang up to replace those that foundered. The success of these local banks in promoting economic development through the provision of credit is beyond the scope of this work; however, it may be noted that their failures were a considerable incentive to the centralization of banking, and note issue (which began with the experiments of individuals and small companies) became the prerogative of central banks and state treasuries.

The twentieth century has witnessed a curious blend of established trends and new departures. As in the past, revol-
utions and wars have necessitated emergency issues of paper 1173
currency, and the German hyperinflation of the 1920s is a 1180
spectacular modern counterpart to the depreciation of the early 1177
notes. In commercial transactions, however, banknotes are 1182
increasingly being replaced by cheques and credit cards. This may be seen not as an innovation, but as a revival of payment by personal promissory notes and receipts, as in the days before paper money became a circulating medium.

Detail from a six pound Bill of Credit, New Jersey, 1776 (**1163**).

1163 During the eighteenth century, the colonies issued notes to finance military expeditions, public works, and, as in this example, public loan offices. The left-hand border of this bill was engraved by David Rittenhouse, later to become the first Director of the United States Mint. New Jersey Bill of Credit, six pounds, 25 March 1776.

1164 The first Polish paper money was also a product of war. This 10 zlotych note of 1794 was issued by the insurrection leader Thaddeus Kosciuszco, in support of the Polish War of Independence.

1165 Founded in 1736, the Bank of Kopenhagen struggled with the familiar difficulties of currency depreciation, excessive note issue, and shortage of specie. In 1791 further note emissions were prohibited and a new Specie Bank created, with limited powers of issue. Bank of Kopenhagen–one riksdaler–1791.

1166 Assignats developed from the attempt to eradicate the national debt by the sale of church lands. Initially the assignats were interest-bearing bonds issued in anticipation of property sales, but in September 1790 they were issued without interest and quickly became circulating currency. After September 1792 the design of the notes significantly ceased to include a royal portrait. France–Assignat–90 livres–29 September 1790.

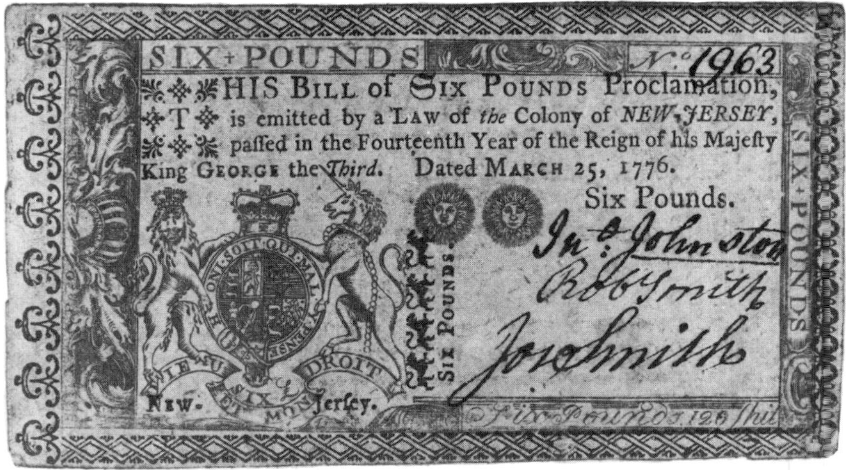

1163

1165 104×157mm

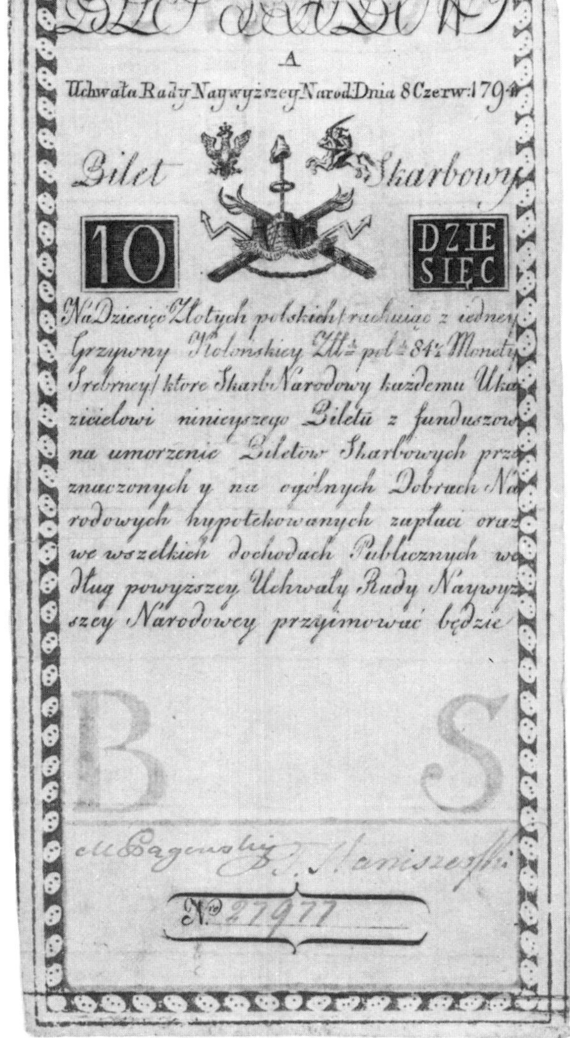

1164 180×95mm

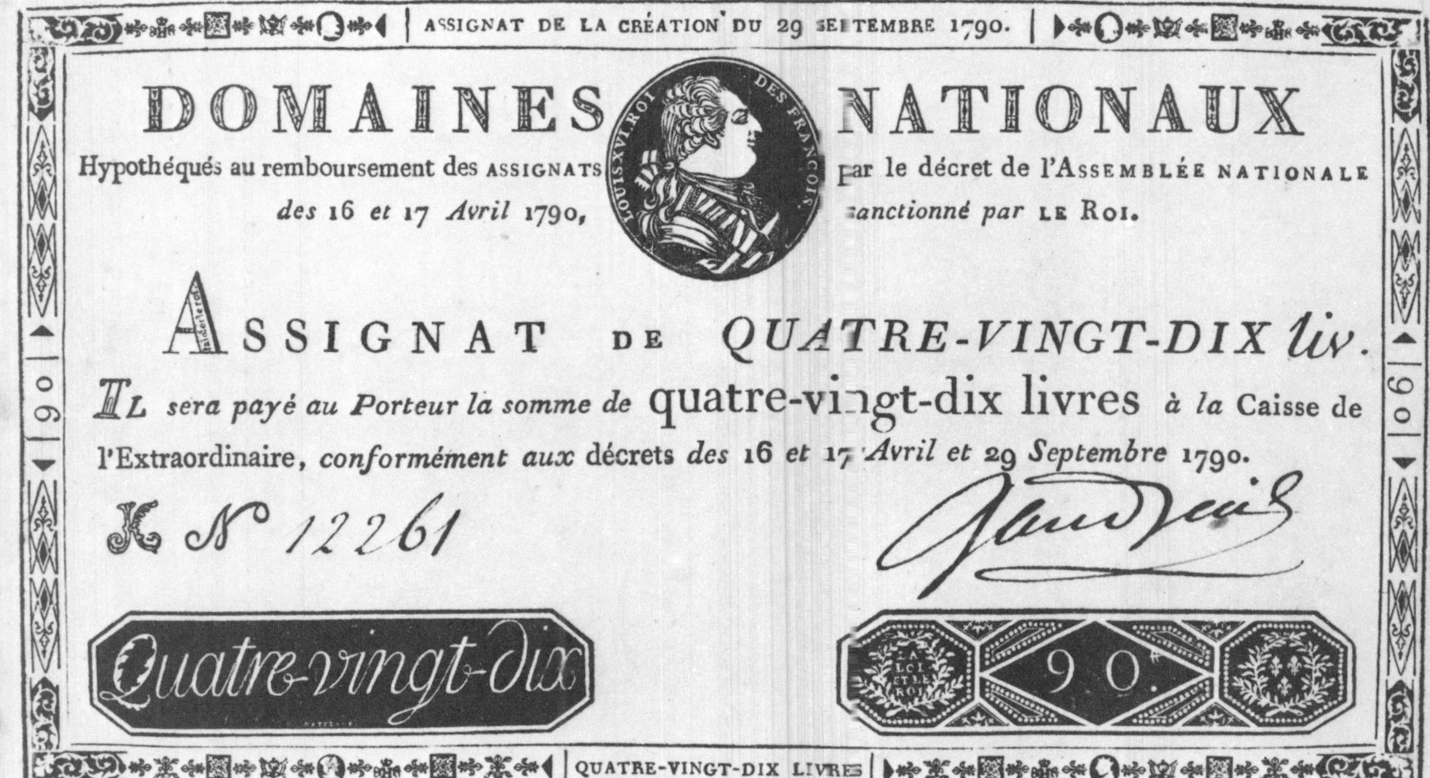

1166

1167 The English provincial banks flourished in the second half of the eighteenth century. However, from the 1790s inadequately controlled note issues, coupled with unstable international relations, caused many crashes. Several acts were passed to regulate banking activities, culminating in the famous Bank Charter Act of 1844, which circumscribed existing note issues and prohibited any provincial bank from issuing notes which was not already doing so. The last English private banknotes were issued in 1921. Great Britain–Pontefract Bank–five guineas–1808.

1168 Great Britain–satirical note denouncing 'Melvillism'–1805. The use of the banknote format for propaganda suggests public familiarity with notes; in this instance it was also an apposite choice. In 1805 a Committee of Naval Inquiry accused First Viscount Melville of mismanaging public funds in his former capacity as treasurer of the Navy. Indeed, the Governor of the Bank of England had complained to Pitt in 1798 that public money was being transferred to private accounts in other banks.

1169 To deter forgery, the design of notes became increasingly sophisticated. The firm which printed this note employed Jacob Perkins and Asa Spencer, both of whom developed the technique of steel engraving to allow more intricate decoration. Bank of North America, Philadelphia–five cents–1815.

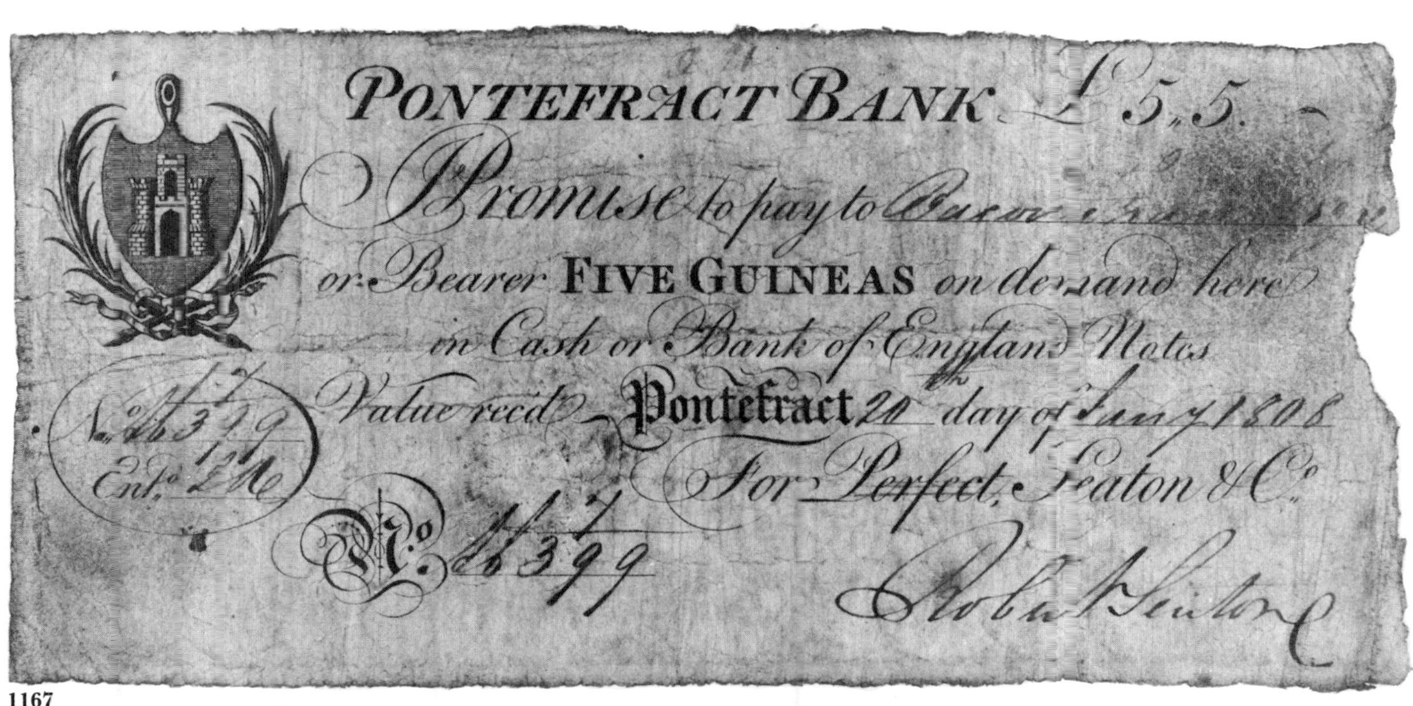

1167

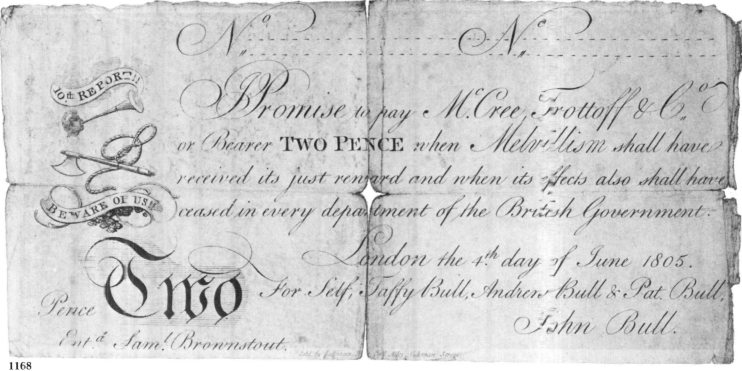

No. No.
I Promise to pay McCree, Frottoff & Co.
or Bearer TWO PENCE when Melvillism shall have received its just reward and when its effects also shall have ceased in every department of the British Government.
London the 4th day of June 1805.
For Self, Taffy Bull, Andrew Bull & Pat Bull,
John Bull.
10th REPORT!!
BEWARE OF US!!
Two Pence
Entd. Saml. Brownstout.

1168

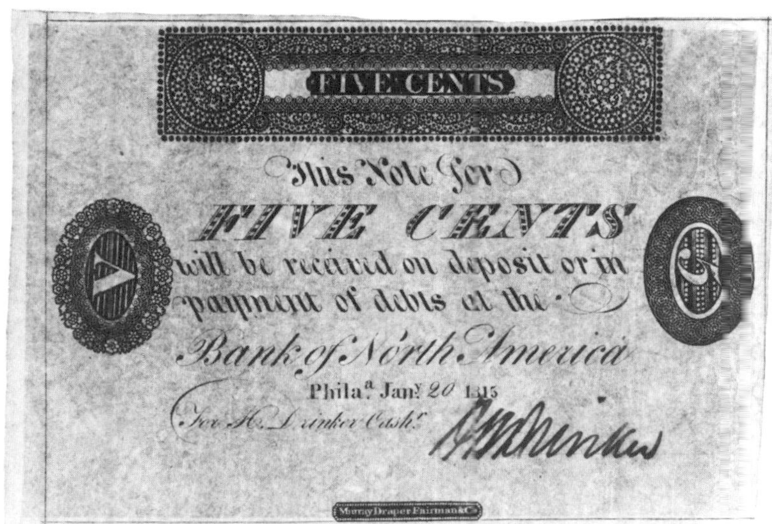

1169

1170 Great Britain–Congreve stamp–1821. Stamp duty was imposed on notes payable on demand from 1793. Its payment was first documented by inkless die stamps until in 1821 the Congreve stamp was printed on the reverse of notes. Originally intended for printing notes, Sir William Congreve's process of two-colour surface printing with interlocking plates was used for stamps as a precaution against forgery. However, the design's very complexity made it easily imitable, not least because the dies could never be reproduced with complete accuracy.

1171 In 1832 the socialist entrepreneur Robert Owen opened an exchange bazaar in London; goods brought to the bazaar were paid for in notes to the value of the number of hours' labour required for their production. An hour's work was reckoned to be worth six pence. Note for one hour's labour, 1832.

1172 These notes, ominously bearing guns, cannonballs and fasces, were issued in support of the War of Italian Independence by Guiseppe Mazzini, founder of Young Italy. Italy–five franchi–1849.

1173 During the Boer War the town of Mafeking was isolated by siege for almost eight months, but the resourceful defenders issued their own currency from an improvized printing works in a bomb shelter. The 10 shilling notes were printed from woodcuts based on a drawing by Colonel Baden-Powell, military commander in the town. Mafeking Siege Note–10 shillings–1900.

1174 In anticipation of gold hoarding, the Treasury issued low denomination notes of one pound and 10 shillings from 1914 to 1928. This third issue 'Bradbury' (named after the Permanent Secretary who signed the notes) was designed by the sculptor and medallist Bertram McKennal. His vignette of Saint George and the dragon was based on a design by Pistrucci on the last coinage of George III (**46**). Great Britain–Treasury note–one pound–1914.

1170

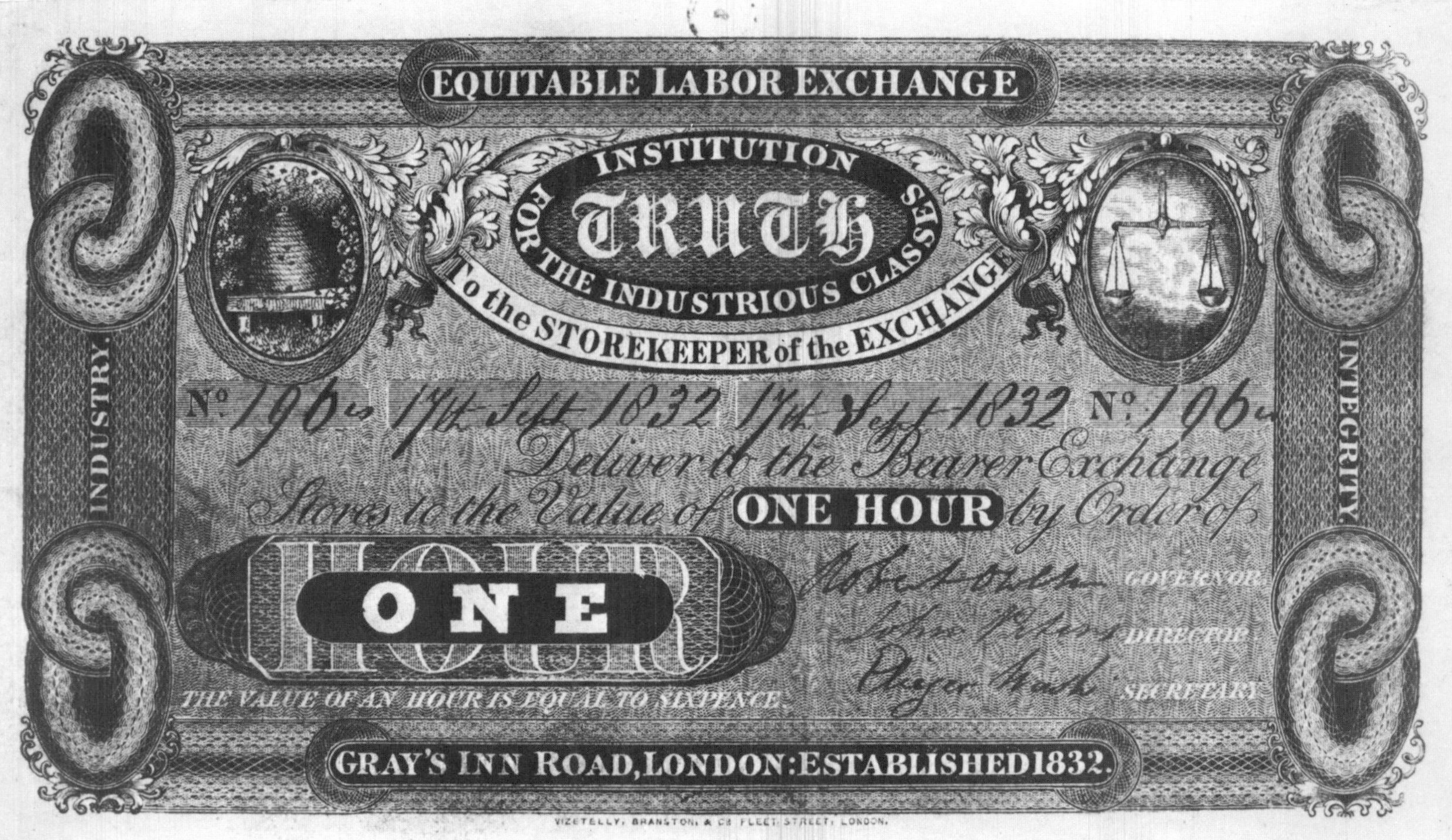

1171

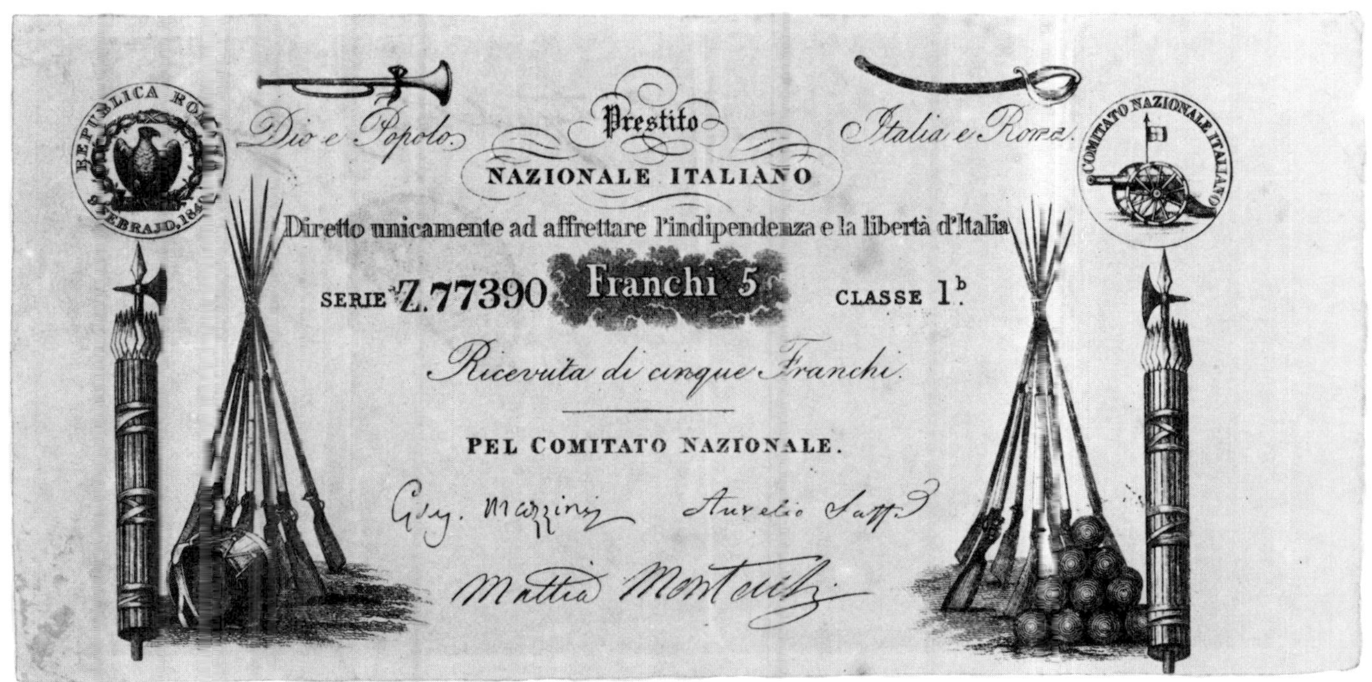
Prestito
Dio e Popolo
Italia e Roma
NAZIONALE ITALIANO
Diretto unicamente ad affrettare l'indipendenza e la libertà d'Italia
SERIE Z.77390
Franchi 5
CLASSE 1.b
Riceruta di cinque Franchi
PEL COMITATO NAZIONALE.
COMITATO NAZIONALE ITALIANO

1172 10[illegible]×208mm

10s.
Mafeking Siege Note.
10s.
March, 1900.
THIS NOTE IS GOOD FOR
Ten Shillings
March, 1900.
5330
(STERLING)
5330
DURING THE SIEGE;
AND WILL BE EXCHANGED FOR COIN ON RESUMPTION OF CIVIL LAW AT THE
Standard Bank,
MAFEKING.
Issued by authority of Col. R. S. S. Baden-Powell, Commanding Frontier Forces
Chief Paymaster.
TOWNSHEND & SON, PRINTERS MAFEKING

1173

UNITED KINGDOM OF GREAT BRITAIN AND IRELAND
CANCELLED
CURRENCY NOTES ARE LEGAL TENDER FOR THE PAYMENT OF ANY AMOUNT
GEORGIVS V. D. G. BRITT: OMN: REX F. D. IND: IMP:
ONE POUND
ISSUED BY THE LORDS COMMISSIONERS OF HIS MAJESTY'S TREASURY UNDER THE AUTHORITY OF ACT OF PARLIAMENT IV. AND V. GEO. V. CH. XIV.
£1
CANCELLED
John Bradbury
SECRETARY TO THE TREASURY

1174

1175-77 These contrasting notes from Germany reflect the upheaval of the First World War and its aftermath. **1175**, a 20 Mark Reichsbanknote of 1915, carries echoes of pre-War optimism with its classical allegory and overflowing cornucopia. **1176** is a 10 Pfennig note issued in Cologne in 1920. This is an example of the Notgeld (emergency money) printed by cities to provide small change. **1177**, by 1923 inflation had rendered notes for sums like 200 million Marks commonplace, and worthless.

1178 After the Revolution the new government issued this note displaying the imperial double-headed eagle to encourage public confidence in their currency. They also resorted to printing notes from Tsarist plates. Russia–250 roubles–1917.

1179 Even in war, care was taken with the design of notes: the low denomination notes issued in Jersey during the German occupation; each value had a different picture on the reverse– the one shilling note bore the silhouette of two elderly gossips. Jersey–one shilling–1940s.

1180 In 1944 the Greek Civil Committee for National Liberation printed a large number of notes to buy provisions for the partisan army.

1181-82 The modern alternatives. **1181**, Sveriges Riksbank– 10 kronor– 1968. The Swedish Stockholm's Banco, which issued the first European banknotes, was taken under government control and chartered as the Sveriges Riksbank in 1668. This note, issued to celebrate the Bank's tercentenary, has on the obverse, the deity Svea (Sweden) sitting against the Bank's first seal. **1182**, Credit Card: Convenient and functional, credit cards are products of their age. Unlike banknotes, however, they are devoid of inscription or illustration to proclaim their origins.

1176

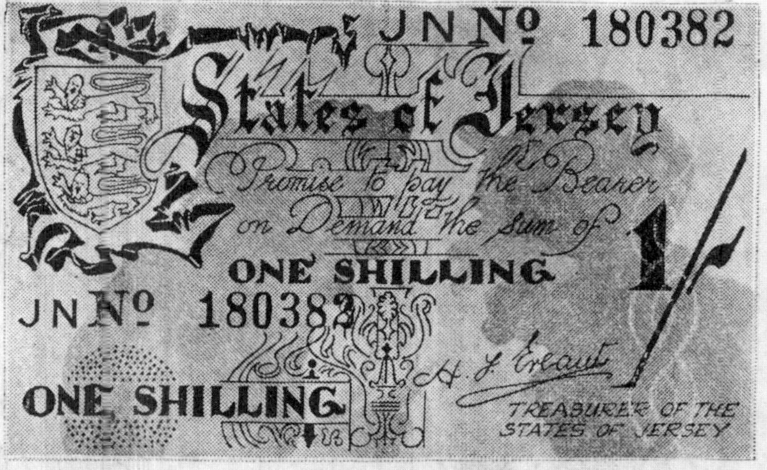

1179

1175

1177

РУБЛЕЙ
РУБЛЕЙ
250
250
РУБЛЕЙ
РУБЛЕЙ
ПОДДѢЛКА КРЕДИТ-
НЫХЪ БИЛЕТОВЪ
ПРЕСЛѢДУЕТСЯ
ЗАКОНОМЪ.

1178

ΠΟΛΙΤΙΚΗ ΕΠΙΤΡΟΠΗ ΕΘΝΙΚΗΣ ΑΠΕΛΕΥΘΕΡΩΣΗΣ
ΕΘΝΙΚΟ ΟΜΟΛΟΓΟ ΑΠΕΛΕΥΘΕΡΩΤΙΚΟΥ ΑΓΩΝΑ
25
25
ΣΤΗΝ ΕΔΡΑ ΤΗΣ ΕΠΙΤΡΟΠΗΣ 5 ΙΟΥΝΗ 1944
ΕΚΤΥΠΩΣΗ ΕΛΕΥΘΕΡΗΣ ΕΛΛΑΔΑΣ

1180

SVERIGES RIKSBANK 1668-1968
10
10
KRONOR
0000000
10

1181

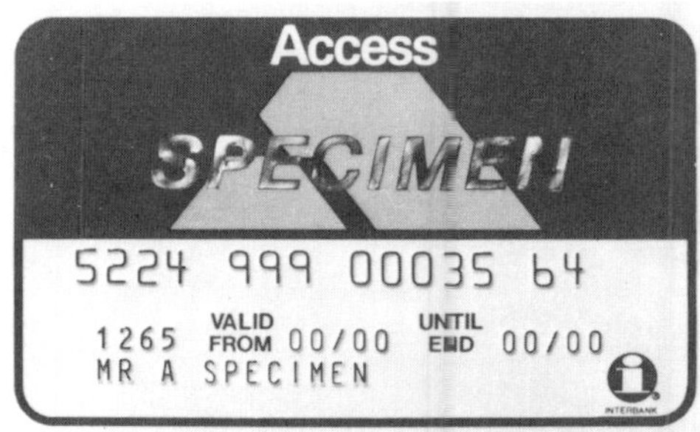
Access
SPECIMEN
5224 999 00035 64
1265 VALID FROM 00/00 UNTIL END 00/00
MR A SPECIMEN

1182 54×86mm

XVI
THE ANCIENT NEAR EAST

David Sellwood

Parthia, equivalent to modern Iraq, Iran and West Afghanistan,
was founded about 230 BC by a tribe of nomads from Central
Asia, and grew on the ruins of the Seleucid empire. The chief
1183 coin of its ruling dynasty, the Arsacids, was the drachma,
weighing about four grammes and struck at mints on the plateau
of Iran, although tetradrachms were current in Mesopotamia. A
few silver obols and vast numbers of bronze chalkoi (weighing
two grammes) and multiples were also issued. The legends were
in Greek supplemented for early issues by Aramaic and for late
ones by Parthian Pahlavi. Dates reckoned according to the
Seleucid era with Macedonian months occur on most tetra-
265 drachms and (with years alone) on the corresponding bronzes.
Monograms on later drachmae indicate the mint-towns. With
few exceptions, the dies of the obverse and reverse were intended
to have coincident axes. Stylistically, the Parthian issues com-
mence in good Hellenistic taste, but later issues tend to be in
very low relief, engraved in a hard linear fashion.

At the time of the rise of Parthia, Persis, in South Iran, was
1202 already independent of the Seleucids. The coins of this little
state, including tetradrachms, drachmae and minor silver, have
the head of the local priest-king on one side and a fire altar with
attendant on the other and include Aramaic or Pahlavi inscrip-
1204 tions. In AD 224, the prince of Persis, Ardashir, overthrew the
Arsacids and set up the Sassanian empire, a much more
aggressive state. Conquests extended from India to Asia Minor.
Sassanian silver drachmae, continuing to weigh about four
grammes, have a characteristically thin flan which often gives
1206 rise to 'dead spots', areas of the design not struck up. Each
monarch has his own crown, allowing relatively easy identification. The Pahlavi of the legends is inherently ambiguous and
although it presents no difficulty with the royal titulature, some
of the mint names on later issues have still not been satisfactorily
1205 read. Gold, chiefly dinars, was added to the range of Parthian
denominations, but relatively few bronze coins were struck,
perhaps because those remaining in circulation from the earlier
period sufficed. Yezdegird III, the last Sassanian ruler was killed
by the Arab invaders in AD 651.

Elymais, a small kingdom in the Zagros foothills, contained
the ancient city of Susa, which was one of its mints. Briefly
independent in the second century BC, it later became feudatory
to the Parthians. Early issues, of good silver, were predominantly 1219
of tetradrachms, but subsequent debasement led to a bronze
coinage of both the latter and 'drachmae'. The style of engraving
became positively un-Greek, while on many specimens the
reverse design was reduced to a field of randomly disseminated 1221
dashes; if an inscription were employed at all, Parthian Pahlavi
was the medium.

The closely neighbouring state of Characene, at the head of
the Persian Gulf had a similar history, short-lived autonomy 1222
before capture by the Arsacids. Here the main denomination was
always the tetradrachm, increasingly debased, and struck at the 1223
capital Spasinu. Legends originally in Greek were finally in 1224
Aramaic. Both Elymais and Characene were incorporated in the
Sassanian empire, their coinage suppressed.

Nabatea was an Arab kingdom based on Petra, probably its
mint. Early issues begin about 100 BC and the Romans finally
incorporated it in their eastern administration in AD 106. Scarce 1225
silver drachmae and more plentiful bronze formed the main
currency. No doubt the population aimed at self-sufficiency for,
according to Diodorus, 'they live in the open air. It is their
custom neither to plant grain, set out any fruit-bearing tree, use
wine nor construct any house... because those who possess these
things are, in order to retain the use of them, compelled by the
powerful to do their bidding'.

The corresponding south Arabian state was under the control
first of the Sabeans and then of the Himyarites. Before about 200
BC, the former struck tetradrachms and drachmae fairly closely 1228,1229
copying in fabric, metal and design fourth century Athenian
currency. Afterwards the Himyarites turned to Roman prototy- 1230
pes and, finally, rulers of the second century AD were responsible for drachmae in the local Semitic script. 1231

Related peoples had set up the kingdom of Axum, across the
Red Sea in Ethiopia. Coins were issued between about AD 250 1232
and the Arab Conquest. For the most part, inscriptions are
notionally in Greek, naturally retained after Christianity was
adopted. An intriguing feature of these issues, whose denominations seem based on a unit of about one gramme, is the use of
gold inlay on silver specimens, and silver inlay on bronze.

An unknown king of Parthia, about 75 BC (**1188**).

1183 The Parthians were a nomadic people originally and they retained many aspects of their former way of life even when they became a great imperial power. Here we have a drachma portraying an early prince (in left profile, the standard position), probably Arsaces II, c. 211-190 BC. He is clean shaven (a Hellenistic convention) and wears a felt bashlik of the type still employed by shepherds in the depth of the central Asian winter.

1184 The greatest expansion of Parthia occurred during the reign of Mithradates I, c. 171-38 BC. About 140 BC he captured Seleucia-on-the-Tigris and used its Greek mint to strike this splendid tetradrachm. For several early issues, this denomination is right-facing, an inheritance from Seleucid practice, and the style of engraving is Westernized also.

1185 With the expansion of Arsacid control, several mints were employed to strike drachmae ranging from Susa and Ecbatana in the west to Margiana (Merv) and Areia (Herat) in the east. This drachma comes from the city of Nisa (now in Turkmenistan) and its name NICAIA appears behind the rather formalized portrait of the young prince Phraates II c. 138-27 BC.

1186 The coins of Artabanus I (c. 127-23 BC) are usually reckoned to be the peak of achievement in Parthian numismatic art. Certainly the details of this drachma portrait (the unique hair style in concentric waves, the straggling beard, the triple-drop ear-ring, the neck torque, the embroidered kandys or cloak) have been engraved on the die by a masterly hand.

1187 The second great Arsacid monarch was Mithradates II (c. 123-88 BC), in whose reign the initial contact with Rome was made. From about 100 BC he is depicted with a realistically prominent nose and also with a new headgear, a tiara shaped like a tea-cosy, having long ear- and neck-flaps and with pearl-embroidered decorations on the side.

1188 From the death of Mithradates II until about 57 BC, the history of Parthia is obscure and we have no general agreement on the attributions. The unknown king depicted on this tetradrachm reigned about 75 BC. With his issues a new hair style, close curled and covering the ear, was adopted, remaining characteristic of Parthian coin portraits.

1189 The seated archer is the almost invariable reverse design of Parthian drachmae. Early issues show him seated on a stool or omphalos (an inverted wickerwork basket) but later ones, as here, employ a high-backed throne. He is often thought to represent Arsaces I, eponymous founder of the dynasty, and he is portrayed in steppe dress, bashlik, cloak, pleated trousers and laced boots, sighting down the bow which was the favourite Parthian weapon. The square arrangement of the legend is another characteristic of Arsacid issues; while the language may be Greek, the employment of a succession of high-flown epithets is more obviously oriental – thus one reads 'Of the great king Arsaces, divinely descended, beneficent.' At the right is a Greek inscription, showing the coin to have been struck at Rhagae, now a suburb of Tehran, c. 75 BC.

1190 Most Parthian coins have the left profile bust and the use of frontality seems to be connected with the occupation of the throne by princes descended through the female line of Arsaces and normally ruling in Media Atropatene, now Azerbaijan. The king depicted here is perhaps that Darius represented in effigy at Pompey's triumph and who ruled c. 70 BC. The craftsman has most competently overcome the difficulties inherent in the 'en face' position.

1191 One of the greatest Roman disasters was the Parthian massacre at Carrhae in 53 BC. The contemporary Arsacid was Orodes II and the drachma illustrated comes towards the end of his reign, c. 40 BC. Already a degree of formalization is evident in its style. A wart occurs on the royal brow and its reappearance became, for later monarchs, a guarantee of true descent. The stars and crescent probably refer to the boast of Parthian kings to be brothers of the sun and moon; however, it is also likely that the increase in use of such symbols during each reign was, for a time, a help to the mint bureaucracy in distinguishing successive issues.

1192 Phraates IV had been persuaded to send his older sons as hostages to the court of Augustus so that

1183×2

1186×2

1184×3

1185×2

1187×2

1188×2

1189×3

the youngest, Praataces, could succeed him. The queen Musa then murdered Phraates and married her son. The Parthian nobility were prepared to stomach this incestuous union in fact a Magian custom) but rebelled against other infringements of their rights and disposed of the pair. In their place, the aristocracy invited back Vonones, one of Phraates' sons. His drachma portrait has a short Roman haircut and he further flouts Arsacid numismatic convention by setting his own name in the nominative on the obverse. Such aberrations reflected too westernized an approach and Vonones himself was expelled c. AD 11.

1193 During the first century AD intermittent warfare with Rome naturally forced Parthia away from its superficial Hellenism, back upon a deeply rooted oriental culture. The drachma of Vologases II (c. AD 78) reflects this, carrying behind the head in Parthian script the first two letters of his name. Such supplementary information was necessary because there were several contenders for the throne at this juncture and all Parthian rulers officially called themselves Arsaces.

1194 During his razzia through Mesopotamia in AD 116 Trajan captured the Parthian capital, Ctesiphon, and with it the golden throne and daughter of Osroes I, whose portrait this is. The strange coiffure, with hair sprouting above the streaming diadem (the symbol of royalty) and in large elaborate bunches below it, foreshadows those of the Sassanian princes. By now the engraving is very flat, there being no attempt to individualize the features.

1195 On later Parthian drachmae the seated archer of the reverse (**1189**) is a mere caricature, while the Greek legend, although retaining its square format, is reduced to near unintelligibility. For the coin illustrated, the top line has been replaced by Parthian script reading MTRDT MLK (king Mithradates); we know nothing historically of this monarch, but stylistically the coin is dated about AD 140. Below the archer's bow is a monogram denoting the mint, Ecbatana.

1196 As compared with the drachmae, Arsacid tetradrachms still attempted to give a readable legend. Unfortunately, as can be seen, the dies were habitually far larger than the flan, so that most of the script is missing. The design shows the enthroned monarch receiving a diadem from the goddess of Seleucia. Above the diadem are the letters of the Seleucid date 493, equivalent to AD 132; in the exergue is the month of issue, Panemcs, approximately June. At the right is the king's name, Vologases (IV). The metal of such issues is frequently highly debased.

1197 The final Parthian drachmae were struck by Artabanus IV (c. AD 216-24). Here we see him wearing the typical Arsacid tiara and he also has a forked beard; behind the head in Parthian script we read the start of his name. By now the engraving is almost wholly linear with no relief, a far cry from that at the beginning of the dynasty.

1198 Because of the Parthians' nomadic background, it was not difficult for fresh invaders to incorporate or be incorporated in the Arsacid feudal system. About AD 50 a small independent kingdom was set up in Margiana (Merv) and the local ruler, Sanabares struck there Parthian-style bronze drachmae. The formalized portrait with its over-emphasized hair-style indicates on the one hand a reaction from Hellenistic naturalism and on the other the Scytho-Celtic artistic continuum extending from Western Europe to the borders of China.

1190×3

1191×2

1192×

1193×3

1194×3

1195×3

1196×2

1197×3

1198×3

1199 An Indo-Parthian state flourished during the first century AD in Arachosia and Sistan i.e. southern Afghanistan. The rulers all bore Iranian names and were probably related to the Arsacids. Their rare silver drachmae all correspond to Parthian exemplars and here we see an issue of Otanes, who wears a tiara identical with that of Vologases II (**1193**) necessarily a contemporary. However, behind the head we meet not a name but a symbol or *tamgha*, which occurs on many other Indo-Parthian issues, some from the Indus Valley (**1361**).

1200 The reverse design of the same coin in an amalgam of Parthian tetradrachm and drachma types, the enthroned king crowned by Nike. In front is the Ecbatana monogram (**1195**), which had, it seems, become fossilized as part of the drachma apparatus. The square format legend, while poorly engraved, can be made out as reading, 'Outanes, king, son of Orthagnes, king.'

1201 The Seleucids were really only concerned to protect the north Iranian trade route with central Asia and the Indus valley. In consequence south Iran was not much affected by Hellenism and the earliest numismatic evidence for an independent Iranian state comes from Persis (modern Fars). The tetradrachm whose reverse is illustrated was struck at Istakhr, close to Persepolis, by Autophradates, one of its priest-kings. The design features him standing before the fire altar dedicated to Ahura-mazda, while the accompanying somewhat ambiguous Aramaic script points to a date about 200 BC and includes the name WTPRDT.

1202 With the rise of Arsacid power, Persis was forced into a feudatory state and indeed adopted many Parthian numismatic conventions. However, the portrait on this drachma owes little to its overlords. It was struck for a Darius, c. 120 BC, who wears a distinctive tiara, based on the flat Macedonian kausia, but additionally decorated with an eagle, an important element in later Sassanian iconography. The high relief head, with its stubbly beard, is a 'tour-de-force' of the engraver's art.

1203 With few silver mines at their disposal, the princes of Persis were obliged to get metal for their coinage by trade. Blanks were then most easily made by beating out flat the currency so obtained. This may account for the typically thin section of later period issues, such as the one shown. It portrays Manuchihr I, who probably reigned c. AD 150; again, the emphasis is on exotic coiffure, the maintenance of which would clearly preclude any strenuous (and hence degrading) activity on the part of its sacrosanct wearer.

1204 For his early issues, c. AD 210, Ardashir, the destroyer of the Arsacid empire, continued to employ the normal Persid techniques. However, the frontality of the portrait impressed on these silver drachmae incorporates a power and determination markedly different from that of the insipid contemporary Arsacid issues (**1197**).

1205 The Arsacids apparently never struck gold coins; but when he succeeded to their empire, Ardashir evidently decided that gold dinars such as that illustrated were a necessary adjunct to his new-found pretensions. Part of his 'de jure' claim to their throne must have been that all those kings after Mithradates II were usurpers, because Ardashir's portrait is an almost exact copy, down to the tiara ornaments, of that employed by his great predecessor (**1187**). The engravers seem to have recovered their old skill too and the portrait is really first-class.

1206 The thin flat flan of the drachma of Ardashir I shown here remained characteristic of all subsequent issues of this, the major Sassanian coin denomination. Struck shortly before his death, c. AD 241, he has now dispensed with Arsacid symbolism and is instead portrayed in another complicated hair style, a 'puff' above the diadem enclosed in a silk bag, while his beard is elaborately curled. The Pahlavi legend refers to him as 'seed of the gods'.

1207 The anti-western policy of Ardashir was taken up with even greater enthusiasm by his son Shapur I (AD 241-72). The emperor Valerian was defeated in battle and died in captivity, such exploits naturally enhancing the standing of Shapur in the eyes of his contemporaries. His numismatic iconography, with artificially arranged streaming hair, a close curled

1199×3

1200×2

1201×2

1202×3

1203×2

1205

beard confined at the bottom by a ring and, especially, the turreted crown were all intended to identify uniquely the 'great king' to his subjects. Many of the drachmae such as that shown were struck on flans made from melted-down Roman antoniniani, which were themselves debased.

1208 Although, as with other oriental dynasties, the harem must have played an important part at the Sassanian court, evidence for it is usually lacking in a male-dominated society. However, Bahram II (AD 276-93) chose for his most common issues to have both a wife and one of his sons portrayed with him. The concept of a unique head-dress now clearly extended to all members of the royal family; the heads of griffins, boars, eagles, etc. form the major feature. The titulature still contains references to the monarch's status as 'king of kings, of the divine seed'.

1209 The major element of the reverse design of nearly all Sassanian drachmae was the fire altar (**1201**). Under Ardashir I, this appeared alone, but with later reigns we find, as on the drachma of Bahram II, two figures, either the monarch and the chief priest or the monarch and a female divinity, presumably Anahita; sometimes the figures are turned outwards holding long sceptres, sometimes inwards with swords or with hand raised in adoration. Symbols, pellets, etc., occur in the field or on the altar and may refer to mints or officinae. The legend associates the altar fire with the monarch.

1210 Minor silver denominations, such as this obol of Shapur II (AD 309-79), were probably much more common at the time of issue than they now seem to be. Together with tiny copper coins, they were perhaps distributed as largesse at coronations. In designs they resemble the drachmae, although a diadem occasionally replaced the fire altar.

1211 In the Iranian epics Bahram Gur (Bahram V, AD 420-38) appears as the 'great hunter.' His drachmae follow established types, but on the reverse at this period we sometimes find a bust in the altar flames; this bust represents Ahura-mazda usually, but other examples include the appropriate crown, implying the royal portrait. The mint name is also incorporated intermittently in the reverse inscription.

1212 Balash (Valkaš or Vologases) AD 484-88 reigned at a time of considerable interplay, peaceful and otherwise, between Iran and the Kushan state of north-west India. It may be that as an indirect result of Buddhist influences, the monarch is depicted with a sacred flame issuing from his shoulder. The legend is reduced to 'Valkaš the happy.'

1213 On the reverse of the same drachma, the style of engraving is now much more perfunctory. The only inscription is the mint name Rhayy.

1214 The reign of Khusru I (AD 531-79) was regarded as one of the most glorious of the Sassanian epoch. He compelled the Byzantines to pay an annual subsidy of 1000 pounds of gold and this was later increased. The dinar illustrated may have been struck from this ever-recurrent booty. The unusual facing bust with its prominently displayed crescent reminds us of the strong Arabian influence.

1215 The major feature of the reverse of **1214** is a standing figure of the king in his pearl-embroidered skirt holding a large diadem. Part of the inscription shows that this was struck in year 44 of the reign.

1216 Such was the veneration accorded to the reigning monarch that, if he were dethroned, even temporarily, he had to receive a second coronation to re-establish the efficacy of his *xwarna*; at the same time his crown was modified. Khusru II, AD 591-628, suffered successful rebellion at the start of his reign and was eventually assassinated. We see him here wearing his second crown, an object so massive that when seated in audience, it was suspended directly above his head on a chain.

1217 The reverse of **1216** depicts the standard fire altar (**1201, 1209**), the attendants with hands clasped on the pommels of vertical swords. As with other contemporary issues, the design is surrounded by three dotted circles, one more than on the obverse. All such drachmae carry year dates at the left and mint names on the right (year 28 and MR = Merv in this case). Upwards of 40 mint signatures, not all deciphered, are known. These coins must have been struck in millions and are still extant in thousands.

1204

1206

1207

1208

1209×3

1210×2

1211

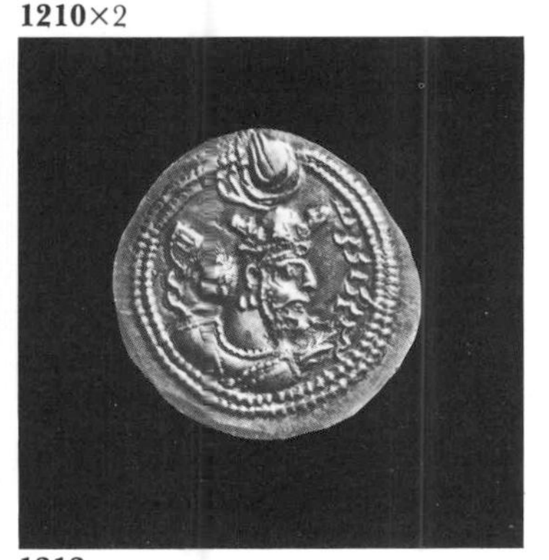
1212

1213

1214×2

1215×2

1216

1217

1224×2

element of the reverse design.

1231 By the second century AD Himyarite coins were no longer obviously derivative. Indeed, the very cupped shape of the silver specimen illustrated, combined with a portrait head adorned by pendent ringlets of hair in Semitic fashion, is unique. This example was struck by 'Amdan Bayyin at the mint of Raidan.

1225×3

1226×3

1227×3

1228×3

1218 After the murder of Khusru II, the Sassanian state existed in near anarchy for several decades until it was overthrown by the Arabs. Several ephemeral reigns occupied the period, among them that of the only Sassanian female sovereign Boran (AD 630-31) whose drachma portrait we see here. She also has her special crown, with long pendant decorations.

1219 Elymaean numismatic traditions derived from both Seleucid and Parthian prototypes. On the tetradrachm illustrated we see the jugate busts of Kamnaskires (II?) and his Queen Anzaze, compare the contemporary issue of Antiochus XI (**212**) but with typically Arsacid coiffures. Behind is an 'anchor' probably the symbol of a local rain-god. The coin was struck in 79 BC, probably at Seleucia-on-the-Hedyphon.

1220 During the first century BC there was a rapid deterioration, both in engraving skill and in metal content; many of the Elymaean 'tetradrachms' such as the one below contain no appreciable proportion of silver. The 'anchor' continues as a dynastic symbol and the issuer was another Kamnaskires, but no date is given on the coin.

1221 Parthian hegemony over Elymais eventually led to a dynasty there of Arsacid stock, rejoicing in such typical names as Phraates. The copper 'drachma' shown was struck by a Kamnaskires-Orodes, perhaps about AD 80. The exotic hair and beard styles as well as the frontality are entirely characteristic of Parthian art.

1222 Although bearing Iranian names, the princes of Characene had a distinctly Semitic cast of features. Tiraios II (78-48 BC), one of whose tetradrachms is illustrated, also adopts a florid coiffure owing something to his Arsacid overlords. A few bronze or lead issues supplemented these large coins which must have been used by those traders who took advantage of Characene's favourable entrepot situation.

1223 One of the most common names in the Characenian king-list is Attambelos, and the first ruler so called struck the tetradrachm shown here. Most such issues carry a reverse design of a seated Heracles holding a club. The legend runs 'Of king Attambelos, the deliverer, beneficent' in Greek with the Seleucid era date B □ Σ (=41 BC) in the exergue. The monogram probably refers, as it does for Arsacid tetradrachms, to the controlling magistrate. This and all later issues are frequently debased.

1224 As in Parthia, so in Characene, Greek fell into disuse and the later coins reverted to an Aramaic inscription. On the bronze 'tetradrachm' shown, this has been read as 'Maga son of Attambelos', but we have no historical record of such a prince, who probably reigned shortly before the accession of Ardashir I, the conqueror of Parthia and its dependencies.

1225 The relatively precarious position of Nabatea, between the hammer of Rome and the anvil of Parthia is reflected in the scarcity of its silver coinage. Naturally, Seleucid exemplars influenced the choice of the jugate position for the busts of Obodas III (30-9 BC) with his queen; the diadem implies royalty as usual and there is a Nabatean letter in the field.

1226 Aretas IV (9 BC–AD 40) was the greatest of the Nabatean kings. The reverse depicts his consort, laureate and veiled; the inscription reads 'Huldu, queen of Nabatea, year 10.' Coins such as this from early in the reign are well made, but subsequently both the standard of engraving and the silver content declined.

1218×3

1219×2

1220×2

XVII

ISLAM AND THE NEAR EAST

Michael Broome

The empire seized by the Arabs in the name of Islam in the seventh century AD contained two separate economies; Persia, with a plentiful supply of indigenous silver, and the Mediterranean coastlands with a Byzantine currency of gold and copper. Initially these two systems were allowed to coexist and a large number of Sassanian mints are known to have struck silver
1233 drachmae for the Arab governors. In contrast, there is little evidence that the only Byzantine mints in the area, Alexandria and Carthage, operated under Arab rule, except for a few copies of Alexandrian 12-nummi pieces possibly struck after the Arab conquests. By AD 690 (70 AH) with the power of the Umayyad Caliphs firmly centred on Damascus an Arab gold currency was needed, both as a trading medium and as visible evidence of the international standing of Islam.

The decision to act was reputedly sparked off by a squabble over the marks of authenticity on the Egyptian papyrus supplied to the Byzantine treasury. Taking as his model the solidus of Heraclius portraying the emperor standing and flanked by his two sons as colleagues, the Caliph 'Abd al-Malik struck similar coins but omitted the bars on the crosses and replaced the legend with the Arabic Kalima or 'Declaration of Faith'. In 693
554 (74 AH) shortly after Justinian II had issued a new solidus with a facing bust of Christ and, on the reverse, the emperor defiantly holding a large cross, 'Abd al-Malik responded with a new and
1234 dated series showing a standing caliph with his hand on his sword. Three years later, perhaps in consequence of the developing study of Muhammad's life and teaching, all images were dropped from the coinage and a new system introduced.

1236 This 'post-reform' coinage had two components, a gold *dinar*
1237 and a silver *dirham*, both names being clearly marked on the coins. They were struck from pure metal, within the refining standards of the time, and 10 dirhams weighed the same as seven dinars, the weight of the dinar being set at 20 Syrian carats or 4·25 grammes. It seems likely that this ratio was chosen to reflect the gold and silver prices then current. Although these soon changed, the standards were to survive for the next 750 years.

The design of the new coins was spartan.

'There is no god but Allah alone'

they proclaimed in the 'Kufic' Arabic script newly developed at Kufa. This central credo of Islam was supported by other phrases from the Holy Quran and set, on the silver coins, within a pattern of circles and annulets. The caliph's role as a follower of Muhammad–al-kalifat Muhammad–rather than a leader of Islam was implied by the complete anonymity of the coins and it was not until a century later – and with the foundation of a new dynasty – that we begin to find the caliph's name on the coins.

In two respects, the dirham followed the Sassanian drachma it supplanted; it was roughly the same size, and the mint and the 'regnal year' of striking were given in words, although the Arabs used the full mint-name rather than an abbreviation. The Hijra lunar era used for both dirham and dinar began in AD 622 with the Prophet's original 'flight' from Mecca to Medina, and is still used over most of the Islamic world. Gold coins in general had no mint-name until 813 (198 AH) but were probably struck at Damascus, the Umayyad capital. The main mints for silver were Damascus and, after 702 (84 AH) Wasit, although over 60 other mints operated.

In 749 (132 AH) the Umayyads were supplanted by the Abbasids and shortly afterwards a new capital was built near
Baghdad, named the City of Peace. The Abbasids maintained 1240
the system of coinage but replaced the long reverse inscription of
the Umayyads with the simple statement: 'Muhammad is the 1239
Prophet of Allah'. While, over the years, additional names and titles appear on the coins, the only change of type during the two centuries of Abbasid rule was the addition in 818 (202 AH) of a second marginal quotation from the Quran.

The copper coinage has no obvious division between the Umayyad and the Abbasid periods. The vast number of Byzantine folles circulating in Syria and North Africa seems to have been sufficient for the first 60 years, but then local mints
were opened to strike a copper *fulus* of the standing caliph type 1234
and even copies of the Byzantine 40-nummi pieces, complete with a large M on the reverse. These were replaced about 696 (77 AH) by purely Arabic designs, the earlier issues often
incorporating a reminder of desert life such as a palm branch or 1238
a desert rat. Abbasid coppers are wholly epigraphical. Initially
anonymous, the legends soon gives the mint, governor and date. 1245
The style of the fulus is quite different from the dirham or dinar, even if from the same mint, until about 770 (153 AH) when it begins to match the silver. Although Abbasid gold and silver was struck mainly at Baghdad until well into the tenth century AD, copper coins died out by about 864 (250 AH).

Numismatically, and after the Abbasid revolution of 749 (132 AH) politically as well, North Africa and Spain pursued an independent course. Dechristianized versions of Heraclian solidi
of Carthage are known with enigmatic inscriptions in Latin 1235
thought to stand for the Arabic Kalima. As their weights accord with the post-reform standard they were probably struck between 696 (77 AH) and 704 (85 AH) when a portraitless dated 565
series begins, some of which were minted in Spain. An Arabic

Mounted archer on a silver dirham of the Seljuq Qilij Arslan V, AD 1248 (**1272**).

1250 A gold quarter dinar of 272 AH struck by the Aghlabid Ibrahim II, probably for use in newly conquered Sicily.

1251 Superficially an Aghlabid coin, this dinar from Qayrawan challenges the Abbasid leader of Islam by naming the Fatimid Abdallah as Commander of the Faithful.

1252 A typical Fatimid dinar in the style of al-Mu'izz but struck triumphantly at the mint of Misr, the newly conquered capital of Egypt, soon after the short-lived Ikshidid dynasty had been swept away.

1253 Silver was scarce in Egypt and had to be imported. These rare silver coins down to 1/16 dirham were struck c. 350 AH.

1254 A glass weight of al-Mustansir, the Fatimid Caliph. Originally intended to check the weights of the new coin, by late Fatimid times they became small change themselves.

1255 The elegant and unusual design used by al-Mustansir for Sicilian quarter dinars 446 AH.

1256 A Zurayhid dinar from Aden of 510 AH struck to the Yemen weight of 2·5 grammes. Note the distinctive spiky calligraphy.

1257 The widespread use of Fatimid gold coins around the Mediterranean led to them being copied. This coin in the style of al-Amin was probably struck by the Crusaders.

1258 One of a curious group of oversize silver dirhams struck near the silver mines of the Hindu Kush in the name of the Samanid Nuh bin Nasr.

1259 Ghaznavid coinage consisted of dumpy base silver dirhams like this; or worse.

1260 This billon dirham of the Qarakhanids struck c. 400 AH at Sughd is one of the earliest examples of a 'looped square' design.

1250×3

1251×2

1252

1253A

1254

1255×3

1256×2

1253B

1257×3

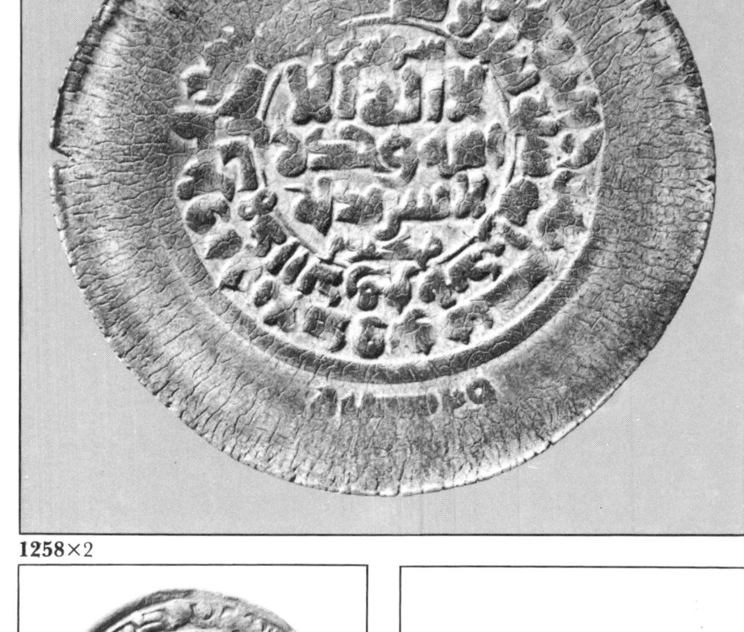

1258×2

1259×2

1260

1261×2

1262

1261 The tribal symbols of bow and mace on this dinar of 448 AH show that power rests with the Turkish Seljuqs from the steppes of Russia.

1262 Careless of the Islamic dislike of images on their coins, the Seljuqs of Syria chose an elephant to identify their copper pieces c. 500 AH.

1263 The scarcity of silver in the Islamic world led to the use of Byzantine copper folles in the adjoining territories as unofficial small change. Some of these pieces were then countermarked, presumably to allow their official use and this led to Islamic coins based on Byzantine designs such as the accompanying Artuqid fals from Amid (**1263B**).

1263A×3

1263B×3

1252 Fatima. Initially based in Tunisia under Caliph al-Mu'izz, they conquered the whole of the North African coastlands and in 969 (358 AH) seized Egypt from the Ikhshidids. The capital was moved to the new city of al-Qahira–Cairo–and Palestine and Arabia were absorbed.

In keeping with their achievement in setting up the first Shi'ite dynasty of any consequence, the Fatimids restyled the coinage,
1255 primarily dinars and quarter-dinars, so that the legends were set out in two or three circles with sometimes a blank anulus between. Each ruler selected a different combination until the
1253 end of the period. Rare fractional dirhams in similar style were
1254 minted, but small change seems to have been provided by glass coin weights found locally in some profusion.

Although the Tahirids served the Caliphs well, they were unable to put down a revolt in Sistan under al-Saffar, the coppersmith, or to prevent the Samanid governor of Transox-
1258 ania from establishing an independent dynasty. Claiming Sassanian descent they made Bukhara a focus for Persian national interests. Both Saffarids and Samanids struck dirhams in the name of the Caliph and when the Tahirids disintegrated in 873 (259 AH) Samanid dinars were minted at Nishapur. In Sistan, where the Saffarids had managed to retain most of their power as Samanid governors fractional gold pieces were struck over a period of some 70 years.

In 940 (328 AH) the final threat to the Abbasids came from the Buyids who stirred the Shi'ite minorities of the Elburz Mountains to mount an attack on Persia and Iraq that completely destroyed the civil power of the Caliph and enforced Shi'ite doctrines on the mullahs. Little of this shows on the coinage. Dinars and dirhams of traditional type were struck in the Caliph's name with the names of the Buyid amirs appearing as the branches of the family gained power. By this time, the concept of a coin having a particular weight had been lost, as surviving specimens vary considerably about the average. This is particularly marked in the dirhams and may be due to the shortage of silver that developed in the Arab world during the tenth century AD. The vast number of dirhams exported to Russia and Scandinavia in trade would have drained the Islamic treasuries and difficulties over the silver mines in the mountains prevented their replenishment.

The Samanid rise to power was paralleled a century later when Mahmud, governor of Ghazna, gained enough power to
replace them by the Ghaznavid dynasty. From this strategic **1386**
position, northern India could be raided as well as Khwarazm and Persia. His coinage began with a brief continuation of the large silver Samanid pieces first struck near the mines of the
Hindu Kush; but the normal currency was of small nondescript **1259**
dirhams with rapidly reducing silver content. A separate series
showing a stylized bull was struck for the Indian provinces. **1383**
Normal gold dinars were struck in some quantity at Ghazna, Herat and Nishapur. Unlike Samanid coins, they recognize al-Qadir as Caliph.

The Turkish Invasion

To maintain control over the vast territories conquered by the Abbasids demanded more troops than could be supplied from Arab or even Persian stock. The only good sources of fighting men were the pagan Turkish tribes that inhabited the steppes of south Russia. On the eastern frontiers of Islam, bands of Turkish mercenaries frequently fought for the Arabs, and male slaves that formed a large proportion of the booty of war were valued as new recruits. Some rose to high positions and for 50 years from 836 (221 AH) the Caliph was virtually controlled by his Turkish bodyguard in Samarra. The Ghaznavid armies were mainly Turkish, but rival bands of Seljuq Turks penetrated Buyid territory further west and in 1038 (429 AH) established a new
dynasty at Nishapur. Their leader Tughril Beg, using the **1261**
unpopularity of the Buyids' Shi'ite policies, advanced to Baghdad to 'free the Caliph' and soon destroyed the Buyids. In spite

1264 The Zangids developed their own designs including a western-style double-headed eagle and an eastern figure holding the new moon from Mosul.

1265 One of the largest copper coins from the Islamic series, this Zangid piece from Jazira dated 600 AH weighs 32 grammes and shows an unusual tamgha.

1266 The Seljuqs of Rum struck their first coinage in copper with a purely Byzantine obverse.

1267 The silver coinage of the Seljuqs of Rum was normally epigraphic, but their nomadic traditions sometimes appear as with this horseman armed with a mace from Kaysariyah.

1268 Typical of the early silver coinage of the Seljuqs of Rum, this dirham with its stubby lettering and elaborate arabesques has a fresh and commanding style. Struck in the Seljuq capital of Qonya in 618 AH.

1264A×3

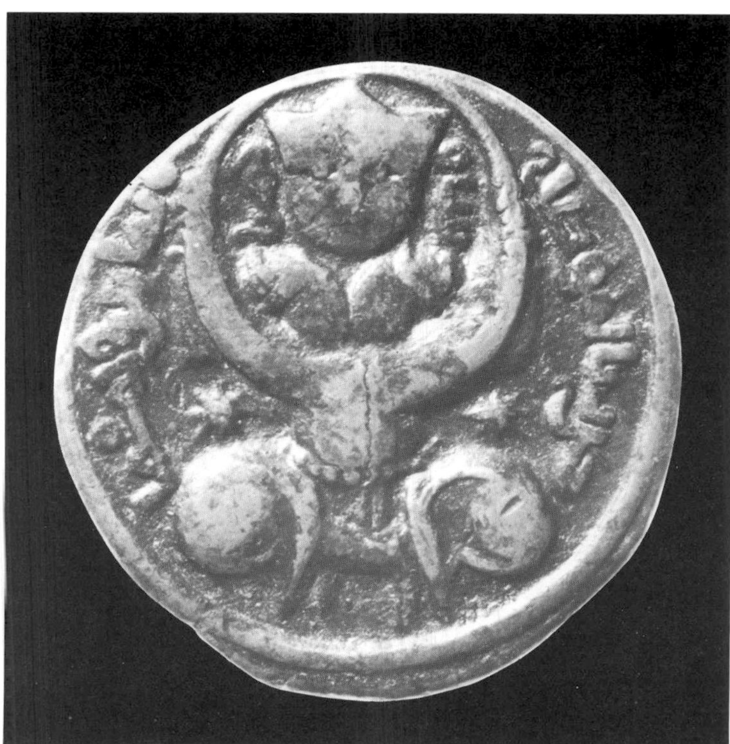

1264B×3

1265×3

1266×2

1267

1268

1269 An unusual bilingual silver coin from Armenia struck by Hethoun I acknowledging the overlordship of the Seljuq Kay Qubad I; no mint, no date but c. 630 AH.

1270 A fairly extensive copper coinage was struck by the Seljuqs of Rum, the later pieces having a typical thick style of lettering.

1271 The forerunner of the royal symbol of Persia, tradition ascribes the origin of this piece to the wish of Kay-Khusru II to honour his beautiful Georgian wife. Her horoscope showed that she was born when the sun was in the constellation of Leo.

1272 This beautiful silver dirham struck in the name of the boy-king Qilij Arslan IV in 646 AH may well have been intended to recall the common ancestry of the Seljuqs and the Mongols whose help was being sought to overthrow Kay Kawus II, his brother and a contender for the Seljuq throne.

1273 In the event the Mongols took over the country and ruled in the name of the three sons of Kay Khusru II. Their names and titles are all squeezed on to this silver coin (no longer called a dirham) of Sivas dated 654 AH.

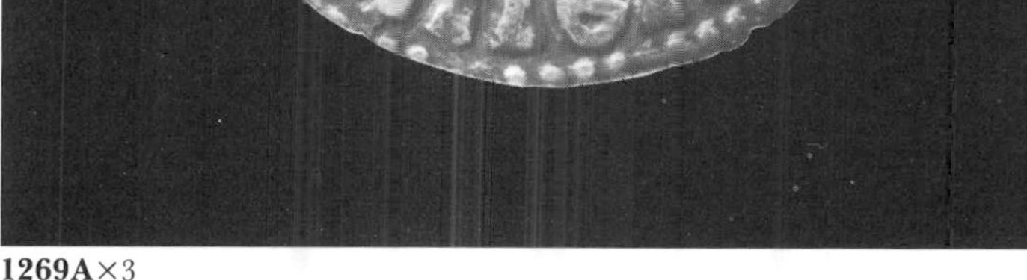

1269A×3

1269B×3

1270×2

1271×2

1272×2

1273×2

of the alien cultural background of the Seljuqs they maintained the coinage on traditional lines. Silver was still scarce and the early coins are mainly dinars with the Seljuq tribal symbols
1261 triumphantly displayed on each side. As time went on even gold became scarce and later issues were struck in debased gold.

1387 To the north, Islam had spread to the Ghurids of Afghanistan who eventually destroyed the Ghaznavids, and to the Ilek Khans or Qarakhanids of Bukhara. Both came under Seljuq control but by 1200 (600 AH) the Seljuq Turkish governors of Khwarazm, under the title of Khwarazm Shahs, superseded the Seljuqs. The Ilek Khans introduced a major change in Islamic design when they struck large copper fulus c. 1000 (400 AH) with the legend
1260 set within cartouches such as the 'looped square', a design that provided the inspiration for many succeeding coins. The Khwarazm Shahs also struck similar large billon coins (some named dirhams) and normal dinars with a billon horseman issue for Afghanistan.

Although the original Seljuq supremacy had waned by 1157 (552 AH) allowing a resurgence of civil power by the Abbasid Caliphs who struck large gold dinars over the next century, the resounding defeat of the Byzantines in 1071 (463 AH) at the battle of Manzikert had opened Anatolia to attack by independent groups of Seljuqs who gradually settled most of the land. Pre-eminent amongst these were the Seljuqs of Rum who, although losing their capital Qonya to Frederick Barbarossa and the Third Crusade, took advantage of the Latin conquest of Constantinople in 1204 (601 AH) to regain almost all Anatolia.

Their coinage marks a complete break with 500 years of
Islamic coin design. Initially in copper, using Byzantine designs 1266
familiar to the people, it soon moved to the use of a mounted warrior as the main feature from about 1200 (600 AH). The predominant coins were silver, some named dirhams or even
dinars. Normally epigraphic, with rare horseman types, they 1267
made good use of the thick flowing script employed, sometimes 1268
adding complex arabesques. The purely Turkish Seljuqs of Rum were probably the originators of the national symbol of Persia,
the lion and sun, found on the common 'astrological' issues of 1271
Kay Khusru II. The quality of the engraving then falls off but new designs were being employed until the dynasty was extinguished in 1300 (700 AH).

250 years earlier in Iraq and Syria, the Seljuq governors or Atabegs overthrew their masters and set up their own dynasties. The Zangids based on Mosul were the most important and
played a large part in the wars of the second Crusade eventually 1264
occupying Egypt and destroying the Fatimids. Their army 1265
commander Yusuf bin Ayyub, known to the west as Saladin,

1274 The last few Seljuq puppet rulers under the Mongols used coins of this type from most of their mints. This specimen of Mas'ud II was struck at the silver mines of Baibirt in the north-east of Anatolia.

1275 The decay of Seljuq power allowed the Abbasid Caliphs to grow in influence and for a century they struck their own gold coins. The later issues like this piece of the last Caliph al-Musta'sim were often very heavy weighing up to 20 grammes.

1276 A full dirham struck in the Syrian town of Hamah in 583 AH by Saladin the Ayyubid.

1277 Other distinctive silver dirhams of the Ayyubids from Damascus and Aleppo.

1274

1276×2

1277A×2

1277B×2

1275

1278 Typical of the later Ayyubid coins of Damascus, this silver piece with the name of al-Salih Ismail was probably struck by the Crusaders in Acre c. 1250 AD. Compare **617**.

1279 The early Ayyubid gold coinage, struck in Egypt, followed the Fatimid style with circular legends. About 620 AH a new style was introduced with the old-fashioned Kufic script replaced by Nashki. Heavy dinar of Alexandria 622 AH weighing 7·4 grammes.

1280 The bird on this Rasulid dirham from the Yemen of 774 AH is the mint mark of Zabid.

1281 The Mamluk Baybars retained the Ayyubid style but added a prowling lion below the legend. Dinar of Alexandria.

1278×2

1279

1280

1281×2

turned on the Zangids in 1169 (564 AH) and established the Ayyubid dynasty based in Damascus.

The Atabegs struck a series of coins unparalleled in Islamic history; large copper coins with designs based on Roman or even
1263 Greek prototypes. Their origin possibly lies in the countermarked Byzantine folles used in the Jazira, or in the use for small change of locally-found hoards of Roman or Greek Imperial bronzes in face of the absence of small denominations towards the end of the Seljuq period.

The Ayyubids, the new rulers of Egypt made little change to the Fatimid coinage of variable weight dinars and 'black dirhams' of low-grade silver, except in Syria where the first good silver coinage for over 200 years was minted. Although they were not named as dirhams the coins were struck to the traditional 2·9 grammes on small flans. Halves were also minted and new bold designs used for both denominations. So successful were the new 'Nasiri coins that they were copied extensively in good silver by
1278 the Crusaders of Acre until forced by Papal edict to change the
617 Islamic inscriptions.

By 1250 (648 AH) the Ayyubids had also succumbed to their Turkish slave army commanders. These 'mamluks' were especially trained as fighting men and formed a powerful
1281 professional army that easily thrust aside the last weak Ayyubid. As the centre of power moved to Cairo, the Syrian silver coinage deteriorated to the Egyptian standards and although of
1282 improved fineness was of poor workmanship. When the Mongol invasion cut off silver supplies the Mamluks turned to copper and produced quantities of lumpy coins with an intriguing
1285 variety of designs. The trade from India and the Far East channelled through Egypt, generated a need for a standardized
1284 gold currency and in consequence Barsbay I introduced in 1425 (829 AH) a gold *ashrafi* or sequin of 3.4 grammes: with a distinctive design which became one of the trading currencies of the Mediterranean. He also attempted to come to terms with the shortage of silver by using silver coins marked with the
1283 denomination of ¾ and ⅜ dirhams, an experiment not followed by his successors who struck only half and quarter dirhams of decreasing weight.

The Mongols

The pressures impelling the Turks westwards were equally
1286 applicable to the Mongols of Siberia. Under Ghengiz Khan, they invaded Tibet and China from their capital of Qarakorum and in 1220 (617 AH) moved into Khwarazm ending the brief empire of the Khwarazm Shahs. After Ghengiz Khan's death in 1227
1295 (624), his lands were divided, with the Blue Horde controlling
Southern Russia, the Giray Khans controlling the Crimea and **1296**
the Chagatayids controlling Khwarazm. The greatest impact on **1297**
the Islamic world came from the Ilkhanids who conquered Persia c. 1250 (650 AH) at about the same time Kublai Khan conquered China. Small silver coins weighing c. 1.5 grammes were struck from 1252 (650 AH) by the Blue Horde, later, by the Golden Horde, and at a lower weight, by the Giray Khans. Rudimentary in style they are nevertheless of interest in displaying the tribal tamghas and introducing c. 1267 (665 AH)
in the Crimea the use of numerals for the date. Few silver coins of **1287**
the Great Khans survive, but the Ilkhanids struck a wide range of types in gold, silver and copper, using up to 200 mints. The economic factors producing such activity also led to the most rapid inflation then known to the Islamic world. Between 1278 (676 AH) and 1352 (753 AH) the weight of a silver dirham was reduced 12 times as it fell from 2·85 to 0·84 grammes. Each new weight standard was signified by a design change and the steps allowed the whole coinage to form part of the same accounting
system. Early Ilkhanid coins used the newly developed Mongol **1290**
script on the reverse although written horizontally instead of **1438**
vertically as on the Mongol Chinese coins. The standard of engraving and production was generally high and the popularity of Abu-Sa'id's 'looped-square' coins was such that they were copied by independent Anatolian and Turkmen tribes for decades after the Ilkhanids had vanished. Considering the strength both of their civil and their military organization it is surprising how short was their period of power.

Abu-Sa'id died in 1335 (736 AH) and the Ilkhanid sultans became mere figureheads, their land soon to be dismembered by
local chieftains. The Jalayrids took the major part with the **1299**
Artuqids rising again in Hisn-Keyfa, the Muzaffarids in Shiraz
and the Sarbardarids, a fiercely Shi'ite group, in Astarabad. **1298**
Each dynasty produced silver coins, mostly double dirhams of 1.5 grammes although the Sarbardarids struck anonymous six and eight dirham coins.

The coming of Timur 'Lenk', called Tamerlane by the western
chroniclers, changed the face of the world of Islam. He was **1300**
originally governor of the area around Samarqand for the Chagatayids, but broke out in imitation of Ghengiz Khan (his claimed ancestor) and uprooted the existing dynasties from Afghanistan to Syria, destroying the established system of irrigation that enabled life to flourish in what are still most inhospitable climates and surroundings. Timur himself left few
coins behind but his son Shah Rukh's coinage of five gramme **1301**
silver *tankahs* was extensive.

The Timurid empire disappeared as rapidly as it had arisen, but the Timurid Hussayn Bayqara from his elegant court at

1296-97 The Giray Khans established themselves in the Crimea c. 760 AH and remained there for over 400 years until it was annexed by Russia. These two coins were struck 300 years apart but show little change. The Giray tamgha appears on both.

1298 The disintegration of the Ilkhanid dynasty allowed smaller 'Alid groups to grow. This anonymous but fiercely Shi'ite coin of the Sarbardarids comes from Sebsevar.

1299 A gold Jalayirid piece from Baghdad copying the 'square Kufic' design introduced by Abu Sa'id the Ilkhanid 50 years earlier (**1294**).

1296×2

1297A×2

1297B×2

1298

1299

1300 Tamarlane who destroyed much of the civilization of the Middle East and ruled in great splendour from Samarqand, placed his symbol of three circles on this eight-dirham coin.

1301 A new silver tankah of Sebsevar struck by Timur's son Shah Rukh at a weight of five grammes.

1302 A tankah of Husayn Bayqara, the last Timurid of any stature, struck at Herat in 897 AH.

1303 The Aq Qoyunlu or White Sheep of Diyarbakr survived Timur's ravages by timely acceptance of his overlordship and became a force to be reckoned with. A silver tankah of Ya'qub with an unusual reverse design and legend.

1304 A rare anonymous silver coin of the Zirids.

1305 The Murabids struck Fatimid-type dinars with a single margin on each side. This piece of Yusuf bin Tashfin shows his name below the obverse and was struck in 487AH at Seville in Spain.

1300

1301×2

1302

1303×2

1304×2

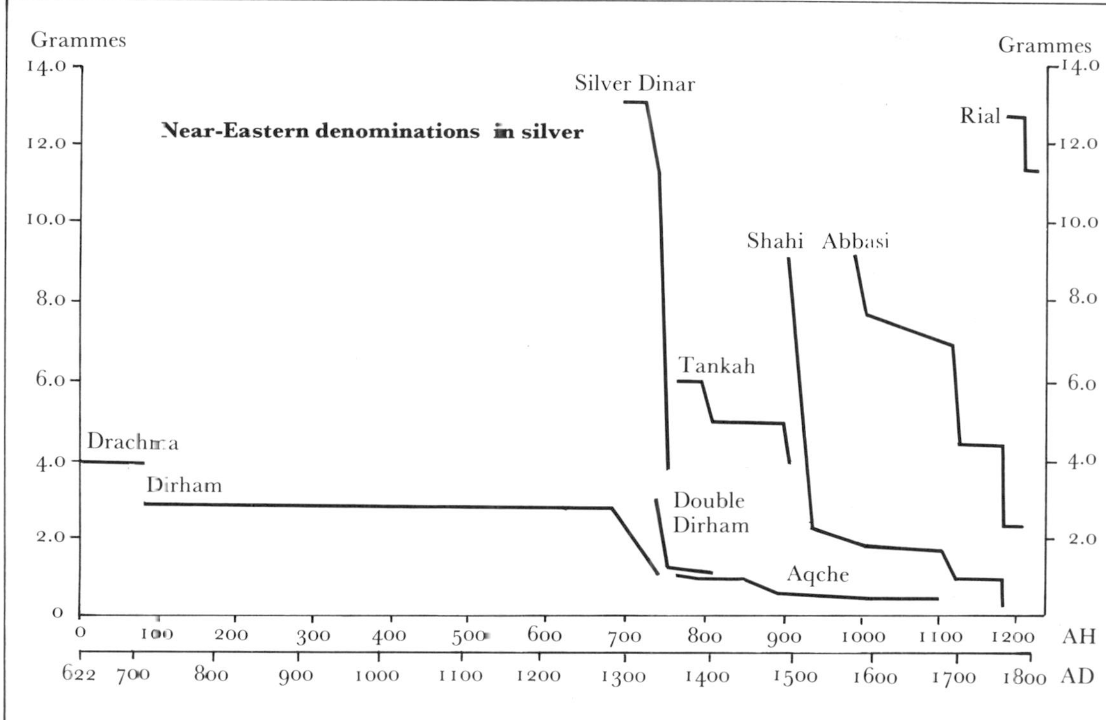

1305

military consequence it provided a tremendous ideological boost.
The coinage struck during the post-Timur civil wars provides
mint-names and dates and reflects the changing fortunes of the
amirs, quick to use the coinage to proclaim their antecedents.
The tughra or ornamental signature of the ruler was first placed
1314 on Ottoman coins by Suleyman bin Bayazid. Mehmet the
Conqueror was the overall victor but during the 31 years of his
1315 second reign the aqche fell to 0·8 grammes. Triumphant gold
1317 *altuns* were struck in Constantinople, but aqches, normally dated
only with the accession year, provided the main medium of
exchange rather like the pre-1279 English penny. Rates of pay
were quoted in aqches and the coins changed hands in sealed
purses of guaranteed contents. Copper *manghirs*, although fre-
1316 quently demonetized, were officially accepted for payment of
local taxes and were struck to definite weights. The intricate
designs of some of these are worthy of study in their own right.

By 1512 (918 AH) when Selim the Grim became Sultan, the Ottomans were the most powerful force in the Islamic world. Five years later the degenerate Mamluk state was absorbed and the powerful army of professional jannisaries thrown at the emerging Safavids in Persia whose Shi'ite views challenged the Sultan's claim to the Caliphate. In consequence of this territorial expansion and the control of trade routes that it brought, gold
coins were struck at more than 20 mints and Suleyman the
Magnificent claimed the proud title of 'Sultan of the two lands
(Europe and Asia) and Qakhan of the two seas' (the Black Sea
and the Mediterranean). The tiny Ottoman aqches proved
unpopular in Syria and Iraq and silver dirhams were minted 1318
there. By c. 1592 (1000 AH) many mints were striking these
heavier coins and using the larger flan for regional designs.

Suleyman died in 1566 (974 AH) and the succession of weak
sultans that followed resulted in an inability to deal either with
the population growth generated by the prosperous times, or the
rise of bandits in central Anatolia. The Ottoman Empire was not
immune to the inflation in Europe caused by the New World
bullion and the silver coinage was constantly being devalued.
The denominations were not given on the coins but in 1687 1320
(1099) Suleyman II struck a *gurush* of 120 aqches weighing 19
grammes with thirds, halves and three-quarters of *zolotas*. A
reorganization of the coinage c. 1703 (1115 AH) produced three
parallel series of gold coins: the old 3·4 grammes ashrafi; a new 1324
zeri mahbub at 2·6 grammes with Constantinople renamed
Islambul, and a north African series at 3.2 grammes. The silver
also was realigned but with a fourth standard for Azerbaijan
more in line with the Persian coinage. By the end of the
seventeenth (eleventh) century only five mints were in regular

1306 A small silver qirat from Cordova of the Murabid Ali bin Yusuf. His name appears below the reverse as Leader of the Muslims.

1307 Square silver dirhams were struck anonymously by the Muwahhids and Hafsids of North Africa for over 150 years and copied extensively by Christian communities. This piece comes from Marrakesh.

1308 A double dinar of the Muwahhids. Undated but struck 646-665 AH at Sijilmasah in south Morocco. This type was used throughout North Africa for the next 500 years.

1309 An anonymous dinar of the Marinids c. 750 AH from Fes. This may represent the "oboli di musc'" of western chroniclers, used as a source of pure gold for presentation to the church.

1310 The first major change in design of North African gold coins, other than Ottoman issues, came with the Filali Sharifs of Morocco. The eight-pointed star of this gold coin from Fes of 1189 became the predominant symbol of all later Moroccan series.

1311 A cast copper three-fulus piece from Fes in Morocco, dated in western numerals.

1312 The Mongol withdrawal from Anatolia allowed local Turkmen dynasties to strike their own coins such as this silver piece of the Saru Khan showing the tughra of Ishaq bin Ilyas.

1313 The Ottoman ruler Bayazid I annexed most of Anatolia in 792 AH. His dumpy silver aqche simply states, 'Bayazid bin Murad' with no titles of any sort.

1314 Timur captured Bayazid and re-established the smaller states leaving Bayazid's sons to fight for the Ottoman territories. His eldest son, the Emir Suleyman, struck this aqche in 806 AH showing his name and descent as a tughra, its first use in the Ottoman series.

1306×3

1307×3

1309

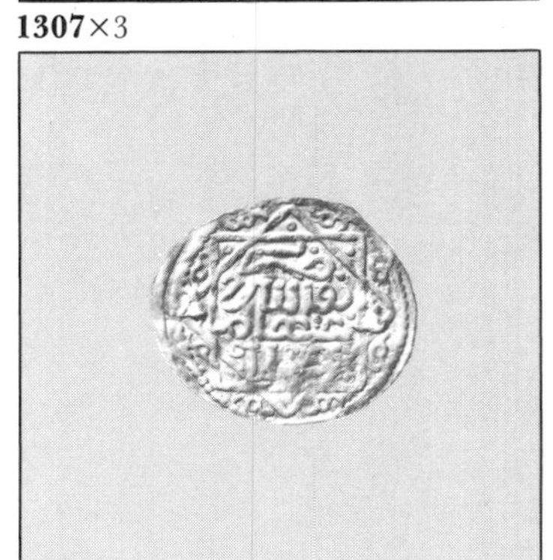

1310

1308×3

1311×3

1312×3

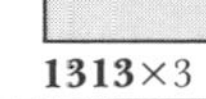

1313×3

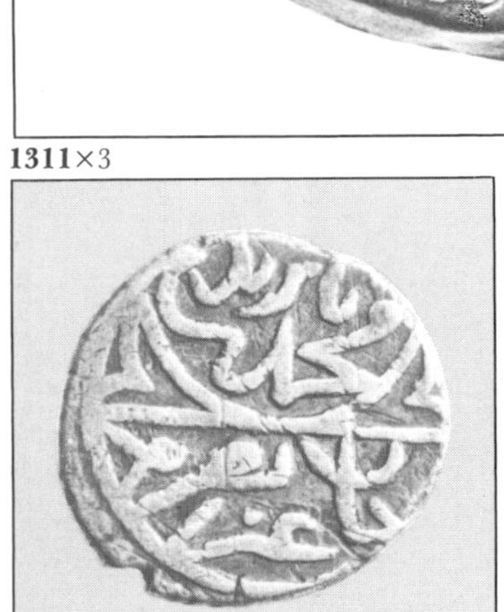

1315A×3

1315B×3

1314×6

1315 An aqche of Mehmet the Conqueror minted at Adrana, the Ottoman capital in Europe.

1316 One of the extensive series of locally struck copper manghirs, of Suleyman I.

1317 The West trembled when Mehmet II conquered Constantinople in 857 AH, but it was 882 before the first gold altun of the Ottoman series was struck there.

1318 The new prosperity of the Ottoman Empire put strains on the traditional use of silver aqches as the basic currency. In the reign of Suleyman the Magnificent some silver dirhams were struck at mints in newly conquered territory like this coin of Baghdad.

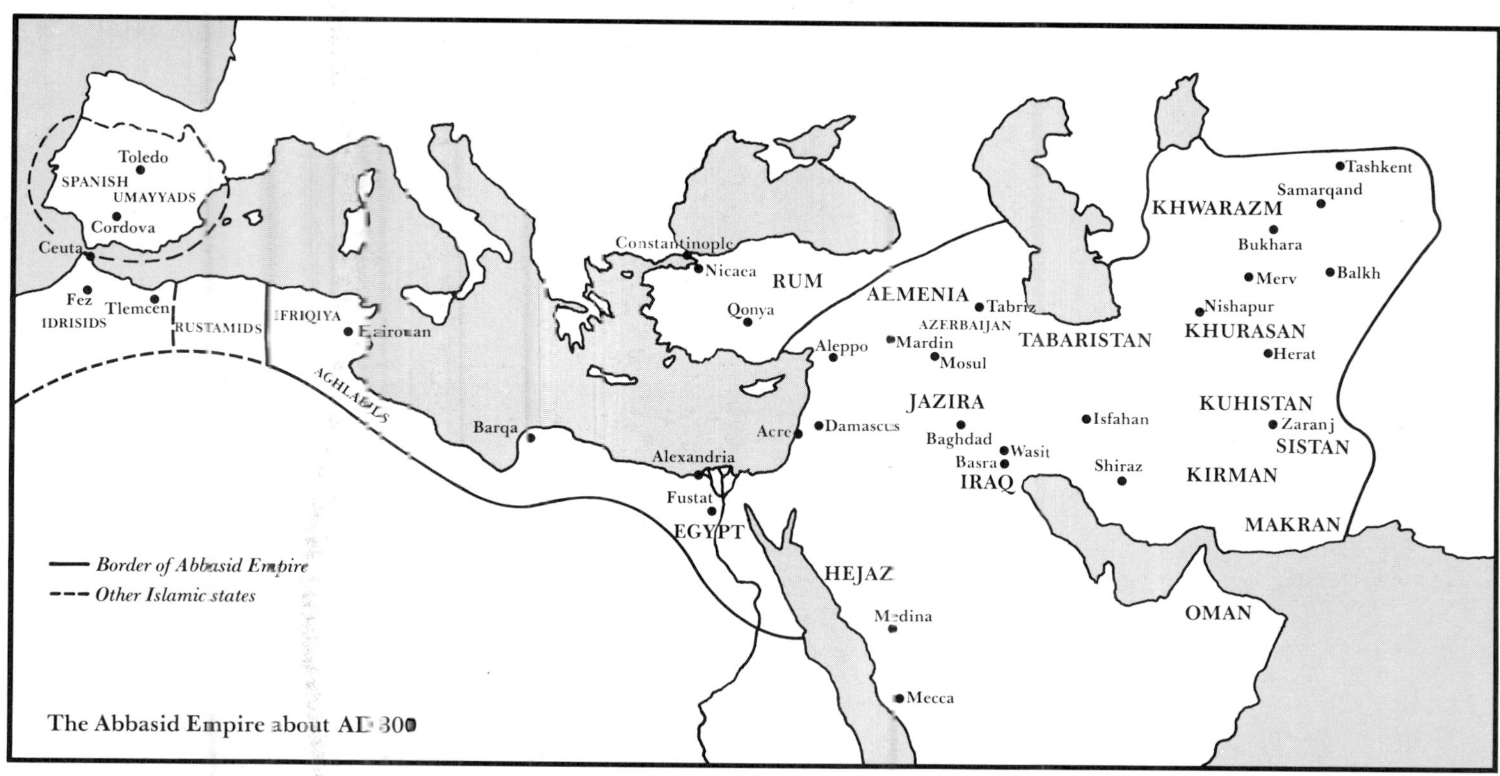

The Abbasid Empire about AD 800

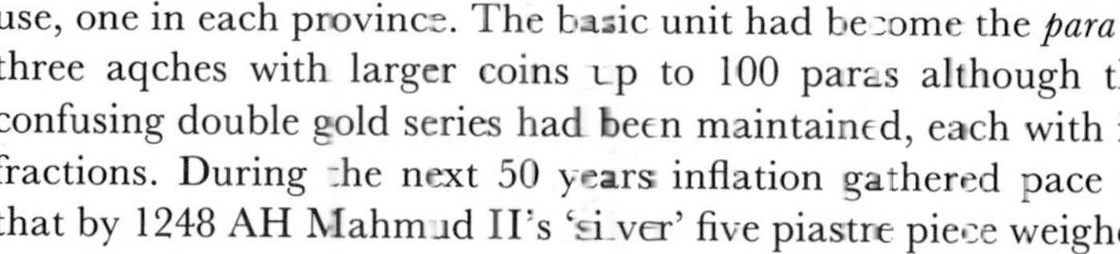

1316×2 1317A×2 1317B×2 1318×2

use, one in each province. The basic unit had become the *para* of three aqches with larger coins up to 100 paras although the confusing double gold series had been maintained, each with its fractions. During the next 50 years inflation gathered pace so that by 1248 AH Mahmud II's 'silver' five piastre piece weighed less than Suleyman's piastre and was almost pure copper.

Persians and Afghans

The newly established Ottoman hold on eastern Anatolia was soon threatened by Shi'ites from Azerbaijan. In 1501 (907 AH)
1326 the Sufi order of the Safavids emerged from Ardabil and with the help of the seven 'red-head' Turkmen tribes known as 'Qizil Bash' drove the Aq Qoyunlu out of Tabriz. Isma'il, the first Shah, went on to establish a Shi'ite state in Iraq and Persia, soon appreciated by western powers as a counterweight to the Ottomans. He also established a completely new series of gold and silver coins based on the *mithqal* of 4·6 grammes. The basic gold coin weighed one mithqal and halves and quarters were also struck. The silver pieces weighed one, two or four mithqals. The
1327 two mithqal piece being known as a *shahi*. A parallel series of gold *ashrafi* to the Mamluk standard were also minted and in time all gold coins became known as ashrafis. Early Safavid coins used a wide variety of designs; almost every mint was different and designs changed frequently. The large flans needed for the two mithqal silver 'shahis' carried Isma'il's full titles and 1328
the names of the 12 Safavid Imams. 15 years later the inexorable laws of supply and demand brought inflation and by AD 1576 1332
(948 AH) the shahi weighed only half of a mithqal. By then the ruler's name was replaced by a distich and the mint names given epithets e.g Dar-al-Sultan – the city of the Sultan. In time almost every mint had such an epithet although confusingly several mints eventually shared the same title. By 1650 (1060 AH), the normal silver coin was an *abbasi* of four shahis and a five-abbasi 1333
silver crown was struck.

The main internal currency of Safavid Persia was silver, but the charges for minting were high and coins circulated at values far above their bullion cost. Even so, large quantities were exported illegally to India. The abbasis were particularly esteemed for their consistent quality and weight. Two subsidiary silver coinages also circulated; low fineness two-shahi pieces of 1335
the Huwayza mint that provided a token currency for everyday use, and bent silver 2½-shahi bars known as larins, from Lar, 1336
and stamped between dies. The use of *larins* was obligatory for foreign merchants trading around the southern coast of Persia from as early as AD 1550 when they were worth about 10

1319 In the year 1003, Mehmet III reintroduced the use of the tughra on Ottoman silver coins after a gap of 200 years. It identified the new low-weight dirhams from Syria and Iraq.

1320 The needs of the economy for silver brought imports of foreign crown-sized coins. To counter this Suleyman II introduced in 1099 AH a new gurush weighing c. 19 grammes.

1321 A magnificent gold presentation piece of Mahmud I.

1322 The aqche had fallen in weight to only ⅛ gramme by the beginning of the twelfth century of the Hijra.

1323 Coins of Mahmud I from the North African provinces of Tunis and Algiers. Unlike normal Ottoman issues the dates on these coins are the actual date of striking. The gold half sequin from Algiers (**a**) has provided the pattern for innumerable copies in brass used as jewellery. The name Mustafa at the top of the 10 para silver coin of Tunis (**b**) is the second half of Mahmud's name, split most unusually between each side of the coin.

1319×3

1320×3

1321×3

1322×3

1323a

1323b

1324 A sequin of Mustafa III showing Islambul, the new title given to Constantinople. Only the last digit of the date is given as Mustafa's accession coincided with the beginning of a new decade.

1325 For a few years Egypt under Pasha Ali Bey was virtually independent and the word 'Al ' is seen at the top of this 20 para silver piece next to the 85 for the date 1185 AH.

1326 After 150 years of preparation the Sufi order of the Safavids threw off the Aq Qoyunlu rulers of Azerbaijan in 907 AH. This anonymous silver tankah from Sari would have been struck at that time.

1327 Once Shah Isma'il had established himself he produced a coinage of large silver pieces. This silver shahi weighing nearly 10 grammes comes from Ardabil, the centre of Safavid power. The interwoven cartouches contain the names and attributes of the 12 Imams accepted by the Safavids.

1328 Examples of Safavid inventiven s in turning the Alid phrases into a coin design.

1324×2

1326×2

1325×3

1327×3

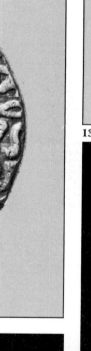

1328B×3

1328A×3

English pence. Small numbers were still in use 300 years later.

The period between 1722 (1135 AH) and 1786 (1209 AH) brought violent changes of power. The governor of Afghanistan declared his independence and then invaded Persia. After a few years the Afghans were dislodged by Nadir, an Afshari who also extinguished the Safavid dynasty. He was murdered in 1747 (1160 AH) and four different groups fought each other for control. Eventually, Afghanistan regained its independence under the Durranis and the Qajars of Tabaristan ruled in Persia, making Tehran their capital.

These changes are quite apparent on the coinage. The rare

1329 A gold quarter ashrafi of Shah Tahmasp.

1330 The Safavids' most hated enemies were the Shirvan Shahs of Shamakhi in what is now Russian Azerbaijan. This coin was struck at Shamakhi by the Shirvan Shah.

1331 Following the decline of the Timurids, Afghanistan was divided between the Moghuls, the Safavids and the Shaybanids from Transoxania who were descendants of Ghengiz Khan. This silver piece of Timurid style was issued by Kochkunju at Asfarayin c. 930 AH.

1332 By the time of Shah Safi I 1038-52 AH the weight of a shahi had fallen to a fifth of its original weight and the inscription had settled down to a shortened and thickened version as seen on this coin of Isfahan.

1333 A silver four-shahi piece from Isfahan struck by Shah Sultan Hussayn showing the high standards of engraving and calligraphy. Around the obverse are arranged the names of the 12 Shia Imams.

1334-36 A wide variety of coinage was in use in various parts of Persia. Here are a rectangular five-shahi piece struck in the north between 1129 and 1131 AH (**1334**), a debased coin of Huwayza which provided coinage for ordinary transactions (**1335**), and a larin from the south, imposed on foreign merchants for trading transactions at a high profit to the authorities (**1336**).

1329×3

1330×3

1331×3

1332×2

1334

1333A×2

1333B×2

1335×2

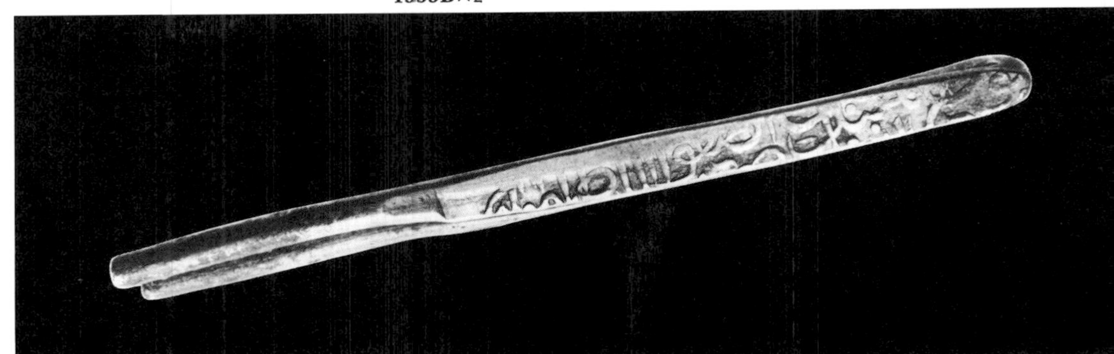

1336×2

1337 An example of the unusual tughra found on some of the coins of Nadir the Afshari.

1338 Many of Nadir's coins employed dies smaller than the flans as for this 10-shahi silver piece from the Sind.

1339 A gold mohur-ashrafi of the Zand ruler Karim Khan from Isfahan. The use of an ornamental cartouche set in a plain surround to display but not restrict the lettering, is an example of the wide range of designs used for the Zandieh coinage.

1340 Most major towns struck their own local coinage in copper and used a wide selection of images to distinguish their products. This mysterious sun face from Abushahr probably has a continuous ancestry back to the exuberant coins of the Artuqids 600 years earlier.

1337×3

1338×3

1339×3

1340×3

Afghan issues omit the Shi'ite names but are still in the Safavid style. The coins of Nadir Shah are quite different, small dumpy pieces omitting the Kalima altogether and in denominations
1337 from 1 to 20 shahis. Nadir's empire extended into northern India
1338 and heavy gold mohur-ashrafis were struck at his Indian mints and later elsewhere. The confusion following Nadir's death led to a complicated series of parallel coinages before the Qajar eunuch Agha Muhammad unified the country. He issued a new *rial* of 25 shahis and replaced the gold mohur-ashrafis with a *toman*, initially equivalent to the contemporary English guinea. All coinage was scarce following the civil war and 'civic' copper *puls* of bewildering variety became the common currency. Most of these pieces show a bird or beast except in Afghanistan where the Durranis, who also minted Indian style rupees, placed a sabre on their coppers.

By 1797 (1203 AH) the multitude of dynasties in the Near and Middle East had been reduced to four; the Durranis in Afghanistan, the Qajars in Persia, and the Filali Sharifs in Morocco with the Ottomans holding all the rest. Each dynasty struck a coinage in gold, silver and bronze in a number of denominations and within a century each had moved to the use of machine-struck token coinage. 48

XVIII
ANCIENT INDIA

David MacDowall

The early coinage of the north-west provinces of India from the sixth to the fourth centuries BC consisted of bent bars of silver, slightly concave, with a wheel symbol struck at each end. Major finds come from Taxila, Charsadda, and Bajaur in North Pakistan and from Gardez, Jelalabad, and Kabul in Afghanis-
1341 tan. Double the weight of the Persian siglos, they were the silver currency of the eastern Achaemenid provinces, while the small round concave silver coin with the same solar symbol provided a
1342 fractional denomination. Silver punch-marked coins circulated in the Gangetic provinces of India from the sixth century BC, and subsequently became the standard currency of the unified
1343 Mauryan empire. The punches were applied separately, but at the same time, by the authority issuing the coinage and not by private individuals. The symbols seem to mark the dynasty, ruler, mint, and perhaps the issue and moneyer. The analysis of finds has established the localities in which particular types circulated. Associated finds, sometimes with Greek, Indo-Greek, and Roman coins, indicate the broad sequence of development.
1344 Uninscribed cast copper coins are among the commonest from Ancient India. They are found especially in Rajputana and the United Provinces on sites which yield punch-marked silver and belong to the same general period – the third century BC. Copper punch-marked coins are much rarer than the silver and seem to
1345 be of one class only – probably the local coinage of Magadha in the Mauryan period.

Many of the inscribed copper coins of Ancient India have a Brahmi legend indicating the tribe by which they were struck; others are closely associated with a particular locality such as Taxila by the pattern of finds. Many of these coins were square in shape with clear traces of the incuse square of the reverse die –
1346 such as the Negama coppers and the Elephant and Lion coins
1347 attributed to Taxila. The issues of some localities are marked by the recurrent use of a distinctive symbol. Some later issues reflect the influence of the coinage of the Indo-Greek or Kushan invaders, while retaining tribal elements from earlier issues. The
1349 Kuninda coinage of Amoghabuti in the first century BC follows the pattern of the Indo-Greek silver drachma. Of particular interest are the square copper coins of Taxila. Its common elephant and lion square coppers are distributed widely and well represented in finds from Begram and Mirzakah in Afghanistan as well as at Taxila. They seem to represent the late Mauryan copper currency of the north-west provinces of that empire.

When the Greeks of Bactria crossed the Hindu Kush mountains and occupied the former Mauryan provinces of Arachosia and the Kabul Valley in the early second century BC, they introduced a fine Greek coinage, modelled on the pattern of currency that had been established there by the Mauryans.
Early Indo-Greek kings such as Agathocles and Pantaleon 1350
copied the form and weight standard of the square copper coins of Taxila, adding a Brahmi legend to their Greek titulature.
Another early king Apollodotus I struck his Indian silver 1351
drachmae to the reduced Indian weight standard of the silver karshapana, using a square shape, influenced no doubt by the silver punch-marked series. His name and titles in Greek on the obverse are repeated in Prakrit (the Indian) language on the reverse – now written in Kharoshthi (not Brahmi) script. Kharoshthi script is derived from that used in Aramaic, the chancelry language of the Achaemenid Persian empire, and it is used for lapidary inscriptions in the north west of India in the two centuries preceding and following the commencement of the Christian era.

Subsequent Indo-Greek kings who controlled Bactria and Aria struck an Attic standard currency with legends in Greek alone for these provinces, but a bilingual Greek and Kharoshthi coinage in silver and copper on the reduced Indian weight standard for their Indian territories. Their Indian coinage, however, retained the Greek tradition of fine portraiture and
strictly classical reverse types – like the Dioscuri used by Euc- 1352
ratides and Pallas Athene employed by the Stratos. In India, as 1355
in Bactria, the coinage was struck on a Seleucid model. 194
Throughout the series most issues have monograms in the
reverse field of the coins, which are normally combinations of 1353
Greek letters. Several scholars have tried to identify monograms with the names of specific mints; but such attributions must remain hypothetical until they can be supported by concrete statistical evidence of the distribution of copper coins with monograms, and this has not yet been done. They probably contain letters from the names of moneyers or magistrates. At one stage Menander introduced a series of Greek letters on his Indian issues to indicate the value of his copper coinage. From this we see that eight chalchoi were equivalent to one obol in his Indian, as in his Attic system. At a later stage there seems to have been a more complicated pattern of sub-kings and separate kingdoms. The sole source for much of the history of this period – the names of the kings and the locality of their kingdoms – is derived from their coinages and the patterns of coin finds. In spite of its fragmentation into separate series, the coinage retains
its purity of silver, fine Greek portraiture, and reverse types until 1354
the Indo-Greek kingdoms are progressively overthrown by the Yue-chi (early Kushans), Indo-Scythians and Indo-Parthians.

The Kushan king Varahan II of Bactria, early fourth century AD (**1363**).

1341 A thick, slightly bent bar of silver stamped with a geometric six-armed symbol at each end, and struck on a weight standard double that of the Persian siglos (**144**). Fifth or fourth century BC.

1342 This round, concave silver coin with a similar geometric six-armed symbol is the quarter denomination of the bent bar silver and is worth half a Persian siglos, fifth or fourth century BC.

1343 On this punchmarked silver coin from Dharawat there are five symbols – the rayed sun, a geometric design of three arrows and three ellipses, two taurine symbols flanking a dot within a circle, a tree within a railing, and an animal. Silver karshapana, fourth century BC.

1344 Uninscribed cast coin in copper of the third century BC with the common Indian symbol of a hill shown schematically by three arches with a crescent above. This specimen is a double coin – two examples cast together and not subsequently separated.

1345 Punchmarked copper coin with five symbols similar to those on the punchmarked silver. These include the sun, a six-armed geometrical design and a hill symbol.

1346 A square inscribed coin in copper with a bold legend in Brahmi script *Negama*, which means either

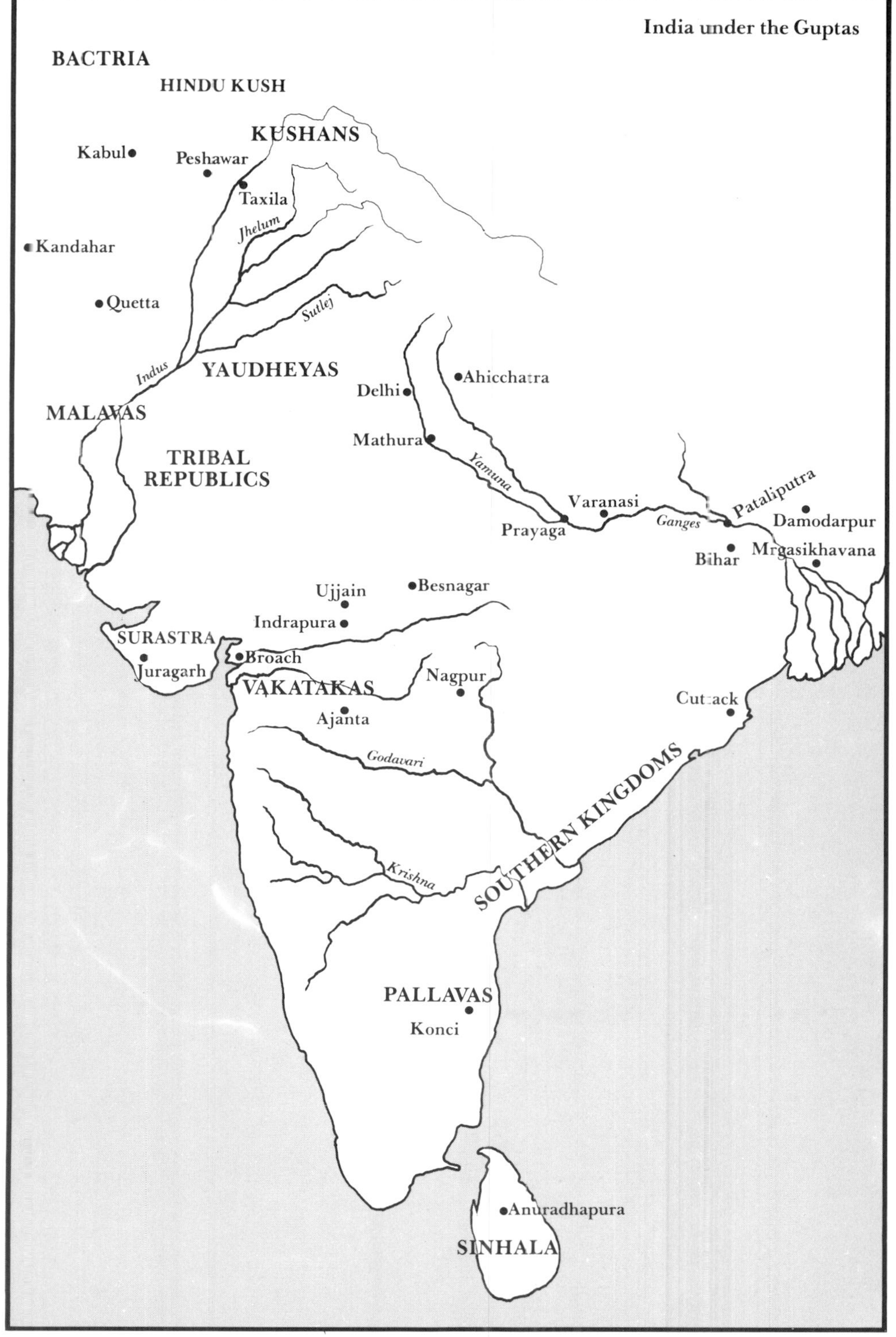

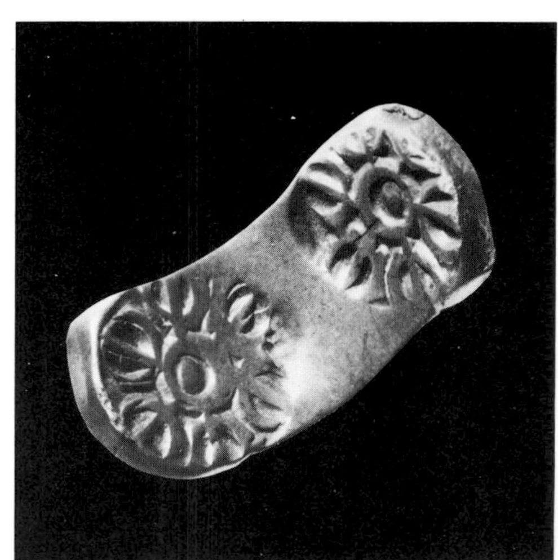
1341×2

1342×3

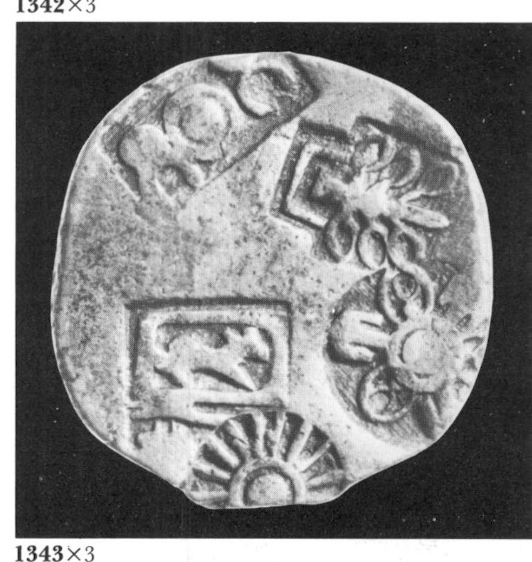

1343×3

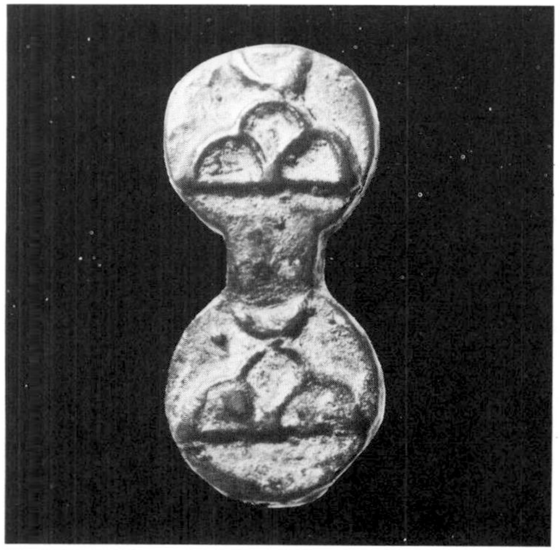
1344×2

1345×2

1346×2

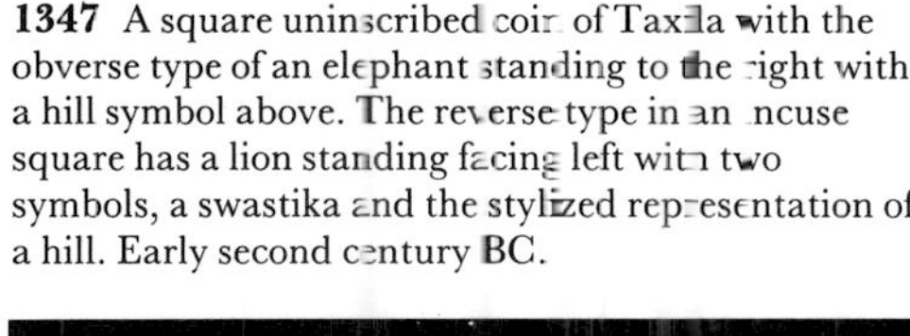

'the traders' or 'market traders guild' i.e. trade token or coin of commerce. It is attributed to Taxila in the early second century BC.

1347 A square uninscribed coin of Taxila with the obverse type of an elephant standing to the right with a hill symbol above. The reverse type in an incuse square has a lion standing facing left with two symbols, a swastika and the stylized representation of a hill. Early second century BC.

1348 This copper coin of Ujjain, probably of the third century BC, has a standing deity holding a spear – probably Karttikeya rather than Siva. Above there is a solar symbol, to the left a tree within a railing and to the right a geometric six-armed symbol. As on the punchmarked silver, some of the symbols change more frequently than others.

1349 Silver drachma of Amoghabuti, king of Kuninda in the first century BC with the obverse type of a deer standing in front of a female figure – probably Lakshmi. There are symbols in the field above, behind and below the deer. This coin has a Brahmi legend on the obverse and a Kharoshthi legend on the reverse, giving the king's name and title of maharaja.

1350 On this square copper coin of Pantaleon about 175 BC the female figure holding a lotus and dressed in oriental trousers is probably a dancing girl. To her left and right is the king's name in Brahmi script. The reverse type of this coin is struck in an incuse square similar to that of **1347**. It shows a sedate, statuesque maneless lion with a neat legend of the king's name in clear Greek letters.

1351 Square silver drachma of the Indo-Greek king Apollodotus I c. 170 BC. It is one of the earliest of the bilingual coins of the Greeks in India with legends in both Greek and Kharoshthi. It copies the square format and the weight standard of the earlier Mauryan punchmarked silver (**1343**). The neat Greek legend on the obverse frames the type of the Indian elephant. Beneath is a monogram incorporating the elements of several Greek letters. Its reverse shows the Indian humped bull framed by a neat Kharoshthi legend which gives the same name and royal titles as in the Greek.

1347A×2

1347B×2

1348×3

1349×3

1350A×2

1351A×3

1351B×3

1350B×2

During the first century BC the Indo-Greeks in the Indus valley were replaced by the powerful empire of the Indo-Scythians (Śakas) – established by Maues and consolidated by Azes I (whose accession was in 58 BC). Azes I, Azilises and Azes II retained the pattern of the Indo-Greek currency, but, instead
1356 of a portrait, normally showed the Śaka King of Kings on horseback. They use a wide range of reverse types, still classical in concept, now with Kharoshthi as well as Greek letters and monograms as issue marks. Towards the end of the reign of Azes II there was a major debasement of the silver coinage. The old denominations with the same types were progressively issued in base silver and billon – presumably because the Yue-chi (Kushan) invaders in the north had interrupted the supply of silver from the mines at Panshir north of Kabul. About this time
1357 there is a further change: each major mint begins to use only one principal reverse type for its silver or billon coinage. After Azes II the empire began to break up; satraps and generals issued coins in their own names with the types that Azes II had employed in that province; and these became much more local coinages with a different pattern in different localities. One of
these late Śaka satraps Rajuvula extended his territory eastward 1359
about AD 15 and struck base silver drachmae imitating the coinage of late Indo-Greek kings of Strato's line.

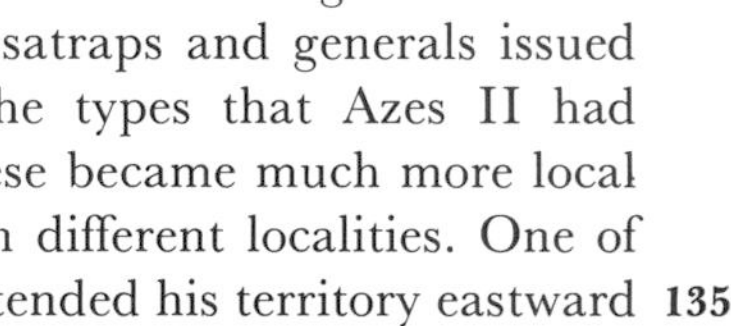

Spalirises and other kings who seem to be Indo-Parthian had 1360
established themselves in the province of Kandahar in the closing years of the first century BC, and issued a distinctive coinage with square coppers, based on the early Indo-Scythian pattern. About AD 20 the greatest of the Indo Parthian kings,
Gondophares, created a major empire that included Arachosia, 1361
the Kabul Valley, the Indus territories and satrapy of Rajuvula.

1352 The reverse of this square copper coin of Eucratides (mid second century BC) shows the Dioscouri charging right on horseback, holding lances and palms. The king's name and titles are in the Kharoshthi legend. To the right is a monogram of several Greek letters that probably conceals the name of a moneyer and distinguishes the issues of one of Eucratides' mints.

1353 This square copper coin of Antialcidas in the later second century BC uses the bust of Zeus with a thunderbolt over his shoulder for its obverse type. The reverse shows the *pilei* (hats) of the Dioscouri surmounted by two stars with two palms between them. The Greek monogram and letter again conceal the name of a moneyer.

1354 Silver tetradrachm of Hermaeus, the last Indo-Greek king to rule in the Kabul valley, first century BC. His Greek titulature calls him 'the Saviour'. The enthroned figure on the reverse seems to be Zeus, but wears the radiate crown of the sun and should probably be regarded as Zeus-Mithra. Again to the right is an issue mark in the form of a monogram.

1355 Silver drachma of Strato, one of the later rulers in the eastern Indo-Greek kingdom of Sagala, first century BC. Its reverse shows Athena holding an aegis and hurling a thunderbolt – a type that was copied by his Saka and Indo-Parthian successors.

1352×2

1353A×3

1353B×3

1354A×3

1354B×3

1355×2

1356A

1356B

1357A

1358A

1358B

1359×3

1357B

1356 Silver tetradrachm of the Indo-Scythian king Azes I, mid-first century BC. This obverse type of the king mounted holding a lance distinguishes the issues of Azes I from his later namesake Azes II. Below the horseman is a Kharoshthi letter which in this period serves as an issue mark. The reverse type remains classical in concept—here Zeus radiate with a long sceptre.

1357 Silver tetradrachm of Azes II, late first century BC. The obverse type of the king on horseback holding a whip distinguishes the silver issues of Azes II from his predecessor and namesake. Zeus holding a victory in his extended right hand has now been recognized as the reverse type used in this period at the mint of Taxila.

1358 Round copper coin of Azes II. The monograms in the obverse and reverse field on copper coins of the Azes dynasty correspond with issue marks known from the silver and help us to attribute the coppers. This issue with an Indian humped bull on the obverse and lion on the reverse is attributed to Azes II and the mint of Gandhara. As on the silver these coppers have bilingual Greek and Kharoshthi legends.

1359 Rajuvula, the Saka satrap of Mathura c. AD 15 copies in this issue the silver drachmae of Strato. This coin has a fine portrait bust of the Saka king diademed, but a bungled Greek legend, 'of the King of Kings Razi the Saviour', whereas the Kharoshthi legend on the reverse is more specific and accurate.

1360 A square copper coin of Spalirises, an Indo-Parthian king who seems to have ruled at Kandahar. Its obverse shows the king holding his battleaxe and has a good Greek legend round the dotted border that frames the type.

1361 Billon tetradrachm about AD 40 of Indo-Parthian king Gondophares, whose name is really a Persian title, 'Winner of Glory.' Gondophares, who established a major empire in Arachosia and the Indus Valley, is shown on horseback being crowned by a winged victory. In the field is the planetary symbol of Gondophares, used on many of the issues of his dynasty that do not have a portrait.

1362 Double gold dinar of Vima Kadphises c. AD 100. The king in royal Kushan dress is seated cross-legged on the clouds. His legend is in good Greek. Vima introduced a gold trading currency that was used by the international traders on the silk route.

1363 A Kushano-Sassanian gold dinar of Varahan II, scyphate (saucer-shaped) early fourth century AD. The king stands sacrificing at a low altar on the obverse (see the frontispiece to this chapter). His name and titles as *Kushan Shah* (King of the Kushans) is given in cursive Bactrian script and he wears Sassanian dress. This currency of Bactria is also based on the Kushan gold dinar, and its types are derived ultimately from the standing king and Siva with his bull that Vasu Deva had utilized (**1375**).

1362

1360×2

1361×2

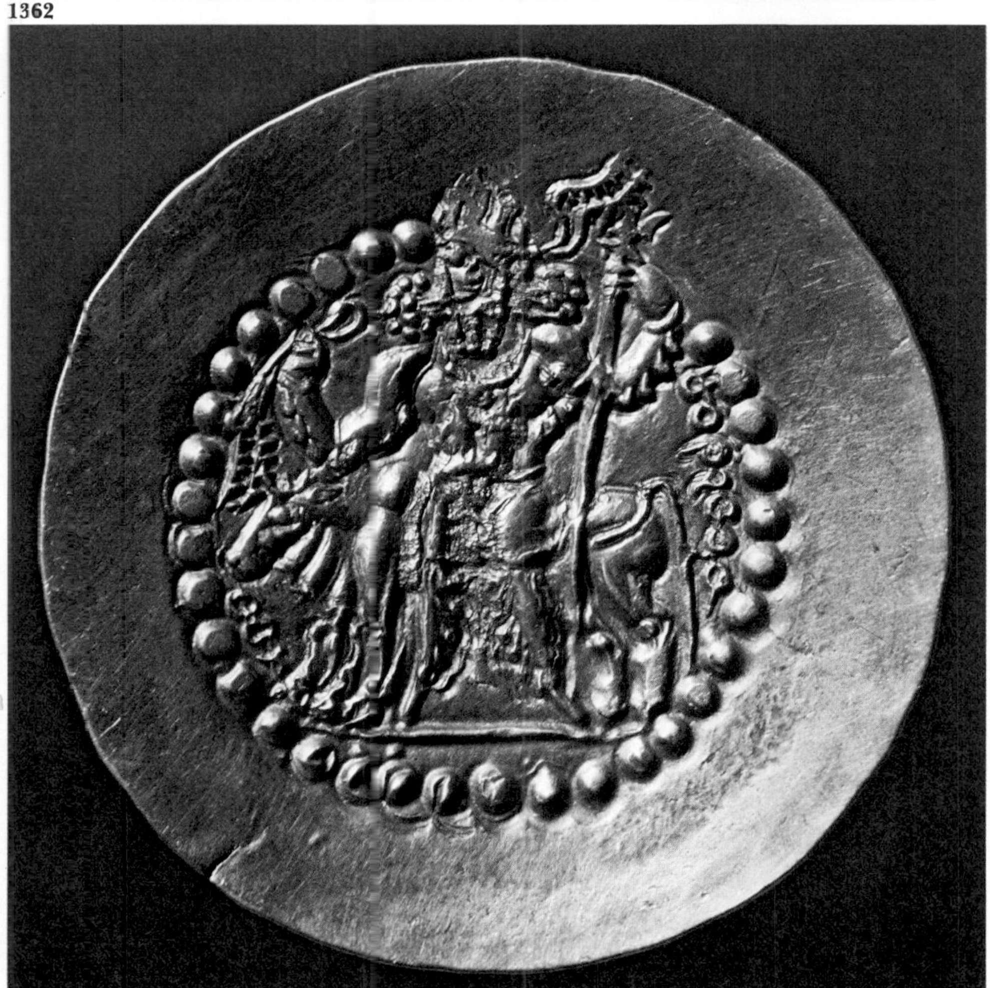

1363

1364 Copper tetradrachm of Kabul and Arachosia with a striking portrait of Gondophares and remains of a Greek legend with his titulature. The reverse type of this coinage has a figure of Nike (Victory) holding a wreath and remains of a legend in Kharoshthi. The denomination and its titulature are derived from the late coinage in copper copying the tetradrachms of Hermaeus.

1365 Copper tetradrachm of Pacores, a later Indo-Parthian king of the second century AD from Kandahar, with a distinctive bust of the king wearing a torquis. After the dynasty lost its extensive empire in the Indus valley, its kings in Arachosia assumed a grander style, 'The King of Kings, the Great', whereas Gondophares was content with 'King Gondophares the Saviour'.

1366 Copper tetradrachm of the early Kushan Kujula Kadphises, early first century AD. Its obverse retains the debased portrait of the copper tetradrachms imitating Hermaeus and their legend in blundered Greek. The reverse legend in Kharoshthi has the titles of Kujula Kara Kadphises and employs the types of Heracles holding his club with a lion skin over his left arm – a Greek divinity with whom the Kushan god of war and death was assimilated.

1367 In this local issue of copper coins found near Taxila, Kujula models his obverse portrait on that of a Roman emperor – with a diademed head closely resembling that of Augustus or Tiberius. The reverse of this coin shows an oriental figure sitting on a Roman curule chair.

1368 A standard copper didrachm of the nameless king 'Soter Megas' i.e. the great, the Saviour, who unified the Kushan confederacy, later first century AD. The king is given the idealized rayed head of Mithra. To the left is the nameless king's tamgha, a three-pronged symbol found on most of his coins.

1369 Copper tetradrachm of Vima Kadphises. This is the obverse found on the common copper coins of Vima and Kanishka. The king in Central Asian dress, extends his right hand over an altar in the act of sacrifice. Its legend is now in Bactrian, an Iranian language written in Greek characters, 'The Shah Kanishka'.

1370 Copper tetradrachm of Kanishka, early second century AD, with the reverse type of Mithra – the sun god with his title in Bactrian, 'Mioro' in the field. To the left is the tamgha used regularly by both Vima and Kanishka.

1371 Kushan gold dinar of Kanishka with one of the first known representations of the Buddha. The Buddha stands in statuesque form and is clearly labelled.

1372 Copper tetradrachm of Huvishka later second century AD – struck to a reduced weight standard. Huvishka as ruler of India is shown riding an elephant. The reverse shows Siva the Indian deity, here two-armed and holding a long trident. The different reverse types on the copper coins of Kanishka and Huvishka seem to be the distinguishing marks of officinae at the Kushan mint.

1373 Copper coin from Puri, third century AD, copying the obverse type of the Kushan copper tetradrachm. These Kushan derivative coins provided the copper currency for the Lower Ganges provinces.

1374 Copper issue of the Yaudheya tribe copying the Kushan denomination and fabric of the reduced coppers of Huvishka. Its reverse shows a female divinity, with a flower vase on one side and an inverted trisul on the other.

1375 The standard copper denomination of Vasu Deva and his successors, third century AD. Siva stands in front of his bull Nandi. Commonly attributed to Vasu Deva, this was the type of a long series of later Kushan copper coins in the Indus Valley and eastern Afghanistan.

1364A 1364B 1365 1366A×2

1367×2 1368×2 1369 1366B×2

1370 1372A

1373 1372B 1371×3

1376 Kushano-Sassanian copper coin of Shapur II of the Indus Valley, dating from his conquests about AD 360. This fine portrait has the cursive Bactrian legend 'Shoboro'. Its reverse has a characteristic Sassanian fire altar, sometimes with the symbol of Gondophares.

1377 Lead coin of the Andhra king Gautamiputra early second century AD. Its reverse shows a bow fitted with an arrow pointing upwards and its Brahmi legend gives the King's name.

1378 Silver drachma of the western satrap Damasena (AD 223-36). Like other coins in the long series issued by the satraps who ruled Surastra, this drachma has an obverse portrait and the reverse type of a hill or shrine shown schematically – and surmounted by a star and crescent – presumably the sun and moon. Round the type there is the Brahmi legend giving the satrap's name and date.

1379 Gupta gold dinar of Chandra Gupta II AD 380-414, from Fyzabad – a denomination derived from the later Kushan gold. The king shoots at a lion that falls backwards. The Brahmi legend has an honorific couplet reconstructed from several specimens, 'The moon among kings brave as a lion whose fame is far spread, invincible on earth, he conquers heaven.'

1374

1375

1376×2

1377

1378×2

1379×2

His coinages retain the existing pattern of denominations and
types in each of these provinces – adding simply his name,
1364 portrait and, on coinages with no portrait, his distinctive tamgha.
Gondophares is mentioned in the Acts of Saint Thomas and
the Takht-i-Bahi inscription of AD 46. His successors continued
to rule in Arachosia and Seistan up to the rise of the Sassanians,
and issued a series of copper tetradrachms with the Nike
(Victory) reverse.

Late in the second century BC the Indo-Greek rulers in
Bactria were overthrown by the Yue-chi nomad tribes who
migrated southward from the steppes of Central Asia. One of its
tribes, the Kushans, welded the Yue-chi into a powerful
confederacy in the first century AD. Its early coinage copied the
denominations and types of the existing currency – notably the
copies in copper of the tetradrachms of the last Indo-Greek king
1354 Hermaeus in the Kabul Valley, to which it added the name of
1366 the Kushan king Kujula Kadphises in the Kharoshthi legend
early in the first century AD. Later in the century the Kushan
nameless king 'Soter Megas' (the great, the saviour) introduced
a uniform coinage in copper through all his territories from
1368 Russian Turkistan across Afghanistan and Pakistan to north-
west India. His successor Vima Kadphises c. AD 100 introduced
1362 a fine gold coinage with legends in Greek and Kharoshthi to
serve as a trading currency for the important traffic on the silk
route. Vima struck no silver, but introduced the standard
1369 Kushan copper tetradrachm of about 16 grammes that is found
in large quantities across the empire. Under Kanishka (early
second century AD) we find evidence of Graeco-Roman
influence in the coinage-types derived from Roman pattern
books, the use through successive issues of multiple reverse
types, which seem to mark the product of officinae as at Roman
mints. Kanishka began to emphasise the Iranian character of his
dynasty, substituting Bactrian titles such as *Shao* for the Greek
Basileus ('King') and *Mioro* ('Mithra') for *Helios* (the 'sun'). 1370

In the gold types of Kanishka and Huvishka we see a
remarkable pantheon of the deities of the cosmopolitan empire
drawn from Iran, India, and the Graeco-Roman world. Eventu- 1371
ally under Huvishka the weight standard of the copper denominations was reduced by 25% creating a fiduciary currency 1372
dependent on the gold. This gave rise to many local copies – until
the coppers of Vasu Deva and the later Kushans returned to a
more traditional Indian pattern.

The Telagu country of Peninsular India, ruled by the Andhras
from the decline of the Mauryans to the third century AD, had a
distinctive coinage in that lead predominated in several 1377
localities.

Contemporaries and probably feudatories of the Kushans in
Surastra, the Western Satraps issued a long series of silver
drachmae mostly dated in the Śaka era of AD 78 – an important
series from which we can reconstruct the sequence of satraps and 1378
mahasatraps and the developments in Brahmi script down to the
Gupta conquest in the fourth century AD in the Gangetic
provinces of India. Kushan rule was limited in both extent and
time; but Kushan copper coinage made a major impact on the
currencies that followed. In Bihar and Orissa there was an
extensive issue of Puri Kushan coins, crudely copying the types 1373
of Kanishka, during the third century AD. In other localities
tribal coinage re-emerged when the power of the Kushans
waned; but was now influenced in its fabric, denominations and
general appearance by the Kushan copper, as in the issues of the
Yaudheyas in the country near Delhi. In eastern Afghanistan 1374
and the Indus Valley Kushan rule continued up to the mid
fourth century using fossilized types such as the standing king 1375
and Śiva with the bull type first introduced by Vasu Deva. The
denomination was progressively reduced in size and weight,
until it was replaced in the time of Shapur II by a copper
currency with Sassanian portraiture and traces of a Sassanian 1376
fire altar (later fourth century AD). The gold dinar, derived from
the Great Kushans, also remained a standard denomination,
evolving into the Kushano-Sassanian gold scyphate during the
fourth century AD in Bactria, and the later Kushan gold of the 1363
Indus Valley and Punjab. The eastern series was in turn copied
and succeeded by the fine and extensive gold coinage of the
Gupta empire which emerged as the major power in North India
in the fourth century AD under the leadership firstly of Chandra 1379
Gupta I and then of Chandra Gupta II.

لا اله الا الله محمد
رسول الله
١٠٦٤

XIX

MEDIEVAL AND MODERN INDIA

Nicholas Rhodes

During the reign of Skanda Gupta (AD 455–80) new invaders
appeared from the north–the White Huns, also known as the
Hepthalites. After an early defeat by the Guptas, they turned to
conquer Iran before invading India again, shortly before 500.
This time the Huns rapidly conquered western and much of
northern India, but they were never able to consolidate their
1380 conquests, and in about 528 their leader Mihirakula was forced
to flee to Kashmir.

Although the Hun occupation was shortlived, it was a turning
point in the history of India, and the following five centuries may
be equated with the contemporary dark ages in Europe. The
1382 previous political and social system was broken up, and numerous dynasties rose and fell. International trade declined, and
such coins as were struck were for local use only, with debased
alloy and little uniformity of standard.

Southern India was politically and economically separate
from the north, and its artistic culture and its currency system
developed along different lines. The area grew wealthy from
seaborne trade with Europe and China, but no coins were struck
between the seventh and tenth centuries, when the trade route to
the west was cut off by the Arabs. After the tenth century,
1388 however, many gold coins were struck by the various dynasties
who vied for control of the Deccan. Few of these coins have
inscriptions long enough to allow proper attribution, although
most have dynastic emblems. In the far south, the Cholas and
the Pandyas were the dominant dynasties, and both sporadically
struck coins in gold, silver and copper between the tenth and
fourteenth centuries.

In the early years of the eleventh century, Mahmud of Ghazna
1259 invaded north-western India from his base in Afghanistan, and
1386 annexed the Punjab. His successors settled in Lahore, where
they struck small copper coins similar in design and fabric to the
bull and horseman coins of the local Hindu rulers.

The real Muslim conquest of India did not begin until the last
quarter of the twelfth century when Muhammad Ghori swept
down from Afghanistan. With fanatical zeal and ferocious
efficiency, he crushed northern India, slaughtering infidels by
1387 the thousand, and reshaping the whole structure of the country
according to his Islamic principles. By the time of his death in
1206, the whole of northern India as far as Bengal had been
annexed, and his conquests were consolidated and extended by
his successors as Sultans of Delhi. By 1340, the Delhi Sultanate
controlled the whole of India as far south as the Deccan, leaving
only the Tamil states in Hindu hands.

Initially, the Ghorids took little interest in the coinage, but
during the reign of Iltutmish (1211-36) a fine new silver coin, the
tankah, appeared with a design that was purely Islamic. The 1389
weight standard of this coin was based on the Indian tola of 96
ratis (the seed of the plant *Abrus Precatorius*) or about 11
grammes, and this standard, changing only slightly from time to
time, still continues as the *rupee*. Following the Islamic practice,
these tankahs had the date and place of minting, and from then
on, the coins became an important source for political history.
The uniform fabric allowed these coins to circulate widely at face
value within the empire, and as bullion further afield.

From this period onwards, India became one of the great coin-
issuing countries of the world. Its hunger for precious metals
became legendary, and much of this was converted into coin
before being hoarded. Base metal, copper or billon coins were
struck in many areas for local use, but the silver and gold were
issued as trade items, and had a wide circulation.

The power of the Delhi Sultanate reached a zenith early in the
reign of Muhammad Tughlaq (1325-51), who has been called
'The Prince of Moneyers', because of his frequent experiments 1390
with the coinage. Apart from changes in weight standard, he
tried on one occasion, to replace the silver coins with copper or
brass tankas. This experiment proved disastrous, as, to quote a
contemporary historian, the 'house of every Hindu was turned
into a mint'. Muhammad's experiments with other aspects of
government were no more successful, and gradually during the
next century, the more prosperous parts of the empire began to
declare their independence. Many of these new states, such as
Bengal, the Bahmanis in the Deccan, Malwa, and Gujerat,
struck much finer coins than the now impoverished Delhi
Sultanate.

In about the year 1336 the Hindu dynasty of Vijayanagar rose
to power in the south, and was able to prevent any further expansion of Muslim rule for over 200 years. Vijayanagar maintained a completely different currency system from the Muslims,
striking only gold coins called *pagoda* (weighing about 3·5 1391
grammes), and its tenth, the *fanam*.

When Zahiruddin Babur became ruler of Kabul in about
1505, northern India was politically weak and vulnerable.
Babur, who was a Mongol, directly descended from Timur and 1392
claiming descent from Ghengiz Khan, was naturally tempted by
the wealth of India. After several reconnoitring forays, he
launched his main attack on India in 1525 with only 12,000 men.
In spite of being heavily outnumbered, he succeeded in defeating
the Sultan of Delhi, and before his death in 1530 he had
conquered most of northern India as far as the frontier of Bengal.

Detail from the gold 200-mohur of the Moghul emperor Shah Jahan,
1628-58 (**1403**).

1380 These silver coins were copied from Sassanian dirhams which reached India in the course of trade. Crude, debased copies were struck as late as the eleventh century. White Huns, Mihirakula (AD 500-28).

1381 Although Bhoja Deva was one of the few Indian rulers to strike silver coins in the ninth century, these pieces, showing the boar incarnation of Vishnu on the obverse, are very common. Gurjara-Pratihara Kingdom of Kanauj, Bhoja Deva (840-90).

1382 Isolated in their Himalayan valley, the Nepalese struck copper coins of Kushan fabric, with designs showing great artistic talent. Nepal, inscribed 'Gunanka', seventh century.

1383 This bull and horseman design was copied by many Hindu and Muslim rulers of north-west India until the thirteenth century. Silver shahis of Kabul and Gandhara, inscribed 'Samanta Deva', ninth century.

1380×2

1381×3

1382A×2

1383A×3

1383B×3

1382B×2

1385A×3

1384×2

1385B×3

1384 These fine silver bracteates are similar in fabric to the German bracteates (**725**) struck over 100 years later. Chandra kings of East Bengal, tenth century.

1385 This Ceylonese coin copies a type first used by the Cholas and the Pandyas of south India. Ceylon, Queen Lilavati (1197-1200 and 1209-11), copper massa.

1386 Mahmud of Ghazna (998-1030) struck this fine silver dirham at Mahmudpur (Lahore) in 1028. The kalima on one side is in Arabic and on the other in Sanskrit. Later Muslim rulers did not show such religious tolerance.

1387 After Muhammed's conquest of Delhi in 1193, gold coins were struck with a seated Lakshmi, and his name in Nagari script on the reverse. A similar design had been used by Hindu rulers on gold coins since the eleventh century. Ghorids, Muhammed bin Sam (1173-1206).

1386A×2

1386B×2

1387A×3

1387B×3

Babur's son Humayun, was not able to hold together the territory gained by his father, and in 1539 he was defeated by
1393 Sher Shah, an Afghan chief from Bihar. Humayun fled to Iran, and Sher Shah reestablished a Delhi sultanate, ruling the whole of northern India from Bengal in the east to the Afghan frontier in the west. Sher Shah was an able administrator, and achieved much during his reign of only six years. He built a new city at Delhi, laid out highroads with accommodation at intervals for travellers and instituted many reforms in the civil administration which were later adopted by the Moghuls.

Sher Shah's successors proved incomptetent, however, and the Sultanate began to disintegrate. Bengal declared its independence in 1553, which encouraged Humayun to return from exile, and he recaptured Delhi in 1555. Although Humayun was to die in 1556, his son Akbar completed the conquest of the Muslim sultanates and established the Moghul Empire.

1395 Akbar was one of the most successful of Indian rulers. He realized that the country could not be effectively governed if the
1396-1400 Hindus were continually persecuted as they had been under the Sultans, and he introduced many reforms to bring justice to his empire. By the time of his death in 1605, he had extended his empire over all northern India and much of Afghanistan. The empire was to be further extended by his successors Jahangir and Shah Jahan. While the Moghuls increased the prosperity of the plains, many of the neighbouring Hindu hill kingdoms to the
1404-07 north and east grew prosperous on increased trade, and they struck their own silver coins.

In 1510, the Portuguese captured Goa, the chief port of the
1394 Sultan of Bijapur. Soon afterwards they captured the important trading post of Hormuz in the Persian Gulf, and with their supremacy at sea, the Portuguese were able to control the
1503 lucrative spice trade for much of the sixteenth century, bringing quantities of silver from Europe in exchange. This influx of silver enabled the Indian rulers to strike greater numbers of silver coins at this time. The power of the Portuguese was not to last, however, and by the end of the sixteenth century they were weakened by political troubles in Europe.

In the early seventeenth century, other European powers were quick to take the place of the Portuguese, and the British and Dutch, the Danish and the French all appeared on the scene. The Dutch concentrated their efforts on Ceylon and the Spice Islands around Java, while the other countries set up trading posts around the coast of the subcontinent. Within these towns, coins were struck, usually with European types for local circulation, although the weight standards were usually taken from the local Indian coins, which also circulated. Sometimes however, the Europeans struck copies of local coins, and circulated these beyond the limits of their jurisdiction.

During the reign of Aurangzeb (1658-1707), the Moghuls continued to make military conquests, and by the end of the century controlled more territory than any previous Indian empire. Aurangzeb was, however, not willing to sacrifice his fanatical religious principles for political expediency as his predecessors had done. His anti-Hindu zeal and his frequently futile military campaigns sowed the seeds of the downfall of Moghul power. During the early eighteenth century, local governors assumed an increasingly independent role, and demanded the Moghul emperor's permission to strike coins in his name. The British and the French also did this, and struck 1409
Moghul type mohurs and rupees, which could circulate throughout India.

During the eighteenth and nineteenth centuries, many local rulers declared complete independence from the Moghuls and struck coins in their own name. Among them were the Sikhs in the Punjab, the Nawabs of Oude in Lucknow, and Haidar Ali in Mysore. Other rulers continued to strike coins, often debased, in the name of the Moghul Emperor, although they were in no other way subservient to him. Most of these independent mints struck rupees to slightly differing standards of weight and fineness, inhibiting the circulation of coinage, which had previously existed.

The trading interests of the British were naturally threatened by the breakdown of political stability, and the East India Company extended its operations into the political arena with a series of astute moves and military victories. In 1765, the British obtained revenue-collecting powers in Bengal from the Moghul governor, and over the next century they gradually spread their power and influence until the whole of the subcontinent acknowledged British supremacy.

In Bengal in 1765 the British inherited a chaotic monetary system. Not only did the various types of rupee have different values according to weight and fineness, but also new coins circulated at a premium over those only two years old. By the end of the century the system was rationalized by striking all new coins with a fixed date of the nineteenth year of Shah Alam (1773), and the old coins were gradually withdrawn without loss. The British continued to strike coins of Moghul type until 1833, with slightly differing standards in the various mints, according to local practice. From 1835, however, a new standard British rupee with the weight fixed at 180 grains and displaying a portrait of William IV, was circulated throughout the areas of India directly ruled by the East India Company, and the former

1388 Many of the gold coins struck in the Deccan at this period use the punchmarking technique, reminiscent of the earliest coins of the subcontinent. Eastern Chalukya, Raja Raja I (1019-59).

1389 Alauddin acquired great wealth during his military campaigns in the south. On his coins he referred to himself as the 'second Alexander', as Alexander the Great of Macedon was still a legend in India. Sultans of Delhi, Alauddin Muhammad Shah Khilji (1296-1306), silver tankah.

1390 The artistic quality of this heavy gold coin is very high. Sultans of Delhi, Muhammad Tughlaq (1325-51), gold dinar, Delhi 726 AH (= AD 1325-26).

1391 The coins of south India are less useful to the historian than those of the north, as they are never dated and do not show the name of the mint. Vijanagar, Krishnaraya (1509-30), gold multiple pagoda.

1392 After his conquest of Delhi, Babur struck silver coins in India and Afghanistan to the Timurid weight standard. Moghul, Babur (in India 1525-30), silver shahrukhi, Qandahar 933 AH (= AD 1526-27).

1393 During this short reign, Sher Shah completely reformed the coinage, introducing the word 'rupee,' which was derived from the Sanskrit *rupya* meaning (wrought silver) Satgaon, Sher Shah Suri (1538-45), silver rupee.

1394 The Portuguese adopted the Apostle Saint Thomas as their patron saint for India, and after 1549 struck gold coins with the figure of the saint, to the weight standard of the contemporary south Indian gold pagodas. Portuguese India, João III, (1521-37), Goa, Gold San Thomé.

1395 After the 30th year of his reign Akbar began dating his coins with his regnal year rather than using the Hijra year. He also reduced the length of the inscription to the essential religious invocation, the mint, and the year and month of issue. Moghul, Akbar (1556-1605), silver rupee, Agra regnal year 50, month Amardad.

1388

1389A

1389B

1390A

1390B

1396 Jahangir ignored the normal orthodox Muslim rule against portraiture, and in his first year struck this fine gold mohur with the portrait of his father Akbar, probably for use as medallic gifts to courtiers. Moghul, Jahangir (1605-28), gold mohur

1397 During the early years of his reign, Jahangir increased the weight of his rupee, but in his sixth year it was reduced to the traditional standard by public demand. Many rupees of the period were struck on square flans. Moghul, Jahangir (1605-28), silver rupee, Agra, year five.

1398-1400 In the thirteenth year of his reign, Jahangir decided that instead of the name of the month of issue, he would sometimes put the figure of the constellation which belonged to the month on his coins (here Libra [**1398**], Aries [**1399**] and Gemini [**1400**]). These are among the most attractive of all Indian coins, are very rare, and are frequently forged. Moghul, Jahangir (1605-28), gold zodiacal mohurs.

1401 The representation of Ardhanarisvara on this rupee is not otherwise known in Hindu art. The reverse inscription commemorates a ritual bath in the river Lakhi, a branch of the Brahmaputra river, well within Muslim territory, so that the coin really commemorates a victorious military expedition. Tripura, Vijaya Manikya (1532-64), silver rupee, dated 1482 Saka (AD 1560).

1402 In the mid-sixteenth century, transHimalayan trade increased considerably to the benefit of border states such as Cooch Behar, which began striking fine silver coins. Cooch Behar, Nara Narayan (1555-77), silver tanka.

1391A×2 **1391B**×2 **1392A**×2 **1392B**×2

1393A **1393B** **1394A**×2 **1394B**×2

1395A **1395B** **1396**×2 **1398**×2

1397A **1397B** **1399**×2 **1400**×2

1401A **1401B** **1402A**×2 **1402B**×2

1403 Several Moghul emperors struck high denomination coins for presentation to ambassadors and favourites. These massive (c. 2200 grammes) gold pieces are thought to be the world's highest denomination coins, although they were too large for normal circulation. According to documentary sources, gold and silver pieces up to the weight, of 1000 ordinary coins were struck. Moghul, Shah Jahan (1628-58), gold 200 mohur.

1404-05 Although the jawa is the smallest coin ever struck (weight 0·01 grammes), it is occasionally found cut into fractions for even smaller change! Nepal, c. 1740, silver jawa (**1404**) and cut quarter (**1405**).

1406 Before 1791, the Tibetans had no coinage of their own, and had an agreement with Nepal, whereby the latter sent coin to Tibet in exchange for silver. Since the Nepalese specially debased the coins sent to Tibet, they were able to make large profits. Nepal, Bhatgaon, Jaya Ranajit Malla (1722-69), base silver mohur.

1407 The Ahom Kings of Assam struck a fine series of octagonal coins, usually with Sanskrit legends, but occasionally they used the traditional Ahom language. Assam, Supungmung (1663-70), silver rupee.

1408 In 1677 and 1678, patterns were prepared in England for a rupee to be struck in Bombay. Unfortunately it was not possible to produce good impressions from the dies in India, and it is doubtful if any of the few pieces struck in Bombay ever circulated. British India, Bombay, Charles II, pattern silver rupee, 1678.

1409 It was in 1717 that the British obtained the permission of the Moghal Emperor to strike coins in his name. British India, Bombay. Rupee in the name of Moghul Emperor Shah Jahan II (1717).

1403

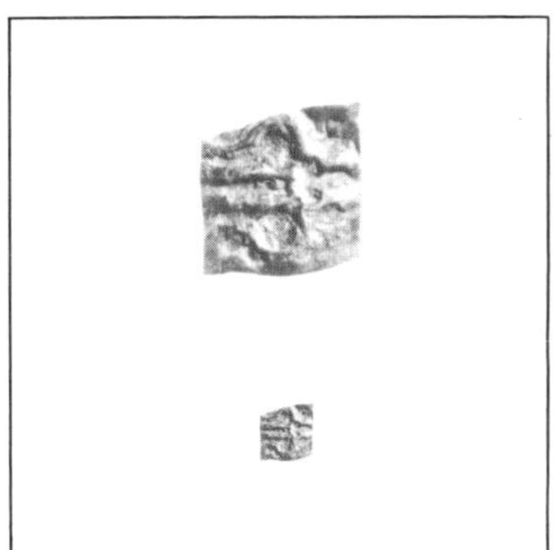

1404×1, ×3

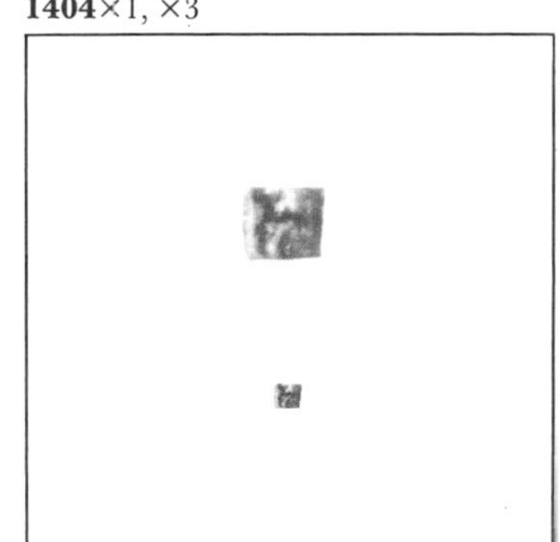

1405×1, ×3

1406

1407

1408A

1408B

1409

1410A×2

1410B×2

1411A

1411B

1410 After striking pagodas similar to those struck by other rulers in the area, it was decided in 1808 to make the design more European. British India, Madras, gold two-pagoda (1808-15).

1411 Nearly 2·5 billion rupees were struck in India during the latter half of Queen Victoria's reign, making this a very familiar coin throughout the world. British India, Queen Victoria, silver rupee, 1862.

1412 These coins on a broad flan, were specially struck for presentation purposes. Jaipur, Nazarana rupee struck by Isvari Singh (1743-60) in the name of Moghul Emperor Alamgir II.

1413 Bharatpur was one of two native mints to put a portrait of Queen Victoria on its coins. Bharatpur, Jaswant Singh, rupee, 1858.

1414 Jodhpur was one of the few states to strike hammered coins in the twentieth century. Jodhpur, Sardar Singh with Edward VII, copper half-anna, 1906.

1415 The capital of the Asoka pillar at Sarnath was chosen as the emblem of the new Republic, and has appeared on all modern coins of India. Indian Republic, aluminium 10-paisa, 1973.

1412A

1412B

1413A

1413B

1414A

1414B

coins were gradually withdrawn. Many of the maharajas, who
maintained local autonomy while acknowledging the suzerainty
1412 of the British, continued to strike their own coins, usually in the
name of the Moghul Emperor.

In 1858, after the Mutiny, the East India Company, which
had until then maintained its position between the Crown and
the Government of India relinquished all political powers, and
the Moghul Emperor was finally 'retired'. Queen Victoria was
proclaimed Queen of India and control throughout India was
1411 firmly in the hands of the British Government. The right of states
to strike their own coinage was reviewed, and whereas there had
been over 100 mints before 1858, the number was reduced to
about 34, and most of the coins struck now acknowledged the
1413 British monarch. By the end of the century, however, the value of
1414 the native coins had fallen so much, relative to the British, that
many mints were closed, and few of those that struck a regular
coinage survived into the twentieth century.

In 1947 independence was granted to a divided India. No
change was immediately made to the currency system, and
although Pakistan struck coins with a star and crescent in 1948,
it was not until 1950 that the new Indian Republic struck coins
of its own. In 1957, the old binary system with 64 *paisa* to the
rupee, was replaced in India with a decimal system of 100 *naye*
paise to the rupee. The decimal system was not new to the
1415 subcontinent, as it had already been used in Ceylon since 1870,
and in Nepal since 1932. In 1971 Bangladesh, the former East
Pakistan, seceded from Pakistan with Indian support, and in
1972 Ceylon changed its name to Sri Lanka and became a full,
independent member of the Commonwealth. The Portuguese
continued to strike coins for Goa until it was finally absorbed
into India in 1961.

1415A×3

1415B×3

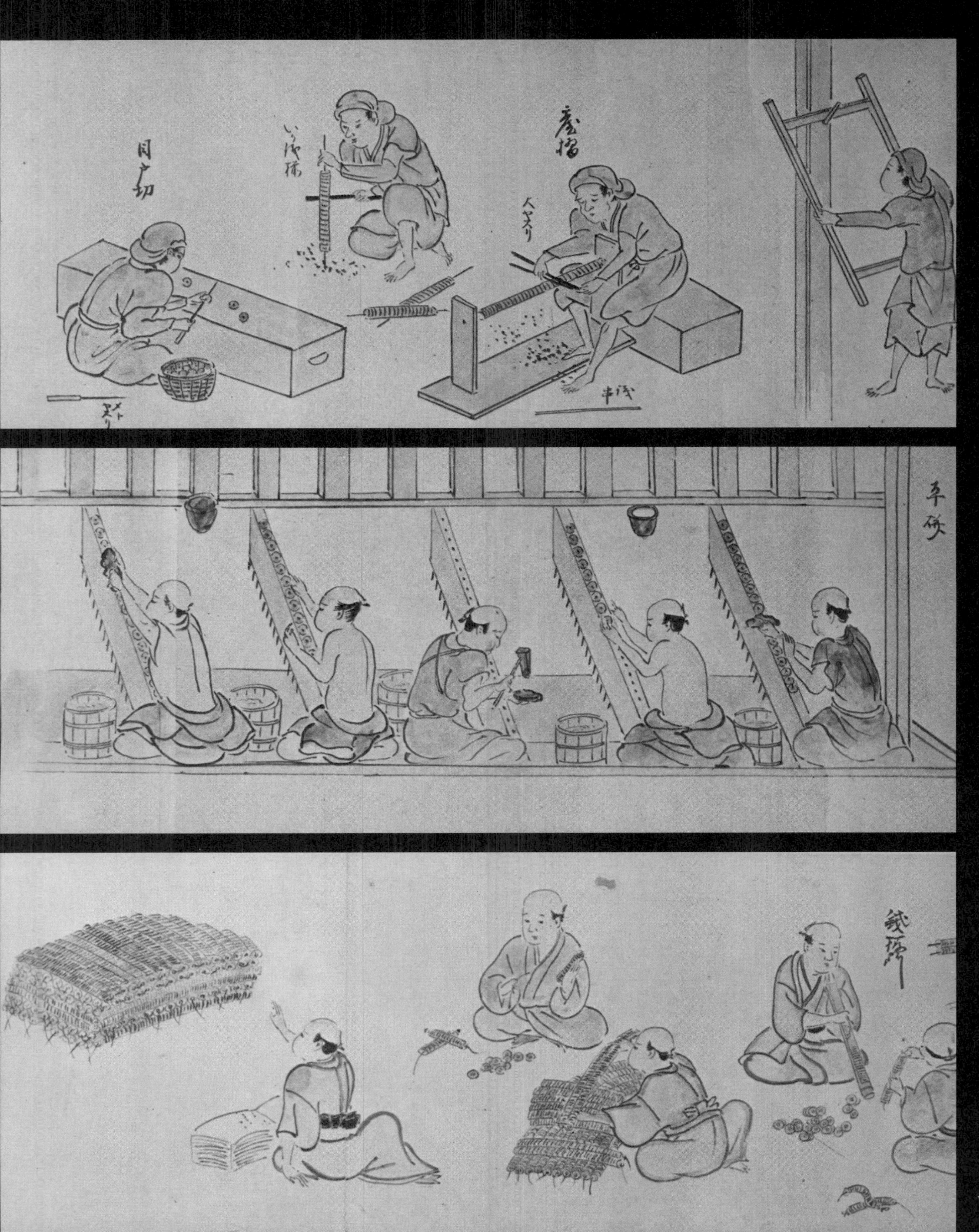
大ヤスリ
串銭

XX

THE FAR EAST

Joe Cribb

Coinage in the Far East has a long history of its own. Shortly after the Lydians invented coins, the Chinese created their own version of the same thing. From this they developed a coinage totally different except in function from that of the West, which not only spread throughout China and to her neighbours, but also circulated in south-east Asia, where trade with India had already introduced coinage. Coins of this tradition were still being issued early this century, but by then trade with Europe and America was leading to their replacement by western-style coins.

Traditional coins of the Far East are characterized by being cast from base metal with only inscriptional designs. Because these coins were of low value and easily imitated, they created a multitude of problems for their users. The inconvenience of moving the huge quantities of them needed in trade and the difficulties faced by their issuers in preventing forgery and acquiring the metal to maintain a national coinage led to the adoption of many alternatives, such as token coinages, paper money and commodity money, all with their own problems.

The invention of coinage in China developed directly from the use as money of various objects. From about the twelfth century BC monetary use was made of grain, cloth, animals, ornaments and metals, most functional of which were cowry shells and bronze tools. The first coins were cast bronze imitations of these monetary objects, hoes, knives and cowries. The earliest coins
1417 were inscribed imitation hoes issued by the Zhou kings in the
late sixth century BC. At that time the Zhou, who had ruled China since the eleventh century BC, were only figureheads ruling a small territory around their capital in northern Henan. The rest of civilized China was controlled by feudal states, some of which in the fifth century BC also began to issue hoe coins.

1418 By the third century BC the use of hoe coins had spread to all
1419 the feudal states, except those in the extreme south and east. In
1422 the south Chu State adopted cast bronze coins which imitated
1421 cowries and in the east Qi State also made bronze coins, but
imitating knives. The economic importance of Qi led other states to issue knife coins alongside their hoe coins.

Gold also played a monetary role in ancient China, but only as ingots, never coined.

In the third century BC a practical solution to the problem of
1424 handling irregularly shaped coins was found by replacing hoe
and knife coins with flat disc-shaped coins with a central hole, so they could be carried in bulk on strings.

The third century BC also saw a political change in China. The ruler of Qin State, through his superior military and political abilities, gradually conquered the other states and made himself emperor. One of his first acts was to reform the economy. He standardized weights and measures, reorganized the tax systems and demonetized the chaotic coinages of Zhou, replacing the hoe, knife, cowry and round coins with his own new **1425**
round coins, which became the model for coinage in China and the Far East for more than 2000 years.

In 206 BC Qin was overthrown by the Han dynasty. Qin and Han changed China's political and economic structure, abolishing feudalism and instituting an absolute monarchy assisted by a bureaucratic administration. This form of government survived, in spite of numerous lapses into anarchy, until the nineteenth century. To manage their economy through this form of government, the Han sought to establish a workable national
coinage but it took almost 100 years to achieve. Han repeatedly **1426**
adjusted the official weight of the coin introduced by Qin until **1428**
an effective standard was hit upon in 118 BC. Following introduction of the new standard, the monetary use of gold ingots was also regularized in 95 BC.

The new standard coins were issued until the end of Han in AD 220 and were still used and occasionally cast until the seventh century AD. After Han rule collapsed, China fragmented into smaller states in conflict with each other, which totally disrupted the coinage by dislocating the copper supply.
Attempts were made to readjust the weight standard and to issue **1429**
token coins. The ineffective rule of the small states thereby worsened the coinage by encouraging forgery, particularly of the token coins. Where copper was scarce, iron and lead coins were issued, while in some states coins had to be banned and commodities, particularly silk, grain and gold replaced them.

The Sui dynasty reunited China in AD 580 and attempted to
reorganize the coinage by issuing new bronze coins on the Han **1430**
standard. All unofficial coins were demonetized.

In 618 the Tang dynasty overthrew Sui and restored China to Han-style bureaucracy. Like Han they needed a stable national coinage for the state to function. They reorganized weights and
measures on a decimal basis and in 621 issued new coins **1431**
weighing a tenth of an ounce and measuring a tenth of a foot across. Successive Chinese governments for the next 1300 years issued similar coins. Although the Tang made massive issues of coins, they were unable to produce enough for their increasingly monetized economy. From the eighth century the government made extensive use of silver ingots as money. In 666 and 758 unsuccessful token coinages were tried. However the establishment of numerous provincial mints in 845 was successful in

Final stages of coin production at the Sendai mint, Japan, 1728:
filing edges; polishing surfaces; stringing the finished coins.

1416 The importance of the cowry as a monetary object in Ancient China is clear from the adoption of its pictograph in the written language to signify money. Many of the Chinese characters referring to monetary activities incorporate the sign for cowry to indicate their meaning. See **1422**.

1417 Bronze hoe coin, sixth century BC, Zhou Imperial Mint, Luoyang, Henan, inscribed 'gu', a personal name. This is the earliest type of hoe coin, still resembling the actual tool it imitated. Like the hoe it has a socket for a wooden handle.

1418 Bronze hoe coin, late fourth century BC, Wuyang City mint, Wei State, inscribed with its mint name, as was usual from the fifth century. The hoe coins of this period no longer have a socket and bear little resemblance to the original tool.

1419 As coins developed in China, they underwent a progressive simplification of shape, so that by the third century they bore little resemblance to the tools they originally imitated. The first changes took place as the Zhou hoe coins (1) were copied, after 425 BC, at civic mints in Liang (2), Zhou (3), Zhao (4) and elsewhere. The hollow handle was soon omitted and as time passed progressive simplification of the modified shapes took place in Liang (5-9) and Zhao (10-13). By the early third century BC the hoe coins had become very stylized. Most of the states using hoe coins adopted the shape developed in Liang (14), as in Yen (15) and Zhao (16). The hoe coins used in the third century were nearly all a half denomination, introduced by Liang and Zhao, which proved more convenient than the larger coins (7).

1420 The knife coins also showed a progressive change in size and shape as they spread. The coinage of Qi (1,2) remained the same shape but became slightly smaller during its three centuries of circulation. The knife coin adopted by Yen was however much smaller (3,4) and continued to shrink as it spread to Zhao (5,6), where coins of a slightly different shape, also grew smaller (7-9).

1421 Bronze knife coin, fourth century BC, Qi City mint, Qi state, inscribed 'legal money of Qi'. This

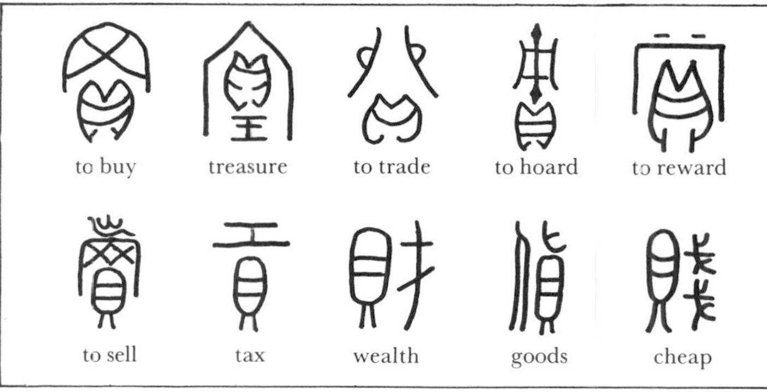

1416

1418×2

1417

1419

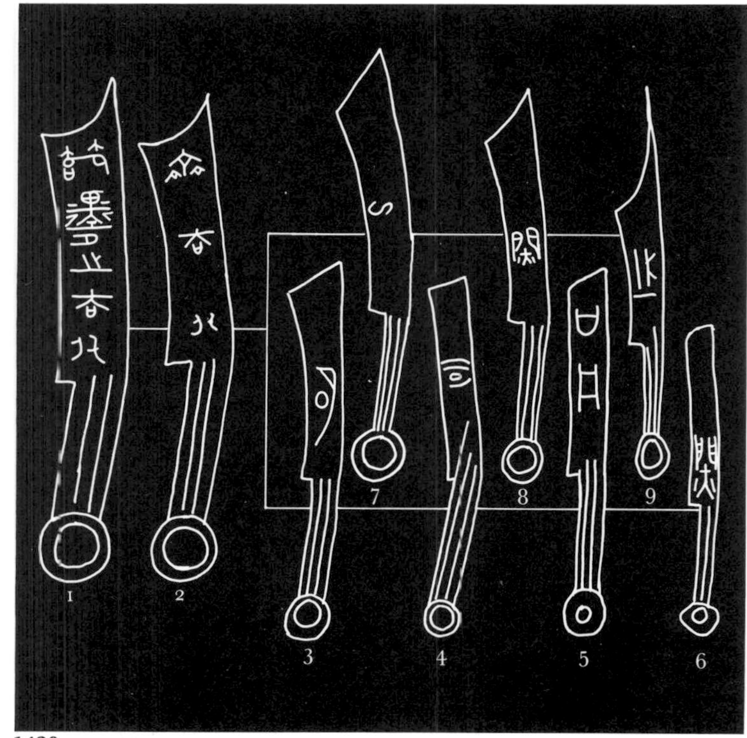

1420

type retains the features of an actual knife, with a ridged handle and finger hole for gripping and a raised edge to strengthen the blade, but the blade is unsharpened because of its different function.

1422 Bronze imitation cowry coin, fourth century BC, with undeciphered inscription. The numerous uninscribed bone, shell, stone and metal cowry imitations found on Zhou sites are probably only ornaments; inscribed pieces, like this, are money.

1423 Gold one pound ingot, fourth century BC, Chu State, with stamps inscribed 'weighed at Ying' (Ying was capital of Chu until 278 BC). The sources of gold during the Zhou period were limited to the state of Chu and all surviving ingots were made in that state.

1424 Bronze round coin, about 250 BC, Yuan City mint, Liang State, inscribed with its mint name. The round coins replacing hoe coins had round holes, those replacing knife coins had square ones. Apart from its practicality, it is not clear why a round shape was adopted.

1425 Bronze half-ounce coin, 221 BC, Qin dynasty. Because Qin's new coinage was a national coinage, its mint-name was omitted from its inscription which now only stated its weight of half an ounce (about eight grammes). The square hole was adopted so that batches of coins could be threaded onto square rods and their edge marks caused by casting removed.

1426 Bronze five-grain coin, 118 BC, Han dynasty. When the Han decided upon an effective standard weight, they changed the coin inscription from 'half ounce' to 'five grain', the new weight equal to about 3.5 grammes. The raised rim discouraged clipping.

1427 Bronze five-grain coin, AD 529, Northern Wei dynasty, inscribed 'five-grain (coin) of the Yongan era.' From AD 338 dates, expressed as the name of the imperial era, began to appear in coin inscriptions, but did not become a permanent feature until the Song dynasty. The dates were introduced along with other new types of inscriptions to distinguish the numerous local issues made during this period.

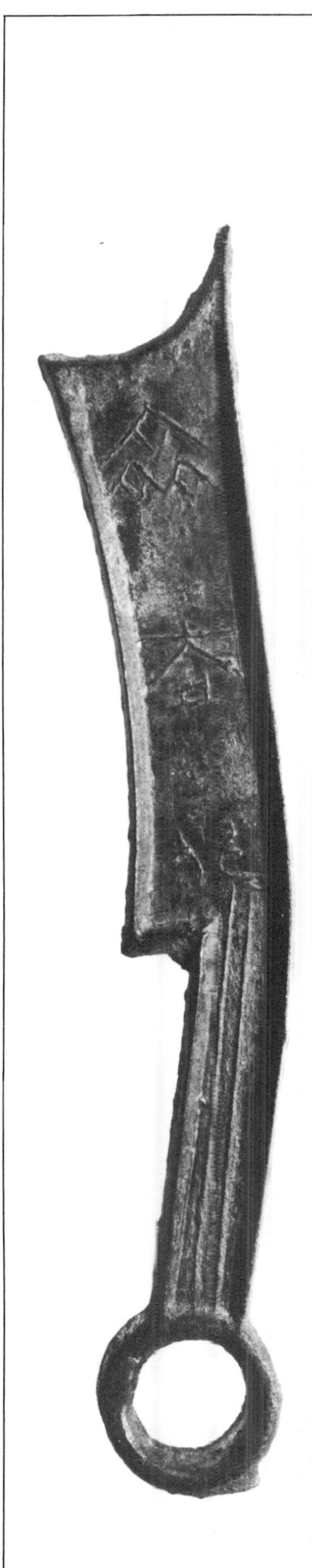

1421

1422×2

1424

1425

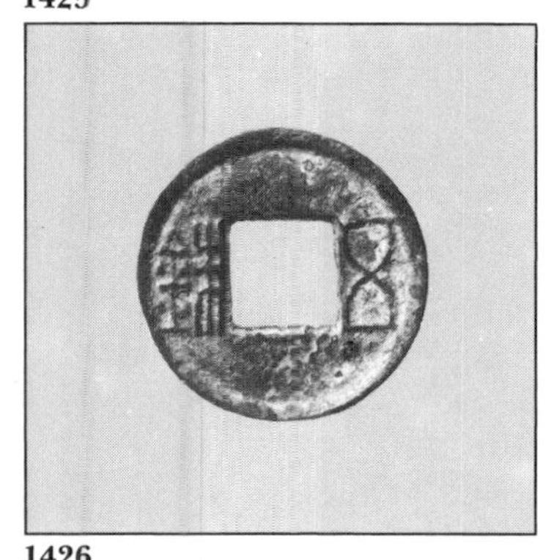

1426

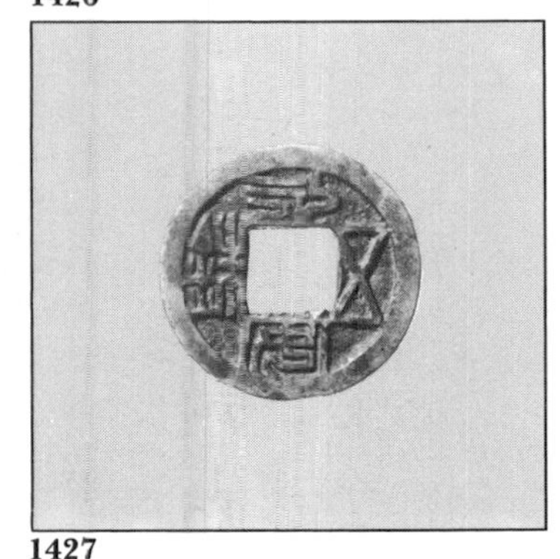

1427

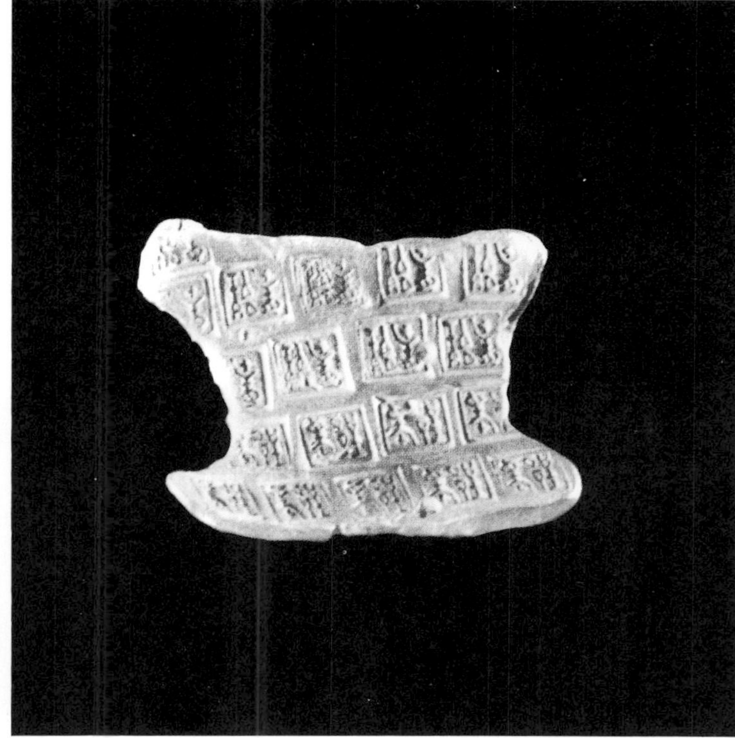

1423

increasing the money supply. By 800 merchants had also adopted a practice which, as well as being convenient, also increased the amount of money in circulation. When conducting long-distance trade, instead of transporting, and thereby removing from circulation, the necessary quantities of coins, they deposited them with other traders and used credit transfer notes instead. In 811 the government monopolized the issue of these notes, which were called 'flying money'.

When Tang fell in 906, China was again divided between small contentious kingdoms and the coinage once again disintegrated. Several states tried to retain the Tang coinage, but most were forced to issue iron or lead coins or give up using coins completely.

When unity was restored by the Song dynasty in 960, China's currency was in chaos. From 968 they started issuing a new bronze coinage on the Tang standard and demonetizing the iron and lead coins. They issued thousands of millions of coins each
year, but failed to eradicate iron coins completely. From 971 1435
Sichuan was declared an iron coinage zone and in 1040 Shaanxi and Shanxi were added to it. The low value of iron coins made them very inconvenient for trade, so merchants deposited them in banks and used their deposit notes as money instead. In 1024 the government closed the banks and replaced their notes with official paper money.

In the rest of China bronze coins were the main currency, but the government also encouraged the use of silver ingots to
facilitate tax collection and trade. The shortage of copper created 1436
by increased coin production led to regular reductions of the copper content of the coins. The shortage was also aggravated by the constant flow of bronze coins out of China to neighbouring states, which started during the Tang dynasty, but only became a problem during the Song period, in spite of government bans. Exported originally as metal, the coins involved were so numerous that they were frequently reused at their destination as currency, thereby increasing the demand for them. However

1428 Bronze coin mould for casting Han five-grain coins, first century BC. Until AD 1890, Chinese coins were cast in moulds. The moulds were made from various materials, but always allowed a number of coins to be cast at one time.

1429 Bronze token coin, AD 579, Northern Zhou dynasty, inscribed 'to circulate forever through 10,000 kingdoms,' official value 500 standard coins. So many people were tempted to forge this coin that within a year it had to be withdrawn.

1430 Bronze five-grain coin, AD 589, Sui dynasty, inscribed with its weight. On introducing their new coins, Sui set up sample coins at each market place and all coins not matching them were confiscated to be melted and recast as official coins.

1431 Bronze coin, AD 621, Tang dynasty, inscribed circulating 'treasure (i.e. coin) of the opening (of the dynasty).' Tang's new standard coin (weighing about four grammes) was called a 'qian,' meaning coin, but translated in English as 'cash,' a pidgin word derived from the South Indian 'kashu,' meaning a small copper coin.

1432 Bronze standard coins of the Xining era (1068-77). To administer the vast coin issues of the Song period a system of control was established using variations in design to distinguish different issues. It is not clear how, but these distinctions related to mint and date of issue. The basic variations were between styles of calligraphy, 1-4 of the illustrated coins are in pattern style, 5-8 in seal style. Each issue was further marked by minor differences in the calligraphy. This system was used until 1189 when a system using year numerals on the reverses was introduced.

1428×½

1429×3

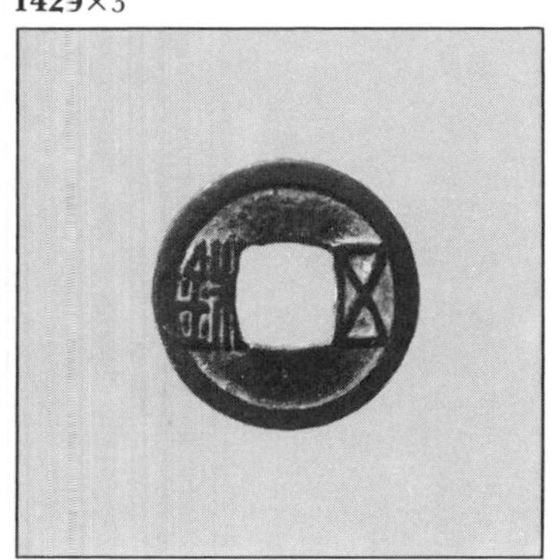

1430

1431

1432

1433×3

1433 Bronze token coin, AD 1072, Song dynasty, inscribed 'heavy coin of the Xining era,' worth two standard coins. From 1072, these token coins circulated alongside the standard coins until the end of the Song dynasty.

1434 Bronze token coin, 1107, Song dynasty, inscribed 'coin of the Daguan era,' worth 10 standard coins. The administrative importance of calligraphy in coin inscriptions prompted Emperor Huizong, a renowned artist, to design his coins with his own hand, using the 'slender gold,' calligraphy he invented.

1435 Iron coin, 1200, Song dynasty, Qichun mint, Hubei, inscribed coin of the Qingyuan era. After Jin occupied north China, Song extended the Sichuan iron coin zone along its northern border as a buffer to limit the export of bronze coins to Jin.

1436 Silver tax ingot, twelfth century, Song dynasty, inscribed with details of its function and weight, 50 ounces (approximately two kilos). Ingots like this were used from the Tang until the Yuan period, originally rectangular in shape, they developed concave sides and then convex ends.

1437 Bronze token coin, 1204, Jin dynasty, inscribed 'heavy coin of the Taihe era,' worth 10 standard coins. Relying on imported Song coins and later paper money, Jin issued few coins, but all were beautifully designed. This elegant coin inscribed in decorative seal script was part of the last significant issue.

1438 Bronze token coin, 1310, Yuan dynasty, inscribed 'coin of the Yuan dynasty,' worth 10 standard coins. The inscription is Chinese phonetically transcribed in Phagspa, the official Yuan script. Chinese coins inscribed with Sogdian, Mongol, Tibetan, Tangut, Manchu and Arabic have also been issued at this and other periods.

The Dynasties of China

Zhou dynasty	11th century BC–256 BC
Spring and Autumn period	770 BC–476 BC
Warring states period	475 BC–221 BC
Qin dynasty	221 BC–207 BC
Han dynasty	206 BC–AD 220
First period of disunity	220–589
Sui dynasty	581–618
Tang dynasty	618–907
Second period of disunity	907–960
Song dynasty	960–1272
Northern Song period	960–1127
Southern Song period	1127–1272
Liao dynasty	916–1125
Western Xia dynasty	1038–1227
Jin dynasty	1115–1234
Yuan (Mongol) dynasty	1271–1368
Ming dynasty	1368–1644
Qing (Manchu) dynasty	1644–1911
Republic	1912–
People's Republic	1949–

1434

1435

1436

1437

1438

in the late eleventh century, by raising production and issuing
1432 acceptable, low denomination token coins, Song was able to
1433,1434 supply virtually all the coins needed by their highly monetized
economy.

In 1126 one of Song's northern neighbours, the Nuchen conquered northern China. Invading northern barbarians were an age-old problem for China, hence the Great Wall. During Song four northern peoples moved into China and set up their own Chinese style empires where standard Chinese bronze coins were issued. They were the Liao (916-1125) founded by the Kitan in Manchuria, Western Xia (1038-1227) founded by the Tangut in Gansu, Jin (1115-1234) founded by the Nuchen who ousted Song from northern China, and Yuan (1280-1367) founded by the Mongols who, after defeating Western Xia and Jin, finally captured the rest of China from Song.

Song in the south and Jin in the north faced similar monetary
problems and sought similar solutions. Shortage of copper
drastically reduced the production of standard coins, but the 1437
demand for currency to serve their thriving economies continued
to grow, prompting them both to increase the monetary use of silver, produce more token coins and adopt on a national basis the previously localized paper money. Poor understanding of the

1439 Impression from engraved bronze block for printing Yuan government notes, issued 1287-1320, worth two coin strings (i.e. 2000 standard coins). The notes were printed in black on paper made from mulberry bark and stamped with vermilion impressions from authorizing seals.

1440 Bronze coin, 1408, Ming dynasty, inscribed 'coin of Yongle era.' When Yongle coins were produced, coins had been officially banned as a boost to paper money circulation. They were cast for overseas trade. Ming coins became an essential part of Japan's economy and have been found as far afield as East Africa.

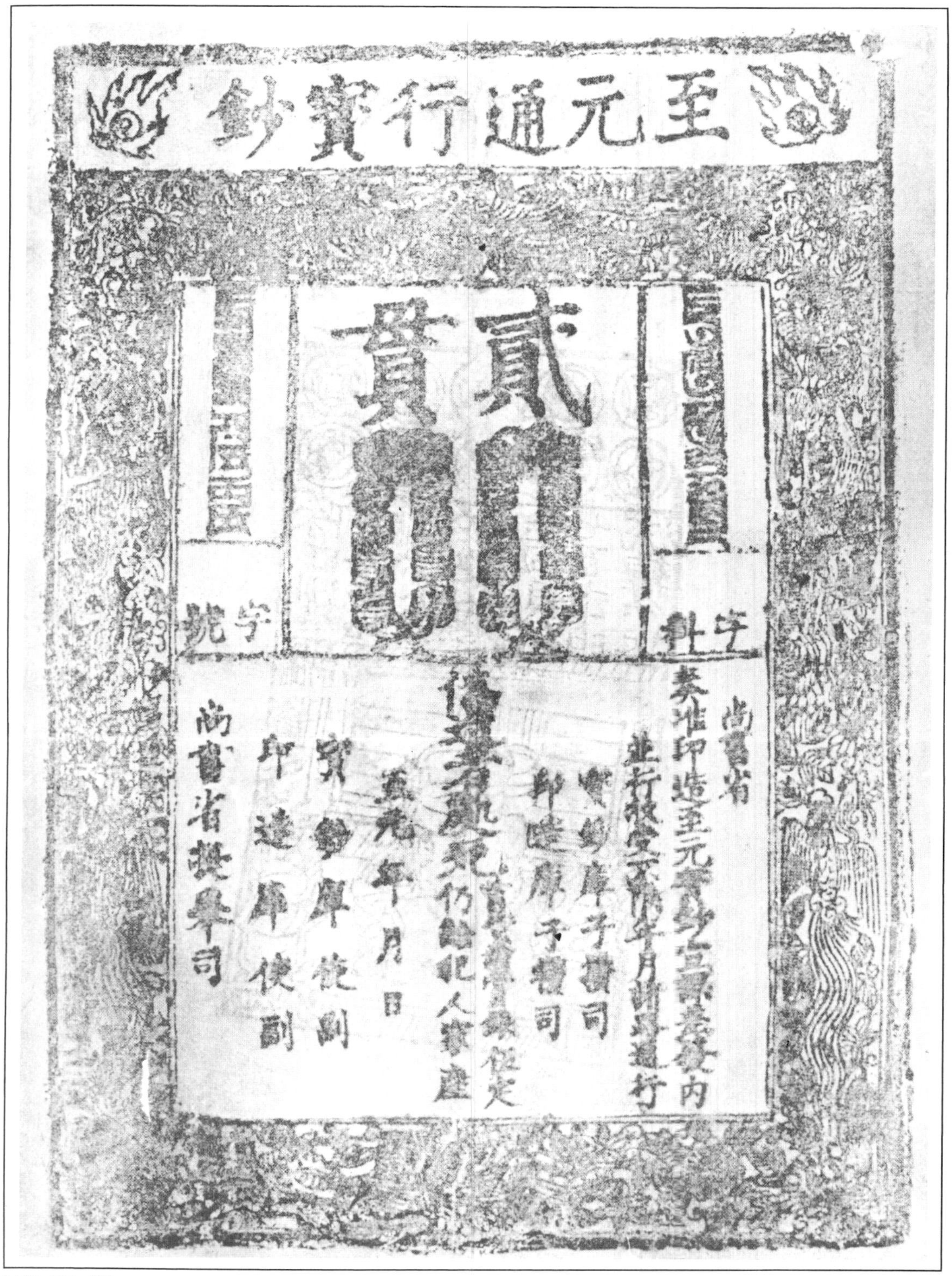

1439 293×222mm

1440A

1440B

1442A

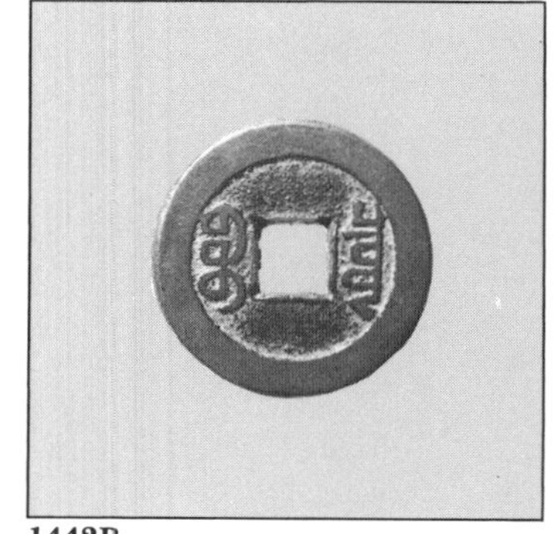

1442B

principles governing paper currency led to uncontrolled issues in both Song and Jin resulting in dramatic inflation. By the fall of China to the Mongols their paper money was virtually worthless.

1439 The invading Mongols found bronze coins so scarce they also had to issue paper money, but unlike Song and Jin they carefully controlled it, issuing notes backed with silver reserves. The first issue made in 1260 circulated until the end of Yuan. Their stability was ensured by bans on the monetary use of bronze coins, gold and silver. At first Yuan had the political authority to enforce paper money circulation, but from 1300 it declined. New notes issued in 1309 and token coinage in 1310 had to be withdrawn within a year. Nevertheless, government notes remained the principal currency, although its gradual depreciation led Yuan to make use of silver ingots to conduct its official business.

On returning China to native rule in 1368 the Ming dynasty
attempted to reinstate the bronze coinage, but, in spite of 1440
relatively large issues of coins and token coins, were forced in 1374 to issue paper money. However, they failed to exercise efficient control over its issue and circulation. The government banned the circulation of coins and silver, but by 1450 the notes had already depreciated to a thousandth of their issue value.

1441 Brass standard coins of the Kangxi era (1662-1722), Board of Revenue Mint, Beijing (Peking). The Qing period was another period of intensive coin issue and, as formerly, calligraphic variations were used as coin issue control marks. Qing coins all bore mint marks on their reverses, so it can be assumed that the differences were used as date indicators. During the 61 years of the Kangxi era the same inscription was used, but each year's issue is distinguishable by its calligraphy. Furthermore from 1702 coins of two different weight distinguished by their size and calligraphy at the Beijing mints.

1442 Brass coin, 1770, Qing dynasty, Board of Revenue mint, Beijing, inscribed 'coin of the Qianlong era' and 'boo ciowan,' its mint name in Manchu script. From 1645 Qing coins were inscribed with their mint name, after 1657 in Manchu.

1443 Bronze token coin, 1853, Qing dynasty, Board of Revenue mint, Beijing, inscribed 'principal coin of the Xianfeng era' and its mint name and value of 1000 standard coins. The copper shortage created by the Taiping rebellion prompted this issue, but extensive forgery lead to its withdrawal the following year.

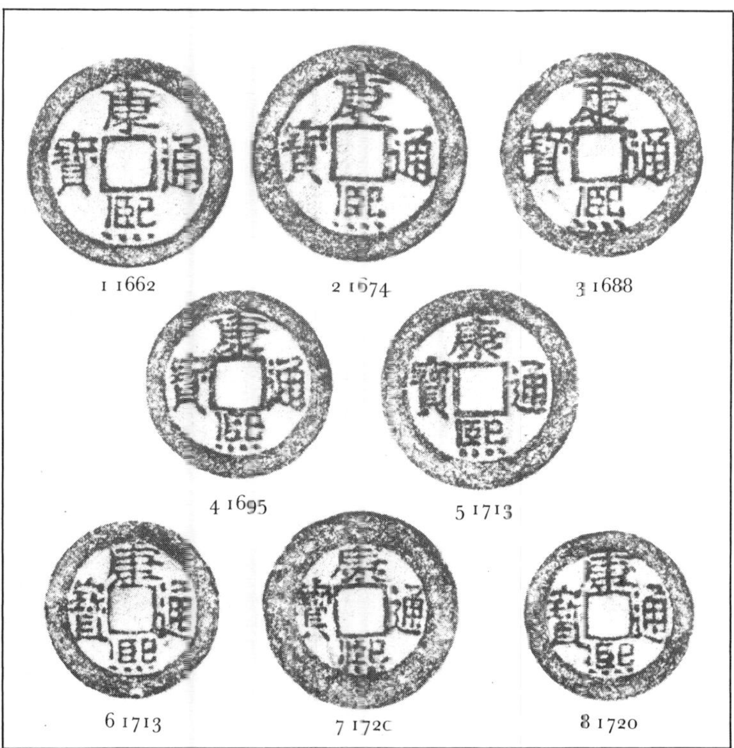

1441

1443

Nevertheless notes were still issued for use in certain official transactions until the early seventeenth century.

The exclusive paper currencies of Yuan and Ming increased the export of coins and although coin issues restarted again from 1527, they were inadequate. With insufficient coins and worthless paper money the government and people turned to silver, which during the last century of Ming rule became the standard currency in many parts of China. This was made possible by large imports of silver, initially from Japan, and later from Latin America via Europe and the Philippines.

American silver came in the form of Spanish coins from her American mints, but was mostly melted on arrival and cast into currency ingots. Eventually, however, the fixed weight and quality of the coins became recognized by the Chinese, who began to use them as they were and thereby coinage of the western traditon spread to China.

In 1644 Ming was overthrown by the Manchu, northern invaders who founded Qing, China's last dynasty. While establishing a powerful military rule they set about successfully restoring the Chinese coinage, by setting up a national network
1441 of mints to cast new standard coins in vast quantities and by
1442 encouraging the monetary use of silver. They left the control of the use of silver in the hands of merchants, who set up their own monetary system based on silver ingots. For everyday purposes the official coins were used, but in trade silver became the normal medium of exchange. Merchants also set up banks issuing paper money. The government, wary of inflation, refrained from doing so, until the Taiping Rebellion (1851-61) caused their monetary system to disintegrate by weakening its control over the provinces and cutting the copper supply. The
1443 government was forced to issue token coins and paper money, both of which rapidly depreciated. The monetary system never recovered.

Another factor was also at work undermining the traditional coinage system. Foreign trade was introducing more and more silver into China. Large areas were abandoning Chinese coins and using foreign silver coins instead. Elsewhere so much silver 1448
was available that the merchants' ingots were becoming very widely used. People, distrusting the official coins, preferred to use bank notes or ingots issued by merchants they trusted. 1451

After the suppression of the Taipings, the interest of foreign trading powers in the monetary system of China grew. In an attempt to simplify trade they struck silver dollars for use in 1450
China and they pressed the Chinese government to reform its coinage. When attempts to do this failed, the Chinese were forced in 1889 to issue western-style coins, silver dollars and 1452
fractions, followed in 1900 by copper cents.

Because the central government was now ineffectual, each provincial mint set up to strike dollars and cents adopted different designs and standards. China now had three inefficient monetary systems, uncontrolled western coinage, localized merchants' notes and ingots and the ailing traditional coinage. The overthrow of Qing by the establishment of a Republic in 1912 did little to improve the situation. In 1911, just before their overthrow, Qing had plans to establish a national dollar coinage, but it took the Republic until 1914 to carry this out. 1455
The new national dollar gradually became widely accepted, but its subsidiary coins failed to oust the locally issued coins which had continued under the Republic, although the merchants notes and ingots and the traditional coins now began to disappear.

Local currencies persisted because the central government could not control the local military leaders who had gained power during the establishment of the Republic. By 1928 the Nationalist Party had succeeded in unifying most of China and started to reform the currency. World recession and their war against the Communists led them to abandon the silver dollar in favour of paper dollars and base metal token coins. The resulting 1457
inflation contributed to their defeat by the Communists in 1949.

The Communists established a People's Republic and, once

1444 Silver trade ingot, 1767, weighing 50 ounces and inscribed with its date, place of manufacture, and the names of the issuing merchant and smith. From the eighteenth century, privately made ingots circulated as money. This shape of ingot originated in the Ming period.

1445 Government note, 1854, Qing dynasty, issued in Beijing by the Board of Revenue, denominated as 10 ounces of silver. The Imperial government failed to get these notes into circulation outside Beijing, because the provincial authorities refused to accept them.

1446 Silver customs ingot, 1884, Guangdong, inscribed with its function, place of issue and maker's name. By this period silver currency ingots were widespread. Each region had its own shape of ingot. Pieces like this were only made in Guangdong, Guangxi and Hunan.

1447 Brass coin, 1889, Qing, Guangzhou mint, inscribed 'coin of the Guangxu era' and with its mint name and weight. The issue of traditional standard coins like this, struck on Western machinery, was the final futile attempt to resuscitate the traditional coinage system.

1448 Silver eight-real piece, 1758, Mexico City mint, stamped with signature marks by Chinese merchants who had checked its weight and fineness before recirculating it. Spanish silver coins were circulated as money in south-east China from the mid-seventeenth century.

1449 Silver dollar, about 1837, Taiwan, issued as military pay. The circulation of Spanish coins in Taiwan and Fujian led to the production of several native imitations like this piece, which portrays the Chinese god of longevity.

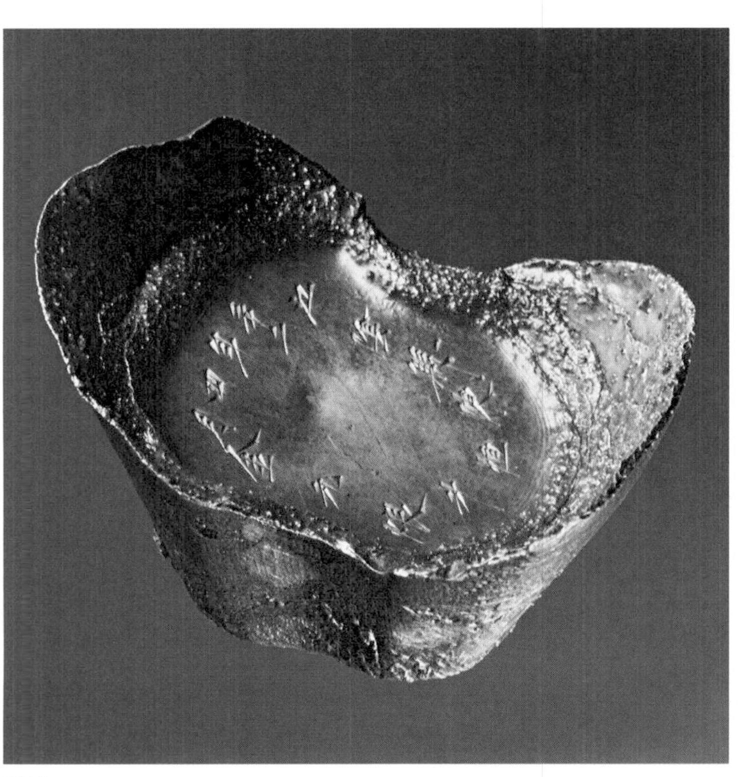

1444

1446

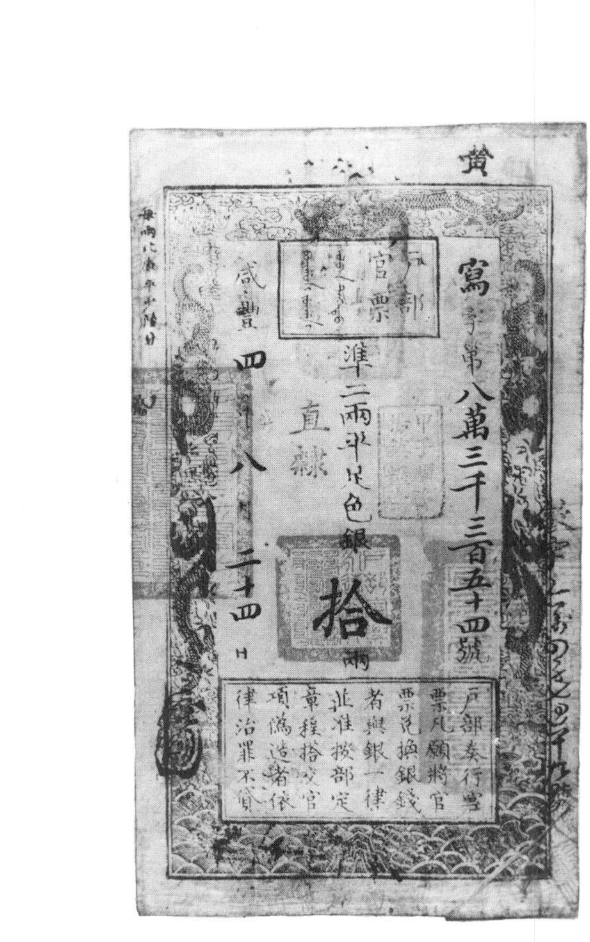

1445 316×178mm

1447

1448

1449

1450

1451

1452

1450 Silver trade dollar, 1874, Japanese Empire. The profit gained from importing American silver coins into China prompted Japan, Britain, France, the U.S.A. and others to make coins for this trade.

1451 Silver trade ingot, nineteenth century, Zhejiang, inscribed with its place of issue, maker's name and weight, 0·72 ounce. The circulation of foreign dollars encouraged local Chinese merchants to cast ingots of the same weight, i.e. 0·72 ounce.

1452 Silver dollar, 1889, Qing dynasty Guangzhou, Guangdong. The first official western-style silver coin issued in China. Although clearly a coin, it is still valued as an ingot by weight, 0·72 ounce.

1453 Provincial government one-dollar note, 1899, issued by the Hubei Silver Dollar Office, printed in Japan. The dragon on the note and the coin decorating it symbolized the Emperor.

1454 Copper cent, 1901, Qing dynasty, Fujian mint. Notionally a cent, this coin was issued officially as 10 standard coins (cash), but had a market value of its own, fluctuating from 80 to over 250 to the dollar.

1455 Silver dollar, 1914, Republic of China, Central Mint, Tianjin. This coin portraying President Yuan Shikai was China's first national dollar.

1456 Silver dollar, 1934, Chinese Soviet Republic, Sichuan and Shaanxi. Several issues of dollars were made in Communist held areas during their struggle with the Nationalist regime. This coin's inscription is the familiar slogan, 'Workers of the World, Unite!'

1457 Nickel 20 cents, 1936, Republic of China, Shanghai mint. This coin portrays President Sun Yatsen, founder of the National Party (Guomindang).

1458 500,000 dollar note, 1949, Central Bank of China. The Nationalist regime's extreme paper money inflation led in 1949 to the issue of notes denominated up to five million dollars, all portraying the Nationalist leader Chiang Kaishek.

1454

1455

1456

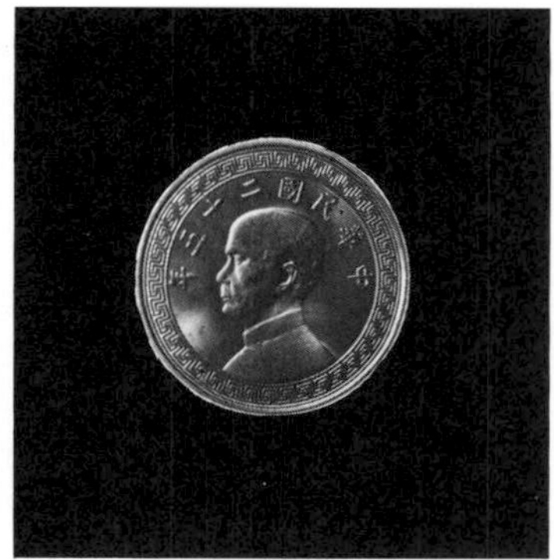

1457

1458

1453 210×133 mm

they had controlled the monetary system by setting up a people's
currency, issued paper dollars and aluminium cents which still 1459
circulate today.

In China today there are two regions which until recently were separate political and economic entities. One of these, Xinjiang (Chinese Turkestan) first came under Chinese rule in the Han and Tang period. Imported Chinese coins circulated there alongside locally issued imitations of Indian and Chinese coins. Following the ninth century Islamic conquest of Turkestan, Islamic coins were used there together with imported Chinese coins until China reconquered the area in the eighteenth century. The Qing monetary system was introduced, but the coins were cast on a different standard and the silver currency was officially controlled.

An Islamic rebellion threw out the Chinese and in 1872
Islamic coins were issued. When the Chinese regained control in
1877, they struck silver coins following the rebels' example.
From 1890 larger silver coins and soon after copper cents were
introduced, but until 1949 and the Communist takeover they 1461
were issued on a separate standard.

The other area, Tibet, began to feel China's influence from the
Tang period, but Tibet used uncoined money and was unaf-
fected by the Chinese monetary system until the Ming period,
when Chinese silver ingots were imported through trade. When
the Manchus entered Tibet in 1791 they found Indian-style coins
imported from Nepal circulating alongside Chinese ingots. The
Chinese struck silver coins there as part of the Indian-style 1460
coinage, which continued as the main currency until the
Communist takeover in 1959.

Several small areas using non-Chinese coinages were also created by foreign powers, particularly the British, Portuguese,

1459 Aluminium cent, 1956, People's Republic of China. In 1957 aluminium coins (dated 1955 or 1956) were issued to replace the low denomination notes of the reformed People's Currency issued in 1953 by the People's Bank of China.

1460 Silver sho (i.e. a tenth of a Chinese ounce), 1793, Tibet, Lhassa mint. When Tibet came under Chinese domination in 1792, a mint was set up by the Chinese at Lhassa to strike Tibetan coins with Chinese inscriptions. The first issue was inscribed 'Tibetan coin of the Qianlong era, year 58,' i.e. 1793. Occasional issues were made until 1836 and again in 1910.

1461 Silver half-ounce coin, 1905, Xinjiang, Kashgar mint, inscribed in Chinese and Arabic. Xinjiang silver coins were denominated by weight as fractions of the Chinese ounce and no dollars were issued as in the rest of China until the year of the Communist takeover in 1949.

1462 Silver dollar, 1866, Hongkong. Acquired by Britain in 1841 Hongkong's currency consisted of Spanish and Mexican dollars. The cost of importing these for local use and for trade with China prompted the Colony to establish a mint in 1866 to strike its own dollars. The Chinese however would only accept them at a discount, and in 1868 the mint was closed.

1463 Silver and bronze coins, AD 708, Japan, inscribed 'coin of the opening of the Wado era.' Japan's first coins were issued under Tang influence and were probably cast by imported Chinese moneyers. Because of forgery the attempt at a bimetallic coinage was abandoned after two years and the silver coins were withdrawn.

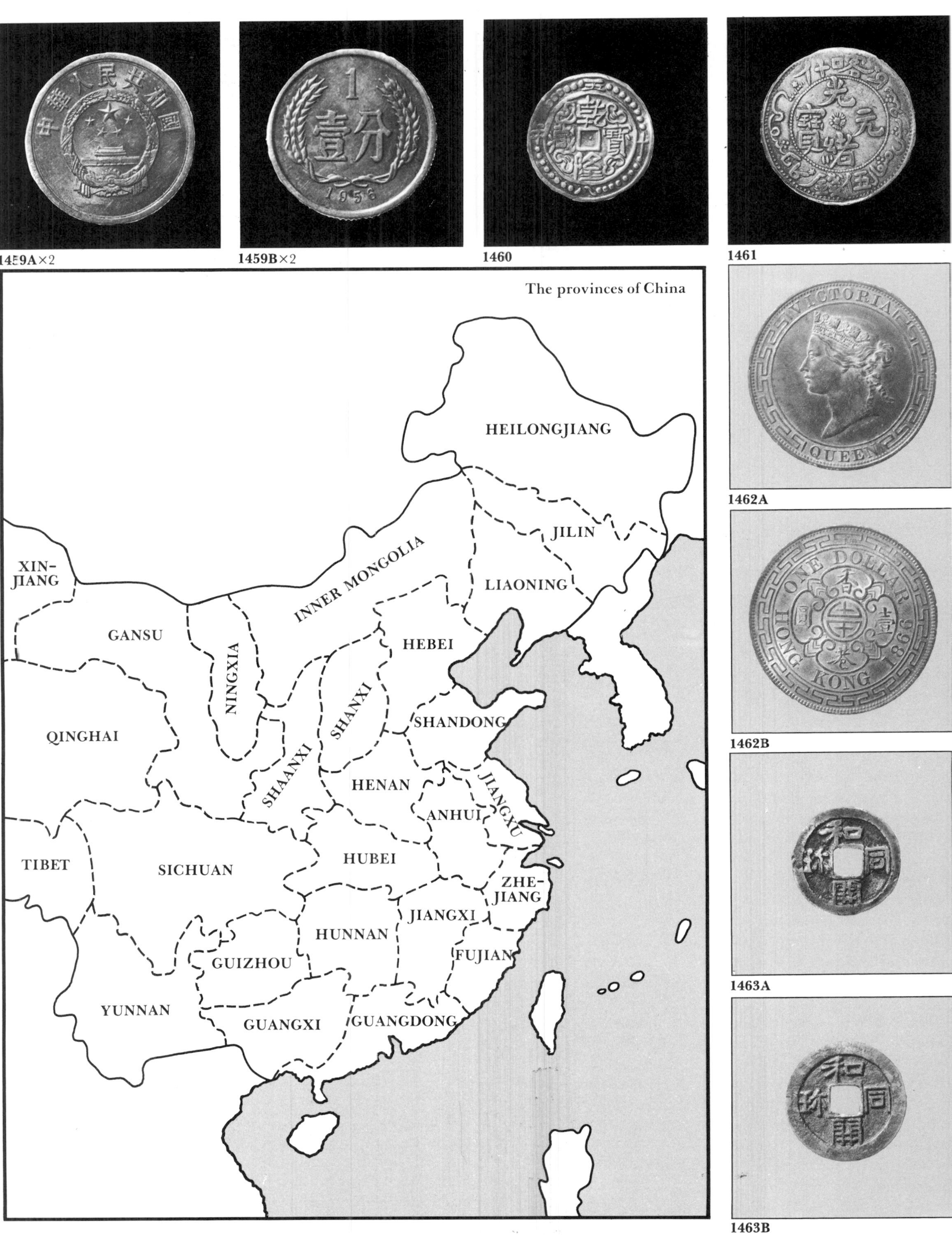

1459A×2

1459B×2

1460

1461

1462A

1462B

1463A

1463B

1464 Bronze forgery, thirteenth century. Japanese copy of Chinese Tang dynasty coin (**1431**). When Chinese coins were not available the Japanese made their own imitations of them, normally by casting, but many were engraved by hand.

1465 Gold coin, 1593, Japanese copy of Chinese Ming dynasty bronze coin. Such pieces cast in gold and silver were made by the military leader Toyotomi Hideyoshi, probably for distribution as rewards. The Ming coin imitated, called in Japan *eiraku sen* was very popular in fifteenth and sixteenth century Japan.

1466 Bronze coin, 1626, Japan, Tokugawa period, inscribed 'coin of the Kanei era.' Coins with this inscription were Japan's first successful issue and were still being issued until 1870, long after the end of the Kanei era (1624-44).

1467 Bronze standard coins, Japan, Tokugawa period. The immense issues of Kanei coins by the Tokugawa shoguns necessitated the adoption of a control system similar to that used in contemporary China. Although mint names were later used, the mint and date of most Kanei coins could only be distinguished by their calligraphy. Thus, all these coins, although they have the same inscription, can be attributed to their exact date and place of issue.

1468 Iron token coin, 1866, Japan, Tokugawa period, inscribed 'coin of the Kanei era' and on the reverse *Mori*, short for its mint name Morioka, worth four standard coins. These coins represent the final degradation of the Tokugawa coinage system. The wave pattern symbolizes the idea that the coin should circulate freely like water.

1464

1466

1465×3

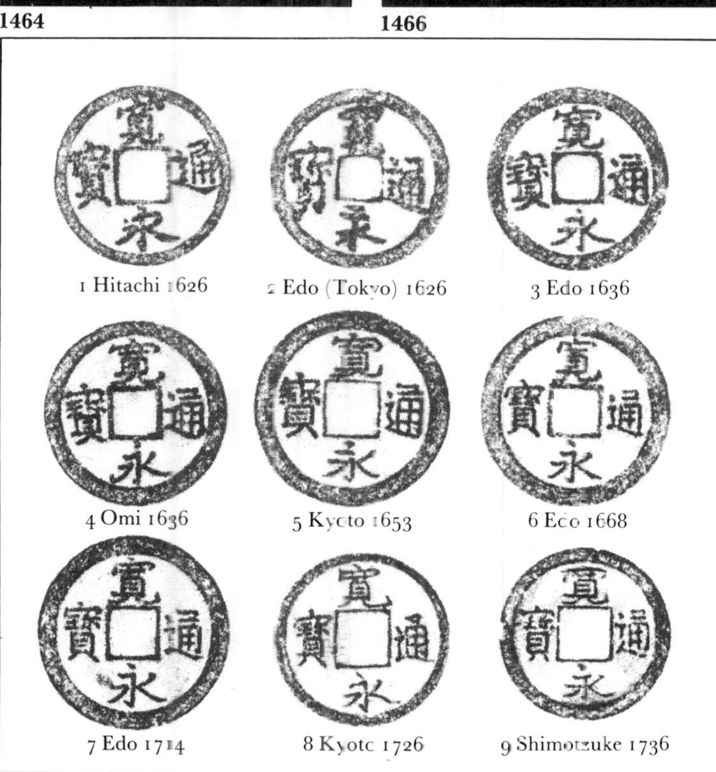

1467

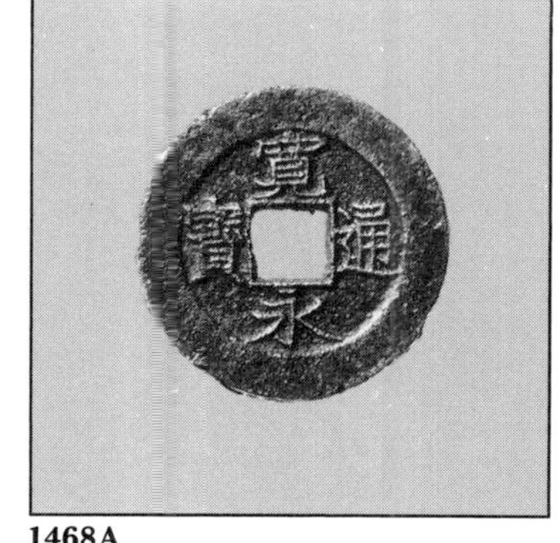

1468A

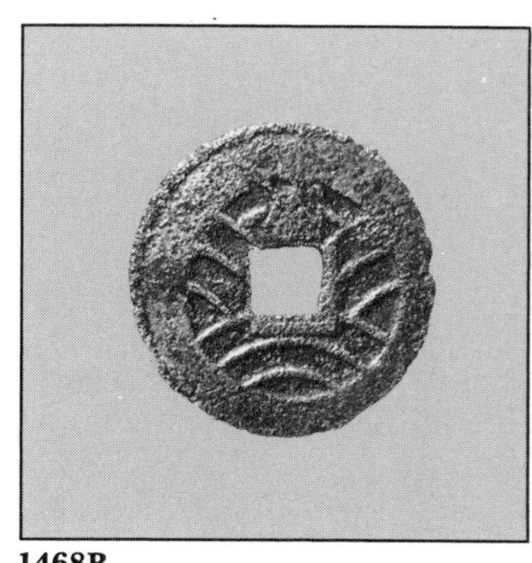

1468B

Germans, Dutch, Russians and Japanese, occupying Chinese territory and introducing their own coins and paper money
1462 there. British Hongkong, Portuguese Macau and Russian-dominated Mongolia still maintain their own separate currency systems. Taiwan's monetary system is also separate, not through foreign rule, but because the Nationalist Party under Chiang Kaishek held out on the island against the Communists and maintained their own currency.

The export of China's economic ideas and coins to its neighbours deeply influenced their monetary systems. The nearer states, Japan, Korea and Vietnam were the most affected, those further away, in south-east Asia and the Indian Archipelago obviously less so.

Japan, before the seventh century, was a tribal society with a primititive economy based on barter and coins were unknown. In 645 under Chinese influence a powerful clan tried to reorganize Japan's political system in imitation of the Tang dynasty and an attempt was made in 708 to monetize the
1463 economy with issues of Chinese style bronze coins. Both the political and economic reforms were unsuccessful because the power of the clans could not be broken and Japan's society was too primitive to need coins outside its cities. Nevertheless the coinage experiment continued for 250 years, during which 11 new issues were made, each baser and lighter but officially worth ten times more than its predecessor. The government could not prevent the resulting inflation, forgery and growing distrust of the whole idea of coins. The use of coins had always been limited and when it died out commodities, such as rice and cloth, continued to serve most monetary functions, but it was not long before coins began to reemerge.

From the late tenth century trade between Japan and China began to grow and Chinese coins became an increasingly popular part of it. The developing Japanese economy began to need coins and Chinese merchants were ready to import them. By the thirteenth century trade in Japan could be conducted with coins, instead of rice, and deposit notes were also beginning to be used as money. Japan's thirst for coins was insatiable and China's development of paper money allowed even more to be imported into Japan, but no efforts were made by the Japanese government to cast its own coins. Instead it opened up official trade with Ming China to increase the import of coins and
allowed private mints to be set up to cast imitations of the 1464
Chinese coins.

The sixteenth century saw a revolution in Japanese political and economic life. A series of military dictators transformed Japanese society and established a new currency. They issued

1469 Gold 10 ounce coin, 1860, Japan, Tokugawa period. Gold coins of this denomination and its fractions were issued from the beginning of the Tokugawa period. The Indian ink inscription consists of its denomination and the Gold Mint Superintendent's signature.

1470a Silver bar coin, 1837, Japan, Tokugawa period, called *chogin* (long silver), first issued 1601. This coin and its lump-shaped fractions circulated by weight, but were nevertheless struck at the official Silver Mint for issue as coins.

1470b Silver quarter-ounce coin, 1837, Japan, Tokugawa period. New fixed-weight coins were issued to rationalize the silver coinage and to replace the small rectangular gold coins which were becoming very small and debased because of the rising price of gold.

1471 Provincial silver coin, 1862, Japan. Akita clan. Actually denominated as 0·92 ounce, this coin circulated as a full ounce. Their abundant mines gave Akita the resources to make large issues of silver, bronze and lead coins. Their silver coins circulated widely outside their territory.

1472 Provincial lead token, 1862, Japan, inscribed with its place of issue, Hosokura, and denomination, 100 coins. Once official coins had become scarce and paper money worthless, several clans issued lead tokens for internal use, simply to allow the purchase of daily necessities.

1473 Local paper money, 1766, Japan, Toyooka clan, denominated as one ounce of silver. Over 250 clans issued paper money denominated in coins or commodities. They were mostly issued because of local shortages of official coin, but sometimes for profit.

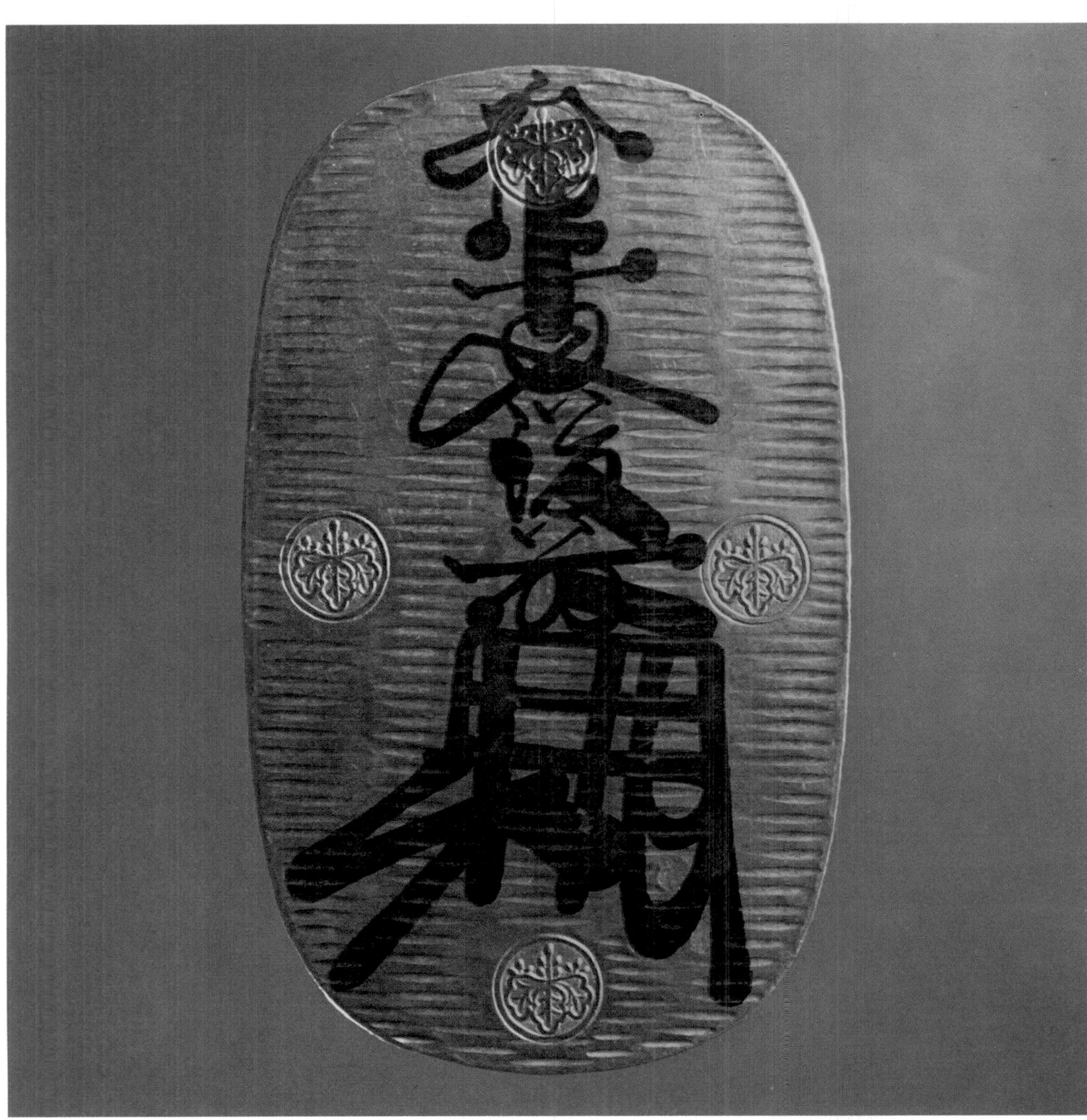

1469

1470a

1470b

1471

1472

1474 Gold 10-dollar (*yen*) coin, 1870 (issued 1871), Japanese Empire, Osaka mint. The coinage initiated by the Meiji Restoration was designed and produced with British help, because the new Osaka mint, bought secondhand from the British government, was in fact the failed Hongkong dollar mint (**1462**).

1475 Government fifty-cent (*sen*) note, 1872, Japanese Empire, printed in Germany. Extensive forgery of the traditionally printed government notes issued in the first years following the Meiji Restoration forced the government to seek foreign help in printing a more secure note.

1476 Brass five-dollar coin, 1961, Japanese Empire. Current Japanese coins are all base metal and have western type designs, buildings, flowers etc. The cog and rice on this coin represent industry and agriculture, typical themes on modern European coins.

1477 Bronze coin, AD 1102, Korea, Koryo dynasty, inscribed 'coin of the Eastern Sea', a name of Korea. The Koryo dynasty made five issues of coins, the first two exactly copied Chinese Tang types but the other three had original types, inscribed, like the contemporary Song coins in a variety of calligraphic styles.

1478 Bronze coin, AD 1423, Korea, Yi dynasty, inscribed 'coin of Korea'. Following the failure of paper money issues in 1401 and 1410 an attempt was made to reintroduce bronze coinage, but the shortage of copper prevented its success and in 1445 paper money was tried again.

1473

1474A

1474B

1476

1475

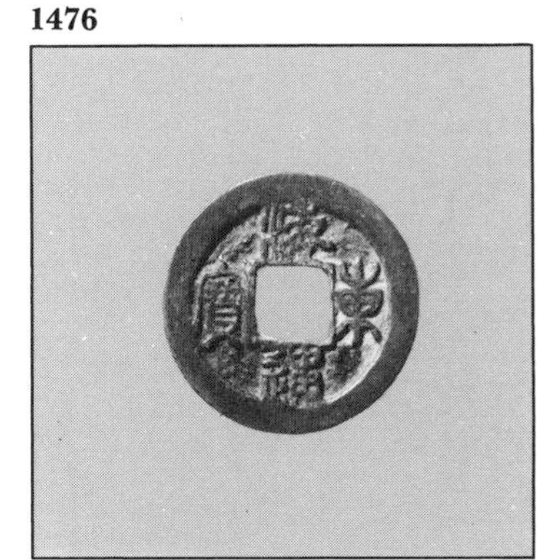
1477

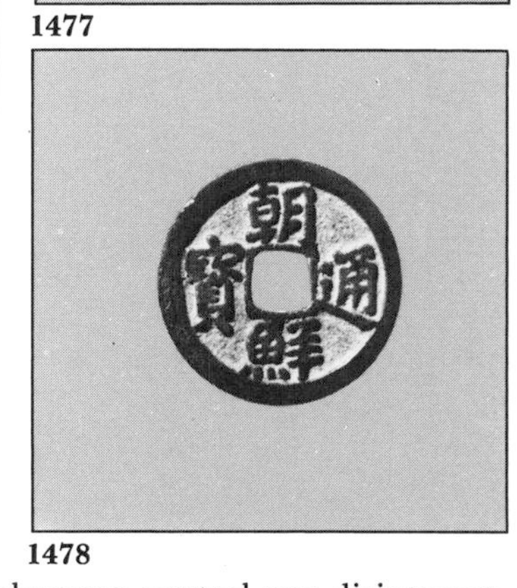

1478

their own Chinese-style coins and demonetized all imported
1466 coins and their imitations. They also supplemented the bronze
coinage with issues of gold and silver coins, at first copying the bronze coins, but by the end of the century in totally new shapes, flat oval and rectangular gold, and silver in crude bars and lumps.

The political system perfected by the last of these dictators, Ieyasu Tokugawa (1601-16), who adopted the title Shogun, kept Japan stable under the rule of his descendants for the next 250 years, during which the economy expanded very quickly. By 1630 privately issued paper money, based on silver, was widely used around Osaka and in 1661 the Tokugawa Shogun gave permission for the clans to issue similar notes. These notes were
1473 being issued until the end of Tokugawa rule in 1868, by which
time they were also being issued by temples, townships, etc.

Tokugawa stability led to stagnation and during the eighteenth century the coinage began to deteriorate. There were issues of token coins and provincial mints not always under full central control cast coins below the official standard. By 1740 iron coins were issued to replace the bronze. As the value of gold rose the gold coins were debased and reduced in weight. The clans also aggravated these problems by overissue of their paper money which quickly diminished in value.

By the nineteenth century Tokugawa control was disintegrating and power was moving into the hands of the local clans, who
were not only making paper money, but by the 1860s had also 1471,1472
begun to issue their own coins in a variety of metals and shapes.

In 1868 the more powerful clans overthrew Tokugawa and established a modernized state and restored imperial rule. As part of this modernization, known as the Meiji Restoration after the new imperial era established in 1868, a new mint was built at
Osaka in 1870 to strike a western-style coinage of gold, silver and 1474
bronze dollars and cents and the government had paper money 1475
printed in Germany. Both coins and notes were backed by gold. Before 1880 the new issues had replaced all the traditional currencies.

In the first half of this century the cost of wars and adherence to the gold standard depreciated Japan's currency. Its gold and
silver coins were demonetized and its economy is now served by 1476
base metal coins and bank notes.

Korea was the first of China's neighbours to come in contact with her coinage. During China's Zhou period knife coins found their way into Korea and later Chinese coins circulated in northern Korea when it came briefly under Han rule, but this had little impact on the Koreans who continued to barter or use commodity money.

1479 Brass coin, 1852, Korea, Yi dynasty, Treasury Department mint, Seoul, inscribed 'coin of permanent stability'. Coins with this inscription, first cast in 1678 AD, were issued until 1890 AD. To control this lengthy production, the coins had on the reverse their mint name and various other marks indicating furnace number and batch.

1480 Silver coin, 1882, Korea, Yi dynasty, Treasury Department mint, Seoul, inscribed 'Great Eastern 0·3 ounce (coin)'. Growing foreign trade encouraged Korea to cast silver coins, but hoarding and export prevented their circulation and the attempt was abandoned.

1481 Silver dollar (*huan*), 1892 (issued 1894), Korea, Yi dynasty, Inchon mint, denominated five ounces. The issues of the Inchon mint, established in 1892 with Japanese help, resemble contemporary Japanese coins. After the Japanese closed it in 1905 they struck coins for Korea denominated in cents at Osaka.

1482 Aluminium cent (*chon*), 1970, Democratic People's Republic of Korea. North Korea's coins, like those of other communist states, have the national emblem as their main type.

1483 Bronze coin, about AD 978, Vietnam, Dinh dynasty, inscribed 'prosperous coin of the Daibinh era'. Vietnam's first coin closely imitates the coins of the contemporary Chinese Taiping era, but is easily distinguished by name of the Dinh dynasty inscribed on its reverse.

1484 Unofficial bronze coin, thirteenth century, imitating a Chinese coin issued AD 1092. Many of the lightweight imitations circulating in medieval Vietnam had confused inscriptions like this coin, copied from more than one coin. Two characters are in seal script and two are cursive.

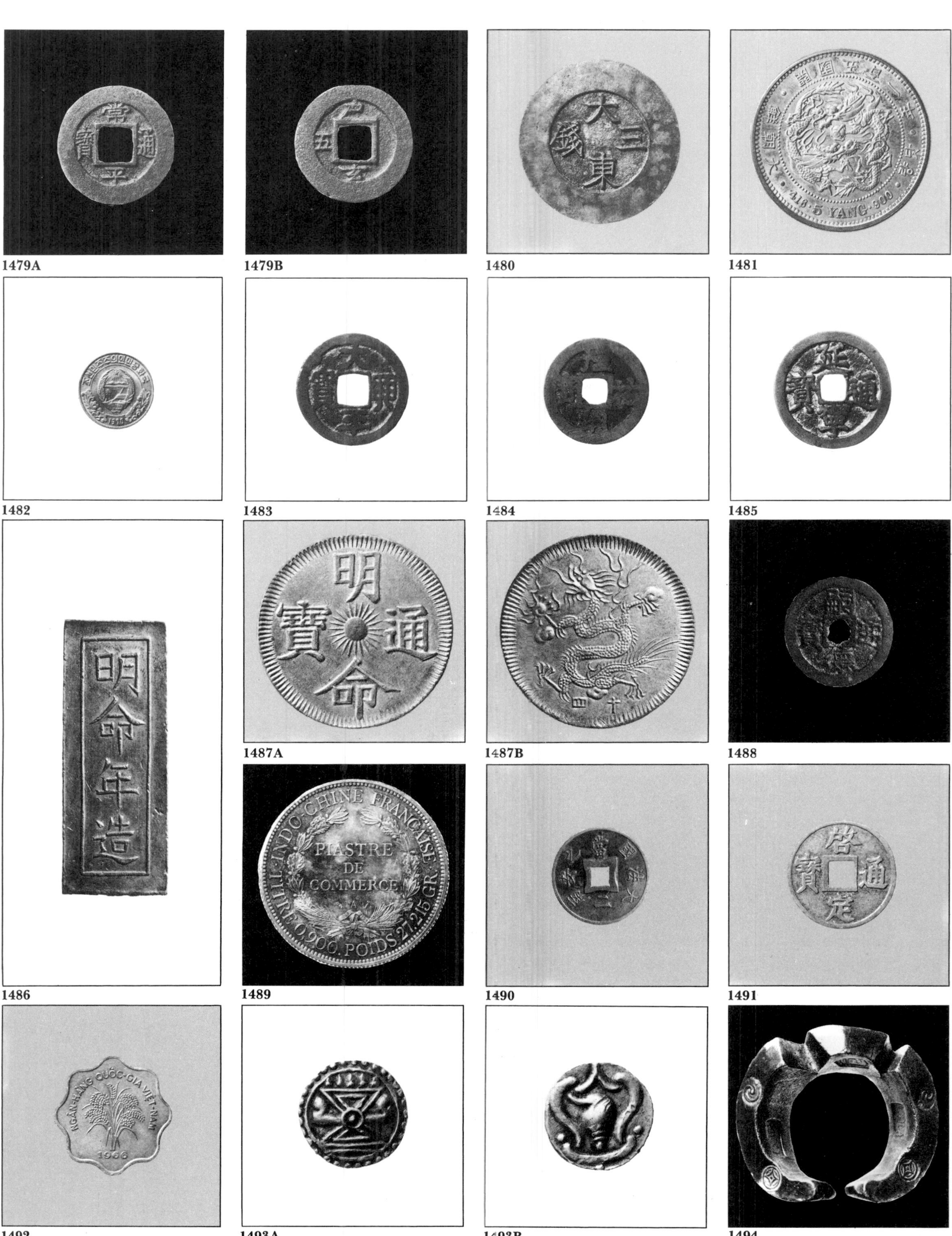
1479A 1479B 1480 1481 1482 1483 1484 1485 1486 1487A 1487B 1488 1489 1490 1491 1492 1493A 1493B 1494

1485 Bronze coin, AD 1454, Vietnam, later Le dynasty, inscribed 'coin of the Dienninh era'. After the expulsion of the Chinese from Vietnam in AD 1428, the Le dynasty made several issues of coins resembling Chinese Ming coins in calligraphic style.

1486 Silver one-ounce bar, 1824, Vietnam, Nguyen dynasty, Before Nguyen silver circulated in Vietnam in the form of ingots, but from 1812 officially struck silver bars denominated by weight were issued for circulation.

1487 Silver dollar, 1833, Vietnam, Nguyen dynasty, inscribed 'coin of the Minhmang era'. As foreign trade led to increasing circulation of Spanish silver coins in Vietnam, the Nguyen emperor was prompted to issue, from 1832, the earliest series of native dollars in the Far East.

1488 Zinc coin, 1847, Vietnam, Nguyen dynasty, inscribed 'coin of the Tuduc era'. From 1802 Nguyen, due to a shortage of copper, issued zinc coins, valued at six to one bronze coin, for circulation in the north.

1489 Silver trade dollar (*piastre de commerce*), 1898, French Indochina. Following their conquest of Vietnam the French issued paper dollars in 1879 and silver and bronze cents. Silver dollars were not issued until 1885.

1490 Bronze coin, 1901, French Indochina. Alongside their issues of dollars and cents the French also struck bronze and zinc coins for native use. This coin, worth a fifth of a cent, was denominated as equal to two traditional Vietnamese coins.

1491 Bronze coin, 1916, Vietnam, Nguyen dynasty, inscribed 'coin of the Khaidinh era'. After the French conquest the Nguyen emperors were still ruling, but with little real power. However they retained their coinage rights until the Second World War and used it to issue the last coins of the Chinese tradition.

1492 Cupronickel five-dollar (*dong*) coin, 1966, Republic of Vietnam. When the French withdrew from Vietnam in 1955, the Communist North already had its own currency, but the South had to make new issues, at first only notes, but from 1960 coins also, struck in London (Royal Mint).

1493 Silver coin, eighth century, Pyu kingdom (in modern Burma). The designs on this coin, a throne and a temple containing a conch shell are Indian religious symbols. Coins with these or related symbols have been attributed to kingdoms in north and south Burma, Bengal, Thailand and Cambodia.

1494 Silver four-bat coin, fifteenth century, Thailand, Chiengmai. In medieval Thailand bar-shaped coins were issued, sometimes cut and bent to show they were not plated. The bar coins of Chiengmai and the other northern Thai kingdoms were replaced in the seventeenth century by the spherical coins of the southern Thais who overthrew them.

1495 Silver four-bat coin, 1851, Thailand, Bangkok dynasty, stamped with the dynastic and royal marks of King Mongkut (1851-68). The southern Thai kingdoms shortened the length of their bar coins until when bent they were spherical. The Ayuttha dynasty (1350-1767) systematized these coins using weight denominations.

1496 Silver one-bat coin, 1860, Thailand, Bangkok dynasty. The disruption of the Thai coinage by the circulation of imported foreign dollars prompted King Mongkut to set up a western-style mint in 1860 to strike a new coinage to replace the traditional spherical coins. This coin was struck with dies personally presented to Mongkut by Queen Victoria to use with his minting machinery manufactured in Birmingham.

1497 Silver one-kyat (*rupee*) coin, 1850 (issued 1865), Burma, King Mindon Min. With British help a mint was set up in Mandalay for the Burmese government in 1865. The gold, silver, bronze, iron, and lead coins struck at this mint were the first national coinage produced for Burma. The peacock is Burma's national emblem.

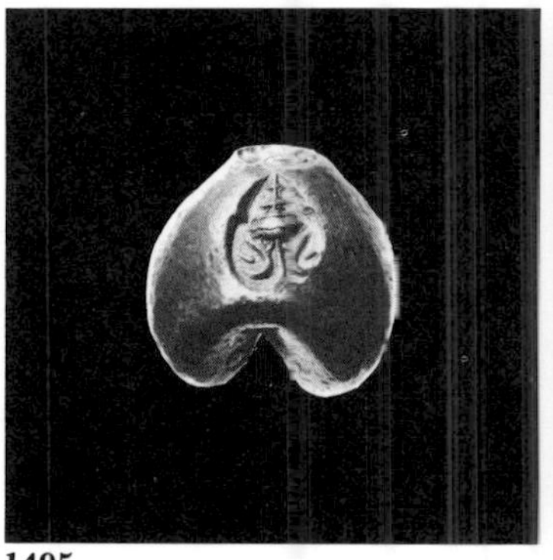
1495

1496A

1496B

1497

Coins were first issued by the Koryo dynasty (918-1392) who
1477 in 996 cast imitations of Tang dynasty coins which they imported from China. During the 11th and 12th centuries Koryo continued to issue coins and import them from China. Like China they also faced a shortage of coins, but found an unusual solution by issuing from 1101 officially stamped silver vases as money. These circulated until demonetized in 1331.

Koryo's coinage was interrupted in the thirteenth century by the Mongols who subjugated Koryo and forced their paper money upon the Koreans.

From 1392 Korea was ruled by a new dynasty, Yi, who ruled until the beginning of this century. Yi imported coins from Ming China and also cast its own coins. In 1401 they also copied Ming paper money issues, but with equal disaster, as it drove coins out of circulation, mostly to Japan, and when it failed the Koreans had to resort to the use of cloth as money.

The abundant coinage of China's Qing dynasty gave Yi the
1479 opportunity of importing coins again and producing its own.

Yi outlawed foreign trade, except with China, and restricted internal commerce causing Korea's economy to stagnate and its coinage to deteriorate with extensive debasements and issues of token coins. When foreign trade was forced upon Korea, the country was so weak that its principal customer, Japan, was able
1481 to take over first its economy and then its government and in 1910 assimilated it into the Japanese Empire.

Japan had western-style silver and bronze coins, closely modelled on its own coinage, struck for Korea and Japanese banks were set up in Korea to issue notes for general circulation. Korea's whole monetary system was controlled from Japan and the traditional coinage quickly disappeared.

Japan ruled Korea until the end of the Second World War, when it came under Allied occupation. For a short period the only currency was that issued by the occupying forces. When Korea was eventually returned to native rule, split in two under the influence of its occupiers, the Russian-dominated north
reformed its currency according to communist economic princi- 1482
ples, while the American dominated south set up a western-style currency system, but both retained the denominations introduced by Japan.

Vietnam was also introduced to Chinese coinage during Chinese rule in the Han period. It remained part of the Chinese Empire and Chinese coins circulated there until 939, when it achieved independence. Chinese coins were still imported and used, but its new rulers also issued their own coins. When these 1483
two sources proved inadequate, vast numbers of lightweight 1484
imitations of Chinese coins were unofficially made.

In the late fourteenth century the Ming attempted to reestablish Chinese rule and during a short occupation imported full-weight standard coins. After their withdrawal the Vietnamese rulers also issued full-weight coins, but never enough to replace the lightweight imitations which remained the bulk of coins in circulation. Official coin issue dwindled as Vietnam's economy was disrupted by civil wars.

In the eighteenth century issues started again, sufficient to drive most of the unofficial coins from circulation by the end of the century.

By the nineteenth century the impact of foreign trade began to change the Vietnamese monetary system. Extensive imports of
foreign dollars prompted the Vietnamese to coin silver, at first in 1486
bars, and from 1832 western-style coins as well. The resulting 1487
expansion of Vietnam's economy also increased demand for 1488
bronze coins, but because enough copper was not available zinc coins were also issued.

The French conquered Vietnam in the 1880s and European-style coins and paper money gradually became the main
currency, although local coins were still issued until the Japanese 1490
invasion in 1942.

After Vietnam was returned to French rule in 1945, their monetary system was briefly resumed. A prolonged guerilla war ensured Vietnam's return to native rule. At first the north and

1498 Silver one-tical coin, 1847, Cambodia, King Angduong. Like its neighbours, Burma and Thailand Cambodia set up a mint to strike western style coins with British help. The coin shows the mythical 'hamsa' bird, a type used on its traditional coinage.

1499 Cupronickel one-bat coin, 1977, Thailand, King Phumipol Adulyalet. The use of royal portraits on current Thai coins originated in the production at the Royal Mint, London in 1887 of a series of bronze coins for Thailand closely modelled on the Victorian penny.

1500 Gold coin, thirteenth century, Java. Small gold and silver coins inscribed with a single Indian letter are found on Sumatra, Java and in the Philippines. Their attribution to individual kingdoms is conjectural.

1501 Tin coin, about 1631, Java, Sultan Aboul Ma'ali of Bantam. This is the earliest of the tin copies of Chinese coins with Islamic or European inscriptions which became widespread in the Indian Archipelago and Malaya in the eighteenth century.

1502 Tin coin (quarter cent), about 1880, Thailand, Patalung Province. In the nineteenth century, tin copies of Chinese coins made by Chinese merchants became widely used in Malaya and the Archipelago and even spread to Thailand's southern provinces.

1503 Tin bastardo, 1511, Portuguese Malacca, King Manuel I. Portugal's role in the Far East was very brief, but in 1511 it cast the first European coinage in South East Asia, multiple denominations of the local Islamic tin coins, with European types and inscriptions.

1498×3

1499×3

1500×1, ×3

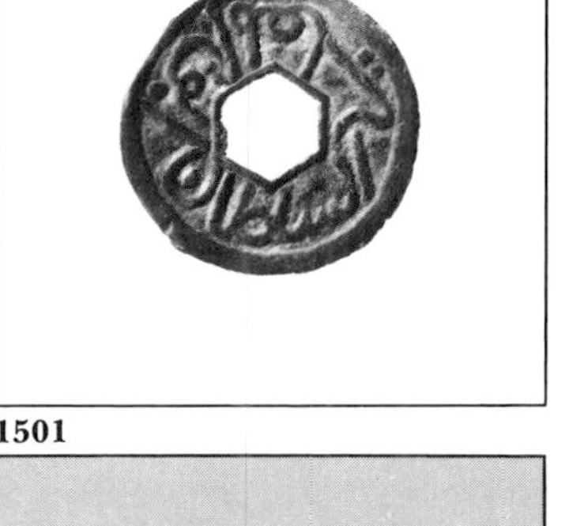
1501

1502×2

1503×2

1505

1506

1504 Tin coin, 1864, Malaya, Pahang Sultanate. Tin coins, deriving their shape from the tin ingots previously circulating as money, began to be issued in Pahang in 1819. Inscribed in Arabic on the base, they were apparently denominated as four-cent pieces.

1505 Silver dollar, 1828, Spanish Philippines, overstruck dollar of Peruvian Republic, 1827. The Latin American independence movements deprived Spain of its silver mints and forced her to import coins from the newly independent republics. On arrival in the Philippines these coins were crudely restruck at Manila for local use.

1506 British Trade Dollar, 1895, Calcutta Mint, India. A shortage of dollars in the Far East due to increased consumption of silver in America encouraged Britain in 1895 to strike new dollars in India for circuation in the Far East. Until 1903 it was the standard dollar of British Malaya.

1507 Copper doit, 1726, Dutch East Indies, Dordrecht mint, Holland. From 1726 the Dutch East India Company had copper coins with its VOC sign specifically made for export to the East Indies to replace the Chinese and Japanese coins which circulated there.

1508 Silver guilder, 1802, Dutch East Indies, Enkhuizen mint, Holland. This coinage was originally made for the Dutch Cape of Good Hope, but the British seizure of the Cape caused it to be forwarded to Java, where it was put into circulation.

1509 Cupronickel ten cents, 1969, Singapore, Royal Mint, London. Singapore gained independence from Britain as part of Malaysia in 1963, but in 1965 it broke away from Malaysia and set up its own currency. Several of its coins show local marine wild life, like the seahorse on this denomination.

1504

1507

1508

1509A×2

1509B×2

south had separate regimes with currencies matching their political attitudes, communist in the north and western-influenced capitalism in the south, but after the communists unified Vietnam, the currencies were united into a system using aluminium coins and paper notes like other members of the communist block.

In the rest of south-east Asia coinage was introduced as a result of trade with India. From the second century AD native kingdoms arose along the coast of mainland south-east Asia and in the Indian archipelago. They were heavily influenced by Indian culture and by the seventh century several mainland kingdoms were striking Indian-style silver coins. In the archipelago gold and silver coins were also issued at a later date. By the fourteenth century these coinages had disappeared, on the mainland when the Indianized kingdoms were weakened or overthrown by migrating northern peoples, the Burmese and Thais, and on the islands by the influx of Chinese coinage.

The northern migrants brought with them more primitive monetary systems. Silver and base metal ingots became the main currencies, with barter serving in everyday trade. The Burmese used crude ingots, but the Thais, probably under Chinese
1494,1495 influence, used stamped silver ingots which were later developed into a coinage. Burma was without coinage until the late eighteenth century, except in the north where coins based on the Islamic coinage of Bengal were struck by the Arakanese. On its southern coast coin-shaped lead ingots were used, but this remained a local currency.

Of the ancient kingdoms of the mainland only Cambodia survived. From the sixteenth century, long after its first coins had disappeared it again issued silver coins, struck with a die only on one side with religious types.

The imports of Chinese coins into the archipelago during the thirteenth and fourteenth century were so extensive that they were used as the legal currency. Although these coins were still circulating on some islands until recently, from the fifteenth century a reduced supply and a new political order created a new monetary system.

The Indian Archipelago was gradually converted to Islam and Indian-style Islamic coins began to be issued, particularly in
Sumatra and Malaya. The shortage of local copper obliged the 1501
local Islamic rulers to issue lightweight tin coins for small 1504
change. These sometimes had a central hole like the Chinese coins they replaced.

The Islamic conversion was followed by another far more important development for the coinage, the arrival of European
traders who, as well as importing vast quantities of their coins, 1505-08
also introduced into the area many new coinages based on their own coinages, those they imported or on the local coins, some of which they allowed to continue. From the late eighteenth century European-style paper money was also introduced.

Western style coinage and paper currency was not issued in mainland south-east Asia until the mid-nineteenth century. With the exception of Vietnam, the new coinages were all struck with European machinery, but on local weight standards.

By the beginning of this century imperialism in its final phase had swept away most of the local currencies on the mainland and in the islands and replaced them with colonial currencies closely based on Western monetary systems. The Japanese invasion during the Second World War, with its vast issues of worthless paper money, destroyed not only western imperial rule, but also its currencies. After the war, as the area gradually threw off the yoke of foreign domination, the newly emerging states initiated their own new currencies, some like Singapore resembling
contemporary European issues, others like Burma based on their 1509
precolonial issues, but all essentially modern systems with base metal coins and paper notes.

LIST OF ILLUSTRATIONS

This list provides necessary information concerning the coins and other objects illustrated, which, for practical reasons, could not always be incorporated into the captions. The information is given all or in part in the following order: illustration number; mint city, people, or country of origin; ruler or dynasty; metal (abbreviations AU = gold, AR = silver, AE = bronze, Al = aluminium, Bill = billon, Cu = copper, CuNi = cupro-nickel, El = electrum, Fe = iron, Pb = lead, Sn = tin); denomination and date; diameter in millimetres and weight in grammes; present location of the object photographed. Each roman numeral refers to the frontispiece of that particular chapter.

Unless otherwise stated all objects are in the British Museum. Other collections cited at the end of each number are:
ANS (American Numismatic Society, New York)
Ash. (Ashmolean Museum, Oxford)
Berlin (Pergamon Museum, East Berlin)
BN (Bibliotheque Nationale, Paris)
Cop (The Royal Coin Collection, The National Museum, Copenhagen)
FW (Fitzwilliam Museum, Cambridge)
PG (Collection of Professor P Grierson in the Fitzwilliam Museum, Cambridge)
Philadelphia (The University Museum, Philadelphia, USA)
Port. (Collection of J Porteous Esq)
Rhod. (Collection of N G Rhodes Esq)
Rome (Museo Nazionale, Rome)
RM (The Royal Mint Museum, London)
Sell. (Collection of D G Sellwood Esq)

Frontispiece: Illuminated frontispiece from Nicolas Oresme, *de Moneta* c.1490; BN
I England, Henry VIII; AU sovereign, 1543; 42/12.94
1 Seychelles, Elizabeth II: CuNi 5-rupees, 1971; 30/13.25; RM
2 Brunswick-Lüneburg, Johann Friedrich; AR gulden, 1676; 38/16.84; Port.
3 Scotland, Mary; AR ryal, 1566; 41/30.34
4 Venice, Doge Pietro Gradenigo; AU ducat, 1289; 20/3.53; PG
5 Mantua, Frederick Gonzaga; AR scudo, 1536-40; 39/25.70; Rome
6 Russia, Nicholas II; AE 3-kopeks, 1915; 28/9.85
7 Russia, Soviet Republic; AE 3-kopeks, 1924; 28/9.79
8 China, Han dynasty; AE 5-grains, 118 BC; 26/3.35
9 China, Qing dynasty; AE standard coin, 1889; 24/3.47
10 North India; AR ingot, 4th cent.BC; 11/3.37
11 India; CuNi 5-pice, 1959; 18/4.02
12 India, Kanishka; AU dinar, 2nd cent.AD; 20/7.04
13 Magnesia, Themistocles; AR didrachm c.460 BC; 20/8.67; BN
14 Ionia, Phanes; EL stater, c.580 BC; 21/14.02
15 Thurii, Italy; AR distater, c.375 BC; 25/15.82
16 Bactria, Antimachus; AR tetradrachm, c.180 BC; 34/16.96
17 Rome; AR didrachm, c.300 BC; 19/7.56
18 Rome; AR denarius, 54 BC; 16/4.01
19 Rome, Augustus; AR denarius, c.20 BC; 19/3.77
20 Rome, Caligula; AE sestertius, c.AD 40; 35/29.07
21 Cologne, Tetricus I; Bill antoninianus, c.AD 272; 18/2.20
22 Siscia, Constantius I; Bill follis, c.AD 300; 31/10.47
23 Siscia, Constantine I; AU medallion, AD 306; 24/6.80
24 Seleucia ad Tigrim, Mithradates I; AR tetradrachm, c.140 BC; 36/15.95; Sell.
25 Persia, Shapur I; AR drachma, c.AD 260; 37/4.28
26 Merv, Umayyad governors; AR drachma, 31 AH (= AD 651-52); 32/4.06
27 Carthage, Arab-Byzantine; AU solidus, 85 AH (= AD 704); 13/4.32
28 Wasit, Umayyad; AR dirham, AD 726-27; 27/2.86
29 Baibirt, Ilkhanid, Abu Sa'id; AR dirham, AD 1331-32; 16/1.21
30 Isfahan, Hussayn; AR 4-shahi, AD 1703-04; 39/17.37
31 Constantinople, Justinian I; AE follis, 538-39; 42/23.59
32 Constantinople, Basil II & Constantine VIII; AU histamenon, 976-1025; 34/4.07; FW
33 London, Wessex, Alfred; AR penny, 871-99; 18/1.56; FW
34 London, John; AR penny, 1216; 20/1.45; FW
35 Bristol, Edward I; AR penny, 1279; 20/1.38; FW
36 Hersfeld, Siegfried; AR pfennig, 1180-1200; 42/0.76; PG
37 France, Philip VI; AU écu-à-la-chaise, 1337; 29/4.50
38 Milan, Galeazzo Maria Sforza; AR testone (lira), 1468-76; 27/9.70
39 Milan, Charles V; AR testone, 1536-56; 31/11.91
40 Florence, Alessandro de Medici, AR testone, 1532-36; 29/9.89
41 France, Henri II; AR mill teston, 1553; 28/9.53
42 France, Louis XIII; AR écu blanc, 1643; 44/27.39
43 England, Commonwealth; AR crown, 1652; 45/29.88
44 Danzig, Sigismund III; AR ort, 1621; obv. 30/6.69 rev. 29/6.26
45 Great Britain, George III; AE penny (pattern), 1797; 35/28.63
46 Great Britain, George III; AU sovereign, 1817; 22/7.99
47 Great Britain, Elizabeth II; AU sovereign, 1979; 22/8.01; RM
48 Saudi Arabia, CuNi 4-gurush, 1956-57 (AH 1376); 30/12.02
49 France; AR 2-francs, 1902; 36/10.02
50 France; CuNi franc, 1960; 23/5.94
II Wall painting from the tomb of Nebamun and Ipuky, Thebes, Egypt, c.1375 BC
51 Hoard from Tell Taya c.2300 BC
52 Clay tablet from Nippur, 21st cent.BC; Philadelphia
53 Scale trays and weights from Ugarit, 14th cent.BC
54 Tomb of Amenemhat, Beni Hasan, 19th cent.BC (from P.E. Newberry, Beni Hasan I pl.xi)
55 AR fragments from Tell el-Amarna, 14th cent.BC
56 Zinjirli, Barrekub; AR ingot, 8th cent.BC; (497.38 gm); Berlin
57 AR fragments from Eshtemoa, 8th cent.BC
58 AR fragments from Nush-i-Jan, 7th cent.BC
59 Jasper seal from Megiddo, 8th cent.BC
60 AR fragments from the Taranto hoard, c.500 BC
III Head of the nymph Arethusa from 95
61 Ionia; EL twelfth stater, c.625 BC; 7/1.16
62 Ionia, Phanes; EL stater, c.600-580 BC; 21/14.02
63 Phocaea; EL stater, c.600 BC; 19/16.51
64 Miletus; EL stater, c.600 BC; 21/14.01
65 Ionia; EL ninety-sixth stater, c.575 BC; 4/0.18
66 Ionia; EL stater, c.575 BC; 22/14.29
67 Sardes, Lydia; EL third stater, c.575 BC; 13/4.73
68 Sardes, Croesus (posthumous); AU stater, c.530 BC; 16/8.05
69 Sybaris, Italy; AR staters, c.530 BC; obv. 30/7.89 rev. 30/8.27
70 Athens; AR didrachm, c.525 BC; 19/8.53
71 Aegina; AR stater, c.540 BC; 20/11.97
72 Corinth; AR stater, c.525 BC; 25/8.51
73 Athens; AR tetradrachm, c.510 BC; 25/17.30
74 Athens; AR drachma, c.425 BC; 15/4.06
75 Athens; AR obol, c.425 BC; 9/0.71
76 Athens; AR eighth obol, c.330 BC; 5/0.10
77 Olbia, S. Russia; AE, c.425 BC; 35/2.98
78 Olbia; AE, c.375 BC; 68/115.01
79 Himera, Sicily; AE hemilitron, c.430 BC; 25/23.84
80 Acragas; AE hemilitron, c.420 BC; 27/17.65
81 Syracuse; AE hemilitron, c.410 BC; 17/3.24
82 Metapontum; AE obol, 360 BC; 19/8.18
83 Cumae, Italy; AR stater, 450 BC; 20/7.64
84 Thurii; AR distater, c.375 BC; 25/15.82
85 Croton; AR stater, c.420 BC; 23/8.09
86 Terina; AR stater, c.400 BC; 19/7.61
87 Acragas, Sicily; AR decadrachm, 412 BC; 37/43.56
88 Catana; AR tetradrachm, c.405 BC; 27/17.26
89 Gela; AR tetradrachm, c.475 BC; 25/17.18
90 Himera; AR tetradrachm, c.464 BC; 24/17 13
91 Himera; AR tetradrachm, c.415 BC; 27/17 18
92 Messana; AR tetradrachm, c.430 BC; 24/17.36
93 Naxos; AR tetradrachm, c.460 BC; 27/17.43
94 Syracuse; AR decadrachm, c.465 BC; 35/44.41
95 Syracuse; AR tetradrachm, c.410 BC; 28/17.26
96 Syracuse; AR tetradrachm, c.410-405 BC; 27/17.20
97 Lycia, Zagaba; AR stater, c.390 BC; 23/9.28; Ash.
98 Syracuse; AR decadrachm, c.405 BC; 34/43.34
99 Syracuse; AR decadrachm, c.400 BC; 33/43.16
100 Syracuse; AU 20-litra, c.405 BC; obv. 10/1.15 rev. 10/1.14
101 Panormus; AR tetradrachm, c.380 BC; 26/16.83
102 Lilybaeum; AR tetradrachm, c.410 BC; 27/16.96
103 Macedonia; AR stater, c.490 BC; 23/16.92
104 Edoni, Getas; AR octadrachm, c.480 BC; 31/28.02
105 Macedonia, Alexander I; AR octadrachm, c.475 BC; 32/28.97
106 Thasos; AR stater, c.490 BC; 22/9.27
107 Abdera; AR tetradrachm, c.375 BC; 23/10.96
108 Amphipolis; AR tetradrachm, c.360 BC; 25/14.28
109 Mende; AR tetradrachm, c.430 BC; 26/17.29
110 Chalcidian League; AU stater, c.350 BC; 15/8.60
111 Peparethus; AR tetradrachm, c.490 BC; 27/16.92
112 Larissa; AR drachma, c.360 BC; 20/6.08
113 Delphi; AR tridrachm, c.480 BC; 30/18.40
114 Delphi; AR stater, 336 BC; 23/12.11
115 Boeotia; AR stater, 370 BC; 20/12.18
116 Athens; AR tetradrachm; 24/17.17
117 Lycia, Täthivaibi, AR stater, c.425 BC, 20/9.64
118 Babylonia, Mazaces; AR tetradrachm, c.330 BC; 24/16.14
119 Egypt, Artaxerxes III; AR tetradrachm, c.340 BC; 22/15.48
120 Ionia, Tissaphernes; AR tetradrachm, c.410 BC; 27/16.68
121 Athens; AU hemidrachm, c.405 BC; 10/2.13
122 Athens; AR (plated) drachma, 406-05 BC; 15/2.85
123 Athens; AE 'kollybos', c.405 BC; 6/0.35
124 Corinth; AR stater, c.500 BC; 16/8.68
125 Ambracia, NW Greece; AR stater, c.360 BC; obv. 22/8.46 rev. 19/8.50
126 Sicyon, Peloponnese; AR stater, c.380 BC; 22/12.26
127 Elis; AR stater, c.380 BC; 25/12.35
128 Elis (Pisa); AU obol, 365-64 BC; 9/1.01
129 Arcadian League; AR stater, 365-64 BC; 23/12.29
130 Pheneus; AR stater, c.360 BC; 23/11.99
131 Cnossus, Crete; AR stater, c.425 BC; 27/11.29
132 Phaestus; AR stater, c.325 BC; 25/11.73
133 Aptera; AR stater, c.350 BC; 25/11.46
134 Melos (Aegean island); AR stater, c.320 BC; 23/13.40
135 Panticapaeum, S. Russia; AU stater, c.350 BC; 18/9.11
136 Cyzicus, Asia Minor; EL stater, c.450 BC; 18/16.06
137 Cyzicus, Pharnabazus; AR tetradrachm, c.395 BC; 25/14.65
138 Lampsacus; AU 'daric', c.350 BC; 18/8.45
139 Clazomenae; AR tetradrachm, c.380 BC; 25/16.96
140 Magnesia, Themistocles; AR didrachm, c.460 BC; 20/8.67; BN
141 Rhodes; AU didrachm, c.330 BC; 18/8.60
142 Caria, Maussollus; AR tetradrachm, c.360 BC; 22/15.15
143 Sardes, Lydia, Darius I; AU daric, c.500 BC; 14/8.27
144 Sardes; AR siglos, c.460 BC; 15/5.42
145 Lycia, Kharai; AR stater, c.420 BC; 22/8.28
146 Lycia, Pericles; AR stater, c.370 BC; 24/9.80
147 Side; AR stater, c.380 BC; 20/10.69
148 Aphrodisias, Cilicia; AR stater, 450 BC; 23/9.89
149 Tarsus, Pharnabazus; AR stater, 397-4 BC; 23/10.88
150 Tarsus, Datames; AR stater, 378-2 BC
151 Tarsus, Mazaeus; AR stater, c.340 BC; 24/11.09
152 Phoenicia; AR tetradrachm, c.350 BC; 20/15.04
153 Marium, Cyprus, Timochares; AR stater, c.390 BC; 28/10.84
154 Sidon, Phoenicia, Balshallim II; AR double shekel, c.375 BC; 30/28.39
155 Tyre; AR stater, c.400 BC; 23/13.41
156 Judaea; AR drachma, c.350 BC; 16/3.28
157 Egypt; AU 'daric', c.350 BC; 16/8.20
158 Cyrene; AR stater, c.360 BC; 26/13.19
159 Macedonia, Philip II; AU stater, c.340 BC; 17/8.62
160 Macedonia, Philip II; AR stater, c.345 BC; 24/14.50
161 Macedonia, Philip II, (posthumous); AR stater, 336-5 BC; 24/14.37
162 Macedonia, Alexander III; AR tetradrachm, 336-5 BC; 24/17.14
163 Macedonia, Alexander; AU stater, c.330 BC; 17/8.63
164 Macedonia, Alexander Sidon; AU stater, 323-22 BC; 17/8.62
165 Macedonia, Alexander Babylonia; AR decadrachm, c.330 BC; 31/39.68
166 Macedonia, Alexander Babylonia; AR tetradrachm, c.330 BC; 25/15.39
IV Head of Alexander the Great from 173
167 Macedonia, Philip III, Babylon; AR tetradrachm, c.320 BC; 28/16.96
168 Alexandria, Egypt, Ptolemy I; AR tetradrachm, c.300 BC; 28/15.61
169 Alexandria, Egypt, Ptolemy I; AR tetradrachm, c.300 BC; 28/14.77
170 Macedonia, Cassander; AE, c.300 BC; 21/4.88
171 Salamis, Cyprus, Demetrius Poliorcetes; AR tetradrachm, c.300 BC; 29/17.20
172 Thebes, Demetrius Poliorcetes; AR tetradrachm, 289-7 BC; 28/16.87
173-174 Pergamum, Lysimachus; AR tetradrachm, 297-81 BC; 30/17.21
175 Aradus, Phoenicia, Seleucus I; AR tetradrachm, c.310 BC; 29/16.78
176 Apamea, Syria, Seleucus I; AE, c.300 BC; 20/7.40
177 Susa, Seleucus I; AR tetradrachm, c.300 BC; 26/16.84
178 Pergamum, Philataerus; AR tetradrachm, c.275 BC; 29/16.98
179 Athens; AU stater, 297-5 BC; 17/8.58
180 Rhodes; AR didrachm, c.300 BC; 20/6.62
181 Cnossus; AR stater, c.300 BC; 23/11.09
182 Egypt, Ptolemy III (probably posthumous); AU octadrachm, c.220 BC; 27/27.76
183 Egypt, Ptolemy III; AU octadrachm, c.225 BC; 27/27.75
184 Alexandria Troas; AE late 3rd cent.BC; 18/4.97
185 Ephesus, Berenice II of Egypt; AU octadrachm (pierced), c.250 BC; 27/27.71
186 Alexandria Troas, Antiochus Hierax; AR tetradrachm, 246-27 BC; 34/16.98
187 Pergamum, Eumenes I; AR tetradrachm, 263-41 BC; 29/16.86
188 Alexandria Troas, Antiochus Hierax; AR tetradrachm, 246-27 BC; 31/16.89
189 Egypt, Ptolemy III; AE, c.240 BC; 42/71.62
190 Macedonia, Antigonus Gonatas; AR tetradrachm, c.265 BC; 31/17.13
191 Pontus, Mithradates III; AR tetradrachm, 220-185 BC; 30/17.16
192 Bithynia, Prusias I; AR tetradrachm, 228-185 BC; 33/17.20
193 Persis, Bagadat; AR tetradrachm, 3rd cent. BC; 30/16.89
194 Bactria, Demetrius I; AR tetradrachm, c.200-185 BC; 32/16.78
195 Bactria, Antimachus; AR tetradrachm, c.190-80 BC; 34/16.96
196 Aetolian League; AR tetradrachm, later 3rd cent.BC; 31/16.79
197 Acarnanian League; AR stater, c.200 BC; 25/10.23
198 Dyrrhachium; AR drachma, 2nd cent.BC; obv. 19/3.47 rev. 20/3.42
199 Sparta, Nabis; AR tetradrachm, 207-192 BC; 29/17.06
200 Macedonia, Philip V; AR tetradrachm, 220-179 BC; 34/16.74
201 Macedonia, T. Quinctius Flamininus; AU stater, c.195 BC; 19/8.42
202 Ecbatana, Antiochus III; AR tetradrachm, c.200 BC; 29/16.96
203 Histiaea, Euboea; AR tetrobol, c.175 BC; obv. 16/2.13 rev. 15/2.05
204 Smyrna, in the name of Alexander; AR tetradrachm, c.190 BC; 33/16.87
205 Byzantium, in the name of Lysimachus; AU stater, c.150 BC; 19/8.50
206 Macedonia, Perseus; AR tetradrachm; 34/16.80
207 Nisibis, Antiochus IV; AE 4-chalkoi, 175-64 BC; 23/9.78
208 Bactria, Menander; AR tetradrachm, c.150 BC; 30/16.15
209 Cappadocia, Ariarathes V; AR drachma, 163-30 BC; obv. 19/4.14 rev. 19/4.17
210 Egypt, Ptolemy VI and Cleopatra I; AU octadrachm, 180-74 BC; 28/27.82
211 Egypt, Ptolemy XII; AR tetradrachm, 55-54 BC; 27/14.03
212 Syria, Antiochus XI and Philip; AR tetradrachm, 93 BC; 28/13.41
V Head of Zeus from 255
213 Syracuse; AR stater, c.340 BC; 22/8.53
214 Carthage; AR 5-shekels, 264-41 BC; 39/36.49
215 Syracuse, Hieron II; AR 25-litrae (?), 275-215 BC; 35/27.74
216 Metapontum; AR didrachm, late 4th cent.BC; 22/7.87
217 Locri; AR stater, 286-82 BC; 22/7.08

218 Rome; AR didrachm, c.300 BC; 19/7.56
219 Rome; AE aes signatum, c.275 BC; 153 × 90/1746
220 Rome; AE as, c.225 BC; 65/c.258
221 Todi; AE quadrans, mid 3rd cent.BC; 43/64.67
222 Carthaginians in Spain; AR 1½ shekel, late 3rd cent.BC; 25/11.17
223 Capua, Italy; AR stater, 216-11 BC; 19/4.93
224 Taranto, Italy; AU stater, c.305 BC; 18/8.60
225 Carthaginians in Italy; AR ½-shekel, late 3rd cent.BC; 18/3.77
226 Sicily; AR denarius, c.210 BC; 19/4.41
227 Rome; AR victoriate, c.210 BC; 16/2.38
228 Teate; AE quincunx, late 3rd cent.BC; 24/12.05
229 Italy; AE as, c.205 BC; 33/47.79
230 Paestum; AE, late 1st cent.BC; 13/4.65
231 Catana; AE, 1st cent.BC; 20/9.01
232 Lepcis Magna, Africa; AE, 1st cent.BC; 19/4.35
233 Osca, Spain; AR denarius, early 2nd cent.BC; 17/3.58
234 Obulco; AE, 2nd cent.BC; 34/31.53
235 Ibiza; AE, 2nd cent.BC; 22/6.81; Cop.
236 Rome; AR denarius, 140 BC; 20/3.79
237 Rome; AE semis, c.130 BC; 24/9.62
238 Rome; AR denarius, 112 BC; 18/3.95
239 Rome; AE quadrans, 112 BC; 20/7.11
240 Rome; AR denarius, 113 BC; 18/3.90
241 Rome; AR quinarius, 101 BC; 14/1.84
242 Rome; AR denarius, 101-100 BC; 18/3.76
243 Rome; AU aureus, 80 BC; 20/10.87
244 Rome; AR denarius, 64 BC; 19/3.96
245 Rome; AR denarius, 58 BC; 18/4.08
246 Rome; AR denarius, 56 BC; 18/3.87
247 Rome; AR denarius, 56 BC; 19/3.83
248 Rome; AR denarius, 54 BC; 17/4.02
249 Italy; AR denarius, 91-87 BC; 20/4.00
250 Rome; AR denarius, 57 BC; 17/4.13
251 Rome; AR denarius, 46 BC; 18/3.89
252 Rome; AR sestertius, 45 BC; 13/0.78
253 Rome; AE strip of three asses, 90 BC; 80/35.92
254 Thessalian League; AR drachma, c.180 BC; 24/6.19
255-256 Samos; AR tetradrachm, c.170 BC; 35/16.72
257 Macedonia, First Republic; AR tetradrachm, 168-7 BC; 31/15.49
258 Achaean League; AR drachma, c.160 BC; 15/2.42
259 Athens; AR tetradrachm, c.160 BC; 36/17.05
260 Tenedos; AR tetradrachm, mid 2nd cent.BC; 29/16.70
261 Pergamum; AR cistophorus, c.165 BC; 31/12.24
262 Rhodes; AR plinthophorus, late 2nd cent.BC; 17/2.99
263 Antioch, Antiochus VI; AR tetradrachm, 144 BC; 35/16.53
264 Antioch, Tryphon; AR tetradrachm, 142-139 BC; 24/12.05
265 Jerusalem, Antiochus VII; AE 132-1 BC; 14/3.52
266 Tyre; AR shekel, 103-2 BC; 28/14.25
267 Amisus, Mithradates VI; AE 90-85 BC; 29/18.52
268 Pontus, Mithradates VI; AR tetradrachm, 75 BC; 34/16.70
269 Athens, Mithradates VI; AU stater, 88-6 BC; 21/8.33
270 Antioch, Tigranes; AR tetradrachm; 29/16.41
271 Macedonia, Aesillas Quaestor; AR tetradrachm, c.80-75 BC; 30/16.66
272 Soli-Pompeiopolis; AE, later 1st cent.BC; 29/10.37
273 Apamea, Asia; AR cistophorus, 56-3 BC; 27/11.50
274 Apamea, Asia; AE 56 BC; 21/14.78
275 Gortyn, Crete; AR tetradrachm, 69-63 BC; 29/15.10
276 Antioch, Syria; AR tetradrachm, 57-55 BC; 26/15.74
277 Numidia, Juba I; AR denarius, c.50 BC; 19/3.75
278 Cappadocia, Ariobarzanes I; AR drachma, 96-63 BC; 17/3.98
279 Cilicia, Tarcondimotus; AE, 64-31 BC; 21/8.10
280 Commagene, Antiochus I; AE, c.50 BC; 21/5.83
281 Nicaea, Bithynia; AE, 62-59 BC; 24/8.90
282 Galatia, Amyntas; AR tetradrachm, c.30 BC; 29/16.05
283 Rome; AU aureus, 46 BC; 20/8.07
284 Rome; AR denarius, 44 BC; 17/4.10
285 Corinth; AE late 40s BC; 23/5.27
286 Greece or Asia; AR denarius, c.43 BC; 18/3.80
287-288 Sicily; AU aureus, 43-40 BC; 20/8.09
289 Greece; AE sestertius, c.35 BC; 35/26.73
290 Phoenicia, Cleopatra; AR shekel, c.34 BC; 27/14.37
291 Ascalon, Cleopatra; AR shekel, 49 BC; 27/13.03
292 Mark Antony; AR denarius, 31 BC; 18/3.79
293 Sparta, Atratinus; AE, c.38 BC; 19/5.81
294 Cyrene; AE, c.35 BC; 32/21.75
295 Magnesia ad Sipylum, Asia; AE, c.25 BC; 25/11.65
296 Rome; AE as, c.38 BC; 35/23.36
297 Rome; AU aureus, late 30s BC; 20/7.94
298 Pella, Macedonia; AE, c.30 BC; 25/13.08
299 Rome; AR denarius, 28 BC; 20/3.89
300 Asia; AE 2-as, c.25 BC; 28/14.77

VI Detail from 323

301 Transylvania; AR tetradrachm, c.200 BC; 22/13.72
302 Danube basin; AR tetradrachm, c.200 BC; 20/12.42
303 Danube basin; AR tetradrachm, c.100 BC; 21/7.43
304 Danube basin; AR tetradrachm, c.200 BC; obv 30/16.07 rev. 28/15.46
305 Insubres; AR drachma, late 3rd cent.BC; 15/2.39
306 Eravisci; AR 'denarius', late 1st cent.BC; 18/3.13
307 Boii; AR tetradrachm, late 1st cent.BC; 27/16.93
308 Noricum; AR tetradrachm, 1st cent.BC; 23/10.11
309 Bohemia; AU stater, 2nd cent.BC; 11/2.73
310 Boii; AU stater, c.60 BC; 16/6.98
311 Vindelici; AU stater, c.100-50 BC; 18/7.17
312 Germani; AR 'quinarius', 1st cent.BC; 13/1.69
313 Pannonia; AR tretradrachm, 2nd cent.BC; 26/12.64
314 Genoa; AR 'minim', 1st cent.BC; 11/0.85
315 South-west Gaul; AR drachma, 2nd cent.BC; 15/4.82
316 Volcae Tectosages; AR drachma 2nd-1st cent.BC; 16/3.29
317 Ruteni; AR 'quinarius', 1st cent.BC; 13/2.18
318 South-west Gaul; AR drachma, 2nd cent.BC; 20/4.42
319 Elusates; AR drachma, 1st cent.BC; 16/2.
320 Gaul; AR drachma, late 2nd cent.BC; 17/2.04
321 East Gaul; AU stater, late 3rd cent.BC; 18/3.37
322 West Gaul; AU stater, 3rd cent.BC; 21/8.
323 Treveri; AU stater, 2nd cent.BC; 20/7.82
324 Ambiani; AU stater, 2nd cent.BC; 26/7.4
325 Central Gaul; AU stater, late 2nd cent.BC; 23/7.94
326 Veneti; AU ¼ stater, 2nd cent.BC; 12/1.
327 Rhone Valley; AR 'quinarius', 2nd cent.BC; 14/2.32
328 Allobroges; AR 'quinarius', late 2nd cent.BC; 15/2.51
329 Eastern Gaul; AR 'quinarius', early 1st cent.BC; 13/1.86
330 East Gaul; AR 'quinarius', 1st cent.BC; 12/1.77
331 Sequani, Togirix; potin, mid 1st cent. BC; 5/2.55
332 Aedui; potin, early 1st cent.BC; 18/4.37
333 Arverni; AU stater, 1st cent.BC; 18/7.51
334 Bituriges Cubi; AR 'quinarius', c.45 BC; 14/1.92
335 Carnutes; AE, mid 1st cent.BC; 17/3.84
336 Armorica; Bill stater, mid 1st cent.BC; 20/5.46
337 Parisii AU stater, early 1st cent.BC; 22/7.39
338 Ambiani; AU stater, c.100-50 BC; 17/6.41
339 Treveri; AU stater, 58-50 BC; 16/6.00
340 Remi, potin, c.50 BC; 19/4.49
341 Pictones, Duratius; AR 'quinarius', c.50 BC; 13/1.88
342 Arverni, Epasnactus; AR 'quinarius' c.50 BC; 14/1.91
343 Britain; AU stater, c.100-50 BC; 20/6.24
344 Britain; potin, mid 1st cent.BC; 18/1.47
345 Atrebates, Verica; AU stater, early 1st cent.AD; 16/5.36
346 Verulamium, Tasciovanus; AR 'denarius' late 1st cent.BC; 13/1.18
347 Camulodunum, Cunobeline; AU stater, early 1st cent.AD; 17/5.53
348 Camulodunum, Epatticus; AR 'minim', c.AD 25; 8/0.30
349 Cantii, Dubnovellaunus; AR, 15-1 BC; 14/0.89
350 Durotriges; AR, 1st cent.BC; 18/5.30
351 Dobunni; AR, 1st cent.BC; 12/0.83
352 Iceni; AR, mid 1st cent.AD; 13/1.22
353 Coritani; AU stater, mid 1st cent.AD; 20/ 40

VII Detail from 378

354 Rome, Augustus; AR denarius, 20-15 BC; 19/3.77
355 Rome, Augustus; AE sestertius, c.22 BC; 35/27.68
356 Lyons, Augustus; AR denarius, c.1 BC; 20/3.84
357 Lyons, Augustus; AE as, 10-2 BC; 27/11.
358 Julia Traducta, Augustus; AE, c.1 BC; 33/16.83
359 Nemausus, Augustus; AE, c.AD 10; 27/13.49
360 Lyons, Tiberius; AR denarius, AD 14-37; 20/3.57
361 Lyons, Tiberius; AU quinarius, AD 31-2; 15/3.79
362 Rome, Tiberius; AE sestertius, AD 22-3; 35/27.71
363 Antioch, Syria, Tiberius; AE, AD 31; 28/13.85
364 Judaea, Pontius Pilate; AE lepton, AD 29-30; obv. 15/2.03 rev. 16/2.20
365 Rome, Caligula; AE as, AD 37-41; 29/11.
366 Rome, Agrippina; AE sestertius, AD 37-41; 36/27.54
367 Rome, Caligula; AE sestertius, AD 37-38; 35/29.07
368 Apamea, Bithynia, Caligula; AE, AD 37-41; 32/12.31
369 Mauretania, Ptolemy II; AU, AD 21-40; 18/3.10
370 Rome, Claudius I; AE quadrans, AD 41; 18/3.43
371 Lyons, Claudius I; AU aureus, AD 46-47; 20/7.71
372 Western empire, Claudius I; AE 'as' c.AD 50; 23/5.10
373 Ephesus, Claudius I; AR cistophorus, c.AD 50; 26/10.79
374 Pergamum, Britannicus; AE, c.AD 50; 19/3.08
375 Lyons, Nero; AU aureus, AD 54; 19/7.60
376 Rome, Nero; AE dupondius, AD 64; 30/1 .24
377 Rome, Nero; AE semis, AD 64; 18/2.93
378 Rome, Nero; AE sestertius, AD 64-66; 34/29.82
379 Lyons, Nero; AE sestertius, AD 64-66; 36/22.61
380 Lyons, Nero; AE sestertius, AD 64-66; 37/22.92
381 Alexandria, Egypt, Nero; Bill tetradrachm AD 63-64; 24/13.21
382 Commagene, Antiochus IV; AE, AD 38-72; 29/14.71
383 Chios; AE obol, 1st-2nd cent.AD; 26/7.13
384 Spain; AR denarius, AD 68; 18/3.39
385 Carthage, Clodius Macer; AR denarius, AD 68; obv. 18/3.49 rev. 18/3.06
386 Lyons, Galba; AE sestertius, AD 69; 34/2 70
387 Rome, Otho; AR denarius, AD 69; 18/3.4
388 Antioch, Syria, Otho; AR tetradrachm, AD 69; 27/14.95
389 Bithynia, Vespasian; AE; 35/24.67
390 Rome, Vespasian; AR denarius, AD 69; 1 3.25
391 Rome, Titus; AE sestertius, AD 72; 33/25.4
392 Rome, Titus; AE sestertius, AD 81; 36/25.3
393 Rome, Titus; AE sestertius, AD 80-1; 33/ .36
394 Rome, Domitian; AE sestertius, AD 95-6; 34/24.64
395 Rome, Domitian; AR denarius, AD 85; 20/3.43
396 Rome, Domitian; AE as, AD 86; 29/10.44
397 Rome, Domitian; AR quinarius, AD 88; 1 /1.66
398 Rome, Vitellius; AE sestertius, AD 69; 34/25.55
399 Cibyra, Asia, Domitian; AE, c.AD 85, c'mk after 96; 27/6.76
400 Rome, Nerva; AU aureus, AD 96; obv. 19/7.53 rev. 19/7.68
401 Rome, Nerva; AE sestertius, AD 97; 34/2 .53
402 Berytus, Syria, Nerva; AE, AD 96-98; 25/ 3.36
403 Rome, Trajan; AR denarius, AD 98-99; 20/3.39
404 Rome, Trajan; AR denarius, AD 106; 20/ 26
405 Rome, Trajan; AE sestertius, AD 104-11; 34/28.42
406 Rome, Trajan; AR denarius, c.AD 107; 19/3.41
407 Arabia (?), Trajan; AR drachma, AD 114-; 19/3.17
408 Ancyra, Galatia, Trajan; AE, AD 98-100; 31/22.66
409 Hatra, Mesopotamia; AE, 2nd cent.AD; /14.15
410 Rome, Hadrian; AR denarius, AD 117; 18/3.05
411 Rome, Hadrian; AR 8-denarii, AD 119; 3 /25.59
412 Rome, Sabina; AU aureus, AD 117-36; 19/7.33
413 Rome, Hadrian; AU aureus, AD 134-8; 2 7.42
414 Rome, Hadrian; AE sestertius, c.AD 127-3; 34/26.86
415 Rome, Verus; AU aureus, AD 161; 19/7.
416 Adramyteum, Mysia, Antinous; AE, c.AD 130-8; 34/26.67
417 Judaea, Bar Cochba; AR shekel, AD 133— 25/14.89
418 Bosphorus, Rhoemetalces; AU stater, AD 131-2; obv. 19/7.66 rev. 20/7.71
419 Rome, Divus Antoninus; AR denarius, AD 161; 22/3.50
420 Rome, Faustina I; AU aureus, AD 139; 18/7.18
421 Rome, Diva Faustina; AE sestertius, AD 141; 33/24.30
422 Rome, Antoninus Pius; AE sestertius, AD 143; 35/29.42
423 Rome, Antoninus Pius; AE as, AD 148; 30/10.70
424 Alexandria, Egypt, Hadrian; AE, AD 134-35
425 Obverse of 420
426 Rome, Verus; AE sestertius, AD 163-4; 33/24.84
427 Rome, Faustina II; AE sestertius, c.AD 161; 34/27.49
428 Rome, Commodus; AU aureus, AD 175; 20/7.24
429 Caesarea, Cappadocia, Aurelius; AR didrachm; 21/6.60
430 Laodiceia-Pergamum 'alliance'; AE, c.AD 160; 40/30.37
431 Rome, Commodus; AE sestertius, AD 186; 30/22.80
432 Rome, Commodus; AE sestertius, AD 190; 32/23.39
433 Rome, Commodus; AE medallion, AD 192; 40/21.38
434 Amaseia, Pontus, Alexander Severus; AE, AD 229; 33/21.38
435 Athens; AE, c.AD 250; 21/6.15
436 Pergamum, Septimius Severus; AE, AD 193-211; 44/42.55
437 Byblos, Macrinus; AE, AD 217-8; 30/16.76
438 Cnidus, Caracalla and Plautilla; AE, c.AD 205; 32/13.96
439 Synnada, Gallienus; AE, AD 253-268; 32/15.82
440 Apameia, Phrygia, Septimius Severus; AE, AD 193-211; 36/23.83
441 Athens; AE, 3rd cent.AD; 21/4.36
442 Ilium, Septimius Severus; AE, AD 193-211; 36/21.87
443 Chios; AE, 1st cent.AD; 16/2.91
444 Abydus, Commodus; AE, c.AD 175; 36/22.28
445 Abonuteichus, Antoninus Pius; AE, AD 138-161; 31/20.22

VIII Portrait of Probus from 475

446 Rome, Septimius Severus; AU aureus, AD 204; 21/7.23
447 Rome, Caracalla; AR antoninianus, AD 215; 24/5.09
448 Laodicea, Syria, Caracalla; AR tetradrachm, c.AD 210; 27/12.82
449 Tarsus, Caracalla; AE, c.AD 215; 34/19.65
450 Augusta Traiana, Thrace, Caracalla; AE, c.AD 200; 30/16.45
451 Antioch (?), Syria, Elagabalus; AR denarius, AD 218-9; 18/3.11
452 Rome, Gordian III; AE sestertius, AD 238; 31/24.01
453 Caesarea, Cappadocia, Gordian III; AR didrachm, AD 240; 24/8.79
454 Antioch, Pisidia, Gordian III; AE, AD 238-244; 34/28.60
455 Edessa, Mesopotamia, Gordian III; AE, AD 238-244; 34/22.48
456 Rome, Philip I, for use in Syria; AR tetradrachm, AD 244-49; 25/11.65
457 Rome, Trajan Decius; AE 2-sestertii, AD 249-51; 36/42.57
458 Rome, Trajan Decius; AR denarius, AD 249-51; 20/3.80
459 Anazarbus, Cilicia, Valerian I; AE, AD 253-8; 30/17.90
460 Panemoteichos, Pisidia, Gallienus; AE, c.AD 256; 34/16.57
461 Rome, Gallienus; AR antoninianus, c.AD 266; 20/3.32
462 Postumus; AU aureus, AD 260-269; 23/6.69
463 Milan, Gallienus; AR antoninianus, c.AD 265; 24/4.07
464 Rome, Claudius II; AU 8-aurei, AD 268; 37/38.64
465 Sparta, Gallienus; AE 8-as, AD 253-68; 30/13.36
466 Emisa, Syria, Uranius Antoninus; AR tetradrachm, c.AD 253; 30/8.40
467 Carnuntum, Austria, Regalian; AR antoninianus; 19/3.20
468 Postumus; Bill antoninianus, AD 260-269; 20/3.81
469 Victorinus; Bill antoninianus; 20/2.53
470 Cologne, Tetricus I; Bill antoninianus, c.AD 272; 18/2.20
471 Barbarous; Bill 'antoninianus'; 13/0.95
472 Rome, Aurelian; Bill antoninianus; 22/4.28
473 Antioch, Syria, Aurelian and Vabalathus; Bill antoninianus; 20/3.52
474 Antioch, Syria, Aurelian and Vabalathus; Bill antoninianus; 21/3.90
475 Siscia, Probus; Bill antoninianus; 22/4.24
476 Reverse of 475
477 Ticinum, Probus; Bill antoninianus; 24/4.33
478 Ticinum, Probus; Bill antoninianus; 22/3.43
479 Serdica, Probus; Bill antoninianus; 21/3.70
480 London, Carausius; Bill antoninianus; 25/4.09
481 Colchester (?), Carausius; Bill antoninianus; 23/4.65
482 Alexandria, Egypt, Diocletian; Bill tetradrachm, AD 285; 20/7.55

IX Detail from 540

483 Nicomedia, Licinius I; AU aureus, AD 308-24; 21/6.80
484 Siscia, Constantine I; AU medallion, AD 336-37; 24/6.80
485 Trier, Valentinian II; AU solidus, AD 375-92; 20/4.42
486 Amiens, Magnentius; AE maiorina, AD 350-53; 28/8.42
487 Siscia, Vetranio; Bill maiorina, AD 350; 22/7.32
488 Rome, Constantius II; AU solidus, AD 357; 21/4.44
489 Antioch, Syria, Galerius; AU aureus, AD 293-305; 18/5.33
490 Antioch, Syria, Constans; AU solidus, AD 333-37; 20/4.43
491 Constantinople, Gratian; AU solidus, AD 367-83; 21/3.12
492 Trier, Valens; AR siliqua, AD 364-78; 17/2.07
493 Arles, Valens; AE, 364-78; 17/2.53
494 Arles, Gratian; AU solidus, AD 367-83; 21/4.46
495 Arles, Constantius II; AR siliqua, AD 353-61; 17/1.95
496 Barbarous; AE, c.AD 355; 18/1.86
497 AE weight for solidus, AD 395-423; 19/4.23
498 Valens; AR siliqua (clipped), AD 364-78; 12/0.89
499 Nicomedia, Diocletian; AU medallion, c.AD 300; 37/53.50
500 Rome, Maximian; Bill medallion, c.AD 300; 41/74.59
501 Pavia, Maximian; AR siliqua, c.AD 295; 17/3.01
502 Siscia, Constantius I; Bill follis, c.AD 300; 31/10.47
503 Carthage, Galerius; Bill follis, c.AD 300; 27/8.82
504 London, Constantine I; Bill centenionalis, AD 318; 20/3.38
505 Lyons; Bill centenionalis, AD 330-35; 18/1.85
506 Trier, Fausta; AU 2-solidus AD 324-26; 24/8.78
507 Trier, Fausta; Bill centenionalis, AD 330-35; 19/2.52
508 Antioch, Syria, Constantius II; Bill maiorina, AD 348-51; 24/4.64
509 Lyons, Constans; Bill maiorina, AD 348-50; 23/5.40

510 Constantinople, Julian; Bill maiorina, AD 363; 28/8.73
511 Constantinople, Theodosius I; AU solidus, c.AD 385; 21/4.38
512 Ravenna, Honorius; AU solidus, c.AD 405; 21/4.44
513 S. Gaul, Visigoths; AU 'solidus', c.AD 420; 20/4.39
514 Rome, Libius Severus; AU solidus, AD 461-65; 21/2.19
515 Ravenna, Libius Severus; AU solidus, AD 461-65; 21/4.39
516 Milan, Libius Severus; AU solidus, AD 461-65; 21/4.35
517 Central Gaul, Majorian; AR, AD 457-61; 12/0.70
518 S. Gaul, Visigoths; AU 'solidus', c.AD 440-50; 19/4.22
519 S. Gaul, Visigoths; AU 'tremissis', c.AD 480; 14/1.42
520 Constantinople, Arcadius; AU solidus, c.AD 400; 20/4.44
521 Constantinople, Anastasius; AU solidus, c.AD 500; 19/2.18
522 Constantinople, Theodosius II; AU solidus, AD 439; 20/4.45
523 Constantinople, Leo I; AU semissis, c.AD 460; 18/2.21
524 Constantinople, Marcian; AE, AD 450-57; 10/4.43
525 Constantinople, Anastasius; AE follis, c.AD 500; 37/18.52
526 Constantinople, Justinian I; AE follis, AD 538-39; 42/23.59
527 Constantinople, Constans II; AE follis, AD 641-42; 23/9.56
528 Rome, Anthemius; AU solidus, c.AD 470; 20/4.44
529 Milan, Julius Nepos; AU solidus, AD 476-80; 21/4.36
530 Ravenna, Odovacar; AR ½-siliqua, c.AD 490; 11/0.82
531 Rome, Zeno; AE follis, c.AD 489; 28/18.39
532 Rome, Theodoric; AU 3-solidi, c.AD 500; 34/13.60; BN
533 Rome, Theodoric; AU solidus, c.AD 500; 19/4.47
534 Rome, Ostrogoths; AU solidus, AD 527-35; 20/4.43
535 Rome, Justinian I; AU solidus, AD 535-46; 22/4.43
536 Rome, Athalaric; AR, AD 526-35; 12/0.69
537 Rome, Justinian I; AR 120-nummi, AD 535-46; 11/0.67
538 Rome, Totila; AE 10-nummi, AD 548-51; 19/7.50
539 Rome, Ostrogoths; AE follis, c.AD 500; 25/9.04
540 Rome, Theodahad; AE follis, AD 534-36; 25/10.60
541 Ravenna, Honorius; AR siliqua, AD 402-23; 17/1.84
542 Africa; AR 'siliqua', early 5th cent.AD; 15/1.86
543 Carthage; AE, AD 400-50; 10/1.21
544 Carthage, Gunthamund; AR 100-denarii, AD 484-96; 15/2.13
545 Carthage, Vandals; AE 42-nummi, c.AD 500; 29/13.00
546 Rome, Vespasian; sestertius reengraved as AE 83-nummi, c.AD 500; 34/23.75
547 Carthage, Justinian I; AE follis, AD 534-38; 28/11.74
548 Constantinople, Justinian I; AU solidus, c.AD 550; 20/4.45
549 Constantinople, Justin II; AU solidus AD 565-78; 20/4.41
550 Constantinople, Tiberius II; AU solidus, AD 578-82; 20/4.26
551 Constantinople, Heraclius; AR hexagram, c.AD 625; 22/6.54
552 Constantinople, Theodosius II; AU solidus, AD 424-25; 21/4.38
553 Constantinople, Theodosius II; AU solidus, AD 425; 20/4.32
554 Constantinople, Justinian II; AU solidus, AD 692-95; 20/4.36
555 Constantinople, Leo II and Zeno; AU solidus, AD 474; 19/4.41
556 Constantinople, Justin I and Justinian I; AU solidus, AD 527; 20/4.49
557 Cyzicus, Justin II and Sophia; AE follis, AD 575-6; 30/11.99
558 Constantinople, Constans II; AU solidus, AD 659-68; 20/4.48
559 Syracuse, Leontius II; AU solidus, AD 695-98; 18/3.92
560 Syracuse, Justinian II; AE follis AD 685-95; 22/3.69
561 Carthage, Maurice Tiberius; AU solidus, AD 586-87; 18/4.38
562 Carthage, Heraclius; AU solidus AD 608-09; 16/4.36
563 Carthage, Constantine IV, Heraclius, Tiberius II; AU solidus, AD 678-79; 13/4.44
564 Sardinia, Tiberius III; AU solidus, AD 698-705; 14/4.25
565 Africa, Arabs; AU solidus, AD 704-05; 11/4.30
566 Ravenna, Maurice Tiberius; AU tremissis, AD 582-602; 17/1.48
567 Lombards; AU tremissis, c.AD 600; 17/1.43
568 Visigoths; AU tremissis, c.AD 550; 15/1.43
569 Seville, Spain, Liuvigild; AU tremissis, AD 568-86; 16/1.06
570 Tarragona, Wamba; AU tremissis, AD 672-80; 20/1.46
571 al-Andalus, Spain, Arabs; AU solidus, AD 716-17; 14/4.10
572 Gaul, Gundobad; AU solidus, AD 491-516; 20/4.47
573 Lyons, Gundobad; AE, c.AD 500; 9/0.77
574 Theudebert; AU solidus, AD 532-48; 19/4.42
575 Lausanne, Franks; AU tremissis, c.AD 580; 15/1.37
576 Marseilles; AU solidus, c.AD 590; 20/3.87
577 Paris, Clovis II; AU tremissis, AD 639-57; 11/1.26
578 Marseilles, Chlothar II; AU solidus, c.AD 615-29; 22/3.75
579 Orléans; AU tremissis, c.AD 610; 10/1.23
580 Sion and Susa; AU tremissis, c.AD 600; 13/1.32
581 Anglo-Saxon; AU tremissis, c.AD 650; 13/1.29
582 London, Crispus; Bill centenionalis, AD 321; 20/2.99

X Detail from 604

583 Leo III, Constantine V; AU solidus, AD 717-41; 19/4.43
584 Constantine V, Leo IV, Rome; AU solidus, AD 741-75; 20/3.97
585 Theophilus, Sicily; AU semissis, AD 829-42; 12/1.62; FW
586 Michael III; AU solidus, AD 842-66; 19/4.30; FW
587 Basil I; AU solidus, AD 867-86; 20/4.36; FW
588 Nicephorus II (Phocas); AR miliaresion, AD 963-69; 22/2.88
589 Constantine VII, Romanus II; AU solidus, AD 945-49; 19/4.41
590 Basil II, Constantine VIII; AU histamenon, AD 976-1025 (clipped); 34/4.07; FW
591A Constantine IX; AU histamenon, AD 1042-55; 27/4.38; FW
591B Constantine IX; AU tetarteron, AD 1042-55; 17/4.02; FW
592 Isaac I, Comnenus; AU histamenon, AD 1057-59; 26/4.41
593 Romanus IV; AU histamenon, AD 1067-71; 25/4.33; FW
594 Constantine VI & Irene; AR miliaresion, AD 781-97; 22/2.66
595 Leo V & Constantine; AR miliaresion, AD 813-20; 22/2.05; FW
596 Constantine VII; AU solidus, AD 945; 19/4.47
597 Irene; AE follis, AD 797-802; 22/3.99
598 Theophilus; AE follis, AD 829-42; 28/8.61; FW
599 Basil I; AE follis, AD 867-86; obv. 25/6.63 rev. 27/10.01
600 Leo VI (886-912); AE follis; 26/7.74; FW
601 Romanus I (919-44); AE follis; 27/5.58; FW
602 Anonymous Follis, Class A2; 32/15.19; FW
603 Anonymous Follis, Class C; 28/6.75; FW
604 Alexius I (1081-1118); AU hyperpyron; 30/4.06; FW
605 Manuel I (1143-80); AU hyperpyron; 28/4.15; FW
606 Isaac II (1185-95); El one-third hyperpyron; 28/3.94; FW
607 Alexius I (1081-1118); AE tetarteron; 17.5/25; FW
608-609 John II (1118-43); AE tetarteron; 16/1.20; FW
610 Isaac of Cyprus; Bill trachy; 28/4.87; FW
611 Michael VIII Palaeologus; AU hyperpyron; 25/4.36; FW
612 John III of Nicaea (1222-54); AU hyperpyron; 26/4.24; FW
613 Antioch, Tancred; AE follis; 17/2.48; PG
614 Beyrout, John of Helin; Bill denier; 16/0.58; PG
615 Antioch, Bohemond III; Bill denier; 16/1.03; PG
616 Jerusalem, Amaury I (1167-73); Bill denier; 17/0.84; PG
617 Acre; AU bezant, 1251; 20/3.05; PG
618 Cyprus, Hugh II (1253-67); El bezant; 25/3.78; PG
619 Cyprus, Henry II; AR besant blanc; 26/4.72; PG
620 Armenia, Leo I (1185-1219); AR tram; 20/3.11; PG
621 Georgia, Rusudan; AR dirham; 20/2.60; PG
622 Trebizond, Manuel I: AR asper; 25/2.86
623 Constantinople, Andronicus II and III; AU hyperpyron; 22/4.15; FW
624 Constantinople, Andronicus II and Michael IX (1282-1328); AR basilicon; 19/2.44; FW
625 Constantinople, John V; AR silver hyperpyron; 26/8.33
626 Constantinople, Manuel II; AR half silver hyperpyron; 29/3.68; FW
627 Mytilene, Giacomo Gattilusio; Bill denier (?); 13/0.94; PG
628 Mytilene, Dosino Gattilusio; AE denier (?); 13/1.17; PG
629 Rhodes, Pierre de Cornillan; AR gigliato; 27/3.80; PG
630 Chios, Maionesi; AR gros, late 15th cent. AD; 25/3.28; PG
631 Cyprus, Henry II; AR gros, 1310-24; 25/4.62; PG

XI Detail from 800

632 Franks, St Martin de Tours; AR denier, late 7th cent.AD; 10/1.10; PG
633 Anglo-Saxon; AR penny, late 7th cent.AD; 11/1.07; FW
634 Anglo-Saxon; AR penny, late 7th cent.AD; 11/1.20; FW
635 Franks, Pepin the Short (751-68); AR denier; 16/1.15; PG
636 Franks, Charlemagne (768-814); AR denier; 16/1.31; PG
637 Franks, Charlemagne; AR denier; 19/1.66; PG
638 Franks, Charlemagne; AR denier; 20/1.65; PG
639 Franks, Louis the Pious (814-41); AR denier; 20/1.58; PG
640 Franks, Louis the Pious; AU solidus; 19/5.65; PG
641 Mercia, Offa (757-96); AR penny; 16/1.26; FW
642 Mercia, Offa and Aethelheard; AR penny; 19/1.43; FW
643 Mercia, Burgred (852-74); AR penny; 20/1.38; FW
644 London, Wessex, Alfred (871-99); AR penny; 18/1.56; FW
645 Vikings, Anlaf Guthfrithsson; AR penny; 20/1.15; FW
646 Lombards, Cunincpert; AU tremissis; 19/1.33; PG
647 Lombards; AU tremissis; 16/1.28; PG
648 Lombards, Aistulf (749-56); AU tremissis; 16/1.15; PG
649 Papacy, Hadrian I (772-95); AR denaro; 19/1.22; PG
650 Papacy, John VIII (872-75); AR denaro; 20/1.15; PG
651 Papacy, Benedict IV; AR denaro; 18/1.29; PG
652 Naples, Sergius I (840-61); AE follaro; 29/8.05; PG
653 Benevento, Grimoald III and Charlemagne; AU tremissis; 16/1.25; PG
654 England, Ethelred II (978-1016); AR penny; 20/1.44; FW
655 England, Harold II; AR penny, 1066; 18/1.38; FW
656 England, William I; AR penny; 18/1.26; FW
657 England, Henry I (1100-35); AR penny; 20/1.38; FW
658 England, John (1199-1216); AR penny; 20/1.45; FW
659 England, Henry III (1216-72); AR penny; 18/1.44; FW
660 England, Edward I (1272-1307); AR penny; 20/1.38; FW
661 Scotland, William I; AR penny; 20/1.52; FW
662 Scotland, Alexander III; AR penny; 19/1.34; FW
663 Ireland, John; AR penny; 18/1.41; FW
664 Bruges; AR denier c.1250; 10/0.45; PG
665 Ghent; AR denier; 10/0.41; PG
666 Utrecht, Dirk van der Aare; AR penny; 15/0.61; PG
667 Holland, Floris V (1256-96); AR penny; 14/0.59; PG
668 Champagne, Thibaud II; Bill denier; 18/0.88; PG
669 Anjou, Charles II; Bill denier; 18/0.98; PG
670 France, Louis VII (1137-80); Bill denier; 20/1.09; PG
671 Vienne; Bill denier, 13th cent. AD; 17/0.99; PG
672 Saint-Aignan; Bill denier; 18/1.16; PG
673 Vendôme; Bill denier, 12th cent. AD; 18/1.05; PG
674 Valence; Bill denier; 18/1.06; PG
675 France, Louis IX; Bill denier tournois; 19/0.86; PG
676 Burgundy, Robert II; Bill denier; 18/0.95; PG
677 Saxony, Otto I; AR sachsenpfennig; 21/1.15; PG
678 Bavaria, Henry III; AR penny; 22/1.70; PG
679 Germany, Henry II (1002-14); AR penny; 20/1.47; PG
680 Frisia, Egbert; AR penny; 18/0.69; PG
681 Cologne, Anno (1056-75); AR penny; 19/1.21; PG
682 Würzburg, Otto I; AR penny; 15/0.82; PG
683 Hesse, Sophia and Henry I; AR penny; 17/0.70; PG
684 Germany, Frederick Barbarossa; AR penny; 17/1.47; PG
685 Osnabrück, Gerhard (1193-1215); AR penny; 21/1.40; PG
686 Dortmund, Rudolf of Habsburg; AR penny; 16/1.40; PG
687 Aachen, Louis IV; AR penny; 17/1.21; PG
688 Augsburg; AR heller, late 13th cent. AD; 16/0.33; PG
689 Bavaria, Otto I; AR penny; 16/0.85; PG
690 Carinthia, Bernhard; AR penny; 17/0.91; PG
691 Passau (?); AR penny c. 1250; 24/0.86; PG
692 Sweden, Olaf Tryggvason; AR penny; 21/2.24; PG
693 Denmark, Harthacnut; AR penny; 17/1.02; PG
694 Denmark, Svend Estruthsson; AR penny; 18/1.10; PG
695 Poland, Boleslas Chrobry; AR penny; 19/1.01; PG
696 Poland, Vladislav II; AR penny; 13/0.59; PG
697 Poland, Vladislav II; AR penny; 13/0.48; PG
698 Kiev, Vladimir (972-1015); AR srebennik; 26/2.97; PG
699 Bohemia, Boleslav II (967-99); AR penny; 20/0.77; PG
700 Bohemia, Bratislav I (1037-55); AR penny; 20/1.07; PG
701 Bohemia, Bratislav I; AR penny; 15/1.04; PG
702 Bohemia, Przemysl Ottocar I; AR penny; 18/1.00; PG
703 Hungary, Solomon; AR penny; 15/0.57; PG
704 Hungary, Bela II (1131-41); AR penny; 11/0.44; PG
705 Hungary, Bela IV; AR penny; 11/0.55; PG
706 Hungary, Louis the Great; AR penny; 14/0.54; PG
707 Slavonia, Ladislas IV; AR denier; 15/0.96; PG
708 Pavia, Henry IV; AR denaro papiensis; 15/1.28; PG
709 Milan, Frederick Barbarossa; AR denaro, c. 1150; 18/0.82; PG
710 Trieste, Givard; AR denaro; c. 1210; 20/1.06; PG
711 Sicily, Roger II (1101-30); AU tari; 13/1.01; PG
712 Amalfi, Roger II; AU tari; 17/0.67; PG
713 Sicily, Frederick II; AU multiple tari; 15/8.76; PG
714 Sicily, Frederick II; AU multiple tari; 12/2.35; PG
715 Sicily, Roger II (1130-54); AR ducalis; 23/2.41; PG
716 Sicily, Roger II; AR one-third ducalis, 1140; 13/0.75; PG
717 Salerno, Robert Guiscard; AE follaro; 15/6.97; PG
718 Sicily, Roger I; AE follaro; 26/10.36; PG
719 Sicily, Frederick II (1220-50); Bill denaro; 14/0.41; PG
720 Sicily, William II; AE follaro; 13/1.94; PG
721 Castile, John I; Bill cornado; 18/0.80; PG
722 Castile, Alfonso VIII; AU alfonsino; 27/3.76; PG
723 Portugal, Sancho I; AU morabitino; 28/3.85; PG
724 Worms, Conrad I (1150-71); AR penny; 27/0.78; PG
725 Meissen, Conrad the Great; AR bracteate; 30/0.86; PG
726 Brandenburg, Albert the Bear; AR bracteate; 27/0.88; PG
727 Brandenburg, Otto I; AR bracteate; 28/0.95; PG
728 Thuringia, Albert the Rude; AR bracteate; 24/0.37; PG
729 Frankfurt am Main, Frederick Barbarossa (1152-90); AR bracteate; 26/0.72; PG
730 Brandenburg, Albert the Bear (1134-70); AR bracteate; 32/0.85; PG
731 Nordhausen, Frederick Barbarossa; AR bracteate; 46/0.66; FW
732 Hersfeld, Siegfried I (1180-1200); AR bracteate; 42/0.76; PG
733 Magdeburg, Wichmann of Seeburg; AR bracteate; 27/0.97; PG
734 Halberstadt, Gero (1160-77); AR bracteate; 27/0.81; PG
735 Erfurt, Archbishop Henry I (1142-53); AR bracteate; 41/0.85; PG
736 Arnstein, Walter II (1133-66); AR bracteate; 28/0.89; PG
737 Lindau, Frederick II (1215-50); AR bracteate; 23/0.48; PG
738 Brunswick, William (1195-1213); AR bracteate; 21/0.46; PG
739 Augsburg, Udalschalk (1184-1202); AR bracteate; 24/0.81; PG
740 Constance, Eberhard II (1248-74); AR bracteate; 20/0.44; PG
741 Zurich, Frauenmünster; AR bracteate; 16/0.37; PG
742 Todtnau, Albert III of Austria (1386-95); AR bracteate; 17/0.20; PG
743 Saxony, Frederick II (1428-64); AR hohlpfennig; 20/0.39; PG
744 Venice, Ranieri Zeno (1253-60); AR grosso; 20/2.18; PG
745 Bologna; AR grosso, c. 1300; 18/1.41; PG
746 Pisa; AR grosso, c. 1250; 19/1.68; PG
747 Florence; AR grosso, c. 1250; 20/1.71; PG
748 Rome, Brancaleone d'Andolo; AR grosso, 1252-55; 23/3.32; PG
749 Rome, Charles of Anjou; AR grosso rinforzato; 16/3.79; PG
750 Naples, Robert the Wise (1309-43); AR gigliato; 29/3.96; PG
751 Bergamo; AR grosso, c. 1250; 20/2.10; PG
752 Milan; AR grosso, c.1250; 12/2.86; PG
753 Venice, Andrea Dandolo (1343-54); AR soldino; 14/0.56; PG
754 Florence; AR grosso guelfo, c.1405-06; 23/2.54; PG
755 Siena; AR grosso, c.AD 1375; 22/2.47; PG
756 France, Louis IX (1226-70); AR gros tournois; 25/4.10; PG
757 Hainaut, Margaret of Constantinople (1244-80); AR petit gros; 21/2.51; PG
758 Barcelona, James II (1291-1307); AR croat; 24/3.30; PG
759 Brabant, John I (1268-94); AR petit gros; 22/2.50; PG
760 Flanders, Louis I (1322-46); AR gros; 27/3.85; PG
761 France, John the Good (1350-64); AR gros à la fleur de lis florencée; 29/3.65; PG
762 Flanders, Louis II (1346-84); AR botdrager; 31/3.59; PG
763 Metz, Thierry of Boppard (1346-84); AR gros; 25/3.33; PG
764 Lorraine, Charles II (1390-1431); AR gros; 24/2.53; PG
765 Cologne, Walram of Jülich (1332-49); AR groschen; 26/3.91; PG
766 Aachen, AR groschen, c.1375; 26/2.17; PG
767 Trier, Werner of Falkenstein (1388-1415); AR albus; 24/2.12; PG
768 Würzburg, Gottfried IV (1443-58); AR schilling; 23/1.99; PG
769 Bohemia, Wenceslas II (1278-1305); AR pragergroschen; 26/3.63; PG
770 Ulm; AR pragergroschen, c.1425; 26/2.56; PG
771 Saxony, Frederick II (1323-49); AR meissnergroschen; 27/3.58; PG
772 Hamburg; AR witten, c.1400; 18/1.24; PG
773 Teutonic Order, Winrich of Kniprode (1351-82); AR schilling; 20/1.72; PG
774 Hungary, Charles Robert (1308-42); AR gros; 26/3.52; PG
775 Serbia, Stephen Decanski (1321-31); AR grosch; 21/2.18; PG
776 Serbia, Stephen Dushan; AR grosch, 1346-55; 19/1.53; PG
777 Wallachia, Vladislav I (1364-77); AR dinar; 17/0.76; PG

778 Bosnia, Stephen II Tomasevick (1461-63); AR groschen; 22/1.42; PG
779 England, Edward III; AR groat, c.1360; 26/4.68; FW
780 Scotland, David II (1329-71); AR groat; 28/4.30; FW
781 Castile, Peter the Cruel (1350-69); AR real; 25/3.43; PG
782 Portugal, Fernando I (1367-83); AR real; 25/3.34; PG
783 Sicily, Frederick II; AU augustale, 1231-50; 19/5.27
784 Naples, Charles I of Anjou; AU reale d'oro, c 1270; 20/5.29; PG
785 Florence; AU florin, 1332; 20/3.53; PG
786 Venice, Pietro Gradenigo (1289-1311); AU ducat; 20/3.53; PG
787 Genoa; AU genovino, c.1275; 19/3.50; PG
788 France, Philip IV; AU petit royal assis, AD 1290; 23/3.54; PG
789 France, Philip IV; AU masse d'or, 1296; 30/7.06 PG
790 France, Philip VI; AU royal d'or, 1328; 26/4.22; PG
791 France, Philip VI; AU écu à la chaise, 1337; 28/4.46
792 France, John the Good; AU mouton, 1355; 29/4.68; PG
793 France, Charles VI; AU écu d'or, c.1385; 29/3.99; PG
794 France, John the Good; AU franc à cheval, 1360; 28/3.76;
795 Flanders, Louis de Male; AU vieil heaume, 1367; 35/6.70; PG
796 Flanders, Louis de Male; AU flandres d'or, 1369; 32/4.16; PG
797 Brabant, Philip the Good (1430-67); AU lion d'or; 30/4.23; PG
798 Poitiers, Edward the Black Prince; AU pavilion d'or, 1360; 33/5.36
799 Castile, Peter the Cruel (1350-69); AU dobla; 26/4.53; PG
800 England, Edward III; AU noble, 1344-60; 35/7.70
801 Cologne, Frederick III of Saarwerden (1371-1414); AU goldgulden; 23/3.50; PG
802 Frankfurt am Main, Sigismund; AU goldgulden, c.1425; 23/3.47; PG
803 Hungary, John Hunyadi (1446-52); AU florin; 21/3.57; PG
804 Bohemia, Charles IV (1346-78); AU florin; 20/3.51; PG
805 Naples, Charles I of Anjou (1266-85); AU carlino d'oro; 23/4.34; PG
806 Sicily, Peter of Aragon (1282-85); AU pierreale; 23/4.37
807 Rome, Eugenius IV (1431-47); AU ducat; 23/3.50; PG
808 Milan, Filippo Maria Visconti; (1412-47); PG
809 Bologna; AU bolognino, c.1390; 20/3.48; AU ducat; 21/3.51; PG
810 Genoa, Simone Boccanegra (1339-44); AU genovino; 21/3.54; PG

XII Detail from 834

811 Venice, Nicolo Tron; AR lira, 1472; 28/6.26
812 Milan, Galeazzo Maria Sforza; AR lira, 1468-76; 29/9.66
813 Milan, Louis XII; AR testone, 1500-23; 29/9.61
814 Milan, Charles V; AR testone, 1536-56; 31/11.91
815 Rome, Sixtus IV; AR grosso, 1471-84; 25/3.82
816 Florence Republic; AR barile, 1509; 28/3.44
817 Florence, Alessandro de Medici; AR testone, 1532-36; 28/9.81
818 Malta, Jean de Vallette; AE 2-tari, 1567; 27/4.65
819 Famagusta, Cyprus, M.A. Bragadin; AE bezant, 1570; 28/4.55
820 Venice, Alvise Pisani; AE osella, 1735; 38/9.49
821 Savoy, Carlo Emanuele I; AR ducatone, 1588; 42/31.70
822 Naples, Ferdinand I; AE cavallo, 1458-94; 18/2.09
823 Freiburg; AR dicken, c 1494; 28/9.54
824 Austria, Sigismund, Hall; AR guldiner, 1486 41/31.60
825 Saxony, Friedrich III, Annaberg; AR guldengroschen, 1500-08; 42/29.07
826 St. Joachimsthal, Schlick Counts; AR guldengroschen, c.1520; 42/28.76
827 Stolberg, Ludwig II, Augsburg; AR reichsgulder, 1554; 41/31.14
828 Saxony-Altenburg-Weimar, Johann Wilhelm; AR reichsthaler, 1569; 41/28.28
829 Trier, Lothar von Metternich, Coblenz; AR albus, 1599-1623; 22/1.45
830 Pfalz-Zweibrucken, Wolfgang; AR schusselpfennig, 1532-69; 13/0.37
831 Hildesheim, Ernst von Bayern; AR groschen, 1606; 21/1.81
832 Habsburg, Ferdinand III, Graz; AR groschen, 1647; 22/1.97
833 Bohemia, Rudolf II, Joachimsthal; AR maley-groschen, 1603; 17/1.02
834 Brunswick-Wolfenbüttel, Heinrich Julius; AR 5-thaler löser, 1609; 83/145.84
835 Kuttenberg, Bohemia, Friedrich; AR 24-kreuzer 1620; 30/7.89
836 Dresden, Saxony, Johann Georg I; AR thaler, 1620; 44/26.90
837 Frankfurt-am-Oder; AE pfennig, 1622; 15/0.21
838 Saxony-Weimar; AR reichsthaler, 1623; 42/28.76
839 Bamberg, Johann Georg II; AR thaler, 1622-33; 44/28.67
840 Friedland, Albrecht von Wallenstein; AR thaler, 1629; 44/28.90
841 Augsburg, Sweden, Gustav Adolf; AR thaler 1632; 43/29.14
842 Brunswick-Wolfenbüttel, August; AR glockenthaler, 1643; 41/28.80
843 Saxony-Weimar, Bernhard (commemorative); AR ¼-thaler, 1655; 31/7.17
844 Brandenburg-Bayreuth, Christian; AU ducat, 1642; 23/3.47
845 Alba Iulia, Transylvania, Georg Rakoczi; AU ducat, 1646; 21/3.46
846 Dresden, Saxony, Johann Georg III; AR 2/3-thaler, 1682; 37/15.61
847 Habsburg, Leopold I; AR thaler, 1671; 45/28.49
848 Sayn-Wittgenstein, Gustav; AR 2/3-thaler, 1676; 38/15.29
849 Anhalt-Bernburg, Victor Friedrich; AR thaler, 1746; 42/29.21
850 Montfort, Anton II; AR gulden, 1690 (c'mkd 1693); 38/15.95
851 Brunswick-Wolfenbüttel, Karl; AE pfennig, 1743; 21/3.19
852 Hanover, Georg III; AR 1/3-thaler, 1789; 27/6.50
853 Nürnberg city; AR conventionsthaler, 1758; 41/28.00
854 Austria, Maria Theresia; AR thaler, 1780; 40/28.00
855 Prussia, Friedrich II; AU doppelfriedrichs d'or, 1750; 29/13.34
856 Vienna besieged; AU ducat, 1529; 17/3.55
857 Jülich besieged; AR, 1621; 34/7.23
858 Hungary, Franz Rakoczi; AE poltura, 1706; 23/3.29
859 Portugal, Alfonso V; AU cruzado, 1457-81; 22/3.35; FW
860 Portugal, Manuel I; AR tostao, 1495-1521; 26/8.41
861 Rio de Janeiro, Portugal, Pedro II; AU moeda, 1703; 30/10.48
862 Portugal, Jose I; AU 4-escudos, 1753; 31/14.26
863 Burgos, Spain, Ferdinand and Isabella; AR real c.1500; 27/3.40
864 Toledo, Spain, Ferdinand and Isabella; AU 2-excelente; 29/6.93
865 Seville, Spain, Philip III; AU pistole, 1611; 22/6.61
866 Segovia, Spain, Philip III; AR 8-reales, 1590; 40/27.34
867 Segovia, Spain, Philip III; AR 50-reales, 1618; 73/168.23
868 Segovia, Spain, Philip IV; AE 8-maravedis, 1625; 27/6.47
869 Spain, Charles III (pretender); AR 2-reales, 1708; 27/5.36
870 Spain, Charles III; AE 8-maravedis, 1773; 31/12.33
871 Valencia, Charles II; AR croat, 1684; 39/1.91
872 Burgundian Netherlands, Maximilian I; AU grote reaal, 1487; 39/14.73
873 Guelders, Karel von Egmond; AR snaphaan, 1509-38; 36/7.76
874 Flanders, Charles V, Bruges; AR karolusgulden, 1540-56; 38/22.83
875 Flanders, Charles V, Bruges; AE korte, 1549; 19/1.78
876 Holland; AR leeuwendaalder, 1604; 40/27.17
877 Overijssl; AU rosenobel, c.1582-86; 36/7.54
878 Guelders; AR 10-stuivers, 1606; 31/5.88
879 Utrecht; AU rijder, 1760; 27/9.94
880 Holland; AR gulden, 1748; 33/10.44
881 Holland; AE duit, 1739; 22/3.05
882 Flanders, AE liard, 1590; 26/5.40
883 Brabant, Albert and Isabella; AR patagon, 1618; 41/27.78
884 Austrian Netherlands, Maria Theresia; AR ½-escalian, 1750; 23/4.35
885 Breda besieged; AR 60-stuivers, 1625; 32/14.99
886 France, Louis XII, Paris; AR teston, 1514-15; 27/9.07
887 France (Dauphiné), Francois I, Romans AR teston, 1515-47; 29/8.96
888 France, Francois I; AU écu à la croisette 1540-47; 26/3.40
889 Paris (Moulin), France, Henri II; AR teston, 1553; 28/9.53
890 Toulouse, France, Henri III; AR franc, 1583; 35/13.87
891 Dinan, France, Charles X; AR ¼-écu, 1594; 29/9.66
892 France, Henri IV; AE double tournois, 1603; 20/3.23
893 France, Louis XIII; AR écu blanc, 1643; 44/27.39
894 France, Louis XIV; AE liards, 1654; 73 × 18/23.00
895 Dijon, France, Louis XIV; AR écu aux palmes, 1695; 41/27.03
896 France, Louis XV, Strassburg; AE sol 1773; 29/11.41
897 France, constitutional coinage; AR 15-sous, 1791; 24/5.04
898 Dombes, Anne-Marie-Louise; AR 1/12 écu, 1664; 21/2.26
899 England, Henry VII; AR testoon, 1504-09; 29/9.17
900 England, Henry VIII, York; AR groat; 24/2.50
901 England, Edward VI; AR crown, 1551; 43/30.59
902 Scotland, Mary and Lord Darnley; AR ryal, 1565; 42/30.45
903 England, Elizabeth I; AU pound, 1594-95; 38/11.18
904 England, James I; AU unite, 1604-05; 37/9.98
905 England, James I; AE farthing token, 1616-23; 16/0.70
906 Scotland, Charles I; AR 12-shillings, 1625-49; 32/5.75
907 England, Charles I, Oxford; AR pattern crown, 1644; 42/29.35
908 England, Pontefract besieged; AR shilling, 1648; 29 x 30/6.15
909 England, Commonwealth; AR shilling, 1652; 32/5.82
910 Towcester, England, W. Bell; AE ½-penny token, 1650-72; 18/2.09
911 England, Charles II; AU guinea, 1663; 25/8.42
912 England, Charles II; Sn farthing, 1684; 23/5.60
913 England, William III, Bristol; AR ½-crown, 1697; 33/1509
914 Great Britain, Anne, Edinburgh; AR shilling, 1709; 26/6.07
915 Great Britain, George I; AR shilling, 1723; 25/5.99
916 Bath, Great Britain, W. Gye; AE ½-penny token, 1794; 29/9.35
917 Great Britain, George III; Au guinea, 1794; 24/8.39
918 Ireland, James II; AE shilling, August 1689; 25/6.50
919 Denmark, Christian IV; AR mark, 1606; 29/6.11
920 Norway, Frederik III and Christiania; AR daler, 1654; 45/28.73
921 Sweden, Christina; AR daler, 1641; 44/28.91
922 Sweden, Karl XII; AE ½-daler plåtmynt, 1710; 125/5.60
923 Sweden, Karl XII; AE daler, 1718; 24/4.60
924 Danzig, Poland, Sigismund I; AR 3-grosze, 1540; 21/2.67
925 Nagybanya, Poland, Stephan Bathori; AR thaler, 1586; 42/28.81
926 Danzig, Poland, Sigismund III; AR 6-grosze, 1599; 28/4.62
927 Torun, Poland, John Casimir; AU ducat, 1654; 24/3.46
928 Lithuania, Poland, John Casimir; AE solidus, 1661; 16/1.28
929 Dresden, Poland, August II; AR 2/3-thaler, 1700; 37/17.34
930 Vienna, Austria, Franz II; AE 3-gross, 1794; 28/11.91
931 Moscow, Russia, Mikhail Feodorovich; AR kopek, 1613-45; 15 × 10/0.51
932 Russia, Alexei Mikhailovich; AR yefimok, 1655; 43/28.87
933 Russia, Peter I; AR rouble, 1705; 43/28.47
934 Russia, Peter II; AU zolotnik, 1727; 20/4.02
935 Kolyvan, Russia, Catherine II; AE 5-kopeks, 1784; 43/49.16

XIII Detail from 936

936 Great Britain, George III; AE 2-pence, 1797; 40/56.45
937 Great Britain, George III; AR dollar, 1804; 40/31.72
938 Great Britain, George IV; AR crown, 1821; 38/28.25
939 Great Britain, Victoria; AU 5-pounds, 1839; 38/39.26
940 Great Britain, Victoria; AR crown, 1847; 38/28.32
941 Great Britain, Victoria; Cu penny, 1860; 34/9.48
942 Great Britain, George V; AR crown, 1935; 38/47.47
943 Great Britain, George VI; AU sovereign, 1937; 21/8.00; RM
944 Great Britain, Elizabeth II; CuNi 50-pence, 1972; 30/13.25; RM
945 Great Britain, Sunderland; AE penny, 1797; 34/18.00
946 Lundy Island; AE puffin, 1929; 29/10.08
947 Guernsey, Elizabeth II; CuNi 25-pence, 1972; 38/28.18
948 Ireland, George IV; AE penny, 1823; 33/17.42
949 Ireland; CuNi shilling, 1930; 22/5.79
950 Iceland; AE 2-kronur, 1930; 35/19.69
951 Norway, Frederik IV; Cu 4-skilling, 1809; 33/23.08
952 Norway, Oscar I; AR speciedaler, 1856; 37/28.94
953 Norway; AR 2-kroner, 1914; 29/15.01
954 Sweden; AU 20-kronor, 1878; 23/8.97
955 Sweden, Charles XV; Cu 5-ore, 1861; 28/8.85
956 Sweden; AR rigsdaler, 1827; 24/8.47
957 Sweden, Gustav V; AR 5-kronor, 1935; 39/24.96
958 Sweden, Charles XIV; AR rigsdaler, 1827; 36/29.22
959 Sweden, Charles XIV; Cu 2-skilling, 1836; 33/19.13
960 Denmark, Christian VIII; AR speciedaler, 1840; 36/28.94
961 Denmark, Christian IX; AU 10-kroner, 1873; 18/4.48
962 Finland, AR 10-markaa, 1967; 35/24.06
963 Finland, AR 10-markaa, 1970; 35/22.33
964 Russia, Soviet Union; AR rouble, 1924; 34/19.98
965 Russia, Nicholas I; AR 1½-rouble, 1836; 40/30.91
966 Russia, Nicholas I; platinum 12-roubles, 1843; 36/41.38
967 Russia, Nicholas II; AR rouble, 1907; 34/20.00
968 Russia, Nicholas I; AE 10-kopeks, 1836; 43/45.51
969 Russia, Alexander I; AR pattern rouble, 1804; 41/30.07
970 Russia, Nicholas I; AR 1½-roubles, 1839; 40/31.06
971 Russia, Alexander II; AU 5-roubles, 1855; 23/6.56
972 Poland; AR 5-zloty, 1831; 31/15.48
973 Poland, Alexander I; AR 5-zloty, 1834; 31/15.48
974 Poland; Fe 20-fenigow, 1917; 22/3.92
975 Poland; CuNi 10-zloty, 1968; 27/9.46
976 Danzig; AU 25-gulden, 1923; 44/7.99
977 Estonia; kroon, 1934; 25/5.87
978 Latvia; AE santing, 1935; 17/1.81
979 Lithuania; AR 5-litai, 1925; 28/13.49
980 Czechoslovakia; AR 10-korun, 1937; 39/11.98
981 Czechoslovakia; AE koruna, 1970; 23/4.15
982 Hungary, Ferdinand I; AR thaler, 1837; 37/28.06
983 Hungary; AE 3-kreuzer, 1849; 32/25.80
984 Hungary, Francis Joseph; AR forint, 1884; 29/12.34
985 Hungary, Horthy; AR pengo, 1930; 35/25.05
986 Hungary; AR 20-forint, 1956; 32/17.61
987 Austria, Francis I; AE kreuzer, 1816; 26/8.73
988 Austria, Francis I; AR ½-thaler, 1834; 33/14.03
989 Austria; AR thaler, 1868; 36/16.89
990 Austria; AR 2-thaler, 1857; 41/37.04
991 Austria, Francis Joseph; AU 100-corona, 1908; 37/33.86
992 Austria, Republic; AU 100-schilling, 1926; 32/23.52
993 Austria, Republic; AR 2-schilling, 1928; 28/12.08
994 Gurk, Austria; AR thaler, 1801; 40/28.10
995 Westphalia, Jerome; AR 5-franken, 1808; 37/25.00
996 Hanover; AR thaler, 1830; 35/23.43
997 Hanover, William IV; AR 2/3-thaler, 1834; 32/13.07
998 Baden; AR kronenthaler, 1832; 39/29.50
999 Bavaria, Ludwig I; AR thaler, 1832; 38/28.06
1000 Bavaria; AR 2-thaler, 1839; 38/31.09
1001 Frankfurt; AR gulden, 1838; 30/10.61
1002 Frankfurt; AR 2-thaler, 1866; 40/37.00
1003 Frankfurt; Bill 6-kreuzer, 1853; 20/2.60
1004 Hamburg; AU ducat, 1867; 21/3.48
1005 Prussia; AR 2-thaler, 1840; 41/37.12
1006 Saxony; AR 2-thaler, 1858; 41/37.00
1007 Saxony; AR thaler, 1871; 33/18.50
1008 Anhalt, Friedrich; AU 20-mark, 1875; 11/7.96
1009 Bavaria; pattern 3-marks, 1913; 33/12.94
1010 Prussia, William II; AU 20-marks, 1896; 22/7.96
1011 Prussia, William II; AR 5-marks, 1901; 38/27.77
1012 Prussia, William II; AR 3-marks, 1913; 33/16.67
1013 Saxe-Meiningen; AR 5-marks, 1902; 38/27.76
1014 Saxe-Weimar; AR 5-marks, 1908; 38/27.81
1015 German East Africa; AE 20-heller, 1916; 29/11.55
1016 German East Africa (Tanganyika); AR rupee, 1890; 30/11.62
1017 German New Guinea; AR 5-marks, 1894; 37/27.75
1018 Germany; Al 200-marks, 1923; 23/1.00
1019 Germany; AE 10-pfennigs, 1937; 21/3.98
1020 Saarland; AE 20-franken, 1954; 23/4.04
1021 Germany; AR 10-marks, 1972; 33/15.37
1022 Germany; silvered AE 1 billion-mark, 1923; 62/81.26
1023 Netherlands, Louis Napoleon; AU 20-gulden, 1810; 26/13.64
1024 Netherlands, Wilhelm I; AU 10-gulden, 1820; 22/6.72
1025 Netherlands, Wilhelm III; AR gulden (proof), 1867; 27/10.00
1026 Netherlands, Wilhelmina; AU gulden, 1897; 22/6.72
1027 Netherlands, Juliana; AR 2½-gulden, 1964; 33/15.02
1028 Belgium, Leopold I; AR 5-francs, 1835; 37/25.04
1029 Antwerp; AE 10-centimes, 1814; 35/26.02
1030 Belgium, Leopold II; AR 5-francs, 1880; 37/25.02
1031 Congo, Leopold II; AR 2-francs, 1887; 27/10.02
1032 Belgium; 25-centimes, 1918; 26/6.48
1033 Belgium; AR 50-francs, 1958; 30/12.46
1034 France, Napoleon; AR 5-francs, 1803; 37/24.95
1035 France, Napoleon; AU 5-francs, (proof), 1807; 37/42.45
1036 France, Louis XVIII; AR 5-francs, 1815; 37/24.96
1037 France, 2nd Republic; AR 5-francs, 1848; 37/25.01
1038 France, 2nd Republic; AR 5-francs, 1849; 37/25.02
1039 France, Napoleon IV; AR 5-francs, 1874; 38/25.43
1040 France, Republic; AR 2-francs, 1902; 26/10.02

1041 France, Republic; Al-AE 2-francs token, 1922; 26/8.21
1042 France, Republic; Bill pattern, 1897; 25/4.90
1043 France, Republic; AU 20-francs, 1874; 20/6.45
1044 France, Republic; CuNi 100-francs, 1954; 23/6.00
1045 Algeria; Al 10-centimes, 1922; 25/1.69
1046 Madagascar; Al 2-francs, 1948; 27/2.18
1047 Tunisia; AU 20-francs, 1900; 42/6.42
1048 Comoro Islands; AR 5-francs, 1890; 37/25.00
1049 Helvetian Republic; AR 4-francs, 1799; 40/32.98
1050 Appenzell, Switzerland; AR 4-francs, 1816; 39/29.04
1051 Geneva, Switzerland; AR 5-francs, 1848; 37/26.05
1052 Switzerland; AR 5-francs, 1850; 36/25.05
1053 Switzerland; AU 20-francs, 1894; 21/6.44
1054 Switzerland; AR 5-francs, 1925; 37/25.00
1055 Switzerland; AR 5-francs, 1881; 37/24.96
1056 Switzerland; AR 2-francs, 1959; 27/10.00
1057 Italy, Napoleon; AU doppia, 1803; 28/12.16
1058 Cisalpine Republic; AR 30-soldi, 1801; 30/7.35
1059 Subalpine Republic; AU 20-francs, 1810; 27/6.42
1060 Cisalpine Republic; AR scudo, 1800; 39/23.10
1061 Ligurian Republic; AU 96-lire, 1805; 33/25.22
1062 Milan; AU 40-lire, 1848; 26/12.91
1063 Venice, Ferdinand I; AR scudo, 1840; 19/25.96
1064 Lucca; AR lira, 1838; 27/5.18
1065 Lucca; AE 5-centesimi, 1806; 28/9.15
1066 Naples and Sicily; AR 12-carlini, 1810; 37/27.58
1067 Sardinia; AR 5-lire, 1820; 37/24.96
1068 Papal States, Leo XIII; AR 5-lire, 1878; 36/26.12
1069 Italy, Umberto I; AU 100-lire, 1880; 35/32.23
1070 Italy, Victor Emanuel II; AR 5-lire, 1861; 36/24.98
1071 Italy, Victor Emanuel III; AR 20-lire, 1928; 35/19.92
1072 Eritrea; AR 5-lire, Ad 1891; 40/28.08
1073 Montenegro, Nicholas I; AU 100-perpera, 1910; 37/33.87
1074 Serbia; CuNi 10-para, 1884; 20/4.06
1075 Yugoslavia, Alexander I; AU 20-dinara, 1925; 21/6.45
1076 Yugoslavia, Republic; Al-AE 10-dinara, 1955; 21/3.00
1077 Albania; AR 2-franka ari, 1926; 27/9.98
1078 Bulgaria; AU 100-leva, 1894; 34/32.37
1079 Bulgaria; AR 50-leva, 1934; 27/9.98
1080 Bulgaria, Republic; AR 5-leva, 1970; 35/20.44
1081 Romania, Carol I; AU 20-lei, 1890; 20/6.42
1082 Romania, Marie; AU 50-lei, 1922; 39/16.13
1083 Greece, Republic; AE 10-lepta, 1828; 35/17.08
1084 Greece, Otto; AR 5-drachmae, 1833; 37/22.34
1085 Greece, Republic; AR 20-drachmae, 1930; 28/11.32
1086 Greece, Constantine; CuNi 5-drachmae, 1971; 28/8.95
1087 Ionian Islands; AE tazeta, 1801; 25/5.00
1088 Crete; AR 5-drachmae, 1901; 37/24.98
1089 Cyprus, Victoria; AR 18-piastres, 1901; 30/11.32
1090 Spain, Joseph Napoleon; AU 320-reales, 1810; 35/26.81
1091 Barcelona; AR 5-pesetas, 1813; 40/26.92
1092 Spain, Ferdinand VII; AR duro, 1808; 40/26.95
1093 Valencia; AR 4-reales, 1823; 26/5.68
1094 Spain, Isabel II; AR 20-reales, 1850; 37/26.02
1095 Cartagena, Spain; AR 5-pesetas, 1873; 37/28.72
1096 Spain, Charles VII; AR 5-pesetas, 1874; 37/24.33
1097 Spain, Alfonso XIII; AU 20-pesetas, 1892; 34/32.20
1098 Port Phillip, Australia; AU ounce, 1853; 28/31.15
1099 Spain, Isabel II; AR 5-pesetas, 1894; 35/20.06
1100 Spain, Republic; AR peseta, 1933; 23/4.98
1101 Spain, Republic; CuNi 25-pesetas, 1959; 26/8.48
1102 Spain, Juan Carlos; CuNi 5-pesetas, 1975; 23/5.62
1103 Portugal, John; AU pesa, 1806; 32/14.33
1104 Portugal, Pedro IV; AU pesa, 1826; 32/14.31
1105 Portugal, Carlos I; AR 1000-reis, 1898; 37/24.93
1106 Portugal, Republic; AR 10-escudos, 1932; 30/12.50
1107 Terceira Island, Maria; AE 80-reis, 1829; 40/25.65
1108 Angola; Ni-AE 50-centavos, 1928; 30/10.49
1109 South Africa; AU pond, 1874; 27/8.00
1110 Ethiopia, Menelik; AR tallero, c.1899; 39/7.06
1111 Katanga; AU 5-francs, 1961; 25/13.30
1112 Brisbane, Australia; AE penny, c.1864; 33/13.51
1113 Australia; AR florin, 1910; 28/11.29
1114 Australia, Elizabeth II; CuNi 50-cents, 1970; 33/15.57

XIV Detail from 1117

1115 Mexico, AR 2-reales, c.1565; 28/6.78
1116 Lima, Peru; AU 8-escudos, 1713; 30/27.00
1117 Mexico; AR 8-reales, 1732; 39/27.13
1118 Mexico; AR 8-reales, 1787; 39/26.83; ANS
1119 Mexico, Ferdinand VI; AU 8-escudos, 1759; 37/26.99; ANS
1120 Mexico, Charles IV; AR medal, 1789; 39/26.86
1121 Chilpaneingo, Mexico; AR 8-reales, c.1813; 39/25.25; ANS
1122 Mexico; AR 8-reales, 1824; 39/26.89; ANS
1123 Mexico; AR dollar, 1866; A 37/26.92; B 37/27.00
1124 Mexico; AR dollar, c.1870; 37/27.07; ANS
1125 Mexico; AE 'hacienda' token, 1842; 30/11.93; ANS
1126 Mexico; AR peso, 1914; 39/21.74; ANS
1127 Mexico; AR 100-pesos, 1977; 39/27.67
1128 Guatemala; AR 8-reales, 1839; 39/27.01; ANS
1129 Honduras; Bill 8-reales, 1857; 39/13.67; ANS
1130 Costa Rica; countermark (1846) on Guatemala AR 8-reales, 1737; 28 × 46/26.08; ANS
1131 Panama; AR 2½-centesimos, 1904; 9/1.23; ANS
1132 Guatemala; AE 5-pesos, 1923; 25/5.82
1133 Bolivia; AR 8-sueldos, 1840; 38/26.92; ANS
1134 Venezuela; AE centavo, 1843; 32/13.59; ANS
1135 Paraguay; AR 300-guaranies, 1968; 38/27.03; ANS
1136 Uruguay; AR 1000-pesos, 1969; 37/24.90; ANS
1137 Chile; Ni-Brass 100-escudos, 1974; 23/5.00; ANS
1138 Brazil, Alfonso VI; AR 600-reis, 1660; 37 × 39/25.79; ANS
1139 Brazil, João V; AU dobra, 1732; 37/28.49
1140 Brazil; AR 4000-reis, 1900; 50/51.19; ANS
1141 Bermuda; AE 6-pence, c.1616; 25/2.36; ANS
1142 Grenada; AR 4-bitts, 1814; 20 × 33/8.43; ANS
1143 Haiti; AE 2-centimes, 1832; 26/6.62; ANS
1144 British Virgin Islands, Elizabeth II; CuNi 50-cents, 1973; 32/4.58
1145 Massachusetts; AR shilling, 1652; A 29/4.22; B 29/4.73
1146 Continental Congress; AR dollar, 1776; 38/17.45
1147 Vermont; AE cent, 1788; 27/7.15; ANS
1148 United States; AE cent, 1793; 27/13.86; ANS
1149 United States; AR ½-dollar A 1861; 30/12.44; B 1863; 30/12.43
1150 Utah; AU 5-dollars, 1860; 23/7.54; ANS
1151 New Orleans; AR ½-dollar, 1861; 30/12.41; ANS
1152 United States; AR dollar, 1878; 38/26.73; ANS
1153 United States; AU 20-dollars, 1907; 34/33.43; ANS
1154 United States; AE cent, 1909; A 19/3.12; B 19/3.07
1155 United States; AR ½-dollar, 1920; 30/12.45; ANS
1156 United States; AR ½-dollar, 1964; 30/12.48; ANS
1157 United States; CuNi dollar, 1979; 26/8.09; ANS
1158 Canada, Louis XIV; AR 5-sols, 1670; 21/2.29; ANS
1159 Montreal, Canada; AE sou, 1857; 27/6.34; ANS
1160 Canada; AR 50-cents, 1908; 30/11.63; ANS
1161 Canada; tombac 5-cents, 1943; 20/4.54; ANS
1162 Canada; AR 10-dollars, 1974; 45/48.39; ANS

XV Detail from 1163

1163 New Jersey, United States; 6-pounds, 1776; 112 × 61
1164 Poland; 10 zloty, 1794; 180 × 96
1165 Denmark, Bank of Copenhagen; riksdaler, 1791; 158 × 103
1166 France; 90 livres assignat, 1790; 192 × 119
1167 Great Britain, Pontefract Bank; 5-guineas, 1808; 184 × 85
1168 Great Britain; 'skit note' 2-pence, 1805; 190 × 94
1169 Philadelphia, Bank of North America; 5-cents, 1815; 100 × 70
1170 Great Britain; Congreve duty stamp 5-pence, 1821; 191 × 100
1171 Great Britain, Robert Owen; labour note 6-pence, 1832; 210 × 112
1172 Italy; 5-franchi, 1849; 208 × 99
1173 Mafeking, South Africa; 10-shillings, 1900; 161 × 118
1174 Great Britain; pound, 1914; 150 × 84
1175 Germany, Reichsbank; 20-marks, 1915; 141 × 90
1176 Germany, Cologne; 10-pfennigs, 1920; 88 × 47
1177 Germany, Cologne; 200 million-marks, 1923; 138 × 89
1178 Russia; 250-roubles, 1917; 175 × 105
1179 Jersey; shilling, c.1943; 105 × 68
1180 Northern Greece; 25-oka, 1944; 133 × 74
1181 Sweden, Riksbank; 10-kroner, 1968; 120 × 68
1182 Great Britain; Access card, 1980; 85 × 54

XVI Detail from 1188

1183 Parthia, Arsaces II: AR drachma, c.211-190 BC; 18/4.06; Sell
1184 Parthia, Mithradates I; AR tetradrachm, c.140 BC; 26/15.95
1185 Parthia, Phraates II; AR drachma, 138-27 BC; 18/3.74; Sell
1186 Parthia, Artabanus I; AR drachma, c.125 BC; 20/4.03; Sell
1187 Parthia, Mithradates II; AR drachma, c.100 BC; 22/4.10; Sell
1188 Parthia; AR tetradrachm, c.75 BC; 31/15.33; Sell
1189 Parthia; AR drachma, c.75 BC; 21/4.10; Sell
1190 Parthia, Darius (?); AR drachma, c.70 BC; 21/4.21; Sell
1191 Parthia, Orodes II; AR drachma, c.40 BC; 22/3.91; Sell
1192 Parthia, Vonones I; AR drachma, AD 10; 21/3.93; Sell
1193 Parthia, Vologases II; AR drachma, c.AD 78; 21/3.41; Sell
1194 Parthia, Osroes I; AR drachma, c.AD 110; 20/3.81; Sell
1195 Parthia, Mithradates IV; AR drachma, c.AD 140; 20/3.75; Sell
1196 Parthia, Vologases IV; AR tetradrachm, AD 182; 23/13.60; Sell
1197 Parthia, Artabanus IV; AR drachma, AD 216-24; 17/3.60; Sell
1198 Indo-Parthians, Sanabares; AE 'drachma', 1st cent. AD; 16/3.67; Sell
1199-1200 Indo-Parthians, Ontanes; AR drachma, c.AD 75; 20/2.57; Sell
1201 Persis, Autophradates; AR tetradrachm, c.200 BC; 26/17.08
1202 Persis, Darius; AR drachma, c.120 BC; 16/4.24; Sell
1203 Persis, Manuchir I; AR drachma, c.AD 150; 20/3.10
1204 Sassanians, Ardashir I; AR drachma, c.AD 210; 22/3.51
1205 Sassanians, Ardashir I; AU dinar, c.AD 210; 21/8.49
1206 Sassanians, Ardashir I; AR drachma, c.AD 240; 25/4.28
1207 Sassanians, Shapur I; AR drachma, AD 241-72; 26/4.28
1208-09 Sassanians, Bahram II; AR drachma, AD 276-93; 26/4.02
1210 Sassanians, Shapur II; AR obol, AD 309-79; 12/0.66
1211 Sassanians, Bahram V; AR drachma, AD 420-38; 30/4.10
1212-13 Sassanians, Balash; AR drachma, AD 484-88; 28/4.11; Sell
1214-15 Sassanians, Khusru I; AU dinar, AD 574; 19/4.43; Sell
1216-17 Sassanians, Khusru II; AR drachma, AD 618; 31/4.16
1218 Sassanians, Boran; AR drachma, AD 630; 30/3.10; Sell
1219 Elymais, Kamnaskires (II?); AR tetradrachm, 79 BC; 27/15.69
1220 Elymais, Kamnaskires (III?); AE tetradrachm, 1st cent. BC; 28/15.39
1221 Elymais, Orodes; AE drachma, c.AD 80; 15/3.50; Sell
1222 Characene, Tiraios II; AR tetradrachm, c.AD 60; 29/13.62
1223 Characene, Attambelos I; AR tetradrachm, 41 BC; 29/13.62
1224 Characene, Maga; AE tetradrachm, c.AD 200; 26/16.27
1225 Nabatea, Obodas III; AR, c.20 BC; 18/6.56
1226 Nabatea, Aretas IV; AR, c.20 AD; 15/4.51
1227 Nabatea, Rabbel II; AR, AD 70-106; 14/7.36
1228-29 Sabeans; AR, 3rd cent. BC; 18/5.39
1230 Himyarites; AR, c.AD 50; A 26/5.41; B 27/5.56
1231 Himyarites; AR, 2nd cent. AD; A 23/1.89; B 21/1.29
1232 Axum, Ezanas; AU, c.AD 325; 17/1.44

XVII Detail from 1272

1233 Arab-Sassanian; AR drachma; 32/4.06
1234 Arab-Byzantine; AE fals; A 20/3.04; B 25/2.93
1235 Arab-Byzantine; AU solidus; 13/4.32
1236 Umayyad, Abd al-Malik; AU dinar, AD 697-98; 19/4.28
1237 Wasit, Umayyad; AR dirham, AD 726-27; 27/2.86
1238 Umayyad; AE fals; A 18/7.25; B 19/6.63
1239 Abbasid; AU dinar, AD 772-73; 19/4.09
1240 Abbasid; AR dirham, AD 763-64; 25/2.88
1241 Tabaristan, Abbasid Governors; AR ½-drachma, AD 738-39; A 23/1.81; B 24/1.76
1242 Ma'adam al Shash, Harun al-Rashid; AR dirham, AD 805-06; 25/2.88
1243 Samarqand, al-Mustamid; AU dinar, AD 884-85; 20/2.91
1244 Samarra, al Muqtadir; AR dirham, AD 913-14; 26/2.98
1245 Hamadan, Abbasid; AE fals, AD 765-66; 25/6.29
1246 Spain, Umayyad; AR dirham, AD 806-07; 26/2.73
1247 Spain, Abd al-Rahman III; AU ¼-dinar, AD 929-30; 13/0.97
1248 Morocco, Idris II; AR dirham, AD 812-13; 22/2.23
1249 Aghlabid, Ibrahim II; AU dinar, AD 895-96; 19/2.17
1250 Aghlabid, Ibrahim II; AU ¼-dinar, AD 885-86; 13/1.06
1251 al-Qayrawan, Fatimid; AU dinar, AD 913-14; 18/3.99
1252 Misr, al-Mu-izz; AU dinar, AD 968-69; 23/4.18
1253A al-Mansuriyah; AR ½-dirham, AD 955-56; 19/1.50
1253B top Fatimid; AR ⅛-dirham, c.AD 960; 14/0.38;
1253B bottom Fatimid; AR 1/16-dirham, c.AD 960; 11/0.20
1254 al-Mustansir, Fatimid; glass-weight 2-dirhams; 27/5.96
1255 Sicily, al-Mustansir, Fatimid; AU ¼-dinar, 1054-55; 14/0.89
1256 Aden, al-Sayyid; AU dinar, 1116-17, 22/2.37
1257 Crusader imitation; AU dinar, c.1125; 22/3.85
1258 Andabah; AR dirham, AD 978-79; 43/8.27
1259 Ghazna, Mahmud; AR dirham, 1004-05; 19/3.12
1260 Sughd, Qarakhanid; Bill dirham, c.1010; 26/2.20
1261 Seljuq, Tughril Beg; AU dinar, 1057-58; 20/4.02
1262 Seljuqs of Syria, Ridwan bin Tutush; AE fals, c.1105; 22/3.15
1263A Artuqids; countermarked 'shams' on Byzantine AE Anon Class C follis, 12th cent. AD; 28/7.59
1263B Artuqids; AE fals, 1152-76; 32/14.93
1264A Singjar, Zangid, Imad al-Din Zangi; AE, 1188-89; 22/7.87
1264B al-Mosul, Zangid, 'Izz al-Din Mas'ud; AE, 1189-90; 27/7.87
1265 Jezira, Mu'izz al-Din Sinjar Shah; AE, 1203-04; 35/33.45
1266 Seljuqs of Rum, Mas'ud I; AE, 1116-56; 20/3.30
1267 Kaysariyah, Seljuqs of Rum, Sulayman II; AR, 1203-04; 23/2.81
1268 Qonya, Seljuqs of Rum, Kay Qubad I; AR dirham, 1221-22; 23/2.91
1269 Armenia, Hethoun I; AR dirham, 1226-36; 22/2.80
1270 Seljuqs of Rum, Kay Qubad I; AE, 1219-36; 20/2.65
1271 Sivas, Seljuqs of Rum, Kay-Khusru II; AR dirham, 1242-43; 21/2.90
1272 Sivas, Seljuqs of Rum, Qilij Arslan IV; AR dirham, 1248-49; 22/2.75
1273 Sivas, Seljuqs of Rum, '3 brothers'; AR, 1256-57; 20/2.60
1274 Ma'dan Baibirt, Mas'ud II; AR, 1288-89; 25/2.97
1275 Madinal al-Salam, Abbasid, al-Musta'sim; AU dinar, 1245-46; 28/8.55
1276 Hamah, Ayyubid, Salah al-Din Yusuf; AR dirham, 1186-87; 21/2.74
1277A Damascus, Ayyubid, al-'Adil; AR dirham, 1208-09; 20/2.99
1277B Aleppo, Ayyubid, al-'Aziz; AR dirham; 1220-21; 20/2.99
1278 Crusader imitation; AR, c.1250; 21/3.10
1279 Alexandria, Ayyubid, al-Kamil; AU dinar, 1225-26; 23/7.41
1280 Zabid, Yemen, al-Afdal; AR dirham, 1372-73; 25/1.82
1281 Alexandria, Mamluk, Barsbay; AU dinar, 1267-68; 23/7.42
1282 Cairo, Mamluk, Qala'un; AR dirham, c.1285; 19/3.39
1283 Burgi Mamluks, Barsbay; AR ¾-dirham, 1422-38; 16/2.29
1284 Cairo, Mamluk, Barsbay; AU sequin, 1425-26; 29/3.38
1285A Damascus, Bahri Mamluks, Abu Bakr; AE; 19/3.31
1285B Burji Mamluks, Temirbugha; AE, 1467-68; 19/5.08
1286 Ghengiz Khan; AR, c.1210; 15/3.07
1287 Tiflis, Turazina; AR, 1244-45; 18/2.75
1288 Mosul, Hulagu; AR dirham, 1270-71; 27/2.59
1289 Irbil, Hulagu; AE, 1262-63; 26/7.07
1290 Tabriz, Arghun; AR, 1285-86; 20/2.20
1291 Tiflis, Arghun and Dimitri II; AR, 1273-89; 21/2.11
1292 Shiraz, Ghazan Mahmud; AU 2-dinars, 1298-99; 26/8.65
1293 Jurjan, Abu Sa'id; AR, 1317-18; 28/11.60
1294 Baibirt, Abu Sa'id; AR, 1331-32; 16/1.76
1295 Mukhshi, Uzbegs (Golden Horde); AR, 1318-19; 16/1.76
1296 Crimea, Hajj Giray; AR aqche, 1454-55; 13/0.69
1297 Crimea, Krim Giray; AR, 1758-59; 19/1.08
1298 Sebsevar, Sarbadarid; AR, 1369-70; 25/4.29
1299 Baghdad, Ahmad; AU, 1386-87; 21/7.72
1300 Samnan, Timur (Tamerlane); AR 8-dirhams, 1388-1402; 26/6.01
1301 Sebsevar, Shah Rukh; AR tankah, 1424-25; 21/5.06
1302 Herat, Husayn Bayqara; AR tankah, 1491-92; 24/5.17
1303 Aq Qoyunlu, Ya'qub; AR tankah, 1486-87; 20/5.15
1304 Zirids; AR, c.1060; 16/1.55
1305 Seville, Yusuf bin Tashfin; AU dinar, 1094-95; 27/4.14
1306 Cordova, Ali bin Yusuf; AR qirat, 1111-12; 12/0.93
1307 Marrakesh, Almohad; AR dirham; 14/1.50
1308 Sijilmasah, Almohad; AU 2-dinars, c.1250; 30/4.55
1309 Fez, Mohammad es Sa'id; AU dinar, c.1372-73; 23/2.31
1310 Fez, Filali Sharifs, Mohammad; AU dinar, 1775-76; 24/2.99 (pierced)
1311 Fez, Filali Sharifs; AE 3-fulus, 1869; 27/10.09
1312 Amirs of Saru Khan, Ishaq bin Ilyas; AR aqche, 1374-75; 14/0.74
1313 Ottomans, Bayazid I; AR aqche, 1389-90; 12/1.17
1314 Ottomans, Emir Suleyman; AR aqche, 1403-04; 14/1.16

1315 Ottomans, Mehmet I; AR aqche, 1419-20; 12/1.08
1316 Constantinople, Suleyman I; AE manghir, 1546-47; 15/1.60
1317 Constantinople, Mehmet II; AU altun, 1478-79; 19/3.51
1318 Baghdad, Suleyman II; AR dirham, 1519-20; 20/3.70
1319 Aleppo, Mehmet III; AR dirham, 1594-95; 22/2.51
1320 Constantinople, Suleyman II; AR gurush, 1687-88; 31/9.33
1321 Constantinople, Mahmud I; AU 6-altuns, 1730-31; 44/15.79
1322 Constantinople, Ahmed III; AR aqche, 1703-04; 10/0.16
1323A Algiers, Mahmud I; AU ½-altun, 1734-35; 18/3.50
1323B Tunis, Mahmud I; AR 10-para, 1737-38; 24/5.91
1324 Constantinople, Mustafa III; AU altun, 1759-60; 18/3.50
1325 Misr, Ali Bey; AR 20-para, 1771-72; 29/6.78
1326 Sari, Safavids; AR tankah, c.1501; 16/3.59
1327 Ardabil, Isma'il I; AR shahi, 1519-20; 24/9.24
1328A Asterabad, Isma'il I; AR shahi, c.1520; 24/9.24
1328B Mashhad, Isma'il I; AR ½-shahi, c.1518; 26/5.12
1329 Kirman, Tahmasp I; AU ¼-ashrafi, 1552-53; 10/1.16
1330 Shamakhi, Shirvan Shahs; AR aqche, 1531-32; 12/0.67
1331 Asfarayin, Kochkunji; AR tankah, c.1523; 22/3.30
1332 Isfahan, Safi I; AR 2½-shahi, 1630-31; 20/7.67
1333 Isfahan, Hussayn; AR 4-shahi, 1703-04; 39/17.37
1334 Isfahan, Hussayn; AR 5-shahi, 1714-15; 29/3.63
1335 Huwayza, Abbas II; AR 2-shahi, 1660-61; 19/3.71
1336 Isfahan, Tahmasp I; AR larin, 16th cent. AD; 61/4.89
1337 Ashfaris, Nadir; AR 2-shahi, 1735-36; 18/2.71
1338 Sind, Nadir; AR 10-shahi, 1740-41; 21/11.50
1339 Isfahan, Karim Khan; AU mohur-ashrafi, 1753-54; 23/10.96
1340 Abushahr; AE fals, c.1800; 21/6.49

XVIII Obverse of 1363

1341 North India; AR bent bar, 5th or 4th cent.BC; 27/11.46
1342 North India; AR ½-siglos, 5th or 4th cent.BC; 15/2.81
1343 North India; AR karshapana, 4th cent.BC; 19/3.42
1344 North India; AE, 3rd cent.BC; 27/4.56
1345 North India; AE, late 4th cent.BC; 27/15.44
1346 Taxila; AE, early 2nd cent.BC; 24/6.92
1347 Taxila; AE, early 2nd cent.BC; 38 × 35/13.22
1348 Ujjain; AE, 3rd cent.BC; 19/7.58
1349 Kuninda, Amoghabuti; AR drachma, 1st cent.BC; 17/2.20
1350 Bactria, Pantaleon; AE, c.175 BC; 21/12.55
1351 Bactria, Apollodotus I; AR drachma, c.170 BC; 16/2.42
1352 Bactria, Eucratides; AE, c.150 BC; 22/7.62
1353 Bactria, Antialcidas; AE c.125 BC; 19/8.95
1354 Bactria, Hermaeus; AR tetradrachm, 1st cent.BC; 24/9.72
1355 Sagala, Strato; AR drachma, 1st cent.BC; 17/2.48
1356 Indo-Scythians, Azes I; AR tetradrachm, c.50 BC; 26/9.46
1357 Taxila, Azes II; AR tetradrachm, c.25 BC; 25/9.30
1358 Gandhara, Azes II; AE, c.25 BC; 30/13.69
1359 Mathura, Rajuvula; AR drachma, c.AD 15; 14/2.46
1360 Kandahar, Spalirises; AE, c.50 BC; 22/8.12
1361 Arachosia, Gondophares; Bill tetradrachm, c.AD 40; 24/9.45
1362 Kushan, Vima Kadphises; AU 2-dinars, c.AD 100; 15.81
1363 Kushano-Sassanians, Varahan II; AU dinar, c.AD 325; 32/7.81
1364 Arachosia, Gondophares; AE tetradrachm, c.AD 40; 23/9.50
1365 Kandahar, Pacores; AE tetradrachm, 2nd cent. AD; 23/7.93
1366 Kushan, Kujula Kadphises; AE tetradrachm, 1st cent.AD; 18/7.76
1367 Kushan, Kujula Kadphises; AE, 1st cent.AD; 18/3.36
1368 Kushan, Soter Megas; AE didrachm, c.AD 75; 19/3.06
1369 Kushan, Vima Kadphises; AE tetradrachm, c.AD 100; 27/16.80
1370 Kushan, Kanishka; AE tetradrachm, c.AD 125; 26/16.80
1371 Kushan, Kanishka; AU dinar, c.AD 125; 20/7.04
1372 Kushan, Huvishka; AE tetradrachm, c.AD 175; 25/9.56
1373 Puri; AE, 3rd cent.AD 23/8.56
1374 Yaudheya; AE, c.200 AD; 24/10.41
1375 Indus Valley, Vasu Deva; AE, 3rd cent.AD; 23/8.60
1376 Kushno-Sassanians, Shapur II; AE, c.AD 360; 18/4.26
1377 Andhras, Gautimaputra; Pb, c.AD 12[illegible]; 30/10.73
1378 Surastra, Damasena; AR drachma, AD 223-36; 15/2.44
1379 Fyzabad, Chandra Gupta II; AU dinar, c.AD 400; 14/7.84

XIX Detail from 1403

1380 White Huns, Mihirakula; AR, AD 500-28; 26/3.51
1381 Kanauj, Bhoja Deva; AR, AD 840-90; 20/4.20
1382 Nepal; AE, 7th cent.AD; 22/8.44
1383 Ohind, Samanta Deva; AR shahi, 9th cent.AD; 19/2.92
1384 East Bengal, Chandra Kings; AR, 10th cent.AD; 44/3.46
1385 Ceylon, Lilavati; AE massa, c.1200; 2[illegible]/4.13
1386 Lahore, Mahmud; AR dirham, 1028; [illegible]8/2.78
1387 Ghorids, Muhammed bin Sam; AU, 1[illegible]93; 15/4.20
1388 Eastern Chalukaya, Raja Raja; AU; 3[illegible]/4.32
1389 Delhi, Alauddin; AR tankah, c.1300; 2[illegible]/10.76
1390 Delhi, Muhammad Tughlaq; AU dinar, 1325-26; 23/12.82
1391 Vijanagar, Krishnaraya; AU, c.1520; [illegible]/7.75
1392 Kandahar, Moghuls, Babur; AR shahrukhi, 1526-27; 23/4.63
1393 Satgaon, Sher Shah; AR rupee, 1543-44; 27/11.40
1394 Goa, João III; AU San Thomé, 1521-[illegible]7; 19/3.22
1395 Agra, Akbar; AR rupee, 1605; 25/11.[illegible]
1396 Agra, Jahangir; AU mohur, 1605; 22/[illegible].85
1397 Agra, Jahangir; AR rupee, 1609; 20/1[illegible].[illegible]7
1398 Agra, Jahangir; AU mohur, 1618-28; [illegible]1/10.92
1399 Agra, Jahangir; AU mohur, 1618-28; [illegible]1/10.88
1400 Agra, Jahangir; AU mohur, 1618-28; [illegible]0/10.90
1401 Tripura, Vijaya Manikya; AR rupee, [illegible]560; 23/10.56; Rhod.
1402 Cooch Behar, Nara Narayan; AR tankah, 1555-57; 15/9.60
1403 Moghul, Shah Jahan; AU 200-mohur 1653-54; 137/2200
1404 Nepal; AR jawa, c.1740; 4/0.01
1405 Nepal; AR ¼-jawa, c.1740; 1/0.002
1406 Nepal, Ranajit Malla; AR mohur, 172[illegible]-59; 31/5.44
1407 Assam, Supungmung; AR rupee, 1663-70; 22/11.18
1408 Bombay, Charles II; AR rupee, 1678; [illegible]/11.79
1409 Bombay, Shah Jahan II; AR rupee, 1[illegible]; 26/11.49
1410 Madras; AU 2-pagodas, 1808-15; 20/[illegible]5
1411 British India, Victoria; AR rupee, 18[illegible]; 30/11.64
1412 Jaipur, Isvari Singh; AR rupee, 1743-[illegible]0; 30/11.21
1413 Bharatpur, Victoria; AR rupee, 1858; [illegible]/11.13
1414 Jodhpur, Edward VII; AE ½-anna, 1[illegible]; 23/21.33
1415 India; Al 10-pice, 1973; 24/2.29

XX Prints from 'Scenes of the Coin Mint at Sendai, Rizuzen Province, Japan, 1728

1416 Drawings of Chinese characters
1417 China; AE hoe coin, 6th cent.BC; 97/[illegible]10
1418 China; AE hoe coin, late 4th cent.BC; [illegible]/4.95
1419 Drawings of hoe coins
1420 Drawings of knife coins
1421 China; AE knife coin, 4th cent.BC; 18[illegible]/[illegible]9.96
1422 China; AE cowry coin, 4th cent.BC; 1[illegible]/[illegible]2.56
1423 China; AU ingot, 4th cent.BC; (c. 280 gm)
1424 China, Yuan City; AE, c.250 BC; 43/[illegible]79
1425 China, Qin; AE ½-ounce, 221 BC; 32/[illegible]33
1426 China, Han; AE 5-grain, 118 BC; 26/[illegible]5
1427 China, northern Wei; AE 5-grain, AD 5[illegible]9; 23/2.68
1428 China, coin mould; AE 1st cent.BC; 2[illegible]/[illegible]94
1429 China, northern Zhou; AE 500 standard 'cash', AD 579; 30/4.28
1430 China, Sui; AE 5-grain, AD 589; 23/2.3[illegible]
1431 China, Tang; AE 'cash', AD 621; 25/[illegible]
1432 Rubbings of Xining coins
1433 China, Song; AE 2-'cash', 1072; 31/7.[illegible]
1434 China, Song; AE 10-'cash', 1107; 41/1[illegible].34
1435 China, Song; Fe, 1200; 24/5.08
1436 China, Song; AR 50-ounce ingot, 12th cent.AD; 20/60.60
1437 China, Jin; AE 10-'cash', 1204; 44/13.[illegible]
1438 China, Yuan; AE 10-'cash', 1310; 41/[illegible]90
1439 China, Yuan; note 2000-'cash', 1287-1[illegible]0; 293 × 222
1440 China, Ming; AE, 1408; 25/3.23
1441 Rubbings of Kangxi coins
1442 China, Qing; AE, 1770; 25/4.75
1443 China, Qing; AE, 1853; 63/78.83
1444 China; AR 50-ounce ingot, 1767; 108/1870.00
1445 China Qing; note 10-ounce of silver, 1854; 316 × 178
1446 Guangdong; AR ingot, 1884; 56/385.00
1447 Guangzhou, Qing; AE 'cash', 1889; 24/3.47
1448 Mexico; AR 8-reales, 1758; 39/27.13
1449 Taiwan; AR dollar, c.1837; 40/26.68
1450 Japan; AR dollar, 1874; 38/27.50
1451 China, Zhejiang; AR ingot, 19th cent.; 27/26.84
1452 Guangzhou, Qing; AR dollar, 1889; 39/26.92
1453 Hubei; note dollar, 1899; 210 × 133
1454 Fujian, Qing; AE cent, 1901; 28/8.59
1455 China, Republic; AR dollar, 1914; 39/26.84
1456 China, Republic; AR dollar, 1934; 39/25.37
1457 China, Republic; Ni 20-cents, 1936; 24/5.88
1458 China, Republic; note 500,000 dollars, 1949; 146 × 62
1459 China, Republic; Al cent, 1956; 18/0.71
1460 Tibet; AR sho, 1793; 26/3.67
1461 Xinjiang; AR ½-ounce, 1905; 33/17.40
1462 Hongkong; AR dollar, 1866; 38/26.97
1463A Japan; AR, AD 708; 23/6.41
1463B Japan; AE, AD 708; 26/4.33
1464 Japan; AE 13th cent.; 24/2.70
1465 Japan; AU, 1593; 24/5.75
1466 Japan; AE, 1626; 25/3.16
1467 Rubbings of Japanese coins
1468 Japan, Tokugawa; Fe, 1866; 28/5.27
1469 Japan, Tokugawa; AU 10-ounce, 1860; 134/112.96
1470A Japan, Tokugawa; AR chogin, 1837; 88/123.61
1470B Japan, Tokugawa; AR ¼-ounce, 1837; 23/8.75
1471 Japan, Akita; AR, 1862; 80/34.32
1472 Japan, Hosokura; Pb token, 1862; 62/146.69
1473 Japan, Toyooka; note ounce of silver, 1766; 136 × 40
1474 Japan; AU 10-dollar, 1870 (1871); 32/16.39
1475 Japan; note 50-cent, 1872; 88 × 53
1476 Japan; AE 5-dollar, 1961; 22/3.74
1477 Korea, Koryo; AE, 1102; 24/3.16
1478 Korea, Yi; AE, 1423; 24/4.62
1479 Korea, Yi; AE, 1852; 24/6.24
1480 Korea, Koryo; AR 0.3-ounce, 1882; 34/11.02
1481 Korea, Koryo; AR dollar, 1892 (1894); 38/27.00
1482 Korea, Republic; Al cent, 1970; 16/0.72
1483 Vietnam, Dinh; AE, AD 978; 23/2.11
1484 Vietnam, unofficial; AE, 13th cent.; 21/1.50
1485 Vietnam; AE, 1454; 24/3.07
1486 Vietnam, Nguyen; AR ounce, 1824; 57/38.34
1487 Vietnam, Nguyen; AR dollar, 1833; 41/27.30
1488 Vietnam, Nguyen; Zinc, 1847; 23/2.31
1489 French Indochina; AR dollar, 1898; 39/27.31
1490 French Indochina; AE ⅕-cent, 1901; 20/1.96
1491 Vietnam, Nguyen; AE, 1916; 22/2.33
1492 Vietnam, Republic; CuNi 5-dollar, 1966; 24/4.04
1493 Pyu (Burma); AR, 8th cent.AD; 22/5.51
1494 Thailand; AR, 4-bat, 15th cent.AD; 41/62.90
1495 Thailand, Mongkut; AR 4-bat, 1851; 24/60.57
1496 Thailand, Mongkut; AR bat, 1860; 32/15.69
1497 Burma, Mindon Min; AR kyat, 1850 (1865); 31/11.90
1498 Cambodia, Angduong; AR tical, 1847; 30/15.50
1499 Thailand, Phumipol Adalyalet; CuNi bat, 1977; 25/7.06
1500 Java; AU, 13th cent.; 7/2.39
1501 Java, Aboul Ma'ali; Sn, c.1631; 24/1.62
1502 Patalung, Thailand; Sn ¼-cent, c.1880; 37/9.61
1503 Malacca, Manuel I; Sn bastardo, 1511; 35/35.51
1504 Pahang, Malaya; Sn, 1864; 74/108.60
1505 Philippines; AR dollar, 1829; 42/25.60
1506 Calcutta, British Imperial issue; AR dollar, 1895; 38/27
1507 Dutch East India Co., Dordrecht; AE doit, 1726; 23/3.23
1508 Dutch East India Co., Enkhuizen; AR guilder, 1802; 31/10.57
1509 Singapore; CuNi 10-cents, 1969; 19/2.81

Acknowledgements

Ashmolean Museum, Oxford 97; Miriam Balmuth 52, 56; Museo Nazionale, Rome 5; Royal Mint, London 1, 47, 944; Weidenfeld and Nicolson, London *frontispiece*.

The photographs of coins in the collection of the American Numismatic Society, New York were supplied by the Society.

The photographs of coins in the Fitzwilliam Museum, Cambridge including those from the collection of Philip Grierson were supplied by the Museum.

The remaining coins including those in the collections of John Porteous, Nicholas Rhodes, David Sellwood and in the British Museum were all photographed for the Hamlyn Group by Ray Gardner.

BIBLIOGRAPHY

An indispensable guide through the maze of numismatic literature is:
Philip Grierson, *Bibliographie Numismatique* (ed. 2, Brussels, 1979).

Bibliographic compilations are published regularly in the perodicals *Numismatic Literature* (the American Numismatic Society, New York, 1947/49–) and *Coin Hoards* (Royal Numismatic Society, London, 1975–).

It has also been the custom at recent International Numismatic Conferences to publish accounts of work published during the previous years:

A survey of Numismatic Research 1960–1965 (3 vols.) Copenhagen, 1967.
A survey of Numismatic Research 1966–1971 (3 vols.) New York, 1973.
A survey of Numismatic Research 1972–1977 Berne, 1979.

General books
R.A.G. Carson, *Coins: Ancient, medieval, and modern* (ed.2, London, 1970, also available in three parts).
P. Grierson, *Numismatics* (Oxford, 1975). Oxford University Press.
J. Porteous, *Coins in History* (London, 1968). Weidenfeld & Nicholson.
F.von Schrötter, *Wörterbuch der Münzkunde* (1930 repr. 1970).
A.R. Frey, *Dictionary of numismatic names* (New York, 1947). Sandford J. Durst.

Ancient coinage
B.V. Head, *Historia Numorum: A manual of Greek numismatics* (1911 repr. 1966). Zeno Publishers.
G.K. Jenkins, *Greek Coins* (London, 1972: also French and German editions) Barrie & Jenkins.
C.M. Kraay, *Archaic and Classical Greek Coins* (London, 1976). Methuen Inc.
D.R. Sear, *Greek Coins and their Values* (2 vols., London, 1978, 1979).
Y. Meshorer, *Jewish coins of the Second Temple period* (Tel-Aviv, 1967).
D.F. Allen, *The Coins of the Ancient Celts* (Edinburgh, 1979).
D. Nash, *Settlements and Coinage in Central Gaul c.200–50 BC* (Oxford, 1979). British Archaeology Reports.
R.P. Mack, *The Coinage of Ancient Britain* (ed.3, London, 1975). Seaby's Numismatic Publications Ltd.
R. Forrer, *Keltische Numismatik der Rhein- und Danaulande* (1908 repr. 1968).
M.H. Crawford, *The Coinage of the Roman Republic* (Cambridge, 1974). Cambridge University Press.
J.P.C. Kent, *Roman Coins* (London, 1978). Thames & Hudson.
H. Mattingly, et al., *The Roman Imperial Coinage* (11 vols. continuing). Spink & Son Ltd.
H. Mattingly and R.A.G. Carson, *The Coins of the Roman Empire in the British Museum* (6 vols. to AD 238). British Museum Publications Ltd.
R.A.G. Carson, *The Principal Coins of the Romans* (2 vols., 1978, 1980). British Museum Publications Ltd.
R.A.G. Carson, P.V. Hill, J.P.C. Kent, *Late Roman Bronze Coinage 324–498* (London, Spink & Son Ltd.).

Medieval and modern coinage
A.R. Bellinger and P. Grierson, *Catalogue of the Byzantine Coins in the Dumbarton Oaks Collection and in the Whittemore Collection* (3 vols., 1966–73).
P.D. Whitting, *Byzantine Coins* (London, 1973, also French and German editions). Barrie & Jenkins.
M.F. Hendy, *Coinage and money in the Byzantine empire 1081–1261* (Washington, 1969).
A. Engel and R. Serrure, *Traite de numismatique du moyen age* (3 vols. repr. Bologna 1964).
P. Grierson, *Monnaies au moyen age* (Fribourg, 1976, also German edition).
G. Schlumberger, *Numismatique de l'Orient latin* (repr. Graz, 1954).
D.M. Metcalf, *Coinage in South-Eastern Europe* (London, 1979).
G.C. Brooke, *English Coins* (ed.3, London, 1966). Spink & Son Ltd.
E.E. and V. Clain-Stefanelli, *Monnaies européennes et monnaies coloniales américaines entre 1450 et 1789* (Fribourg, 1978).
H.F. Burzio, *Diccionario de la moneda hispano-american* (Santiago, 1956–58).
T.V. Buttrey, *Coinage of the Americas* (New York, 1973). American Numismatic Society.
P. Vilar, *A history of gold and money 1450–1920* (London, 1976). New Left Books.
H. Rittmann, *Moderne Munzen* (Munich, 1974, also French edition by A. Dowle and A. Clermont, Fribourg, 1972).
W.D. Craig, *Coins of the World 1750–1850*, (ed.3, Racine, 1976). Wehman Brothers Inc.
C.L. Krause and C. Mishler, *Standard catalog of world coins 1800–1976* (ed.4, Iola, 1977). Krause Publications Inc.
F. Pridmore, *The coins of the British Commonwealth of Nations* (4 vols. 1960–75). Spink & Son Ltd.

Paper money
M. McKerchar, *A Papermoney Bibliography* (London, 1979).
A. Pick, *Standard Catalog of World Paper Money* (Iola, 1977). Krause Publications Inc.

Eastern coinage
D. Sellwood, *An introduction to the Coinage of Parthia* (London, 1971). Spink & Son Ltd.
R. Gobl, *Sassanian Numismatics* (Brunswick, 1971, also German edition).
S. Lane-Poole, *Oriental Coins in the British Museum* (Microfiche repr. OR/, 1980).
M. Mitchiner, *The world of Islam: Oriental coins and their values* (London, 1977).
M. Mitchiner, *The Ancient and Classical World 600BC–AD650* (London, 1978). Hawkins Publications.
A. Berman, *Islamic Coins* (Jerusalem, 1976).
I. and C. Artuk, *Istanbul Arkeoloji Muzeleri Teshirdeki Islami Sikkeler Kataloğu* (2 vols. Istanbul, 1971–1974).
P.L. Gupta, *Coins* (New Delhi, 1969).
M. Mitchiner, *Indo Greek and Indo-Scythian Coinage* (9 vols. 1975–76) Hawkins Publications.
B. Chattopadhaya, *Coins and Currency systems of South India AD 225–1300* (New Delhi, 1977).
J.H.S. Lockhart, *The Stewart Lockhart Collection of Chinese Copper Coins* (1915, repr. 1975).
Y.C. Wang, *Early Chinese Coinage* (New York, 1951).
L-S. Yang, *Money and Credit in China* (Cambridge, Mass., 1952).
C. Scholten, *The coins of the Dutch overseas territories, 1601–1948* (Amsterdam, 1953).

INDEX

Numbers in roman type refer to pages; numbers in *italics* refer to caption numbers.

Aachen *684, 687, 766*
'Abd al-Malik 259; *1236*
Abd al-Rahman III 261, *1247*
Abdera 33, 37; *107*
Aboul Ma'ali of Bantam *1501*
Abu Sa'id 267; *29, 1293, 1294, 1299*
Abushahr *1340*
Acanthus 37
Acragas *80, 87*
Acre 267; *1278*
Actium 69, 70, 71; *197, 297, 298*
Aden *1256*
Adrana 269
Aegina 27, 33; *71*
Aethelheard of Canterbury, Archbishop *642*
Aetolia *196*
Afghanistan 251, 265, 275, 279, 285, 287, 289; *1199, 1351, 1379*
Agathocles 57, 279
Agha Muhammad 275
Agrippa *359, 365*
Agrippina the Elder *366*
Agrippina the Younger *373, 375*
Aistulf 145; *648*
Akbar 289; *1395*
Akenaton *55*
Akkadia 21
Alamgir II *1412*
al-Amin *1257*
al-Andalus 261
Alauddin Muhammad Shah Khiliji *1389*
Albania *1077*
Albinus 103
Albert III of Austria *742*
Albert the Bear *726, 730*
Albert the Rude *728*
Alcaeus 27
Aleppo *1277*
Alexander I 37; *105*
Alexander III the Great 23, 41, 43, 44, 55, 67, 69, 75; *141, 162, 163, 165, 167, 168, 194, 304, 309, 1228, 1389*
Alexander III of Scotland *662*
Alexander IV *167*
Alexander Severus *434*
Alexander Zabinas 55
Alexandria 87, 99, 105, 259; *168, 169, 210, 211, 381, 482, 1279, 1281*
Alexandria Troas *185*
Alexius I Comnenus 131
Alfonso V *859*
Alfonso VIII of Castile *722*
Alfonso X of Castile 163
Alfred the Great *33, 644*
Algeria 261, 269; *1323*
Ali bin Yusuf *1306*
al-Mahdiyya 269
al-Mansur, Caliph *1240*
al-Mu'izz, Caliph 263; *1252*
al-Mustansir *1254, 1255*
al-Musta'sim *1275*
'Amdan Bayyin *1231*
Amiens *486*
Ammon, Samuel 18
Amoghabuti 279; *1349*
Amphipolis *108, 257*
Anastasius 16; *525, 526, 533*
Anatolia 265, 269, 271, 273; *1312, 1313*
Andrea Dandolo *753*
Andriscus 69
Angduong *1498*
Anjou *669*
Anlaf Guthfrithsson *645*
Anne-Marie-Louise *898*
Anne, Queen *914*
Anno of Cologne, Archbishop *681*
Anquara *269*
Anthemius 121; *528*
Antialcidas *1353*
Antigonus 43
Antimachus *16, 195*
Antinous *416*
Antioch 55, 103; *212, 263, 270, 276, 451, 454, 489, 490, 508*
Antiochus I *186, 280*
Antiochus III *202*
Antiochus III of Syria 51
Antiochus IV *207, 382*
Antiochus VII *265*
Antiochus XI *212, 1219*
Antiochus Hierax *188*
Anthony, Susan B. *1157*
Antoninius Pius *419, 422, 423, 445*
Apamea *176*
Apollodatus I 279; *1351*
Aptera *133*
Aquileia *710*
Arabia 251, 263; *245*
Arachosia 279, 281, 285; *1199, 1364, 1365*
Aradus *175*
Aragon 164; *758, 806*
Aratinus *293*
Arcadin *30*
Ardashir 251; *1204-07, 1209, 1224*
Areia (Herat) *1185*
Aretas III *245*
Aretas IV *1226*
Aria 279
Ariarathes V *209*
Aristotle 21
Arsaces I *1189, 1190*
Arsaces I *1183*
Artabanus *1186*
Artabanus IV *1197*
Arzinjan 269
Assan *1467*
Astarabad 267
Athens 27, 33, 35, 37, 41; *70, 73-76, 108, 109, 116, 120, 121-123, 152, 178, 179, 259, 269*
Attambelos I *1223*
Augsburg *739, 827, 841*
Augustus 14, 57, 61, 65, 66, 67, 71, 87, 95, 103; *29, 295, 298, 306, 346, 354, 355-359, 827, 842, 1192, 1230, 1367*
Aulus Gabinius *275*
Aurangzeb 289
Aurelian 103, 105; *472, 502*
Australia *1098, 1112-14*
Austria 159; *832, 833, 853, 884, 982, 985, 987-994*
Autophradates *1201*
Avesta 265
Axum 253; *1232*
Azerbaijan 273; *1190, 1326, 1339*
Azes I 283; *1356*
Azes II 281; *1356-58*
Azilises 281

Babylon *24, 165, 157*
Bactria 15, 43, 279, 285; *16, 194, 206, 1363, 1369, 1370, 1376*
Baden-Powell, Robert *1173*
Baghdad 259, 261, 263; *1240, 1299, 1328*
Bahram I *1208, 1209*
Bahram (Gur) V *1211*
Bahrein 2
Bajaur 27
Balash *1222*
Ba'lshallim II *154*
Bangladesh 293
Bank of England 243
Barcelona 161; *758, 869*
Barrekub, King 24; *56*
Barsbay, al-Ashraf 267; *1283, 1284*
Basil I *587*
Basil II *32, 590*
Bath *916*
Bathori, Stefan *925*
Bavaria 149, 179; *689, 699, 853, 999, 1007, 1009*
Bayazid I *1313, 1314*
von Bayern, Ernst *331*
Begram 279
Beijing (Peking) *1442, 1443, 1445*
Bela IV *765*
Belgium *874, 1028-33*
Bell, William *910*
Benedict III *651*
Benevento 145; *653*
Bengal 28 , 289; *1384, 1493*
Beni-Hasan *54*
Bergamo 161; *751*
Beth Shan 23
Bhoja Deva *1381*
Bihar 285, 289
Birmingham *1134, 1496*
Bithynia 69; *192, 277, 368*
Blampied, Edmund *1179*
Blondeau, Peter 18
Bohemia 149, 154, 176, 179, 201; *765, 770, 804, 833, 835, 840*
Boleslav I *699*
Bolivar, Simon *1133*
Bolivia *1133*
Bologna 161, 177; *745, 747, 748, 809*
Bombay 1 ; *1408*
Boran *1214*
Bordeaux *722*
Bosnia 165; *778*
Bosphorus 89
Boudicca *352*
Boulton, Matthew 19, 201, 221, 227
Brabant, 161; *759, 779, 797*
Bragadin, M.A. *819*
Brancaleone d'Andolò *748*
Brandenburg 154; *726, 837, 848*
Bratislav I *700, 701*
Brazil 205, 231, 232; *1138-40*
Breda *885*
Bremen 163
Brenner, Victor D 240
Brindisi *75*
Briot, Nicholas 18
Bristol *35, 950*
Britain 91, 103, 113, 243; *343-353, 371, 480, 496, 936-947, 1167-74*
Bruges *664, 875*
Brunswick 9, 155, 179, 193; *2, 738, 834, 842, 851*
Brutus 69; *282, 286*
Bukhara 263, 265
Bulgaria 163, 269; *304, 1078-80*
Burebista 8
Burgred of Mercia *643*
Burgundy 17; *797*
Burma 311; *1493-98*
Busel 176
Byzantium 6, 131-141, 145, 163; *205, 507, 583-609, 638, 1225*

Caepio *242*
Caesarea 87, 89, 103, 105; *429, 453*
Cairo 263
Calcutta *1506*
Caligula *29, 365, 367, 382*
Cambodia 311; *1493, 1498*
Canada 254, 240; *1158-62*
Cappadocia 69, 87; *209, 429, 453*
Capua 51; *223*
Caracalla 103, 105; *447-450*
Caratacus 81; *348*
Carausius 103, 109; *480, 481*
Carinthia *590*
T. Carisius *251*
Carlo Emanuele I 189; *821*
Carrhae *1'94*
Carthage 37, 41, 55, 57, 61, 116, 124, 125, 259; *27, 96, 100-102, 214, 225, 227, 503, 545-545, 547-563*
Casimir, John 203; *927, 928*
Cassander 43; *170*
Cassius 69
Castile 176; *781, 999*
Catana *23*
Catherine II *935*
Cellini, Benvenuto 18, 189; *817*
Ceylon 289, 293; *1385*
Champagne *668*
Chandra Gupta I 285
Chandra Gupta II 285; *1379*
Characene 251; *1222-24*
Charlemagne 143, 145; *635-639, 653, 634, 766*
Charles I of Anjou 161, 163, 176
Charles I of England 18, 201; *906, 908*
Charles II of Anjou 161; *774*
Charles II of England *911, 912, 1408*
Charles III of Spain *870*
Charles IV *804*
Charles V Emperor 189, 200, 201; *39, 814, 818, 865, 874*
Charles V of France *793*
Charles X *891*
Charles Robert of Hungary *774*
Charsadda 279
Chaucer, Geoffrey *194*
Chiang Kaishek 305; *1458*
Chichester 31
Chiengma *1494*
Chile 231; *1137*
China 11, 12, 243, 267, 295-311; *3, 9, 1416-1509*
Chios 91; *187, 443*
Chlothar II *578*
Christian IV *919*
Christina of Sweden 205; *921*
Chu State 295; *1423*
Cicero *233, 281*
Cilicia 69; *148, 149, 449, 459*
Claudius 65, 87; *370-372, 378*
Claudius II 103, 105; *464*
Clazomenae 14; *139*
Clement VII 18, 189
Cleonymus of Sparta *224*
Cleopatra 59; *290, 299, 369*
Clodius Macer *385*
Clovis II *577*
Cnossus *151, 181*
Coblenz *823*
Colchester 81; *347*
Cologne 21; *470, 765, 801, 1176, 1177*
Commius 81; *345*
Commodus 87, 103, 105; *428, 431-433, 493*
Como 161
Congreve, Sir William *1170*
Conrad the Great *725*
Constans *496, 509, 558*
Constans II 125, 145; *527*
Constantine I the Great 15, 117, 125, 131; *23, 484, 504, 507*
Constantine IV *558, 562*
Constantine V 131, 132; *583, 584*
Constantine VI *594, 596*
Constantine VIII *32, 589, 590*
Constantine IX *591*
Constantinople 121, 125, 131, 265, 269, 271; *31, 32, 490, 507, 510, 516, 520-527, 548-556, 584*
Constantius I *22, 502*
Constantius II *488, 495, 508, 510*
Continental Congress 243
Copenhagen *765*
Cordova *1246, 1306*
Corinth 27, 33, 37, 57; *72, 124, 125, 214-216, 258, 285*
Costa Rica *1128, 1130*
Crete 27; *132-133, 153, 181, 275, 1128, 1130*
Crimea 267; *1296, 1297*
Crispus *129, 532*
Croesus of Lydia 27; *68*
Cromwell, Oliver *908, 909*
Crondall hoard 129
Croton *85*
Crusade, Second 265
Crusade, Third 265
Ctesiphon *1194*
Cumae *83*
Cunincpert 145; *646*
Cunobeline 81; *347*
Cynoscephalae *201*
Cyprus *819*
Cyrenaica 69; *294*
Cyrene *158*
Cyzicus 33, 103; *136, 137, 557*
Czechoslovakia *980, 981*

Dalames *156*
Damascus 253, 267; *1277, 1278*
Damasena *1273*
Danelaw 145; *545*
Danzig 18; *44, 924, 926*
Darius I 23; *113*
David, King 24
David II of Scotland *780*
Deccan 12, 287; *1383*
Decius *458*
Delhi 287, 289
Delphi 41; *115, 114, 196*
Demetrius I of Bactria *194*
Demetrius Poliorcetes 43; *171, 172, 179, 180*
Denmark 149, 233; *693, 694, 919, 920, 960, 961, 1164*
Diocletian 15, 103, 109, 111, 113, 116; *22, 482, 499, 504*
Diodorus 25
Diogenes 33
Dirk of Utrecht, Bishop *666*
Domitian 91, 95; *390, 394-400*
Dordrecht *872*
Dortmund *696*
Dublin *663*
Dubnovellaunus *349*
Dupré, A. *857*
Dutch East Indies *1507, 1509*

East India Company 289, 293
Eberhard of Constance *740*
Ecbatana *202, 1185, 1195, 1200*
Edinburgh *780*
Edward I *660*
Edward III 163; *779, 798, 800*
Edward VI 18, 189; *901*
Edward VII *1114*
van Egmond, Duke Karel *873*
Egypt 22, 23, 43, 55, 87, 105, 111, 261, 267, 269; *54, 119, 149, 150, 157, 299, 416, 1252, 1253, 1279, 1325*
Elagabulus 105; *451*
Eligius *577*
Elis *127, 128*
Elizabeth I 200; *903*
Elizabeth II *1147*
Elymais 251; *1219-21*
Emporiae 75; *318, 319, 320*
England 17-19, 129, 143, 145, 147, 163, 164, 169, 176, 193, 200, 205, 223, 234, 240; *641-660, 779, 895-917*
Enna *293*
Epaminondas *115*
Epasnactus *346*
Epatticus 81
Ephesus 25, 27; *184, 374*
Epillus 81
Erz Gebirge 179
Eshtemoa 24; *57*
Estonia *977*
Ethelred the Unready *654*
Ethiopia 251; *1110*
Euainetos 14; *89*
Eucratides 279; *1352*
Eudocia Macrembolitissa *593*
Eugenius IV *827*
Eukleidas *96*
Eumenes 68; *187*
Ezanas *1232*

Falkenstein 155; *767*
Famagusta *819*
Fausta *506*
Faustina I *420, 421, 425*
Faustina II *427*
Feodorovich, Mikhail *931*
Ferdinand I 200
Ferdinand III *832*
Fernando of Portugal *782*
Ferrara 18, 19, 183
Fez *1309-11*
Finland *962, 963*
Flanders 148, 161, 169; *757, 759, 760, 762, 874, 875, 882*
Florence 18, 163, 164, 177, 183, 189; *40, 747, 754, 785, 816, 817*
Foppa, Cristoforo 18
France 17-19, 129, 145, 149, 161, 164, 169, 181, 183, 193, 200, 205, 243; *49, 50, 788-794, 812, 1034-45, 1166*
Francois I *887, 888*
Franconia 163
Frankfurt am Main 176; *729, 802, 1001-03*
Frankfurt am Oder *837*
Franklin, Benjamin *1146*
Franz II *930*
Frederick I Barbarossa 159; *684, 709, 729, 731, 746*
Frederick II, Emperor 18, 163; *713, 714, 719, 731, 751, 783, 806*
Frederick II of Saxony *771*
Frederick III of Denmark *920*
Frederick III of Saarwerden *801*
Freiburg 189; *823*
Friedrich II of Prussia *855*
Friedrich III der Weise *825*
Frisia 143
Fyzabad 1379

Galatia *282, 408*
Galba *386*
Galerius *489, 503*
Gallienus 103, 105, 111; *439, 459-465*
C. Gallius Lupercus *355*
Gandhara *358, 1383*
Gansu 299
Gänzberg *853*
Gardez 279
Gaul *496*
de Gaulle, Charles 19
Gautimiputra *1377*
Genoa 161, 177; *787, 810*
George I 9, *915*
George II *915*
George III *45, 46, 852, 917, 1147, 1174*
Gerhard of Osnabrück *685*
Germanicus *366*
Germany 17, 18, 143-154, 176, 179, 189, 201, 203, 307; *823, 995-1022, 1175-79, 1475*
Ghazan Mahmud *1292*
Ghazna 263
Ghengiz Khan 267, 287; *1286, 1331*
Ghent *665*
Goa 12, 289, 293
Gondemar 126
Gondophares 281, 285; *1361, 1365, 1376*
Gonzaga, Duke Frederick *5*
Gordian 103
Gordian II *452*
Gordian III 103, *453-455*
Görtz, Baron 205, *923*
Gottfried IV *768*
Gradenigo, Pietro *4*
Gratian *490, 491, 494*
Graz *832*
Greece 13, 14, 18, 23-25, 55, 67, 69, 89; *258, 1083-87, 1180*
Grenada *1142*
Grimoald III 145; *653*
Guandong *1446*
Guangxi *1446*
Guatemala *1128, 1132*
Guelders *873, 878*
Gujerat 287
Gundobad 126; *572, 573*
Gunthamund *544*
Gustav Adolf *841*
Gustav of Sayn-Wittgenstein *848*
Guyenne 169

Hadrian *410-418, 424*
Hadrian I, Pope 145; *649*
Haidar Ali 289
Hainaut 17, 161; *757, 759*
Haiti 233; *1143*
Hall 18, 193; *823*
Hamah *1276*
Hamburg 163, 176; *772, 1004*
Hannibal 55; *222*
Hanover 9, 179; *852, 996, 997*
Harington, Lord *905*
Harold II *655*
Harthacnut *693*
Harun-al-Rashid *1242*
Henan 295; *1417*
Henri II of France *41*
Henri III of France *890, 891*
Henry the Lion, Duke of Saxony *738*
Henry II of England *658*
Henry II, Emperor *679*
Henry III of England 164; *659*
Henry IV, Emperor *680*
Henry VI, Emperor *745*
Henry VII of England 181, 189; *872, 899*
Henry VIII of England 9; *1, 900, 901*
Heraclius 125, 259; *551, 554, 562*
Herat 263, 269; *1302*
Hermaeus 285; *1354*
Herodotus 23, 27
Hesse 161; *683, 732*
Hikesias of Sinope 33
Hildesheim *831*
Himera *79, 90, 91*
Hindu Kush 263, 279; *1258*
Hisn-Keyfa 267
Histiaea *203*
Homer 25; *443*
Hongkong 305; *1462, 1474*
Honorius 120, 124; *497, 512, 513, 541*
Hormuz 289
Hosokura *1472*
Hubei *1435*
Huerta, General *1126*
Hulagu *1288, 1289*
Humayun 287
Hunan *1446*
Hungary 149, 163, 176, 179, 201; *703-707, 803, 833, 858, 982-986*
Hussayn Bayqara 267; *1302*
Huvishka 285; *1372*
Huwayza *1335*

Ibiza 87; *235*
Ibrahim II *1250*
Iceland *950*
Ifriqiyah 261
Ile de la Cité 18
Illyria 67; *198*
Iltutmish 287
Inchon *1481*
India 12, 251, 267, 279-293, 295; *10, 11, 12, 1341-1415, 1506*
Indus Valley *1199, 1201*
Ionia *61-66, 140, 204*
Iran 243, 251, 287, 289; *1212*
Iraq 251, 263, 265, 271, 273; *1289, 1319*
Ireland 148, 149, 201; *663, 918, 948, 949*
Isaac I Comnenus *592*
Isfahan *1339*
Islanbul 271; *1323*
Isma'il 273
Istakhr *1201*
Italy 17, 18, 27, 61, 111-126, 145, 151, 159, 161, 163, 181, 189; *15, 60, 69, 82, 1057-72, 1172*

Jahangir 12, 289; *1396-1400*
James I of England 200, 201; *903*
James II of Aragon *758*
James II of England *918*
Japan 243, 301, 305-307, 309, 311; *XX, 1450, 1463-76, 1501, 1508*
Java 289
Jazira *1265*
Jelalabad 279
Jersey 1179
Jerusalem *265, 391, 719*
Jin 299
Joao III *1394*
Joao V 189; *862, 1139*
Jodhpur *1414*
Johann Friedrich, Duke 9; *2*
Johann Georg I *836*
Johann Georg II *839*
Johann Georg III *846*
John, King of England *34, 658, 663*
John the Good, King of France *761, 792, 794*
John I of Castile *721*
John I, Emperor 131
John VIII Palaeologus 183
John VIII, Pope *650*
Jose I *862*
Juba I 281
Judaea *156, 265, 364, 417*
Jugurtha *246*
Julian the Apostate 120; *497, 510*
Julianus 103
Julius III 18
Julius Caesar 65, 69, 70, 81; *283-285, 341*
Julius Duratius *341*
Julius Togirix *331*
Justin I 121, 125, 126; *556*
Justin II *549, 557*
Justinian I 16, 20, 125, 126; *32, 526, 534-537, 547, 548, 556, 568*
Justinian II 16, 125, 259; *554, 560, 586*